An Introduction to
Sociolinguistics

LEARNING ABOUT LANGUAGE

General Editors:
Geoffrey Leech & Mick Short, Lancaster University

An Introduction to
Sociolinguistics

Third Edition

Janet Holmes

PEARSON
Longman

Harlow, England • London • New York • Boston • San Francisco • Toronto
Sydney • Tokyo • Singapore • Hong Kong • Seoul • Taipei • New Delhi
Cape Town • Madrid • Mexico City • Amsterdam • Munich • Paris • Milan

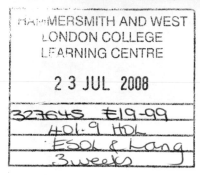
Pearson Education Limited

Edinburgh Gate
Harlow
Essex CM20 2JE
England

and Associated Companies throughout the world

Visit us on the World Wide Web at:
www.pearsoned.co.uk

First published 1992
Second edition published 2001
Third edition published 2008

© Longman Group UK Limited 1992
© Pearson Education Limited 2001, 2008

ISBN: 978-1-4058-2131-5

British Library Cataloguing-in-Publication Data
A catalogue record for this book is available from the British Library

Library of Congress Cataloging-in-Publication Data
Holmes, Janet, 1947–
   An introduction to sociolinguistics / Janet Holmes. – 3rd ed.
      p. cm.
   ISBN 978-1-4058-2131-5
   1. Sociolinguistics.   I. Title.
   P40.H66 2008
   306.44—dc22
                              2007036870

10 9 8 7 6 5 4 3 2 1
12 11 10 09 08

Typeset in 10.5/13pt Minion by 35
Printed and bound in Malaysia (CTP-VVP)

The publisher's policy is to use paper manufactured from sustainable forests.

For Rob

Brief contents

Contents

Preface

The third edition of my textbook has provided a further opportunity to respond to some of the many valuable suggestions that readers have sent to me over the last 10 years. I have added some new examples, updated the references and recommended readings once again, and in response to many requests I have added a new chapter on approaches to the analysis of discourse. I have also added some additional sociolinguistic concepts, and expanded the discussion of material in places.

This book uses many examples from a range of sources. When no explicit source is provided, the examples are based on my own experience, and especially on corpora of recorded materials that I have accumulated over many years of teaching and research. The examples are generally 'cleaned up' and edited for presentation in this introductory book, but almost all are 'authentic' in that I began from a genuine interaction.

A number of teachers have told me that they find this book useful for teaching socio-linguistics to students for whom English is an additional language. Since the book was written, inevitably, with an English-speaking audience in mind, I encourage teachers to adapt the exercises to the situations of their students.

I hope the new chapter proves useful and that the amendments and additions increase the value of the book both for students and teachers.

Janet Holmes
Wellington, New Zealand
April 2007

Author's acknowledgements

I would like to express my appreciation to my many colleagues and friends who have cheerfully answered my queries, provided me with material, checked my examples, and assisted me in a myriad ways with the writing and revision of this book. The list of those who have helped in some way includes at least the following: Tim Beaglehole, Mike Bennett, Mary Boyce, David Britain, Duncan Campbell, Jenny Cheshire, Jennifer Coates, Averil Coxhead, Terry Crowley, Diana Eades, Caroline Everest, Jackie Ferry, Richard Gwyn, Ray Harlow, Dick Hudson, Anke Hoffmann, Al Hunkin, Yushi Ito, Graeme Kennedy, Chris Lane, Uta Lenk, John Makeham, Caroline McGhie, Brian Morris, Paul Nation, John Newman, Harry Orsman, Caroline Quirk, Christopher Quirk, John Read, Silvia Rey, Mary Roberts, Donna Starks, Maria Stubbe, Yukako Sunaoshi, Vivien Trott, Maria Verivaki, Jeffrey Waite, Paul Warren, Geirr Wiggen, Teresa Wong, and Walt Wolfram. I apologise for inadvertent omissions. I am also very grateful to Meg Sloane who typed out many of the examples in the first edition, and to Miriam Meyerhoff and Rob Holmes who helped me construct a number of the figures and tables.

I must thank particularly Laurie Bauer, Miriam Meyerhoff and Allan Bell, who each patiently read and helpfully commented on earlier drafts of this book, and Anke Hoffmann who carefully proof-read and commented on the second edition. Geoffrey Leech was a positive and encouraging editor who provided detailed comments and suggestions at every stage. Elizabeth Mann and Casey Mein were supportive publisher's advisers. Finally I must thank Tony, Rob and David Holmes for their good humour and support throughout the production and revision process. A dedicated computer is one outcome we have all benefited from.

For assistance with the revisions in this third edition, I would like to express appreciation to Bob Good for suggestions for improvement, to Julia de Bres, Paul Kerswill, Martin Paviour-Smith, and Stephanie Schnurr for assistance with improvements, and to Meredith Marra and Sharon Marsden for a wide range of support and editorial assistance.

Publisher's acknowledgements

We are grateful to the following for permission to reproduce copyright material:

Table 2.4 from 'Bilingualism with and without diglossia: Diglossia with and without bilingualism', *Sociolinguistics: The Essential Readings*, edited by C. Bratt Paulston and G.R. Tucker, Blackwell, Maldon, MA (Fishman J.A. 2003); Figure 3.1 from 'A model for the evaluation of bilingual education', *International Review of Education*, Vol. 24, No. 3, Springer (Spolsky, B. 1978), with kind permission of Professor B. Spolsky; Figure 4.1 from 'Standards, codification and sociolinguistic realism: the English language in the outer circle', *English in the World*, edited by R. Quirk and H.G. Widdowson, Cambridge University Press, Cambridge (Kachru, B.B. 1985); Table 4.1 from *Pidgins and Creoles*, Routledge and Kegan Paul, London (Todd, L. 1974); Figure 6.1 from *Dialects*, p. 21, Routledge, London and New York (Trudgill, P. 1994); Figures 6.2 and 6.3 from *Sociolinguistics*, Penguin, London (Trudgill, P. 1983) reproduced with permission of Penguin Books; Figures 6.7 and 7.5 from 'Phonology, grammar and discourse in dialect convergence', *Dialect Change*, edited by P. Auer, F. Hinskens and P. Kerswill, Cambridge University Press, Cambridge (Cheshire, J., Kerswill, P. and Williams, A. 2005); Table 6.1 Adapted with the permission of The Free Press, a Division of Simon & Schuster Adult Publishing Group, from THE RELIGION OF JAVA by Clifford Geertz. Copyright © 1960 by The Free Press. Copyright © renewed 1988 by Clifford Geertz. All rights reserved; Figure 7.2 from *The Sociolinguistics of Language*, Blackwell, Oxford (Fasold, R. 1990); Table 7.1 from 'Pronunciation of intervocalic and final stops in New Zealand English: a pilot project', unpublished terms project, Victoria University, Wellington (Hui, S. 1989); Figure 9.3 from *Variation and Linguistics Theory*, Center for Applied Linguistics, Washington (Bailey, C.J. 1973); Figure 9.4 from *Language Change, 3rd Edition*, Cambridge University Press, Cambridge (Aitchison, J. 2001); Figure 10.1 from *The Social Differentiation of English in Norwich*, Cambridge University Press, Cambridge (Trudgill, P. 1974); Figure 10.2 from *The Social Stratification of English in New York City*, Center for Applied Linguistics, Washington (Labov, W. 1966) with permission from Cambridge University Press; Figure 10.4 from 'They're off and racing now: the speech of the New Zealand race caller', *New Zealand Ways of Speaking English*, edited by A. Bell and J. Holmes, Multilingual Matters, Clevedon, Avon (Kuiper, K. and Austin, P. 1990); Table 10.1 from *The Language of the News Media*, Blackwell, Oxford (Bell, A. 1991); Figure 11.1 from 'Linguistic routines and politeness in greeting and parting', *Conversational Routine*, edited by F. Coulmas, Mouton, The Hague, (Laver, J. 1981) © 1981 Walter de Gruyter GmbH & Co. KG, D-10785 Berlin; Figure 11.2 from 'Rituals of encounter among the Maori', *Explorations in the Ethnography of Speaking*, edited by R. Bauman and J. Sherzer, Cambridge University Press, Cambridge (Salmond, A. 1974); Table 12.1 based on 'Hedging your bets and sitting on the fence: some evidence for hedges as support structures' in *Teo Reo*, Vol. 27, Linguistic Society of New Zealand, Christchurch (Holmes, J. 1984); Table 12.3 from 'Verbal turn taking and exchanges in faulty dialogue', *The Sociology of the Languages of American Women*, edited by B. L. Dobois and I. Crouch, Trinity University Press, San Antonio, Texas (Eakins, B. and Gene-Eakins, R. 1979).

PUBLISHER'S ACKNOWLEDGEMENTS

We are grateful to the following for permission to reproduce photographs:

Paul Kerswill for the photograph of Hemnesberget in Chapter 1 (page 6).

We are grateful to the following for permission to reproduce cartoons:

Pages 34 and 162 DENNIS THE MENACE ® used by permission of Hank Ketcham Enterprises and © North America Syndicate; Page 63 Flann O'Riain's 'Cartoon of Irish Language' from *Lazy Way to Gaelic* is reproduced by permission of Birlinn Ltd (www.birlinn.co.uk); Page 147 © 1986 United Feature Syndicate, Inc. Reproduced by permission; Page 314 © New Zealand Herald; Page 331 'Well actually Doreen, . . .' The Far Side ®; Page 349 from *Teo Reo*, used by permission of the Linguistic Society of New Zealand.

Chapter 4 Example 9, Exercise 6 and 7 extracts from *Pidgin and Creole Languages*, Longman, London (Romaine, S. 1988); Chapter 5 Example 4 extract from 'Thousands Threaten Strike over Language Rights in Moldavia', *Reuters News*, 30 July 1989 © 1989 Reuters Limited; Chapter 5 Example 7 extract from 'It's Greek to Them', *San Francisco Chronicle*, 26.12.82 © San Francisco Chronicle reprinted with permission; Chapter 5 Example 9 extract from a letter to the Editor of the *New Zealand Listener*, 5/4/86; Chapter 7 Example 6 extract from *The Story of New Zealand*, Reed Methuen, Auckland (Bassett, J., Sinclair, K. and Stenson, M. 1985); Chapter 10 Example 3 extract from Monty Python's Flying Circus, Episode 28, © Python (Monty) Pictures LTD; Chapter 10 Example 11 extract from *New Zealand Herald*, 31 December 1986; Chapter 10 Example 20 extract from *Structure and Style in Javanese: A Semiotic View of Linguistic Etiquette*, Philadelphia, University of Pennsylvania Press, pp. 89–90 (Errington, J. Joseph 1988), reprinted with permission of the University of Pennsylvania Press; Chapter 11 Example 2(a) ® Mars slogan is a registered trademark, reproduced with permission of Mars UK Ltd; Chapter 12 Example 12 extract from 'Women's place in everyday talk: reflections on parent–child inter-action', *Social Problems*, 24, The University of California Press (West, C. and Zimmerman, D. 1977); Chapter 14 Example 4 a transcript from Shortland Street copyright © South Pacific Pictures Serials Limited 1995; Chapter 14 Examples 33, 34, 36, 37, 40 and 41 from Wellington Language in the Workplace Corpus with permission of Janet Holmes, Director.

In some instances we have been unable to trace the owners of copyright material, and we would appreciate any information that would enable us to do so.

1 What do sociolinguists study?

WHAT IS A SOCIOLINGUIST?

Sociolinguists study the relationship between language and society. They are interested in explaining why we speak differently in different social contexts, and they are concerned with identifying the social functions of language and the ways it is used to convey social meaning. Examining the way people use language in different social contexts provides a wealth of information about the way language works, as well as about the social relationships in a community, and the way people signal aspects of their social identity through their language. This book will explore all these aspects of sociolinguistic study.

Example 1

Ray: Hi mum.
Mum: Hi. You're late.
Ray: Yeah, that bastard Sootbucket kept us in again.
Mum: Nana's here.
Ray: Oh sorry. Where is she?

Ray's description of his teacher would have been expressed differently if he had realised his grandmother could hear him. The way people talk is influenced by the social context in which they are talking. It matters who can hear us and where we are talking, as well as how we are feeling. The same message may be expressed very differently to different people. We use different styles in different social contexts. Leaving school Ray had run into the school principal.

Example 2

Ray: Good afternoon, sir.
Principal: What are you doing here at this time?
Ray: Mr Sutton kept us in, sir.

This response reflects Ray's awareness of the social factors which influence the choice of appropriate ways of speaking in different social contexts. *Sociolinguistics* is concerned with the relationship between language and the context in which it is used.

The conversation between Ray and his mother also illustrates the fact that language serves a range of functions. We use language to ask for and give people information. We use it to express indignation and annoyance, as well as admiration and respect. Often one utterance will simultaneously both convey information and express feelings. Ray's utterance

Yeah, that bastard Sootbucket kept us in again

not only tells his mother why he is late, his choice of words also tells her how he feels about the teacher concerned, and tells us something about his relationship with his mother (he can use words like *bastard* talking to her) compared to his grandmother and the principal (to whom he uses *sir*). The relationship with his mother is an intimate and friendly one, rather than a formal, distant or respectful one.

Exercise 1

(a) Identify the words in examples 1 and 2 which reflect the fact that Ray's relationship with his mother is a friendly one compared to his relationship with the principal.

What does this suggest about the social significance of choice of words?

(b) Ray greeted the principal with the words *Good afternoon, sir.*

How do or did you greet your school principal? Would you use the same words to your father? Would you use the same greeting to your best friend? Why (not)?

Answers at end of chapter

We also indicate aspects of our social identity through the way we talk. Our speech provides clues to others about who we are, where we come from, and perhaps what kind of social experiences we have had. Written transcripts provide no auditory clues to readers, and examples 1 and 2 are also too short to provide reliable clues to speaker gender or ethnicity, but we can deduce Ray's age reasonably accurately from his linguistic choices (he is in his early teens), as well as make a reasonable guess about his social background. Later chapters will examine in some detail the ways that we express different aspects of our social identity through our linguistic choices.

WHY DO WE SAY THE SAME THING IN DIFFERENT WAYS?

Example 3

Every afternoon my friend packs her bag and leaves her Cardiff office in southern Wales at about 5 o'clock. As she leaves, her business partner says *goodbye Margaret,* (she replies *goodbye Mike*), her secretary says *see you tomorrow* (she replies *bye Jill*), and the caretaker says *Bye Mrs Walker* (to which she responds *goodbye Andy*). As she arrives home she is greeted by *Hi mum* from her daughter, Jenny, *hello dear, have a good day?* from her mother, and simply *you're late again!* from her husband. Later in the evening the president of the local flower club calls to ask if she would like to join the club. *Good evening, is that Mrs Billington?* she asks. *No, it's Margaret Walker, but my husband's name is David Billington,* Margaret answers. *What can I do for you?* Finally a friend calls *Hello Meg, sut wyt ti?*

My friend lives in a predominantly monolingual speech community and yet she has been called all sorts of names in the space of three hours. What's more, none of them are deliberately insulting! If she had managed to embroil herself in an argument or a passionate encounter of a different kind she might have been called a whole lot more names – some very nasty, some very nice! In most languages, there are many different ways of addressing people. What are the reasons for choosing a particular form?

Languages provide a variety of ways of saying the same thing – addressing and greeting others, describing things, paying compliments. As in examples 1 and 2, the final choice reflects factors such as the relationship between the people in the particular situation, and how the speaker feels about the person addressed. In example 3, her mother's choice of *dear* reflects her affectionate feelings towards Margaret. If she had been annoyed with her daughter, she would have used her full name *Margaret*. Her friend's use of *sut wyt ti?* ('how are you?') as a greeting reflects her Welsh ethnicity. The choice of one linguistic form rather than another is a useful clue to non-linguistic information. Linguistic variation can provide social information.

Exercise 2

Make a list of all the names you are called by people who know you. For each name note who uses it to you and when or where.

　Do some people call you by more than one name?

　What are the reasons why people choose one name rather than another for you?

Answer at end of chapter

Exercise 3

We often have different names for people when we are addressing them directly, as opposed to when we are referring to them in different contexts.

Note what you call your mother in different contexts:

(a) addressing her
   (i) at home alone with her
   (ii) on the telephone with friends listening
   (iii) in a shop.
(b) referring to her
   (i) at home to another family member when she is present
   (ii) at home to another family member when she isn't present
   (iii) to an acquaintance who doesn't know her
   (iv) to a sales assistant in a shop when she is present.

What influences your choice of address form and reference form in each of these contexts?

Answers at end of chapter

WHAT ARE THE DIFFERENT WAYS WE SAY THINGS?

Example 4[1]

Sam: You seen our 'enry's new 'ouse yet? It's in 'alton you know.

Jim: I have indeed. I could hardly miss it Sam. Your Henry now owns the biggest house in Halton.

The examples discussed so far have illustrated a range of *social* influences on language choice. Sociolinguists are also interested in the different types of *linguistic* variation used to express and reflect social factors. Vocabulary or word choice is one area of linguistic variation (e.g. *that bastard Sootbucket* vs *my teacher Mr Sutton, Margaret* vs *dear*). But linguistic variation occurs at other levels of linguistic analysis too: sounds, word-structure (or morphology), and grammar (or syntax) as well as vocabulary. Within each of these linguistic levels there is variation which offers the speaker a choice of ways of expression. They provide us with different linguistic styles for use in different social contexts. Choices may even involve different dialects of a language, or quite different languages, as we shall see.

In example 4, the most obvious linguistic variation involves pronunciation. Sam 'drops his aitches' while Jim doesn't. Just as vocabulary choices convey social information, so using different pronunciation conveys social information too. Sam is a coal-miner and Jim is an old friend of Sam's son, Henry. Jim is also the local MP and he has dropped in to see Sam on one of his regular visits from London where he now spends most of his time. The difference in Sam's and Jim's [h]-dropping behaviour reflects their different educations and occupations. In other words, despite their common regional origins they have different social backgrounds and that is reflected in their speech.

Example 5

(a) Refuse should be deposited in the receptacle provided.
(b) Put your rubbish in the bin, Jilly.
(c) Please tender exact fare and state destination.
(d) Give me the right money and tell me where you're going.

The sentences in example 5 illustrate language variation in grammar and vocabulary. The first, (a), uses a passive grammatical structure *should be deposited*, for example, which avoids any mention of the people involved. By contrast (b) uses an imperative verb form, *put*, and an address form, *Jilly*. This utterance is much more direct and it specifies whose rubbish is the focus of the directive. *Refuse, deposited* and *receptacle* are all more formal and less frequent words than *rubbish, put* and *bin*. Both sentences express the same message or speech function: they give a directive. But they are not interchangeable. If your mother said (a) to you as you dropped a bit of paper on the floor, it is likely you would find it odd. You might assume she was being sarcastic or humorous, but you would not be likely to consider it a normal way of speaking to someone she knew well.

Exercise 4

(i) Identify the linguistic features which distinguish (c) and (d).
     What levels of linguistic analysis does the variation involve?
(ii) What non-linguistic and social factors are likely to account for the different
     ways of saying the same thing illustrated in example 5?

Answers at end of chapter

Example 6

In northern Norway there is a village, Hemnesberget, which has become famous among sociolinguists because the language used by the villagers was described in great detail by two sociolinguists, Blom and Gumperz, in the late 1960s. Blom and Gumperz reported that the Hemnesberget villagers knew and used two distinct kinds of Norwegian: firstly, the local dialect, Ranamål (*Rana* is the district, *mål* is the Norwegian word for 'language'), and secondly the standard dialect or standard Norwegian, Bokmål (literally 'book-language'). Bokmål was used by the teachers in school, it was the language of the textbooks and after a little exposure it was the kind of Norwegian that the pupils used to discuss school topics in school too. Bokmål was used in church services and sermons. It was used when people went into the local government offices to transact official business. It was used on radio and television. And it was used to strangers and visitors from outside Hemnesberget. So what did that leave for Ranamål?

Ranamål was the kind of Norwegian that people spoke to their family, friends and neighbours most of the time. As the local dialect, it signalled membership in the local speech community. People used Ranamål to each other at breakfast, to local shopkeepers when buying their newspapers and vegetables, to the mechanic in the local garage, and to the local people they met in the street. A local person who used Bokmål to buy her petrol would be regarded as 'stuck up' or 'putting on airs'.[2]

In this example the linguistic variation involves two dialects. In other words it is not just a matter of pronunciation differences, or vocabulary choices, or grammatical variation. All these levels of linguistic analysis are involved in the variation noted.

Hemnesberget in Norway

Source: Photo courtesy of Paul Kerswill. Reproduced with permission

Ranamål, the local dialect, differs from Bokmål, the standard dialect, in a number of quite specific ways. Each has its own pronunciation features: Ranamål, for instance, has a palatal nasal sound [ɲ] (as in Spanish *señor*), which Bokmål does not have. Each dialect has distinctive word-forms or morphological features: the plural of *the horses* is *hestene* in Bokmål but *hæstan* in Ranamål. And there are other words which differ between the dialects too: the Bokmål word for *she* is *hun*, while in Ranamål *she* is *ho*; the Bokmål word for *but* is *men*, the Ranamål word is *mænn*.

The reasons why people chose Ranamål as opposed to Bokmål are similar to the reasons that lead people to select *Meg* as opposed to *Mrs Billington* in addressing an English woman. Factors such as who is being talked to, where and for what reasons are important. There is another factor which may also be relevant, namely the topic of a discussion. It is clearly illustrated in Hemnesberget in the linguistic behaviour of university students who tend to switch dialect when they discuss certain topics. They generally use Ranamål in the village, like everyone else, when they come home during vacations, but when they begin to discuss national politics with each other, it was found they tended to switch unconsciously to Bokmål. The topic was one they associated with discussions outside the village in the standard dialect, and so they switched to the linguistic forms they would normally use to discuss it.

The linguistic variation involved in Hemnesberget is not different in kind from the variation which distinguished Sam and Jim's accents in example 4, or the choice of vocabulary and grammar in example 5; it is simply a matter of scale. And the reasons for the choice of one dialect rather than another involve the same kind of social considerations – the participants, the social setting, and the topic or purpose of the interaction.

Because of these similarities sociolinguists use the term *variety* (or sometimes *code*) to refer to any set of linguistic forms which patterns according to social factors. Variety is a sociolinguistic term referring to language in context. A variety is a set of linguistic forms used under specific social circumstances, i.e., with a distinctive social distribution. Variety is therefore a broad term which includes different accents, different linguistic styles, different dialects and even different languages which contrast with each other for social reasons. It has proved a very useful sociolinguistic term because it is linguistically neutral and covers all the different realisations of the abstract concept 'language' in different social contexts.

Example 7

In a mountain village, Sauris, in north-east Italy, a sociolinguist reported in 1971 that the adults were all trilingual. Before 1866 the village had been part of the Austrian empire, and its villagers all spoke German. In the late 1960s they still used a German dialect in the home, and to neighbours and fellow villagers. They also used the regional language Friulian with people from the surrounding area outside the village, and the young men, in particular, tended to use it to each other in ▶

the pub. These men had gone to secondary school together in Ampezzo, a nearby town, and Friulian had become for them a language of friendship and solidarity. Italian was the language people used to talk to those from beyond the region, and for reading and writing. Because their village was now part of Italy, Italian was the language of the church and the school.

In this example the different linguistic varieties used in Sauris are distinct languages. They are distinguishable from each other in their sounds, their grammar and their vocabulary. Italians from outside the area would not be able to understand the German dialect, nor even the Friulian, although, like Italian, it is a Romance language. The varieties are also distinguishable by the way they are used – their social distribution is different. The local people select the appropriate variety for any particular interaction according to similar social factors to those identified in earlier examples: who they are talking to, in what kind of setting, and for what purposes. Using German in the pub is generally not appropriate, for example, though it has been done. One angry woman used German very effectively to berate her husband for ending up in the pub when he was supposed to be at the dairy with their milk, making cheese. Her use of German isolated him from his friends in the pub and emphasised her point that he was neglecting his domestic responsibilities. People may manipulate the norms to make a point – something we shall see more of in later chapters.

These examples illustrate the range of linguistic variation which can be observed in different speech communities. People may use different pronunciations, vocabulary, grammar, or styles of a language for different purposes. They may use different dialects of a language in different contexts. And in some communities they will select different languages according to the situation in which they are speaking.

In any community the distinguishable varieties (or codes) which are available for use in different social contexts form a kind of repertoire of available options. The members of each community have their distinctive *linguistic repertoires*. In other words in every community there is a range of varieties from which people select according to the context in which they are communicating. In monolingual communities these take the form of different styles and dialects.

In a small Lancashire village my mother's linguistic repertoire includes the styles of English she needs in the social contexts in which she operates. The way she talks to the woman selling bread in the baker's shop is different from the way she talks to her bank manager, and that is different again from the way she talks to her grandchildren, and from the language she uses in church. In Malaysia, for similar reasons, a woman's linguistic repertoire may include two varieties of English, two different dialects of Chinese and different styles within these, as well as standard or Bahasa Malay and a colloquial variety known as Bazaar Malay. As elsewhere, choosing the appropriate variety from this wide linguistic repertoire depends on social factors.

On the whole people acquire their knowledge of varieties and how to use them appropriately in the same way that they acquire their knowledge of most other aspects of language – by extensive exposure and a process of osmosis. The Chinese Malaysian, like my Lancashire-born mother, built up her linguistic repertoire by hearing the different varieties in use in the community she lives in. More formal varieties – and especially distinctive written varieties – may involve more conscious learning, but most varieties in a person's linguistic repertoire are acquired with little conscious effort.

SOCIAL FACTORS, DIMENSIONS AND EXPLANATIONS

Social factors

In each of the examples discussed, certain social factors have been relevant in accounting for the particular variety used. Some relate to the users of language – the participants; others relate to its uses – the social setting and function of the interaction. Who is talking to whom (e.g. wife – husband, customer – shop-keeper, boss – worker) is an important factor. The setting or social context (e.g. home, work, school) is generally a relevant factor too. The aim or purpose of the interaction (informative, social) may be important. And in some cases the topic has proved an influence on language choice. University students in countries which use English for tertiary education, such as Tanzania, Indonesia and Papua New Guinea, often find it easier to discuss their university subjects using English, for example, just as the students from Hemnesberget used standard Norwegian rather than the local dialect to discuss national politics.

Not all factors are relevant in any particular context but they can be grouped in ways which are helpful. In any situation linguistic choices will generally reflect the influence of one or more of the following components:

1. The **participants:**
   a. **who** is speaking and
   b. **who** are they speaking **to**?
2. The **setting** or social context of the interaction: **where** are they speaking?
3. The **topic: what** is being talked about?
4. The **function: why** are they speaking?

In this book the focus will be on speech, but the same questions can be asked about written communication, as example 5 illustrated. Throughout this book, these social factors will prove important in describing and analysing all kinds of interaction. They are basic components in sociolinguistic explanations of why we don't all speak the same way, and why we don't all speak in the same way all of the time.

▓ Social dimensions

In addition to these components it is useful to take account of four different dimensions for analysis which relate to the factors above and which have been only implicit in the discussion so far. These are:

1. A *social distance* scale concerned with participant relationships
2. A *status* scale concerned with participant relationships
3. A *formality* scale relating to the setting or type of interaction
4. Two *functional* scales relating to the purposes or topic of interaction.

The solidarity – social distance scale

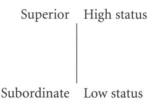

Intimate   Distant

High solidarity   Low solidarity

This scale is useful in emphasising that how well we know someone is a relevant factor in linguistic choice. In Wales, the choice of *Meg* vs *Mrs Billington* reflects consideration of this dimension, for instance. People's choice of Ranamål vs Bokmål in Hemnesberget, or German rather than Italian in Sauris, similarly reflects judgements about a relationship on this dimension.

The status scale

Superior   High status

Subordinate   Low status

This scale points to the relevance of relative status in some linguistic choices. The choice of *sir* by Ray in the first example, for instance, signalled that the school principal was of higher status and entitled to a respect term. Similarly the name avoidance by her secretary and the use of *Mrs* by the caretaker reflected the higher status of Margaret Walker-Billington, since she called both of these people by their first names. Sam's [h]-dropping in example 4 reflected his lower social group status in the society as a whole, while the educationally and occupationally higher-status Jim dropped none.

The formality scale

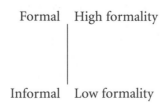

Formal   High formality

Informal   Low formality

This scale is useful in assessing the influence of the social setting or type of interaction on language choice. In a formal transaction such as one with the bank manager in his office, or at a ritual service in church, the language used will be influenced by the formality of the setting. For a friendly chat, people use colloquial language. In Hemnesberget, Bokmål was the language of school and government offices. Ranamål was the language of the home. The written language of notices is often very formal and impersonal, as example 5 illustrates. Often degrees of formality are largely determined by solidarity and status relationships. But not always. A very formal setting, such as a law court, will influence language choice regardless of the personal relationships between the speakers.

The referential and affective function scales

Though language serves many functions, the two identified in these scales are particularly pervasive and basic. Language can convey objective information of a referential kind; and it can also express how someone is feeling. Ray's utterance *Yeah, that bastard Sootbucket kept us in again* simultaneously expresses information about why he is late, while also conveying his feelings about the teacher referred to. Gossip may provide a great deal of new referential information, while also clearly conveying how the speaker feels about those referred to. It is very common for utterances to work like this, though often one function will dominate. In general the more referentially oriented an interaction is, the less it tends to express the feelings of the speaker. Radio broadcasts of the weather forecast tend to put the emphasis on information or the referential function, for instance. By contrast, interactions which are more concerned with expressing feelings often have little in the way of new information to communicate. Talk between neighbours over the fence at the weekend about the weather, for instance, is more likely to be mainly affective in function, and intended to convey goodwill towards the neighbour rather than important new information. In fact the specific content of the conversation is rarely important.

These scales will be referred to and illustrated further in subsequent chapters. Together with the social components identified in the previous section they provide a useful framework for discussing language in its social context in different speech communities, and for discussing the ways in which language reflects its users and the uses they put it to.

Referentia l

High   Low
information ——————————— information
content   content

Affective

Low   High
affective ——————————— affective
content   content

Exercise 5

Answer the following two questions for each of utterances a, b, and c, below.

(i) What information does the utterance provide about the relationship between the people talking in the context of their talk?
(ii) What is the function of the utterance in the context?

Does it convey primarily affective or referential information?

(a) Here is the forecast for the Wellington district until midnight Tuesday issued by the meteorological service at 6 o'clock on Monday evening. It will be rather cloudy overnight with some drizzle, becoming fine again on Tuesday morning. The outlook for Wednesday – a few morning showers then fine.
(b) Good morning little one – you had a good big sleep, didn't you, pet?
(c) Excuse me, Mr Clayton. I've finished your letters, sir.

Answers at end of chapter

Exercise 6

Your local walking club is discussing the preparations for their next weekend away.
   Using the four dimensions of sociolinguistic analysis proposed in this chapter, identify four linguistic features likely to characterise their discussions in each of these situations:

(a) during an organised meeting in the club meeting room and
(b) when they discuss the details over a drink in the local bar.

Looking for explanations

Sociolinguists aim to describe sociolinguistic variation and, if possible, explain why it happens. Why, for example, should Ray describe a teacher differently when talking to his mother and when answering the school principal? Why do different people call my friend Margaret by different names? Why should a formal grammatical construction with formal vocabulary sound sarcastic when used by your mother?
   The first two steps which need to be taken are:

1. to identify clearly the linguistic variation involved (e.g. vocabulary, sounds, grammatical constructions, dialects, languages)
2. to identify clearly the different social or non-linguistic factors which lead speakers to use one form rather than another (e.g. features relating to participants, setting or function of the interaction).

Then we can begin to look for patterns which will help to formulate an *explanation* of why people use one set of forms in some contexts, but different forms in others.

When the two sociolinguists Blom and Gumperz visited Hemnesberget what did they ask? First of all, 'what are the linguistic forms used in this village?' Secondly, 'what are the social factors which lead people to use one set of forms rather than the other?' And finally, 'can we explain why particular social factors lead to the use of one set of forms rather than another?'

In other words the sociolinguist's aim is to move towards a theory which provides a motivated account of the way language is used in a community, and of the choices people make when they use language.

The relationship between linguistic choices and the social contexts in which they are made is sometimes easiest to see when different languages are involved. The first section of this book focusses on multilingual speech communities and describes some of the ways in which social considerations affect language choice. But there is plenty of language variation in monolingual communities too, and it is just as socially meaningful. The second section of the book focusses on social features of the language user. It explores the range of social information conveyed about participants by their linguistic choices within one language. In the third section the focus shifts to the uses of language, and the influence on language of the social context in which it is used and the functions it expresses.

ANSWERS TO EXERCISES IN CHAPTER 1

Answer to exercise 1 (a)

Ray greets his mother with the friendly form *hi*, compared to the more distant and formal *good afternoon* used to the school principal. He uses *mum*, an address form which indicates that he gets on well with her. He could have used no address form at all. Note that he uses the respectful address form *sir* to the principal. Finally he refers to his teacher as *that bastard* and uses a nickname *Sootbucket* for him, an indication that he is treating his mother as an intimate. This contrasts with the way he refers to the teacher when talking to the principal, when he uses *Mr Sutton*.

We choose our words carefully according to whom we are talking to. Language choices convey information about the social relationships between people as well as about the topic of discussion. The kind of information which is relevant to language choice includes how well we know the other person and whether they are socially superior.

Answer to exercise 1 (b)

Most people greet friends and family differently from those they do not know so well, and from those who are in a superior relationship to them, such as the school principal or the boss at work. Often nicknames or endearments are used between people who know each other well (e.g. *mornin' sweetheart, hello love*). It is common to avoid names and use only a formal greeting, such as *good morning*, to superiors. The particular forms you use may vary from those suggested, but the general patterns described here should apply.

Answer to exercise 2

This is just an example of the kind of list you might make.

Name	Speaker	When/where
Robert	grandparents	home, letters
	teachers	school
	doctor	surgery, hospital
	mother	when annoyed
Robbie	mother, father	most of the time
Robbie-Bob	mother	when feeling affectionate
Rob	friends, brother	most of the time
Bob	friends	outside home to annoy me
Robert Harris	parents	when very annoyed
Mr Harris	strangers	letters, shops

Parents often call children by a variety of names depending on how they feel towards them. The person in the example above is called *Robbie* by his mother in most circumstances, but when she is annoyed with him she calls him *Robert* or even *Robert Harris*. Friends often have a range of names for each other too. Friends call him *Rob* most of the time, but *Bob* when they want to tease or annoy him.

In some cultures people have one name which is used only in the family and another for use outside. In some cultures people have a ceremonial name used only on very formal occasions. Marital status is sometimes relevant to choice of address form (e.g. Miss vs Mrs and choice of surname).

Answers to exercise 3

Possible answers:

(a) addressing your mother
    (i) at home alone with her: *mum, mummy, mom, ma, Tess*
    (ii) on the telephone with friends listening: *mother, mater, Tess*
    (iii) in a shop: *mother*
(b) referring to your mother
    (i) at home to another family member when she is present: *mum, mom*
    (ii) at home to another family member when she isn't present: *the old lady, our mam*
    (iii) to a friend who doesn't know her: *my mum*
    (iv) to a sales assistant in a shop when she is present: *my mother*

In addressing and referring to your mother, the term you use is likely to reflect your social background, and may differ according to which country you live in. In England, for instance, some members of high social groups use *mummy* well beyond childhood, while others use *mater* or *mama*, especially in reference. Members of lower social groups sometimes use *ma*, especially for address. Some members of middle social groups use their mother's first name in address, especially when they become adults. Some use her first name in referring to her in front of others. In some families *mum* changes to *mother* as she and the children grow older.

In general the following factors are among those relevant in selecting appropriate terms of address: family norms of address between children and parents at different stages; audience (who is listening?); social context (is it formal or public, or private and personal, for instance).

In reference the relationship between the speaker and the addressee is also relevant as well as how well they know the person being referred to.

Answers to exercise 4

(i) **Vocabulary choices**. *Tender* vs *give*, *state* vs *tell*, *destination* vs *where you're going*, *exact* vs *right*. Use of *please* in (c).

   Syntax. Both sentences use imperative structures, but the more formal verbs in (c) assist in avoiding the use of the personal pronouns *me* and *you* which occur in (d). The determiner is omitted before *exact fare* and *destination*, which increases the impersonality of the expression. These are both places where *your* could have occurred, for instance.

(ii) The medium of expression is relevant since (a) and (c) are much more likely in writing than in speech. Written and spoken language differ in many specific ways. Whether spoken or written, sentences (a) and (c) are also more formal and distancing. If they were spoken they would be appropriate only in the most formal context, between strangers or people who did not know each other well, or where the speaker was far superior or more powerful than the addressee. Sentences (b) and (d) would be appropriate in speech in informal contexts. The address form in sentence (b) shows the speaker knows the addressee and suggests they know each other well. It could be seen as softening the directive, making it gentler.

Answers to exercise 5

(a) (i) This is a recorded telephone message and therefore the speaker does not know the hearer. This is reflected in the lack of address term and the formal syntax.

   (ii) Its primary function is to provide referential information. It is not intended to provide information on how the speaker is feeling.

(b) (i) Despite the initial greeting *good morning* which can be used to strangers and acquaintances, the speaker clearly knows the addressee well. Two affectionate endearment terms are used (*little one, pet*). These are terms appropriately used downwards in status (e.g. mother to child, older person to younger, nurse to young patient).

   (ii) The use of the tag form (*didn't you?*) is an attempt to elicit a response. However it is not a request for information – the answer is self-evident since it is provided in the utterance itself. This is clearly an utterance with a high affective content.

(c) (i) The address forms (*Mr Clayton, sir*), as well as the initial phrase, as apology for interruption (*Excuse me*), suggest this is an utterance from a subordinate to a superior and that the two do not know each other well.

   (ii) The primary intention of this utterance appears to be to provide referential information. Note, however, that it might have other functions too if we knew more about the context. The secretary might be indirectly (and therefore politely) asking if s/he might leave since s/he has finished a particular task. Utterances often serve more than one function.

▮ Concepts introduced (in the order they occur in the chapter)

Style
Dialect
Variety/code
Linguistic repertoire
Speech function

■ References

Hemnesberget in example 6 is based on Blom and Gumperz (1972).
The Sauris community described in example 7 is based on Denison (1972).

■ Useful additional reading

These references provide more information on the topics discussed in this chapter.

Downes (1998), Ch. 2
Hudson (1996), Ch. 2
Saville-Troike (2003), Ch. 3
Trudgill (2000), Ch. 1
Trudgill (1992)
Wardhaugh (2006), Chs 1 and 2

■ Notes

1. Where possible, as in this example, for ease of reading I will use conventional spelling to reflect a particular pronunciation. However, the English spelling system is not suitable for representing many important sound contrasts, nor for representing the sounds of other languages. It will therefore be necessary to use phonetic symbols too. The symbols used for the sounds of English are described in the Appendix at the end of the book. For sounds from other languages I have used symbols from the International Phonetic Alphabet which are also listed in the Appendix with a gloss to describe how they sound.
2. It has been suggested that the distinction between Bokmål and Ranamål is not as clear as Blom and Gumperz claimed. See Mæhlum (1996). On a visit to Hemnesberget in 2005, Paul Kerswill, a social dialectologist who speaks Norwegian, confirmed this view. He also noted that while older people used some Bokmål forms in their dialect while speaking to him, young people used only dialect forms.

Section A

Multilingual speech communities

2 Language choice in multilingual communities

CHOOSING YOUR VARIETY OR CODE

What is your linguistic repertoire?

Example 1

Kalala is 16 years old. He lives in Bukavu, an African city in eastern Zaire with a population of about 220,000. It is a multicultural, multilingual city with more people coming and going for work and business reasons than people who live there permanently. Over forty groups speaking different languages can be found in the city. Kalala, like many of his friends, is unemployed. He spends his days roaming the streets, stopping off periodically at regular meeting places in the market-place, in the park, or at a friend's place. During a normal day he uses at least three different varieties or codes, and sometimes more.

Kalala speaks an informal style of Shi, his tribal language, at home with his family, and he is familiar with the formal Shi used for weddings and funerals. He uses informal Shi in the market-place when he deals with vendors from his own ethnic group. When he wants to communicate with people from a different tribal group, he uses the lingua franca of the area, Swahili. He learned standard Zairean Swahili at school but the local market-place variety is a little different. It has its own distinct linguistic features and even its own name – Kingwana. He uses Kingwana to younger children and to adults he meets in the streets, as well as to people in the market-place.

Standard Zairean Swahili, one of the national languages, is the language used in Bukavu for most official transactions, despite the fact that French is the official language of Zaire. Kalala knows almost no French and, like most other people in Bukavu, he uses standard Zairean Swahili with officials in government offices when he has to fill in a form or pay a bill. He uses it when he tries for a job in a shop or an office, but there are very few jobs around. He spends most of his time with his friends, and with them he uses a special variety or code called Indoubil. This is a variety which is used among the young people in Bukavu, regardless of their ethnic backgrounds or tribal affiliations.

It is used like in-group slang between young people in monolingual communities. Indoubil is based on Swahili but it has developed into a distinct variety or code in Zaire by drawing on languages like French, English, and Italian – all languages which can be read or heard in the multilingual city of Bukavu.

If we list the varieties or codes he uses regularly, we find that Kalala's linguistic repertoire includes three varieties of Swahili (standard Zairean, local Swahili or Kingwana, and Indoubil) and two varieties of his tribal language, Shi (a formal and an informal or casual style). The factors that lead Kalala to choose one code rather than another are the kinds of social factors identified in the previous chapter as relevant to language choice in speech communities throughout the world. Characteristics of the users or participants are relevant. Kalala's own linguistic repertoire and the repertoire of the person he is talking to are basic limiting factors, for instance.

Table 2.1 illustrates the possibilities for communication when Kalala wanted to talk to a soldier who had recently arrived in Bukavu with his unit. Since he and his addressee share only one code or variety, standard Swahili, there is not much choice if he wants to communicate referential content (as opposed to, say, insult, abuse or admiration, where any variety could carry the affective message).

Table 2.1 Two linguistic repertoires in Zaire

Kalala's linguistic repertoire	Addressee's linguistic repertoire
Shi: informal style	Rega: informal style
formal style	formal style
Indoubil	Lingala
Kingwana	
Standard Zairean Swahili	Standard Zairean Swahili

Source: Based on Goyvaerts et al. 1983 and Goyvaerts 1988

Exercise 1

(i) There are many degrees of 'knowing' a language. Table 2.1 is a simplification since it does not take account of how well Kalala and his addressee know any particular variety.

Consider how well you know a language other than your mother tongue. How would you rate your knowledge? What factors are relevant to your assessment? How does your rating reflect social factors?

(ii) Using the information provided in the section above, which varieties do you think Kalala will use to

(a) talk to his younger brother at home?

(b) plan the morning's activities with his best friend?

(c) greet a stranger from a different tribe whom he met in the street?

Answers at end of chapter

Domains of language use

Example 2

'Anahina is a bilingual Tongan New Zealander living in Auckland. At home with her family she uses Tongan almost exclusively for a wide range of topics. She often talks to her grandmother about Tongan customs, for instance. With her mother she exchanges gossip about Tongan friends and relatives. Tongan is the language the family uses at meal-times. They discuss what they have been doing, plan family outings, and share information about Tongan social events. It is only with her older sisters that she uses some English words when they are talking about school or doing their homework.

Certain social factors – who you are talking to, the social context of the talk, the function and topic of the discussion – turn out to be important in accounting for language choice in many different kinds of speech community. It has proved very useful, particularly when describing code choice in large speech communities, to look at 'typical' interactions which involve these factors. We can imagine, for instance, a 'typical' family interaction. It would be located in the setting of the home; the typical participants will obviously be family members; and typical topics would be family activities. 'Anahina's family's meal-time conversations, described in example 2, illustrate this pattern well. A number of such typical interactions have been identified as relevant in describing patterns of code choice in many speech communities. They are known as *domains* of language use, a term popularised by an American sociolinguist, Joshua Fishman. A domain involves typical interactions between typical participants in typical settings.

Table 2.2 describes five domains which can be identified in many communities.

Table 2.2 Domains of language use

Domain	Addressee	Setting	Topic	Variety/Code
Family	Parent	Home	Planning a family party	_____
Friendship	Friend	Beach	How to play beach tennis	_____
Religion	Priest	Church	Choosing the Sunday liturgy	_____
Education	Teacher	School	Solving a maths problem	_____
Employment	Employer	Workplace	Applying for a promotion	_____

Source: Based on Fishman 1972: 22

Exercise 2

(a) Fill in the column labelled variety/code for your speech community. If your community is monolingual remember that the term variety includes different dialects and styles of language.

▶

A

Multilingual speech communities

(b) Ask a bilingual friend or neighbour which languages they would use in the different domains. It is useful to guess in advance how they will answer and then check your predictions against their responses. When you are wrong see if you can identify the reason for your error.

If you do not know anyone who is bilingual think of where you might meet people who are bilingual. In Wellington, New Zealand, students have found that bilingual people in local shops and takeaway bars are very interested in this topic, and are pleased to talk about their language use. You could consider asking a bilingual worker in a takeaway shop, a delicatessen or corner shop about their patterns of language use. But don't ask when they are busy!

Example 3

In Paraguay, a small South American country, two languages are used – Spanish, the language of the colonisers, and Guaraní, the American Indian indigenous language. People in Paraguay are proud that they have their own language which distinguishes them from the rest of South America. Many rural Paraguayans are monolingual in Guaraní, but those who live in the cities are usually bilingual. They read Spanish literature, but they gossip in both Spanish and Guaraní.

A study by Joan Rubin in the 1960s identified complementary patterns of language use in different domains. Urban bilingual Paraguayans selected different codes in different situations, and their use of Spanish and Guaraní fell into a pattern for different domains (see table 2.3). This was useful though it still leaves considerable areas of language use unspecified. Faced, for example, in the countryside by a woman in a long black skirt

Table 2.3 Domains of language use in Paraguay

Domain	Addressee	Setting	Topic	Language
Family	Parent	Home	Planning a family party	*Guaraní*
Friendship	Friend	Café	Funny anecdote	*Guaraní*
Religion	Priest	Church	Choosing the Sunday liturgy	*Spanish*
Education	Teacher	Primary school	Telling a story	*Guaraní*
Education	Lecturer	University	Solving a maths problem	*Spanish*
Administration	Official	Office	Getting an import licence	*Spanish*

(I compiled this table from data given in Rubin 1968.)

This table describes the situation 40 years ago, but patterns of language use have steadily changed in Paraguay, especially in the urban areas. The complementary patterns of language use identified by Joan Rubin in the 1960s have given way to much greater bilingualism in most domains in twenty-first century Paraguay. City dwellers use both Spanish and Guaraní in the home as well as in school, and some fear that Guaraní may eventually be displaced in urban areas.

smoking a cigar what language should you use? (The answer will be based on your predictions about her linguistic repertoire.)

Modelling variety or code choice

Example 4

Maria is a teenager whose Portuguese parents came to London in the 1960s. She uses mainly Portuguese at home and to older people at the Portuguese Catholic church and community centre, but English is the appropriate variety or code for her to use at school. She uses mostly English at her after-school job serving in a local café, though occasionally older customers greet her in Portuguese.

Domain is clearly a very general concept which draws on three important social factors in code choice – participants, setting and topic. It is useful for capturing broad generalisations about any speech community. Using information about the domains of use in a community it is possible to draw a very simple model summarising the norms of language use for the community. This is often particularly useful for bilingual and multilingual speech communities.

The information provided in example 4, for instance, identifies four domains and describes the variety or code appropriate to each.

Domain	Variety/code
Home/family	Portuguese
Church/religion	Portuguese
Work/employment	English
School/education	English

This information can also be summarised in a diagram or model, as figure 2.1 illustrates. While it obviously oversimplifies the complexity of bilingual interaction, nevertheless a model like this is useful in a number of ways. First, it forces us to be very clear about which domains and varieties are relevant to language choice. The model summarises what we know about the patterns of language use in the community. It is not an account of the choices a person *must* make or of the process they go through in selecting a code. It is simply a description of the community's norms which can be altered or added to if we discover more information. It would be possible, for instance, to add other domains after 'school', for instance, such as 'the pub' or 'the law court'.

A second reason why an explicit model is useful is that it provides a clear basis for comparing patterns of code choice in different speech communities. Models make it easy to compare the varieties appropriate in similar domains in different speech communities. And a model is also useful to a newcomer in a community as a summary of the appropriate patterns of code use in the community. A model describes which code or codes are usually selected for use in different situations. A model for Sauris,

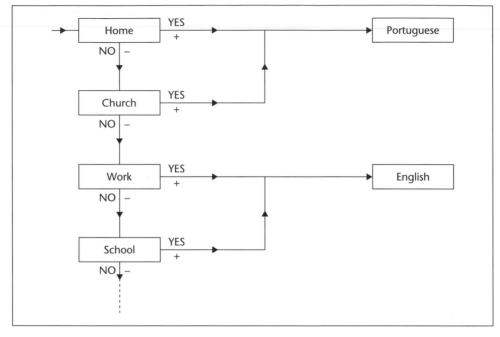

Figure 2.1 Appropriate code choice in different domains among the Portuguese community in London

the Italian mountain community described in example 7 in chapter 1, would show that Friulian is normally used to order a beer in the local bar. And in Bukavu, if you want to be able to buy vegetables in the local market-place at a reasonable price, a model would inform you that you need to know how to use Kingwana.

Exercise 3(a)

Consider example 2 above. What does it suggest about the limitations of a domain-based approach to language choice?

Answer at end of chapter

Example 5

Oi Lin Tan, a 20-year-old Chinese Singaporean, uses three languages regularly. At home she uses Cantonese to her mother and to her grandfather who lives with them. With her friends she generally uses Singapore English. She learned to understand Hokkien, another Chinese language, in the smaller shops and market-place but in large department stores she again uses Singapore English. At primary school she was taught for just over half the time in Mandarin Chinese, and so she often watches Channel 8, the Mandarin television station, and she regularly reads a Chinese newspaper *Liánhé Zǎobào*, which is written in Mandarin Chinese. During the other part of the time at primary school she was taught in a formal variety of Singapore English. This is the code she uses when she has to deal with government officials, or when she applies for an office job during the university holidays. She went to an English-medium secondary school and she is now studying geography and economics at an English-medium university. Her textbooks are all in English.

Exercise 3(b)

Although Oi Lin Tan uses Cantonese to her mother, she uses Singapore English to her sisters. On the other hand, she uses Cantonese at the market to elderly Cantonese vegetable sellers. What factors might account for these code choices?

Answer at end of chapter

Other social factors affecting code choice

Though I have used domains as useful summaries of relevant social factors in the model provided above, it is often necessary to examine more specific social factors if a model is to be a useful description of code choices in a community. The components of a domain do not always fit with each other. They are not always 'congruent'. In other words, within any domain, individual interactions may not be 'typical' in the sense in which 'typical' is used in the domain concept. They may, nevertheless, be perfectly normal, and occur regularly. This is illustrated by Oi Lin Tan's use of Singapore English to her sisters as described in example 5. People may select a particular variety or code because it makes it easier to discuss a particular topic, regardless of where they are speaking. At home, people often discuss work or school, for instance, using the language associated with those domains, rather than the language of the family domain. Some describe this as 'leakage', suggesting it is in some way irregular – the code associated with one domain is 'leaking' into another. In fact it is quite normal and very common. Particular topics may regularly be discussed in one code rather than another, regardless of the setting or addressee.

The dimensions introduced in chapter 1 illustrate this point nicely. Any or all of them may be relevant in accounting for the choice of variety or code in a particular situation. When both participants share more than one variety, then other factors will contribute to the appropriate choice. The **social distance** dimension is relevant, for instance. How well do they know each other, i.e. what is the social distance between the participants? Are they strangers, friends, brothers? Kalala, for example, would use a different code to each.

The **status** relationship between people may be relevant in selecting the appropriate code. A high-status official in Bukavu will be addressed in standard Swahili in many contexts. In Singapore, English is the most frequently selected code for official trans-actions, regardless of the speaker's ethnicity. Social role may also be important and is often a factor contributing to status differences between people. Typical role relationships are teacher–pupil, doctor–patient, soldier–civilian, priest–parishioner, official–citizen. The first-named role is often the more statusful. You can no doubt think of many more examples of role pairs like these. The same person may be spoken to in a different code depending on whether they are acting as a teacher, as a father or as a customer in the market-place. In Bukavu for instance, Mr Mukala, a teacher, insists on standard Swahili from his pupils, his wife uses Kongo, their tribal language, to talk to him, while in the market-place he is addressed in Kingwana, the local variety of Swahili.

Features of the setting and the dimension of **formality** may also be important in select-ing an appropriate variety or code. In church, at a formal ceremony, the appropriate variety will be different from that used afterwards in the church porch. The variety used for a formal radio lecture will differ from that used for the adverts. In Paraguay whether the interaction takes place in a rural as opposed to an urban setting is crucial to appropriate language choice. Other relevant factors relate to the social dimensions of formality and status: Spanish is the appropriate language for formal interactions.

Another important factor is the **function** or goal of the interaction. What is the lan-guage being used for? Is the speaker asking a favour or giving orders to someone? When Kalala applies for an office job he uses his 'best' standard written Swahili on the applica-tion form, and his most formal style of standard Swahili at the interview. When he abuses his younger brother he uses Indoubil, the code in which his vocabulary of 'insult' is most extensive. The function is exclusively affective, and Kalala transmits his feelings effectively, despite the fact that his brother doesn't understand much Indoubil yet.

So in describing the patterns of code use of particular communities, the relevant social factors may not fit neatly into institutionalised domains. As we have seen, more specific social factors often need to be included, and a range of social dimensions may need to be considered too. The aim of any description is to represent the language patterns of the community accurately. If the model does not do that, it needs to be modified. The only limitation is one of usefulness. If a model gets too complicated and includes too many specific points, it loses its value as a method of capturing generalisations.

Exercise 4

Using the information provided in example 1, draw a diagram like that in figure 2.1 summarising the factors relevant to code choice for Kalala in Bukavu.

Answer at end of chapter

Models can usefully go beyond the social factors summarised in the domain concept to take account of social dimensions such as social distance (stranger vs friend), relative status or role (doctor–patient), degrees of formality and the function or goal of the interaction (getting a bargain). Nevertheless, because they are concerned to capture broad generalisations, there are obvious limits to the usefulness of such models in describing the complexities of language choice. Interactions where people switch between codes within a domain cannot always be captured even by diagrams which consider the relevance of topic or social dimensions such as formality and social distance. This kind of linguistic behaviour is better described by a more detailed analysis of particular interactions. This point will be developed further in the section on code-switching and mixing below.

Before considering code-switching, however, it is useful to relate the patterns described so far to the important sociolinguistic concept of *diglossia*.

DIGLOSSIA

A linguistic division of labour

Example 6

In Eggenwil, a town in the Aargau canton of Switzerland, Silvia, a bank-teller, knows two very distinct varieties of German. One is the local Swiss German dialect of her canton which she uses in her everyday interactions. The other is standard German which she learnt at school, and though she understands it very well indeed, she rarely uses it in speech. Newspapers are written in standard German, and when she occasionally goes to hear a lecture at the university it may be in standard German. The national TV news is broadcast in standard German, but weather broadcasts now use dialect. The sermons her mother listens to in church are generally in standard German too, though more radical clerics use Swiss German dialect. The novels Silvia reads also use standard German.

The pattern of code or variety choice in Eggenwil is one which has been described with the term *diglossia*. This term has been used both in a narrow sense and in a much broader sense and I will describe both. In the narrow and original sense of the term, diglossia has three crucial features:

1. Two distinct varieties of the same language are used in the community, with one regarded as a high (or H) variety and the other a low (or L) variety.
2. Each variety is used for quite distinct functions; H and L complement each other.
3. No one uses the H variety in everyday conversation.

The situation in Eggenwil fits these three criteria for narrow or 'classic' diglossia perfectly. There are a number of other communities which fit this narrow definition too. Arabic-speaking countries use classical Arabic as their H variety and regional colloquial varieties as L varieties. In Greece there still exists an H variety Katharévousa, alongside an L variety, Dhimotiki, which is steadily displacing it (as described below).

Multilingual speech communities

A

In Europe in the Middle Ages, Latin was the H variety alongside daughter languages, such as Italian, French and Spanish, which had developed from its more colloquial form. These communities all satisfy the three criteria.

In these communities while the two varieties are (or were) linguistically related, the relationship is closer in some cases than others. The degree of difference in the pronunciation of H and L varies from place to place, for example. The sounds of Swiss German are quite different from those of standard German, while Greek Katharévousa is much closer to Dhimotiki in its pronunciation. The grammar of the two linguistically related varieties differs too. Often the grammar of H is morphologically more complicated. So standard German, for instance, uses more case markers on nouns and tense inflections on verbs than Swiss German; and standard French, the H variety in Haiti, uses more markers of number and gender on nouns than Haitian Creole, the L variety.

Most of the vocabulary of H and L is the same. But, not surprisingly since it is used in more formal domains, the H vocabulary includes many more formal and technical terms such as *conservation* and *psychometric*, while the L variety has words for everyday objects such as *saucepan* and *shoe*. There are also some interesting paired items for frequently referred to concepts. Where standard German uses *Kartoffel* for 'potato', and *Dachboden* for 'attic', Swiss German uses *Härdopfel* and *Estrich*. Where Katharévousa uses *ikías* for 'house', Dhimotiki uses *spiti*.

We have some choices in English which give the flavour of these differences. Choosing between words like *perused* and *read*, or *affluent* and *rich*, for instance, or between expressions such as *having finally despatched the missive* and *when I had posted the letter at last* captures the kind of differences involved. But while either would be perfectly possible in written or spoken English, in most diglossia situations the H form would not occur in everyday conversation, and the L form would generally seem odd in writing.

Exercise 5

Fill in the following table on the basis of your predictions about when H will be used and when L will be used in diglossic communities.

	H(igh) Variety	L(ow) Variety
Religion (sermon, prayers)		
Literature (novels, non-fiction)		
Newspaper (editorial)		
Broadcasting: TV news		
Education (written material, lectures)		
Education (lesson discussion)		
Broadcasting: radio		
Shopping		
Gossiping		

Answer at end of chapter

No one uses H for everyday interaction. In Arabic-speaking countries, for instance, classical Arabic is revered as the language of the Koran. It is taught in school and used for very formal interactions and in writing. But for most everyday conversations in Arabic-speaking countries people use the everyday colloquial variety. A friend of mine went to Morocco having learned classical Arabic at university in England. When he arrived and used his classical variety some people were very impressed. People generally respect and admire those who have mastered classical Arabic. But most of them couldn't understand what he was saying. His colleagues warned him that he would be laughed at or regarded as sacrilegious if he went about trying to buy food in classical Arabic. It would be a bit like asking for steaks at the butcher's using Shakespearian English.

■ Attitudes to H vs L in a diglossia situation

> ### Example 7
> A century and a half ago a Swiss traveller in Haiti expressed his annoyance at the fond complacency with which the white creoles regarded their patois. He was sharply answered by a creole, who declared: 'There are a thousand things one dares not say in French, a thousand voluptuous images which one can hardly render successfully, which the Créole expresses or renders with infinite grace.'

Haiti has been described as another diglossic situation by some linguists, with French as the H variety and Haitian Creole as the L variety. As the quotation in example 7 suggests, attitudes towards the two codes in a diglossia situation are complicated. People generally admire the H variety even when they can't understand it. Attitudes to it are usually very respectful. It has prestige in the sense of high status. These attitudes are reinforced by the fact that the H variety is the one which is described and 'fixed', or standardised, in grammar books and dictionaries. People generally do not think of the L variety as worth describing. However, attitudes to the L variety are varied and often ambivalent. In many parts of Switzerland, people are quite comfortable with their L variety and use it all the time – even to strangers. In other countries where the H variety is a language used in another country as a normal means of communication, and the L variety is used only locally, people may rate the L variety very low indeed. In Haiti, although both French and the Creole were declared national languages in the 1983 constitution, many people still regard French, the H variety, as the only real language of the country. They ignore the existence of Haitian Creole, which in fact everyone uses at home and with friends for all their everyday interactions. On the other hand the quotation in example 7 suggests that even here the L variety is highly valued by some speakers. So while its very existence is denied by some, others may regard the L variety as the best way of expressing their real feelings.

A

Multilingual speech communities

Exercise 6

(a) Using the information provided above, summarise what you now know about the differences between H and L in diglossic communities.

   (i) How are they linguistically related? Are they distinct languages or varieties of the same language?

   (ii) How are they used in the community?

   (iii) Which is used for conversation with family and friends?

   (iv) How is each variety learned?

   (v) Which has most prestige?

   (vi) Which is codified in grammar books and dictionaries?

   (vii) In which variety is literature usually written?

(b) Judged by these seven features would you say that Hemnesberget described in example 6 in chapter 1 qualified as a diglossic community? Why (not)?

Answers at end of chapter

Diglossia with and without bilingualism

Diglossia is a characteristic of speech communities rather than individuals. Individuals may be bilingual. Societies or communities are diglossic. In other words, the term diglossia describes societal or institutionalised bilingualism, where two varieties are required to cover all the community's domains. There are some diglossic communities where there is very limited individual bilingualism; e.g. in Haiti more than 90 per cent of the population is monolingual in Haitian Creole. Consequently they cannot actively contribute in more formal domains.

Table 2.4 is one way of considering the range of potential relationships between diglossia and bilingualism. It is an idealised model but it usefully identifies the extreme positions that are possible. If we restrict the terms diglossia and bilingualism to refer to different languages (rather than dialects or styles), then no. 1 refers to a situation where the society is diglossic, two languages are required to cover the full range of domains, and (most) individuals are bilingual. Those communities in Vanuatu where individuals speak the local village language (e.g. Erromangan, Aulua), as well as Bislama, the lingua franca of Vanuatu, would illustrate this box. No. 2 describes situations where individuals

Table 2.4 Relationship between diglossia and bilingualism

		DIGLOSSIA	
		+	−
BILINGUALISM	+	1. Both diglossia and bilingualism	2. Bilingualism without diglossia
	−	3. Diglossia without bilingualism	4. Neither diglossia nor bilingualism

Source: Fishman (2003: 360). Reproduced with permission

are bilingual, but there is no community-wide functional differentiation in the use of their languages. Many English-speaking countries fit this description. Individuals may be bilingual in Australia, the United States of America, England, and New Zealand, but their two languages are not used by the whole community in different domains.

No. 3 describes the situation of politically united groups where two languages are used for different functions, but by largely different speech communities. This is true for Haiti, since most people are monolingual in Haitian Creole. This situation tends to characterise colonised countries with a clear-cut social class division: i.e. the elite speak one language and the lower classes use another: e.g. the French speaking elite in nineteenth-century Russia and eleventh-century Norman England. There will, of course, always be some bilingual individuals who act as go-betweens, but the overall pattern is one of diglossia without bilingualism. No. 4 describes the situation of monolingual groups, and Fishman suggests this is typical of isolated ethnic communities where there is little contact with other linguistic groups. Iceland, especially before the twentieth century, serves as an example of such a community, but there are also communities like this in places such as Papua New Guinea and the Amazon basin.

The criteria which identify diglossic communities were initially interpreted very stringently, so that few communities qualified as diglossic. Soon, however, it became clear that some sociolinguists felt that the term could usefully be extended.

Extending the scope of 'diglossia'

As table 2.4 suggests, the way H and L varieties of German function in places like Eggenwil is very similar to the ways in which distinct languages operate in other communities, such as Sauris in the Italian Alps. Each code or language is used in different situations from the other. In earlier decades in Paraguay, the domains where Guaraní was used were quite distinct from those where Spanish was appropriate. Because of this similarity it was suggested that bilingual communities like Sauris and Paraguay should also be considered as examples of diglossia. 'Diglossia' is here being used in a broader sense which gives most weight to feature or criterion (ii) – the complementary functions of two varieties or codes in a community. Features (i) and (iii) are dispensed with and the term diglossia is generalised to cover any situation where two languages are used for different functions in a speech community, especially where one language is used for H functions and the other for L functions. There is a division of labour between the languages.

Other features of the 'classic' diglossia situations are also often relevant, but they are not regarded as crucial to the definition. So the H variety is generally the prestige variety, but people may also be attached to and admire the L variety, as in Paraguay where people are typically proud of Guaraní. L is learned at home and the H variety in school, but some people may use H in the home too, as in Sauris where parents used Italian to children in order to prepare them for school. Literature is generally written in H rather than L, but there may be a rich oral literature in L. Though H has generally been standardised and codified in grammar books and dictionaries for centuries, L languages are also increasingly being codified and standardised.

A

Multilingual speech communities

Exercise 7

(a) Fill in the following table using the description of twentieth-century Paraguayan patterns of language use outlined in example 3 and table 2.3 above as a basis for predicting which language is likely to be the main one associated with different domains.

	Spanish	Guaraní
Religion		
Literature		
Schooling		
Broadcasting		
Shopping		
Gossiping		

(b) Does twentieth-century Paraguay qualify as a diglossic society if criterion (ii) is regarded as the only important one?

Answers at end of chapter

Polyglossia

Diglossic situations involve two contrasting varieties, H and L. Sometimes, however, a more sophisticated concept is needed to describe the functional distribution of different varieties in a community. People like Kalala in Bukavu, for instance, use many different codes for different purposes. The term polyglossia has been used for situations like this where a community regularly uses more than two languages. Kalala's linguistic repertoire described in table 2.1 provides a nice example of polyglossic relationships.

Oi Lin Tan's Cantonese-speaking community in Singapore, described in example 5, can similarly be described as polyglossic, but the relationships between the various codes or varieties are not at all straightforward. Table 2.5 represents one way of describing them.

Both Mandarin and formal Singapore English can be considered H varieties alongside different L varieties. Mandarin functions as an H variety in relation to at least two L varieties, Hokkien and Cantonese. Informal Singapore English is an L variety alongside the more formal H variety. So for this speech community there are two H varieties and a number of L varieties in a complex relationship.

Polyglossia is thus a useful term for describing situations where more than two distinct codes or varieties are used for clearly distinct purposes or in clearly distinguishable situations.

Table 2.5 Polyglossia in Singapore

H		Mandarin		Singapore English formal variety
L	Cantonese		Hokkien	Singapore English informal variety

Changes in a diglossia situation

Diglossia has been described as a stable situation. It is possible for two varieties to continue to exist side by side for centuries, as they have in Arabic-speaking countries and in Haiti for example. Alternatively one variety may gradually displace the other. Latin was ousted from its position as the H language in Europe, for example, as the L varieties gradually expanded or leaked up into more formal domains. England was diglossic (in the broad sense) after 1066 when the Normans were in control. French was the language of the court, administration, the legal system, and high society in general. English was the language of the peasants in the fields and the streets. The following words provide a nice illustration of this relationship:

English	French		English
ox	boeuf	→	beef
sheep	mouton	→	mutton
calf	veau	→	veal
pig	porc	→	pork

The English *calf* becomes French *veau* as it moves from the farm to the dinner table. However, by the end of the fourteenth century English had displaced French (while absorbing huge numbers of French words such as *beef*, *mutton*, *veal* and *pork*) so there were no longer domains in which French was the appropriate language to use.

In Greece the relationship between Dhimotiki (L) and Katharévousa (H) has changed in the twentieth century. At the turn of the century the relative roles of the two varieties were still quite distinct. Katharévousa was regarded very highly and was the appropriate variety for serious speeches or writing. Dhimotiki was used for informal conversation. There was a language riot in Athens in 1901 when the New Testament was published in Dhimotiki. Many people felt it was totally unsuited for such a serious purpose. More recently, however, the choice of Katharévousa or Dhimotiki has taken on political significance. Katharévousa was the only official language of Greece during the period from 1967 to 1974 when the right-wing military government was in power. Since then the Athenian variety of Dhimotiki, labelled 'the people's language', has been adopted as the official standard language by the democratic government. As mentioned above, attitudes to the H variety in a typical diglossia situation are usually respectful and admiring. The following quotation indicates that things in Greece have changed. Katharévousa was denounced in the 1980s by a student leader as 'the old-fashioned medium of an educated elite . . . archaic and tediously demanding', with 'freakish diction . . . antiquated rhetorical devices and . . . insufferable verbosity'. By the 1990s Katharévousa was no longer used in schools or even in school textbooks. It seems likely that in the twenty-first century it will disappear from all but the most conservative written contexts.

Finally, it is worth considering whether the term diglossia or perhaps polyglossia should be used to describe complementary code use in *all* communities. In all speech communities people use different varieties or codes in formal contexts, such as religious

A

Multilingual speech communities

DENNIS THE MENACE

"GINA IS *BY LINGAL*... THAT MEANS SHE CAN SAY THE SAME THING *TWICE*, BUT YOU CAN ONLY UNDERSTAND IT *ONCE*."

Source: DENNIS THE MENACE ® used by permission of Hank Ketcham Enterprises and © North America Syndicate

and legal ceremonies, as opposed to relaxed casual situations. In multilingual situations the codes selected are generally distinct languages, e.g. French or Swahili for formal situations vs a vernacular tribal language such as Shi for casual interactions in Zaire. In predominantly monolingual speech communities, such as those of many English-speaking people in Britain or New Zealand, the contrasting codes are different styles of one language. As we shall see in later chapters, there are clearly identifiable linguistic differences between the more formal and the more colloquial styles of a language. But they are often a matter of degree. Nevertheless, there is a sense in which the variety at the formal end of the scale could be regarded as an H variety, while the most casual variety could be labelled L. Adopting this approach, the colloquial Maori used to talk to friends and family and in local shops in Maori townships in the early twentieth century could be described as the L variety. In addition, these communities made use of two H varieties. They used a formal variety of Maori for ceremonial purposes and for formal interaction on the marae (the formal meeting area). English was the other H variety. It was the language of the school, the government, the courts and for all official transactions with the Pakeha (non-Maori New Zealanders). So, if we expand the concept of diglossia to encompass different contextual varieties as well as distinct languages, the situation in these townships could also be described as polyglossic rather than diglossic.

CODE-SWITCHING OR CODE-MIXING

Participants, solidarity and status

A

Multilingual speech communities

Example 8

[*The Maori is in italics.* THE TRANSLATION IS IN SMALL CAPITALS]

Sarah: I think everyone's here except Mere.

John: She said she might be a bit late but actually I think that's her arriving now.

Sarah: You're right. *Kia ora Mere. Haere mai. Kei te pehea koe?*
                [HI MERE.   COME IN.   HOW ARE YOU?]

Mere: *Kia ora e hoa. Kei te pai.* Have you started yet?
            [HELLO MY FRIEND. I'M FINE]

People sometimes switch code within a domain or social situation. When there is some obvious change in the situation, such as the arrival of a new person, it is easy to explain the switch. In example 8, Mere is Maori and although the rest of the meeting will be conducted in English, Sarah switches to Maori to greet her. The Maori greeting is an expression of solidarity. So a code-switch may be related to a particular participant or addressee. In a Polish family living in Lancashire in the 1950s the family used Polish in the home. When the local English-speaking priest called, however, everyone switched to English. In both of these cases the switch reflects a change in the social situation and takes positive account of the presence of a new participant.

A speaker may similarly switch to another language as a signal of group membership and shared ethnicity with an addressee. Even speakers who are not very proficient in a second language may use brief phrases and words for this purpose. Scottish Highlanders who are not proficient speakers of Gaelic nevertheless express their identification with the local Gaelic speech community by using Gaelic tags and phrases interspersed with their English. Maori people often use Maori words and phrases in this way too, whether their knowledge of Maori is extensive or not. Such switches are often very short and they are made primarily for social reasons – to signal the speaker's ethnic identity and solidarity with the addressee. Here are some examples.

Example 9

(a) Tamati: *Engari* [so] now we turn to more important matters.
(Switch between Maori and English)

(b) Ming: Confiscated by Customs, dà gài [PROBABLY]
(Switch between English and Mandarin Chinese)

(c) A: Well I'm glad I met you. OK?

M: ándale pues [OK SWELL], and do come again. Mm?
(Switch between Spanish and English)

In (a), Tamati uses a Maori tag at the beginning of his utterance while the Mandarin speaker in (b) uses a final tag. This kind of switching is sometimes called emblematic switching or tag switching. The switch is simply an interjection or a linguistic tag in the other language which serves as an ethnic identity marker. The exchange in (c), for instance, occurred between two Mexican Americans or Chicanos in the United States. By using the Spanish tag, M signalled to A that she recognised the relevance of their shared ethnic background to their future relationship. The tag served as a solidarity marker between two minority ethnic group members whose previous conversation has been entirely in English.

Switches motivated by the identity and relationship between participants often express a move along the solidarity/social distance dimension introduced in chapter 1. While example 9(c) illustrates a tag expressing solidarity, switches can also distance a speaker from those they are talking to. In Pamaka, a village in Suriname, young people switch between their local community language, Pamaka, and Sranan Tongo, the language of Suriname urban centres. Pamaka is the usual language of interaction in the community, but young people often switch to Sranan Tongo to signal their sophistication and identification with modernity. In one conversation, two young women and a young man are discussing local music. While the women use Pamaka, their community language, the young man deliberately switches to Sranan Tongo and avoids Pamaka. His language switch distances him from the other participants, while also signalling his alignment with the urban western world.

A switch may also reflect a change in the other dimensions mentioned in the first chapter, such as the status relations between people or the formality of their interaction. The examples above have illustrated that different kinds of relationships are often expressed through different codes. More formal relationships, which sometimes involve status differences too, such as doctor–patient or administrator–client, are often expressed in the H variety or code: e.g. Bokmål in Hemnesberget, Spanish in Paraguay, standard Zairean Swahili in Bukavu. Friendly relationships involving minimal social distance, such as neighbour or friend, are generally expressed in an L code: e.g. Ranamål in Hemnesberget, Guaraní in Paraguay, Kingwana or a tribal language such as Shi in Bukavu.

In the little village of Hemnesberget (described in example 6 in the first chapter) Bokmål or standard Norwegian is the variety to use when you go to the tax office to sort out your tax forms. But the person you will deal with may also be your neighbour. The conversation might look like this.

Example 10

[BOKMÅL IS IN SMALL CAPITALS. Ranamål in lower case.]

Jan: Hello Petter. How is your wife now?

Petter: Oh she's much better thank you Jan. She's out of hospital and convalescing well.

Jan: That's good I'm pleased to hear it. DO YOU THINK YOU COULD HELP ME WITH THIS PESKY FORM? I AM HAVING A GREAT DEAL OF DIFFICULTY WITH IT.

Petter: OF COURSE. GIVE IT HERE . . .

Nothing appears to change except the topic of discussion and with it the code. In fact the change of topic here symbolises a change in the relationship between the men. They switch from their roles as neighbours to their roles as bureaucrat and member of the public. In other words they switch from a personal interaction to a more formal transaction. This kind of role switch is commonly associated with a code switch in multilingual communities. Exactly the same kind of switching occurs in Belgium when a government clerk deals with a query from someone she went to school with. They switch from a local variety of Flemish to French when they turn from exchanging stories about what has happened to their schoolmates to sorting out their business. And in shops in bilingual communities, salespeople often switch to the language of their customers. In Strasbourg, for instance, a city in Eastern France, where French is the official language and Alsatian (a Germanic dialect) is the local variety which marks Alsatian identity, salespeople switch between the two varieties according to the preferred language of the shoppers they are serving.

Exercise 8

When people switch from one code to another for reasons which can be identified, it is sometimes called *situational switching*. If we knew the relevant situational or social factors in advance in such cases, we could predict the switches. Which code would you predict the speaker will switch from and which code will they switch to in the following situations and why?

A

Multilingual speech communities

(a) A Hemnesberget resident chatting to a friend in the queue at the community administration office gets to the counter and speaks to the clerk.
(b) Three students from the Chinese province of Guangdong are sharing a flat together in London. They are discussing the ingredients of the stir-fry vegetable dish they are cooking. One of them starts to discuss the chemical composition of the different ingredients.

Answers at end of chapter

▨ Topic

Example 10 illustrated that people may switch code within a speech event to discuss a particular topic. Bilinguals often find it easier to discuss particular topics in one code rather than another. In Hemnesberget, Bokmål is the more appropriate variety for discussing a business matter. Topic relates to the function dimension introduced in chapter 1. For many bilinguals certain kinds of referential content are more appropriately or more easily expressed in one language than the other. Japanese war brides in America, for instance, found it easier to use Japanese for topics they associated with Japan such as 'fish' and 'New Year's Day'. Chinese students sharing a flat in English-speaking countries tend to use Cantonese with each other, except to discuss their studies when they switch to English. This is partly because they have learned the vocabulary of economics or linguistics or physics in English, so they do not always know the words for 'capital formation' or 'morpheme' or 'electron' in Cantonese. But it goes further than simply borrowing words from English. They often switch to English for considerable stretches of speech. The technical topics are firmly associated with a particular code and the topic itself can trigger a switch to the appropriate code.

Another example of a referentially oriented code switch is when a speaker switches code to quote a person.

Example 11

[*The Maori is in italics.* THE TRANSLATION IS IN SMALL CAPITALS]
A Maori person is recalling the visit of a respected elder to a nearby town.

'That's what he said in Blenheim. *Ki a mātou Ngāti Porou, te Māoritanga i papi ake i te whenua.* [WE OF THE NGĀTI POROU TRIBE BELIEVE THE ORIGINS OF MĀORITANGA ARE IN THE EARTH.] And those Blenheim people listened carefully to him too.'

The switch involves just the words that the speaker is claiming the quoted person said. So the switch acts like a set of quotation marks. The speaker gives the impression – which may or may not be accurate – that these are the exact words the speaker used.

A related reason for switching is to quote a proverb or a well-known saying in another language, as illustrated in the following example.

Example 12

[*The Mandarin Chinese is in italics.* THE TRANSLATION IS IN SMALL CAPITALS]
A group of Chinese students are discussing Chinese customs.

Li: People here get divorced too easily. Like exchanging faulty goods. In China it's not the same. *Jià goǔ súi goǔ, jià jī súi jī.* [IF YOU HAVE MARRIED A DOG, YOU FOLLOW A DOG, IF YOU'VE MARRIED A CHICKEN, YOU FOLLOW A CHICKEN.]

The code switch corresponds exactly to the proverb being recited from Chinese. The similarity of quotation and proverb recitation is very clear. Both are referentially motivated switches in that the speaker wishes to be accurate – the exact words are important. But switches often serve several functions at once. In these examples the switches not only emphasise the precise message content, they also signal ethnic identity. In other words they have an affective as well as a referential function.

Switching for affective functions

The use of Jamaican Creole or Patois alongside standard English by those who belong to the Afro-Caribbean or West Indian Black communities in Britain follows similar patterns to those described above for a range of multilingual and bilingual communities. At school, for instance, Black British children use Patois to their friends and standard English to their teachers.

Example 13

Polly is a young British Black woman. She speaks standard English with a West Midlands accent, as well as Patois, a variety of Jamaican Creole. On one occasion a schoolteacher annoyed her intensely by criticising a story she had written about British West Indians. In particular, he corrected the use of Patois by one of her characters – something he knew nothing about. Her response was to abuse him in Patois, swearing at him only just below her breath. The effect was electrifying. He was terrified. He threatened to send her to the headmaster but in fact he didn't, and she noted with satisfaction that he left her alone after that.

Polly's switch to Patois was here used to express affective rather than referential meaning. The teacher didn't need to understand the words – he simply needed to get the affective message. In other contexts too switching between Patois and standard English can achieve

A

Multilingual speech communities

a range of interesting rhetorical effects. Just as the use of ethnic tags signalled ethnic group membership for speakers in the utterances in example 9, a switch from Patois to standard English with the local British regional pronunciation can signal a person's identity as a West Midlander in a conversation where local regional values are relevant. In an argument with a West Indian from another area over the best soccer team, for instance, the use of the localised English accent can serve just this kind of function.

Example 14 demonstrates not only Polly's code-switching ability – it also illustrates her rhetorical skills.

Example 14

[Patois is written in italics]
With Melanie right you have to say she speaks *tri different sort of language when she wants to. Cos she speak half Patois, half English and when im ready im will come out wid,* 'I day and I bay and I ay this and I ay that. I day have it and I day know where it is' . . . And then she goes *'Lord God, I so hot'.* Now she'll be sitting there right and she'll go. 'It's hot isn't it?', you know, and you think which one is she going to grow up speaking?

This is not simply code-switching for the purposes of accurate quotation. The Patois is being used here for amusement and dramatic effect. Melanie is being parodied and sent up. Polly is again using her ability in the two codes for affective purposes.

Many bilinguals and multilinguals are adept at exploiting the rhetorical possibilities of their linguistic repertoires. Standard Norwegian is the language of the school, for instance, but while they are in class children may make rude remarks or jokes about the teacher in their local dialect. In Paraguay too, Guaraní, the L variety, is considered more appropriate for joking and humorous anecdotes. So while discussing a serious political issue in Spanish a Paraguayan might switch to Guaraní with a humorous example or a witty aside. Fijian people switch from Fijian to Hindi for joking, and because Hindi is not normally used for communication between Fijians, just the switch itself is often considered to be amusing.

A language switch in the opposite direction, from the L to the H variety, is often used to express disapproval. So a person may code switch because they are angry.

Example 15

[The German is in italics. THE TRANSLATION IS IN SMALL CAPITALS*]*
In the town of Oberwart two little Hungarian-speaking children were playing in the woodshed and knocked over a carefully stacked pile of firewood. Their grandfather walked in and said in Hungarian, the language he usually used to them:
  'Szo! ide dzüni! jeszt jerámunyi mind e kettüötök, no hát akkor!'

[WELL COME HERE! PUT ALL THIS AWAY, BOTH OF YOU, WELL NOW.]
When they did not respond quickly enough he switched to (dialectal) German:
'*Kum her!*'
[COME HERE!]

Exactly the same content is expressed first in Hungarian and then in German. The children in fact know only Hungarian so the reason for the switch is clearly not to convey referential content. In Oberwart, German is the language of the school and officialdom. So in families where Hungarian is the usual language of the home, a switch to German is significant. In these homes Hungarian expresses friendship and solidarity, and a switch to German puts the addressee at a distance. German symbolises authority, and so by using German the grandfather emphasises his anger and disapproval of the children's behaviour.

Example 16 illustrates a similar code switch between two different styles of English. Its purpose is similarly to reprimand a child and the switch involves a move from an intimate and friendly style to a formal style which distances the speaker from the addressee.

Example 16

Father: Tea's ready Robbie.
          (*Robbie ignores him and carries on skate-boarding.*)
Father: Mr Robert Harris if you do not come in immediately there will be consequences which you will regret.

Exercise 9

Identify the linguistic features in example 16 which signal that Robbie's father has switched code between his first and second utterance.

Answer at end of chapter

Metaphorical switching

Example 17

At a village meeting among the Buang people in Papua New Guinea, Mr Rupa, the main village entrepreneur and 'bigman', is trying to persuade people who have put money into a village store to leave it there. This is a section from his skilful speech.

▶

A

Multilingual speech communities

[*Tok Pisin is in italics.* Buang is not italicised.]

Ikamap travel o wonem, mi ken stretim olgeta toktok. Orait. Pasin ke ken be, *meni* ti ken nyep la, su lok lam *memba* re, olo ba *miting autim olgeta tok* . . . *moni* ti ken nyep ega, rek mu su rek ogoko nam be, one *moni* rek, . . . *moni* ti ken *bak stua* lam vu Mambump re, m nzom agon. *Orait, bihain, bihainim bilong wok long bisnis, orait, moni bilong stua bai ibekim olgeta ples.*

English Translation

If any problem comes up, I will be able to settle all the arguments. OK. This is the way – the money that is there can't go back to the shareholders, and the meeting brought up all these arguments . . . the money that's there you won't take back, your money will . . . this money from the bulk store will come back to Mambump, and we'll hold on to it. Now later, if we continue these business activities, then the store money will be repaid to everyone.

In many of the examples discussed so far the specific reason for a switch can be identified with reasonable confidence. Though it would not be possible to predict when a switch will occur without knowing what a speaker intended to say next, it is often possible to account for switches after they have occurred (i.e. post hoc). Example 17, however, moves switching into a different dimension. It is an example of what can be achieved by a really skilled bilingual. In this situation there are no obvious explanatory factors accounting for the specific switches between Buang and Tok Pisin. No new person joined the audience at any point. There was no change in the setting or in the topic – 'bisnis'. There are no quotations or even angry or humorous utterances. What is the social meaning of these rapid switches?

By switching between codes with such rapidity the village bigman effectively draws on the different associations of the two codes. Buang is the local tribal language. By using it Mr Rupa is emphasising his membership of the Buang community – he belongs here and everyone knows him. But he is also a skilled businessman with contacts in the outside world of money and marketing. Mr Rupa's use of Tok Pisin ('talk pidgin'), a creole which is a valuable lingua franca and an official language in Papua New Guinea, emphasises this role of entrepreneur, as well as his superior knowledge and experience as a man of the wider world. Buang symbolises high solidarity, equal status and friendly feelings. Tok Pisin represents social distance, status and the referential information of the business world. Mr Rupa is getting the best of both worlds. He is code-switching for rhetorical reasons, drawing on the associations of both codes. This type of switching has sometimes been called *metaphorical switching*. Each of the codes represents or symbolises a set of social meanings, and the speaker draws on the associations of each, just as people use metaphors to represent complex meanings. The term also reflects the fact that this kind of switching involves rhetorical skill. Skilful code-switching operates like metaphor to enrich the communication.

Example 18

[THE WORDS ORIGINALLY SPOKEN IN SAMOAN ARE IN SMALL CAPITALS.]

Alf is 55 and overweight. He is talking to a fellow Samoan at work about his attempt to go on a diet.

My doctor told me to go on a diet. She said I was overweight. So I tried. BUT IT WAS SO HARD. I'D KEEP THINKING ABOUT FOOD ALL THE TIME. Even when I was at work. And in bed at night I'D GET DESPERATE. I COULDN'T GET TO SLEEP. So I'd get up and RAID THE FRIDGE. THEN I'D FEEL GUILTY AND SICK AND WHEN I WOKE UP NEXT DAY I WOULD BE SO DEPRESSED because I had to start the diet all over again. The doctor wasn't sympathetic. She just shrugged and said 'well it's your funeral!'

In this example the speaker draws on his two languages to express his ambivalent feelings about the topic he is discussing. Though there is no exact and one-to-one correspondence, it is possible to see that in general personal feelings are expressed in Samoan while English provides some distance and objectivity about the topic. English is used for referential content such as 'My doctor told me to go on a diet', while Samoan expresses his shame and embarrassment ('I'd get desperate', 'I would be so depressed'). Similarly, in Swiss Germany, people in internet chat rooms switch between Swiss German dialects and Standard German to indicate their attitudes to chat messages. The switches serve as a subtle means of conveying their approval or disagreement or ambivalence about previous messages.

Some people call the kind of rapid switching illustrated in the last few examples 'code-mixing', but I prefer the term metaphorical switching. Code-mixing suggests the speaker is mixing up codes indiscriminately or perhaps because of incompetence, whereas the switches are very well motivated in relation to the symbolic or social meanings of the two codes. This kind of rapid switching is itself a specific sociolinguistic variety; it has been labelled a *fused lect*. It is a distinctive conversational style used among bilinguals and multilinguals – a rich additional linguistic resource available to them. By switching between two or more codes, the speakers convey affective meaning as well as information.

Lexical borrowing

It is obviously important to distinguish this kind of switching from switches which reflect lack of vocabulary in a language. When speaking a second language, for instance, people will often use a term from their mother tongue or first language because they don't know the appropriate word in their second language. These 'switches' are triggered by lack of vocabulary. People may also borrow words from another language to express a concept or describe an object for which there is no obvious word available in the language they are using. Borrowing of this kind generally involves single words – mainly nouns – and it is motivated by lexical need. It is very different from switching where speakers have a genuine choice about which words or phrases they will use in which language.

Borrowings often differ from code switches in form too. Borrowed words are usually adapted to the speaker's first language. They are pronounced and used grammatically as if they were part of the speaker's first language. New Zealand English has borrowed the word *mana* from Maori, for instance. There is no exact equivalent to its meaning in English, although it is sometimes translated as meaning 'prestige' or 'high status'. It is pronounced [ma:nə] by most New Zealanders.[1] The Maori pronunciation is quite different with a short *a* in both syllables. The word *Māori* is similarly adapted by most English speakers. They use an English diphthong [au] rather than a longer [a:o] sound, and they pluralise the word by adding the English plural inflection *s* and talk of the *Maoris*. In the Maori language the plural is not marked by an inflection on the noun. By contrast, people who are rapidly code-switching – as opposed to borrowing the odd word – tend to switch completely between two linguistic systems – sounds, grammar and vocabulary.

Exercise 10

Where possible insert in the appropriate column an example number from this chapter which illustrates the relevant reason for switching

Reasons for code-switching	Quote an example number from this chapter
Change in a feature of the domain or social situation	
Setting	_____
Participant features	
Addressee specification	_____
Ethnic identity marker	_____
Express solidarity	_____
Express social distance	_____
Assert social status	_____
Topic	_____
Quoting someone	_____
Proverb	_____
Aspect of the function or purpose of interaction	
Add emphasis	_____
Add authority	_____
Express feelings (vs describing facts)	_____
Can you add any further reasons for code-switching?	

Because there are several possible acceptable answers to this exercise I have not supplied any one answer. You may find it interesting to discuss your answers with fellow students.

Linguistic constraints

Sociolinguists who study the kind of rapid code-switching described in the previous section have been interested in identifying not only the functions or meaning of switches, and the stylistic motivations for switches, but also the points at which switches occur in utterances. Some believe there are very general rules for switching which apply to all switching behaviour regardless of the codes or varieties involved. They are searching for universal linguistic constraints on switching. It has been suggested for example that switches only occur within sentences (*intra-sentential switching*) at points where the grammars of both languages match each other. This is called 'the equivalence constraint'. So you may only switch between an adjective and a noun if both languages use the same order for that adjective and noun, as illustrated in example 19.

Example 19

English	French	Possible switch point?
red boat	bateau rouge	NO
big house	grande maison	YES: i.e. 'big maison' or 'grande house'

Another suggestion is that there is always a 'matrix language frame' (MLF) which imposes structural constraints on code-switched utterances. So, for example, system morphemes (such as tense and aspect inflections) will always come from the *matrix language*; and the order in which morphemes may occur in code-switched utterances will be determined by the MLF. The other language is called the *embedded language*. In example 20, the content words (the verb and the noun in capitals) are from English, the embedded language, but the system morphemes, the prefixes signalling negation, subject, person, number and gender, are from Swahili, the matrix language; and they occur in the order which is normal in Swahili.

Example 20

Leo si-ku-COME na-BOOK z-angu
'Today I didn't come with my books'

Other sociolinguists argue that it is unlikely that there are universal and absolute rules of this kind. It is more likely that these rules simply reflect the limited data which has been examined so far. They also criticise the extreme complexity of some of the rules, and point to the large numbers of exceptions. These sociolinguists argue for greater attention to social, stylistic and contextual factors. The points at which people switch codes are likely to vary according to many different factors such as which codes are involved, the functions of the particular switch, and the level of proficiency in each

A

Multilingual speech communities

45

code of the people switching. So, it is suggested, only very proficient bilinguals such as Mr Rupa will switch within sentences, intra-sententially, whereas people who are less proficient will tend to switch at sentence boundaries (*inter-sentential switching*), or use only short fixed phrases or tags in one language on the end of sentences in the other language, as illustrated in the utterances in example 9.

It is easy to see how these issues generate more questions. Is all code-switching rule-governed? How do social and linguistic factors interact? What kind of grammar or grammars are involved when people code-switch? When people switch rapidly from phrase to phrase for instance, are they switching between the two different grammars of the codes they are using, or do they develop a distinct code-switching grammar which has its own rules? There are still no generally accepted answers to these questions.

◼ Attitudes to code-switching

Example 21

(a) In Hemnesberget, two linguists recorded university students home on vacation. The students unconsciously switched between the local dialect and standard Norwegian according to the topic. When they later heard the tapes some were appalled and promised they would not switch in this way in the future.

(b) 'When I switch (inadvertently), I usually realise soon afterwards and correct myself, but it is still embarrassing.'

(c) 'Code switching is not very pure.'

(d) 'My attitude towards code-switching is a very relaxed one.'

People are often unaware of the fact that they code-switch. When their attention is drawn to this behaviour, however, most tend to apologise for it, condemn it and generally indicate disapproval of mixing languages. Among Mexican Americans the derogatory term *Tex Mex* is used to describe rapid code-switching between Spanish and English. In parts of French-speaking Canada *joual* is a similar put-down label for switching between French and English, and in Britain [tuṭi fuṭi] ('broken up') Panjabi refers to a style which switches between Panjabi and English. In Hemnesberget, the speech of young students who were switching between the local dialect and the standard was condemned as *knot* or 'artificial speech'. Reactions to code-switching styles are negative in many communities, despite the fact that proficiency in intra-sentential code-switching requires good control of both codes. This may reflect the attitudes of the majority monolingual group in places like North America and Britain. In places such as Papua New Guinea (PNG) and East Africa where multilingualism is the norm, attitudes to proficient code-switching are much more positive. The PNG bigman's status is undoubtedly enhanced by his ability to manipulate two or more codes proficiently. It seems possible that an increase in ethnic self-consciousness and confidence may alter attitudes among minority group members in other communities over time.

These issues will be discussed further in the next chapter. Attitudes to a minority language are very important in determining not only its use in a code-switching style, but also its very chances of survival.

ANSWERS TO EXERCISES IN CHAPTER 2

Answer to exercise 1 (i)

You need to consider a number of factors in assessing how well you know a language. Can you both understand and speak the language? Can you read and write it? And how well? Rate yourself on a scale of 1 to 5 for each skill: speaking, understanding, reading, writing.

Here is an example of a scale for speaking skills.

1. Complete fluency in a wide range of contexts.
2. Cope with most everyday conversations.
3. Cope with very simple conversation.
4. A few words and phrases such as simple greetings, thanks etc.
5. No knowledge.

Generally, the degree of linguistic skill we develop reflects our social experience with a language. If, for example, we use a language only in speaking to others in the market-place, the vocabulary and grammar we use will be restricted to such contexts. If we use a language only for reading the newspaper, we may not be able to speak it fluently.

Answers to exercise 1 (ii)

(a) Kalala would probably use informal Shi, especially if his parents were present. If his brother was close in age and they got on well they would be likely to use Indoubil to each other. If his brother was much younger he would not yet know much Indoubil.

(b) Indoubil, the language of peer-group friendship.

(c) This would depend on his assessment of what languages the stranger knew. He would probably use Kingwana if he guessed the person lived in Bukavu, but standard Swahili if he thought they came from out of town. However, his assessment of the stranger's social status, or the function of the interaction might also be relevant, as discussed in the next section.

Answer to exercise 3 (a)

The domain-based approach allows for only one choice of language per domain, namely the language used most of the time in that domain. Clearly more than one language may occur in any domain. Different people may use different languages in the same domain. We will see below that for a variety of reasons (such as who they are talking to) the same person may also use different languages in the same domain.

Answer to exercise 3 (b)

Oi Lin's choices illustrate further factors which may influence code choice. The particular addressee may influence code choice within a domain. She uses Singapore English to her sisters and friends of the same age – it is the code commonly used by young people to each other, partly because they use it so much at school, partly because they feel positive about it. She uses Cantonese to elderly vegetable sellers, perhaps because she wants to emphasise their common ethnicity so they will feel well-disposed towards her and she may get a better bargain, perhaps also because she judges that Cantonese is the language they are most proficient in and she wants the exchange to be as comfortable as possible for them. A model which took account of these factors would be much more complicated than that illustrated above.

Answer to exercise 4

Figure 2.2 illustrates one way of representing language choice in Bukavu for Kalala. (Other arrangements of the relevant factors are also possible.)

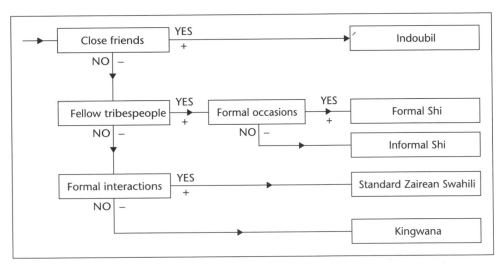

Figure 2.2 Model of appropriate code choice in Bukavu

Answer to exercise 5

	H(igh) variety	L(ow) variety
Religion (sermon, prayers)	H	
Literature (novels, non-fiction)	H	
Newspaper (editorial)	H	
Broadcasting: TV news	H	
Education (written material, lectures)	H	
Education (lesson discussion)		L
Broadcasting: radio		L
Shopping		L
Gossiping		L

Answers to exercise 6 (a)

(i)   They are different varieties of the same language.

(ii) They are used in mutually exclusive situations. Where H is appropriate, L is not, and vice versa. H is used in more formal contexts and L in less formal contexts.

(iii) Only L is used for conversation with family and friends.

(iv) L is learned 'naturally' in the home. H is learned more formally – usually in school.

(v) This is a tricky question. In the usual sense of prestige – i.e. high status – the answer is H. However, people are often more attached to L emotionally. When people have this kind of fondness for a variety, the variety is sometimes described as having 'covert prestige' (see chapter 15).

(vi) H is generally codified in grammar books and dictionaries. More recently linguists have also begun to codify the L variety in some places such as Haiti.

(vii) Literature is usually written in H, but when the L variety begins to gain status people begin to use it to write in too.

Answer to exercise 6 (b)

The use of Ranamål and Bokmål by members of the Hemnesberget speech community, as described by Blom and Gumperz, qualifies as diglossic on all criteria. One apparent exception is the fact that people used Bokmål or standard Norwegian for everyday conversation to those from outside the village. To fellow villagers it would be considered snobbish, but it was normal to outsiders. This simply emphasises that the diglossic pattern characterises the Hemnesberget speech community as Blom and Gumperz described it, but does not necessarily extend outside it. Note, however, that in a 'classic' diglossic community, H would not generally be used comfortably for everyday conversation even to outsiders.

Answer to exercise 7 (a)

	Spanish	Guaraní
Religion	✓	
Literature	✓ (serious)	✓ (magazines)
Schooling	✓	
Broadcasting	✓	✓ (e.g. farming)
Shopping		✓
Gossiping		✓

Answer to exercise 7 (b)

Yes, on the whole. In some domains, as discussed above, choice of language depended on factors such as the particular topic or function of the interaction. In rural areas lack of proficiency in Spanish may (still) lead to the use of Guaraní in situations where Spanish would be appropriate in the town. Nevertheless, in general in the 1960s, people were still clear that one code rather than the other is most appropriate in particular interactions. In the twenty-first century, however, interactions in urban homes typically involve both languages.

Answers to exercise 8

(a) From Ranamål to Bokmål because Ranamål is the variety used for personal interactions while Bokmål is appropriate for official transactions.

(b) From their Chinese dialect, Cantonese, to English because the topic of Chinese food is appropriately discussed in Cantonese but the technical topic introduced is more easily discussed in English, the language in which they are studying.

A

Multilingual speech communities

Answer to exercise 9

The use of title and full name (*Mr Robert Harris*) rather than affectionate nickname (*Robbie*). The very full and formal construction with a subordinate clause (*if . . . immediately*) preceding the main clause. The use of a distancing construction (*there will be consequences which you will regret* rather than, say, the more familiar *you'll be sorry*). The use of relatively formal vocabulary (e.g. *consequences, immediately* rather than, say, *right now, regret* rather than *be sorry*).

■ Concepts introduced

Domain
Diglossia
H and L varieties
Bilingualism with and without diglossia
Polyglossia
Code-switching
Situational switching
Metaphorical switching
Code-mixing
Fused lect
Lexical borrowing
Intra-sentential code switching
Embedded and matrix language
Inter-sentential code switching

■ References

The basic concepts introduced in this chapter are discussed further in the following sources:

Ferguson (1959) reprinted in Giglioli (1972)
Fishman (1971, 1972, 2003)
Gumperz (1971, 1977)
Myers-Scotton (1993, 1997)
Platt (1977)
Poplack (1980)
Rampton (1995)

The following source provided material for this chapter:

'Aipolo and Holmes (1990) on Tongan in New Zealand
Auer (1999) introduces the term 'fused lect'
Blom and Gumperz (1972) on Hemnesberget, Norway
Browning (1982) on Greece
Choi (2005) on Paraguay in the twenty-first century
Dorian (1982) on Gaelic, Scottish Highlands
Ervin-Tripp (1968) on Japanese war-brides
Gal (1979) on Oberwart, Hungary

Gardner-Chloros (1997) on code-switching in Strasbourg stores
Goyvaerts (1988), and Goyvaerts et al. (1983) on Bukavu, Zaire
Gumperz (1977) on code-switching
Migge (2007) on Pamaka and Sranan Tongo in Suriname
Rubin (1968, 1985) on Paraguay
Santarita and Martin-Jones (1990) on Portuguese in London
Siebenhaar (2006) on Swiss-German internet chat
Siegel (1995) on Fijian-Hindi code-switching for humour
Valdman (1988) on Haiti

Quotations

Example 7 is from Reinecke (1964: 540).
Example 9 (3) is adapted from Gumperz (1977: 1).
Example 11 is from Smith (1971: 4).
Example 14 is from Edwards (1986: 90–1).
Example 15 is from Gal (1979: 112).
Example 17 is an excerpt from Sankoff (1972: 45–6) where a full analysis of the complete text from which this excerpt is taken is provided, demonstrating the complexities of analysing code-switching behaviour.
Example 20 is adapted from Myers-Scotton (1997: 80).
Example 21 (b) is a Kurdish–Arabic bilingual, example 21 (c) is a Hebrew–Arabic–English trilingual, and example 21 (d) is a French–English bilingual. All are quoted in Grosjean (1982: 148).
Quotation about current attitudes to Katharévousa is from Dimitropoulos (1983), cited in *Linguistic Minorities Project* (1985: 68).

Useful additional reading

Fasold (1984), Chs 1 and 2
Mesthrie et al. (2000), Ch. 4
Meyerhoff (2006), Ch. 6
Myers-Scotton (2006), Ch. 6
Romaine (2000), Ch. 2
Saville-Troike (2003), Ch. 3
Wardhaugh (2006), Ch. 4

Note

1. I have used the system for representing sounds (rather than letters) which is described in the Appendix. Linguists provide representations of the way people pronounce words, as opposed to their spellings, in square brackets. Individual sounds are also represented in square brackets, to distinguish them from letters.

A

Multilingual speech communities

3 Language maintenance and shift

There are many different social reasons for choosing a particular code or variety in a multilingual community, as chapter 2 illustrated. But what real choice is there for those who speak lesser-used languages in a community where the people in power use a world language such as English? How do economic and political factors influence language choices? The various constraints on language choice faced by different communities are explored in this chapter, as well as the potential longer-term effects of these choices – language shift or language death. In the final part of the chapter, attempts to reverse these consequences through language revival efforts are described.

LANGUAGE SHIFT IN DIFFERENT COMMUNITIES

Migrant minorities

Example 1

Maniben is a young British Hindu woman who lives in Coventry. Her family moved to Britain from Uganda in 1970, when she was 5 years old. She started work on the shop floor in a bicycle factory when she was 16. At home Maniben speaks Gujerati with her parents and grandparents. Although she had learned English at school, she found she didn't need much at work. Many of the girls working with her also spoke Gujerati, so when it wasn't too noisy they would talk to each other in their home language. Maniben was good at her job and she got promoted to floor supervisor. In that job she needed to use English more of the time, though she could still use some Gujerati with her old workmates. She went to evening classes and learned to type. Then, because she was interested, she went on to learn how to operate a word-processor. Now she works in the main office and she uses English all the time at work.

Maniben's pattern of language use at work has gradually shifted over a period of ten years. At one stage she used mainly Gujerati; now she uses English almost exclusively. Maniben's experience is typical for those who use a minority language in a predominantly mono-lingual culture and society. The order of domains in which language shift occurs may differ for different individuals and different groups, but gradually over time the language of the wider society displaces the minority language mother tongue. There are many different social factors which can lead a community to shift from using one language for most purposes to using a different language, or from using two distinct codes in differ-ent domains, to using different varieties of just one language for their communicative needs. Migrant families provide an obvious example of this process of language shift.

In countries like England, Australia, New Zealand and the United States, one of the first domains in which children of migrant families meet English is the school. They may have watched English TV programmes and heard English used in shops before starting school, but at school they are expected to interact in English. They have to use English because it is the only means of communicating with the teacher and other children. For many children of migrants, English soon becomes the normal language for talking to other children – including their brothers and sisters. Because her grandparents knew little English, Maniben continued to use mainly Gujerati at home, even though she had learned English at school and used it more and more at work. In many families, however, English gradually infiltrates the home through the children. Children discuss school and friends in English with each other, and gradually their parents begin to use English to them too, especially if they are working in jobs where they use English.

There is pressure from the wider society too. Immigrants who look and sound 'different' are often regarded as threatening by majority group members. There is pres-sure to conform in all kinds of ways. Language shift to English, for instance, has often been expected of migrants in predominantly monolingual countries such as England, the United States, Australia and New Zealand. Speaking good English has been regarded as a sign of successful assimilation, and it was widely assumed that meant abandoning the minority language. So most migrant families gradually shift from using Gujerati, or Italian, or Vietnamese to each other most of the time, to using English. This may take three or four generations, but sometimes language shift is completed in just two generations. Typically migrants are virtually monolingual in their mother tongue, their children are bilingual, and their grandchildren are often monolingual in the language of the 'host' country. We can observe the shift by noting the change in people's patterns of language use in different domains over time.

Exercise 1

(a) If you have a friend or acquaintance who belongs to an ethnic minority with a distinct language, they may be willing to share their family history with you. It is very important to be polite and not to put any pressure on someone who is reluctant, however. They may have good reason to feel unwilling to share experiences which may have been painful.

A

Multilingual speech communities

If they are willing to talk to you, find out whether they themselves migrated to the country you live in, or whether it was their parents or grandparents who made the journey. When did they arrive, and why did they come? Try to trace the language history of each generation. What languages do their grandparents/parents/brothers and sisters speak in different domains? Does your friend still speak the ethnic language? If so, who to and in what contexts?

(b) People are often unaware of the range of ethnic minority groups living in their area. How could you find out how many minority ethnic groups there are in the area where you live?

Answers at end of chapter

Non-migrant communities

Language shift is not always the result of migration. Political, economic and social changes can occur within a community, and this may result in linguistic changes too. In Oberwart, an Austrian town on the border of Hungary, the community has been gradually shifting from Hungarian to German for some time.

Example 2

Before World War I the town of Oberwart (known then by its Hungarian name, Felsöör) was part of Hungary, and most of the townspeople used Hungarian most of the time. However, because the town had been surrounded by German-speaking villages for over 400 years, many people also knew some German. At the end of the war, Oberwart became part of Austria, and German became the official language. Hungarian was banned in schools. This marked the beginning of a period of language shift.

In the 1920s Oberwart was a small place and the peasants used Hungarian to each other, and German with outsiders. As Oberwart grew and industry replaced farming as the main source of jobs, the functions of German expanded. German became the high language in a broad diglossia situation in Oberwart. German was the language of the school, official transactions and economic advancement. It expressed formality and social distance. Hungarian was the low language, used in most homes and for friendly interaction between townspeople. Hungarian was the language of solidarity, used for social and affective functions. Soon it became clear that to 'get on' meant learning German, and so knowledge of German became associated with social and economic progress. Speaking Hungarian was increasingly associated with 'peasantness' and was considered old-fashioned. Young people began to use German to their friends in the pub. Parents began to use German instead of Hungarian to their children. In other words the domains in which German was appropriate continued to expand and those where Hungarian was used contracted. Soon God was one of the few addressees to whom young people still used Hungarian when they said their prayers or went to church.

The patterns of language use for any individual in Oberwart depend on their social networks. Who do they interact with? Table 3.1 overleaf shows that interactions between older people and 'peasants' (those working in jobs associated with the land) tend still to be in Hungarian. These are in the top left-hand side of the table. Towards the right and bottom of the table are interactions between younger people and those working in jobs associated with the new industries or in professional jobs. Here German predominates. The pattern in the table suggests that gradually German will completely displace Hungarian in Oberwart, unless something unexpected happens.

A

Exercise 2

(a) Assuming the direction of shift remains constant, add another two rows (H and L) to table 3.1 predicting a possible pattern of language use for 10-year-olds in Oberwart for columns 1–6.

(b) This first section has shown how the patterns of use of a minority language shift over time. In which domains might a minority language group realistically hope to maintain their language?

Answers at end of chapter

Migrant majorities

The examples discussed so far in this chapter have illustrated that language shift often reflects the influence of political factors and economic factors, such as the need for work. People may shift both location and language for this reason. Over the last couple of centuries, many speakers of Irish, Scottish Gaelic and Welsh, for instance, have shifted to England, and consequently to English, primarily in order to get work. They need English both for their job success and for their social well-being – to make friends. But we find the outcome is the same when it is the majority group who do the physical moving.

When colonial powers invade other countries their languages often become dominant. Countries such as Portugal, Spain, France and England have generally imposed their languages along with their rule. This has not always resulted in linguistic subjugation and language shift. Multilingualism was too well-established as normal in countries like India and Papua New Guinea, and in many African countries. It was not possible for a single alien and imported language to displace and eradicate hundreds of indigenous vernacular languages. But when multilingualism was not widespread in an area, or where just one indigenous language had been used before the colonisers arrived, languages were often under threat. In this context English has been described as a 'killer

Multilingual speech communities

Table 3.1 Choice of language in Oberwart

Speaker	Age of speaker	1 To God	2 To older peasants (grandparents' generation)	3 To parents	4 To friends and workmates of same age	5 To children	6 To doctor and government officials
A	63	Hu	Hu	Hu	Hu	GHu	G
B	61	Hu	Hu	Hu	Hu	GHu	G
C	58	Hu	Hu	Hu	GHu	GHu	G
D	52	Hu	Hu	Hu	GHu	GHu	G
E	27	Hu	Hu	GHu	G	G	G
F	25	Hu	Hu	GHu	G	G	G
G	22	Hu	Hu	G	G	G	G

Source: Adapted from Gal 1979

language'. Where one group arrogates political power and imposes its language along with its institutions – government administration, law courts, education, religion – it is likely that minority groups will find themselves under increasing pressure to adopt the language of the dominant group.

Example 3

Tamati lives in Wanganui, a large New Zealand town. He is 10 years old and he speaks and understands only English, though he knows a few Maori phrases. None of his mates know any Maori either. His grandfather speaks Maori, however. Whenever there is a big gathering, such as a funeral or an important tribal meeting, his grandfather is one of the best speakers. Tamati's mother and father understand Maori, but they are not fluent speakers. They can manage a short simple conversation, but that's about it. Tamati's little sister, Miriama, has just started at a pre-school where Maori is used, so he thinks maybe he'll learn a bit from her.

In New Zealand, Maori people have overwhelmingly moved from monolingualism in Maori in the late nineteenth century, through bilingualism in Maori and English, to monolingualism in English in the second half of the twentieth century. Although the 2006 Census figures, as well as a 2006 survey of the health of the Maori language, report a small increase in the number of Maori people able to speak the language, still only 14 per cent of Maori adults claim to speak Maori fluently, and there are very few domains in which it is possible to use the language.

Most Aboriginal people in Australia, and many American Indian people in the United States, have similarly lost their languages over four or five generations of colonial rule. The indigenous people were swamped by English, the language of the dominant group, and their numbers were decimated by warfare and disease. The result of colonial economic and political control was not diglossia with varying degrees of bilingualism, as found in many African, Asian and South American countries, but the more or less complete eradication of the many indigenous languages. Over time the communities shifted to the coloniser's language, English, and their own languages died out.

When language shift occurs, it is almost always shift towards the language of the dominant powerful group. A dominant group has little incentive to adopt the language of a minority. The dominant language is associated with status, prestige and social success. It is used in the 'glamour' contexts in the wider society – for formal speeches on ceremonial occasions, by newsreaders on television and radio, and by those whom young people admire – pop stars, fashion models and disc jockeys. It is scarcely surprising that many young minority group speakers should see its advantages and abandon their own language.

LANGUAGE DEATH AND LANGUAGE LOSS

When all the people who speak a language die, the language dies with them. Sometimes this fact is crystal clear. Manx has now completely died out in the Isle of Man – the last native speaker, Ned Maddrell, died in 1974. Despite recent attempts to revive it, most people agree that Cornish effectively disappeared from Cornwall in the eighteenth century when Dolly Pentreath of Mousehole died in 1777. Less than half of the 250–300 Aboriginal languages spoken in Australia when the Europeans arrived have survived, and fewer than two dozen are being actively passed on to younger generations. Many disappeared as a direct result of the massacre of the Aboriginal people, or their death from diseases introduced by Europeans. In Tasmania, for instance, the whole indigenous population of between 3000 and 4000 people was exterminated within 75 years. Their languages died with them. These are cases of language death rather than language shift. These languages are no longer spoken anywhere.

A community, such as the Turkish community in England, may shift to English voluntarily over a couple of generations. This involves the loss of the language for the individuals concerned, and even for the community in Britain. But Turkish is not under threat of disappearing because of this shift. It will continue to thrive in Turkey. But when the last native speaker (a male) of Martuthunira dies, this Australian Aboriginal language will die with him. Indeed it was predicted that almost all Australian Aboriginal languages would be extinct by the year 2000, a prediction which fortunately has not been completely fulfilled.

When a language dies gradually, as opposed to all its speakers being wiped out by a massacre or epidemic, the process is similar to that of language shift. The functions of the language are taken over in one domain after another by another language. As the domains in which speakers use the language shrink, the speakers of the dying language become gradually less proficient in it.

Example 4

Annie at 20 is a young speaker of Dyirbal, an Australian Aboriginal language. She also speaks English which she learned at school. There is no written Dyirbal material for her to read, and there are fewer and fewer contexts in which she can appropriately hear and speak the language. So she is steadily becoming less proficient in it. She can understand the Dyirbal she hears used by older people in her community, and she uses it to speak to her grandmother. But her grandmother is scathing about her ability in Dyirbal, saying Annie doesn't speak the language properly.

Annie is experiencing language loss. This is the reflection, in the individual's experience, of wide-scale language death. Because she uses English for most purposes, her vocabulary in Dyirbal has shrunk and shrunk. When she is talking to her grandmother she keeps finding herself substituting English words like *cook* in her Dyirbal, because she can't remember the Dyirbal word. She can't remember all the complicated endings on Dyirbal nouns. They vary depending on the sound at the end of the noun, but she uses just one ending *-gu* for all of them. For other words she simply omits the affix because she can't remember it. Her grandmother complains vociferously about her word order. Annie finds herself putting words in the order they come in English instead of in the order her grandmother uses in Dyirbal. It is clear that Annie's Dyirbal is very different from traditional Dyirbal.

Because English is now so widely used in her community it seems unlikely that Dyirbal will survive in a new form based on the variety Annie speaks. It is on its way to extinction. When Annie's generation die it is pretty certain Dyirbal will die with them. The process of language death for the language comes about through this kind of gradual loss of fluency and competence by its speakers. Competence in the language does not disappear overnight. It gradually erodes over time.

With the spread of a majority group language into more and more domains, the number of contexts in which individuals use the ethnic language diminishes. The language usually retreats till it is used only in the home, and finally it is restricted to such personal activities as counting, praying, and dreaming. The stylistic range that people acquire when they use a language in a wider range of domains disappears. Even in the contexts where the language is still used, there is a gradual reduction in the complexity and diversity of structural features of the language – speakers' sound rules get simplified, their grammatical patterns become less complex, and their vocabulary in the language gets smaller and smaller.

In the wider community the language may survive for ritual or ceremonial occasions, but those who use it in these contexts will be few in number and their fluency is often restricted to prayers and set speeches or incantations. In many Maori communities in New Zealand, for instance, the amount of Maori used in ceremonies is entirely dependent on the availability of respected elders who still retain some knowledge of the appropriate discourse. Maori is now used in some communities only for formal ceremonial speeches, prayers for the sick, and perhaps for a prayer to open a meeting.

A

Multilingual speech communities

Exercise 3

(a) What is the difference between language shift and language death?

(b) When language shift occurs in a diglossia situation H sometimes displaces L, while in other contexts L displaces H. Can you think of examples of each of these processes?

Answers at end of chapter

FACTORS CONTRIBUTING TO LANGUAGE SHIFT

Economic, social and political factors

What factors lead a community to shift from using one language to using another? Initially, the most obvious factor is that the community sees an important reason for learning the second language. The reasons are often economic, but they may also be political – as in the case of Israel. Obtaining work is the most obvious economic reason for learning another language. In English-dominated countries, for instance, people learn English in order to get good jobs. This results in bilingualism. Bilingualism is always a necessary precursor of language shift, although, as stable diglossic communities demonstrate, it does not always result in shift.

The second important factor, then, seems to be that the community sees no reason to take active steps to maintain their ethnic language. They may not see it as offering any advantages to their children, for example, or they may not realise that it is in any danger of disappearing. Without active language maintenance, shift is almost inevitable in many contexts. For example, where a migrant minority group moves to a predominantly monolingual society dominated by one majority group language in all the major institutional domains – school, TV, radio, newspapers, government administration, courts, work – language shift will be unavoidable unless the community takes active steps to prevent it. Very often, without consciously deciding to abandon their ethnic language, a community will lose it because they did not perceive any threat. At first it appears very important to learn the majority language in order to achieve social and economic success. The minority language seems safe because 'we all speak it'. Yet, without conscious maintenance it can and probably will disappear in as few as three generations.

The social and economic goals of individuals in a community are very important in accounting for the speed of shift. Rapid shift occurs when people are anxious to 'get on' in a society where knowledge of the second language is a prerequisite for success. Young upwardly mobile people are likely to shift fastest. It has also been noticed that the shift to another language may be led by women or by men depending on where the new jobs lie and the gender roles in the society. Young women in Oberwart, for example, are leading the shift to German there, because they are the ones taking most advantage of the new jobs offered by the industrial changes. Newly arrived immigrant women in New Zealand, on the other hand, often have less education than their husbands. They tend to stay home, at least initially, maintaining the minority language. When they get work it is often in low-paid jobs such as night-cleaning or in bakeries. There they work with others from their own ethnic group and so they can use their ethnic language in the work domain too.

Demographic factors

Demographic factors are also relevant in accounting for the speed of language shift. Resistance to language shift tends to last longer in rural than in urban areas. This is partly a reflection of the fact that rural groups tend to be isolated from the centres of political power for longer, and they can meet most of their social needs in the ethnic or minority language. So, for example, because of their relative social isolation, Ukrainians in Canada who live out of town on farms have maintained their ethnic language better than those in the towns.

Although some younger urban people now speak Maori as a second language, the communities in New Zealand where Maori survives as a language of everyday communication are relatively inaccessible rural areas, populated almost entirely by Maori people. In these communities there are older native speakers who still use the language to talk to each other in their homes and in the streets, as well as for formal Maori speech events. In fact, before television became widespread, the school was the only domain where English was regularly used in these communities. Everyday interactions between Maori people were in Maori. Maori was used at church, in the shops, for community meetings and in the pub. Improved roads, bus services, television in every home – and even in the pub – has changed all that. Richard Benton, a sociolinguist who has surveyed the use of Maori in New Zealand, sums up the situation by saying that even in these isolated communities Maori is now a language which can only be used between consenting adults!

Example 5

In 1974 a Chilean refugee family went to live in a small provincial New Zealand town where there was work but no opportunity at all to use their mother tongue, Spanish. Their 8-year-old daughter, Crystal, quickly realised that her knowledge of Spanish made her seem odd to her school friends and she rapidly refused to use Spanish even at home. Language shift from Spanish to English for Crystal was almost complete by the age of 13. She retained some understanding of Spanish (i.e. some passive knowledge) but she refused to speak it under any circumstances.

Shift tends to occur faster in some groups than in others. The size of the group is sometimes a critical factor. In Australia, the areas with the largest groups of Maltese speakers (Victoria and New South Wales) had the lowest rates of shift towards English. Spanish has survived well in the United States due partly to the large numbers of speakers. On the other hand, an isolated migrant family will have few opportunities to use their mother tongue, and language maintenance will be much more difficult. Isolation is no advantage when it is as extreme as this.

To maintain a language you must have people you can use it with on a regular basis. Crystal's family had nowhere they could use Spanish except in the home, and no one they could talk to in Spanish except each other. They were both isolated and 'odd' in the eyes of others. Maintaining a language is near impossible under these conditions. Crystal's solution to her integration problem was to marry a monolingual New Zealander.

A

Multilingual speech communities

Exercise 4

What would you predict as the effect of intermarriage on language maintenance and shift? If, in England, an English-speaking woman marries a Gujerati-speaking man, for instance, which language will they use to their children?

Answers at end of chapter

Intermarriage between groups can accelerate language shift. Unless multilingualism is normal in a community, one language tends to predominate in the home. German immigrants in Australia are typical. Despite its multicultural composition, Australia is predominantly a monolingual society. When a German-speaking man marries an English-speaking Australian woman, English is usually the dominant language of the home, and the main language used to the children. The same pattern has been observed in many communities. In Oklahoma in America, for instance, in every family where a Cherokee speaker has married outside the Cherokee community, the children speak only English.

A mother whose English is not strong, or who consciously wants to pass on the minority language to her children, may slow down the process of shift to English by using the language to the children. And there are some strongly patriarchal groups where the father's support for the use of the minority language in the home proves effective – Greek and Italian fathers in Australia, for example, and Samoan fathers in New Zealand, actively encourage the use of their languages in the home. Maori men have also expressed concern that their sons should learn Maori, since they will need it to speak formally on the marae in later life. But once the children of mixed marriages start school, it takes a very determined parent to succeed in maintaining the minority language in the home – especially if the other parent doesn't speak the minority language well – or at all!

Attitudes and values

Example 6

Ione is a young Samoan boy living in Australia. His family are very proud of their Samoan identity and culture and they take every opportunity to do things the Samoan way. They are part of an active Samoan community where the language is used regularly for church services and social events. Ione belongs to a Samoan Youth Club attached to the church. They play sport, organise dances, sing and write their own songs, and go on regular trips – all of which he loves. Ione is proud to be Samoan and is pleased his family taught him his language. For him, being Samoan means knowing how to speak Samoan.

Language shift tends to be slower among communities where the minority language is highly valued. When the language is seen as an important symbol of ethnic identity, it is generally maintained longer. Positive attitudes support efforts to use the minority language in a variety of domains, and this helps people resist the pressure from the majority group to switch to their language.

The status of a language internationally can contribute to these positive attitudes. Maintaining French in Canada and the United States is easier because French is a language with international status. It is obvious to French-Americans in Maine, for instance, that French is a good language to know. It has international prestige. Immigrant Greeks are proud of the contribution of Greek to Western philosophy and culture, and this awareness of the importance of their language helps them resist language shift to English. For similar reasons we would expect a language with the international status of Spanish to have a better chance of resisting shift than languages with few speakers such as Maori or Dyirbal. But even the high status of Spanish as a world language could not offset the attitudes of the local community to Crystal's family's 'oddness' described in example 5. Pride in their ethnic identity and their language can be important factors

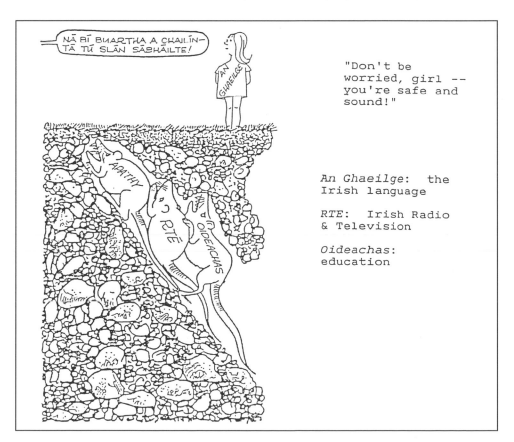

Source: Flann O'Riain's 'Cartoon of Irish Language' from *Lazy Way to Gaelic* is reproduced by permission of Birlinn Ltd (www.birlinn.co.uk)

63

which contribute to language maintenance, provided there is a strong community to support and encourage these attitudes.

> ### Exercise 5
> (a) Why do you think people might want to maintain their minority language when they move to a new country?
> (b) Make a list of the factors which seem to contribute to language maintenance as opposed to those which favour language shift.
>
> *Answers at end of chapter*

HOW CAN A MINORITY LANGUAGE BE MAINTAINED?

> ### Example 7
> '... nothing benefits a country more than to treasure the languages and cultures of its various peoples because in doing so, it fosters intergroup understanding and realises greater dividends in the form of originality, creativity and versatility.'

There are certain social factors which seem to retard wholesale language shift for a minority language group, at least for a time. Where language is considered an important symbol of a minority group's identity, for example, the language is likely to be maintained longer. Polish people have regarded language as very important for preserving their identity in the many countries they have migrated to, and they have consequently maintained Polish for three to four generations. The same is true for Greek migrants in places like Australia, New Zealand and the United States.

If families from a minority group live near each other and see each other frequently, this also helps them maintain their language. Members of the Greek community in Wellington, New Zealand, for instance, belong to a common church, the Greek Orthodox church, where Greek is used. They have established shops where they sell foodstuffs imported from Greece and where they use Greek to each other. There are Indian and Pakistani communities in Britain who have established the same kind of communities within cities, and you can often hear Panjabi or Gujerati spoken in their shops. In America, Chinese people who live in the Chinatown areas of big cities are much more likely to maintain a Chinese dialect as their mother tongue through to the third generation than those who move outside the Chinatown area.

Another factor which may contribute to language maintenance for those who emigrate is the degree and frequency of contact with the homeland. A regular stream of new migrants or even visitors will keep the need for using the language alive. Polynesian migrants from the islands of Niue, Tokelau, Tonga and Samoa arrive in New Zealand regularly. New Zealand Polynesians provide them with hospitality, and the new arrivals provide new linguistic input for the New Zealand communities. The prospect of regular trips back 'home' provides a similar motivation to maintain fluency for many groups. Samoan men in New Zealand, for instance, often expect to return home to take up family and community responsibilities at a later stage in their lives. Greek migrants also see a trip back to Greece as a high priority for themselves and their children. Most Greek New Zealanders regard a trip back to Greece as essential at some point in their lives, and many young Greek girls take the trip with the express aim of securing a good Greek husband. Clearly this provides a very strong incentive to maintain proficiency in Greek.

Example 8

Josie goes to a Catholic secondary school in Bradford. Her best friend is a Polish girl, Danuta. Josie thinks Danuta has a hard life. Danuta's father is a dentist and he is very strict and, in Josie's opinion, very bossy. He insists that everyone speaks Polish in his house. Josie has only been to visit once and even when she was there Danuta's Dad used Polish to his wife and the rest of the children. Danuta has to go to Polish Saturday School too. Josie doesn't envy Danuta, but Danuta doesn't seem to mind. In fact she is very proud of being Polish and of her bilingualism.

Although the pressures to shift are strong, members of a minority community can take active steps to protect its language. If we consider the influence of social factors such as participants and setting, for instance, on language choice, it is clear that social factors may help resist the influence of economic pressures. Where the normal family organisation for an ethnic group is the extended family with grandparents and unmarried relatives living in the same house as the nuclear family, for example, there is good reason to continue using the minority language at home. Similarly groups which discourage intermarriage, such as the Greek and the Chinese communities, contribute to language maintenance in this way. Marriage to a majority group member is the quickest way of ensuring shift to the majority group language for the children.

Obviously a group who manage to ensure their language is used in settings such as school or their place of worship will increase the chances of language maintenance. Tongan people in New Zealand attend church services in Tongan. Heritage language programmes in Canada use the minority language in school for part of each day in order to maintain the languages of groups such as Canadian Ukrainians and Canadian Germans. In Wales bilingual education is available throughout the education system in many areas. In such cases the community has taken steps to try to maintain their language, though the continued influx of English speakers to Wales means that Welsh will never be 'safe'.

Institutional support generally makes the difference between success and failure in maintaining a minority group language. Education, law and administration, religion and the media are crucial domains from this point of view. The minority group which can mobilise these institutions to support language maintenance has some chance of

A

Multilingual speech communities

succeeding. When the government of a country is committed to maintaining or reviving a language, it is possible to legislate for its use in all these domains, as happened in Israel with Hebrew. When Wales achieved self-government in 1999, the Welsh National Assembly made Welsh a compulsory subject in school for children up to the age of 16. (This topic is discussed further in chapter 5 in the section on language planning.) In the final section of this chapter I will discuss just one area – education – where institutional support can contribute to language maintenance and even language revival.

Exercise 6

List the different kinds of institutional support which can be sought by a community of people who want to maintain their minority language within a society where English is the language of the majority. Provide an example of each.

Answer at end of chapter

Many of the factors discussed in this section as relevant to language maintenance have been integrated by Howard Giles and his colleagues, using the concept of 'ethnolinguistic vitality'. These social psychologists suggest that we can predict the likelihood that a language will be maintained by measuring its ethnolinguistic vitality. Three components are involved: firstly, the status of the language as reflected in attitudes towards it, secondly, the size of the group who uses the language and their distribution (e.g. concentrated or scattered), and thirdly, the extent to which the language enjoys institutional support. The concept of ethnolinguistic vitality is clearly very useful in studying language maintenance and shift, though devising satisfactory ways to measure the components is proving a challenge. The concept of ethnolinguistic vitality also provides some ideas for those interested in slowing down or reversing language shift.

LANGUAGE REVIVAL

Sometimes a community becomes aware that its language is in danger of disappearing and takes deliberate steps to revitalise it. Attempts have been made in Ireland, Wales and Scotland, for example, to preserve the indigenous languages, and in New Zealand steps are being taken to attempt to reverse language shift and revitalise Maori. It is sometimes argued that the success of such efforts will depend on how far language loss has occurred – that there is a point of no return. But it seems very likely that more important are attitudinal factors such as how strongly people want to revive the language, and their reasons for doing so. Hebrew was revived in Israel after being effectively dead for nearly 1700 years. It had survived only for prayers and reading sacred texts (much as Latin was used in Catholic services until the 1960s) and that was all. Yet strong feelings of nationalism led to determined efforts by Israeli adults to use it to children, and as a result it has been successfully revived.

The story of Welsh is also interesting. Welsh was a flourishing language in the nineteenth century. It had survived well as the L language in a diglossia situation where the ruling elite used English for administration. Even industrialisation in the nineteenth century initially supported the language, since it provided work for the Welsh speakers in the coal-mining valleys. Welsh people used the language for their everyday communication with each other. But the invasion of Wales by English industrialists had in fact begun a process of language erosion. The work available in mines and iron works attracted English immigrants, and as a result the Welsh language was overwhelmed by the flood of English they spoke. The situation was then exacerbated by the fact that many Welsh-speaking miners left their Welsh valleys during the depression of the 1930s. So the number of Welsh speakers in Wales was being reduced by the effects of both in-migration and out-migration. Language shift to English in public domains was also apparent – especially in industrialised South Wales. It has been said that in 1840 over two-thirds of the population of Wales spoke Welsh, and half of them spoke only Welsh. By the 1980s only 20 per cent of the population spoke the language. But the rate of decline has become less rapid. In 2001, for the third time, the census results indicated an increase in the number of young people speaking Welsh. And a 2004 survey reported that 22 per cent of those sampled could speak Welsh, and 57 per cent of those considered themselves fluent, with 88 per cent reporting that they used Welsh daily.

It has taken a conscious and concerted effort on the part of many Welsh people to slow down the process of language loss. This has included obtaining a Welsh-language television channel and establishing successful bilingual education programmes which extend from pre-school to tertiary level in areas such as Gwynedd. Effective bilingual schooling has generally involved a process known as 'immersion'. Children are immersed in the language (like a warm bath), and it is used to teach them science, maths and social studies, for instance. They are not 'taught' the language. It is rather used as a medium of instruction to teach them the normal school curriculum. This method has proved very successful in many different countries as a means of learning a second language.

Example 9

David is Welsh and he lives in Llandudno in Gwynedd. He is 14 and he goes to a Welsh-medium boys' secondary school where he is taught maths, physics and chemistry in English, and history, geography and social studies in Welsh. Like most of the boys in his class he went to a Welsh-medium primary school where almost all the teaching and learning was in Welsh. His parents speak some Welsh but they are not fluent, and he reckons he now knows a lot more Welsh vocabulary than they do. His little sister attends the local Welsh primary school and she has been complaining to their parents that there are some 'foreigners' from Liverpool in her class who make fun of the sounds of Welsh. David has threatened to come and sort them out but so far his parents have managed to restrain his enthusiasm.

A

Multilingual speech communities

In at least some areas Welsh–English bilingualism has become a reality for children who are taught in Welsh at school. Now, ironically, it appears the success of these programmes may again be under threat as a result of the economic situation of the English. Poor and unemployed families from areas such as Liverpool are moving to Wales because it is cheaper to live in the countryside than in the towns. At the other end of the social scale richer people are exchanging small townhouses in the south for much larger houses and land in Wales. The children of these English people are a threat to the success of bilingual programmes since they see no point in learning Welsh. Once again economic factors are likely to be important in assessing the long-term outcomes of efforts at language maintenance and revival.

Exercise 7

The scales introduced in chapter 1 provide a useful framework for considering the different factors which lead to language maintenance or language shift in different contexts. Consider one minority group situation with which you are familiar.

(a) What is the status of the minority group compared to the majority group?
(b) Which is the language of solidarity for the group and which language expresses social distance or formality?
(c) How formal are the different situations each language is used in?
(d) Which language expresses referential meaning most satisfactorily and most frequently and which expresses social or affective meaning most often?
(e) Which patterns are likely to result in language maintenance and which in language shift?

Answer at end of chapter

Exercise 8

Figure 3.1 provides another useful way of analysing the relationship between linguistic and non-linguistic factors in relation to language maintenance and shift. Consider how each of the factors in the wheel is relevant in favouring or inhibiting language shift in relation to a minority language in your country.

Exercise 9

Yoruba, the language of people living in the state of Lagos in Nigeria, West Africa, is increasingly threatened by the spread of English. In November 2006, Chief Olusoji Smith led a group of tribal elders who recommended that Yoruba be made compulsory as an admission criterion into tertiary institutions. How much of a contribution do you think this will make to encouraging parents to use Yoruba in the home?

Answer at end of chapter

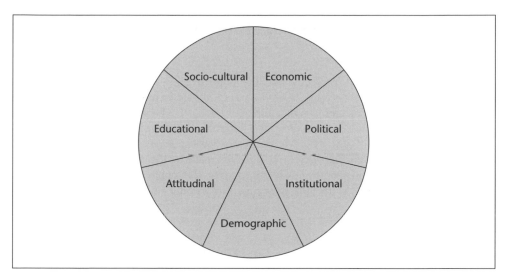

Figure 3.1 Dimensions for analysing language maintenance and shift
Source: Developed from Spolsky, 1978. Reproduced with permission

There is clearly no magic formula for guaranteeing language maintenance or for predicting language shift or death. Different factors combine in different ways in each social context, and the results are rarely predictable. Similar factors apparently result in a stable bilingual situation in some communities but language shift in others. This account has stressed the importance of economic, social, demographic and attitudinal factors. Economic factors are very influential and rarely work in favour of maintaining small minority group languages. Where new jobs are created by industrialisation, they are often introduced by groups using a majority group language with status – often a world language such as English, Spanish or French. Globalisation also contributes to this trend. Along with the global spread of concepts, artifacts and ways of doing things, comes the global language which labels them. The degree of success a group has in resisting the intrusion of such a language into all domains, and especially the family domain, will generally account for the speed of language shift. Successful resistance requires a conscious and determined effort to maintain the minority language. 'Wishing will not make it so.'

Though economic and political imperatives tend to eliminate minority languages, it is important to remember examples like Welsh and Hebrew which demonstrate that languages can be maintained, and even revived, when a group values their distinct identity highly and regards language as an important symbol of that identity. Finally, it is also important to realise that pressures towards language shift occur mainly in countries where monolingualism is regarded as normal, and bilingualism is considered unusual. For most of the world it is bilingualism and multilingualism which is normal. In countries like Zaire or India, the idea that you should stop speaking one language when you start learning another is inconceivable.

A

Multilingual speech communities

ANSWERS TO EXERCISES IN CHAPTER 3

Answer to exercise 1 (b)

There are many possible ways. You could note the range of takeaway bars, restaurants and shops which cater for ethnic minority tastes. (A New Zealand student identified 12 different languages used in 16 different takeaway bars in Wellington city centre.) The range of non-indigenous names in the telephone directory provides additional information. You could ask at the local community centre, the citizens' advice bureau, the library, local churches, and the local schools and kindergartens. You could look for evidence of provision made for the language needs of minority language groups – notices in minority ethnic languages on community notice boards, for instance, religious services in minority languages, newspapers in minority ethnic languages, and so on.

Answer to exercise 2 (a)

Speaker	Age	1	2	3	4	5	6
H	10	Hu	GHu	G	G	G	G
I	10	Hu	G	G	G	G	G

A number of alternatives are possible but your pattern should show only German in column 3 and the spread of German into column 2.

Answer to exercise 2 (b)

In general the more domains in which a minority language is used, the more likely it will be maintained. Domain compartmentalisation – keeping the domains of use of the two languages quite separate – also assists resistance to infiltration from the dominant language. Where minority languages have resisted shift longest, there has been at least one domain in which the minority language is used exclusively. The *home* is the one most under any family's control and, especially where there are grandparents and older family members who use the language, language maintenance has sometimes been possible. In larger minority communities the minority language may be maintained in more domains than just the home. *Religious services* may be held in the minority group language; some *education* (e.g. out-of-school classes) may take place in the language. There may even be some *work* available which allows the use of the minority language.

Answer to exercise 3 (a)

Language shift generally refers to the process by which one language displaces another in the linguistic repertoire of a community. It also refers to the result of this process.

Language death has occurred when a language is no longer spoken naturally anywhere in the world. Language shift for the Chinese community may result in Cantonese being no longer spoken in New Zealand or Britain, but Cantonese will not suffer language death while there are millions of native speakers in China and South-East Asia. If Welsh was no longer spoken in Wales, however, it would be a dead language.

Answer to exercise 3 (b)

In most of the examples given above, a dominant language, which initially serves only H functions for a community, has gradually displaced the minority language in the domains where it served L functions. So English, the H language for many immigrant communities, tends to displace their ethnic language. In Oberwart too, it is the H variety, German, which is displacing the L variety, Hungarian. In Sauris, described in chapter 1, example 7, Italian, the H variety, was displacing the German dialect which served L functions. In cases such as these, where the H variety is a fully developed language used elsewhere by another community, extending it into L domains presents no linguistic problems. The required grammar and vocabulary is already available. Moreover the high status of the H variety favours such a shift.

It is possible, however, for a vigorous L variety to gradually expand its functions upwards into H domains and take over the functions of H in literature, administration, the law and so on. Examples of this process are provided in the next section and in chapter 5. Indonesian is a well-known example of a language which began as a language of the market-place, but which expanded into all domains, and is now the national language of Indonesia.

The story of Hebrew shows that it is also possible, through hard work, to take a highly codified H variety which is not used for everyday conversation anywhere else and expand its linguistic resources so that it can be used in L domains too. Hebrew expanded from a narrow range of religious (H) functions to become the national language of Israel, and it is now used for all functions by many native speakers.

The reasons for the different directions that language shift may take involve more than just economic factors, such as where the jobs are. The number of speakers of a language, or the extent of a group's political influence or power, may be crucial. Attitudes and values are important too. Factors such as the status of a language and its importance as an identity marker may be crucial, as the Hebrew example suggests. These factors will be discussed further in the next section.

Answer to exercise 4

When marriage partners use different languages, the majority group language almost always displaces the minority language. Most often in such families, parents use the majority language to their children. When the minority language is the mother's language it may survive longer, but in the end shift to the majority language seems inevitable. This is discussed further in the next section.

Answer to exercise 5 (a)

Language is an important component of identity and culture for many groups. Maintaining their distinct identity and culture is usually important to a minority group member's self-esteem and this will affect the degree of success achieved in the society.

Answer to exercise 5 (b)

It is possible to make a very long list of factors which in some places seem to contribute to language maintenance, but the same factors may elsewhere have little effect or even be associated with shift. In other words there are no absolute answers to this exercise.

On the basis of what you have read so far you might have identified some factors which fit into one of the following categories and which could contribute to language maintenance.

1. *The patterns of language use*: the more domains in which the minority language can be used, the more chance there is of its being maintained. The possibilities will be largely determined by socio-economic factors, such as where the jobs are.
2. *Demographic factors*: where a group is large enough to provide plenty of speakers and reasonably able to isolate itself from contact with the majority, at least in some domains, there is more chance of language maintenance. Where members of ethnic communities are living in the same area this too helps maintain minority languages longer. The frequency of contact with the homeland can also be important – a large number of new immigrants, visitors, or visits to the 'mother country' tend to contribute to language maintenance.
3. *Attitudes to the minority language*: where it is valued and regarded with pride as identifying the minority group and expressing its distinctive culture, there is more chance of it being maintained. Where it has status in the community this will help too.

A

Multilingual speech communities

Support for language maintenance from bilingual peers can contribute to maintenance (just as pressure from monolingual majority group peers can lead to shift).

Answer to exercise 6

Institutional support can be sought in domains such as education, religion, law and administration, and the media.

Examples of this kind of support are:

(i) the use of the minority language in education, e.g. bilingual education programmes, using or teaching the minority language in school, in pre-school, and in after-school programmes,

(ii) support by the law and administration, e.g. the right to use the language in court, the House of Assembly, in dealing with government officials etc.,

(iii) the use of the language in places of worship, e.g. for services, sermons, hymns, chants,

(iv) use of and support for the language in the media, e.g. TV programmes, radio programmes, newspapers, magazines.

Bilingual education as a means of minority language support is discussed further in the next section.

Answer to exercise 7

The patterns identified will vary according to the minority group selected. Very often the answers will be complicated. Scottish Gaelic in Britain, for instance, has different status in the eyes of different people – even the Scots. For some it is the language of solidarity and the language with which they identify. It is an effective vehicle of referential meaning as well as positive affective meaning for such people. Others regard Scottish Gaelic as irrelevant and useless. For them it has low status especially compared to English. Whether Scottish Gaelic can be used in formal contexts, such as a school board meeting, depends on which part of Scotland a person lives in, and how many proficient speakers are present.

Where a language is rated as high in status by its users, and yet also regarded as a language of solidarity to be used between minority group members, where it is regarded as appropriate for expressing referential as well as affective or social meaning, and where it is able to be used in a wide range of contexts both formal and informal, it is much more likely to be maintained. Welsh would fit this description in the opinion of those who support Welsh language maintenance. A language confined to informal contexts, conversations between friends, and used for expressing predominantly social functions is vulnerable to replacement by the higher status, more widely used language of the wider society.

Answer to exercise 9

Though it may contribute to the prestige of Yoruba and encourage more positive attitudes to its maintenance, it seems unlikely that a requirement of Yoruba for entrance to tertiary institutions will make much difference to the use of Yoruba in the home. To encourage the more widespread use of Yoruba it would probably be more useful to require that it be *used* more extensively in educational institutions at all levels. ·

▮ Concepts introduced

Language shift
Language death
Language loss

Language maintenance
Bilingual education
Ethnolinguistic vitality
Language revival

References

The following sources provided material for this chapter:

Aboriginal languages, including Dyirbal: Schmidt (1985, 1990)
Australian ethnic minorities: Clyne (1982, 1985)
Cherokee: Appel and Müysken (1987: 35)
England: Linguistic Minorities Project (1985)
English: Leith (1983)
Manx: Edwards (1985)
Maori: Benton (1991, 2001), *Survey of the Health of the Maori Language* (2006)
New Zealand minority groups: Bell et al. 2000, Fairbairn-Dunlop (1984), Hirsh (1987), Jamieson (1980), Roberts (1991, 2001), Verivaki (1991)
Oberwart: Gal (1979)
Spolsky (1978, 2003)
Wales: Appel and Müysken (1987), Baker (1992), Lewis (1978); Welsh Language Board (2006), http://www.wales.gov.uk/organipo/index.htm, http://www.statistics.gov.uk/census2001/profiles/commentaries/ethnicity.asp
Yoruba: Email circulated by AILA Research Network on Language Policy, 1 December 2006.

Quotations

Example 7 is a quotation from Herder cited in Fishman (1978: 49–50).

Useful additional reading

Crystal (2000)
Fasold (1984), Ch. 8
Fishman (2001)
Harris (2007)
Linguistic Minorities Project (1985)
May (2001)
Mesthrie et al. (2000), Ch. 8
Myers-Scotton (2005)
Myers-Scotton (2006), Ch. 4
Romaine and Nettle (2000)

A

Multilingual speech communities

4 Linguistic varieties and multilingual nations

Over half the world's population is bilingual and many people are multilingual. They acquire a number of languages because they need them for different purposes in their everyday interactions. Kalala's experience in Zaire, described at the beginning of chapter 2, illustrated this. One language was his ethnic or tribal language, another was the language of his education, another served as a useful language of wider communication in particular contexts, such as the market-place, or with outsiders or tourists. In this chapter I will examine the labels and the criteria sociolinguists use to distinguish between different varieties or codes in multilingual communities.

Example 1

Mr Patel is a spice merchant who lives in Bombay. When he gets up he talks to his wife and children in Kathiawari, their dialect of Gujerati. Every morning he goes to the local market where he uses Marathi to buy his vegetables. At the railway station he buys his ticket into Bombay city using Hindustani, the working person's lingua franca. He reads his Gujerati newspaper on the train, and when he gets to work he uses Kacchi, the language of the spice trade, all day. He knows enough English to enjoy an English cricket commentary on the radio, but he would find an English film difficult to follow. However, since the spice business is flourishing, his children go to an English-medium school, so he expects them to be more proficient in English than he is.

The fact that India is one of the most multilingual nations in the world is reflected in Mr Patel's linguistic repertoire, just as the linguistic heterogeneity of Zaire was reflected in Kalala's repertoire. With a population of over a billion, Indians use hundreds of different languages – the exact number depends on what counts as a distinct language, and what is rather a dialect of another language. With this kind of linguistic diversity it is easy to understand the problems facing the country at the national level. Should a country use the same language for internal administration and for official communications with other nations? Which language or languages should be used by the government and the courts? In order to assess the relative claims of different languages it is necessary to look at their status and the functions which they serve.

Sociolinguists have developed a number of ways of categorising languages, according to their status and social functions. The distinction between a vernacular language and a standard language is a useful place to start.

VERNACULAR LANGUAGES

The term *vernacular* is used in a number of ways. It generally refers to a language which has not been standardised and which does not have official status. There are hundreds of vernacular languages, such as Buang in Papua New Guinea, Hindustani in India, and Bumbar in Vanuatu, many of which have never been written down or described. In a multilingual speech community, the many different ethnic or tribal languages used by different groups are referred to as vernacular languages. Vernaculars are usually the first languages learned by people in multilingual communities, and they are often used for a relatively narrow range of informal functions.

There are three components of the meaning of the term vernacular, then. The most basic refers to the fact that a vernacular is an uncodified or unstandardised variety. The second refers to the way it is acquired – in the home, as a first variety. The third is the fact that it is used for relatively circumscribed functions. The first component has been most widely used as the defining criterion, but emphasis on one or other of the components has led to the use of the term vernacular with somewhat different meanings.

Some have extended the term to refer to any language which is not the official language of a country. An influential 1951 UNESCO report, for instance, defined a vernacular language as the first language of a group socially or politically dominated by a group with a different language. So in countries such as the United States where English is the language of the dominant group, a language like Spanish is referred to as a Chicano child's vernacular. But Spanish would not be regarded as a vernacular language in Spain, Uruguay or Chile, where it is an official language. In this sense Greek is a vernacular language in Australia and New Zealand, but not in Greece or Cyprus. The term vernacular simply means a language which is not an official language in a particular context. When people talk about education in a vernacular language, for instance, they are usually referring to education in an ethnic minority language in a particular country.

The term vernacular generally refers to the most colloquial variety in a person's linguistic repertoire. In a multilingual community this variety will often be an unstandardised ethnic or tribal language. The vernacular is the variety used for communication in the home and with close friends. It is the language of solidarity between people from the same ethnic group. By extension the term has been used to refer in a monolingual community to the most informal and colloquial variety of a language which may also have a standardised variety. The term 'vernacular' is used with this meaning by sociolinguists studying social dialects, as we will see in chapter 6.

A

Multilingual speech communities

Finally, the term vernacular is sometimes used to indicate that a language is used for everyday interaction, without implying that it is appropriate only in informal domains. Hebrew, for example, used to be a language of ritual and religion with no native speakers. It was no one's 'parental tongue', and was certainly not considered a vernacular language. Sociolinguists have described the process of developing it for use as the national language of Israel as 'vernacularisation'. Its functions were extended from exclusively H functions to include L functions. From being a language of ritual, Hebrew became a language of everyday communication – a vernacular language. In this sense, vernacular contrasts with ritual or classical language. The Catholic church at one time used Latin for church services, rather than vernacular languages such as English, French and Italian. Using this definition, any language which has native speakers would be considered a vernacular. This is a very broad definition, and it is generally not as useful as the more specific definition which contrasts vernacular languages with standardised languages used for more formal functions.

Exercise 1

(a) Using the first definition above, which of the languages used by Kalala in chapter 2, example 1, and Mr Patel in example 1 above, qualifies as a vernacular language?

(b) Is Dyirbal, described in chapter 3, example 4, a vernacular language?

Answers at end of chapter

STANDARD LANGUAGES

Example 2

Do not take the termes of Northern-men, such as they use in dayly talke, whether they be noblemen or gentlemen, or of their best clarkes all is a matter; nor in effect any speach used beyond the river Trent, though no man can deny but that theirs is the purer English Saxon at this day, yet it is not so Courtly nor so currant as our Southern English is, no more is the far Westerne mans speach; ye shall therefore take the usuall speach of the Court, and that of London and the shires lying about London within LX myles, and not much above.

This is George Puttenham's sixteenth-century view of where young authors would find the most acceptable variety of English. Good English speech was to be heard, in Puttenham's opinion, at Court and from gentlemen who lived within 60 miles of London. He was largely right in identifying the social and regional origins of the variety which we now regard as standard British English.

The term *standard* is even more slippery than vernacular because it too is used in many different ways by linguists. Here is one definition which can serve as a useful starting point. A standard variety is generally one which is written, and which has undergone some degree of regularisation or codification (for example, in a grammar and a dictionary); it is recognised as a prestigious variety or code by a community, and it is used for H functions alongside a diversity of L varieties. This is a very general definition and it immediately excludes most of the world's four or five thousand languages. Only a minority of the world's languages are written, and an even smaller minority are standardised in the sense of codified and accepted by the community as suitable for formal functions. It will be useful to look at an example to illustrate what the definition means in a particular context.

Standard English emerged 'naturally' in the fifteenth century from a variety of regional English dialects, largely because it was the variety used by the English Court and the influential merchants of London, as Puttenham noted. The area where the largest proportion of the English population lived at that time was in a neat triangle containing London, where the Court was based, and the two universities, Oxford and Cambridge. In addition, the East Midlands was an important agricultural and business area, and London was the hub of international trade and exports to Calais. It was also the centre of political, social and intellectual life in England.

So it was the dialect used in this area which was the basis for what we now think of as standard English. It was prestigious because of its use in Court. It was influential because it was used by the economically powerful merchant class. People who came to London from the provinces recognised this and often learned it, and this of course made it useful. The more people who used it, the less effort people had to make to understand regional varieties. It is easy to see how such a code would rapidly develop formal H functions in the context of administration and government.

Standard varieties are codified varieties. Codification is usually achieved through grammars and dictionaries which record, and sometimes prescribe, the standard forms of the language. Dictionary writers (or lexicographers) have to decide which words to include in the dictionary as part of the standard variety, which forms to mark as dialectal, and which to omit altogether. They generally take the usage of educated and socially prestigious members of the community as their criterion.

The codification process, which is part of the development of every standard variety, was accelerated in the case of English by the introduction of printing. In 1476, William Caxton, the first English printer, set up his printing press in Westminster. He used the speech of the London area – the newly emerging standard dialect – as the basis for his translations. In other words, he used the vocabulary, the grammar and the pronunciation of this dialect when looking for words, constructions and spellings to translate works from French. Selecting forms was not always straightforward, however. Caxton comments, for instance, on the problems of deciding between *egges* and *eyren*, alternative forms used for 'eggs' at the time. This choice involved grammar as well as pronunciation since these forms represented alternative ways of pluralising words (the *-en* plural marker has survived in *oxen*, for instance). Like other codifiers,

A

Multilingual speech communities

77

he reported that he consulted the best writers of the upper class for judgements on usage problems.

The development of standard English illustrates the three essential criteria which characterise a standard: it was an influential or *prestigious* variety, it was *codified and stabilised*, and it *served H functions* in that it was used for communication at Court, for literature and for administration. It also illustrates that what we refer to as a standard language is always a particular dialect which has gained its special position as a result of social, economic and political influences. A standard dialect has no particular linguistic merits, whether in vocabulary, grammar or pronunciation. It is simply the dialect of those who are politically powerful and socially prestigious. Once it begins to serve as a norm or standard for a wider group, however, it is likely to develop the wider vocabulary needed to express the new functions it is required to serve.

Standard languages developed in a similar way in many other European countries during the fifteenth, sixteenth and seventeenth centuries. In Italy, Spain, France and Romania, for example, there were a variety of dialects of the vernacular languages (which all derived from varieties of colloquial Latin) which served the L functions of their communities, alongside classical Latin, the H language. From these dialects there gradually emerged a standard, generally based on the dialect of the political, economic and social centre of the country. Some dialects had extra help – the Italians, for example, established a language academy as early as 1582 to make pronouncements on what counted as standard Italian – but most were natural births.

Exercise 2

Look up the meaning of 'standard' in a good dictionary. Which of the meanings listed seems closest to the definition provided in this section?

Answer at end of chapter

World Englishes

Once a standard dialect develops or is developed, it generally provides a very useful means of communication across areas of dialect diversity. Its status as a prestige variety guarantees it will spread. Standard English has served as a useful variety for communication between areas of dialect diversity, not only within Britain but also in countries where the British have had a colonial influence. Local varieties of English, with distinctive linguistic features, have developed in many multilingual countries such as Malaysia, Singapore, Hong Kong, India, and many African countries, where English has served as a valuable language of wider communication in a multilingual context.

The term 'world Englishes' has been used to emphasise the range of different varieties of English that have developed since the nineteenth century. In contexts where multilingualism is the norm, relatively standard varieties, such as formal Singapore English, expressing global concepts shared across nations, coexist alongside more 'nativised' varieties of English, influenced by local languages. Singlish (a colloquial variety of Singapore English) is a good and well-described example. These nativised varieties express the local aspirations and identities of a wide range of communities, and this is reflected in linguistic characteristics such as stress patterns, vocabulary from local languages, grammatical features which reflect the influence of local languages, and semantic concepts drawn from the other languages spoken in the communities where they are used. Singlish has a frequently occurring ethnic final tag *lah*, for example, as well as distinctive intonation patterns, grammar and vocabulary. For example, *chin chye lah* in answer to a query means something like 'it's up to you, I don't mind'. Indian English also has a very distinctive stress pattern, an end-tag *kya* meaning 'right?', and many words from local languages are woven into Indian English conversations. These nativised varieties, used by those for whom English is a second language, have been labelled by Braj Kachru as *outer-circle* varieties of English to distinguish them from varieties used by native speakers or *inner-circle* varieties (see figure 4.1).

The local varieties of English which have developed in New Zealand, Australia, Canada and the United States, where most of the populations are monolingual English speakers, are examples of inner-circle English varieties. Kachru also identified an *expanding circle*

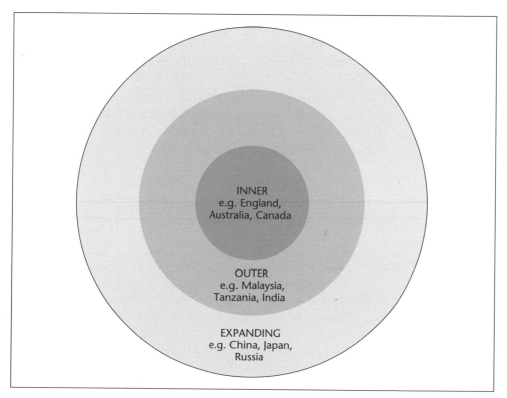

Figure 4.1 Inner, outer and expanding circles of English
Source: Adapted from Kachru, 1985. Reproduced with permission

of those who were learning English as an additional, adjunct or foreign language for a wide range of reasons such as trade or access to higher education, as in China or Japan. English is a foreign language in the expanding circle, serving no crucial communication functions within a country.

Exercise 3

The concept of inner, outer and expanding circles of English presents some problems when we think about the way English is used in countries such as India and Singapore, where it is the first language of some people. Can you think of a better way of distinguishing between different varieties of English across the world?

Answer at end of chapter

While there is a range of variation in spoken varieties at all linguistic levels of analysis, the degree of variation in the written standard varieties has not been so great. And though countries like Australia and New Zealand have established their own standard Englishes, in many countries the standard English of the UK has served as a norm until relatively recently. In Singapore, for instance, British English is still endorsed, at least tacitly, by the government as the appropriate target variety in schools and official communications. The dialect which emerged as the standard in Caxton's time – the ancestor of all standard Englishes – has been influential well beyond the borders of its original dialect area.

English has clearly served as a language of wider communication in many pluralistic contexts, and in many multilingual countries. Alternatively a particular vernacular or local language may develop the role of a language of wider communication in a multilingual area. Such languages are labelled *lingua francas*, and they are the topic of the next section.

LINGUA FRANCAS

Example 3

In the 1960s, a Catholic nun, Sister Dominic, was sent to Rome for a meeting between nuns from different countries. She spoke no Italian but she had been managing pretty well with her French and English until she lost her purse one evening. She simply could not explain what had happened to the local police officer. A priest overheard her struggles and came to her rescue. They proceeded to explore their linguistic repertoires trying to find a language they shared. He came from Brazil and spoke Portuguese and Spanish, but he had been living in Rome for some time, and so he was by then familiar with the local variety of

---

Italian. Finally they found a language in which they could communicate – Latin! At that time Latin was still the language of church services and both had learned Latin to university level. As Sister Dominic described it, the result was a very funny encounter, with her explaining her predicament in formal Latin and the priest then translating into the local Italian dialect.

In this particular encounter, Latin functioned as a lingua franca – a language of communication between two people. In the meeting Sister Dominic was attending between nuns from South America, Africa, Ireland and France, the language of wider communication or lingua franca was English. When academics and experts meet at international conferences, or when politicians arrange summit meetings, a world language such as English, French or Spanish is often used as the lingua franca. In these examples, a particular language serves as a lingua franca in a particular situation. More generally, however, the term lingua franca describes a language serving as a regular means of communication between different linguistic groups in a multilingual speech community.

A

Multilingual speech communities

Example 4

In the heart of the north-west Amazon near the border between Colombia and Brazil, there is a group of Indians who live along the Vaupés river. The river is their food source as well as their communication line with other Indians and the outside world. Tuka is a young Indian girl who lives with her family and five other families in a longhouse on the river. The language of her longhouse and the language she learnt first is her father's language, Tuyuka. In a sense then, in this community, the father's language is what is usually referred to as the 'mother tongue' (i.e. the first language learned). Tuka has learnt her mother's language, Paneroa, as well, however, and speaks it fluently. She knows some Spanish which she learned from a couple of the older men who spent time working on rubber plantations when they were younger and then returned to the longhouse. And she knows Tukano, the language used along the river to communicate with Indians who do not speak the longhouse language. Since there are over 20 languages used by other longhouses within reasonable paddling distance of her longhouse, Tukano is a very useful language for communicating with a wider group. It is the lingua franca of her area of the Vaupés. When a group of visitors arrive in their canoes they begin by giving the ritual greetings in their own language, providing information such as where they have come from, and how long they have been travelling. Then, if they do not know Tuyuka, in order to communicate more specific information and to exchange gossip, they switch to Tukano, the lingua franca for Tuka's area.

A lingua franca is a language used for communication between people whose first languages differ. Between the Colombian Indians, Tukano is the main lingua franca, and it can be used with Indians who live in the Vaupés area of the north-west Amazon on both sides of the border between Colombia and Brazil. If Indians want to communicate with non-Indians in the area they need a second lingua franca, since non-Indians rarely learn Tukano. Colombians use Spanish, and Brazilians use Portuguese.

In some countries the most useful and widely used lingua franca is an official language or the national language. In Tanzania, for instance, Swahili is the language people tend to choose first when they are speaking to someone from a different tribal group. In Papua New Guinea, Tok Pisin (or Neo-Melanesian) is the most widespread lingua franca though, not surprisingly in a country with over 700 different vernaculars, there are also other regional lingua francas, such as Hiri Motu, which is used widely in the province of Papua. In the former Soviet Union, where about a hundred different vernaculars were spoken, Russian served as a lingua franca as well as being the national and official language of the USSR. Throughout the Arabic-speaking world, varieties of Classical Arabic, the sacred language of Islam, are used as a lingua franca among the educated. In other countries educated people often use the language of the former colonial power as a lingua franca.

In multilingual communities lingua francas are so useful they may eventually displace the vernaculars. When people from different ethnic groups marry in Zaire or Tanzania or Papua New Guinea, they often use the lingua franca of their area as the language of the home, and their children may therefore learn very little of their father's and mother's vernaculars. The reason that this has not happened in the Vaupés area, i.e. that Tukano has not displaced the many languages of the different longhouses, is related to the marriage patterns, which are exogamous. People must marry outside their language and longhouse group, and the taboo against marrying someone who speaks the same language is very strong. So a husband will speak to his wife in the longhouse language, while the wife replies in her own language. Maintaining linguistic distinctiveness is important in this multilingual community. If linguistic distinctiveness is an important identifying value for a group, then ethnic languages and vernaculars tend to survive, often for a considerable time. But, as discussed in chapter 3, there are many factors which may contribute to their replacement, and the usefulness of lingua francas in multilingual areas is certainly one relevant factor.

Lingua francas often develop initially as trade languages – illustrating again the influence of economic factors on language change. In West Africa, Hausa is learned as a second language and used in nearly every market-place. In East Africa, Swahili is the most widely used trade language and it was this – the fact that it was known and used so widely – which led the Tanzanian government to select it for promotion as the country's national language. (Swahili's progress to national language is described in the next chapter.) The history of Tok Pisin is similar. It spread as a useful lingua franca for trade in Papua New Guinea and became so widely known and used that it was adopted as an official language. Some believe it is the front runner as a choice for national language, though others think this unlikely in the current political climate. Tok Pisin began life as a pidgin language.

Exercise 4

The usefulness of lingua francas which have emerged naturally in a multilingual context has often resulted in them being selected as national or official languages.

What factors do you think will be relevant when selecting a language to promote as an official or national language? Are they likely to be mainly linguistic or non-linguistic factors?

Answer at end of chapter

There have been many successful attempts to create a language for communication between people who use different languages. From a linguistic and sociolinguistic point of view, the most interesting lingua francas in many respects are pidgin and creole languages.

PIDGINS AND CREOLES

Pidgins

Example 5

Bipo tru igat wanpela liklik meri nau nem bilong em Liklik Retpela Hat. Em i save slip wantaim Mama na Papa bilong em long wanpela liklik haus. Papa i save wok long bus, i save katim paiawut na ol man save baim long em. Orait i gat lapun meri i stap long narapela haus. Dispela lapun emi Tumbuna Mama.

Translation

A long time ago, there was a little girl named Little Red Riding Hood. She lived with her mother and father in a little house. Father worked in the bush, cutting trees for firewood, which he sold to people. Now there was a very old lady who lived in another house. This old lady was Little Red Riding Hood's grandmother.

Most people have a predictable reaction to pidgin languages. They find them amusing. If you read a children's story in a variety of pidgin English, it is easy to understand why – it sounds a lot like baby-talk. But even if we take a serious article from the newspaper, many speakers of English still find pidgin languages humorous or babyish. It is very difficult for native speakers of a language to overcome these attitudes to pidgins which are based partly on their language. Yet pidgins and creoles are real languages, not baby-talk. They are used for serious purposes, and each has a describable and distinctive linguistic structure.

A

Multilingual speech communities

Why do pidgins develop?

A *pidgin* is a language which has no native speakers. Pidgins develop as a means of communication between people who do not have a common language. So a pidgin is no one's native language. Pidgins seem particularly likely to arise when two groups with different languages are communicating in a situation where there is also a third dominant language. On Caribbean slave plantations in the seventeenth and eighteenth centuries, West African people were deliberately separated from others who used the same language so as to reduce the risk of their plotting to escape or rebel. In order to communicate with each other, as well as with their overseers, they developed pidgins based on the language of the plantation bosses as well as their own languages.

On sea-coasts in multilingual contexts, pidgins developed as languages of trade between the traders – who used a colonial language such as Portuguese, or Spanish, or English – and the Indians, Chinese, Africans or American Indians that they were trading with. In fact many of the meanings which have been suggested for the word *pidgin* reflect its use as a means of communication between traders. It may derive from the word 'business' as pronounced in the pidgin English which developed in China, or perhaps from Hebrew *pidjom* meaning 'trade or exchange', or perhaps from the combination of two Chinese characters *péi* and *tsī n* meaning 'paying money'.

Example 6

Bislama is a variety of Melanesian Pidgin which is used by nearly everyone in Vanuatu, an archipelago of about 80 islands in the south-west Pacific. Like the Caribbean pidgins, it originated because of the need for a lingua franca among plantation workers. But the Melanesians who worked in the nineteenth century on the sugar-cane plantations of Queensland (Australia), and later Fiji, were not slaves. They were 'indentured' or contract workers. The pidgin then spread because it was so useful to traders in sandalwood and seaslugs (or *beche de mer*, from which its name derives). The usefulness of a lingua franca in Vanuatu, a country with around 100 different vernacular languages, guaranteed its survival there. Today it is a fully functioning creole which has been adopted as Vanuatu's national language, as we will see in chapter 5.

Initially, then, pidgins develop with a narrow range of functions. Those who use them speak other languages, so the pidgin is an addition to their linguistic repertoire used for a specific purpose, such as trade or perhaps administration. In terms of the dimensions identified in chapter 1, pidgins are used almost exclusively for referential rather than affective functions. They are typically used for quite specific functions like buying and selling grain, or animal hides, rather than to signal social distinctions or express politeness. Consequently the structure of a pidgin is generally no more complicated than it needs to be to express these functions. Nobody uses a pidgin as a means of group identification, or to express social distance, and so there is no pressure to maintain referentially redundant features of a language or complicated pronunciations whose main purpose is to signal how well educated you are.

What kind of linguistic structure does a pidgin language have?

Example 7

Juba Arabic is a pidgin language spoken in the southern Sudan. It has a small vocabulary of words for trade and basic communication, and borrows when necessary from native languages of the Sudan or from colloquial Arabic. It has a very simple sound system and has almost entirely eliminated the complicated morphology of Arabic (which has inflections for gender, number and person on the noun, and tense and negation on the verb). Juba Arabic has its own distinct structure, and it is a stable variety. Though it is easier for an Arabic person to learn than for an English speaker, it does require learning and cannot be just improvised for an occasion.

Pidgin languages are created from the combined efforts of people who speak different languages. All languages involved may contribute to the sounds, the vocabulary, and the grammatical features, but to different extents, and some additional features may emerge which are unique to the new variety. Nevertheless it has been found that when one group speaks a prestigious world language and the other groups use local vernaculars, the prestige language tends to supply more of the vocabulary, while vernacular languages have more influence on the grammar of the developing pidgin. The proportion of vocabulary contributed to Tok Pisin by English, for example, has been estimated at 77 per cent, compared to about 11 per cent from Tolai, the local vernacular which has contributed the largest amount of vocabulary. The language which supplies most of the vocabulary is known as the *lexifier* (or sometimes *superstrate*) language, while the languages which influence the grammatical structure are called the *substrate*. So in Papua New Guinea, English is the lexifier language for Tok Pisin, while Tolai contributes to the substrate.

Because pidgins develop to serve a very narrow range of functions in a very restricted set of domains, they tend to have a simplified structure and a small vocabulary compared with fully developed languages. Words generally do not have inflections, as in English, to mark the plural, or to signal the tense of the verb. Nor are affixes used to mark gender, as in Spanish and Italian. Affixes are dispensed with. Often the information they convey is signalled more specifically elsewhere in the sentence, or it can be deduced from the context, or it is unnecessary. Every learner of French or Spanish, for example, knows that the grammatical gender of objects is strictly dispensable if you are interested in communication as opposed to impressing people.

Exercise 5

Consider table 4.1. What evidence can you find to support the claim that pidgin languages signal only a minimum of grammatical information explicitly?

Table 4.1 Comparison of verb forms in four languages

French	English	Tok Pisin		Cameroon pidgin	
je vais	I go	mi	⎫	a	⎫
tu vas	you go	yu		yu	
elle/il/va	she/he/it goes	em		i	
nous allons	we go	yumi	⎬ go	wi	⎬ go
		mipela	⎭		
vous allez		yupela		wuna	
elles/ils vont	they go	ol	⎭	dem	⎭

Source: From Todd 1974: 2. Reproduced with permission

Answer at end of chapter

The discussion of inflections has illustrated that pidgin languages tend to reduce grammatical signals to a minimum. This makes them easier to learn and to use for the speaker, although it puts a greater burden on the listener. In other respects, pidgins are difficult for the learner, since they tend to be full of structural irregularities.

The vocabulary needed for a trade language is very small compared to the vocabulary of a fully fledged language. While estimates vary widely, it has been suggested that the average monolingual English-speaking adult has a vocabulary of around 20,000 word families. For a pidgin language which is used only for trade, a few hundred words is sufficient. But, as in fully developed languages, one form may do a great deal of work. Tok Pisin *pas* can mean *a pass, a letter, a permit, ahead, fast, firmly, to be dense, crowded,* or *tight, to be blocked*, or *shut*. This feature is particularly characteristic of the vocabulary of pidgin languages. Every form earns its place.

Attitudes

Example 8

Young visitor to Papua New Guinea
When I first heard Pidgin English I just thought it was baby-talk. I thought anyone can do that. It had words like *liklik* for 'little' and *cranky* for wrong and *nogut* for 'bad'. It just made me laugh. Then I began to realise it wasn't as easy as I'd thought. People kept correcting me when I tried, and they got annoyed if I didn't take it seriously. I soon learned better.

Pidgin languages do not have high status or prestige and, to those who do not speak them, they often seem ridiculous languages. They have been described as mongrel jargons and macaroni lingos. They are often the butt of comedy routines and a number of apocryphal definitions are widely quoted. It has been falsely claimed, for example, that *piano* in pidgin English is 'big fella bakis (box) yu faitim he cry'.

Because of the large number of pidgin words which derive from a European language in a pidgin such as Tok Pisin, many Europeans consider pidgins to be a debased form of their own language. They assume they can guess the meanings. This can lead to misunderstandings which can be very serious, as the following example demonstrates.

Example 9

A Papua New Guinean stumbled against a white woman coming out of the theatre. When questioned about what had happened, the Papua New Guinean replied: 'Mi putim han long baksait bilong misis' ['I touched the woman's back with my hand']. As Suzanne Romaine reports: 'The answer cost him half a tooth, his job, and three months in prison, due to the confusion between the meaning of Tok Pisin *baksait* meaning "back", and English *backside*.'

To sum up, a pidgin language has three identifying characteristics:

1. it is used in restricted domains and functions
2. it has a simplified structure compared to the source languages
3. it generally has low prestige and attracts negative attitudes – especially from outsiders.

Pidgins often have a short life. If they develop for a restricted function, they disappear when the function disappears. In Vietnam a pidgin English developed for use between the American troops and the Vietnamese, but it subsequently died out. A trading pidgin usually disappears when trade between the groups dies out. Alternatively, if trade grows, then more contact will generally lead to at least one side learning the other's language, and so the need for the pidgin disappears. In some cases, however, pidgins go on to develop into fully fledged languages or creoles.

Exercise 6

Can you guess which European languages have contributed to the vocabulary of the languages illustrated in the following sentences?

(a) mô pe aste sa banan	I am buying the banana
(b) de bin alde luk dat big tri	they always looked for a big tree
(c) a waka go a osu	he walked home
(d) olmaan i kas-im chek	the old man is cashing a cheque
(e) li pote sa bay mo	he brought that for me
(f) ja fruher wir bleiben	yes at first we remained
(g) dis smol swain i bin go fo maket	this little pig went to market

Answers at end of chapter

Creoles

Example 10

Excerpt from the Pepa Bilong Inkam Takis of the Government of Papua New Guinea.

Tok Tru Olgeta
Olgeta tok hia mekim long dispela pepa emi tru tasol. Mi soim pinis olgeta pei
mani bilong mi bilong dispela yia . . .

Declaration
I, the person making this return, declare that the particulars shown herein are
true in every particular and disclose a full and complete statement of the total
income derived by me during the twelve months from . . .

A *creole* is a pidgin which has acquired native speakers. Many of the languages which
are called pidgins are in fact now creole languages. They are learned by children as their
first language and used in a wide range of domains. Tok Pisin (which was used to illustrate some of the features of pidgins in the previous section) is one obvious example of
a pidgin which has developed into a creole language. This makes it clear that the label
of a language is not an accurate guide to its status as pidgin or creole. Despite its name,
Tok Pisin is a creole because it has been learned as a first language by a large number
of speakers, and has developed accordingly to meet their linguistic needs.

As a result of their status as some group's first language, creoles also differ from
pidgins in their range of functions, in their structure and in some cases in the attitudes
expressed towards them. A creole is a pidgin which has expanded in structure and
vocabulary to express the range of meanings and serve the range of functions required
of a first language.

Structural features

Example 11

Australian Roper River Creole

(a) im megim ginu	he makes a canoe	[present tense]
(b) im bin megim ginu	he made a canoe	[past tense]
(c) im megimbad ginu	he is making a canoe	[present continuous]
(d) im bin megimbad ginu	he was making a canoe	[past continuous]

The linguistic complexity of creole languages is often not appreciated by outsiders.
I mentioned above that pidgin languages do not use affixes to signal meanings such as

the tense of a verb or the number of a noun. Creole languages, however, do develop ways of systematically signalling meanings such as verb tenses, and these may develop into inflections or affixes over time. By comparing the different sentences from Roper River Creole in example 11, you should be able to work out how the past tense and the continuous aspect are expressed.

The past tense is signalled by the particle *bin*, while the progressive aspect is marked by the suffix *-bad* which is attached to the verb. An example from Tok Pisin can illustrate the process by which a creole develops systematic ways of concisely expressing additional meanings as the demands made on the language by the speakers increase.

Example 12

Tok Pisin at different stages

(a) baimbai yu go   you will go
(b) bambai yu go   you will go
(c) bai yu go   you will go
(d) yu bai go   you will go
(e) yu bəgo   you will go

In its pidgin stage reference to future events in Tok Pisin used the adverb *baimbai* which derived from the English phrase *by and by*.

This is illustrated in sentence (a) *baimbai yu go*. As the pidgin developed into a creole, the adverb gradually shortened to *bambai* or *bai* as in (b) and (c). Sentence (d) illustrates an alternative position used for *bai* while (e) shows how it eventually became attached to the verb as a regular prefix signalling future tense. The meaning is expressed more concisely but also less obviously – a common outcome.

The substrate is another source of structural complexity for a creole. Table 4.1 showed that Tok Pisin has two first person plural pronouns, *yumi* and *mipela*. Most Oceanic languages make a distinction between an inclusive plural form, such as *yumi*, which refers to the speaker and the addressee, and an exclusive plural form, such as *mipela*, which refers to the speaker and some third party, but not the addressee. Since this inclusive/exclusive distinction does not occur in English (the lexifier language), it is a clear example of substrate influence on Tok Pisin, and it is found widely in Pacific pidgins and creoles.

Pidgins become more structurally regular as they undergo *creolisation*, the process by which a pidgin becomes a creole. The lists in table 4.2 illustrate a linguistic strategy which regularises the structure of words with related meanings, and so makes the forms easier to learn and easier to understand.

The meaning relationship between the words in the first column and the third column is exactly the same and this is reflected in the form of the creole, but not in English. So if you recognise the pattern it is possible to form new words in the creole language,

A

Multilingual speech communities

Table 4.2 Tok Pisin forms

Tok Pisin	English	Tok Pisin	English
bik	big, large	bikim	to enlarge, make large
brait	wide	braitim	to make wide, widen
daun	low	daunim	to lower
nogut	bad	nogutim	to spoil, damage
pret	afraid	pretim	to frighten, scare
doti	dirty	dotim	–

and to guess the English translation. If you knew the Tok Pisin word for 'hot' was *hat* you could predict that the word meaning 'to make hot' or 'to heat' would be *hatim*. You can similarly guess that the English verb missing from the list above is 'to dirty' or 'make dirty'. Notice that English is nowhere near so regular in form. While we can sometimes find patterns like *black/blacken, soft/soften, wide/widen*, it is not long before an irregular form trips up the unwary learner of English. While there is a word *shorten* in English, there is no word *longen*, for instance.

Exercise 7

Can you work out the patterns and fill in the gaps in the following list?

Tok Pisin	English
gras	grass
mausgras	moustache
gras bilong fes	beard
gras bilong hed	_____
gras antap long ai	eyebrow
gras nogut	weed
pisin	bird
gras bilong pisin	_____
gras bilong dog	_____
gras bilong pusi	_____
han	hand
han bilong pisin	wing of a bird

Answer at end of chapter

As the creole develops, paraphrases like these become more compact and concise, often at the cost of semantic 'transparency'. This is clearly a normal process in language. So *washman* is a combination of elements meaning 'man employed to do the washing' (a bit like English 'washerwoman' – an interesting example of a cultural difference in gender roles too). But though its meaning is clear when you know it, and therefore easy to remember, there is no reason why it could not mean 'man who washes the streets', for instance, and have derived from a longer phrase spelling out that meaning more explicitly. Once it has compacted into *washman* its precise meaning has to be learned. Similarly *daiman* could mean 'executioner' or 'hangman', but in fact means 'corpse'. When concise compounds like these develop from longer phrases they become less transparent and this is a common process in the development of languages.

In fact one of the reasons linguists find the study of pidgins and creoles so fascinating is precisely that they provide laboratories of language change in progress, and for testing hypotheses about universal linguistic features and processes. Pidgins and creoles also demonstrate the crucial role of social factors in the development of languages – since it is the meanings which motivate the structural changes, and the functional demands which lead to linguistic elaboration.

Functions

Example 13

Cameroon Pidgin English

Foh di foh dis graun oh foh no bi sehf – dat na di ting wei i di bring plenti hambag.
Wehda na sohm behta sehns sei mek man i tai hat
Foh di shap ston an shap stik dehm foh bad lohk wei dehm di wohri man foh dis graun,
Oh foh kari wowo ting foh fait dis trohbul wei i big laik sohlwata so?

To be, or not to be – that is the question;
Whether 'tis nobler in the mind to suffer
The slings and arrows of outrageous fortune
Or to take arms against a sea of troubles
And by opposing end them?
[*Hamlet*, III. i]

Many present-day creoles are spoken by descendants of the African slaves in the United States of America and the Caribbean. As mentioned above, the common language of the plantation was generally a pidgin, and children naturally acquired the pidgin as a first language. As the families' communicative needs expanded, so did the resources of the language they used. The pidgin developed into a creole.

Alternatively a pidgin can become so useful as a lingua franca that it may be expanded and used even by people who share a tribal language. In multilingual speech communities, parents may use a pidgin so extensively during the day, in the market, at church, in offices and on public transport, that it becomes normal for them to use it at home too. In this case, too, children will often acquire it as their first language and it will develop into a creole. Tok Pisin is the first language of many children in Papua New Guinea.

A

Multilingual speech communities

Once a creole has developed it can be used for all the functions of any language – politics, education, administration (including tax forms, as illustrated in example 10), original literature (and translations of Shakespeare too, as in example 13), and so on. Tok Pisin is the most frequently used language of debate in the Papua New Guinea Parliament. Creoles have become accepted standard and even national and official languages, as will be seen in the next chapter. Once developed there is no evidence in their linguistic structure to reveal their pidgin origins. A linguist doing a present-day (or synchronic) analysis of, say, Afrikaans would not be able to identify it as a creole, though many believe it has creole origins. The features which might suggest such origins are all features which can be found in other well-established languages with no history of creolisation that we can know about. (Even English has been described by some as a latter-day creole, with French vocabulary superimposed on a Celtic/Old English base.) This is fascinating and provocative since, as mentioned above, it suggests that the processes of pidginisation and creolisation may be universal processes which reveal a great deal about the origins of language and the ways in which languages develop.

Attitudes

Though outsiders' attitudes to creoles are often as negative as their attitudes to pidgins, this is not always the case for those who speak the language. Tok Pisin has status and prestige for people in Papua New Guinea who recognise its usefulness as a means of communication with a wide range of influential people as well as in getting a decent job. The code-switching example 17 in chapter 2 demonstrated its use as a language signalling the speaker's community status, even though it was not strictly necessary for communication purposes. The Buang Taxi Truck Company similarly use Tok Pisin for their meetings, even though all present speak Buang. It is also a language of solidarity between Papua New Guineans with different vernaculars. Though Haitian Creole is the L language alongside prestigious French in Haiti, nevertheless the majority of the people who are monolingual in the creole express strong loyalty to it as the language which best expresses their feelings.

Origins and endings

Example 14

Some words seem to turn up in many different pidgin languages. The Portuguese word *savi* meaning 'know', for instance, and *palava* meaning 'trouble' are found in many English-based pidgins and creoles. The word *bell* is heard in both Tok Pisin and Chinese Pidgin. *Grease* is rendered as *glease* in Chinese Pidgin, and in an American pidgin known as Chinook Jargon, and as *gris* in Tok Pisin.

Despite their huge geographical spread – they are found in every continent – many similarities are found among pidgins and creoles. Over a hundred have been identified, but the lexifier language for most (about 85) is one of seven European languages: English (35), French (15), Portuguese (14), Spanish (7), German (6), Dutch (5), and Italian (3). So perhaps the similarities are not surprising.

But the fact that similarities have been found between pidgins from quite different geographical regions, and in pidgins where quite different languages have contributed to their development, suggests things are not quite so straightforward. Some have argued that all pidgins and creoles had a common origin. They claim that most pidgins can be traced back to a single fifteenth-century Portuguese pidgin, and perhaps further to a Mediterranean lingua franca, Sabir. Others argue that each pidgin arises and develops independently. They account for the similarities by pointing to two types of constraints on their development which they all share. First, pidgins arise in different contexts but for the same kinds of basic functions – trade, barter, and other essentially transactional and referentially oriented functions. Secondly, these functions are expressed through structural processes which seem universal to all situations of language development – processes such as simplification and reduction of redundant features (like gender markers). It is argued that these processes will be found in any context where basic communication is the aim, so there is no need to argue for a common origin for all pidgins. It is easy to see the fascination of the debate – and it is one which seems likely to continue for some time.

There is almost as much debate about what ultimately happens to a creole. There are a variety of answers depending on the social context. In societies with rigid social divisions, a creole may remain as a stable L variety alongside an officially sanctioned H variety, a situation illustrated in diglossic Haiti where Haitian Creole is the L variety alongside French. Where social barriers are more fluid, the creole may develop towards the standard language from which it has derived large amounts of vocabulary. When a creole is used side-by-side with the standard variety in a community where social barriers are not insuperable, features of the creole tend to change in the direction of the standard variety. This process is described as *decreolisation*.

Eventually there may exist a continuum of varieties between the standard language and the creole – sometimes described as a post-creole continuum. In this situation, linguists label the variety closest to the standard an acrolect (where *acro* means 'high'), whereas the variety closest to the creole is labelled the basilect or 'deep' creole. These two varieties are often mutually unintelligible. Varieties in between these two extremes are described as mesolects or intermediate varieties. Examples can be found in Jamaica and Guyana. Over time a creole in this situation may be engulfed by the standard language, as Negerhollands has been by Dutch in the Dutch West Indies. One further possibility, as we shall see in the next chapter, is that a creole may be standardised and adopted as an official language, as Tok Pisin was in Papua New Guinea, or become a national language, as did Indonesian, a language which developed from pidgin Malay.

A

Multilingual speech communities

Exercise 8

Using the social dimensions introduced in chapter 1 – solidarity, status, formality, and function – consider the social characteristics of the following linguistic varieties described in this chapter.

(a) vernacular
(b) standard
(c) lingua franca
(d) pidgin
(e) creole

Answer at end of chapter

Exercise 9

Most research on creoles has focussed on the relationship between the creole and the (usually European) lexifier language. But in the East Maroon community of Pamaka, the lexifier language (English) is never heard in daily interaction and nor is it an official language of Suriname. Rather people switch regularly between two creole languages, one the local rural community language Pamaka, and the other an urban creole, Sranan Tonga. What are the implications for decreolisation in such a context?

Answer at end of chapter

ANSWERS TO EXERCISES IN CHAPTER 4

Answer to exercise 1 (a)

(a) Shi is Kalala's vernacular. It is his tribal language, learned first and used in the home and with members of his ethnic group. In this sense, Kathiawari, a dialect of Gujerati, is Mr Patel's vernacular (even though Gujerati is a written language with a literary tradition).

Answer to exercise 1 (b)

(b) Dyirbal can be classified as a vernacular language on a number of criteria. It is unstandardised and unwritten. It is, or was, acquired in the home and is used between members of the same tribe for everyday interaction. Its functions are relatively circumscribed.

Answer to exercise 2

The following definition is the closest in the *Collins Dictionary of the English Language* (1991).

Standard: 'an accepted or approved example of something against which others are judged or measured'.

Note the definition stresses the notion of a model or norm without giving any indication of how that norm is determined or where it derives its status from. Sociolinguists emphasise the social and non-linguistic factors which determine the emergence of a particular variety as the standard. They point out that purely linguistic considerations are rarely important. Though linguists may be involved in codification, their recommendations are generally guided by cultural or social factors such as prestige and usage, rather than by the intrinsic linguistic features of alternatives. This point is illustrated in the next chapter.

Answer to exercise 3

Over time, it has been recognised that the distinctions between the circles are very difficult to maintain using the criterion of native vs non-native speakers. An alternative approach is to think of the circles as reflecting different degrees of proficiency: those in the inner circle are those with high or native-like proficiency (whether they are native speakers or not), and the outer and expanding circles represent decreasing levels of proficiency, usually reflecting a more limited range of functions and less frequent use. Another approach would focus on the range of functions English serves, from all functions for those in the inner circle, through to a more limited range of functions as one moves out to the expanding circle.

Answer to exercise 4

Possible answers to this question are provided in the next chapter and you will find that the relevant factors are almost entirely non-linguistic. Any linguistic problems can be resolved relatively easily after the selection is made on other grounds.

Answer to exercise 5

Note that the verb in French changes its form with each pronoun (though in speech there would be no distinction between *vas* and *va*). Grammatical information about the subject is expressed twice therefore, once by the form of the pronoun and once by the verb form. In English the verb has two different forms (*go/goes*) distinguishing the third person singular verb form from the form with other subjects. In Tok Pisin and Cameroon Pidgin the form of the verb is the same throughout. The pronoun alone signals the change in person and number of the subject.

Answers to exercise 6

(a) Seychelles Creole: French based/French is the lexifier language.
(b) Roper River Creole: English-based/English is the lexifier language.
(c) Sranan: English-based/English is the lexifier language.
(d) Cape York Creole: English-based/English is the lexifier language.
(e) Guyanais: French-based/French is the lexifier language.
(f) Papua New Guinea Pidgin German: German-based/German is the lexifier language.
(g) Cameroon Pidgin: English-based/English is the lexifier language.

Answers to exercise 7

hair
feather
dog's fur
cat's fur

Answer to exercise 8

Vernacular languages contrast with standardised varieties predominantly on the status and formality dimensions. Vernaculars are generally low status varieties used to express solidarity or identity in informal contexts. Standard dialects are prestigious varieties which may be used in more formal situations.

Lingua francas and pidgin languages can perhaps be best described in terms of their functions. They are both primarily means of expressing referential functions – they are associated with informal but information-oriented contexts.

Pidgins and creoles are generally regarded as low status linguistic varieties, though we will see in the next chapter that steps can be taken to raise the status of creoles which have been selected for promotion for political reasons.

Answer to exercise 9

Decreolisation is most unlikely in a situation where the lexifier language, English, is not in regular use in the community.

◼ Concepts introduced

Vernacular
Standard
Inner-circle, outer circle and expanded circle varieties of English
Lingua franca
Pidgin
Lexifier or superstrate
Substrate
Creole
Creolisation
Acrolect, basilect and mesolect
Decreolisation

◼ References

The concepts introduced in this chapter are discussed further in the following sources:

Crystal (1988, 1997)
Fasold (1990)
Romaine (1988, 1989)
Todd (1974)

The following sources provided material for this chapter:

Collins Dictionary of the English Language (1991: 1504–5) for definition of 'standard'
Crowley (1990) for example 6
De Camp (1977) for example 7
Ethnologue: http://www.ethnologue.com/. This is an encyclopedic reference work cataloguing the world's known living languages
Hancock (1977) for statistics on pidgin and creole languages
Kachru (1992, 1997) on inner-circle and outer-circle Englishes
Mihalic (1971) and Romaine (1988) on Tok Pisin

Migge (2007) on Suriname creoles (exercise 8)
Nation (2001) on average adult vocabulary size
Pandit (1979) for example 1
Romaine (1988) for list used in exercise 6 and most of examples in exercise 5
Sharpe and Sandefur (1976) for data from Roper River Creole
Sorensen (1972) on Northwest Amazon
UNESCO (1953)
Valdman (1988) on Haiti

Quotations

Example 2 is an excerpt from George Puttenham *The Art of Poesie*, 1589, which is quoted in Shaklee (1980: 46).
Example 5 has been attributed to Paul Freyburg, who worked as a translator for Kristen Press in Papua New Guinea in 1963. Despite efforts, no published source has been located.
Example 9 is from Nelson (1972), reported in Romaine (1988: 11–12).
The speech from *Hamlet* in example 13 was translated by R. Awa and is quoted in Crystal (1988: 14).

Useful additional reading

Coupland and Jaworski (1997), Section VI
Crystal (1997), Ch. 55
Mesthrie et al. (2000), Ch. 9
Meyerhoff (2006), Ch. 11
Myers-Scotton (2006), Ch. 5
Romaine (2000), Ch. 4
Wardhaugh (2006), Ch. 3

A

Multilingual speech communities

5　National languages and language planning

Example 1

Reinaldo Decoud Larrosa is a highly educated Paraguayan who lives in Asunción, the capital city. He has spent many years fighting to develop and encourage pride in Guaraní, the indigenous language, among Paraguayans from all social backgrounds. Upper-class Paraguayans have always regarded Spanish as the language of culture, education and civilisation, and in the past they tended to belittle Guaraní as the language of the ill-bred and uneducated. Larrosa has pointed to the linguistic richness of Guaraní, with its 14 indicative tenses, and extensive vocabulary in areas such as botany, medicine and agriculture. He has also emphasised its importance as the only language which can adequately express Paraguayan national identity. As a result of his efforts and those of others, Guaraní is now a language most Paraguayans are proud of.

Paraguay is the only Latin American nation with a distinctive national language – Guaraní. Guaraní is an indigenous American Indian language spoken by over 90 per cent of the population, and it has coexisted for the past 300 years with Spanish (which is spoken by no more than 60 per cent of the people). Paraguay provides a clear case of stable broad diglossia, with Spanish, the H language, used in formal contexts, for administration, a great deal of education, and legal business, and Guaraní, the L language of solidarity, the language of love, humour and poetry.

In Paraguay we find an interesting example of the competing claims of an indigenous language and a world language for the status of national language. Paraguayans are generally happy to recognise Spanish as a useful language for official business. But though Spanish and Guaraní both have official status, it is Guaraní which most people regard as their real national language. Guaraní is felt to be the language which best expresses their distinctive culture and traditions. These positive feelings towards Guaraní make Paraguay unique among Latin American countries. In other countries the indigenous languages have little status compared to Spanish or Portuguese, the colonial languages.

Many Paraguayans consider that Guaraní is an important symbol of Paraguayan identity. People feel that you cannot be a true Paraguayan unless you can speak the language. Some claim that there are things they can say in Guaraní which are more diffi-cult to express in Spanish. So while people find Spanish a useful language for formal and business interactions, and it is increasingly heard in urban Paraguayan homes, most are proud of Guaraní and express strong loyalty towards it. Paraguayans who meet overseas, for instance, often use Guaraní to each other.

Exercise 1

Which of the following factors do you consider most relevant in assessing the suitability of Guaraní as the national language of Paraguay? Order the factors according to their importance in relation to this issue.

(a) Guaraní is a linguistically interesting language with a complex tense system.
(b) Guaraní is spoken by over 90 per cent of Paraguayans and is the only language of many rural people.
(c) Guaraní has an extensive vocabulary, especially in areas such as botany, medicine and agriculture.
(d) Guaraní expresses solidarity between Paraguayans both at home and abroad.
(e) Guaraní is considered a melodious language, especially appropriate for expressions of love.
(f) Guaraní is an indigenous language which attracts a great deal of language loyalty from Paraguayans.
(g) Guaraní is a morphologically interesting language which forms words using additive and synthetic processes.
(h) Every president of Paraguay has been able to speak Guaraní.

Answer at end of chapter

NATIONAL AND OFFICIAL LANGUAGES

Example 2

Vanuatu is a multilingual Pacific republic consisting of about 80 islands with a population of around 180,000. It declared independence from a joint British and French colonial administration in 1980. Vanuatu is unique in the Pacific because it has adopted a non-European language, a former pidgin, Bislama, as its sole national language. Bislama is an English-lexified creole with origins in a Melanesian plantation pidgin. It is an invaluable lingua franca in Vanuatu, and a very politically acceptable national language.

A

Multilingual speech communities

In the 1960s, the Paraguayan government used two different terms to distinguish between the status of Spanish and Guaraní: Guaraní was declared the 'national' language while Spanish was an 'official' language of Paraguay. In sociolinguistics the distinction between a national language and an official language is generally made along the affective–referential dimension, or more precisely in this context, the ideological–instrumental dimension. A *national language* is the language of a political, cultural and social unit. It is generally developed and used as a symbol of national unity. Its functions are to identify the nation and unite its people. An *official language*, by contrast, is simply a language which may be used for government business. Its function is primarily utilitarian rather than symbolic. It is possible, of course, for one language to serve both functions.

Not surprisingly, governments do not always recognise the distinctions made by sociolinguists. They use the terms 'official' and 'national' to suit their political ends, as the Paraguayan case described above illustrates. However, the Paraguayan situation changed again in 1992, when Guaraní was granted official status alongside Spanish. So Paraguay now has two official languages and one national language, Guaraní. The same pattern is found in multilingual Tanzania with one national language, Swahili, but two official languages, Swahili and English. Similarly, in Vanuatu, the national language is Bislama, a Pacific creole, and it is also an official language alongside French and English, the languages of the previous colonial administrators. Many countries make no distinction between a national language and an official language. In countries which regard themselves as monolingual nations, the same language serves both purposes. In multilingual communities, however, all kinds of permutations have been used in order to satisfy both political and social goals on the one hand, and more practical and utilitarian needs on the other.

In multilingual countries, the government often declares a particular language to be the national language for political reasons. The declaration may be a step in the process of asserting the nationhood of a newly independent or established nation, for instance, as in the case of Swahili in Tanzania, Hebrew in Israel, Malay in Malaysia, and Indonesian in Indonesia. Where this national language cannot serve all the internal and external functions of government business, however, it has then been necessary to identify one or more official languages as well. So French is an official language in many countries, such as the Ivory Coast and Chad, where France was previously a colonial power, and Arabic is an official language in Israel alongside Hebrew.

The identification of official languages may also be necessary when the choice of national language is problematic. In multilingual India, for example, attempts to give Hindi sole status as the national language have not succeeded. Fourteen regional Indian languages are recognised as official languages alongside English and Hindi for the country as a whole, and in addition different states each have their own official languages. Telegu, for instance, is the official language of the state of Andhra Pradesh. Some multilingual countries have nominated more than one national language. The Democratic Republic of the Congo, for instance (formerly Zaire), has four African languages as national languages, Lingala, Swahili, Tshiluba, and Kikongo, alongside French as an official language. Lingala is, however, the official language of the army. In Haiti, the 1983 constitution declared Haitian Creole a national language alongside French, but it was not until 1987 that the Creole was granted official status.

Exercise 2

Can you fill in the following table?
Why do you think some countries have more than one language with official status?

Country	Official language(s)
Australia	
Belgium	
Brazil	
Canada	
Finland	
France	
Haiti	
India	
Indonesia	
Kenya	
New Zealand	
Norway	
Papua New Guinea	
Paraguay	
Philippines	
Singapore	
Tanzania	
Uruguay	
Vanuatu	

Answer at end of chapter

A

Multilingual speech communities

▨ Official status and minority languages

Because of its colonial history, as well as its value as a world language and international lingua franca, English is an official language in many countries throughout the world, such as Pakistan, Fiji, Vanuatu, Jamaica and the Bahamas, as well as those listed above. Often it shares this official status with an indigenous language such as Malay in Malaysia, Swahili in Tanzania, and Gilbertese in Kiribati. But, interestingly, English is not legally an official language of England, the United States of America, or New Zealand. In these countries it has not been considered necessary to legislate that the language of the majority is an official language. In New Zealand, ironically, although English is *de facto* (in fact or actuality) the official language of government and education, Maori and New Zealand Sign Language are the two languages which have legal or *de jure* status as official languages.

Example 3

Te Ringa Mangu is one of a number of Maori activists who have campaigned for many years for Maori rights. An articulate, stimulating and abrasive public speaker, he has often ended up in court on charges of breaching the peace as a result of his protests. There he has insisted on addressing the court in Maori – a language which until recently was not recognised by the New Zealand courts. Now he has the right to address the court in Maori – and the court will provide a person to translate his words into English.

Maori was declared an official language of New Zealand in 1987. What that means, however, is far from clear. Cynics have described it as merely a cosmetic procedure aimed at quietening the demands of Maori activists. But the declaration clearly gives the language a status it did not have previously, and acknowledges its symbolic importance to the country as a whole, as well as to the indigenous Maori people in particular. It can also be regarded as a positive statement of intent – a first step in a process which may encourage the use of Maori in an increasing number of official institutional domains such as the law courts, official government ceremonies and trans-actions, and in education.

Maori activists campaigned for many years for the right to use Maori in official and administrative contexts. Most used peaceful means but minority groups have often taken very radical action in order to get official recognition for their languages. In Wales the Welsh administration recognises Welsh as a language of government and education, but it has no official status in Britain. In the late twentieth century, Welsh activists painted out English road signs in protest against the dominance of English and the English, and the President of Plaid Cymru (the Welsh Nationalist Party) promised to 'fast to the death' to get a Welsh television channel.

Elsewhere there have been riots over language issues. Linguistic minorities in India have rioted when their demands have fallen on deaf ears. In Belgium, French and Flemish have had legal equality since 1963, but language riots in 1968 caused the fall of the government when they proposed to extend the French-speaking section of the University of Louvain (or, in Flemish, Leuven). Though the 1968–69 Official Languages Act declared both French and English official languages in Canada, and gave them equal status in all aspects of federal administration, the Quebec government has been far from satisfied with the reality of English domination and has threatened to secede over language-related issues. In the former Soviet Union *glasnost* and *perestroika* brought in their wake a desire for increased independence among minority language groups, as example 4(a) illustrates. But Russian speakers have also felt concerned about their language rights, as shown in 4(b).

Example 4

(a) Thousands of Moldavians demonstrated in the republic's capital Kishinev yesterday and threatened a general strike if Soviet leaders failed to meet their demands for language concessions . . . Demonstrators, many waving Romanian flags, repeated demands for a return to the Latin alphabet from the Cyrillic imposed by Soviet dictator Josef Stalin.

(b) Russian-speaking workers in Estonia on the Gulf of Finland struck for four days last week against language and election laws, saying they discriminate against them.

© 1989 Reuters Limited

Many minorities would like to gain official status for their languages, but the costs in terms of providing services and information in all official languages are considerable, and most governments count them carefully. In Canada, for instance, as well as French speakers and the indigenous Canadian peoples, such as the Cree and Mohawk, there are many other Canadian minorities – Italians, Portuguese, Chinese and Ukrainians, for instance. Together they make up about 27 per cent of the total Canadian population. Many resent the special status of the French, who make up only 28 per cent of the population. Providing services, information, legal representation and, in some places, education in just two official languages is an expensive business. It seems unlikely other minorities will earn such rights easily.

Exercise 3

In 1855 Dean Trench, a leading architect of the *Oxford English Dictionary*, expressed the hope that studying the dictionary would 'lead through a more intimate knowledge of English into a greater love of England'. In the 1980s this attitude was expressed once again in relation to the standard dialect of English. The British Secretary of State for Education pointed to the importance of the English language as a symbol of nationhood.

What do you think of the claims of these men that studying standard English will develop a sense of national pride in England?

Answer at end of chapter

What price a national language?

Many countries have regarded the development of a single national language as a way of symbolising the unity of a nation. 'One nation, one language' has been a popular and effective slogan. In earlier centuries the national language of a political entity often

A

Multilingual speech communities

103

emerged naturally and relatively unselfconsciously over a period of time. English in England, French in France, Japanese in Japan, Spanish in Spain seem obvious examples. There were very few languages with this kind of status before about 1500. Then the number increased dramatically, especially in the nineteenth century as linguistic nationalism in Europe grew. It has almost doubled again in the twentieth century with the emergence of colonised countries from colonial rule into independent nation-states.

Over the last hundred years nationhood and independence have been very important political issues throughout the world. In the struggle to establish a distinct national identity, and to secure independence from colonial rule, the development of a national language has often played an important part. The symbolic value of a national language as a unifying rallying point in the fight for independence was quickly appreciated in countries such as Tanzania, where more than 120 languages are spoken. In other multilingual countries, such as China, the Philippines and Indonesia, where there are large populations speaking hundreds of different vernaculars, a national language is not only a useful lingua franca and official language, it also serves a symbolic unifying function for these nations.

Where there is a single dominant group, the issue of which language to choose as the official language to represent the nation generally doesn't arise. Somali is the first language of 90 per cent of the people of Somalia and the national official language of the country. Danish is the national language of Denmark, and the first language of 98 per cent of the people. Numerical dominance is not always what counts, however. Political power is the crucial factor.

In multilingual countries the significance of political power in the choice of national language is particularly clear. There are over one hundred vernacular languages spoken in the Philippines. When they gained independence in 1946, Pilipino (now Filipino) was declared the national language. It was so closely based on Tagalog, however, the ethnic language of one particular group, that it has never been unanimously accepted. Tagalog has around twelve million native speakers, but Cebuana, for example, has over ten million speakers, and Ilocano, another indigenous language, over five million speakers. The choice of Tagalog reflected the political and economic power of its speakers who were concentrated in the area which included the capital, Manila. Its relabelling as Filipino was an attempt to help it gain acceptance more widely, but resentment at the advantages it gives to a particular ethnic group is still keenly felt.

In Indonesia by contrast, the government did not select the language of the political and social elite, the Javanese, as the national language. Instead they developed and standardised a variety of Malay which was widely used in Indonesia as a trade language. Since Javanese has a complex linguistically marked politeness system based on assessments of relative status (see chapters 6 and 10), this was an eminently sensible decision. Indeed, the successful spread of Indonesian owes a great deal to the fact that it is a very useful neutral choice in many situations.

Like India, some African countries have avoided selecting just one language as the national language, since the wrong choice could easily lead to riots and even war. Tanzania, however, successfully adopted Swahili as its national language, and the story of how this was achieved illustrates nicely what is involved when a country decides to develop an indigenous language for use as a national language. Linguists are often involved in this process of language planning. In the next section we will examine the steps which must be taken.

PLANNING FOR A NATIONAL OFFICIAL LANGUAGE

Form, functions and attitudes

What is involved in developing a code or variety (whether dialect or language) so that it is suitable for official use? Addressing this challenge involves issues relating to the form of the variety, the functions it serves, and the attitudes people hold towards it.

There are generally four interrelated steps:

1. *Selection*: choosing the variety or code to be developed.
2. *Codification*: standardising its structural or linguistic features. This kind of 'linguistic processing' is known as *corpus planning*.
3. *Elaboration*: extending its functions for use in new domains. This involves developing the necessary linguistic resources for handling new concepts and contexts.
4. *Securing its acceptance.* The status of the new variety is important, and so people's attitudes to the variety being developed must be considered. Steps may be needed to enhance its prestige, for instance, and to encourage people to develop pride in the language or loyalty towards it. This is known as *status planning* or *prestige planning*.

The relationship between the steps is summarised in table 5.1.

Selecting the code to be developed is often an entirely political decision, though linguists may point out the different linguistic problems presented by selecting one variety rather than another. Acceptance by the people will generally require endorsement by politicians and socially prestigious groups. So selection and acceptance are steps which involve social and political factors. Codification and elaborating the code to handle a wider range of functions are, by contrast, essentially linguistic processes. Producing a dictionary and ensuring there are words available for teaching maths in the variety, for instance, are problems for linguists. In practice, however, all these steps are closely interrelated, as the examples below will demonstrate.

Table 5.1 Steps in language planning

	Form	Function and Attitudes
Social	Selection	Acceptance
Linguistic	Codification	Elaboration

Source: From Haugen 1966a: 934

▊ Tanzania

Selecting a code

When Tanzania gained independence in 1961, the government faced the dilemma of which language to choose as its official national language. Choosing one language from over a hundred indigenous languages, each associated with a particular tribe, would have simply provoked discontent, if not inter-tribal warfare. Choosing English for a newly independent nation seemed inappropriate (though many other nations have had little choice but to use the language of the colonisers as their only official language). The first President of Tanzania, Julius Nyerere, chose Swahili, a language of the Bantu language family, which was widely used throughout the country as a lingua franca in many contexts. There were some obvious reasons for his choice. Some were pragmatic. Swahili was already the medium of primary education, for instance, and so all Tanzanians learned the language at school. Other obvious reasons were more ideological. Ninety-six per cent of Tanzania's languages are Bantu languages, like Swahili, so it could be clearly identified as an African language. Moreover Swahili had served as the lingua franca of the anti-colonial political movement for independence. In this role it had acted as a kind of social cement between very disparate groups. It could hardly have had better credentials from a political and social point of view.

Codifying and elaborating Swahili

The process of standardising Swahili was begun by the British administration well before independence. In the 1920s a southern variety of Swahili, used in Zanzibar, was selected as the basis for the standard. The fact that it was being used in primary education and for administration meant standardisation was essential. Its codification involved developing a standard spelling system, describing the grammar of the variety selected as the new standard, and writing a dictionary to record its vocabulary.

Following Tanzanian independence in 1961, Swahili was used in more and more contexts for education, administration, politics and law. Its vocabulary was expanded to meet the demands of new contexts by borrowing freely from Arabic and English as appropriate. President Nyerere intended that eventually it should be used for post-primary education, in the Higher Courts, and in all areas of government. This meant intensive work in order to develop the necessary vocabulary and technical terms, and an enormous amount was achieved in a short space of time. In 1984, however, the government decided not to extend Swahili-medium education to secondary and tertiary education. English is being retained for these levels.

Exercise 4

Why do you think English might be regarded by some politicians as more suitable than Swahili for secondary and tertiary education in Tanzania? What are the counter-arguments?

Answer at end of chapter

Attitudes to Swahili

The role of Swahili in unifying the people of Tanzania to work for independence guaranteed it prestige and positive attitudes. The charisma of Nyerere himself carried over to the language he used extensively in his speeches and his political writings. He used it in domains where formerly English had been used exclusively – he also translated Shakespeare's *Julius Caesar* and *The Merchant of Venice* into Swahili – and this too increased its status. People have often seen the success of Swahili as the national language in Tanzania as due to its 'neutral' status – it is not identified with a particular tribe. But its widespread acceptance was also due to the fact that Tanzanians developed a strong loyalty towards the language which united them in working towards *uhuru* ('freedom').

The story of the acceptance of Swahili as the national language of Tanzania is therefore an interesting one. Swahili serves as a lingua franca in a country with hundreds of different tribal vernaculars. It provides an economical solution to the problem of which language to use for local administration and primary education. It provides a culturally acceptable symbol of unity. Linguistic diversity can seem problematic to those working for political unification. It is potentially divisive. Swahili has provided a very convenient compromise in Tanzania. But finally it is important to remember that the story of how Swahili became the national language of Tanzania might be told rather differently by a group whose tribal vernacular was a competing lingua franca.

In this section the steps involved in developing a particular code or variety for use as a national language have been discussed in relation to a large multilingual country, Tanzania, where the competing varieties are distinct languages. Exactly the same processes and steps are relevant in the deliberate development of a particular dialect for use as national language in a monolingual country, as we shall see in the next section in relation to Norway, a country with a relatively small and homogeneous population.

A

Multilingual speech communities

Exercise 5

A successful national language needs to serve a variety of functions. The following have been identified as important.

Unifying: it must unify the nation, and offer advantages to speakers over their dialects and vernaculars.

Separatist: it must set the nation off from surrounding nations. It should be an appropriate symbol of separate national identity.

Prestige: it should be recognised as a proper or 'real' language with higher status than local dialects and vernacular languages.

Frame-of-reference function: the standard variety serves as a yardstick for correctness. Other varieties will be regarded as non-standard in some respect.

Are all these functions served for the Tanzanian nation by Swahili?

Answer at end of chapter

Exercise 6

The Academy of the Hebrew Language in Israel was faced with the reverse of the task facing language planners in Tanzania, namely to revive an ancient written language to serve the daily colloquial needs of a modern people. Describe each of the four steps outlined above (code selection, codification, elaboration and acceptance) in relation to the development of a national language for Israel, and identify any problems you think the language planners faced.

Answer at end of chapter

DEVELOPING A STANDARD VARIETY IN NORWAY

Example 5

Two competing varieties of Norwegian (Bm *is Bokmål*; Nn *is Nynorsk.*)

Bm Det rette hjemlige mål i landet er det som landets folk
Nn   heimlege   folket i landet
Bm har arvet fra forfedrene, fra den ene ætt til den andre
Nn   arva frå   frå   eine ætta
'The right native tongue in (this) country is that which (the) country's people
have inherited from ancestors, from the one generation to the next.'

In 1814 Norway became independent after being ruled by Denmark for four centuries. The government was then faced with a diglossia situation with Danish as the H language and a range of Norwegian dialects as the L varieties, but no standard Norwegian language. Upper-class people spoke Danish with Norwegian pronunciation in formal situations, and a compromise between that and local Norwegian dialects in informal contexts. Lower-class and rural people used Norwegian dialects, with Danish influence evident in the speech of townspeople. Where was the government to look for an official national language for Norway?

Selecting a code

Essentially the Norwegian government had the choice of developing a national language from standard Danish or from local Norwegian dialects. While Danish offered all the advantages of being codified in dictionaries and grammars, it was the language of H domains and of the 'oppressors' from whom Norway had gained independence. So although choosing Danish would have reduced the linguistic problems facing the planners, it presented different kinds of problems. Standard Danish was not used widely for informal interaction, especially in rural areas, and people's attitudes towards the language were generally at least ambivalent, if not hostile. On the other hand, choosing a variety from among the regional Norwegian dialects raised problems relating to the form and new functions required of a standard language. Any dialect selected would need codifying and would require extensive functional elaboration. And the problem of *which* dialect to select raised obvious headaches in relation to people's attitudes.

Two different approaches were taken to developing a standard written variety of Norwegian. One approach selected a variety based on Danish, with some orthographic and morphological modifications reflecting educated urban Norwegian speech. This eventually developed into Bokmål, the variety mentioned in the description of Hemnesberget in example 6 in the first chapter. The other approach created a new Norwegian written standard by drawing on a range of rural Norwegian dialects. It

A

Multilingual speech communities

was first called Landsmål ('language of the country'), and later, after several reforms, Nynorsk ('new Norwegian').

Codification and elaboration

The Nynorsk solution, which involved amalgamating features from several dialects, is the most intriguing from a linguistic point of view. This composite variety was essentially the brainchild of Ivar Aasen, a schoolteacher who had studied Norwegian dialects. He wrote a grammar and a 40,000-word dictionary of the variety he was advocating as the new Norwegian standard. As a result this constructed variety turned out to be one of the best described languages around at the time. Aasen identified common grammatical patterns in different dialects, and he chose vocabulary from a range of different regions. Where there was a choice of word forms he selected those he considered least 'corrupted' or 'contaminated' by Danish. Rural dialect resources also solved the problem of functional elaboration, or extending the use of Norwegian into domains where Danish had previously been the only appropriate code. New words were needed for many concepts which had previously been discussed only in Danish. Dialect forms were Aasen's main resource for creating new words.

Since the late nineteenth century, then, Norway has had these two competing official written varieties. During the first half of the twentieth century, language planners tried to bring the two closer together (into Samnorsk or 'united Norwegian') through continued codification efforts. After World War II, however, political differences led to a change in attitude among Bokmål supporters in particular. The official policy of amalgamation was no longer pursued so vigorously, and another spelling reform in 1981 introduced more conservative forms into Bokmål. So Bokmål and Nynorsk continue to exist, and in fact they had become even more polarised by the 1990s, with arguments continuing about the appropriate form of a written Norwegian standard.

Nevertheless, it is important to recognise that although Norwegians regard Nynorsk and Bokmål as distinct written varieties, they continue to have much in common – as example 5 shows. Their syntax is almost identical. They differ mainly in the form of particular words (e.g. *hjemlige* vs *heimlege*), and in spelling (e.g. *frå* vs *fra*), but they also share many morphological variants. From a linguistic point of view, they are very similar indeed (though, of course, Norwegians speak Bokmål and Nynorsk with a wide range of regional and social accents).

Pronouncements are regularly made by the Norwegian Language Council about which spellings of particular words are officially sanctioned. Official documents are printed in both varieties, and schoolchildren are taught to read and write both, though local councils decide which variety is to be used as the main vehicle of instruction in the local schools.

Acceptance

What about the problem of attitudes to these two varieties? Though Norwegian nationalists enthusiastically welcomed Nynorsk, the Norwegian-based variety, and rejected the modified Danish alternative, many influential educated city-dwellers did not. They regarded a standard based on rural dialects as rustic and uncivilised. If Nynorsk was to be accepted at all, government support was essential. And it was also necessary to persuade influential public figures to endorse and to use the new variety in public contexts. Aasen succeeded in this to the extent that in 1885 Landsmål was voted official equality with Danish, in 1929 it was relabelled Nynorsk, and at its peak in 1944 it was the chief language of instruction for 34.1 per cent of all schoolchildren. Since then, Nynorsk has had mixed fortunes and in 1993 it was the language of instruction for only 17 per cent of primary school pupils. By the 1990s no more than 25 per cent of all Norwegians used Nynorsk, and many people used both Bokmål and Nynorsk depending on the context. What is more, Bokmål forms continue to displace Nynorsk forms rather than vice versa.

In practice, then, it is clear that Bokmål rather than Nynorsk has been winning out. It is used in most books and by most schools as a medium of instruction. Though some people insist on Nynorsk as the only possible variety for a 'true' Norwegian to use, and stress its significance as a more democratic variety, many dislike its 'country bumpkin' associations. Bokmål has urban and sophisticated connotations. These attitudes are now widespread and their effects on people's usage are likely to make government intervention and language planning irrelevant in the long run.

In some countries a standard dialect of a language, suitable for official uses and acceptable as a national symbol, has emerged naturally, with little or no help from government agencies or linguistic experts. In Norway, as in many more recently developing nations, things have not been so simple. It has been necessary to make deliberate choices, to accelerate the process of language standardisation, and to legislate on the status of particular varieties. It is clear that language planning is a fascinating mixture of political and social considerations, as well as linguistic ones. In the final section of this chapter, however, we will change focus from telescope to microscope, and examine a few of the nitty-gritty linguistic issues that language planners deal with when they get involved in codifying a variety.

A

Multilingual speech communities

Exercise 7

The development of a standard language has sometimes been described as involving the following two steps:

(a) create a model for imitation
(b) promote it over its rivals.

Linguists are often involved as advisers at both stages. Some people have argued that linguists can provide useful linguistic expertise for achieving step (a) but they have no contribution to make to step (b). Do you agree?

Answer at end of chapter

THE LINGUIST'S ROLE IN LANGUAGE PLANNING

Example 6

Lexicographer: a writer of dictionaries, a harmless drudge.
(Johnson, Samuel (1755). *Dictionary of the English Language.*)

Language academies have existed for centuries, but it is also true that individuals have often had an enormous influence on language planning, and especially on the standardisation or codification of a particular variety. Samuel Johnson's 40,000-word dictionary was a landmark in the codification of English, though, as example 6 demonstrates, he had few illusions about the lexicographer's role. Ivar Aasen in Norway created a composite variety of Norwegian (Landsmål/Nynorsk) from a range of dialects. In Israel, Eliezer Ben-Yehuda was the most influential proponent of the vernacularisation of Hebrew. Francis Mihalic wrote the first authoritative grammar and dictionary of Tok Pisin in the 1950s. And in New Zealand Harry Orsman completed the first dictionary of New Zealand English on historical principles in 1997.

More often these days, the nuts and bolts of language planning are handled by committees, commissions or academies. Moreover, the focus of much language planning activity has altered from the promotion of national and official languages in countries trying to establish their autonomy, to include concern for minority and endangered languages. The Kanak Languages Academy, for example, has recently been established to preserve the indigenous languages of New Caledonia. Codification and vocabulary expansion are typically of prime concern for language academies, and in the next section I briefly illustrate these processes, drawing mainly on Maori for exemplification.

Codification of orthography

Example 7

In January 1982, the Greek government passed a law to implement a new writing system called MONOTONY. MONOTONY replaced a complicated system of symbols with a single stroke to indicate pronunciation. Until this law was passed, the Greeks used a system introduced after Alexander the Great spread the Empire, to make Athenian pronunciation clearer to foreigners. In the earlier system there were five rules for placing accents, seven for accenting nouns and pronouns, and five rules for accenting verbs. Each rule had dozens of exceptions. It was estimated that it took average Greek schoolchildren 4500 hours to learn to write their language. With MONOTONY in place, it is estimated that millions will be saved in printing expenses, and typing time will be reduced by up to 35 per cent.

Like the Norwegian example discussed above, example 7 illustrates that governments often get involved with spelling reform. In the past the church was probably the main influence on the written form of previously unwritten languages. Missionaries were trained to translate the Bible into the local language of the place where they were working, and this usually meant first developing a spelling system for the language. In the United States, for instance, Navajo, the Athabaskan language of about 150,000 Navajos, was first written down by missionaries in the early twentieth century. A century earlier in New Zealand, Thomas Kendall, the first resident missionary, produced a rough attempt at an orthography for Maori in 1815.

Missionaries were often good linguists who produced a spelling system which closely reflected the pronunciation of the language. Inevitably there were problems, however. In Samoan, for instance, the sound [ŋ] represented in English as *ng* was accurately identified as a single sound rather than two separable sounds. So, as example 8 illustrates, it was written simply as *g*.

A

Multilingual speech communities

Example 8

Samoan	English
laga	weave
gagana	language
galu	wave, breaker
mogamoga	cockroach
tagi	weep, cry

Samoans therefore write *laga* ('weave') but say something which sounds to English ears like *langa*. They write *galu* but say something which sounds like *ngalu*. Consequently English speakers generally mispronounce words like *mogamoga* when they first see Samoan written down. In Maori, however, where [ŋ] also occurs, this single sound was written as two letters, *ng*. As a result Maori words like *tangi* ('weep'), which are almost identical in pronunciation to Samoan *tagi*, are nevertheless spelt differently. The Samoan orthography is strictly a more precise reflection of its sound system – one symbol is used for one sound. This example illustrates the influence a missionary could have on the codification process.

A recent problem in standardising the spelling of Maori is the choice between a macron over the top of a vowel letter marking its length, ā, vs a double vowel, *aa*. Wellington printers have preferred the macron, while Auckland printers have favoured the double vowel. When it came to making decisions about which to use when printing materials for use in schools or for government notices, there was a great deal of argument by the advocates of each system about why theirs was the better system, as example 9 demonstrates.

Example 9

Letter to the Editor of the New Zealand Listener

Sir

... most of the arguments for using double vowels have been demolished as people have learnt more about the sound systems of Polynesian languages ... The double-vowel writing system has always been awkward. It greatly complicates the learner's task of using a dictionary, and has the added disadvantage of making many familiar words look unfamiliar ...

As for the statement that the use of a diacritical mark is 'impossible with most word-processors', one can only wonder how the French and Germans (among others) cope with computers ...

(Albert J. Schütz, Professor of Linguistics, University of Hawaii)

In New Zealand the Maori Language Act of 1987 established the Maori Language Commission to advise on the development of Maori as an official language of New Zealand. On the long vowel issue it has come down in favour of the systematic use of the macron, describing it as simpler, easier to read, more economical and less likely to result in ambiguity. Ultimately, however, the capabilities of word-processors will probably have as much influence as anything else in determining usage in this area. This is not so true of the introduction of new vocabulary, where social and cultural factors may be as relevant in choosing forms, as linguistic and technological ones.

Developing vocabulary

Example 10

The Academy of the Hebrew Language in Israel has tried to select indigenous words where possible, but widespread usage has led them to accept *lipstick*, and *pajama*, for instance. Borrowed words are often integrated into Hebrew structure, however, so that *check-im*, 'bank checks', uses the Hebrew plural suffix *-im*. (Note too the adoption of American spellings rather than British for *pyjama* and *cheque*.)

Hebrew faced the problem of finding words for everyday colloquial things which had previously been referred to in people's vernacular languages. More often a language will need vocabulary for more specialised or formal domains, as was the case with Swahili, Tok Pisin and Malay, or for concepts and objects introduced from another culture, as with Navajo in the USA. In New Zealand the Maori Language Commission has often been asked for advice on vocabulary for new contexts and uses of Maori, as people want to use it for new functions such as writing official documents, and teaching mathematics and geography.

Example 11

Te Kōmihana mō Te Reo Māori or
Te Taura Whiri i te Reo Māori

A specific example of the kinds of choices which faced the Maori Language Commission in this area is illustrated by the problem of providing Maori names for government institutions, including themselves. They were called at first *Te Kōmihana mō Te Reo Māori*. *Te reo* is a widely known Maori phrase meaning 'the language', but the title also includes the word *kōmihana* which simply borrows the English word *commission* and adapts it to the Maori sound system. The transliteration is quite predictable, with *k* substituting for *c*, *h* substituting for *s* (since Maori has no [s], and [h] is the usual fricative substitution), and a final vowel, since Maori is a language in which all syllables end in vowels. The Commission changed its name however to *Te Taura Whiri i te Reo Māori* (literally 'the rope binding together (the many strands of) the Maori language'). This is a Maori name for the Commission – not one borrowed from English. The commissioners felt that such a label had greater linguistic and cultural integrity, and this provides an insight into how they see their task. In advising others on usage, they are often faced with the dilemma of which of these options to recommend:

1. a word borrowed from English
2. an equivalent Maori word which is perhaps not well known or with a slightly different meaning which could be adapted
3. a word newly created from Maori resources.

The Commission takes the view that its task is not simply a mechanical one of making Maori a suitable instrument for official communication. It recognises another more symbolic and less instrumental dimension to its task. Consequently where possible the Commission uses native resources, trying to 'remain true to the spirit of the language'; but of course this is not always achievable.

The *Tiriti* ('Treaty') *o Waitangi*, for example, involved too well established a borrowing to attempt a change at this stage. The National Library, however, was translated rather metaphorically as *Te Puna Mātauranga o Aotearoa* (literally 'the fount of knowledge of New Zealand').

A nice example of the adaptation of an older Maori word with a slightly different meaning is the use of *rangapū* which has been officially adopted to translate the important concept of 'partnership' – important in the current political debate about the relationship between Maori and Pakeha in New Zealand. It is a word which meant 'group' or 'company' but which was not widely known and was little used.

A

Multilingual speech communities

Coining words is another solution. The term *reo irirangi*, literally 'spirit voice', uses native resources to label a modern object, the radio. Another example which demonstrates that even a Commission can have a sense of humour is the coinage *pūkoro ure* to translate 'condom'. *Pūkoro* means literally 'a long thin bag-shaped net for catching eels' and *ure* is the word for 'penis'.

Exercise 8

Can you identify which of the following words have been borrowed into Maori from English and guess the reasons for the borrowings?

(a)	neke	snake
(b)	weka	native woodhen
(c)	parau	plough
(d)	pihikete	biscuit
(e)	whare	house, hut
(f)	pia	beer
(g)	wai	water
(h)	pahi	bus
(i)	kuia	old woman
(j)	kūmara	sweet potato

Answer at end of chapter

Acceptance

I have provided some very specific examples in this section of the kinds of linguistic issues language planners get involved with, illustrating mainly from Maori. The same issues have been faced by those involved in the development of the Navajo language in the USA, Aboriginal languages in Australia, Swahili in Tanzania and standard Norwegian in Norway. The next step in the process involves the politicians and the people as much as the sociolinguist.

Example 12

- Getting a separate TV Channel was a major triumph for Welsh language activists. This contributed greatly to the status of Welsh as a language to be taken seriously.
- Radio Vanuatu, a crucial means of inter-island communication, uses mainly Bislama, the national language. This enhances its status and inevitably contributes to the process of standardisation.
- Maori language supporters have been arguing for years that Maori should be allocated more media time. In 2000, only 2.5 per cent of national radio programmes were broadcast entirely in Maori, and there was even less Maori on New Zealand television although these figures are increasing.

The Maori Language Commission can recommend that certain linguistic forms be adopted by the media and used in schools, just as the Norwegian government regularly publishes its lists of approved words. But people have to accept and use them. This is what finally determines whether a proposed form succeeds or not, and this applies as much to an individual word as to a new code selected to serve as a standard official language. The adoption of forms by the media can contribute to the process. But finally the people will decide. The Norwegian government's ambivalence between Bokmål and Nynorsk in Norway has been a source of irritation to people. And the government's regular pronouncements in the media on new 'official usages' which represent attempts at compromise have not always been accepted. It is said that people often ignore the newspaper lists of officially approved forms and use the ones they happen to have learned in school. In such a situation people finally vote with their tongues, and it seems Bokmål is emerging as the *de facto* written standard in many areas.

Nevertheless it is generally true that government support plays an important part in gaining acceptance for a code. In China, Putonghua (or Mandarin) has been promoted by the Chinese government as the standard variety of Chinese since 1949 when the People's Republic was established. The fact that many Chinese people already spoke this variety no doubt helped, but the government's unwavering attitude and deliberate efforts to promote its use in a wide variety of contexts have led to its gaining wide acceptance among the 1300 million or so Chinese who make up the Republic. Putonghua uses the pronunciation of the Beijing dialect, the capital city, together with the grammar of the highly valued Northern Chinese dialects, and the vocabulary of modern colloquial Chinese. These choices have also helped people to accept it. A variety which begins with some status always has a useful head-start.

Exercise 9

What steps could a government take to spread the knowledge, use and acceptance of a language?

Answer at end of chapter

Acquisition planning

Having considered the linguist's role at the micro-level of codification, it is useful finally to return to the macro-level of language planning activities. In addition to corpus planning and status or prestige planning, which were discussed above, sociolinguists may also make a contribution to organised efforts to spread a language by increasing the number of its users. This is sometimes called *acquisition planning*, and, since the most widespread method of encouraging the acquisition of a language is to use the education system, it is also known as language-in-education planning. Language planners may be asked to advise about a range of issues such as who should be the target of the language promotion efforts, the most effective language teaching methods in particular contexts,

A

Multilingual speech communities

what materials should be used, and how the programmes should be evaluated. Should everyone have access to language teaching, for instance? How much say should a local community have in the way a language is taught, or the materials used, as opposed to a top-down uniform approach monitored by the government?

In China, newspapers and radio contributed to early efforts to promote knowledge of Mandarin: a demonstration radio programme promoted the approved pronunciation, while newspapers in Mandarin printed in transcribed characters. In Japan, although there are substantial minority groups speaking Korean and Chinese, Japanese is the only official language. Acquisition planning currently focusses only on English which all children are required to study throughout the school system. In Tanzania, Norway, Singapore, and many other countries, the education system plays a crucial role in acquisition planning, and issues of access, curriculum, methodology and evaluation are decided by government departments. 'Absorption centers' in Israel, where immigrants live while sorting out employment and housing, offer government subsidised, on-site Hebrew classes. By way of contrast, in the early days of attempts to revive Maori, people from the Maori community took the initiative to establish their own pre-schools where Maori was used. They sought advice from sociolinguists who had studied similar programmes overseas, but the early *kohanga reo* (language nests) were under the control of the local community and used local resources and materials. Classes were also held in many Maori communities, using a range of different methods and materials, in order to provide opportunities for adults to improve their Maori language knowledge and proficiency. These two examples illustrate different ways of approaching acquisition planning.

Exercise 10

This chapter has emphasised the political basis of many language planning activities. Imagine you were a speaker of the minority language, Capiznon, in the Philippines when the government decided to develop Tagalog as the national language and rename it Pilipino. What costs would this entail for you and your community?

Conclusion

Example 13

A New Zealander who had moved to England decided to prepare a dessert of fruit which in her New Zealand childhood had been called *chinese gooseberries*. As a result of successful linguistic engineering, followed by a good promotional campaign, she knew they were now known in New Zealand and overseas as *kiwifruit*. She was somewhat dismayed, however, on opening her English recipe book to read the first instruction 'Slice up 6 Kiwis'. In New Zealand *Kiwi* refers to a New Zealander!

Language planning is defined most simply as deliberate language change. This covers a wide variety of activities including the introduction of new labels for fruit, the reform of spelling systems, and the provision of advice on non-sexist terminology such as *Ms* and *chairperson*, a topic discussed in chapter 12. It also includes the development of national languages and standard dialects, as illustrated in this chapter.

Language planners generally focus on specific language problems. Their role is to develop a policy of language use which will solve the problems appropriately in particular speech communities. In this chapter I have focussed in some detail on a few specific cases of language planning in order to exemplify some of the issues which have to be resolved by language planners, and some of the ways which have been used to resolve them. We have seen, for instance, that language planners may need to develop a variety upwards into new H domains, as with Swahili, Tok Pisin, Indonesian, and Nynorsk, or alternatively downwards into new L domains as in the case of Hebrew, Bokmål, and to some extent Mandarin Chinese.

This chapter has been concerned mainly with the language policies of countries and states rather than the language behaviour of individuals. Yet it has been clear that ultimately it is the patterns of linguistic behaviour of individual language users that determine whether a national policy will succeed or not. If people do not use an official language then it will simply wither away. If recommendations about approved or preferred spellings are ignored, they will become defunct. The reasons why people adopt one form and not another are complicated. Language expresses identity and membership of particular groups as well as nationhood.

Multilingualism highlights linguistic diversity and makes it easier to perceive, as we have seen in the first part of this book. But it is clear that there is rich linguistic diversity within languages too. Members of monolingual speech communities use this diversity to signal their attitudes and allegiances, just as multilingual people use their different languages for these purposes. Kalala (in chapter 2, example 1) signalled his ethnic group membership when he used Shi. He signalled his friendship group and age when he used Indoubil. His variety of Swahili reflected his regional and social background. In section B of this book we will look in some detail at the ways in which monolinguals signal such non-linguistic information.

A

Multilingual speech communities

ANSWERS TO EXERCISES IN CHAPTER 5

Answer to exercise 1

This is a good question to discuss with others since an exchange of views is likely to be helpful. There can certainly be no definitive answer to such a question. Nevertheless, linguistic features of the language are less relevant than attitudinal, political and social factors. So statements (a) and (g) are probably least relevant to the adoption of the language as a national language, and statements (c) and (e) are relevant only to the extent that they express Paraguayans' attitudes to their language and suggest that it could be developed relatively easily if adopted for other reasons. Statements (b), (d) and (f) are the ones I would rate highest, with (h) an interesting indication of the political value of knowing the language. Overall it must be recognised that the preservation and maintenance of the language has owed much to political factors. Guaraní has proved useful politically as a unifying symbol for the nation.

Answer to exercise 2

The list below is based on the status given these languages by the governments of the relevant countries. In many countries there is no one language which can adequately serve as the only official language. A world language such as English is often used as an official language for external official functions, alongside a local language which serves internal official functions (e.g. Philippines, Tanzania). In some countries, giving more than one language the status of official language is a way of recognising the linguistic and cultural diversity within the country (e.g. India, Papua New Guinea, Singapore).

Country	Official language(s)
Australia	English
Belgium	Dutch (Flemish), French, German
Brazil	Portuguese
Canada	English, French
Finland	Finnish, Swedish
France	French
Haiti	French, Haitian Creole
India	Hindi, English, 14 regional languages
Indonesia	Indonesian
Kenya	Swahili, English
New Zealand	Maori, New Zealand Sign Language, English ('de facto')
Norway	Norwegian (Nynorsk, Bokmål)
Papua New Guinea	English, Tok Pisin, Hiri Motu
Paraguay	Guaraní, Spanish
Philippines	Filipino, English
Singapore	Malay, Mandarin, Tamil, English
Tanzania	Swahili, English
Uruguay	Spanish
Vanuatu	Bislama, French, English

Answer to exercise 3

Your answer will reflect your views about the relationship between language and nation. The attitudes expressed by the men quoted reflect the tendency to see language and nation as synonymous – one language = one nation. This view of the 'ideal' nation-state as a single people using a single language is very widely held. To some extent it is reflected in the descriptions (derived from those of sociolinguists involved) of the language situations in Paraguay presented above and Tanzania below. Alternative views are possible, however. Some sociolinguists have pointed out, for example, that the 'one nation-one language' view reflects the impact of predominantly monolingual cultures such as those of France and England. They suggest that studying standard English is not likely to lead to a love of England for a British Black whose home language variety is ridiculed and repressed, and whose economic prospects are depressing. Nor is it likely that linguistic minorities in Britain, such as speakers of Panjabi, Polish and Greek, will be very enthusiastic about a 'one nation-one language' viewpoint.

Answer to exercise 4

The obvious answer is the fact that materials are already available in English for teaching at these levels, and it will clearly be cheaper to use these than to develop materials in Swahili. As a world language, English will also give students access to a wider information base.

The counter-arguments involve considering the level of linguistic competence in a language which is necessary before it is possible to learn effectively through it at secondary and tertiary level. Most Tanzanians identify strongly with Swahili and they are fluent in it by the end of secondary school. The switch to English as the medium for education is likely to create a barrier for at least some Tanzanians. Those from poor backgrounds and rural areas are most vulnerable. Not all will succeed in mastering English well enough to gain the benefits it offers.

Answer to exercise 5

The discussion of Swahili illustrates that it can be regarded as serving all these functions in Tanzania.

Unifying: Swahili serves to unify Tanzanians, since it is not the language of a particular tribe. It offers advantages over tribal languages as a means of communication, education and access to government jobs, for instance.

Separatist: Since Swahili is used throughout East Africa as a lingua franca, this function is not so clearly realised as others. Guaraní in Paraguay is a better example of a language serving this separatist function, since it clearly distinguishes Paraguay from other South American nations. Swahili sets the country off from surrounding countries only to the extent that it is *the* national language of Tanzania. However, the standard used is a distinctly Tanzanian variety of Swahili. It is certainly regarded by many Tanzanians as a symbol of their separate national identity.

Prestige: There is no doubt about the status of Swahili as a proper or 'real' language. It has much greater status in the nation as a whole than any tribal vernacular language.

Frame of reference function: There is a standard variety of Swahili which exists alongside a range of regional varieties. The standard was developed from the variety spoken in Zanzibar town. The standard is clearly recognised as the norm and other varieties are regarded as regionally marked.

Answer to exercise 6

Selecting a code: The chosen language had to act as a Jewish symbol and therefore had to be a Jewish language. Hence the only real choices for the people of Israel were Yiddish or Hebrew. The selection of Hebrew was basically a political decision. It was considered the only possible choice for the great majority of Israeli Jews. Not all Jews spoke Yiddish and it had little prestige. For many the associations of Yiddish – especially the variety closely related to German linguistically – were simply unacceptable.

Codification: Like Latin, Hebrew is a highly codified variety. Grammars and dictionaries already existed. Spelling and pronunciation rules based on classical texts existed too. Codification of the modern variety of Hebrew which has now emerged is still in progress.

Elaboration: This is where most work needed to be done. The selection of forms for use in everyday conversation involved drawing on a variety of literary dialects of Hebrew, as well as the various mainly European vernaculars spoken by immigrants to Israel.

Acceptance: Hebrew had great prestige. People respected it and revered it as the language of religion and literature. An extensive literary revival of Hebrew in the eighteenth and nineteenth centuries meant it was used for new and broader functions by writers. This prepared the ground for its being seen as the obvious candidate for national language. It was adopted as a vernacular first in the 1880s by enthusiasts who persuaded people to teach it to their children as a first language, though some felt it was too sacred for everyday use. Its advantages as a lingua franca

A

Multilingual speech communities

between immigrants who spoke many different languages generally added to its attractions. So its prestige, its unifying function and its usefulness all contributed to its acceptance.

This answer, and the account of the establishment of Hebrew as the national language of Israel, is based on the sources listed below. An alternative analysis regards Hebrew as a creole with a Yiddish as the substrate language and Hebrew as the superstrate or lexifier language. An even more radical position labels the language as Israeli and regards it as a creole with input from Hebrew, Yiddish and a number of European languages including Russian and Polish.

Answer to exercise 7

While linguists have obvious expertise in developing the form of a standard variety, the task of promoting the variety will require a variety of skills and resources which are not particularly linguistic. However, sociolinguists have a role to play in advising on the relative advantages and disadvantages of different varieties from the point of view of their likelihood of acceptance. Some varieties begin with a head start – Swahili in Tanzania, for instance, had a great deal going for it in terms of acceptance compared with English, and was therefore easier to promote. Promoting Yiddish would have been very problematic in Israel.

Answer to exercise 8

Items (d) and (f) are obvious borrowings referring to foodstuffs introduced by Europeans. Item (a) is a borrowing: there are no snakes in New Zealand and the concept was introduced with the English language. Similarly items (c) and (h) refer to imported objects. The Maori Language Commission would not try to alter or replace well established borrowings such as these with native Maori words.

The remaining words (b), (e), (g), (i) and (j) are Maori words, as you might have guessed since they refer to New Zealand items, or to concepts which are basic in most cultures.

Answer to exercise 9

In implementing a language policy to extend the use of a particular variety or code, most governments use both the education system and the mass media – newspapers, radio, TV. They also encourage and approve the use of the language in official spheres of administration. An effective education system can be a very powerful means of extending the functions of a particular variety, spreading proficiency in the variety, and giving it status which increases its acceptability, as both the Chinese and the Tanzanian examples illustrate. Organised efforts to promote the learning of a language have been labelled *acquisition planning*.

▪ Concepts introduced

National language
Official language
De facto and *de jure* status of languages
Language planning
Status or prestige planning
Corpus planning
Acquisition planning
Codification

References

The basic concepts introduced in this chapter are discussed further in the following sources:

Cooper (1989)
Crystal (1997)
Eastman (1983)
Garvin and Mathiot (1956)
Haugen (1966a)
Kaplan and Baldauf (2005)
Rubin and Jernudd (1971)
Trudgill (2000)

The following sources provided material for this chapter:

Blanc (1968), Cooper (1989), Gold (1989) on Hebrew
Bourhis (1983) on French in Quebec
Cameron and Bourne (1989) on English
Choi (2005), Rubin (1968, 1985) on Paraguay
Crowley (1990) on Bislama in Vanuatu
Haugen (1959, 1965, 1966b) on Norwegian
Jahr (1989) on Norwegian
Kirkwood (1989) on the Soviet Union
Russell (1989) on Swahili in Tanzania
Trudgill (2000) on Norwegian
Vikør (1995) on Norwegian
Whiteley (1968, 1969) on Swahili in Tanzania
Wiggen (1997) on Norwegian
Wurm (1985) on Tok Pisin
www.cal.org/co/haiti/hlang.html on Haiti
Zuckermann (2003) on Israeli and alternative approaches to Hebrew

Quotations

Example 4 is taken from the *Dominion* (a daily newspaper published in Wellington, New Zealand), 1/8/89. The original source of this extract is 'Thousands threaten strike over language rights in Moldavia', *Reuters News*, 30 July 1989, © 1989 Reuters Limited.
Example 7 is from the *San Francisco Chronicle*, 26/12/82.
Example 9 is from the *New Zealand Listener*, 5/4/86.

Useful additional reading

Eastman (1983)
Fasold (1984), Chs 2 and 9
McColl Millar (2005)

A

Multilingual speech communities

Mesthrie et al. (2000), Ch. 12
Myers-Scotton (2006), Ch. 12
Paulston and Tucker (2003), Parts X and XI
Wardhaugh (1987)
Wardhaugh (2006), Ch. 15

Section B

Language variation: focus on users

6 Regional and social dialects

In the previous section of this book the focus has been on language variation in multilingual communities. In this section the focus moves to language variation in monolingual communities. People often use a language to signal their membership of particular groups and to construct different aspects of their social identity. Social status, gender, age, ethnicity and the kinds of social networks people belong to turn out to be important dimensions of identity in many communities. I will illustrate the way people use language to signal such affiliations in this second section of this book.

Example 1

Telephone rings.

Pat: Hello.
Caller: Hello, is Mark there?
Pat: Yes. Just hold on a minute.
Pat (to Mark):   There's a rather well-educated young lady from Scotland on the
                  phone for you.

When you answer the telephone, you can often make some pretty accurate guesses about various characteristics of the speaker. Pat was able to deduce quite a lot about Mark's caller, even though the caller had said nothing explicitly about herself. Most listeners can identify children's voices without any problem. When the caller is an adult it is usually easy to tell whether a speaker is female or male. If the person has a distinctive regional accent, then their regional origins will be evident even from a short utterance. And it may also be possible to make a reasonable guess about the person's socio-economic or educational background, as Pat did.

No two people speak exactly the same. There are infinite sources of variation in speech. A sound spectrograph, a machine which represents the sound waves of speech in visual form, shows that even a single vowel may be pronounced in hundreds of minutely different ways, most of which listeners do not even register. Some features of speech, however, are shared by groups, and become important because they differentiate one group from another. Just as different languages often serve a unifying and separating function for their speakers, so do speech characteristics within languages. The pronunciation, grammar, and vocabulary of Scottish speakers of English is in some respects quite distinct from that of people from England, for example. Though there is variation within Scotland, there are also some features which perform an overall unifying function. The letter *r* in words like *girl* and *star* is pronounced in a number of English-speaking areas, and Scotland is certainly one of them. And a Scot is far more likely to say *I'll not do it* than *I won't do it*.

Similarly the pronunciation of *bath* with the same vowel as in *sat* distinguishes a speaker from the north of England from a southerner. And while many speakers of English use the same vowel in the three words *bag*, *map* and *bad*, workers in Belfast pronounce them in a way that sounds like [beg], [ma:rp] and [bod] to English people. Speech provides social information too. Dropping the initial [h] in words like *house* and *heaven* often indicates a lower socio-economic background. And so does the use of grammatical patterns such as *they don't know nothing them kids* or *I done it last week*. We signal our group affiliations and our social identities by the speech forms we use.

REGIONAL VARIATION

International varieties

Example 2

A British visitor to New Zealand decided while he was in Auckland he would look up an old friend from his war days. He found the address, walked up the path and knocked on the door.

'Gidday,' said the young man who opened the door. 'What can I do for you?'

'I've called to see me old mate Don Stone,' said the visitor.

'Oh he's dead now mate,' said the young man.

The visitor was about to express condolences when he was thumped on the back by Don Stone himself. The young man had said, 'Here's dad now mate', as his father came in the gate.

There are many such stories – some no doubt apocryphal – of mistakes based on regional accent differences. To British ears a New Zealander's *dad* sounds like an English person's *dead*, and *bad* sounds like *bed*. Americans and Australians, as well as New Zealanders, tell of British visitors who were given *pens* instead of *pins* and *pans* instead of *pens*. On the other hand an American's *god* sounds like an English person's *guard*, and an American's *ladder* is pronounced identically with *latter*.

There are vocabulary differences in the varieties spoken in different regions too. Australians talk of *sole parents*, for example, while people in England call them *single parents*, and New Zealanders call them *solo parents*. South Africans use the term *robot* for British *traffic-light*. British *wellies* (*Wellington boots*) are New Zealand *gummies* (*gumboots*), while the word *togs* refers to very different types of clothes in different places. In New Zealand *togs* are what you swim in. In Britain you might wear them to a formal dinner.

Exercise 1

You may like to check out the extent of American vs British influence on vocabulary in your region. The following questions provide a simple way of measuring this. Ask ten of your friends to answer them and work out how many American items vs how many British items they choose. You should allow for the fact that some may use both. If you are not sure which is the British item and which the American, check in a big reference dictionary such as Webster's *Third New International Dictionary* or the big *Oxford English Dictionary*.

(a) When you go window-shopping do you walk on the *pavement* or the *sidewalk*?
(b) Do you put your shopping in the car's *trunk* or in the *boot*?
(c) When the car's engine needs oil do you open the *bonnet* or the *hood*?
(d) Do you fill up the car with *gas* or with *petrol*?
(e) When it is cold do you put on a *jersey* or a *sweater*?
(f) When the baby is wet does it need a dry *diaper* or *nappy*?
(g) Do you get to the top of the building in an *elevator* or a *lift*?
(h) When the children are hungry do you open a *can* or a *tin* of beans?
(i) When you go on holiday do you take *luggage* or *baggage*?
(j) When you've made an error do you remove it with an *eraser* or a *rubber*?

Example 3

1. Do you have a match?
2. Have you got a cigarette?
3. She has gotten used to the noise.
4. She's got used to the noise.
5. He dove in, head first.
6. He dived in head first.
7. Did you eat yet?
8. Have you eaten yet?

Pronunciation and vocabulary differences are probably the differences people are most aware of between different dialects of English, but there are grammatical differences too. Can you distinguish the preferred American from the traditional British usages in the sentences in example 3?

Americans prefer *do you have*, though this can now also be heard in Britain alongside the traditional British English *have you got*. Americans say *gotten* where people in

England use *got*. Many Americans use *dove* while most British English speakers prefer *dived*. Americans ask *did you eat*? while the English ask *have you eaten*? Are the American or the British usages predominant where you live?

The differences that English speakers throughout the world notice when they meet English speakers from other nations are similar to those noted by speakers of other languages too. Spanish and French, for example, are languages which are extensively used in a variety of countries besides Spain and France. Speakers of Spanish can hear differences of pronunciation, vocabulary and grammar in the varieties of Spanish spoken in Mexico, Spain, Argentina and Paraguay, for example. Native speakers of French can distinguish the French used in Montreal from Parisian and Haitian French. There are differences in the vocabulary of different varieties. So, for example, a Parisian's *travail* ('work') is a *djobe* in Montreal. The word for 'beggar' is *mendiant* in France but *quêteux* in Quebec. And Canadians like *aller aux vues* when they want to see a film, while Parisians like *aller au cinéma*. Even grammatical gender assignment differs in the two varieties. *Appétit* ('appetite') and *midi* ('midday'), for instance, are feminine in Canada, but masculine in France, while the opposite is true for *automobile* and *oreille* ('ear'). Clearly Canadian French and Parisian French are different dialects.

Sometimes the differences between dialects are a matter of the frequencies with which particular features occur, rather than completely different ways of saying things. People in Montreal, for example, do not always pronounce the *l* in phrases like *il pleut* and *il fait*. Parisians omit the *l* too – but less often. If you learned French in school you probably struggled to learn which verbs used *avoir* and which used *être* in marking the perfect aspect. Getting control of these patterns generally causes all kinds of headaches. It would probably have caused you even more pain if you had realised that the patterns for using *avoir* and *être* are different in Montreal and Paris.

Exercise 2

How do you pronounce *batter*? How many different pronunciations of this word have you noticed? Use any method you like to represent the different pronunciations.

Answer at end of chapter

◼ Intra-national or intra-continental variation

Example 4

Rob: This wheel's completely disjaskit.
Alan: I might could get it changed.
Rob: You couldn't do nothing of the sort. It needs dumped.

This conversation between two Geordies (people from Tyneside in England) is likely to perplex many English speakers. The double modal *might could* is typical Geordie, though it is also heard in some parts of the Southern USA. The expression *needs dumped* is also typical Tyneside, though also used in Scotland, as is the vocabulary item *disjasket*, meaning 'worn out' or 'completely ruined'. The pronunciation is quite distinctive of Tyneside too, and perhaps especially the intonation patterns. Because they like the speech heard in television programmes such as *Auf Wiedersehen Pet* or *Byker Grove*, some people can imitate the tune of Geordie speech – if nothing else. We are dealing here not just with different accents but with dialect differences within a country, since the distinguishing forms involve grammatical usages and lexical items as well as pronunciation.

Regional variation takes time to develop. British and American English, for instance, provide much more evidence of regional variation than New Zealand or Australian English. Dialectologists can distinguish regional varieties for almost every English county, e.g. Yorkshire, Lancashire, Northumberland, Somerset, Cornwall and so on, and for many towns too. Some British dialects, such as Scouse (heard in Liverpool), Cockney and Geordie, even have distinct names showing how significant they are in distinguishing groups from one another. Within the London area, the Cockney dialect is quite distinctive with its glottal stop [ʔ] instead of [t] in words like *bitter* and *butter*, and its rhyming slang: e.g. *apples and pears* for 'stairs', *lean and lurch* for 'church', the undoubtedly sexist *trouble and strife* for 'wife' and the more ambiguous *cows and kisses* for 'the missus'.

In the USA, too, dialectologists can identify distinguishing features of the speech of people from different regions. Northern, Midland and Southern are the main divisions, and within those three areas a number of further divisions can be made. Different towns and even parts of towns can be distinguished. Within the Midland area, for example, the Eastern States can be distinguished; and within those the Boston dialect is different from that of New York City; and within New York City, Brooklynese is quite distinctive. Again, pronunciation, grammar, and vocabulary distinguish these dialects. In the rural Appalachians, one can hear pronunciations such as *acrosst* and *clifft*, as well as verbs with *a*-prefixes, such as *a-fishin'* and *a-comin'*. Words for *dragonfly* in the Eastern States include *darning needle*, *mosquito hawk*, *spindle*, *snake feeder*, *snake doctor*, and *snake waiter*, but of these only *darning needle* is used in New York. From *darning needle*, however, New York has developed two new variants *dining needle* and *diamond needle*. (It becomes difficult at this point to remember that these are all names for an insect not a sewing implement!)

In areas where English has been introduced more recently, such as Australia and New Zealand, there seems to be considerably less regional variation – though there is evidence of social variation. The high level of intra-national communication, together with the relatively small populations, may have inhibited the development of marked regional differences in these countries. In New Zealand, for instance, there are greater differences among the Maori dialects than within English, reflecting the longer period of settlement and more restricted means of communication between people

B

Language variation: focus on users

from different Maori tribes before European settlers arrived. Maori pronunciation of words written with an initial *wh*, for example, differs from one place to another. The Maori word for 'fish' is *ika* in most areas but *ngohi* in the far North, and *kirikiri* refers to 'gravel' in the west but 'sand' in the east of New Zealand. There are many more such differences.

Exercise 3

Can you guess what the following words and phrases mean?

They are all words collected from regional dialects of British English. A good British English dialect dictionary will provide information about their meanings and where they are used.

(a) snowblossom
(b) time for our snap
(c) mask the tea
(d) the place was all frousted
(e) clinker bells
(f) a great mawther
(g) I'm really stalled
(h) a bairn
(i) an effet
(j) I'll fill up your piggy, it's time for bed

Answers at end of chapter

Figure 6.1 is a map of England showing where different dialect words are used for the standard English word *splinter*. The boundary lines are called *isoglosses*. This is just one word out of thousands of linguistic features which vary in different dialects.

When all the information on linguistic regional variation is gathered together on a map, with isoglosses drawn between areas where different vocabulary, or grammatical usages or pronunciations occur, the result looks something like a spider's web. Some of the web's lines are thicker than others because a number of boundaries between features coincide. But there is also a great deal of overlap between areas. The line between an area where people use [a] rather than [a:] in a word like *path*, for example, does not coincide with the line which separates areas using *have you any sugar?* rather than *have you got any sugar?* Areas which use the word *elevenses* rather than *snap* or *snack* do not all use different words for *brew* or *snowflake* or *manure* or *splinter*. The same vocabulary may be used throughout an area where contrasts in the pronunciation of words are quite dramatic. In other words, defining linguistic areas is not at all straightforward – a point which is illustrated very clearly in example 5.

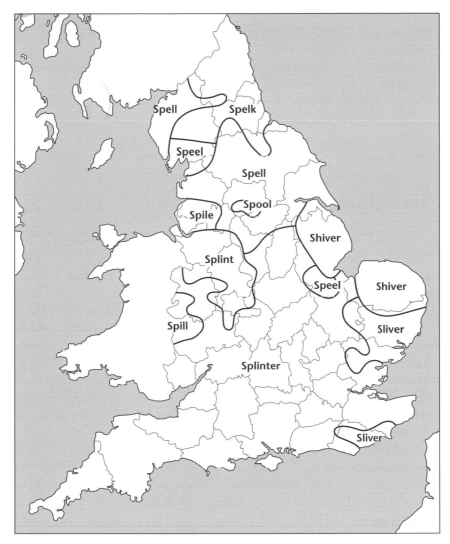

Figure 6.1 Words for *splinter* in English Dialects

Source: Trudgill, 1994: 21. Reproduced with permission

B

Language variation: focus on users

Exercise 4

Where there are differences between regions, it is interesting to discover the local names for particular objects. There are often regional differences in the words used for standard English *scarecrow*, *stream*, and *cowpat*, for instance. When asking people what they call these items, you should phrase your question so as to avoid using the word you are interested in. To exemplify I have provided four questions aimed at eliciting labels for four more objects which often vary regionally:

▶

133

(a) What do you call a small round sweet cake with a hole in the middle?
(b) What do you call the vehicles people push babies round in?
(c) What do you call an item of clothing worn to protect clothing especially while cooking?
(d) What do you call the shoes people wear for tennis or running?

Collect information from a range of people on what they call these objects and where possible include older people who were born outside your area.

Cross-continental variation: dialect chains

Example 5

Miriam learnt French and Italian at university and was a fluent speaker of both. As part of her course she was required to study for three months in Paris and three months in Rome. Her time in Paris went well and she decided to take a holiday on her way to Rome, travelling across France to Italy. She was keen to hear the varieties of French and Italian spoken in provincial towns. She stayed in cheap pensions (French 'bed-and-breakfast' places), and she made a special effort to talk to the local people rather than tourists. Her Parisian accent was admired and she could understand the French of Dijon and Lyon. But as she moved further from Paris she found the French more difficult to follow. Near the border between France and Italy, in the town of Chambéry, she could not be sure what she was hearing. Was it Italian French or French Italian? Whatever it was, it was difficult for her to understand, though she had no trouble making herself understood. Most people thought she spoke beautifully – especially for a foreigner! In Italy she found that the Italian spoken in Turin and Milan was very different from the Italian she had learned. As she approached Rome, however, she gradually began to comprehend more of what she heard. And finally in Rome she found some kind of match between the way she spoke and the way the Italians around her spoke.

Though a map suggests the languages of Europe or Italy are tidily compartmentalised, in reality they 'blend' into one another. The varieties of French spoken in the border towns and villages of Italy, Spain and Switzerland have more in common with the language of the next village than the language of Paris. From one village and town to the next there is a chain or continuum.

Dialect chains are very common across the whole of Europe. One chain links all the dialects of German, Dutch and Flemish from Switzerland through Austria and Germany, to the Netherlands and Belgium, and there is another which links dialects of

Portuguese, Spanish, Catalan, French, and Italian. A Scandinavian chain links dialects of Norwegian, Swedish and Danish, so that Swedes and Norwegians in adjacent areas can communicate more easily than fellow-Swedes from southern and northern Sweden. The same kind of dialect chains are found throughout India and China. They illustrate very clearly the arbitrariness of the distinction between 'language' and 'dialect'.

It is easy to see that if we try to define what counts as German vs Dutch or Swedish vs Norwegian or Italian vs French using only linguistic features, the task will be fraught with problems. Where are the boundaries between one dialect and the next, or one language and the next, to be drawn? The linguistic features overlap, and usage in one area merges into the next. Intelligibility is no help either. Most Norwegians claim they can understand Swedish, for instance, although two distinct languages are involved, while Chinese who speak only Cantonese cannot understand those who speak Mandarin, despite the fact that both are described as dialects of the Chinese language.

Example 6

Ming is an old woman who lives with her son in a rural village near the town of Yingde in Guangdong Province in southern China. The family grows vegetables for the local market. Ming speaks only her provincial dialect of Chinese, Cantonese. Last summer, Gong, an official from Beijing in the north, visited her village to check on the level of rice and ginger production. Gong also spoke Chinese, but his dialect was Mandarin or *putonghua*. Ming could not understand a single word Gong said.

Languages are not purely linguistic entities. They serve social functions. In order to define a language, it is important to look to its social and political functions, as well as its linguistic features. So a *language* can be thought of as a collection of dialects that are usually linguistically similar, used by different social groups who *choose* to say that they are speakers of one language which functions to unite and represent them to other groups. This definition reflects sociolinguistic reality by including all the linguistically very different Chinese dialects, which the Chinese define as one language, while separating the languages of Scandinavia which are linguistically very similar, but politically quite distinct varieties.

Exercise 5

(a) Define the difference between a regional accent and a regional dialect.
(b) What do you think is the difference between a regional and a social dialect?

Answers at end of chapter

B

Language variation: focus on users

SOCIAL VARIATION

RP: a social accent

Example 7

Diana: Have you heard – Jonathan's engaged to that northern girl – from Cumbria!

Reg: She may be northern but I assure you she is very acceptable. Her father is a lord, and a rich one at that! She has had the best education money can buy. Those traces of northern accent are fashionable these days my dear!

In earlier centuries you could tell where an English lord or lady came from by their regional form of English. But by the early twentieth century a person who spoke with a regional accent in England was most unlikely to belong to the upper class. Upper-class people had an upper-class education, and that generally meant a public (i.e. private!) school where they learned to speak RP. RP stands not for 'Real Posh' (as suggested to me by a young friend), but rather for Received Pronunciation – the accent of the best educated and most prestigious members of English society. It is claimed the label derives from the accent which was 'received' at the royal court, and it is sometimes identified with 'the Queen's English', although the accent used by Queen Elizabeth II, as portrayed so brilliantly by Helen Mirren in the movie *The Queen*, is a rather old-fashioned variety of RP.

RP was promoted by the BBC for decades. It is essentially a social accent not a regional one. Indeed, it *conceals* a speaker's regional origins. This is nicely illustrated in figure 6.2, the accent triangle.

As the triangle suggests, the linguist will find most linguistic variation at the lowest socio-economic level where regional differences abound. Further up the social ladder the amount of observable variation reduces till one reaches the pinnacle of RP – an accent used by less than 5 per cent of the British population. So a linguist travelling round Britain may collect over a dozen different pronunciations of the word *grass* from the working-class people she meets in different regions. She will hear very much less variation from the lower-middle- and middle-class people. And, at least until recently, the upper classes would pronounce the word as [gra:s] wherever they came from in England. Things are changing, however, as the exchange in example 7 suggests.

Figure 6.2 captured the distribution of accents in England until recently. Today a more accurate diagram might have a somewhat flatter top, suggesting accents other than RP can be heard amongst those who belong to the highest social class. (See figure 6.3 on page 138.) In other speech communities it is certainly possible to hear more than just one accent associated with the highest social group. Most well-educated Scots,

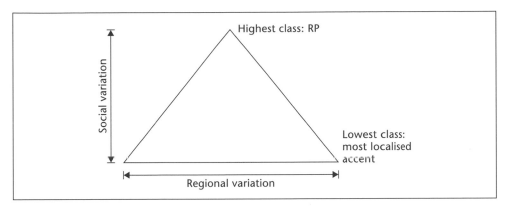

Figure 6.2 Social and regional accent variation

Source: From Peter Trudgill (1983) *Sociolinguistics*. Penguin: London. Page 42. Copyright © Peter Trudgill, 1974, 1983, 1995, 2000. Reproduced by permission of Penguin Books Ltd

Irish and Welsh speakers do not use RP, and there is more than one socially prestigious accent in these countries. And in ex-colonies of Britain such as Australia and Canada, other accents have displaced RP from its former position as the most admired accent of English. In fact RP now tends to be perceived by many people as somewhat affected (or 'real posh'!).

SOCIAL DIALECTS

The stereotypical 'dialect' speaker is an elderly rural person who is all but unintelligible to modern city dwellers. But dialects are simply linguistic varieties which are distinguishable by their vocabulary, grammar and pronunciation; the speech of people from different social, as well as regional, groups may differ in these ways. Just as RP is a social accent, so standard English is a social dialect. It is the dialect used by well-educated English speakers throughout the world. It is the variety used for national news broadcasts and in print, and it is the variety generally taught in English-medium schools.

Standard English

Example 8
(a) I've not washed the dishes yet today.
(b) I haven't washed the dishes yet today.

Standard English is more accommodating than RP and allows for some variation within its boundaries. This is reflected in figure 6.3, the trapezium or table-topped mountain.

Language variation: focus on users

B

137

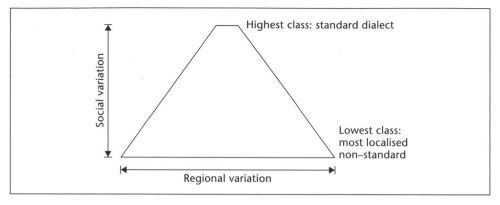

Figure 6.3 Social and regional dialect variation

Source: From Peter Trudgill (1983) *Sociolinguistics*. Penguin: London. Page 41. Copyright © Peter Trudgill, 1974, 1983, 1995, 2000. Reproduced by permission of Penguin Books Ltd

The flat top reflects the broader range of variants (alternative linguistic forms) which qualify as part of the standard dialect of English in any country. It is estimated that up to 15 per cent of the British regularly use standard British English. So in standard English, a limited amount of grammatical variation is acceptable. A speaker of standard English might produce either of the sentences in example 8 above.

The dialect we grace with the name standard English is spoken with many different accents. But, as illustrated in the discussion of regional dialects, there are also many standard Englishes. American standard English is distinguishable from Australian standard English, for instance, and both differ from the British standard dialect.

In social terms, linguistic forms which are not part of standard English are by definition non-standard. Because the standard dialect is always the first to be codified, it is difficult to avoid defining other dialects without contrasting them with the standard.

And then, because such non-standard forms are associated with the speech of less prestigious social groups, the label inevitably acquires negative connotations. But it should be clear that there is nothing linguistically inferior about non-standard forms. They are simply different from the forms which happen to be used by more socially prestigious speakers. To avoid the implication that non-standard forms are inadequate deviations from the standard, some sociolinguists use the term *vernacular* as an alternative to non-standard, and I will follow this practice.

Vernacular is a term which is used with a variety of meanings in sociolinguistics, but the meanings have something in common. Just as vernacular languages contrast with standard languages, vernacular dialect features contrast with standard dialect features. Vernacular forms tend to be learned at home and used in informal contexts. So all uses of the term vernacular share this sense of the first variety acquired in the home and used in casual contexts. Vernacular dialects, like vernacular languages, lack public or overt prestige, though they are generally valued by their users, especially as means of expressing solidarity and affective meaning – a point I will return to in the discussion of attitudes to language in chapter 15.

So far I have been discussing accents and dialects as if the linguistic features which identify them were stable, fixed and absolute. But, as with the notion of distinguishable languages, this is just a convenient fiction. The way people speak is characterised by patterned variation. The patterns are fascinating and reflect the social factors which are significant in a society. To illustrate this in the rest of this chapter I will discuss the relationship between speech and social status or class.

■ Caste dialects

People can be grouped together on the basis of similar social and economic factors. Their language generally reflects these groupings – they use different social dialects. It is easiest to see the evidence for social dialects in places such as Indonesia and India where social divisions are very clear-cut. In these countries, there are caste systems determined by birth, and strict social rules govern the kind of behaviour appropriate to each group. The rules cover such matters as the kind of job people can have, who they can marry, how they should dress, what they should eat, and how they should behave in a range of social situations. Not surprisingly, these social distinctions are also reflected in speech differences. A person's dialect reflects their social background.

There are quite clear differences in Indian languages, for example, between the speech of the Brahmins and non-Brahmin castes. The Brahmin word for 'milk' in the Kannada language, for instance, is *haalu*, while non-Brahmin dialects say *aalu*. The Tamil Brahmin word for 'sleep' is *tuungu*, while non-Brahmin dialects use the word *orangu*. And in Tulu, the Brahmin dialect makes gender, number and person distinctions in negative tenses of the verb which are not made in non-Brahmin dialects. In Javanese, too, linguistic differences reflect very clear-cut social or caste divisions.

Example 9

An Indonesian student at a British university was trying to explain to her English friend the complications of social dialects in Java and the ways in which Javanese speakers signal their social background. 'It is much harder than in English', she said. 'It is not just a matter of saying *sofa* instead of *couch*, or *house* rather than *'ouse*. Every time you talk to a different person you have to choose exactly the right words and the right pronunciations. Almost every word is different and they fit together in patterns or levels, depending on who we are talking to. Because I am well-educated and come from a rich family, I use five different levels of language.'

Javanese social status is reflected not just in choice of linguistic forms but also in the particular combinations of forms which each social group customarily uses, i.e. the varieties or stylistic levels that together make up the group's distinctive dialect. In English, stylistic variation involves choices such as *ta mate* vs *thank you so much*. In Javanese things are very complicated. There are six distinguishable stylistic levels. Table 6.1 provides a couple of words from each level to show the overlap and intermeshing of forms involved. (This example is discussed further in chapter 10 where the reasons for the numbering system are made clear.)

There are three distinct Javanese social groups and three associated dialects (see table 6.1).

1. The dialect of the lowest status group, the peasants and uneducated townspeople, consists of three stylistic levels: 1, 1a and 2.
2. The dialect of urbanised people with some education consists of five stylistic levels: 1, 1a, 2, 3 and 3a.
3. The dialect of the highly educated highest status group also consists of five levels, but they are different from those of the second social group: 1, 1a, 1b, 3 and 3a.

Table 6.1 Two Javanese words at different stylistic levels

'You'	'Now'	Stylistic level
padjenengan	samenika	3a
sampéjan	samenika	3
sampéjan	saniki	2
sampéjan	saiki	1a
pandjenengan	saiki	1a
kowé	saiki	1

Source: Adapted with the permission of The Free Press, a Division of Simon & Schuster Adult Publishing Group, from THE RELIGION OF JAVA by Clifford Geertz. Copyright © 1960 by The Free Press. Copyright © renewed 1988 by Clifford Geertz. All rights reserved

In Javanese, then, a particular social dialect can be defined as a particular combination of styles or levels each of which has its distinctive patterns of vocabulary, grammar and pronunciation, though there are many forms which are shared by different stylistic levels.

Social class dialects

Vocabulary

The term social class is used here as a shorthand term for differences between people which are associated with differences in social prestige, wealth and education. Bank managers do not talk like office cleaners, lawyers do not speak in the same way as the burglars they defend. Class divisions are based on such status differences. Status refers to the deference or respect people give someone – or don't give them, as the case may be – and status generally derives in Western society from the material resources a person can command, though there are other sources too. Family background may be a source of status independently of wealth (the youngest child of an earl may be poor but respected!). So class is used here as a convenient label for groups of people who share similarities in economic and social status.

Social dialect research in many different countries has revealed a consistent relationship between social class and language patterns. People from different social classes speak differently. The most obvious differences – in vocabulary – are in many ways the least illuminating from a sociolinguistic point of view, though they clearly capture the public imagination. In the 1950s in England many pairs of words were identified which, it was claimed, distinguished the speech of upper-class English people ('U speakers') from the rest ('non-U speakers'). U speakers used *sitting room* rather than *lounge* (non-U), and referred to the *lavatory* rather than the (non-U) *toilet*. The following excerpt from a Nancy Mitford novel provides an illustration.

Example 10

Uncle Matthew: 'I hope poor Fanny's school (the word school pronounced in tones of withering scorn) is doing her all the good you think it is. Certainly she picks up some dreadful expressions there.'

Aunty Emily, calmly, but on the defensive: 'Very likely she does. She also picks up a good deal of education.'

Uncle Matthew: 'Education! I was always led to believe that no educated person ever spoke of notepaper, and yet I hear poor Fanny asking Sadie for notepaper. What is this education? Fanny talks about mirrors and mantlepieces, handbags and perfume, she takes sugar in her coffee, has a tassel on her umbrella, and I have no doubt that, if she is ever fortunate enough to catch a husband, she will call his father and mother Father and Mother. Will the wonderful education she is getting make up to the unhappy brute for all these endless pinpricks? Fancy hearing one's wife talking about notepaper – the irritation!'

Aunty Emily: 'A lot of men would find it more irritating to have a wife who had never heard of George III. (All the same, Fanny darling, it is called writing paper you know – don't let's hear any more about note, please.)'

B

Language variation: focus on users

If these vocabulary differences exist at all, they are rather like those which distinguish Brahmin and non-Brahmin castes – they distinguish social groups on a categorical basis. You either use the U term or you don't! It is not quite that simple, of course, since as the U terms spread beyond the boundaries of the U group new terms are introduced. By the 1970s only non-U speakers, it was claimed, used 'handbag' for U 'bag', a non-U 'settee' was a U 'sofa' and your non-U 'relatives' were U 'relations'. There is no empirical research to back up these claims, but even if they exist, vocabulary clues are superficial and conceal the complexity and relative fluidity of social class membership in places like Britain. The barriers between groups are not insurmountable as in caste-based societies. People can move up or down the social ladder, and this potential mobility is mirrored more accurately in other aspects of their speech – such as pronunciation.

Exercise 6

A preference for different vocabulary by different social groups is relatively easy to identify and always fascinates people.

Can you produce a list of words for your speech community that divides people up according to their social background? Words for *death, lavatory, really good,* and *under the influence of alcohol* often vary from one social group to another.

Pronunciation

Example 11

Kim: Only uneducated people drop their 'h's.

Stephen: Let's hear you say 'Have you heard about Hilda's new house that her husband left her? It cost her a heck of a lot to fix up.' If you don't drop a single 'h' in that sentence you'll sound like one of Monty Python's upper-class twits!

In describing differences between Canadian and Parisian French, I mentioned that the differences are often not absolute, but rather matters of frequencies. Exactly the same is true for the speech of different social groups. Groups are often distinguished by the frequency with which they use particular features, rather than by their use of completely different forms. This important point can be illustrated with a simple example. Usha Pragji, a New Zealand student, taped a radio broadcast of two elderly people's accounts of their childhood in Edwardian Wellington, the capital city of New Zealand. The two speakers contrasted on a range of social variables.

Example 12

Marjorie Lee lived in what she described as 'a new large hideous Edwardian mansion'. Her father was a lawyer. Her mother had been one of the first women students at Canterbury College, part of the University of New Zealand. Marjorie went to Miss Barber's Private School until her early teens when she was provided with a governess.

George Davies lived with four members of his family in a small house. His mother was a solo parent whose only steady income came from 'keeping grandmother'. As George said, 'we weren't hard-up, we were absolutely poverty-stricken'. Illustrating this he recounted that they sometimes took palings off the fence for firewood, and 'you could pretty well tell the state of the family finances by whether Grandma's inlaid brooch was in the pawn shop or not'.

The two recordings were analysed to see whether there were differences between the speakers in terms of the numbers of [h]s they 'dropped' in words like *house*. Usha found that Marjorie Lee did not omit a single [h] while George Davies dropped 83 per cent of the [h]s which occurred in his interview. The speakers' different social backgrounds were clearly reflected in this feature of their speech.

This speech variable is widely called [h]-dropping – a label which you should note reflects the viewpoint of speakers of the standard. It has been analysed in many social dialect studies of English. Figure 6.4 shows the average [h]-dropping scores for five different social groups in two different places in England: West Yorkshire and Norwich. Different studies use different labels for different classes so wherever I compare data from different studies I have simply used numbers. In this figure (and throughout the book), group 1 refers to the highest social group (often called the upper middle class or UMC) and group 5 to the lowest (usually called the lower or working class).

In both areas the highest social group drops the least number of [h]s and the lowest group omits the most. The regularity of the patterns from one group to the next seems quite remarkable when you first see a diagram of this kind, but it is quite typical. The average scores for socially differentiated groups generally follow exactly this kind of pattern for any linguistic variable where there are clearly identifiable standard and vernacular variants.

There are regional differences in that the West Yorkshire scores are systematically higher than the Norwich scores, but the overall pattern remains the same. We also need to remember that these are averages and within each social group there is always a great deal of individual variation. In the West Yorkshire study, for example, one person who

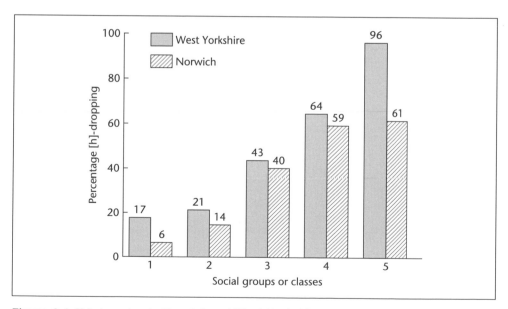

Figure 6.4 [h]-dropping in Norwich and West Yorkshire social groups
Source: This diagram was constructed from data in Trudgill, 1974 and Petyt, 1985

B

Language variation: focus on users

belonged socially in the middle group (3) dropped every [h]. From a linguistic point of view, taking account only of [h]-dropping, they sounded as if they came from a lower social group. Averaging may conceal considerable variation within a group.

The way different pronunciations fall into a pattern reflecting the social class of their speakers was first demonstrated by William Labov in a study of New York City speech which is now regarded as a classic in sociolinguistics. He designed a socio-linguistic interview to elicit a range of speech styles from 120 people from different social backgrounds, and then he analysed their pronunciations of a number of differ-ent consonants and vowels. He found regular patterns relating the social class of the speakers to the percentage of standard as opposed to vernacular pronunciations they produced. Some of the linguistic features he studied have been found to pattern socially in English-speaking communities all over the world. The pronunciation -ing vs -in' ([ɪŋ] vs [ɪn]) at the end of words like *sleeping* and *swimming*, for instance, distinguishes social groups in every English-speaking community in which it has been investigated. The figures in table 6.2 demonstrate that, as with [h]-dropping, there are regional variations between communities, but the regularity of the sociolinguistic pattern in all four communities is quite clear.[1] The Brisbane data was collected from adolescents, but the data from the other communities is representative of the communities as a whole. In each community, people from lower social groups use more of the vernacular [in] variant than those from higher groups.

Table 6.2 Percentage of vernacular [in] pronunciation for four social groups in speech communities in Britain, America, and Australia

Social group	1	2	3	4
Norwich	31	42	91	100
West Yorkshire	5	34	61	83
New York	7	32	45	75
Brisbane	17	31	49	63

Example 13

In New York City in 1964 a man was observed in three different department stores asking one store worker after another: 'where are the women's shoes?'. The man appeared not only to have a short memory, since he repeated his question to a shop assistant in each aisle on several different floors, he also appeared to be slightly deaf since he asked each person to repeat their answer to him. After receiving the answer he would scurry away and scribble something in his notebook. Oddest of all, when he finally made it to the fourth floor where the women's shoes were, he showed absolutely no interest in them whatsoever but wandered around the floor asking, 'Excuse me, what floor is this?'. When questioned by a puzzled store detective he said he was a sociolinguist!

One linguistic form which has proved particularly interesting to sociolinguists studying English-speaking speech communities is the variable pronunciation of [r] in words like *car* and *card*, *for* and *form*. For our purposes, there are two possible variants of [r]. Either it is present and pronounced [r], or it is absent. If you listen to a range of dialects you will find that sometimes people pronounce [r] following a vowel, and sometimes they don't. In some regions pronouncing [r] is part of the standard prestige dialect – in Scotland, for example, in Ireland, and in the Boston and New York areas of the eastern United States. In other areas, standard dialect speakers do not pronounce [r] after vowels (or 'post-vocalically' as linguists describe it) in words like *car* and *card*.[2] In areas where [r] pronunciation is prestigious, sociolinguists have found patterns like those described above for [h]-dropping and -*in'* vs -*ing* ([in] vs [iŋ]) pronunciation. The higher a person's social group, the more [r] they pronounce.

In New York City, Labov conducted an interesting experiment demonstrating in a neat and economical way that pronunciation of post-vocalic [r] varied in the city according to social group. As example 13 describes, he asked a number of people in different department stores where to find an item which he knew was sold on the fourth floor. Then, pretending he hadn't heard the answer, he said, 'Excuse me?' People repeated their answers and he obtained a second and more careful pronunciation. So each person had the chance to pronounce [r] four times: twice in *fourth* and twice in *floor*. This ingenious rapid and anonymous survey technique provided some interesting patterns.

The results showed clear social stratification of [r] pronunciation. Overall the 'posher' the store, the more people used post-vocalic [r]. And even within stores a pattern was evident. In one store, for instance, nearly half the socially superior supervisors used post-vocalic [r] consistently, while only 18 per cent of the less statusful salespeople did, and the stock boys rarely used it at all.

Post-vocalic [r] illustrates very clearly the arbitrariness of the particular forms which are considered standard and prestigious. There is nothing inherently bad or good about the pronunciation of any sound, as the different status of [r]-pronunciation in different cities illustrates. In New York City, pronouncing [r] is considered prestigious. In Reading in England it is not. This is reflected in the patterns for different social groups in the two cities illustrated in figure 6.5.

In one city the higher your social class the more you pronounce post-vocalic [r]. In the other, the higher your social class the fewer you pronounce.

Example 14

Cholmondley: Which 'otel are you staying at old chap?

The same point is illustrated by [h]-dropping. Kim's comment in example 11 expresses a widely held viewpoint – only uneducated people drop their [h]s. Some claim that [h]-dropping is evidence of laziness or slovenly speech. Yet well into this century the top

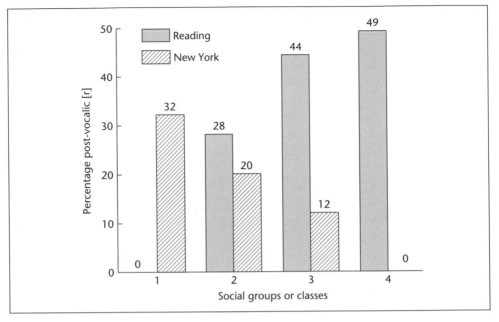

Figure 6.5 Post-vocalic [r] in Reading and New York social group

Source: This diagram was constructed from data in Romaine, 1984: 86

social classes in England dropped the [h] at the beginning of words like *hotel* and *herb*. Interestingly, initial [h] has recently reappeared in the speech of young Londoners who belong to ethnic minority groups. Clearly, the particular linguistic forms which people regard as prestigious or stigmatised are in general totally arbitrary. This is probably most obvious in the pronunciation of vowels where the precise values of the standard forms are entirely determined by the speech of the most prestigious social group.

Example 15

Sir – What is happening to the humble letter 'i' in New Zealandese? In many mouths HIM becomes HUM, JIM is JUM and TILL is TULL. I overheard a young girl telling her friend on the phone that she had been to a doctor and had to take six different PULLS a day. After four repetitions, she had to spell it to be understood.

In this letter the writer is complaining about the way New Zealanders pronounce their vowels. The examples illustrate the difficulty of precisely describing differences in the pronunciation of vowels without the aid of a phonetic script. Measuring slight differences in the way speakers pronounce the 'same' vowels is also a challenging task. In his pioneering study of New York speech, Labov measured people's pronunciation of five

Source: © 1986 United Feature Syndicate, Inc. Reproduced by permission

vowels as well as a number of consonants. Measuring the presence or absence of [h] or [r], or the difference between [in] and [iŋ], is difficult enough when you are listening to tapes of interviews. Measuring small but significant differences in vowel pronunciations can seem a nightmare. Labov developed a method which involved giving a score to different pronunciations according to how close they were to the prestige pronunciation or standard in the community.

The scoring system is most easily understood by giving an example. In New Zealand a survey of 141 people living in the South Island distinguished three different social groups on the basis of the way speakers pronounced the diphthongs in words such as *boat*, *bite*, and *bout*. Four points on a scale were used to measure the different pronunciations. A score of 4 was allocated to pronunciations closest to RP, and a score of 1 to the 'broadest' New Zealand pronunciations, with two points in between. A pattern emerged with the highest social group scoring 60 or more (out of a possible 100) for these diphthongs, the middle group scoring between 50 and 55, while the lowest social group scored less than 43 (where 25 was the minimum possible score).

Many New Zealanders consider RP an inappropriate standard accent for New Zealand, but in practice it is still an influential prestige norm. The systematically patterned scores for diphthong pronunciation in different social groups clearly revealed the social basis of New Zealand patterns of pronunciation. The higher a person's social class, the closer their pronunciation was to RP. The scoring system allowed comparison of the way different social groups pronounced these vowels.

Exercise 7

You will find that you can collect examples yourself to illustrate the patterns described, though it takes a bit of practice to accurately identify the sounds you are listening for.

Tape record the best-educated person you know, and the person with the least education. Ask them to describe the first school they went to. Then count the number of [in]s they use compared to the number of [iŋ]s at the end of words like *swimming* and *running*. Check whether any differences you find between your speakers in the numbers of [in] vs [iŋ] are consistent with the findings reported in this chapter.

Example 16

Jean Charmier is a young Parisian who works as a labourer on a construction site. His speech is quite different in many ways from the speech of the news announcers on national television. One difference involves his pronunciation of the *as* in words like *casser* ('break') and *pas* ('not'). He says something which sounds more like *cosser* for *casser* and instead of *je ne sais pas* for 'I don't know', he omits the *ne* (as most now do in colloquial French) and pronounces the phrase as something which sounds like *shpo*.

Although the sociolinguistic patterns described in the preceding section have been most extensively researched in English-speaking communities, they have been found in other languages too. In fact we would expect to find such patterns in all communities which can be divided into different social groups. In Paris the pronunciation of the first vowel in words like *casser* and *pas* varies from one social group to another. In Montreal the frequency with which [l] is deleted distinguishes the French of two social groups, as illustrated in table 6.3.

This table also introduces another interesting influence on linguistic variation. The pronunciation of a linguistic form often alters in different linguistic contexts. Table 6.3 shows that not only does [l]-deletion differ between the social classes, it also differs according to the grammatical status of the word in which it occurs. [l] has almost disappeared in Montreal French in impersonal *il*.

The surrounding sounds also affect the likelihood of [l]-deletion. It is much more likely to disappear before a consonant than before a vowel. This is the point being made by Stephen in example 11. Most people 'drop their hs' in an unstressed syllable. So linguistic as well as social factors are relevant in accounting for patterns of pronunciation. But within each linguistic context the social differences are still quite clear.

Similar patterns can be found in any speech community where there is social stratification. In Tehrani Persian, as well as in the Swahili used in Mombasa, the same relationship is found between speech and social class. The higher social groups use more of the standard forms, while the lowest groups use the fewest standard forms.

Table 6.3 Percentage [l]-deletion in two social classes in Montreal French

	Professional	Working Class
il (impersonal)	89.8	99.6
e.g. il pleut 'it is raining'		
il (personal)	71.6	100.0
e.g. il part 'he is leaving'		
elle	29.8	82.0

Source: Reproduced from Sankoff and Cedergren 1971: 81

Grammatical patterns

> **Example 17**
>
> *Whina is 8 years old and she is telling a visitor the story of a film she has seen.*
>   'And then these little flies went to go and they made a house by theirself, and this big fly was playing his guitar. He play and play. Then the little flies was making the house, and then the flies um sew um these leaves up all together.'

This is a slightly edited extract from a tape-recorded interview. Whina was one of eighty New Zealand children who were recorded telling the story of a film they had seen. As the extract shows, this was a good way of providing a natural context for the children to use a large number of past tense forms of verbs. It was then possible to compare the proportion of standard verb forms in the speech of children from different social groups. On average it was found that children from lower-class families used more vernacular verb forms than children from middle-class families.

This pattern has been noted for a variety of grammatical variables. Here are some examples of standard and vernacular grammatical forms which have been identified in several English-speaking communities.

Form	Example
Past tense verb forms	1. I finished that book yesterday.
	2. I finish that book yesterday.
Present tense verb forms	3. Rose walks to school every day.
	4. Rose walk to school every day.
Negative forms	5. Nobody wants any chips.
	6. Nobody don't want no chips.
Ain't	7. Jim isn't stupid.
	8. Jim ain't stupid.

As with pronunciation, there is a clear pattern to the relationship between the grammatical speech forms and the social groups who use them. Figure 6.6 illustrates this. The higher social groups use more of the standard grammatical form and fewer instances of the vernacular or non-standard form. With the grammatical pattern illustrated in figure 6.6, the third person singular form of the present tense regular verb (e.g. standard *she walks* vs vernacular *she walk*), there is a sharp distinction between the middle-class groups and the lower-class groups. People are often more aware of social stigma in relation to vernacular grammatical forms, and this is reflected in the lower incidence of vernacular forms among middle-class speakers in particular. Note that this pattern is found both in a variety of American English in Detroit, and in a variety of British English in Norwich.

Sentence (6) in the list illustrates a pattern of negation which is sometimes called 'negative concord' or 'multiple negation'. Where standard English allows only one

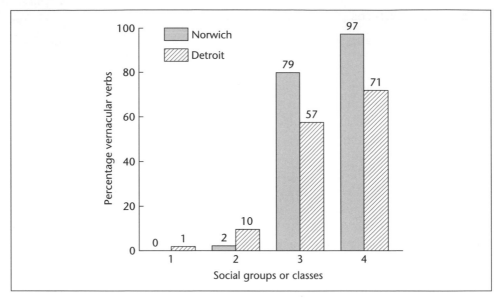

Figure 6.6 Vernacular present tense verb forms (3rd person singular: *she walk*) in Norwich and Detroit

Source: This diagram was constructed from data in Trudgill 1983a: 44 and Wolfram and Fasold, 1974

negative in each clause, most vernacular dialects can have two or more. In some dialects every possible form which can be negated is negated. An adolescent gang member in New York produced the following:

9. It ain't no cat can't get in no coop.
   Translated into standard English, the meaning of this utterance in context was
10. There isn't any cat that can get into any (pigeon) coop
    or, more simply, no cat can get into any coop.
    Sentence (11) comes from an adolescent in Detroit:
11. We ain't had no trouble about none of us pulling out no knife.

Multiple negation is a grammatical construction which has been found in all English-speaking communities where a social dialect study has been done. In every community studied it is much more frequent in lower-class speech than in middle-class speech. In fact there is usually a dramatic contrast between the groups in the amount of multiple negation used. It is rare in middle-class speech.

Multiple negation is a very 'salient' vernacular form. People notice it when it is used even once, unlike say the use of a glottal stop for the standard pronunciation [t] at the end of a word, where the percentage of glottal stops generally needs to be quite high before people register them. The dramatic split evident between middle-class and lower-class usage of multiple negation reflects this salience. Middle-class speakers tend to avoid it, while lower class speakers use it more comfortably.

In reporting patterns relating linguistic features to social status I have inevitably simplified a great deal. Many factors interact in determining the proportion of vernacular or standard forms a person uses. Some of these are social factors such as the age or gender of the speaker, and they will be examined in the next couple of chapters. Another factor, however, which was mentioned briefly above, is the linguistic environment in which a word occurs. Table 6.3, for example, provided information on the effect of the linguistic environment in which [l]-deletion in French occurred. In English it has been found that people omit the auxiliary verb *have* more often before *got* (e.g. *you got to go*) than before other verbs (e.g. *you've done that*). The lexical context appears to be relevant. Before analysing the effects of social variation, then, social dialectologists must take into account the effects of the linguistic environment in which the linguistic feature occurs.

B

Language variation: focus on users

Exercise 8

(a) Make three points about the distribution of non-standard or vernacular forms in British urban dialects which are supported by figure 6.7.

(b) Figure 6.7 shows values for three towns in England. Similar diagrams can be drawn for social classes. If the labels 'Hull', 'Milton Keynes', and 'Reading' referred to social classes, which would be the lowest social class? How do you know?

Answer at end of chapter

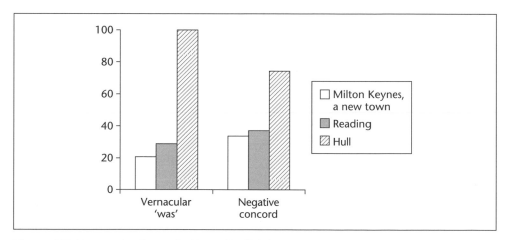

Figure 6.7 Vernacular forms in three English towns

Note: Vernacular 'was' = use of *was* where standard English uses *were*: e.g. *you was late again*. Negative concord = multiple negation.

Milton Keynes, Reading and Hull are British towns. Milton Keynes is a relatively new town 80 kilometres north of London. Reading is 60 kilometres west of London and Hull is the furthest north and over 200 kilometres from London.

Source: Cheshire, Kerswill and Williams, 2005. Reproduced with permission

◼ A note about methodology

> ### Example 18
>
> My friend Terry taught sociolinguistics at a New Zealand university. He described to his students how I and my colleagues Allan Bell and Mary Boyce designed our sample for the Wellington social dialect survey by establishing a quota of five people per cell for each of our target groups: young Pakeha women, middle-aged Maori men, and so on. After the exams, he rang to tell me that some of his students had clearly misunderstood our method of collecting data. In their exam answers they described how we had put people in cells before interviewing them!

The term 'cell' is used to describe the box in a diagram which indicates the target numbers for each group in a sample. Our goal was a minimum of five people in each box or cell in the diagram to represent each group, including women and men, three age groups, two ethnic groups (Maori and Pakeha), and two social groups. We managed to reach our target, but not by capturing people and putting them in cells till they agreed to be interviewed! Table 6.4 illustrates a sample of 20 people divided by age and gender with a quota of five people per cell.

Collecting good-quality social dialect data requires considerable skill. Some of the challenges and pitfalls which face the social dialectologist will emerge during the discussion in the next few chapters. In this chapter I have mentioned the use of rapid and anonymous surveys as one useful technique for collecting a lot of data very quickly. Labov used this method when he asked 'where are the women's shoes?' in the New York department store. Another example is the use of a street survey to ask people to pronounce certain words (ideally presenting them in written or visual form to prevent bias). This method can give the researcher an idea of what is worth studying in more detail. But it has obvious limitations. Though patterns of gender and age and even ethnic variation can be detected using this approach, since we can usually guess these features when we meet someone, it is harder to be sure about the social background of speakers when no social information is collected from them.

Table 6.4 A sample of 20 by age and gender with a quota of 5 people per cell

		Age	
		Young	Middle-aged
Gender	Male	5 young males	5 middle-aged males
	Female	5 young females	5 middle-aged females

And, of course, the data is limited in quantity and style. A sociolinguistic interview which attempts to elicit a range of styles as well as collect background information from the interviewee is thus much more useful. This is by far the most widespread method of collecting social dialect data. But of course it is much more time-consuming and thus expensive.

Conclusion

The way you speak is usually a good indicator of your social background. And there are many speech features which can be used as clues. Sociolinguists have found that almost any linguistic feature in a community which shows variation will differ in frequency from one social group to another in a patterned and predictable way. Some features are stable and their patterns of use seem to have correlated with member-ship of particular social groups in a predictable way for many years. Variation in pronunciation of the suffix -ing and [h]-dropping are examples of features which are usually stable. Grammatical features, such as multiple negation and tense markers, are often stable too. This means they are good ones to include in any study of an English-speaking community. They are reliable indicators of sociolinguistic patterning in a community.

Social dialect surveys have demonstrated that stable variables tend to divide English-speaking communities sharply between the middle class and lower or working classes. So patterns of [h]-dropping and [iŋ] vs [in] pronunciation sharply divide the middle-class groups from the lower-class groups in Norwich. Grammatical variables do the same, as figure 6.6 illustrated. There is a sharp rise in the number of vernacular forms between the middle-class groups and the lower-class groups both in Detroit and in Norwich, and the same pattern has been observed in many other communities. This pattern has been labelled *sharp stratification*.

Not all variation is stable over time, however. In fact variation is often used as an indicator of language change in progress. New linguistic forms don't sweep through a community overnight. They spread gradually from person to person and from group to group and they often stratify the population very delicately or finely. Unstable variation is thus associated with *fine stratification* and is a clue to linguistic changes in progress in the community, as we will see in chapter 9.

In exploring the relationship between language and society, this chapter has been concerned almost exclusively with the dimension of social status or class. It is clear from all the evidence discussed that the social class someone belongs to is reflected in their speech patterns. Many people, however, are not very conscious of belonging to a particular social class. They are much more aware of other factors about the people they meet regularly than their social class membership. A person's gender and age are probably the first things we notice about them. The next chapter explores ways in which women and men speak differently, and describes speech differences associated with age.

B

Language variation: focus on users

ANSWERS TO EXERCISES IN CHAPTER 6

Answer to exercise 2

Using the system for representing sounds in Appendix 1, your answer for *batter* might include:

[batə] the pronunciation considered standard in Britain
[batər] a pronunciation considered standard in North America
[baʔə] a Cockney pronunciation
[baʔər] and [badər] pronunciations heard in the West Country of England

There are many other possible pronunciations, including one common in Liverpool which sounds like [batsə] with affrication after the [t], and another which occurs in New Zealand English which sounds like [betə] to British ears.

Answers to exercise 3

(a) 'snowflake' (Somerset)
(b) 'time for a snack' (Norfolk and elsewhere too)
(c) 'infuse or brew the tea' (Cumberland, Durham, Northumberland, Yorkshire, Scotland)
(d) 'the place was all untidy, disordered' (Lincolnshire)
(e) 'icicles' (Somerset)
(f) 'a great rough awkward girl' (Essex, East Anglia and elsewhere)
(g) 'I'm really fed up, weary' (Yorkshire)
(h) 'child' (Scottish)
(i) 'newt' (south-east)
(j) a *piggy* is a 'hot water bottle' (Scotland, Northumberland)

Answers to exercise 5

(a) Accents are distinguished from each other by pronunciation alone. Different dialects are generally distinguishable in pronunciation and vocabulary and grammar.
(b) Regional dialects involve features of pronunciation, vocabulary and grammar which differ according to the geographical area the speakers come from. Social dialects are distinguished by features of pronunciation, vocabulary and grammar according to the social group of the speakers. Social group is usually determined by a range of features, such as education, occupation, residential area, and income level. So people who come from different social groups speak different social dialects if they use different words, pronunciations, and grammatical features. Examples of these are discussed in the next section.

Answers to exercise 6

(a) Example of points you might have made:
   – the pattern of vernacular usage is consistent for both variables in all three places
   – negative concord is slightly more frequent than non-standard *was* in two of the three places
   – vernacular *was* is particularly distinctive of Hull speech, where it reaches almost 100 per cent or categorical status
   – the further north you go the higher the percentage of vernacular forms
   – this table suggests that regional variation intersects with class variation since, as the section preceding this exercise indicates, these vernacular forms typically stratify urban populations socially.
(b) Hull would be the equivalent of the lowest social class because the percentages of vernacular forms are highest in Hull and lower social groups tend to use more vernacular forms.

▓ Concepts introduced

Accent
Regional dialect
Isogloss
Dialect chain
Social dialect
Vernacular
Sociolinguistic patterns
Methodology
Sharp and fine stratification

▓ References

The following sources provided material for this chapter:

Bayard (1987) for New Zealand data
Bright (1966) on Indian languages
Bright and Ramanujan (1964) on Indian languages
Chambers and Trudgill (1980)
Cheshire, Kerswill and Williams (2005) is the source of figure 6.7
Eisikovits (1989a) on *have* deletion
Feagin (1979) for data on Anniston and West Virginia
Finegan and Besnier (1989: 383) for definition of a language
Gordon and Deverson (1985, 1989)
Guy (1988: 37) on 'social class'
Labov (1966, 1972a, 1972b), especially data on New York City
Lee (1989) on Brisbane adolescents' speech
McCallum (1978) on New Zealand past tense usage
Mitford and Ross (1980) and Wales (1994) on 'U' speech
Petyt (1985) for West Yorkshire dialect data
Pragji (1980) on [h] dropping
Romaine (1984)
Sankoff and Cedergren (1971) on Montreal French
Shuy, Wolfram and Riley (1967) for Detroit data
Trudgill (1974, 1983a), especially data on Norwich
Wolfram and Fasold (1974) for Detroit data
Wolfram and Schilling-Estes (1998) for Appalachian data

▓ Quotations

Example 10 is from Mitford (1949: 29)
Example 15 is from Gordon and Deverson (1989: 35)

B

Language variation: focus on users

◼ Useful additional reading

Chambers and Trudgill (1980)
Milroy (1987)
Trudgill (1990)
Trudgill (2000), Ch. 2
Wardhaugh (2006), Chs 2 and 7
Wolfram (1991)
Wolfram and Schilling-Estes (1998)

◼ Notes

1. Here and elsewhere I have combined data from groups 3 (upper working class) and 4 (middle working class) in Norwich and West Yorkshire for ease of comparison with communities which were analysed into only four social groups.
2. 'Post-vocalic' is the term widely used for the [r] in words like *car* and *card* which is not pronounced in many varieties of English, and I use this term throughout the book Note, however, that strictly speaking one should refer to non-pre-vocalic (r) in such contexts, since [r] is always pronounced between vowels in words such as *wary* and *carry*.

7 Gender and age

Do women and men speak differently? Do children speak differently from adults? English speakers are often not aware that the answer to both these questions is almost certainly 'yes' for all speech communities.

The linguistic forms used by women and men contrast – to different degrees – in all speech communities. There are other ways too in which the linguistic behaviour of women and men differs. It is claimed women are more linguistically polite than men, for instance, and that women and men emphasise different speech functions. These claims will be explored in later chapters. In the first section of this chapter the focus will be on evidence that women and men from the same speech community use different linguistic forms.

First a brief comment on the meaning of the terms *sex* and *gender* in sociolinguistics. I have used the term *gender* rather than *sex* because *sex* has come to refer to categories distinguished by biological characteristics, while *gender* is more appropriate for distinguishing people on the basis of their socio-cultural behaviour, including speech. The discussion of *gender* in this chapter focusses on contrasts between features of women's and men's speech. The concept of gender allows, however, for describing masculine and feminine behaviours in terms of scales or continua rather than absolute categories. This is something which will be discussed further in chapter 12.

GENDER-EXCLUSIVE SPEECH DIFFERENCES: HIGHLY STRUCTURED COMMUNITIES

Example 1

Tayana is a young Amazonian Indian woman from the north-west Amazon Basin. She lives with her husband and children and a number of other families in a longhouse beside the river. The language of her longhouse is Tuyuka, which is the language of all the men in this tribe, and the language she uses to talk to her children. She comes from a different tribe and her first language is Desano. She uses Desano to her husband, and he replies in Tuyuka.

Women and men do not speak in exactly the same way as each other in any community. The Amazon Indians provide an extreme example. As described in chapter 4, in any longhouse the language used by a child's mother is different from her father's language, because men must marry outside their own tribe, and each tribe is distinguished by a different language. In this community women and men speak different languages.

Less dramatically, there are communities where the language is shared by women and men, but particular linguistic features occur only in the women's speech or only in the men's speech. These features are usually small differences in pronunciation or word-shape (morphology). In Montana, for instance, there are pronunciation differences in the Gros Ventre American Indian tribe. Where the women say [kja'tsa] for 'bread' the men say [dʒa'tsa]. In this community if a person uses the wrong form for their gender, the older members of the community may consider them bisexual. In Bengali, a language of India, the women use an initial [l] where the men use an initial [n] in some words.

Word-shapes in other languages contrast because women and men use different affixes. In Yana, a North American Indian language, and Chiquita, a South American Indian language, some of the words used between men are longer than the equivalent words used by women and to women, because the men's forms sometimes add a suffix, as illustrated in example 2.

Example 2

Yana

Women's form	Men's form	
ba	ba-na	'deer'
yaa	yaa-na	'person'
ʔau	ʔau-na	'fire'
nisaaklu	nisaaklu-ʔi	'he might go away'

In traditional and conservative styles of Japanese, forms of nouns considered appropriate for women are frequently prefixed by *o-*, a marker of polite or formal style.

In some languages there are also differences between the vocabulary items used by women and men, though these are never very extensive. Traditional Japanese provides some clear examples.

Example 3

Japanese

Women's form	Men's form	
otoosan	oyaji	'father'
onaka	hara	'stomach'
oishii	umai	'delicious'
taberu	kuu	'eat'

In modern Japanese, these distinctions are more a matter of degrees of formality or politeness than gender; so the 'men's' forms are restricted to casual contexts and considered macho or coarse, while the 'women's' forms are used by everyone in public contexts.

Some languages signal the gender of the speaker in the pronoun system. In Japanese, for instance, there are a number of words for 'I' varying primarily in formality (a point explored further in chapter 10), but women are generally restricted to the more formal variants. So *ore* is used only by men in casual contexts and *boku*, the next most casual form, is used mainly by men, while women are traditionally expected to use only the more formal variants, *atashi* and *watashi*, and the most formal *watakushi*. However, modern young Japanese women are increasingly challenging such restrictions.

Exercise 1

Do English pronouns encode the gender of the speaker?

Answer at end of chapter

Gender differences in language are often just one aspect of more pervasive linguistic differences in the society reflecting social status or power differences. If a community is very hierarchical, for instance, and within each level of the hierarchy men are more powerful than women, then linguistic differences between the speech of women and men may be just one dimension of more extensive differences reflecting the social hierarchy as a whole. In Bengali society, for instance, a younger person should not address a superior by first name. Similarly a wife, being subordinate to her husband, is not permitted to use his name. She addresses him with a term such as *suncho* 'do you hear?' When she refers to him she uses a circumlocution. One nice example of this practice is provided by the Bengali wife whose husband's name was *tara*, which also means 'star'. Since she could not call him *tara*, his wife used the term *nokkhotro* or 'heavenly body' to refer to him. This point – the interrelationship of gender with other social factors – is illustrated even more clearly in the next section.

The fact that there are clearly identifiable differences between women's and men's speech in the communities discussed in this section reflects the clearly demarcated gender roles in these communities. Gender-exclusive speech forms (i.e. some forms are used *only* by women and others are used *only* by men) reflect gender-exclusive social roles. The responsibilities of women and men are different in such communities, and everyone knows that, and knows what they are. There are no arguments over who prepares the dinner and who puts the children to bed.

GENDER-PREFERENTIAL SPEECH FEATURES: SOCIAL DIALECT RESEARCH

> ### Example 4
>
> Keith was a 7-year-old Canadian from Vancouver whose parents were working for six months in the city of Leeds in Yorkshire, England. He had been enrolled at the local school, and after his first day Keith came home very confused. 'What's your teacher's name?' asked his father. '*She* says she's Mrs Hall,' said Keith, 'but when the boys call her *Mizall* she still answers them. And the girls sometimes call her *Mrs Hall* and sometimes *Mizall*. It sounds very funny.'

Not surprisingly in Western urban communities where women's and men's social roles overlap, the speech forms they use also overlap. In other words women and men do not use completely different forms. They use different quantities or frequencies of the same forms. In all the English-speaking cities where speech data has been collected, for instance, women use more *-ing* [iŋ] pronunciations and fewer *-in'* [in] pronunciations than men in words like *swimming* and *typing*. In Montreal, the French used by women and men is distinguished by the frequencies with which they pronounce [l] in phrases such as *il y a* and *il fait*. Both women and men delete [l], but men do so more often than women. In Sydney, some women and men pronounce the initial sound in *thing* as [f], but the men use this pronunciation more than the women. Both the social and the linguistic patterns in these communities are gender-preferential (rather than gender-exclusive). Though both women and men use particular forms, one gender shows a greater preference for them than the other.

In all these examples women tend to use more of the standard forms than men do, while men use more of the vernacular forms than women do. In Australia, interviews with people in Sydney revealed gender-differentiated patterns of [h]-dropping.

> ### Exercise 2
> What would you predict for [h]-dropping patterns? Is it more likely that women or men drop most [h]s?
>
> *Answer at end of chapter*

GENDER AND SOCIAL CLASS

> **Example 5**
>
> Linda lives in the south of England and her dad is a lawyer. When she was 10 years old she went to stay for a whole school term with her uncle Tom and auntie Bet in Wigan, a Lancashire town, while her mother was recovering from a car accident. She was made to feel very welcome both in her auntie's house and at the local school. When she went home she tried to describe to her teacher what she had noticed about the way her uncle and auntie talked. 'Uncle Tom is a plumber' she told Mrs Button 'and he talks just like the other men on the building site where he works – a bit broad. He says *'ouse* and *'ome* and [kup] and [bus]. When she's at home auntie Bet talks a bit like uncle Tom. She says "Me feet are killin' me [luv]. I've 'ad enough standin' [up] for today". But she works in a shop and when she's talking to customers she talks more like you do Mrs Button. She says *house* and *home* and she talks real nice – just like a lady.'

The linguistic features which differ in the speech of women and men in Western communities are usually features which also distinguish the speech of people from different social classes. So how does gender interact with social class? Does the speech of women in one social class resemble that of women from different classes, or does it more closely resemble the speech of the men from their own social class? The answer to this question is quite complicated, and is different for different linguistic features. There are, however, some general patterns which can be identified.

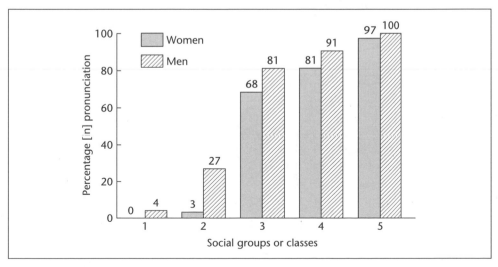

Figure 7.1 Vernacular [in] by sex and social group in Norwich
Source: This diagram was devised from data in Trudgill, 1983a

In every social class men use more vernacular forms than women. Figure 7.1 shows, for instance, that in social dialect interviews in Norwich, men used more of the vernacular [in] form at the end of words like *speaking* and *walking* than women. And this pattern was quite consistent across five distinct social groups. (Group 1 represents the highest social group.)

Source: DENNIS THE MENACE ® used by permission of Hank Ketcham Enterprises and © North America Syndicate

Notice, too, that in the lowest and the highest social groups the women's speech is closer to that of the men in the same group than to that of women in other groups. In these groups class membership seems to be more important than gender identity. But this is not so true of women in group 2. Their score (of 3 per cent) for vernacular forms is closer to that of women in group 1 than it is to that of men from their own group. This may indicate they identify more strongly with women from the next social group than with men from their own social group. Possible reasons for this will be discussed below.

Exercise 3

Recent research suggests that Japanese women and men may use grammatical patterns with different frequencies. Are you aware of any differences in the grammar of English-speaking women and men? What pattern of gender differences would you predict for grammatical variables such as multiple negation, which was discussed in chapter 6?

Answer at end of chapter

Across all social groups women generally use more standard forms than men and so, correspondingly, men use more vernacular forms than women. In Detroit, for instance, multiple negation (e.g. *I don't know nothing about it*), a vernacular feature of speech, is more frequent in men's speech than in women's. This is true in every social group but the difference is most dramatic in the second highest (the lower middle class) where the men's multiple negation score is 32 per cent compared to only 1 per cent for women. Even in the lowest social group, however, men use a third more instances of multiple negation than women (90 vs 59 per cent).

This pattern is typical for many grammatical features. In many speech communities, when women use more of a linguistic form than men, it is generally the standard form – the overtly prestigious form – that women favour. When men use a form more often than women, it is usually a vernacular form, one which is not admired overtly by the society as a whole, and which is not cited as the 'correct' form. This pattern has been found in Western speech communities all over the world. It was described in 1983 by Peter Trudgill, the sociolinguist who collected the Norwich data, as 'the single most consistent finding to emerge from sociolinguistic studies over the past 20 years'.

This widespread pattern is also evident from a very young age. It was first identified over thirty years ago in a study of American children's speech in a semi-rural New England village, where it was found that the boys used more [in] and the girls more [iŋ] forms. Later studies in Boston and Detroit identified the same pattern. Boys used more vernacular forms such as consonant cluster simplification: e.g. *las'* [las] and *tol'* [toul], rather than standard *last* [last] and *told* [tould]. Boys pronounced *th* [ð] in words like *the* and *then* as [d] more often than girls did. In Edinburgh, differences of this sort were observed in the pronunciation of girls and boys as young as six years old.

The pattern is clear, consistent and widespread and it is evident from a very early age. What is the explanation for it? Why does female and male speech differ in this way?

Exercise 4

Before you read the next section, consider some possible explanations for the finding of social dialect surveys that women use more standard forms than men. Consider the possible influence of the dimensions discussed in chapter 1: social status, social distance or solidarity, the formality of the context and the functions of speech. How might these affect the speech used by an interviewee in a social dialect survey? Bear in mind that no single explanation is likely to fit all cases.

EXPLANATIONS OF WOMEN'S LINGUISTIC BEHAVIOUR

'Why can't a woman be more like a man?' (*My Fair Lady*)

When this pattern first emerged, social dialectologists asked: 'why do women use more standard forms than men?' At least four different (though not mutually exclusive) explanations were suggested. The first appeals to social class and its related status for an explanation, the second refers to women's role in society, the third to women's status as a subordinate group, and the fourth to the function of speech in expressing gender identity, and especially masculinity.

The social status explanation

Some linguists have suggested that women use more standard speech forms than men because they are more status-conscious than men. The claim is that women are more aware of the fact that the way they speak signals their social class background or social status in the community. Standard speech forms are generally associated with high social status, and so, according to this explanation, women use more standard speech forms as a way of claiming such status. It has been suggested that this is especially true for women who do not have paid employment, since they cannot use their occupations as a basis for signalling social status.

The fact that women interviewed in New York and in Norwich reported that they used more standard forms than they actually did has also been used to support this explanation. Women generally lack status in the society, and so, it is suggested, some try to acquire it by using standard speech forms, and by reporting that they use even more of these forms than they actually do.

Though it sounds superficially plausible, there is at least some indirect evidence which throws doubt on this as the main explanation for gender differences in social dialect data. It is suggested that women who are not in paid employment are most likely to claim high social status by using more standard forms. This implies that women in the paid workforce should use fewer standard forms than women working in the home. But the little evidence that we have in fact suggests that just the opposite may be true. An American study compared the speech of women in service occupations, working in garages and hotels, for instance, with the speech of women working in the home. Those in paid employment used more standard forms than those working in the home. In the course of their jobs, the first group of women were interacting with people who used more standard forms, and this interaction had its effect on their own usage. By contrast, the women who stayed home interacted mainly with each other, and this reinforced their preference for vernacular forms.

Exactly the same pattern was found in an Irish working-class community. The younger women in Ballymacarrett, a suburb of Belfast, found work outside the community, and used a much higher percentage of linguistic features associated with high status groups than the older women who were working at home. This evidence throws some doubt, then, on suggestions that women without paid employment are more likely to use standard forms than those with jobs, and so indirectly questions the social status explanation for women's speech patterns.

Woman's role as guardian of society's values

'A woman's place is in the home.'

Example 6

Mrs Godley, an early New Zealand settler, believed in the civilising influence of women. When two young men she knew were about to begin work on a sheep station in the South Island province of Canterbury in 1852, she warned them that they would become 'semi-barbarous'. She begged them to have a 'lay figure of a lady, carefully draped, set up in their usual sitting-room, and always behave before it as if it was their mother'.

A second explanation for the fact that women use more standard forms than men points to the way society tends to expect 'better' behaviour from women than from men. Little boys are generally allowed more freedom than little girls. Misbehaviour from boys is tolerated where girls are more quickly corrected. Similarly, rule-breaking of any kind by women is frowned on more severely than rule-breaking by men. Women are designated the role of modelling correct behaviour in the community. Predictably then, following this argument, society expects women to speak more correctly and standardly than men, especially when they are serving as models for children's speech.

This explanation of why women use more standard forms than men may be relevant in some social groups, but it is certainly not true for all. Interactions between a mother and her child are likely to be very relaxed and informal, and it is in relaxed informal contexts that vernacular forms occur most often in everyone's speech. Standard forms are typically associated with more formal and less personal interactions. It seems odd to explain women's greater use of more standard speech forms (collected in formal tape-recorded interviews) by referring to a woman's role as a speech model in her very intimate and mainly unobserved interactions with her child.

▧ Subordinate groups must be polite

Example 7

'You are an intolerable bore Mr Brown. Why don't you simply shut up and let someone speak who has more interesting ideas to contribute', said Lord Huntly in the well-educated and cultured accent of the over-privileged.

A third explanation which has been proposed for women's use of more standard forms is that people who are subordinate must be polite. Children are expected to be polite to adults. Women as a subordinate group, it is argued, must avoid offending men – and so they must speak carefully and politely.

It is not immediately apparent why *polite* speech should be equated with *standard* speech. It is perfectly possible to express yourself politely using a vernacular Liverpool or Glaswegian accent, and it is equally possible to be very insulting using RP, as example 7 illustrates. A more sophisticated version of this explanation, however, which links it to the social status explanation, suggests that by using more standard speech forms women are looking after their own need to be valued by the society. By using standard forms a woman is protecting her 'face' (a technical term used by sociolinguists with approximately the same meaning as in the phrase *to lose face*). She is also avoiding offence to others.

Suggesting that a woman uses standard forms in order to protect her 'face' is not very different from saying she is claiming more status than she is entitled to, compared to men from the same social group. On the other hand the suggestion that women's greater use of standard forms may relate not only to their own face-protection needs, but also to those of the people they are talking to, is more promising. It is consistent with other evidence of women's sensitivity to their addressees, which is discussed more fully in chapter 12.

Like most of the explanations presented, this explanation also begins from the assumption that it is women's behaviour which is aberrant and has to be explained. Men's usage is being taken as the norm against which women's is being measured. Yet this seems odd when we remember that what people are trying to explain is why women are using the standard forms or the norms. Why should standard or 'correct' behaviour need explaining? It is men's speech which uses fewer standard forms – not women's. Instead of asking 'why do women use more standard speech forms than men?', it makes more sense to ask 'why don't men use more standard forms?'

Exercise 5

Before you read the next section, can you think of possible reasons why men in social dialect studies might use more vernacular forms than women?

▓ Vernacular forms express machismo

Example 8

Knocker: Comin' down the club Jim?

Jim: Not friggin' likely. It's rubbish that club.

Knocker: It ain't that bad. Music's cool. I seen a couple of sharp judies there too. If we plays our cards right . . . Anyways you was keen enough las' week.

Jim: The music's last Knocker. I'm off down the Pier 'ead if there ain't nothin' better on offer.

Knocker: Bleedin' rozzers crawlin' round down there. Come down ours instead.

[Vernacular lexical items in the Liverpool dialect Scouse: *judies* ('girls'), *last* ('hopeless') *rozzers* ('police').]

One answer which has been suggested to the question 'why don't men use more standard forms?' is that men prefer vernacular forms because they carry macho connotations of masculinity and toughness. If this is true it would also explain why women might *not* want to use such forms.

There is some evidence to support the suggestion. The speakers on a tape who were identified as most likely to win in a street fight were those who used most vernacular forms. The fact that Norwich men tended to claim that they used more vernacular forms than they actually did, while the women didn't, supports this explanation too. The men apparently wanted to sound less standard than they actually were. This suggests these men regard vernacular forms positively and value them highly, even if they don't always openly admit to doing so. It has been suggested, then, that these forms have 'covert prestige' by contrast with the overt prestige of the standard forms which are cited as models of correctness. (See chapter 15 for a further discussion of covert and overt prestige.)

The converse of this claim is that standard forms tend to be associated with female values and femininity. Some linguists have pointed to the association of standard forms with female teachers and the norms they impose in the classroom, with the suggestion that boys may reject this female domination, and the speech forms associated with it, more vigorously than girls. More generally in the society, a preference for vernacular forms may be a reaction to what is perceived as overly influential female norms.

This explanation seems consistent with much of the sociolinguistic evidence which has accumulated. It is worth asking, however, what it implies about the values expressed by working-class women's speech. The taped voices that people were asked to assess in terms of their likely abilities in a street fight were men's voices. How do people respond to working-class women's speech? Would her listeners consider the high frequency of vernacular forms in the speech of the 70-year-old woman in example 9 as evidence that she was a tough and masculine old woman?

Example 9

C'mere an Ah'll tell ye a wee laugh – ma twin – ma brother an me's twins – he's ten i a family, Ah've nane, Mary – an ma other niece's daughter, she was up visitin er mother an oor Andy was in, as we just cawed im Aundra – Scoatch – but it's Andrew – [. . .] Ah think e'll maybe be aboot ten, Scott – e says, 'Uncle Andrew, are you French?' E says, 'Away, an don't be daft! A'm Brigton!' E says, 'Where's that? Is that abroad? Fae Brigton!'

Or would they consider her a promiscuous old tart? One New Zealand study suggested that women avoid vernacular forms because they are associated with promiscuous women and 'loose morals'.

There are other problems too. If a higher frequency of vernacular forms conveys connotations of masculinity (or promiscuity), then why do *all* speakers from *all* social classes use more vernacular forms in less formal contexts? (See chapter 10 for examples of this pattern.) Women use more vernacular forms in relaxed situations, as example 5 suggested. Why should forms most typically associated with informal relaxed contexts be identified as 'masculine'?

Some alternative explanations

'. . . women continue to be one of the mysteries of the universe.' (Shuy 1969: 14)

Example 10

It was widely considered that Rose had married beneath her. Her parents were both doctors, as she was herself. She had been educated at a private girls' school and had proceeded on the basis of an outstanding exam performance to Oxford University. She was earning a very respectable salary from her practice when she married Bruce. Bruce worked in his father's sports shop and, while it was clear he would eventually inherit the business, at the time of their marriage he seemed no match for Rose intellectually, financially or socially. Nevertheless the marriage seemed to work – despite these apparent disparities.

How are women categorised?

There are alternative ways of accounting for at least some of the social dialect evidence that women's and men's speech differs. Consider, for example, the data on which these generalisations have been made. In assigning women to a particular social class, researchers in early social dialect studies often used the woman's husband's occupation as their major criterion. Not all women marry men from the same social class, however. It is perfectly possible for a woman to be better educated than the man she marries, or even to have a more prestigious job than him, as illustrated in example 10. In such cases women's use of more standard forms would require no explanation at all. They would simply be using appropriate forms which accurately reflected their social background. When women are classified by their husband's social group, miscategorisation is one plausible explanation of their speech behaviour.

The influence of the interviewer and the context

In many social dialect studies the interviewers are middle-class, well-educated academics. When people wish to be cooperative they tend to accommodate to the speech of the person they are talking to. In other words their speech becomes more like that of their addressee (as will be illustrated more fully in chapter 10). Women tend to be more cooperative conversationalists than men, as we shall see in chapter 12. Hence one factor accounting for women's use of more standard forms in social dialect interviews may be their greater accommodation to the middle-class speech of their interviewers. There is clear evidence of speech accommodation, for instance, in Swahili data collected in Mombasa, a town in Kenya. The women interviewed shifted much more dramatically than the men did from more to less standard forms when they were speaking to a friend rather than a stranger.

Men on the other hand tend to be less responsive to the speech of others, and to their conversational needs. In fact it seems perfectly possible that working-class men might react against the speech of a middle-class academic from the university, and so in their interviews they may have diverged in their speech forms, using more vernacular forms precisely to distinguish themselves from the interviewer. An Australian study demonstrated that this was exactly how adolescent boys reacted in an interview with a stranger. The differences between women's and men's speech behaviour would then be explicable in terms of their different responses to the interviewer collecting the data.

B

Exercise 6

How do you think you would speak in a social dialect interview? What would be the effect of the context and the interviewer's status on your speech? With your friend's permission, tape yourself talking to a friend in a relaxed context. Then select three questions from those in the appendix to this chapter and interview your friend.

▶

Can you hear any differences in your speech or that of your friend in the two contexts? Pay attention to [h]-dropping and [ɪn] vs [ɪŋ] variation.

Would you respond differently to a female vs a male interviewer? Why might women respond differently from men in a formal interview situation with a male interviewer?

Answer at end of chapter

Many of the interviewers who collected the social dialect data discussed in the previous sections were male. The interview context was therefore different for men and women. Women were being interviewed by a male stranger, a highly educated member of the dominant group in the society. Men were being interviewed by a member of their own gender. In such circumstances it is likely that the interview context would be considerably more comfortable for men than for women, especially for middle-class men. Male solidarity would reduce the formality of the context. This too might account for men's greater use of vernacular forms.

In one of the earliest social dialect surveys, the male interviewers asked different questions of women and men in order to elicit a casual style of speech in which vernacular forms were more likely to occur. The women were asked about childhood games and skipping rhymes, while the men were asked about fights, terms for girls and, in some cases, terms for a girl's sexual organs. As one pair of commentators note, 'With the best will in the world, it seems unlikely that a discussion of skipping rhymes could induce the rapport of two men talking about smutty words.' The fact that men used more vernacular forms than women in these interviews does not then seem so surprising. It can be accounted for by the fact that the interview context was different for women and men.

Women's greater use of standard speech forms may then be an indication of their sensitivity to contextual factors. Standard speech forms are used in more formal contexts. They reflect social distance. They are used in contexts where people operate primarily in terms of social status and role. When people do not know each other well, they tend to speak in ways that reflect their social roles (e.g. customer–shopkeeper, teacher–pupil, interviewer–interviewee) rather than relating as individuals. Standard speech forms are appropriate to such transactional roles. Where women use more standard speech forms than men in social dialect interviews, this may be due to the fact that they experienced the interview as a relatively formal interaction with a stranger.

This explanation accounts for the difference in women's and men's speech forms by referring to the relationship between the people concerned in the context in which they are operating. It provides a thought-provoking alternative to explanations which characterise women as status-conscious individuals who use more standard speech forms to ensure they are perceived as socially statusful.

Exercise 7

My young German friend, Anke, thinks that the explanations suggested above for differences in women's and men's speech are biased against men. Do you agree?

What does this suggest about interpretations of social dialect data?

Discuss with your teacher how you might test alternative explanations for gender differences in speech observed in your community.

This discussion of alternative explanations of women's linguistic behaviour also illustrates another important point. The 'same' behaviour may be interpreted quite differently by different researchers. Identifying linguistic differences between groups is just the first step. Interpreting their significance is another, and any interpretation will be influenced by a researcher's theoretical framework and beliefs about the relationship between language and social factors. A researcher who believes the status dimension is more influential in accounting for linguistic differences than the solidarity dimension, for instance, will provide a different explanation from one who sees a person's social contacts as more influential in accounting for their speech than their social class background. This point will be illustrated further in chapter 8.

In concluding this section it is worth noting that although gender generally interacts with other social factors, such as status, class, the role of the speaker in an interaction, and the formality of the context, there are cases where the gender of the speaker seems to be the most influential factor accounting for speech patterns. In some communities, a woman's social status and her gender interact to reinforce differential speech patterns between women and men. In others, different factors modify one another to produce more complex patterns. But in a number of communities, for some linguistic forms, gender can itself be a primary factor accounting for speech variation. The gender of the speaker can override social class differences, for instance, in accounting for speech patterns. In these communities, expressing masculine or feminine identity seems to be very important.

The social dialect survey of the Sydney community, mentioned above, provides some support for this view of gender as an important factor in its own right, as does data from a recent study in Tyneside, an area in the north-east of England. Glottalisation of [p], [t] and [k], for instance, is characteristic of the Tyneside vernacular. (Glottalisation involves cutting off the air at the vocal cords while producing the sounds [p], [t], [k].) It is better described as a masculine norm than a working-class norm, since men use these glottalised sounds across all styles regardless of their social class, whereas glottalisation varies in the speech of women from different classes. Figure 7.2 makes the point graphically.

There is similar evidence from Reading where Jenny Cheshire, dressed in her motorbike gear, recorded the speech of adolescent girls and boys in an adventure playground. She found the usual pattern of gender-differentiation in grammatical patterns such as multiple negation, and the use of forms such as *ain't*. Overall boys used vernacular

B

Language variation: focus on users

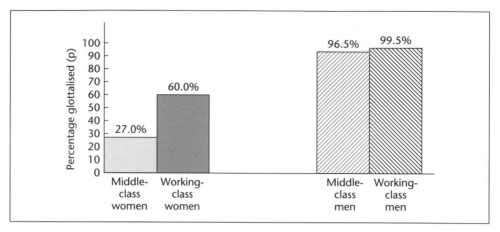

Figure 7.2 Glottalised [p] in speech of Tyneside women and men from two social classes

Source: Reproduced with permission from Fasold, 1990: 101

forms more frequently than girls did. The boys who used most vernacular forms had the highest scores on a scale based on toughness (ability to fight and steal), peer group status, and ambition to do a 'tough' job, such as slaughterer. But interestingly the speech of tough girls – those capable of swearing, stealing or setting fire to the adventure playground – was quite distinguishable from that of the boys on a number of grammatical features. So toughness was here not the distinguishing factor. Gender identity itself was an influential explanatory factor accounting for different speech patterns which were observed. Penny Eckert's research with adolescents in playgrounds in Detroit suggests that, while social group is a fundamental dimension, the symbolic value of speech is often more important for the girls than the boys. In these communities, specific linguistic forms may signal membership of the group 'male' or 'female' in particular.

Overall, then, the nature of the relationship between gender and speech is complex, and the way gender interacts with a range of other factors needs careful examination in each speech community. The social roles that women and men play, their different values and social networks (who they talk to most), the social categories they identify with and the social identities they wish to construct, and their sensitivity to contextual factors, including characteristics of the person they are talking to, are relevant factors accounting for people's speech patterns which will be explored in more detail in the next few chapters. But signalling gender-affiliation or constructing gender identity cannot be ignored as factors in their own right.

This section has focussed on the widespread evidence that men use more vernacular forms than women, but there are exceptions to this pattern. Figure 7.1 showed that women from the lower social groups in Norwich used almost as many vernacular forms as the men. And there are some communities, such as Pont-rhyd-y-fen, a small Welsh mining community, and Brazlândia, a satellite city of Brasília, where the women use more vernacular forms than the men. A high frequency of vernacular forms may have a much wider range of associations than the explanation which identifies them with masculinity and toughness suggests, as we shall see in the next few chapters. To give just two contrasting examples, vernacular forms may express conservative, non-urban values (where the standard is the urban norm), or alternatively vernacular forms may reflect anti-establishment attitudes (where the standard is the middle-class adult norm). In the next section we will see examples of young people's use of vernacular forms expressing the latter.

AGE-GRADED FEATURES OF SPEECH

Example 11

I was listening to New Zealand radio recently when they announced that they were going to be interviewing the Minister of Health after the news. I couldn't think who the Minister was. So I listened to the interview and I was very impressed with the policies he outlined, and particularly with his sensitive and sympathetic attitudes to the need for cervical screening for women. 'How sensible,' I thought, 'what an intelligent man!' I waited for the end of the interview to find out who he was. 'And that was an interview with the Minister of Health, Helen Clark,' announced the interviewer. Well at least that explained the sympathetic attitude to women's health issues!

One of the most obvious speech differences between women and men is in the pitch of their voices. Most people believe this difference develops at puberty. It is thought to be as difficult to guess the gender of a 5-year-old on the phone as it is to identify the gender of a swaddled infant from its wails and coos. It is certainly true that young boys' voices often 'break' at puberty and become noticeably lower in pitch. Their voice quality reflects their physical growth. Boys' vocal cords generally grow faster and bigger than girls' at puberty. Men's heads and lungs are also larger than women's, just as older people's are bigger than children's. As a result male voices generally sound lower in pitch than women's, just as adult voices sound deeper than children's. Differences are relative, however, and the pitch ranges of women and men overlap to a considerable extent. In any community there will always be some women whose natural speaking pitch is deeper than that of some men.

This physical explanation is only part of the reason for gender differences in voice pitch however. Social and cultural factors contribute too. Young boys' voices often become lower in pitch than girls' voices well before there is any physical basis for the change. It is more masculine to speak with a lower-pitched voice, and so young boys often develop this masculine feature, along with other more obviously sociolinguistic features of male speech such as the greater use of vernacular forms described above.

B

Language variation: focus on users

173

Influence in public domains has been a male prerogative until relatively recently. The fact that women politicians, like Helen Clark in example 11, often have deeper voices than average may reflect the public's preference for voices with masculine associations in politics; or perhaps women politicians are using male models in order to gain acceptance in spheres previously dominated by males. These norms are culturally relative too. There are cultures where the average pitch of men's voices is considerably higher than that of the average American male, for instance, and the upper reaches of some Japanese women's pitch range are out of sight compared to those of English-speaking women. Only a young child could compete.

Example 12

G is a teenage Australian girl and I is a female interviewer.

G: We went – I've seen 'One Flew Over the Cuckoo's Nest' – can't even say 'cuckoo' properly. That was a good show. The only thing is they swear a lot in it.

I: And that really bothers you?

G: Mm. Sometimes, like, sometimes I'll be in the mood for it an other times I'll think, you, know 'I don't wanna say that.' Cause when you listen t'other people it sounds terrible, you know . . .

I: You don't think about that when you're 13 or 14 doing it yourself.

G: No, you don't. When you get older, you think, 'Oh Jesus, what did I ever say that for?'

There are other features of people's speech which vary at different ages too. Not only pitch, but vocabulary, pronunciation, and grammar can differentiate age groups. There are patterns which are appropriate for 10-year-olds or teenagers which disappear as they grow older. These are age-graded patterns. Between the ages of 10 and 15, and typically with encouragement from their teachers and parents, middle-class Glaswegians learn to substitute [t] for the vernacular glottal stop variant in words like *water* and *matter*. The extensive swear word vocabulary which some teenagers use is similarly likely to change over time, as example 12 suggests. The frequency with which they use such words tends to diminish, especially as they begin to have children and socialise with others with young families. It seems possible that adult men restrict swearing largely to all-male settings, whereas females reduce their swearing in all settings as they move into adulthood.

Slang is another area of vocabulary which reflects a person's age. Current slang is the linguistic prerogative of young people and generally sounds odd in the mouth of an older person. It signals membership of a particular group – the young. In New Zealand young people currently use the terms *wicked*, *choice* and *cool* to describe something they approve of. Earlier generations of New Zealanders used *bosker* and *bonzer*. *Grouse* is another such word that has reappeared in the early twenty-first century after previously being fashionable in the 1970s. Rich Californian Valley girls use *mondo*. Because slang is so ephemeral, vocabulary can be a real give-away if you are trying to guess a person's age on the telephone or radio. Out-of-date slang words like *spiffing*, *topping*, *super*, *groovy*, and *fab* identify a British person as a member of the older generation as accurately as an old-fashioned RP pronunciation such as [o:fən] for *often*.

Exercise 8

Ask five people over 70 years old and five people aged between 15 and 25 from similar social backgrounds to tell you what words they would use in the following contexts:

(a) I've just got a new car. It's _____.
    (Ask for two or three words meaning they like it and think it is good.)
(b) The Australians were beaten by six wickets and I'm not surprised. Their playing was _____.
    (Ask for two or three words meaning it was terrible.)
(c) I heard a talk about personality types on the radio today. The speaker didn't know a thing about the subject. It was _____.
    (Ask for two or three words meaning it was wrong or misleading.)

You could add another couple of sentences if there are particular slang words you would like to check out in this way.

Is there any pattern in the forms you have collected?

Are some words used only by the older people and others used only by young people? Are there any words you had not heard before? Are there any words used by one group which you think members of the other group would not understand?

B

AGE AND SOCIAL DIALECT DATA

Social dialect research has provided a great deal of information about patterns of pronunciation and grammar for different age groups. A common pattern for stable vernacular forms, such as the use of [in] for standard [iŋ], in *walking*, or [d] for [ð] in *then*, or multiple negation, is represented by the curve in figure 7.3. The graph suggests the relative frequency of vernacular forms in different age groups. It indicates that they are high in childhood and adolescence, and then steadily reduce as people approach middle age when societal pressures to conform are greatest. Vernacular usage gradually increases again in old age as social pressures reduce, with people moving out of the workforce and into a more relaxed phase of their lives.

In other words the model suggests that as people get older their speech becomes gradually more standard, and then later it becomes less standard and is once again characterised by vernacular forms.

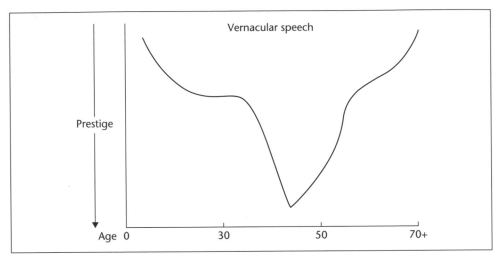

Figure 7.3 Relationship between use of vernacular forms and age
Source: Reproduced from Downes 1998: 191

In a New Zealand survey, the pattern in figure 7.3 was particularly clear in men's use of the [in] vs [iŋ] variants at different ages. Those in their 40s used fewer instances of [in] than those in their 20s, or than those over 70. The first part of the pattern is illustrated in figure 7.4 in relation to the variable of multiple negation. Young children in both Detroit and the Appalachian region of America use multiple negation more frequently than adolescents, and adolescents use it more frequently than adults. Children gradually acquire standard forms in the same way as they gradually acquire new vocabulary and control of grammatical constructions. It is likely that this process reflects an expansion of the child's stylistic range. In other words, the child gradually acquires standard forms alongside vernacular forms. The data probably also reflects the fact that, once acquired, these more standard forms are likely to be used more often in an interview with a sociolinguist.

Many social dialectologists have found that adolescents use particularly high frequencies of vernacular forms, especially if they are forms such as *ain't* and multiple negation which people clearly recognise and identify as non-standard. This provides empirical support for a proposed peak during adolescence when peer group pressure not to conform to society's norms is greatest. However, this pattern is not attributable to age alone. Like slang, vernacular forms act as solidarity markers; they can indicate membership of close-knit social groups, as we will see in the next chapter. New York gang members, for instance, delete the *-ed* which signals past tense at the ends of words much more often than adults from the same social group, but also more often than those labelled 'lames', young people who do not belong to gangs. Gang members more often say *miss* for *missed* (in utterances like *he miss the bus yesterday*) and *pass* for *passed* (*it pass me*) than 'lames' or adults. And they use more multiple negation than adults and 'lames' in the same social class. As we will see in the next chapter,

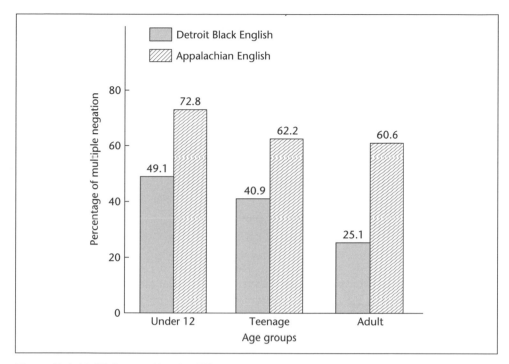

Figure 7.4 Multiple negation in different age groups in two communities

Source: This diagram was constructed from data in Romaine, 1984: 108–9

membership of a close-knit social group is more important than age alone in accounting for these patterns.

Patterns for particular linguistic features may vary between communities, but there is general agreement that, all other things being equal, in their middle years people are most likely to respond to the wider society's speech norms by using fewer vernacular forms. Conversely, it is in middle age that they are most likely to use more standard forms. The use of standard or prestige forms peaks between the ages of 30 and 55 when people experience maximum societal pressure to conform. So standard vowels and [ɪŋ] pronunciations of words like *working* are usually highest in this period of people's lives. An interesting parallel in the multilingual context of Montreal is the level of bilingualism reported by French Canadians at different ages. Young people begin life monolingual in French. Then as they grow older, through school and work they become increasingly bilingual. Bilingualism is clearly an asset during their working lives so the level of reported bilingualism rises to a peak between the ages of 30 and 50 while people are in the workforce. After retirement many revert to French monolingualism with their family and close friends. Bilingualism clearly functions as the equivalent of a linguistic prestige form in a monolingual community, while the reversion to French monolingualism parallels the greater use of vernacular forms among older people illustrated in figure 7.3.

AGE GRADING AND LANGUAGE CHANGE

Before leaving considerations of the relationship between age and speech patterns it is important to notice how easy it is to confuse patterns of language change with speech patterns which vary with different age groups.

Exercise 9

There are at least two alternative explanations for the pattern shown in table 7.1. What are they?

Answer at end of chapter

Table 7.1 Vernacular pronunciation of standard [t] in medial and final position in New Zealand English

Linguistic form	Age group	
	20–30 years (%)	40+ years (%)
Glottal stop [ʔ] for final [t] (e.g. [baʔ] *bat*)	82	33
Flap for medial [t] (e.g. [leder] for *letter*)	35	6

Source: From Hui 1989: 6. Reproduced with permission

When a linguistic change is spreading through a community, there will be a regular increase or decrease in the use of the linguistic form over time. For an innovation – a form on the increase – this will show up in a graph as a low use of the form by older people and a higher use among younger people. For a form which is disappearing just the opposite will be true. Younger people will use less of the form and older people more.

Milton Keynes is Britain's fastest-growing new town. It was founded in 1967 and by 2005 its population had more than quadrupled. A social dialect study of teenage speech in the town indicates that [f] is rapidly replacing standard [θ] in words like *thought* and *mouth*, and [v] is replacing standard [ð] in words like *mother* and *brother*. This feature has been called (th)-fronting since the standard sound is pronounced a little further back against the teeth, while the lips are involved in [f] and [v]. Is this a feature of adolescent speech or is it a change in progress? The evidence suggests that this is a change which began in London as long ago as 1850, and though it took a while to get started it is now accelerating as it spreads northwards.

Exercise 10

Look at figure 7.5.
   Are there any differences in the patterns of use of the three sounds in the three towns?
   Does the figure support or challenge the claim that (th)-fronting is spreading north in England?

Answer at end of chapter

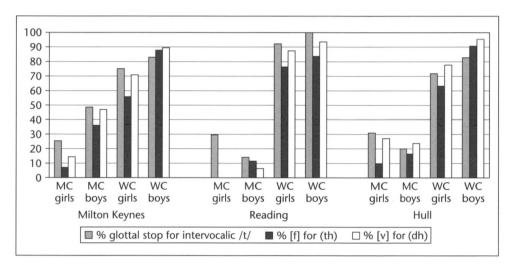

Figure 7.5 Three vernacular features in girls' and boys' speech in three English towns

Note: Milton Keynes is 80 kilometres north of London, Reading is 60 kilometres west of London, and Hull is the furthest north and over 200 kilometres from London.

Source: Cheshire, Kerswill and Williams 2005: 146. Reproduced with permission

We will look at patterns of linguistic change in chapter 9 and consider how information about what different age groups are saying can provide clues to changes in progress. The discussion in this section shows that before studying patterns of change it is important to know the normal distribution of stable forms through a community. Without this it would be easy to make a wrong deduction. It would be possible, for instance, to interpret the pattern of language use reported in Montreal as evidence of linguistic change in progress. We would project forward the monolingualism of the young and treat it as the in-coming pattern. We would then see the bilingualism of the middle-aged group as likely to be displaced over time and predict a language shift to French, with loss of English. All this would be totally misleading in terms of what was really happening. In fact the pattern of shift from monolingualism to bilingualism and back is one which is stable, and it simply repeats itself for different individuals over time.

B

Language variation: focus on users

This example also highlights the relationship between language and ethnicity which is so apparent in a community where a particular language is associated with a particular ethnic group. In the next chapter we will see that even in monolingual communities, ethnicity is often signalled by the way people speak.

ANSWERS TO EXERCISES IN CHAPTER 7

Answer to exercise 1

No. English pronouns do not reflect the gender of the speaker. The third person singular pronouns encode the gender of the referent, i.e. *she* vs *he*, but all other pronouns can be used to refer to either gender. You might like to consider whether, and if so how, the pronouns used in other languages with which you are familiar encode gender.

Answer to exercise 2

In Sydney, as in all other English-speaking communities where a social dialect survey has studied this feature, men drop more [h]s than women. The differences were not very great in Sydney, however. Men dropped 16 per cent in the interview context, compared to women's 5 per cent. In the North of England [h]-dropping is much more frequent. Hence Keith's confusion in example 4. When asked to say her name on its own, Mrs Hall carefully pronounced the [h] at the beginning of *Hall*, though in other contexts she would omit it, as the boys in her class always did, and the girls usually did when addressing her.

Answer to exercise 3

There is evidence that women use fewer instances than men of all the vernacular grammatical features discussed in the previous chapter. The pattern for multiple negation in Detroit is discussed below. Similar patterns have been observed in other English-speaking communities all over the world. The forms of present and past tense verbs, the use of past participles such as *seen* and *done* as past tense forms, and the use of *ain't* are other grammatical variables which reveal the same patterns. Further grammatical variables which are used differently by women and men are discussed in chapter 12.

Answer to exercise 6

As we will see in chapter 10, most people use more vernacular forms in more relaxed contexts. So it is likely that you used more [in] forms and dropped more [h]s in casual speech than in the interview situation.

Some possible answers to the other questions are discussed in the next section.

Answer to exercise 9

Two possible interpretations of the data in table 7.1.

(a) The pronunciation of standard [t] in medial and final position may be an age-graded feature. As people approach middle age their pronunciation of this sound may become more standard and less vernacular. This is a common pattern for a vernacular feature. If this were an accurate interpretation of the data, one would predict that the percentage of vernacular forms would increase again in old age, so the incidence of vernacular forms for people of retirement age would be higher than for the 40–60 age group.

(b) Alternatively the pronunciation of standard [t] may be changing in New Zealand speech. If this is the case then the data suggests that the vernacular pronunciations (medial flap and glottal stop) are gradually displacing standard [t] in the speech of younger people. One would then predict that scores for those above 60 years of age would show a lower incidence of vernacular forms than those for the 40–60 age group.

Answer to exercise 10

(a) The pattern of use for all three vernacular variants is similar in that they are most frequent in the usage of working-class boys in all three towns. The pattern for MC boys and girls is less clear-cut, but middle-class boys in Milton Keynes use more vernacular forms than middle-class girls, which is not the case in the other towns.

(b) If (th)-fronting is spreading north we would expect it to be most frequent in Reading and Milton Keynes and least frequent in Hull, the northernmost town. Though it is more frequent in middle-class boys' speech in Milton Keynes, overall, this is not clearly the case. There are a number of possible explanations for this, one of which is that the change is too well established in working-class speech for this data to show its progress northwards. Since vernacular changes tend to be established in working-class speech before middle-class speech, the fact that it is more evident in middle-class boys' speech in Milton Keynes than in middle-class Hull speech supports the claim, but the Reading data does not.

◼ Concepts introduced

Gender-exclusive features
Gender-preferential features
Gender and social class
Age grading

◼ References

The following sources provided material for this chapter:

Bodine (1975) on Chiquita
Bortoni-Ricardo (1985) on Brasília
Cheshire (1982) on Reading speech
Cheshire, Kerswill and Williams (2005) on (th)-fronting
Coates and Cameron (1988) on explanation in social dialectology
Downes (1998) on age-grading
Eckert and McConnell-Ginet (2003) Ch. 8 on Detroit adolescents' speech
Eisikovits (1989b) on divergence from standard Australian English in adolescent boys' speech
Gordon (1997) on New Zealand vernacular forms and 'loose morals'
Graddol and Swann (1989) on pitch ranges
Holmes et al. (1991) for New Zealand data on vernacular [in] usage
Horvath (1985) for Sydney data
Hui (1989) on New Zealand English
Labov (1972b: 264–9) on the linguistic consequences of being a 'lame'

Language variation: focus on users

B

Macauley (1977) on Glasgow speech
Milroy (1982) for Belfast data
Milroy (1989) for Newcastle data
Nichols (1983) on service occupations and speech
Romaine (1984) on Edinburgh children's speech
Russell (1982) for Mombasa Swahili data
Shibamoto (1987) for Japanese data
Shuy, Wolfram and Riley (1967) for Detroit data
Sorensen (1972) on Amazon Indians
Thomas (1988) on Pont-rhyd-y-fen speech
Trudgill (1992, 2000) especially data on Norwich

Quotations

Example 6 is adapted from Bassett et al. (1985: 67).
Example 8 is an edited excerpt from Cheshire (1989: 61).
Example 9 is from Macafee (1989: 194).
Example 12 is from Eisikovits (1989b: 43).
Graddol and Swann (1989: 57) on the topics used with women and men in social dialect surveys.
Trudgill (1983a: 162): 'the single most consistent finding to emerge from sociolinguistic studies over the past 20 years'.

Useful additional reading

Coates (1993)
Eckert and McConnell-Ginet (2003)
Fasold (1990), Ch. 4
Meyerhoff (2006), Ch. 10
Romaine (2000), Ch. 4
Trudgill (2000), Ch. 4
Wardhaugh (2006), Ch. 13

APPENDIX

Here are some questions which you could use to collect data in an informal interview.

(a) What do you like doing best in your spare time?
(b) What did you do last weekend?
(c) Do you play any sport or get any regular exercise?
(d) Have you ever seen a fight around here? What happened?
(e) Do you remember your first day at school? How did you get there? What was it like?

(f) What's the worst experience you've ever had at school – a really awful day or a day when something really horrible happened?

(g) What do you think of the standard of driving round here?

(h) Do you think old/young people are better drivers? Why?

(i) Have you ever seen a bad accident around here? What happened?

(j) What does your family do at Christmas?

(k) What did you do on Christmas Day last year?

8 Ethnicity and social networks

When people belong to the same group, they often speak similarly. But there are many different groups in a community, and so any individual may share linguistic features with a range of other speakers. Some features indicate a person's social status, as we saw in chapter 6; others distinguish women and men or identify a person as a teenager rather than as a middle-aged citizen, as illustrated in chapter 7. There are also linguistic clues to a person's ethnicity, and closely related to all these are linguistic features which reflect the regular interactions people have – those they talk to most often. Individuals draw on all these resources when they construct their social identities. This chapter illustrates the relevance of ethnicity and social networks in accounting for people's speech patterns, as well as briefly introducing a related concept, the community of practice.

ETHNICITY

Example 1

When I was in Montreal I found a small restaurant in the old French quarter where the menu looked affordable and attractive. I was greeted in French by the waiter and I responded in French, though my accent clearly signalled that I was a native English speaker. At this point the waiter, who was undoubtedly bilingual, had a choice. He chose to continue in French and, though I cannot be sure of his reasons, I interpreted this choice as expressing his wish to be identified as a French Canadian.

Many ethnic groups use a distinctive language associated with their ethnic identity, as demonstrated in the examples discussed in the first section of this book, as well as in example 1 above. Where a choice of language is available for communication, it is often possible for an individual to signal their ethnicity by the language they choose to use. Even when a complete conversation in an ethnic language is not possible, people may use short phrases, verbal fillers or linguistic tags, which signal ethnicity. So interactions which appear to be in English, for example, may incorporate linguistic signals of the speakers' ethnic identity, as illustrated in example 2.

Example 2

Lee: *Kia ora* June. Where you been? Not seen you round for a while.

June: *Kia ora*. I've just come back from my Nanny's *tangi* [FUNERAL]. Been up in Rotorua for a week.

Lee: *E kī* [IS THAT SO!] a sad time for you, *e hoa* [MY FRIEND] and for all your family, *ne* [ISN'T IT]

June: *Ae* [YES]. We'll all miss Nanny. She was a wonderful woman.

In New Zealand many Maori people routinely use Maori greetings such as *kia ora*, and a conversation between two Maori people may include emphatic phrases, such as *e kī*, softening tags such as *ne*, and responses such as *ae*, even when neither speaks the Maori language fluently. Bargaining with Chinese retailers in the shopping centres, Chinese Singaporeans similarly often signal their ethnic background with linguistic tags, such as the untranslatable but expressive *la*, and phrases or words from their ethnic language. Emphasising common ethnicity may mean they get a better bargain!

Exercise 1

Consider the following utterances. Can you identify any of the linguistic clues to the speaker's ethnicity?

(a) Yo mama so bowlegged, she looks like the bite out of a donut.
(b) I cannae mind the place where those bairns are from.
(c) Dem want me fi go up dere go tell dem.
(d) Kia ora Hemi. Time to broom the floor eh.
(e) Already you're discouraged! Goyim like bagels so why not this.
(f) My brother really hungry la. Let's go for makan.

Answers at end of chapter

As we saw in chapter 3, when a group adopts, willingly or perforce, the dominant language of the society, an important symbol of their distinct ethnicity – their language – often disappears. Italians in Sydney and New York, African Americans and Hispanics in Chicago, Indians, Pakistanis and Jamaicans in London are in this situation. For different reasons, so are most Scots, Irish and Welsh people in Britain, Aboriginal people in Australia, and Maori people in New Zealand. Ethnic groups often respond to this situation by using the majority language in a way which signals and actively constructs their ethnic identity. For groups where there are no identifying physical features to

B

Language variation: focus on users

distinguish them from others in the society, these distinctive linguistic features may be an important remaining symbol of ethnicity once their ethnic language has disappeared. Food, religion, dress and a distinctive speech style are all ways that ethnic minorities may use to distinguish themselves from the majority group.

Italians in Boston use a particularly high percentage of vernacular pronunciations of certain vowels, such as the vowel in words like *short* and *horse*. Similarly, both first and second generation Italians in Sydney are distinguishable in different ways by their pronunciation of Australian English vowels. In New Zealand, as elsewhere in the world, Scots people tend to retain features of their Scottish English. The pronunciation of [r] in words like *part* and *star* is widely noted as a marker of Scottish ethnicity. American Jewish people often signal their ethnicity with a distinctive accent of English within any city in which they have settled. Studies of Jewish people in Boston and New York have identified distinctive pronunciations of some vowels. Jewish Americans also use ethnically marked linguistic tags such as *oy vay*, and occasional Yiddish vocabulary items, many of which, such as *schmaltz, bagel, glitch* and *shlemiel*, have passed into general American English.

African American Vernacular English

Example 3

Jo: This ain' that ba', bu' look at your hands. It ain't get on you either. Asle, look at mine. This all my clay ... In your ear wi' Rosie Greer ... I ain' gone do that one ... Did you hear about the fire at the shoe store? It wan't a *soul* lef'.

In the United States, though their distinct languages disappeared centuries ago, African Americans do not need a distinct variety or code as a symbolic way of differentiating themselves from the majority group. They are visibly different. Nevertheless, this group has developed a distinct variety of English known as African American Vernacular English (I will use the abbreviation AAVE). This dialect has a number of features which do not occur in standard mainstream American English, and others which occur very much less frequently in the standard variety. These linguistic differences act as symbols of ethnicity. They express the sense of cultural distinctiveness of many African Americans.

AAVE is heard especially in the northern cities of the United States. One of its most distinctive features is the complete absence of the copula verb *be* in some social and linguistic contexts. In most speech contexts, speakers of standard English use shortened or reduced forms of the verb *be*. In other words, people do not usually say *She is very nice* but rather *She's very nice*. They reduce or contract the *is* to *s*. In the same kinds of context speakers of AAVE omit the verb *be*, as illustrated in example 4.

Example 4

African American Vernacular English	American Standard English
She very nice	She's very nice
He a teacher	He's a teacher
That my book	That's my book
The beer warm	The beer's warm

In recordings of Detroit speech, for instance, white Americans never omitted the copula verb *be*, whereas African Americans – especially those from the lower socio-economic groups – regularly did.

Another distinctive grammatical feature of AAVE is the use of invariant *be* to signal recurring or repeated actions, as in example 5.

Example 5

African American Vernacular English	American Standard English
She be at school on weekdays	She's always at school on weekdays
The children do be messin' around a lot	The children do mess around a lot
I run when I bees on my way to school	I always run when I'm on my way to school
The beer be warm at that place	The beer's always warm at that place

---

Clearly the grammar of AAVE has some features which simply do not occur in the grammar of white Americans. However, there are many features of the English used by lower socio-economic groups in the United States which also occur in AAVE. Most AAVE speakers simply use these features more frequently than most white Americans. Multiple negation was identified in chapter 6, for instance, as a feature of the English of many lower socio-economic groups. It is also a feature of AAVE, as figure 8.1 illustrates. In every social group interviewed in Detroit, African Americans used more multiple negation than white Americans did.

Consonant cluster simplification is another feature which distinguishes the speech of white and African Americans. All English speakers simplify consonant clusters in some contexts. It would sound very formal, for instance, in a phrase such as *last time* to pronounce both [t]s distinctly. Most people drop the first [t] so the consonant cluster [st] at the end of *last* becomes simply [s]. AAVE speakers also simplify the consonant clusters at the ends of words, but they do so much more frequently and extensively than speakers of standard and regional dialects of English.

AAVE is different from the English of white Americans, then, in a number of ways. There are features which clearly distinguish the two dialects, such as the omission of the verb *be* and distinct meanings of *be*, as illustrated in example 5. And there are other

B

Language variation: focus on users

features, such as multiple negation and consonant cluster simplification, where AAVE uses higher frequencies than are found in the English of most white Americans.

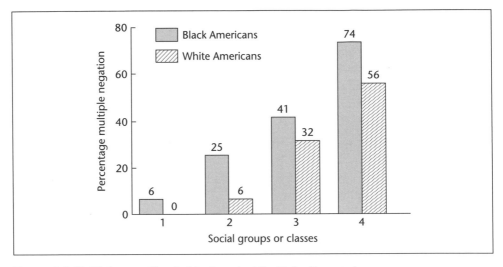

Figure 8.1 Multiple negation in black and white Detroit speech

Source: This diagram was constructed from data in Shuy, Wolfram and Riley, 1967

Exercise 2

(a) Using figure 8.1 as data, what is the relationship between ethnicity and social class in relation to the vernacular features of speech?

(b) Identify the features of the following passage which distinguish it from standard English. These are all features of AAVE, though some also occur in other vernacular varieties.

It's a girl name Shirley Jones live in Washington. 'Most everybody on her street like her, 'cause she a nice girl. Shirley like a boy name Charles. But she keep away from him and Charles don't hardly say nothing to her neither.

(c) Look at sentences 1–8. * = ungrammatical utterance

What is the rule for the occurrence of *be*?

1. They usually be tired when they come home.
2. *They be tired right now.
3. James always be coming to school.
4. *James be coming to school right now.
5. Sometimes my ears be itching.
6. *My ankle be broken from the fall.

Which of these is grammatical in this dialect?

7. Linguists always be asking silly questions about language.
8. The students don't be talking right now.

Answers at end of chapter

▊ British Black English

In Britain the way different ethnic minorities speak English is often equally distinctive. The English of those who speak minority languages such as Gujerati, Panjabi and Turkish generally signals their ethnic background. And people of West Indian or African Caribbean origin use a range of varieties, depending on where they live in England, and how long their families have lived in Britain. Those born in Britain are usually described as members of the British Black community and most speak a variety of Jamaican Creole as well as a variety of English.

The variety of Jamaican Creole used by many British Blacks is known as Patois. London Jamaican, for instance, is the London variety of Patois. It derives from Jamaican Creole, but it has a number of features which distinguish it from the Jamaican variety.

Example 6

Polly is a young British Black teenager who lives in the West Midlands. Her parents came to Britain from Jamaica in 1963 looking for jobs. Though Polly's mother had a good education in Jamaica, the only work she was able to find in Dudley was cleaning offices at night. Polly's father used to work in a factory but he was laid off and has been unemployed for nearly two years now. They live in a predominantly Black neighbourhood and almost all Polly's friends are young Black people. She and her parents attend the local Pentecostal church. Her older brother used to attend too, but he has stopped since he left school.

Polly's verbal repertoire includes standard English spoken with a West Midlands accent, an informal variety of English with some Patois features which could be described as Midlands Black English, and Patois, the variety of Jamaican Creole used by Black people in Dudley, which was described in the section on creoles in chapter 4.

Polly's patterns of language use are not simple. While her parents use Patois to her and her brother, she is expected to use English in response. At home she uses Midlands Black English, but she uses a more standard variety to her teachers at the college where she is doing a hairdressing course. With her friends she uses Patois. In most shops she uses standard English with the local accent, unless she knows the young Black person behind the counter, in which case she might use Midlands Black English.

Polly's ethnicity is signalled not so much by her knowledge of any particular variety, but by the way she uses the varieties in her linguistic repertoire. Many young British Blacks use Patois for in-group talk as a symbol of their ethnicity, but not all are proficient users. In contexts where Patois is appropriate, those who do not know much Patois will use a variety of English which is clearly marked as Black by the fact that it incorporates some Patois features. The use of Patois, as well as the use of Patois features in informal varieties of English, obviously has an important symbolic function. These varieties signal a person's ethnicity as British Black. Between Polly and her black friends,

B

Language variation: focus on users

189

Patois signals friendship or solidarity. It reflects the fact that they belong together as a group of young Black British people. Someone who used standard English in this group when they were talking in the cafeteria between lessons, for example, would be labelled 'prissy' or 'snobby'.

There are a number of linguistic features which characterise Patois. It is a creole and as such it is quite distinct from standard English. There are lexical items such as *lick* meaning 'hit' and *kenge* meaning 'weak, puny'. There are many features of pronunciation, including stress and intonation patterns, which differ from those of standard English. The vowel sound in a word like *home* is sometimes pronounced as in Jamaican Creole, rather than as in the local variety of English. Words like *then* and *thin* are pronounced [den] and [tin]. Plural forms don't have *s* on the end. Tenses aren't marked by suffixes on verbs, so forms like *walk* and *jump* are used rather than *walked*, *walks*, *jumped*, and *jumps*. The form *mi* is used for *I*, *me* and *my* (e.g. *mi niem* for 'my name') and the form *dem* is used for *they*, *them* and *their* (e.g. *dem niem*). Not surprisingly, given the patterns we have found elsewhere, some speakers use more of these features than others. Midlands Black English uses some of these features too, together with a distinctively Midlands accent of English.

There are a number of regional varieties of British Black English, such as Polly's Midlands variety and a London variety, as well as regional varieties of Patois, though many of them have not yet been described. The function of these varieties as symbols of ethnicity among Black British people is quite clear however. They could even be regarded as examples of 'anti-language', a term which has been used to reflect their function of expressing opposition to the mainstream values of white British society which exclude Black people and their culture.

Exercise 3

Teachers have reported that some children who show no sign of Patois features in their speech during their early years at school, start using noticeably Black speech during adolescence. Why do you think this might happen?

Answer at end of chapter

Social dialect researchers in Hackney, an inner city area of London, and an ethnically very diverse area, have identified a new ethnic speech variety used by local teenagers. It has been labelled Multicultural London English because it is used by adolescents from a range of ethnic backgrounds, including Jamaican, African and Asian backgrounds. As well as using monophthongs where other varieties use diphthongs (e.g. [fe:s] for *face* and [go:] for *go*), these teenagers have developed a distinctive vocabulary. They call their friends [blud] *blood* rather than *mate*, *nang* is their word for *good*, *buff* means *attractive*, while *butters* means *ugly*. In Multicultural London English a *house* is referred to as a *yard*, *nuff* means *very*, and *trainers* are *creps*. *People* are referred to as *mandem*. The researchers believe that the new variety has developed as a result of high levels of immigration in the inner city area along with the typical desire of young people to distinguish themselves from other groups, and develop a distinctive identity. Though it is strongly associated with Black British teenagers, it is in fact used much more widely and it is rapidly spreading.

Maori New Zealanders

Example 7

An' den an old ant came – there was a old kuia. She went and walk to de ant's house. An' den she went and knock at the window. An' den de ant started to open his window. An' den he's told the old kuia to go back. An' den de old kuia was talking. An' den de old kuia went and walk back.

In New Zealand there has been considerable discussion about whether a Maori dialect of English exists. Many people assert firmly that there is such a variety, but there is little evidence so far of linguistic features which occur *only* in the speech of Maori people. The alternation between [d] and [ð] at the beginning of words like *the* and *then*, which is indicated in example 7, for instance, is by no means confined to the speech of Maori people. Greetings like *kia ora*, and vocabulary items like *tangi* ('funeral'), illustrated in example 2, are used by Pakeha (New Zealanders of European origin) as well as Maori in New Zealand. However, in general, Maori people use Maori words more frequently in their speech than Pakeha people do. The word *kuia* in example 7 illustrates this. *Kuia* is a Maori word meaning 'old woman', which is widely known in New Zealand. Nevertheless, its occurrence in the child's story suggests the speaker is more likely to be Maori than Pakeha.

There are also grammatical features which occur more frequently in Maori people's speech. In a study of 8-year-old children's speech, vernacular verb forms (such as *walk* for *walked*) occurred more often in the speech of the Maori children than the Pakeha. There were also some distinctive uses of verbs, such as *went and*, which seemed to be used as a narrative past tense marker by the Maori children, as illustrated in example 7.

A comparison of the speech of a small group of New Zealand women also found that the Maori women were more likely to use vernacular past tense forms of some verbs, as illustrated in sentences (a) and (b) in example 8. Moreover, Maori women were more likely than Pakeha to use present tense forms with *s* as in (c) and (d), and much more likely to omit *have*, as in (e) and (f).

Example 8

(a) She *seen* it happen and she stopped and picked Jo up off the bloody road.
(b) Well next I *rung* up the police.
(c) I *says* you wanna bet.
(d) So I *gets* home and I waited a couple of weeks.
(e) Yeah well you * seen him dancing eh so you understand.
(f) See I * been through all that rigmarole before.

* indicates where *have/had* has been omitted.

Exercise 4

Identify the clues in the following excerpt of transcribed speech which suggest that the speaker is Maori.

He's a hell of a good teacher and everything eh. And um I sit in with him sometimes, and 'cause all of a sudden he'll come out speaking Pakeha you know, just it was only, it was only a sentence that he'll speak, you know, one line of it, and the rest is just Maori eh.

Answer at end of chapter

In this section I have focussed on features of people's language which may signal and contribute to the dynamic construction of ethnic identity. People from different ethnic groups often *use* language differently too. Particular groups develop ways of speaking which are distinctive to their culture. The fast repartee known as *soundin'*, for example, is a distinctive use of language by African American gang members, as is the ritual insult illustrated above by utterance (a) in exercise 1. In New Zealand the greeting routines exchanged between Maori people, even in informal contexts, are similarly distinctive. And in more formal Maori contexts the rules for greeting people are very different from those used in Pakeha formal meetings, as we will see in chapter 11. Even patterns of pausing, silence and conversational feedback may differ between ethnic groups, and this can sometimes result in misunderstandings. If you expect your interlocutor to give frequent signals that they are listening and interested (e.g. *mm, yea*), then the absence of feedback can be disconcerting.

In everyday interaction, speech differences may also be reflected in people's social networks, a concept which has proved extremely valuable in accounting for some speech patterns. Social networks move the focus from social features of the speaker alone, such as status, gender, age and ethnicity, to characteristics of the interaction between people.

"No, Timmy, not 'I sawed the chair'. 'I saw the chair' or 'I have seen the chair'."

B

Language variation: focus on users

SOCIAL NETWORKS

Example 9

Tom lives in Ballymacarrett, a Protestant area east of the River Lagan in Belfast. He is 18 years old and works as an apprentice in the shipyard. He got the job through his uncle Bob who works at the shipyard, and he has a cousin Mike, who works there too. He and Mike live in the same street and most nights they have a beer together after work. They also run a disco with two friends, Jo and Gerry, and that means that several nights a week they travel across town to perform at different venues.

The way Tom and his cousin speak reflects the fact that they belong to a small closely knit working-class community. The men they work with and mix with outside work are also their relations and neighbours, and they all speak alike. The patterns noted in the previous sections suggest that, as members of the working class, they will tend to use more vernacular forms than other social groups. And they do. Tom and his mates use a high number of vernacular speech forms.

They frequently delete the *th* [ð] in *mother* and *brother*, for example, and pronounce *man* as [moːn], and *map* as [maːp]. By contrast people in Tom's community who are not so much a part of the kinship, neighbourhood and work networks – who are more marginal – tend to speak less 'broadly' (i.e. with less distinctively Belfast pronunciations). Sandy, for instance, a man who lives on the edge of Ballymacarrett, works for the civil service. He comes from Southern Ireland and doesn't have any family in Belfast. He sees people like Tom only occasionally in the pub. He is not really a part of the close-knit Ballymacarrett male network, and his speech reveals this. He uses far fewer vernacular forms than Tom and Mike.

Figure 8.2 provides a visual representation of Tom's social network. Networks in sociolinguistics refer to the pattern of informal relationships people are involved in on a regular basis. There are two technical terms which have proved very useful for describing different types of networks – *density* and *plexity*. Density refers to whether members of a person's network are in touch with each other. Do your friends know each other independently of you? If so your network is a dense one. Tom's friends and relations know and interact regularly with each other, as well as with him. He clearly belongs to a dense network. This is reflected in the various connections between Mike and Tom and Uncle Bob in figure 8.2.

Plexity is a measure of the range of different types of transaction people are involved in with different individuals. A *uniplex* relationship is one where the link with the other person is in only one area. You could be linked to someone else only because

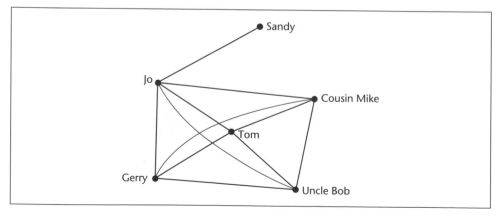

Figure 8.2 An example of a social network

Source: This diagram was constructed from data based on a similar one in Milroy, 1980: 48

you work together, for example, or you might only play badminton together, and never meet in any other context. If most transactions in a community are of this type the network would be characterised as uniplex. *Multiplex* relationships, by contrast, involve interactions with others along several dimensions. A workmate might also be someone you play tennis with and meet at church regularly. If most transactions in a community are of this type, the network would be considered multiplex. Tom's network is multiplex since the people he works with are also his pub-mates, his relations and his neighbours.

It is not surprising that people's speech should reflect the types of networks they belong to. The people we interact with are one important influence on our speech. When the people we mix with regularly belong to a homogeneous group, we will generally speak the way the rest of the group does, provided we want to belong to the group and like the people in it. (This point is developed further in chapter 10 in the section on accommodation theory.) Parents notice this when their children's speech begins to resemble the speech of the other kids at school rather than that of the family. Those children in the new town of Milton Keynes in England who had the strongest school-based networks were using the most innovative features of the new variety that was developing in the town. Their pronunciations of some sounds were quite different from their parents. Adolescent gangs typically have quite distinctive ways of talking which signal their gang membership. In New York, for instance, a study of the speech of African American male gang members showed that the more involved a boy was with the gang, the more vernacular speech forms he used. Boys on the periphery of the gangs used more standard forms than those who were more central or core members. In Britain, too, the speech of young Black people reflects the extent to which they mix with other Black people or with white people in their work and play.

When adults belong to more than one network, they may signal this by unconsciously altering their speech forms as they move from one context to another. A student, for example, may find she uses more standard forms with her friends at university, and more local, vernacular forms when she goes home to the small town or village where her family lives.

B

Language variation: focus on users

Exercise 5

Using figure 8.2 as a model, draw a network for yourself based on your interactions on an average weekday or a weekend. Identify the three people you talk to most. Link them to yourself by lines on the diagram. Then if those people know each other join up the lines as appropriate. Then think who are the three people each of them talk to most. Do *they* know each other? If so link them up – and so on.

Do you think your social network would provide any clues to the way you speak? Would it identify the people whose speech your speech most resembles?

If not, what would provide a more accurate reflection of the influences on your speech?

A study which examined language shift in Oberwart, an Austrian town on the Austrian–Hungarian border, made good use of the concept of social networks. Susan Gal noted who talked to whom over a set period of time. The patterns of social interaction which emerged accounted for people's language preferences. Some people in the Oberwart area worked in the fields and kept farm animals as their parents had before them – they continued to cling to a peasant way of life. Others worked in the industries which had become established in the town. Those people who interacted more with peasants were more likely to prefer Hungarian as their primary language, while those who had more contacts with people involved in industrial jobs tended to prefer German.

In Brazil a similar pattern was found in the speech of rural Brazilian people who had moved to the city of Brasilia. People who adapted to the city, and took advantage of what it offered, developed a wide range of relationships and tended to use more standard forms of Portuguese, while those who kept themselves to themselves, interacting mainly with kinfolk and friends from the country, tended to retain their vernacular rural accents.

In Ballymacarrett, the working-class area of Belfast referred to in example 9, the women's networks are more open than the men's. The men, like Tom, work in the local shipyard with their relations, their neighbours and their mates. Their networks are dense. Young Ballymacarrett women work on the far side of the city where they have found better-paid jobs. The people they work with are not their neighbours or relations, and so they are mixing with a more diverse group of people than their menfolk are. These women's networks are therefore less dense and less closed than the men's, and correspondingly their speech has fewer vernacular forms.

By contrast, in the Clonard, another area of Belfast, the men's traditional source of employment – the linen industry – has disappeared, but the women have sought and found work together. Their networks therefore resemble those of the men in Ballymacarrett – they are dense and multiplex or closely-knit, and this too is reflected in the women's high use of vernacular speech forms. In Belfast, then, male and female speech differences are best explained in terms of the type of networks women and men belong to.

Example 10

Mary is a teenage girl who lives in a working-class African American community on an island in the Waccamaw river in South Carolina. Most of the men work at construction jobs on the mainland to which they commute daily across the river. The women work in the seasonal tourist industry on the mainland as servants or clerks. No one in Mary's community is very well off. She has seven brothers and sisters. Like everyone else on the island, Mary's family own a small motor boat which her mother and father use to travel to the mainland for work each day. She goes to school on the schoolboat, and, like almost all her island friends, she qualifies for a free lunch.

> In her class at school she meets Tracy, who comes from the mainland white community up the river. Tracy has three younger brothers and her mother doesn't have a paid job. She stays home and looks after the boys and the house. Tracy's grandad was a cotton farmer and her dad had expected to carry on working the farm, but the cotton farming business went bust and they had to sell the farm, like most others in the area. So her father works as a supervisor at one of the hotels in the tourist area. They aren't rich, but they're a bit better off than Mary's family. They have a reliable car and they can afford regular holidays.

If we examine the speech of Mary's parents and Tracy's parents in an interview with a white teacher visiting the community, we find some interesting patterns. There are differences between the women's and the men's speech. There are also differences between the speech of the African American parents and the white parents. But not the differences you might predict without thinking a little about their social networks. Tracy's father's speech is much closer to Mary's mother's speech than it is to Tracy's mother's speech. Both Tracy's Dad and Mary's Mum use more standard forms than their spouses. Mary's Dad uses a great many creole forms, while Tracy's mother uses local vernacular dialect forms.

The patterns in these communities are best explained not by gender or by ethnicity, but by the interactive networks the two sets of parents are involved in. African American women interact in their daily work with tourists and middle-class Americans who use high frequencies of standard English forms. White men and young white women similarly work in service industries, interacting not with members of their own community but with strangers and outsiders. Their networks are neither dense nor multiplex. The people they work with are different from the people they live with and 'play' with. Their speech is correspondingly more standard, and they use fewer vernacular or creole forms than the white middle-aged women and the African American men.

Many white middle-aged women, on the other hand, work as housewives in their own communities, and they interact with each other regularly at the shops, for coffee, on the phone and in shared community and child-caring activities. African American men also interact with each other in their work on construction sites. Both these groups have much denser and more multiplex networks than the white men, the young white women, and the African American women. Like the Ballymacarrett men and Clonard women, they use more vernacular and fewer standard forms.

This example draws together a range of the social factors covered in this section of the book. The social class background, gender, age, and ethnicity of the speakers are all relevant, but the example also illustrates clearly the overriding influence which social interaction plays in accounting for patterns of speech. Who we talk and listen to regularly is a very important influence on the way we speak, a point which will be pursued further in chapter 10. It is also illustrated in the final social concept to be considered in this chapter, the community of practice.

B

Language variation: focus on users

◼ Communities of practice and the construction of social identity

---

Example 11

OK, us, you know, like the burnout . . . the burnout chicks, they sit over here, you know, and like jocky chicks stand right here . . . And then there's like um the guys, you know, you know, like weirdos that think they're cool. They just stand like on the steps, and hang out at that little heater . . . And then the poins are inside in the cafeteria, because they're probably afraid to come out into the courtyard.

Jo, an American high school girl, is describing the social organisation of space in the school courtyard. In the process, she positions her own group, the female *burnouts*, in relation to other groups in the school. Penelope Eckert, a sociolinguist who spent many months at this American high school, uses the term 'community of practice' to capture the complexities of what it means to belong to a social group like the burnouts. The burnouts are mainly, but not exclusively, from low-income families. They socialise in the local urban neighbourhood and their friendships extend beyond the school. They reject school values and they are aiming to join the workforce immediately on leaving school. Their behaviour, both linguistic and non-linguistic, distinguishes them clearly from the *jocks*, a much more conformist group who largely accept school values and are heading for college. Groups like these exist in every school community, though the names are different – *nerds, bums, greasers, hoods, cholos, gangsters, drop-outs,* and so on.

The concept 'community of practice' has been adopted by some sociolinguists to permit a focus on social categories like these which make more sense to participants than abstract categories such as class and gender. Communities of practice develop around the activities which group members engage in together, and their shared objectives and attitudes. We all belong to many communities of practice which share particular goals and ways of interacting – family, sports team, work group, hiking group, and so on. Some may be relatively long-term; others, such as a group organising a party, a dance, a school fair, or a conference, will be more temporary.

This approach highlights the extent to which we use language to construct different identities in different social interactions. At school, Jo constructs her *burnout* identity, using particular vocabulary (e.g. *poins*) and innovative variants of vowels in the pronunciation of words like *fun* and *line*. At home with her family or in her after-school job, she may emphasise different aspects of her social identity, again using linguistic choices to indicate her affiliations and values. Using this more ethnographic approach, the researcher focusses on the ways in which individuals 'perform' particular aspects of their social identity in specific situations.

Different aspects of an individual's social identity will be more or less relevant in specific social contexts, and even at different points within the same interaction. So, for instance, a young African American male talking to an African American female is likely to highlight his masculinity at certain points in the conversation, but their shared ethnicity at others. Similarly Jo constructs her identity as a super-cool, non-conformist burnout when she interacts with jock guys, but at certain points in the interaction her linguistic choices may emphasise her gender identity, or her low income background. In example 12, the speaker performs a rather tough 'masculine' identity.

Example 12

I says you better put those fuckin' arms down because that's fightin' material for me . . . she says you can't fuckin' do nothin' to me and I says you wanna bet?

The speaker in example 12 is Geraldine, a young working-class Maori woman, describing a fight in which she was involved. In this brief snippet, talking to a much better educated and very feminine-looking Maori woman, she selects consistently vernacular variants of the -*ing* variable, and vernacular present tense forms of the verb *say*, as well as using swear words. While [in] variants indicate her working-class background, the consistency and concentration of vernacular linguistic features also make Geraldine sound tough and masculine. High frequencies of the [in] variant are associated not only with working-class speech but also with male speech, as we saw in chapter 7. Hence, Geraldine seems to be constructing a tough, masculine gender identity to contrast with the educated feminine identity of her addressee. This is a nice example of how social meaning is a dynamic mutual linguistic construction between different participants in an interaction.

Exercise 6

In example 12, Geraldine's frequent use of [in] variants is discussed using a number of terms: working-class, tough, masculine.
    Do you think it makes sense to separate out non-linguistic variables in this way?

Sociolinguists need to describe the linguistic patterns that correlate with the macro-level abstract categories of class, age, ethnicity, and gender, but for describing the detail and complexity of what goes on in day-to-day interactions between individuals, the concepts of social network and community of practice are particularly useful. They allow us to examine the ways in which individuals use linguistic resources in dynamic and constructive ways to express various social identities – identities which draw on macro-level social categories, such as class and gender, as well as micro-level categories

B

Language variation: focus on users

such as new gang member, or feisty friend, or youngest child in the family. Indeed, it is these moment-to-moment linguistic choices which ultimately create the larger-scale patterns, a point which will become evident in the next chapter.

Conclusion

> 'When it comes to linguistic form, Plato walks with the Macedonian swineherd, Confucius with the head-hunting savage of Assam.'

This famous quotation from Edward Sapir expresses a very fundamental belief held by linguists. All language varieties are equal: there is no significant difference in the complexity of their linguistic structure; they all have resources for creating new vocabulary as it is needed, and for developing the grammatical constructions their speakers require. Any variety can be developed for use in any situation. A language used by a tribe buried in the mountains of Papua New Guinea or the depths of the Amazonian rain forests has the potential for use at the nuclear physics conferences of the Western world, or in the most sensitive diplomatic negotiations between warring nations. There are no differences of linguistic form between varieties which would prevent them developing the language required for such purposes. The barriers are social and cultural.

Though linguists present this ideal of equality between the languages and dialects used by different ethnic and social groups, it has no social reality. Varieties acquire the social status of their users, and the divisions of dialects along racial, ethnic and social lines have been only too apparent in many countries, including the United States of America and Britain. I have used the terms standard and vernacular in describing features which characterise the speech of different social and ethnic groups. Some people have used the term sub-standard for vernacular features, with all the implications of deviance and inadequacy which that term carries, and this has often influenced people's views of the linguistic features involved.

It should be clear from the description of linguistic features provided in chapters 6, 7 and 8, that the difference between those features which happen to characterise the standard dialect and those which occur in vernacular dialects is entirely arbitrary. Indeed, the evidence reviewed demonstrates that the difference between the two is most often simply a matter of the frequency of different forms in the speech of different groups. In chapter 10, it will become clear that no one – not even the Queen of England or the President of the United States of America – uses standard forms all the time.

Before looking at the way people use language in different situations, however, it will be useful to explore a little further the relationship between some of the social factors considered in these three chapters and the process of language change. Since the 1960s, when sociolinguists began to contribute to studies of language change, explanations of the process have been increasingly illuminated by an understanding of the contribution of social factors. In the next chapter the relationship between age-grading and linguistic change will be explored further, and the influence of speakers' social class and gender on the process of language change will be discussed.

ANSWERS TO EXERCISES IN CHAPTER 8

Answer to exercise 1

Some of these examples will be discussed further in the next section.

(a) This is an example of a young African American male 'playing the dozens', a competitive style of speech which consists of ritual insults usually referring to the opponent's mother. The use of *mama* is typical of African American dialect, and the pronunciation suggested by *yo* provides another ethnic clue. A grammatical clue is the omission of the verb form *is* after the word *mama*, another feature frequently found in the English of Black Americans.

(b) This is Scottish speech. There are lexical clues – *bairns* for standard *children* and *mind* for *remember*, and a grammatical clue – the use of *cannae* for standard *can't* or *cannot*.

(c) This is an example of the Patois used by British Blacks with Jamaican origins. The crucial clue is the use of *fi* where standard English uses *to*. The use of *d* [d] where standard English uses *th* [ð] is another clue, but this is also found in many other dialects of English.

(d) Two lexical features suggest the speaker is Maori: the greeting *kia ora* and the name *Hemi* (the English equivalent is *Jim*). The use of the word *broom* as a verb and the final tag *eh* are additional features which have been noted particularly in the speech of Maori people.

(e) This speaker is a Jewish American as indicated by the words *goyim* to refer to non-Jewish people or Gentiles, and *bagels*, a Jewish doughnut-shaped bread roll. The syntactic pattern of the exclamation is also heard more frequently in Jewish discourse.

(f) The speaker is either from Singapore or Malaysia, and probably Chinese or Malay in ethnicity. The omission of *is* provides a clue since this verb is variably present in Singapore and Malaysian English, but this is a feature of many dialects of English. The speaker is identifiable as Singaporean or Malaysian by the use of the particle *la* and the Malay word *makan* for 'meal'.

Answer to exercise 2 (a)

Each social group uses more multiple negation than the group above it, and within social groups African Americans from Detroit consistently use more multiple negation than do white Detroiters. The amount of multiple negation used by African Americans from the highest social group is the same as that used by white speakers from the next social group down, for instance, showing clearly that social and ethnic features interact with linguistic features in a complex way in signalling information about speakers.

Answer to exercise 2 (b)

Features of AAVE:

- the use of *it's* for standard *there was* to introduce the story
- *name* for standard *named*, *live* for *lived*, *like* for *liked*, etc.
- deletion of *who* in the clause *live in Washington*
- *'most* for standard *almost*
- multiple negation *don't . . . nothing . . . neither*.

Answer to exercise 2 (c)

The form *be* has a habitual meaning in these sentences so it cannot occur in constructions which indicate the action took place at a particular point in time.

Hence sentence 8 is ungrammatical and should be marked with *.

Answer to exercise 3

As mentioned in the previous chapter, young people's awareness of society's attitudes, including attitudes to speech, becomes particularly acute during adolescence. So it is usually in their early teenage years that a person's stylistic repertoire expands. Majority group children often learn more standard speech forms for use in more formal situations at this stage, as mentioned in the discussion of age-graded features in chapter 7. For minority group adolescents, however, the pattern is likely to be just the opposite. They become aware at this stage of the wider society's valuation and prejudice against their group, and this often leads to a rejection of the standard speech forms associated with the majority group. It seems likely that for those who used relatively few Patois features as children (at least in school), a greater use of Patois features in adolescence may serve the function of expressing negative attitudes towards the majority culture, while positively asserting their Black British identity.

Answer to exercise 4

There are a number of different types of clue. The expression 'speaking Pakeha' for 'speaking English' is more frequently used by Maori than Pakeha people. The pragmatic particle *eh* is another feature which tends to be more frequent in the speech of Maori people. The other interesting feature is the tense switching which has also been noted more frequently in Maori narratives. Note that the features discussed are matters of frequencies. They do not occur exclusively in the speech of Maori speakers.

▮ Concepts introduced

Ethnicity
African American Vernacular English (AAVE)
British Black English
Maori English
Social network
Network density
Uniplex and multiplex networks
Community of practice
Constructions of social identity

▮ References

The following sources provided material for this chapter:

Bell (2000), Holmes (1997a), McCallum (1978), Jacob (1990) for data on Maori English
Bortoni-Ricardo (1985) data on Brasilia
Downes (1998) on ethnic differences in language use
Eckert and McConnell-Ginet (1992, 1995) on jocks and burnouts
Edwards (1986) data on Patois in Britain
Gal (1979) data on Oberwart
Kerswill and Williams (2000) on Milton Keynes
Kerswill et al. (2006) on Multicultural London English

Labov (1972a, 1972b, 1972c) data on American Black English
Milroy (1980) and Milroy and Gordon (2002) on Belfast, and networks
Nichols (1984) data on South Carolina communities
Shuy, Wolfram and Riley (1967) data on Detroit
Wolfram (1998) data for exercise 2(c)

Quotations

Exercise 1 sentence (a) from Kochman (1972: 261); sentence (c) from Edwards (1986: 144).
Example 3 is from Bryen, Hartman and Tait (1978: 2).
Example 7 is from data collected for McCallum's (1978) research.
Example 8 and quotation in exercise 4 from Jacob (1990).
Example 11 is from Eckert and McConnell-Ginet (1995: 495).
Example 12 uses material collected by Jacob (1990).
Sapir quotation from Sapir (1921: 219).

Useful additional reading

Chambers (2003), Ch. 2
Downes (1998), Chs 4 and 6
Labov (1972b) and (1972c)
Meyerhoff (2006), Ch. 9
Milroy (1980), Ch. 3
Milroy and Gordon (2002), Ch. 5
Trudgill (2000), Ch. 3
Wolfram and Schilling-Estes (1998)

B

Language variation: focus on users

9 Language change

Example 1

Peter: Why is English so illogical! Look at these words *knight* and *thorough*. How can I possibly explain those spellings to my Spanish friend? And why does *changeable* have an *e* in the middle when *argument* doesn't?

Helen: It's not just the spellings that are a problem. It's the meanings of words too. My teacher told me that the real meaning of *nice* is 'precise', and I shouldn't write 'we had a nice holiday'.

Michelle: What about pronunciation? English sounds are really hard to pin down. I heard this old guy on the radio and he was talking about an 'orphan with a korf in winter'. I couldn't make out a word of it till my dad explained the guy was saying that he often had a cough in the winter. Talk about weird!!

It is very easy to demonstrate to English speakers that languages change over time. At the point where English spelling became relatively fixed by printing, the printers recorded the pronunciations current at the time. So the *k* in *knit* and *knife* was not 'silent' in the fifteenth century, and *knight* not only began with a [k], it had a fricative sound in the middle represented by the letters *gh*.

Similarly, if you look up a good etymological dictionary you will find that the word *nice* once meant 'precise', and before that it meant 'fastidious' and earlier still it meant 'ignorant'. Reading Shakespeare turns up many words, such as *hie* ('hurry'), *stilly* ('softly') and *arrant* ('thorough'), which have disappeared or, more treacherously, changed their meaning. *Entertain*, for instance, meant 'keep occupied', so entertaining the invading troops in Shakespeare's time referred not to the efforts of singers and comedians, but to the success of the local army in keeping the foreigners at bay. Even since Jane Austen's time the meanings of words have changed. In her books, a 'pleasing prospect' refers to a landscape more often than an expectation, and to be 'sensible' means to be aware or perceptive.

Talk of language change, like the discussion between the young people at the beginning of this section, often treats language as an entity independent of its speakers and writers. In reality it is not so much that language itself changes, as that speakers and writers change the way they use the language. *Speaker innovation* is a more accurate description than language change. Speakers innovate, sometimes spontaneously, but more often by imitating speakers from other communities. If their innovations are adopted by others and diffuse through their local community and beyond into other communities then linguistic change is the result.

VARIATION AND CHANGE

Language varies in three major ways which are interestingly interrelated – over time, in physical space, and socially. Language change – variation over time – has its origins in spatial (or regional) and social variation. The source of change over time is always current variation. So the regional and social variants described in the previous three chapters provide the basis for language change over time. We will see how this works.

Example 2

'Children these days are putting the language at risk with their careless and sloppy pronunciations. From many possible examples I select just one. The distinctions between *which* and *witch*, and *whether* and *weather*, are slowly but surely disappearing in children's speech. Do other listeners regret this loss as I do? When I heard a child asking *which witch*? recently, it sounded as if she had a stutter.'

Within a monolingual community the superficial impression may be that everyone speaks the same. In a small town it often seems that everyone uses the same language. But a little thought will soon identify areas of variation, most obviously in vocabulary and pronunciation. A good source of information on changes which are currently in progress is the 'Letters to the Editor' section of any newspaper or magazine. People often write about language changes they have observed – usually to complain about them. Many of these changes will be ephemeral, but some will persist and become incorporated into the standard dialect. *Mob* was once condemned as a vulgar word, *bus* was once regarded as a vulgar shortening of *omnibus*, *'otel* was once considered the only acceptable way of pronouncing *hotel*, and the vowel sound in *go* has changed quite radically in the speech of BBC newsreaders over the last 30 years.

All language change has its origins in variation. The possibility of a linguistic change exists as soon as a new form develops and begins to be used alongside an existing form.

If the new form spreads, the change is in progress. If it eventually displaces the old form, the change has become a 'fait accompli' – it has gone to completion. One area of vocabulary where this is very easy to see is in the slang words used by young people to mean 'really good'. As mentioned in the section on age differences in chapter 7, there is a constant turnover of such words in any speech community: *super, spiffing, bonzer, groovy, cool, neat, fantastic, magic, excellent, wicked, hot, rad*. A particular word, such as *wicked*, may first develop this meaning of 'really good' in the usage of a particular sub-group – say young men. If the young men have some kind of status within the speech community – in other words, if other groups (such as young boys or young women) admire them – then the new word will begin to spread. It may eventually spread through the whole community and become the new norm or standard for expressing the concept 'really good'. More often it will spread through a number of groups and then fail to spread further. It may then survive, serving as a marker of the language of those groups, or it may be replaced by the next in-word for 'really good'.

Similarly, a sound change occurs when one sound is replaced in people's speech by another over a period of time, or when a sound disappears, as will be illustrated below. The process is the same. In New Zealand, for example, words like *new* and *nuclear* were once pronounced *nyew* [nju:] and *nyuklear* [nju:kliə]. Right now there is variation in the community. A new norm has been introduced. Young people are increasingly using an American pronunciation without the [j]: i.e. [nu:] and [nu:kliə]. Over time it seems likely that the pronunciation without [j] will displace the [j] pronunciation in most people's speech.

Exercise 1

Look in newspapers and magazines for Letters to the Editor on the subject of language. Do the letters provide clues to changes in progress in your community?

Divide them into comments on vocabulary or word meaning, comments on grammar, and comments on pronunciation.

Which area attracts most comments?

What is the attitude of the writers to the changes which are noted?

Answer at end of chapter

The sorts of questions sociolinguists ask about such changes are 'why do particular changes spread?', and 'how do linguistic changes spread through a community?' Sociolinguists try to identify the particular social factors which are responsible for spreading specific linguistic changes, and they try to explain how these factors influence the spread of the change. In addressing these questions, I will first look at a linguistic change which involves the spread of a prestige form – though interestingly the particular form which has prestige is exactly the opposite in London and New York.

■ Post-vocalic [r] – its spread and its status

> ### Example 3
>
> Elizabeth lives in the town of Ryde on the Isle of Wight, a popular British holiday resort off the south coast and frequent choice for retirement. Her family has lived there for three generations, originally farming, but they now run a small grocery business. Elizabeth's grandfather pronounces [r] pretty consistently in words like *start* and *car*. Elizabeth's parents pronounce [ɹ] in such words too, though not all the time. Her mother uses fewer than her father, and both tend to use fewer when serving the mainland visitors in the shop than when they are talking to the locals. They use most when talking to older relatives and friends at home. Elizabeth, however, doesn't use post-vocalic [r] at all. She did occasionally when she started school, but she soon stopped. Kids from London and the south who have moved to the island in recent years never use [r], and they know what's what!

In many parts of England and Wales, standard English has lost the pronunciation of [r] following vowels in words like *star* and *start*. Post-vocalic [r] does not occur in RP nor in the London Cockney dialect. The loss of post-vocalic [r] seems to have begun in the seventeenth century in the south-east of England, and it is still in progress, since there are areas, such as the south-west of England, where [r] is still regularly pronounced. As example 3 suggests, the change seems to be moving slowly westwards. (Post-vocalic [r] is also pronounced in Scotland and Ireland.)

Accents with post-vocalic [r] are called 'rhotic'. In large areas of England rhotic English accents are regarded as rural and uneducated. In large parts of America, on the other hand, post-vocalic [r] is alive and well and extensively used. Many American accents (though not AAVE) are rhotic. Under the influence of southern British norms, however, Eastern New England (e.g. Massachusetts, Connecticut) is generally non-rhotic. But there is also a conflicting pattern. A survey in the 1960s found that rhoticism was increasing in New York, where it was regarded as prestigious. Post-vocalic [r] was used by almost all New Yorkers in their most formal and careful speech, and young people from the upper middle class pronounced it even in their most casual speech – a sure signal that it was spreading.

So the pronunciation of [r] in English-speaking communities provides a wealth of examples of the complexity of linguistic variation and language change, as well as the arbitrariness of the forms which happen to be standard in any community. While [r]-less speech is the prestigious form which is still spreading in England, in some parts of America it is the rhotic variety which is increasing.

Changes which people are aware of have been described as 'changes from above'. These are changes where people are conscious of their social significance as desirable or prestige features of speech. People evaluate the speech of those who use such features highly. So in a social dialect survey undertaken by Labov, even New Yorkers who did not use post-vocalic (r) in conversation recognised it as a prestigious feature in the speech

Language variation: focus on users

of those who did use it and evaluated their speech positively. A second meaning of 'change from above' refers to the source of the change. In this sense, 'above' refers to the fact that a feature is generally spreading downwards through the social groups in a speech community. So it appears that post-vocalic (r) appeared first in the speech of upper-middle-class New Yorkers, and then gradually filtered down through the different social classes until it reached the speech of the lowest social class in the community. It is important to keep these two meanings distinct even though they often coincide.

Exercise 2

Mix the following words and phrases up with some others which do not involve the letter *r*. This will reduce the likelihood of people guessing which particular sounds you are interested in, which could lead them to pronounce them in an unusual way. Tape record 10 people reading your list. Note whether they pronounce [r] or not in each context.

Can you account for the [r]-pronunciations you identified?

star
start
soaring
drawing
law
lore
law and order
folklore and mythology

Answer at end of chapter

◼ The spread of vernacular forms

It is easy to understand that a pronunciation which is considered prestigious will be imitated, and will spread through a community. But there are also many examples of vernacular pronunciations which have spread throughout speech communities. It is possible for changes to proceed from a variety of starting points in a variety of directions.

Example 4

Martha's Vineyard is a little island about three miles off the coast of Massachusetts and within reach of people from Boston and New York as a holiday retreat. Every summer the island is flooded with visitors who outnumber the residents about seven to one. In the mid twentieth century, these visitors were resented by the locals, despite the fact that they had become increasingly dependent on tourists for their income. The attitudes of the locals towards the visitors was reflected in the Vineyarders' speech.

On Martha's Vineyard those who had lived on the island for generations, and especially those men who fished for their livelihood, resented the fact that the island has been invaded by more recent immigrants, and especially by summer tourists. A 1960s linguistic survey by Labov revealed that these attitudes were reflected in the way they pronounced the (ay) and (aw) sounds in words like *light* and *house*. Their pronunciation of the vowels in these words had gradually become more and more centralised. (The position of the tongue at the start of the vowel had moved towards the centre of the mouth.) So *light* was pronounced [ləit] (it sounds a bit like *layeet*) and *house* was pronounced [həus] (a bit like *heyuuse*). This sound change, which seemed to be unconscious, was a change to a more conservative pronunciation which used to be associated with the area in the past. It had been dying out, but it was revitalised to express solidarity between those who identified with the island and felt loyalty to its rural values and peaceful lifestyle. The centralisation of the vowel in *light* was particularly significant for signalling Islander identity.

Other groups on the island with similar attitudes imitated the fishermen, and so the use of centralised vowels spread. A group of Portuguese Americans, for instance, who had been on the island for several generations and who identified strongly with it, used centralised vowels too. And, not surprisingly, the American Indians – the indigenous inhabitants of the island – also asserted their status as permanent residents of the island through their speech.

So not all linguistic changes involve adopting new forms from outside the speech community. Nor do they always involve forms which people are conscious of as prestigious forms. Vowel centralisation is not an overtly prestigious sound in American speech. On Martha's Vineyard, however, it was clear that people unconsciously valued this speech feature. The spread of centralised vowels illustrates how a vernacular feature can acquire social significance and spread through a community. It acquired covert prestige as a marker of a person's status as a Vineyarder.

Replications of Labov's Martha's Vineyard study between 1997 and 2002 indicate that the (ay) vowel appears to be decentralising so this sound is no longer such a strong marker of island identity. But vowel centralisation in words like *house* has taken on a stronger role as a signal of Vineyarder status or identity and a positive attitude to the island. It is hard to know how to explain such a reversal. The decentralisation of (ay) could indicate that the locals recognise the importance of tourists to their economy and so their antagonism has abated, but the greater centralisation of (aw) suggests that the islanders still want to differentiate themselves from the summer visitors. Language change is always interesting, but not always predictable.

Changes in the pronunciation of vowels are often *changes from below*, in that they are changes below people's level of conscious awareness. In New Zealand the vowel merger of the sounds in *beer* and *bear* was a change from below in this sense. Again it is important to be aware that this is a different meaning of change from below from a change which spreads from a lower social groups upwards through to higher social groups. Such changes may or may not be above the level of conscious awareness. People may adopt new speech features, and especially slang, from lower social groups

B

Language variation: focus on users

relatively consciously. It seems likely that the spread of (th)-fronting in British English (i.e. the substitution of [f] for [θ] and [v] for [ð]) is an example of a vernacular change which is spreading upwards through different social groups, and which is above the level of conscious awareness for most speakers, while the spread of the glottal stop as a substitute for [t] in final position seems to be below the level of consciousness for most speakers.

Exercise 3

The HRT or high rise terminal (a rising intonation pattern on utterances which function as statements) is a vernacular feature which is increasing in Sydney speech. For instance, statements such as *I went to school in Sydney* or *we played tennis* might be uttered with an HRT or rising intonation. These utterances remain statements, not questions, in dialects in which the HRT occurs. Have you heard this intonation pattern in your region? It has been informally noted in a number of English-speaking communities.

A number of alternative explanations have been suggested for its appearance in Sydney. Most interesting is the suggestion that it may have arisen as a feature of the English of Australians responding to the influx of migrants from Europe to Australia in the 1950s. It could be seen as a somewhat negative or defensive response – a way of asserting Australian identity in the face of an influx of new ethnic groups. Alternatively it could be seen more positively – as a way of responding to the communicative needs of new immigrants – an efficient and economical way of checking people were following and understanding utterances. For those who believe that it arose as a way of asserting Australian identity, that still leaves the question of where it originated and why. It seems very likely that the feature has spread from some other region. At least two alternative sources have been suggested.

1. Some Australian researchers regard the HRT as distinctive of Australian English, and they speculate that it has spread to Sydney from other areas of Australia.
2. New Zealand researchers think it more likely that this long-recognised feature of New Zealand English has spread to Australia.

Which of these explanations is supported by the following facts?

(a) The HRT was noted in the speech of New Zealanders before its identification in Australian speech.
(b) A small sample of lower-class New Zealand speakers recorded in 1989 used twice as many HRTs as the Australians recorded in the Sydney survey.
(c) There are a large number of New Zealanders living in Sydney.

Answer at end of chapter

HOW DO CHANGES SPREAD?

Example 5

When she was about seven years old, Greg's daughter Sue started describing any-thing that she really liked as *utter*. Not *utterly great* or *utterly fantastic* – just *utter*! It sounded so weird. But her friends used it too, and her little brother soon began to describe things as *utter*. Greg gradually got used to it. He noticed Sue had even used it in a story and the teacher hadn't corrected it. He wondered if it would spread beyond her school – all the kids seemed to use it at the school. But in fact it just sort of died out eventually. Now Sue describes everything as *cool*. Greg comments that at least that's grammatical.

From group to group

Many linguists have used the metaphor of waves to explain how linguistic changes spread through a community. Any particular change typically spreads simultane-ously in different directions, though not necessarily at the same rate in all directions. Social factors such as age, status, gender and region affect the rates of change and the directions in which the waves roll most swiftly. The wave metaphor is one useful way of visualising the spread of a change from one group to another – as figure 9.1 demonstrates.

In any speech community different sets of waves intersect. You belong simultaneously to a particular age group, region, and social group. A change may spread along any of these dimensions and into another group. Linguistic changes infiltrate groups from the speech of people on the margins between social or regional groups – via the 'middle' people who have contacts in more than one group. These people seem to act as linguistic stockbrokers or entrepreneurs. I will illustrate this point in more detail below when we look at the reasons for linguistic change.

From style to style

One theory of how a change spreads presents the process as a very systematic one. In the speech of a particular individual it suggests the change spreads from one style to another (say from more formal speech to more casual speech), while at the same time it spreads from one individual to another within a social group, and subsequently from one social group to another. Using this model we would trace the spread of prestigious post-vocalic [r] pronunciation in New York, for instance, first in the most formal style of the young people in the most socially statusful group in the commun-ity. Then it would spread to a less formal style for that group, while also spreading to

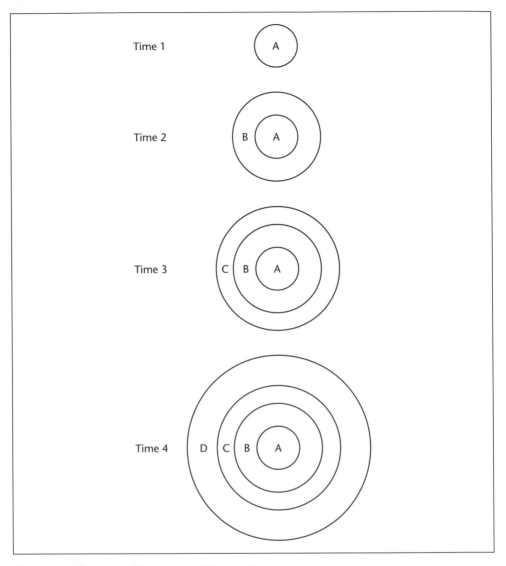

Figure 9.1 The wave-like spread of linguistic changes

Note: ABCD represent different age groups, social groups or regional groups.

Source: This diagram is based on Bailey 1973a: 159

the most formal style of other groups, such as to older people's speech, and to the speech of people from a lower social group. The change gradually spreads from style to style and from group to group, till eventually, if it goes to completion, everyone uses the new form in all their speech styles. Figure 9.2 provides a visual representation of this process.

When a change is a prestigious one it usually starts at the top of the speech community – in the most formal style of the highest status group and spreads downwards.

Time 1

	Social group		
Style	1	2	3
Formal	+	×	−
Casual	×	−	−

The new form is used consistently (+) in the formal style of
group 1. It is variable (×) in their casual style. and variable in the
formal style of group 2. Group 3 do not use the form (−).

Time 2

	Social group		
Style	1	2	3
Formal	+	+	×
Casual	+	×	−

The new form is used consistently by group 1. It has spread to the
casual style of group 2, and to the formal style of group 3, where
it is variable.

Time 3

	Social group		
Style	1	2	3
Formal	+	+	+
Casual	+	+	×

The new form is fully established in both styles of groups 1 and 2,
and in the formal style of group 3. It is variable in group 3's
casual speech.

**Figure 9.2 A model of the spread of a vernacular change through two speech styles
and three social groups**

Source: This diagram is simplified from a more complicated one in Bailey 1973a: 176

(As discussed earlier, it is a change from above). A vernacular change, such as centralisation in Martha's Vineyard, or the spread of glottal stop for [t] in the middle and
at the end of words, tends to begin in people's more casual styles. If it is a form
which is considered very non-standard it may take a long time to spread, and it
may never gain acceptance by the highest status social groups or in formal speech.
Innovating groups who introduce new vernacular sound changes tend to be around
the middle of the social class range – in the upper working class, for instance. And,
as one might expect, younger people tend to adopt new forms more quickly than
older people do and they use them more extensively. So in the London area and East
Anglia, for instance, the use of glottal stop for final [t] has spread very fast in recent
years, and it is now heard very frequently even in the more formal styles of young
people.

Exercise 4

Many studies of the spread of a linguistic change through a population (including the spread of a new variety such as a pidgin or lingua franca) have used an S-shaped wave to represent the progress of the change, as illustrated in figure 9.3. How do you interpret this graph? What does it indicate about the relative rate of progress of a linguistic change at different points in time?

Answer at end of chapter

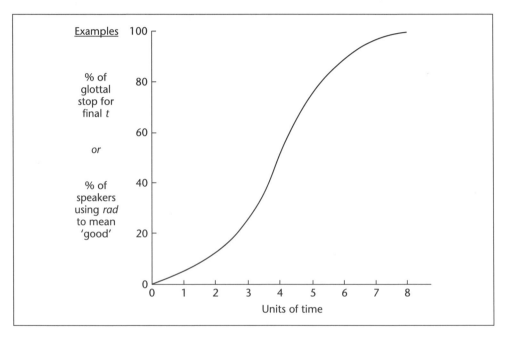

Figure 9.3 The progress of linguistic change

Source: This diagram is modified from one in Bailey, 1973b. Reproduced with permission

From word to word – lexical diffusion

It seems to be the case that sound changes not only spread from one person to another and from one style to another style, they also spread from one word to another. Sound changes spread through different words one by one. This is called *lexical diffusion*. When a sound change begins, all the words with a particular vowel don't change at once in the speech of a community. People don't go to bed one night using the sound [u:] and wake up using [au] in *house*, *pouch*, *how* and *out*. Instead, the sound change occurs first in one word, and then later in another, and so on. In Belfast, for instance, a vowel change affected the vowel in the word *pull* before *put*, and *put* before *should*. And in

East Anglia the vowel in *must* changed before the vowel in *come*, which changed before the vowel in *uncle*, although they all started off with the same vowel, and they all ended up with the identical *different* vowel at a later point.

In New Zealand a vowel change which is currently in progress is the merging of the vowels in word pairs like *beer* and *bear*, which used to be distinct. This change, too, seems to be proceeding by this process of lexical diffusion. A recent study suggested that the distinction had disappeared completely for most young people in the pair *really/rarely*, while *fear* and *fair* were still distinct in many young people's speech.

Exercise 5

A sound change may take many decades or even many centuries to complete. The loss of final [n] in French words such as *an* 'year', *bon* 'good', and *fin* 'end' provides an example. Nowadays the preceding vowel is nasalised (pronounced with the air expelled partly through the nose), and the [n] has disappeared. This change began in the tenth century, and took about five centuries to spread through the French language.

Given the following information on the way this sound change diffused or spread through the vocabulary of French over the years, can you identify the linguistic factor which seems to account for the order in which the change proceeded through different words?

Century	French word	English translation		Nasalised vowel
14th	chacun	'each'	→	[œ̃]
10th	an	'year'	→	[ã]
11th	en	'in'	→	[ã]
12th	non	'no'	→	[õː]
13th	magasin	'shop'	→	[ɛ̃]
10th	sans	'without'	→	[ã]
12th	bon	'good'	→	[õː]
10th	dans	'in'	→	[ã]
14th	un	'one'	→	[œ̃]
12th	bonbon	'sweet'	→	[õː]
13th	pin	'pine'	→	[ɛ̃]
13th	fin	'end'	→	[ɛ̃]
14th	brun	'brown'	→	[œ̃]

Answer at end of chapter

This French example illustrates nicely that language change is more accurately thought of as an accumulation of changes in the speech of individuals, rather than something which occurs in the language independently of its speakers.

HOW DO WE STUDY LANGUAGE CHANGE?

Apparent-time studies of language change

Example 6

I discovered one day that my 11-year-old son, David, did not know what the word *wireless* meant. Neither did his friends. On the other hand my great-grandmother never heard the word *radio*, and, while my grandmother knew what a radio was, she considered the term new-fangled. My mother used both *wireless* and *radio* to refer to the same object, and though I understood both terms I have always used *radio* for preference.

This rather simple example illustrates the way in which information on the language use of different age groups may reveal the direction of linguistic change in a community.

A great deal of linguistic variation is stable but some is an indication of linguistic change in progress. The patterns of deletion of the regular past tense affix (*-ed*) are stable in English-speaking communities. In Norwich, as elsewhere, the forms [in] vs [iŋ], and [h]-dropping, discussed in chapter 6, are also examples of stable variants. The patterns noted for different groups in the community have not changed over the last 50 or 60 years. The substitution of a glottal stop for [t] in certain positions, on the other hand, is increasing in Norwich. The use of [d] for the initial sound in *then* and *than* is an example of stable variation in New York. There is no evidence that the vernacular pronunciation with [d] is increasing. The challenge is to identify the clues which make it possible to predict which current variation will result in change and which won't.

A steady increase or steady decline in the frequency of a form by age group suggests to a sociolinguist that a change may be in progress in the speech community, whereas a bell-shaped pattern is more typical of stable variation. It is apparent that [r] is a prestigious pronunciation in New York, for instance, since higher social groups use more of it than lower social groups. It seems likely that it is spreading through the community, because younger people are using more of it than older people. At this point it is important to compare this pattern with the normal patterns of different ways of speaking at different ages. In chapter 7, I pointed out that the normal pattern for standard or prestige forms was that people used more of them in their middle years, as illustrated in figure 7.3. Their frequency is low in adolescence and declines again in old age. So when a standard or prestige form occurs more often in the speech of younger people than older people, this suggests that it is a new form which is being introduced and adopted by young people.

Comparing the speech of people from different age groups can be a useful clue, then, to language change. This has been called the *apparent-time* method of studying change. Differences between the speech of older people and younger people are interpreted as indications of changes in progress. Younger speakers tend to use more of the newer or innovative forms, and the older speakers use more of the older, conservative forms, the ones they adopted in their own teenage years. When the change involves the spread of a prestige form or an admired usage, then, it is easy to see the evidence of its spread. An increase in the use of these forms in the speech of younger people is a clue that a new form is being introduced.

It is much more difficult to identify a change when it involves the introduction and spread of a less prestigious form, a vernacular form – and these are by far the most frequent kinds of changes in any language. The spread of a swear word, for example, or a slang word, the spread of a vernacular pronunciation such as glottal stop for [t], or the use of the same vowel in words like *beer* and *bear* – which of these will result in a linguistic change is very difficult to spot accurately at an early stage. The regular or normal age-grading pattern for any form involves a higher incidence of vernacular forms among younger people. People normally use more vernacular forms while they are young, and tend to use more standard forms as they get older and respond to the pressure of the society's expectations. This makes it difficult to spot the spread of new vernacular forms by using the distribution of a form in different age groups as a clue. The normal age-graded distributional pattern is very similar to the pattern for a new form which is spreading – greater use by younger people (see figure 7.3). In other words, someone looking at the normal pattern for a stable vernacular feature like consonant cluster simplification might think this was spreading because young people simplify clusters more than older people. In fact the high use of these forms by young people is a function of their age (an age-grading pattern) and the amount of consonant cluster simplification in their speech is likely to reduce as they get older.

In a social dialect survey of the Sydney community, HRTs (described in exercise 3 above) were used far more often by teenagers than adults. This suggested that over time HRTs would become well-established as a feature of Sydney speech. But the researcher had to ensure, before interpreting the pattern in this way, that this was not simply a regular pattern which would repeat itself with each generation. Interpreting it as a clue to change assumes that the teenagers will continue to use the forms they use now as they grow older, so that these forms will become the norms of the adult community over time. In order to resolve such problems we need to examine the reasons for linguistic change, and to identify factors other than age as clues to the direction of changes in progress. I will return to these issues below.

Exercise 6

A pattern which showed the frequency of occurrence of a linguistic form peaking in adolescence would be very difficult to interpret accurately without further information.
    It could be

(a) the typical (age-graded) pattern for a stable vernacular variable or
(b) the pattern for a vernacular variable which is being replaced by a standard or prestige variable (with young people resisting the new standard) or

▶

(c) the pattern for a new vernacular variable which is spreading and replacing a standard variable.

The following patterns are much less ambiguous however.

How would you interpret a graph which showed a peak for the frequency of occurrence of a linguistic form

(i) in young adults' speech?
(ii) in middle age?
(iii) in old age?

Answers at end of chapter

Language change in real time

Example 7

In 1970 an American visiting New Zealand noticed with surprise that some children pronounced words like *milk* and *fill* with a vowel where he expected to hear [l]. Twenty years later he revisited the country and was fascinated to find that the pronunciation he had perceived as so odd on his earlier visit was now widespread throughout the community. Most people seemed to be using a vowel where he used [l] in words like *feel, real, fool, fail, silk* and *salt*. He had in the meantime discovered that this process of replacing post-vocalic [l] with a vowel was well-established in the south of England. 'Would America be next?' he wondered.

The apparent-time method of studying language change is a useful short-cut for sociolinguists who generally cannot afford to wait around for twenty years to see what happens in real time. Sometimes, however, it is possible to build on the work of earlier linguists when studying change. Dictionaries which provide the date when a form was first noted can assist in tracing changes in vocabulary over time. The study of Martha's Vineyard described above built on earlier descriptions of the Vineyarders' speech. The *Linguistic Atlas of New England* provided a description of the pronunciations of an earlier generation, and so changes in pronunciation which had occurred on the island over a 20- to 30-year period could be identified.

One very interesting real-time study was reported by Peter Trudgill, who returned to Norwich 15 years after his original study of the speech patterns of Norwich people. He discovered that some of the variation he had noted had led to linguistic change, as predicted. The vowels of *beer* and *bear*, for instance, which were still distinct for many speakers in 1968, had completely merged by 1983 for all speakers except those from the highest social group.

There were other changes, however, that were well under way by 1983 but which had not been noticed in the 1968 speech sample. As many as 30 per cent of young Norwich people had completely lost the *th* [θ] sound in *thing* from their inventory of consonants by 1983. They substituted [f] for *th* [θ] in words like *thing* and *thin*. This seemed to have been a very rapid and dramatic sound change.

These changes were identified by comparing a sample of people in 1968 and another similar sample 15 years later. In other words this was a study done in real time: a very reliable method of identifying changes. But where do they start and how do they spread? Why do some instances of variation become the source of change while other variations do not? Why do some changes spread and others die out? To begin to answer these questions we need to consider the social factors which affect language use. In what follows I will briefly discuss just three social factors and their relevance to language change – social status, gender, and interaction.

REASONS FOR LANGUAGE CHANGE

Social status and language change

Example 8

'during the 1960s . . . many public schoolboys, in an effort to identify with their peer group in the less privileged (but more exciting) world outside, struggled to shake free of RP and to take on exotic accents like the Liverpool "Scouse" of the Beatles generation . . . all this to the dismay of their parents.' (Note: British 'public' schools are equivalent to private schools elsewhere; they are expensive fee-paying schools.)

There is still a great deal of research and discussion about which social groups introduce linguistic changes. One answer seems to be that a linguistic change may enter a speech community through any social group, but that different types of change are associated with different groups.

Members of the group with most social status, for example, tend to introduce changes into a speech community from neighbouring communities which have greater status and prestige in their eyes. So upper-class London speech has prestige in the eyes of many people from outside London. Middle-class people in Norwich who visit London regularly are therefore likely to introduce prestigious new London pronunciations or 'in' words from London to Norwich. The pronunciation of the vowel in *top* and *dog*, for instance, has changed in Norwich from [ta:p] and [da:g] to RP [top] and [dog]. Middle-class speakers – and especially women (a point I will return to below) – have been among the leaders in this change. Similarly French words such as *sangfroid* and *savoir faire* have been introduced into English by educated middle-class people who know some French. And the much-discussed post-vocalic [r] pronunciation in New York was introduced by younger upper-middle-class speakers imitating the speech of rhotic communities which had prestige for them.

Lower-class speakers are more influential in spreading less conscious linguistic changes. Lower-class men in particular often adopt speech forms from nearby local workers to express solidarity, rather than status or prestige. Interestingly it is not the people at the bottom of the social heap who tend to innovate in this way, but rather those in the middle of the pile. The upper working class is how this group has sometimes been described. It may be that this is the group whose networks have the particular combination of openness which provides exposure to alternative linguistic forms, together with a level of density which gives the forms an opportunity to get established. This group has introduced into Norwich speech, for instance, a change in the pronunciation of the vowel sound in words like *hell* and *tell* which is used by people from the surrounding countryside. Using the new pronunciation *hell* sounds something like [hʌl]. Whether this change will spread upwards depends on whether it infiltrates the speech of the upper middle class in Norwich before they are aware of its low status compared to RP.

In Australia the HRT, mentioned above, seems to be spreading among lower socio-economic groups. People in lower-paid jobs use this intonation most frequently, and it clearly functions as a solidarity marker for this group. However, it is currently regarded by many older higher status speakers, in particular, as vulgar, and so it may remain within the lower social echelons. Alternatively, it may spread into the informal speech of young people from the higher social groups, and so gradually spread upwards in this way.

Exercise 7

On the basis of what you read in chapter 7, do you think women or men are most likely to lead a linguistic change?

Answer at end of chapter

Gender and language change

Example 9

At the beginning of the twentieth century, Gauchat, a French linguist, decided to study the dialect of Charmey, a small remote village in Switzerland. He chose Charmey because he thought the dialect would have little or no variation, but in fact his study ended up as a study of sound change. He found that young people were using new pronunciations, and that among people of the same age women were leading the changes. In the speech of the over-40s *only* women used some of the new variants he identified.

Differences in women's and men's speech are another source of variation which can result in linguistic change. Sometimes women are the innovators, leading a linguistic change, and sometimes men. Women tend to be associated with changes towards both prestige and vernacular norms, whereas men more often introduce vernacular changes.

In Ucieda, a small village in Spain near the provincial capital of Santander, men have been forced to look outside the village to find wives. Many of the village women will not marry the local working dairy farmers because they don't want to remain in the farming villages. The prospect of being stuck at home, as their mothers were, with the cows and the children simply isn't very attractive. The women's speech reflects their social aspirations. They use more of the standard Castilian final [o] pronunciations on words, and fewer of the dialectal final [u] pronunciations, than the men do. In general in this village, then, the women's speech is closer to the standard or prestige pronunciation of Spanish than the men's. The women have had enough of peasant village life. They have seen different lifestyles and been exposed to the standard dialect in their jobs as cooks for upper-class families or as university students. They use more standard forms with people outside the village, and gradually these forms extend throughout their speech, reflecting not only their social contacts but also their values and aspirations. Women in Ucieda are leading change towards Castilian Spanish and introducing prestige variants into Ucieda speech.

Exercise 8

In chapter 3, I discussed changes in the language use patterns of the town of Oberwart. German is gradually displacing Hungarian as the usual language of interaction in many families. Which gender do you think is most likely to be leading changes towards greater use of German in this community and why?

Answer at end of chapter

Martha's Vineyard, by contrast, provides an example of men leading a change. As described above, it was the fishermen who led the change to a more centralised pronunciation of certain vowels. The change involved the revitalisation of an older, more conservative pronunciation, which was re-invested with a new meaning in the light of social changes on the island. It was a change away from the standard to a more vernacular pronunciation, a pronunciation which expressed the men's loyalty to an older set of values which they regarded as threatened by the influx of tourists to their island home.

We find a similar pattern in Norwich in England, as mentioned above. Upper-working-class men are leading a sound change away from the RP standard pronunciation of words like *hell* towards the vernacular norms of the surrounding rural area ([hʌl]). These speech norms appear to express the working-class men's loyalty to local values, and the solidarity of working men as a group. The Norwich women, by contrast, are leading change towards RP in a different vowel. In Belfast the same pattern recurs. Women are leading changes towards the standard, while men are introducing new vernacular variants.

B

Language variation: focus on users

These generalisations account for differences in women's and men's role in relation to language change in a variety of communities. But there are at least two types of exception to these patterns. First, women sometimes introduce vernacular changes into a community, and, secondly, there are communities where women are not leading linguistic change in any direction.

The Belfast communities described in chapters 7 and 8 illustrate the first of these points, as well as the complexity of the processes of change, and the slipperiness of a word like prestige. Contrary to what one might expect, young Clonard women are introducing into the Clonard speech community vernacular pronunciations such as [ba:d] for *bad*, which are associated with the Ballymacarrett community. Why? A number of factors seem to be involved in accounting for this apparently unusual pattern. First it must be noted that prestige is a relative concept. In general, middle-class speech has prestige and working-class speech does not. But within the working-class communities of Belfast, there is another hierarchy based on factors such as where jobs are available and where they are not. Within these communities Ballymacarrett is more prestigious than the Clonard, partly because it has relatively full employment compared to other areas. So the Clonard women are introducing into their community a speech feature which they are imitating from the more prestigious Ballymacarrett community. Although this is a change towards the vernacular not towards the standard dialect, it is a vernacular form used by an admired group within the Belfast context.

A second relevant factor accounting for the role of Clonard women in relation to these vernacular forms is their social networks, a factor discussed in chapter 8. Where women work in jobs which favour the development of multiplex networks (for example, at jobs which involve them in interaction with their friends, kin and neighbours), then they are likely to develop strong solidarity ties with those people. This will be reflected in their speech patterns. So when women develop social networks which are close-knit and multiplex, it seems that they too may introduce changes in the direction of vernacular norms.

The young women studied in the Clonard district were employed in a rather poor central city store in a shopping area serving both Catholic and Protestant communities. In other words it was at a kind of community intersection. This is a typical situation for the introduction of a speech innovation. These women had also developed work and leisure patterns which resembled those of traditionally male groups. So the introduction of vernacular forms into their community by these young women reflected their daily networks and broader range of contacts through their work. It also indicates the importance of solidarity in favouring and consolidating vernacular forms in the speech of any group, male or female, who both work and play together.

Finally, the generalisation about women leading change towards the standard dialect applies only where women play some role in public social life. In Iran and India, for instance, it has been found that Muslim women's speech does not follow the Western pattern. In these places the status of women is relatively fixed and there is no motivation for them to lead linguistic change. It will not lead them anywhere socially. In these societies women do not lead linguistic innovation in any direction.

Exercise 9

The high rise terminal (HRT) has been discussed as an example of a change in progress in some English-speaking speech communities. Which gender would you predict is leading this change? Why?

Answer at end of chapter

Interaction and language change

Interaction and contact between people is crucial in providing the channels for linguistic change, as previous examples have implied. In this final section I will briefly identify more explicitly the ways in which interaction – or lack of it – has affected the progress of linguistic changes in a number of communities.

Linguistic change generally progresses most slowly in tightly knit communities which have little contact with the outside world. There are plenty of examples of places where isolation has contributed to linguistic conservatism. Scottish Gaelic has survived best in the Western Isles of Scotland. The far north and East Cape of New Zealand is where Maori has survived best. Little mountain villages in Italy, Switzerland and Spain are places where older dialects of Italian, French and Spanish are preserved. Sardinia is another example of a relatively isolated area which is renowned for its conservative linguistic forms compared to other Italian dialects such as Sicilian.

One of the best-known examples of linguistic conservatism is Iceland. Icelandic has altered relatively little since the thirteenth century, and it has developed very little dialectal variation. By contrast, during the same period English has changed radically and has been characterised by gross dialectal variation. What explains this contrast? Iceland is much more geographically isolated than England, and so it has been much freer from outside influences, but this is not a sufficient explanation for the relative lack of variation in the language. The glaciated middle of the country means that Icelandic communities are scattered around the coast, and communication between them was very difficult in the past, especially in winter. This kind of geographical situation norm-ally leads to a great deal of dialect divergence. Why has Icelandic remained so stable and so conservative?

One answer to this question seems to be that although they were geographically separated, the Icelandic communities had very strong political and cultural ties, and, against all the odds, they therefore maintained contact with each other. They held regular annual assemblies at which all the important chiefs gathered. They attached great importance to kinship and friendship links and so people kept in close contact from generation to generation and over long distances. They talked to each other a lot. Interaction was the crucial factor which prevented the development of differences in Icelandic.

Example 10

At the age of seven, Frank moved from Cincinnati in the United States of America to Te Awamutu, a small town in New Zealand. The children in Frank's class at school were fascinated by the way he spoke. When he found something interesting, for example, he said *far out*! Frank's schoolmates had only heard Americans on TV say *far out* before. But evidently real people said it too! The expression soon spread and *far out* became well-entrenched as a positive response in children's speech in Te Awamutu.

Is face-to-face interaction crucial for linguistic change? Or is exposure to new forms of the media sufficient? Linguists are not yet sure about the extent to which the media can influence people's speech habits. Some believe that frequent exposure to a pronunciation on television can bring about change. Others argue that face-to-face interaction is necessary before change occurs. A popular compromise is the view that the media can soften listeners up by exposing them to new forms in the speech of admired pop stars or TV personalities. When people are subsequently exposed to a particular form in the speech of a real person, they are then more likely to adopt it.

Example 11

Sam lives in Norwich but he travels to London twice a week, staying overnight with a group of mates there at least once. He works for a small shop which hires out videos and sells tapes and CDs. His job involves collecting orders from the shop's supplier in London, but also keeping in touch with current video material and the pop music scene to pick up the latest trends. In London he goes to rock concerts and discos with his mates, and they watch new videos together. In Norwich he is much envied and admired by his old school mates. He goes to football matches with them at the weekend when Norwich are playing at home, and they play snooker and drink together. Sam's speech is influenced by his London contacts. He uses all the latest Cockney slang, his speech is liberally sprinkled with glottal stops, and he talks about *'avin' a bi' of bovver*, not *bother*.

In Norwich many young people now say *bovver* [bovə] instead of *bother* and *togevver* [təgevə] for *together*. This is a change for them, but Cockneys have used these forms for decades. Has this change spread from London through the influence of young people who spend a lot of time in London? It is a vernacular form which has covert prestige – it expresses solidarity with a particular sub-culture represented by pop music, for example, and negative attitudes to the 'establishment' – older, socially more statusful groups.

As I have indicated throughout this chapter, many linguists believe that linguistic changes spread through the social networks of individuals. Particularly important are people like Sam who acts as a kind of linguistic entrepreneur moving between groups. He serves an important linking function between two distinct but closely knit social networks. As a link-person, he also acts as a kind of bridge or channel for the spread of new linguistic forms from one group to the other. People like Sam act as linguistic innovators within social groups. Innovators are often marginal rather than core members of the groups adopting an innovation. So for an innovation to have a good chance of adoption by the central members of a group it will generally need to be transmitted through a number of different links or bridges. One person is rarely adequate as the only source of a linguistic change. And the change will also need to have some sort of prestige attached to it – whether overt (expressing social status) or covert (expressing solidarity).

New forms can gain prestige from the media. TV may have played a part in explaining at least the speed with which pronunciations like [bovə] have spread. The use of such forms by admired individuals on TV may have softened up Norwich people for the adoption of these forms which are well established in Cockney speech. The fact that a form is used in the vernacular speech of the capital city is probably another factor contributing to its prestige or attractiveness to the ears of young people in other places. Vernacular London speech is generally seen as more desirable than the speech of other cities. But it seems likely that the actual process of diffusion or the spread of forms involves marginal people like Sam who move between groups in each place.

The spread of glottal stops in words such as *bit* and *bitter* where RP uses [t] seems to have followed a similar route. This is a change which is spreading very rapidly out of London in all directions. Here too there is some evidence that the change is spreading by face-to-face contact rather than via the media. Areas closer to London have adopted this change more quickly than areas further away. If the media were the main factor influencing change, there is no reason why glottal stops shouldn't be heard in Liverpool and Newcastle as quickly as in Oxford, Bristol and Norwich. But this isn't what has happened. There is evidence that glottal stops were heard in the speech of young people in cities closer to London before they were heard in the speech of those further away. The influence of the media may again explain the speed of the change, however. Cockney TV heroes help promote positive attitudes to the form in advance – but the actual changes in people's speech seem to require face-to-face contact.

Exercise 10

Look again at example 10 in chapter 8. In this community linguistic change is being led by women like Mary's mother. Compare Sam's contribution to linguistic change (example 11 above) with that of Mary's mother in the South Carolina community. What similarities and differences can you identify?

Answer at end of chapter

B

Language variation: focus on users

Exercise 11

Compare the different words used to introduce quoted speech in the following utterances.

(a) So she says 'why not?'
(b) So she goes 'why not?'
(c) So she's all 'why not?'
(d) So she's like 'why not?'

If you speak English, have you heard these phrases used to introduce quoted speech by people in your speech community? Which do you consider to be new forms and which are established forms? How do you think the new forms are spreading?

Answer at end of chapter

Example 12

Kupwar

Urdu	pala	jəra	kat	ke	le	ke	a		ya
Marathi	pala	jəra	kap	un	ghe	un	a	l	o
Kannada	tapla	jəra	khod	i	təgond	i	bə		yn
	greens	a little	cut	having	taken	having	come	past	I

'I cut some greens and brought them.'

At first glance you would guess that these three sentences were from three dialects of the same language. But this is not the case. They are from three different languages of India, and they do not even all belong to the same language family. The three languages are Kannada, a Dravidian language, and two Indo-European languages, Urdu, which is related to Hindi, and Marathi, a regional language of India. In many places these languages are quite distinct and word-for-word translation of the kind illustrated in the example would be considered impossible. In Kupwar, however, a small Indian village on the border between these two language families, regular and long interaction has resulted in the merging of the structure of the three languages which is illustrated above.

Kupwar has about 3000 people and for centuries three socially distinct groups have lived together there, each speaking a different language as their home language. The Jains use Kannada, the Muslims use Urdu and the Dalit (now considered a more acceptable term for a group formally labelled the Untouchables and more recently Harijan) speak Marathi, the regional language and principal literary language of the area. The villagers regularly use all three languages in their daily activities. Over time, with constant switching between at least two languages in any interaction, the languages have become more and more alike. The word order is now identical, and there are extensive similarities in the structure of words and use of inflections too. A word-for-word translation is easy between the different languages.

It is the communicative needs of the people – their need to be able to interact easily – which has led to a merging of the grammars. On the other hand each group also wants to be identifiably distinct, and this has led to the maintenance of differences at the vocabulary level. One pair of linguists commented that this is the linguistic equivalent of having your cake and eating it too.

This last example illustrates a general point: language change often operates within clear limits. Language serves two very basic functions, as mentioned in chapter 1: a referential or informative function and a social or affective function. In most of this chapter I have focussed on the contribution of social factors to linguistic change – examining how and why it proceeds as it does. The functions of linguistic forms as markers of social status or as signals of solidarity have been extensively discussed. In this last example the requirement that language convey referential meaning as well as expressing social or affective functions, such as group identity, imposes another constraint on the linguistic developments in Kupwar. Language change does not proceed at a rate which results in unintelligibility between groups in contact – the referential requirements are always present. Though parents often complain they cannot understand their children's slang, there is never any real danger that members of groups who interact regularly will lose linguistic contact.

Tracing the progress of a linguistic change through the speech of a community is a fascinating exercise. It involves considering the influence of a wide range of social factors. This chapter has obviously drawn on the discussions of social class, age, gender and interaction in earlier chapters. Any of these factors may be relevant in accounting for where a particular change starts or how it spreads through a community. The discussion in this chapter has also demonstrated that identifying changes in progress involves considering different speech styles as well as the speech of people from different groups. A change which introduces a vernacular variant into a community (such as glottal stop for final [t] in Britain) will infiltrate people's more casual speech styles first. A new prestige variant (such as post-vocalic [r] in New York speech), on the other hand, will be heard first in people's most formal and careful speech styles. In the next chapter we will look in more detail at how a sociolinguist might distinguish different speech styles, and at the effect of a range of contextual factors on people's speech.

B

Language variation: focus on users

ANSWERS TO EXERCISES IN CHAPTER 9

Answer to exercise 1

Many letters comment on linguistic changes in progress. In my observation, most letters comment on variant pronunciations, with word meaning changes next most frequent, and fewer letters concerned with grammatical points. This probably reflects the amount of variation to be heard in the language at any point, rather than the relative salience or noticeability of these different levels of linguistic analysis. In many languages there is a wider range of variation in pronunciation at any one time than at other levels of analysis.

Though there is generally less grammatical variation than variation in pronunciation, grammatical variation is usually more noticeable or attention-grabbing. So the use of one vernacular grammatical form, such as multiple negation, may be enough for a listener to classify a speaker as uneducated.

Finally, it is interesting to note that few letters to the paper welcome language change or comment positively on a linguistic change in progress. Most deplore change and condemn new pronunciations and usages as abominations.

Answer to exercise 2

A number of factors affect the likelihood of [r] pronunciation in the words and phrases provided. You may be able to identify some of them in the data you have collected. First there are some people who have rhotic accents. Most Scottish and Irish people, for instance, will pronounce *r* wherever it is written. Secondly, the influence of the written form means that people who do not usually pronounce [r] in a word like *lore* may do so when they see it written down, especially when it is near to the word *law*. They may wish to make the contrast between the two words clear. Thirdly, people often introduce an [r] between vowels not only in a phrase such as *folklore and mythology* where there is an *r* in the spelling, but also in a phrase like *law and order*. Reasons such as analogy and ease of articulation have been suggested for this linking [r]. It has been labelled 'intrusive (r)' and it is often the focus of letters of complaint in newspapers.

Answer to exercise 3

All these facts support the second explanation. The earlier identification of the HRT in New Zealand speech suggests this feature migrated to Sydney from New Zealand. The frequency with which the HRT was heard in the speech of lower-class New Zealanders suggests it has a longer history in New Zealand than in Australia. It seems possible that the HRT has been imported to Australia from New Zealand, since Sydney in particular has a large New Zealand population. Further support for the notion of an influence from New Zealand to Australia comes from recent comments reported by Australian sociolinguists that some residents of Sydney and Brisbane are adopting New Zealand pronunciations of vowels. More research is clearly needed, however, since there is very little reliable data on HRT usage at present. So this discussion should be regarded as providing suggestions rather than as in any way definitive. It illustrates the ways in which theories and hypotheses about linguistic changes develop.

Answer to exercise 4

The percentage of potential adopters to accept an innovation rises slowly at first, then gathers speed, and then slackens off until it reaches a ceiling or limit. This has been described as a slow-quick-quick-slow progression. It has been suggested that the pattern for the rate of spread of a change in the language, and the pattern of change in the speech of an individual may be much the same S-type curve.

Answer to exercise 5

The sound change began in words where the final *n* (or *ns*) was preceded by *a*. Next it spread to words where the final *n* was preceded by *e*. So the progress of the change can be described as follows:

(a) words ending in *-an(s)*
(b) words ending in *-en*
(c) words ending in *-on*

(d) words ending in *-in*
(e) words ending in *-un*

Although this presents the progression in a way that suggests the sound change went to completion in each group before proceeding to the next group, this is in fact not the way these changes would have progressed. There would have been overlap, as suggested by the wave model. Changes in the pronunciation of group 2 words would have begun before all the group 1 words had changed their pronunciation, and so on. This overlapping pattern describes the progress of changes in an individual's speech as well as in the language as a whole. Figure 9.4 captures this well.

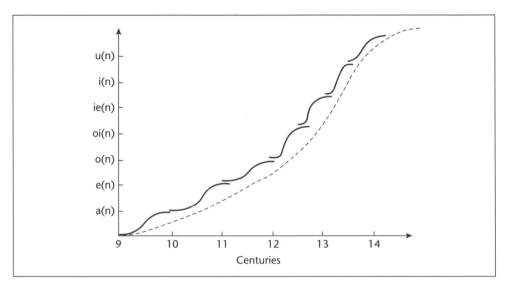

Figure 9.4 Overlapping S-curves: French words ending in *-n* affected by sound change

Source: Reproduced from Aitchison 2000: 93

Answer to exercise 6

(i) *A peak in young adults' speech*: This is a likely pattern for a socially prestigious form entering a community. Little children are not socially conscious so it won't be high in their speech, and adolescents are less likely to adopt it because of their tendency to hold anti-society values.
(ii) *A peak in middle age*: This is the normal pattern for a stable standard variable.
(iii) *A peak in old age*: This suggests a change in progress with old people using the highest frequencies of a form which is disappearing.

Answer to exercise 7

The answer depends on what kind of linguistic change is being discussed. As a broad generalisation women more often lead changes in the direction of the standard or prestige norms; when men lead changes, they generally involve vernacular variants. But things are generally not so simple, as we will see.

Answer to exercise 8

In Oberwart, women are leading the change towards German monolingualism. Hungarian is associated with peasant networks and a rural lifestyle. German is the language of industrial progress and high status well-paid jobs for women and men. Most young women in Oberwart want to marry non-peasant German-speaking men ('peasant men can't get wives!' is how one sociolinguistic researcher put it).

This example illustrates that the same social forces are relevant in accounting for language change in multilingual and in monolingual speech communities. The ways in which language changes spread and the social reasons for change are essentially similar in all speech communities.

Answer to exercise 9

Since the HRT is a vernacular rather than a standard variant, it is difficult to predict whether its introduction is more likely to be led by women or by men. While women tend to lead prestige changes, vernacular changes may be led by either gender.

Data from the Sydney sociolinguistic survey demonstrate that the HRT is used three times as often by young people as by older people. The data also suggest that women are leading this change.

One possible reason for women's lead in relation to this change is the affective *function* which the HRT serves in discourse. It has been suggested that the HRT is a facilitating device, inviting the addressee to participate in the conversation. Such facilitative forms seem to be more frequent in women's speech. The discourse function of the HRT may therefore account for its greater frequency in women's speech. This point will be explored further in chapter 12.

Answer to exercise 10

Though both Sam and Mary's mother are acting as agents of linguistic change, they are leading change in different directions. Sam is introducing a change towards the vernacular into Norwich young men's speech. Mary's mother is introducing a change towards the standard into the speech of her island community. Note in both cases the importance of (a) economic factors – their jobs are the reasons for their moving between two communities on a regular basis; (b) interaction – it is the speech of the people they interact with which is the source of the new linguistic variants; (c) attitudes – the speech forms they adopt and import into their home communities are those of a group they see as having something they admire and aspire to – status, wealth, influence and so on.

Answer to exercise 11

The words *says* and *goes* are older, colloquial quotative forms for introducing reported speech. The newer quotative forms are *be all* and *be like*. Since these forms were first noted in the speech of young Americans, it seems likely that American television programmes, movies and music, together with increased mobility, especially among young people, are all factors which have contributed to their spread. There is some evidence that although these forms occur in the speech of teenage boys and girls, they are most frequent in the girls' usage, and girls appear to be leading the spread of the forms. This is a nice, specific example of the globalisation of English.

Concepts introduced

Speaker innovation
Change from above
Change from below
Wave theory

Lexical diffusion
Apparent-time change
Real-time change

References

The following sources provided material for this chapter:

Allan (1990) on HRT in New Zealand English
Cooper (1982) on language change
Gal (1978) on Hungarian
Gordon and Maclagan (1990) on vowel merging in New Zealand English
Gumperz and Wilson (1971) on Kupwar
Holmquist (1985) on Ucieda
Horvath (1985) for Sydney data
Khan (1991) on women's linguistic patterns in India
Labov (1963), Pope (2002), Blake and Josey (2003) on Martha's Vineyard
Labov (1966) for New York data
Labov (1972a) on Gauchat's study of Charmey
Labov (1981) and (1990) on sound change
Lass (1987) on rhotic accents
Milroy and Milroy (1985) on language change and Icelandic
Tagliamonte and D'Arcy (2004), Meyerhoff (2006) Ch. 11 on quotatives
Trudgill (1974, 1988) for data on Norwich
Williams (1990) on Isle of Wight
Example 2 is based on a contribution to 'Listeners' Views' heard on a New Zealand radio programme.

Quotations

Example 8 is from Honey (1989: 33).
The quotation 'peasant men can't get wives' is from Gal (1978).
The comment on Kupwar residents enjoying 'the linguistic equivalent of having your cake and eating it too' is from Finegan and Besnier (1989: 386).

Useful additional reading

Aitchison (2000)
Bauer and Trudgill (1999)
Chambers (2003), Ch. 4
Downes (1998), Chs 5, 6 and 7
Meyerhoff (2006), Ch. 7
Romaine (2000), Ch. 9
Wardhaugh (2006), Ch. 8

B

Language variation: focus on users

Section C

Language variation: focus on uses

10 Style, context and register

> **Example 1**
>
> Three different requests for information:
>
> 1. *From a friend*
>   Where were you last night? I rang to see if you wanted to come to the movies.
> 2. *In court from a lawyer*
>   Could you tell the court where you were on the night of Friday the seventeenth of March?
> 3. *From a teacher to his pupils in school on the day after Halloween.*
>   I know some of you went 'trick-or-treating' last night and so I thought we might talk a bit today about how you got on. Did you go out last night Jimmy?

In each of these three utterances the speaker is trying to elicit the 'same' information from the addressee, but the context dramatically influences the form of the query. Each request for information is expressed quite differently.

Language varies according to its uses as well as its users, according to where it is used and to whom, as well as according to who is using it. The addressees and the context affect our choice of code or variety, whether language, dialect or *style*. The differences between the three utterances in example 1 are stylistic differences, and it is style which is the focus of this chapter.

In the second section of this book we looked at ways in which people's speech reflects and expresses their group membership. These features are also sometimes described as stylistic features. People talk of an ethnic style or a female register, for instance, referring to the way people speak by virtue of their ethnicity or gender, regardless of context. In this chapter, however, the focus will be on the ways in which speech reflects and constructs the *contexts* in which language is used, rather than characteristics of the speakers. I will first consider the influence of the addressee on the speaker's language, exemplifying from less formal contexts where the solidarity between participants is an important factor contributing to choice of speech style. Then I will examine features of speech style in a range of contexts which vary in formality, looking at the interaction of the formality and status dimensions. Finally, I will consider the way distinctive styles or registers may be shaped by the functional demands of particular situations or occupations.

Exercise 1

Tape-record a friend telling a story from their own personal experience (i.e. something interesting that has happened to them) first to an adult, and then to a child of about five who is the same gender as the adult. Note any differences in the vocabulary chosen and the grammatical patterns used in the different contexts. Can you account for the differences in style by considering the characteristics of the different people they were talking to?

Some of the features you may have noted are discussed in the next section.

ADDRESSEE AS AN INFLUENCE ON STYLE

Example 2

(a) Excuse me. Could I have a look at your photos too, Mrs Hall?
(b) C'mon Tony, gizzalook, gizzalook.

The first utterance in example 2 was addressed by a teenage boy to his friend's mother when she was showing the photos of their skiing holiday to an adult friend. The second utterance was addressed to his friend when he brought round his own photos of the holiday. The better you know someone, the more casual and relaxed the speech style you will use to them. People use considerably more standard forms to those they don't know well, and more vernacular forms to their friends. In a study in Northern Ireland, for instance, people used more standard English forms with an English stranger visiting their village than they did talking to a fellow villager.

This generalisation holds across different languages, though I will illustrate mainly with English in this chapter. In Mombasa, a city in Kenya, the kind of Swahili that people use when talking to their friends is quite different from the variety they use to a Swahili-speaking visitor from outside the community. The same pattern has been reported from research in a range of different places, including Sweden and Hawai'i. The speaker's relationship to the addressee is crucial in determining the appropriate style of speaking. And how well you know someone or how close you feel to them – relative social distance/solidarity – is one important dimension of social relationships.

Many factors may contribute in determining the degree of social distance or solidarity between people – relative age, gender, social roles, whether people work together, or are part of the same family, and so on. These factors may also be relevant to people's relative social status. I will illustrate by discussing how the age of the person addressed may influence a speaker's style.

▉ Age of addressee

Example 3

Mrs N: Oooh, he's walking already.

Mother: Oh, yes, he's such a clever little fellow aren't you?

Mrs N: Hullo coogieboo. Eeeee . . . loo, diddle diddle dur. Ohh eechy, weechy poo poo. Ohh eechy, peachy poo poo. There look at him laughing. Oh he's a chirpy little fellow. Yeees. Whoooo's a chirpy little fellow eh? Yes. Ooooh, can he talk? Can he talk eh eh?

Uttered with high pitch and a sing-song intonation, there is little doubt about the appropriate addressee of utterances such as those in example 3. This example comes, however, from a Monty Python sketch where these utterances are addressed to the speaker's adult son, who responds with 'Yes, of *course* I can talk, I'm Minister for Overseas Development'. The humour depends on the audience's perception of the inappropriateness of addressing a statusful adult in this way.

People generally talk differently to children and to adults – though some adjust their speech style or 'accommodate' more than others. Talking to younger brothers and sisters, even 3-year-olds have been heard using sing-song intonation and 'baby-talk' words like *doggie*, which they no longer use themselves. When talking or writing to a 6-year-old as opposed to a 30-year-old, most people choose simpler vocabulary and grammatical constructions. Compare the excerpts in example 4 and guess which letter was addressed to the child, and which to the adult. Note the different ways in which the same ideas are expressed to the different addressees.

Example 4

1. Dear Paul

   Thanks for your last letter and the subsequent postcards from exotic resorts. We were all green with envy over your trip to Rio with all expenses paid! How do you get to be so lucky!

   Thanks also for the great T-shirt you sent for Rob's birthday. He has vowed to write to you in order to express his gratitude personally – but don't hold your breath! He is particularly embroiled in some new complex computer game at present which is absorbing every spare moment.

▶

Language variation: focus on uses

C

2. Dear Michael

Thank you very much for the letter you sent me. It was beautifully written and I enjoyed reading it. I liked the postcards you sent me from your holidays too. What a lovely time you had swimming and surfing. I wished I was there too.

Robbie liked the T-shirt you chose for him very much. He has been wearing it a lot. He has promised to write to you soon to say thank you but he is very busy playing with his computer at the moment. So you may have to wait a little while for his letter. I hope mine will do instead for now.

Most of the sentences in the letter to the child are short and grammatically simple. Longer ones consist of simple sentences linked by coordination (*and*, *but*). The sentences are also more explicit. Little is left for the child to infer. There are more complex sentences in the letter to the adult with more subordinate clauses: e.g. *He has vowed [to write to you [in order to express his gratitude]]*. The brackets indicate the beginning and end of the subordinate clauses.

The vocabulary in the two letters is different too. In the first letter low frequency words such as *subsequent, exotic, resorts, vowed, gratitude, embroiled*, and *absorbing* suggest the addressee is not a 6-year-old. In the second letter simpler and more common words are used, such as *like, play* and *too*, with phrases like *a lot* and *a little while*. The different addressees clearly influence the language used, even though the message in each letter is very similar.

Many speakers also use a different style in addressing elderly people, often with features similar to those which characterise their speech to children – a simpler range of vocabulary and less complex grammar, the use of *we* rather than *you* to refer to the addressee, and sometimes even the sing-song intonation which characterises baby-talk! The effect is generally patronising, as illustrated in example 5 which was sing-sung by a nursing aid to an elderly woman in a private hospital.

Example 5

It's time for our [i.e. your] lunch now isn't it Mary. We [i.e. you] better wash our [i.e. your] hands.

Exercise 2

The speech used by native speakers to foreigners who do not speak English well is also distinctive. It has been labelled 'foreigner talk'. It has features similar to those which characterise adults' speech to young children. If you have the opportunity, tape someone talking to a learner of English. Note characteristics of the native speaker's speech which are similar to those heard in speech to young children.

Answer at end of chapter

238

In this section, I have shown how the age of the addressee may affect a speaker's style. Most people use language differently to the very young and the very old. In the next section you will see that the social background of the people you talk to also influences the language you use.

Social background of addressee

Example 6

(a) Last week the British Prime Minister Mrs Margaret Thatcher met the Australian Premier Mr Bob Hawke in Canberra . . . Their next meeting will not be for several months.

(b) Las' week British Prime Minister Margaret Thatcher met Australian Premier Bob Hawke in Canberra . . . Their nex' meeding won't be for sev'ral months.

These utterances illustrate a number of linguistic features which distinguish the pronunciations of newsreaders on different radio stations. In (b) there is simplification of consonant clusters, so [la:st] becomes [la:s] and [nekst] becomes [neks]. The pronunciation of [t] between vowels is voiced so it sounds like a [d]. Hence *meeting* sounds like *meeding*. The definite article *the* is omitted before the titles *Prime Minister* and *Premier* and the honorifics *Mrs* and *Mr* disappear. And finally, utterance (b) contracts *will not* to *won't*.

All these features have been identified as typical of the contrasting styles of newsreaders on different New Zealand radio stations. Figure 10.1 shows the contrast between the newsreader on a middle-of-the-road station (ZB) with an audience from the lower end of the social spectrum, compared to the prestigious National Radio network (YA) with its older, generally better-heeled audience.

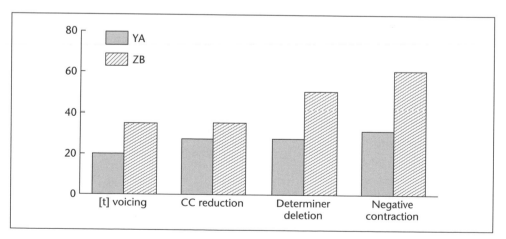

Figure 10.1 Linguistic features of radio announcers' speech on different stations
Source: This diagram was constructed from data in Bell, 1984

This is strong support for the importance of *audience design*: the influence of the addressee or audience on a speaker's style. The most convincing evidence comes from the behaviour of the same newsreader on different radio stations. Where the stations share studios, a person may read the same news on two different stations during the same day. In this situation newsreaders produce consistently different styles for each audience. The news is the same and the context is identical except for one factor – the addressees. So the same person reading the news on the middle-level station reads in a very much less formal style than on the higher-brow radio station.

Exercise 3

Which of the following sentences would have been most likely to have been produced by a newsreader on highbrow British Radio 3, as opposed to a newsreader on Radio 1, a pop station. What linguistic clues can you identify?

(i)   Despite repeated efforts to contact him, the Home Secretary, Mr David Waddington, was not available for comment this morning.

(ii) The las' time Maggie Thatcher visited Australia the weather wasn't much to write home about. This time it has been much bedder according to reports from Sydney.

(iii) Enquiries have not yet provided any new leads in the investigation of the latest postbox robbery, according to the official police spokesman, Detective Superintendent Ray Huntley.

Answers at end of chapter

Exercise 4

Variation in linguistic features is patterned or structured in written as well as spoken texts. The intended audiences of newspapers as well as radio and TV stations affect the language used. Determiner deletion, for instance, is very much more frequent in some British newspapers than others. (Determiners are words such as *the, a, this* which typically precede a noun.) There are two columns of newspapers below. In which would you expect to find most determiner deletion?

1	2
The Times	*Daily Mail*
The Guardian	*Daily Express*
The Daily Telegraph	*The Mirror*
	The Sun

If you can get access to copies of these papers, compare 1000 words from one newspaper from each of the columns above, and calculate the number of determiners which have been deleted as a percentage of the total number of determiners which could have been used.

Answer at end of chapter

> **Example 7**
>
> June works in a travel agent's in Cardiff, the capital city of Wales. She sees a wide range of people in the course of her job. Last Tuesday she saw an accountant, an old friend from school, a woman who works for the council as a cleaner, and a local schoolteacher. As she spoke to each person she pronounced words like *better* and *matter* differently, depending on the way her customer pronounced those words.

When June is speaking to people from the same social background as her own she pronounces the consonant in the middle of *better* as [d] about a quarter of the time. We could say that this is her 'normal' level of [d] pronunciation between vowels. But when she is talking to customers from a lower social class, she adapts her pronunciation to their speech. For the lowest social class in Cardiff the average amount of [d] pronunciation in the middle of words like *better* is about 78 per cent. When June was planning the cleaner's holiday for her, June shifted from her normal 26 per cent of [d] pronunciations to over 60 per cent. In other words, she went over halfway towards the cleaner's speech style. It is June's job to get on well with her clients and encourage them to book with her firm. Accommodating to their speech style is one way she signals her desire to get on well with them and make them feel comfortable.

There are many other examples of responsive shifts of this kind in the way a person speaks. Some of the most interesting from a social dialectologist's point of view are those which show how people's speech changes in response to the interviewer's speech. I noted in chapter 7 that the speech data collected in social dialect surveys is inevitably influenced by the addressee's speech style. An American study demonstrated that features of AAVE occurred more frequently in an interviewee's speech when she was interviewed by an African-American as opposed to a white female fieldworker. On the other hand Peter Trudgill, interviewing people in his home town, Norwich, found that his own speech shifted towards that of the people he was interviewing. In different interviews, the number of glottal stops he used instead of [t] in words like *better* and *bet* reflected very accurately indeed the level of glottal stop usage in the speech of his interviewee. Interviewing a lower-class person who used 100 per cent glottal stops in these contexts, for instance, Peter Trudgill used glottal stops in 98 per cent of the possible contexts. But when he was interviewing a person from a higher social group whose glottal stop level was only 25 per cent, his own level dropped to just over 30 per cent. This is pretty clear evidence that the interviewer was accommodating his speech to the speech of interviewees from different social backgrounds. Most people do this to a greater or lesser extent in different contexts. In the next section we will look at some of the reasons which have been proposed for this speech behaviour.

C

Language variation: focus on uses

ACCOMMODATION THEORY

Speech convergence

The examples in the previous section have demonstrated that when people talk to each other their speech often becomes more similar. In other words, each person's speech converges towards the speech of the person they are talking to. This process is called *speech accommodation*. It tends to happen when the speakers like one another, or where one speaker has a vested interest in pleasing the other or putting them at ease. So the travel agent wanted to gain her customers' orders, and the interviewer wanted to gain his interviewee's cooperation.

Converging towards the speech of another person is usually considered a polite speech strategy. It implies that the addressee's speech is acceptable and worth imitating. Using the same pronunciation and the same sort of vocabulary, for instance, is a way of signalling that you are on the same wavelength.

Exercise 5

There are many different ways in which a person may accommodate to the speech of another. Make a list of as many features as you can think of.

Answer at end of chapter

How do speakers accommodate?

At a party when you respond to and develop a topic introduced by your addressee, you are converging in the content of your speech. When people simplify their vocabulary and grammar in talking to foreigners or children, they are converging downwards towards the lesser linguistic proficiency of their addressees. When a complicated technical message is 'translated' for the benefit of someone who does not know the jargon, speech accommodation is involved. When, in an interview with the hospital matron, a nurse adopts some of the matron's pronunciation features, she is converging upwards in her speech.

In multilingual countries, such as Singapore, India or Zaire, with many varieties to choose from, people may accommodate to others by selecting the code or variety that is most comfortable for their addressees. In the market-place people sometimes accommodate to the language of the person selling goods in order to secure goodwill and, hopefully, a good bargain. Conversely, in a bilingual city like Montreal, French Canadians in cafés and stores often use English to customers that they identify as English speakers in order to improve their chances of a good sale.

Exercise 6

Look at the examples provided above on the influence of the addressee on a person's speech style. Can you identify two clear examples of upward convergence and two examples of downward convergence? Treat 'upward convergence' for the purposes of this exercise as referring to convergence towards the speech of someone with more power or status, or someone deserving respect in the context. Treat 'downward convergence' as referring to convergence towards the speech of someone with less status or power. In order to answer this with accuracy you ideally need some idea of the baseline or 'normal' style of each participant in a particular context – a somewhat debatable concept and one that is difficult to define. Nevertheless, it is possible to make some reasonable deductions about upward and downward convergence from the information provided.

Answers at end of chapter

Speech divergence

Example 8

A number of people who were learning Welsh were asked to help with a survey. In their separate booths in the language laboratory, they were asked a number of questions by an RP-sounding English speaker. At one point this speaker arrogantly challenged the learners' reasons for trying to acquire Welsh which he called a 'dying language which had a dismal future'. In responding to this statement the learners generally broadened their Welsh accents. Some introduced Welsh words into their answers, while others used an aggressive tone. One woman did not reply for a while, and then she was heard conjugating Welsh verbs very gently into the microphone.

Though the situation in which this example occurred – a language laboratory – is somewhat artificial, it provides a very clear example of speech divergence. For obvious reasons, the respondents deliberately diverged from the speech style, and even the language, of the person addressing them. They disagreed with his sentiments and had no desire to accommodate to his speech.

Deliberately choosing a language not used by one's addressee is the clearest example of speech divergence. When the Arab nations issued an oil communiqué to the world not in English, but in Arabic, they were making a clear political statement. They no longer wished to be seen as accommodating to the Western English-speaking powers. Similarly, minority ethnic groups who want to maintain and display their cultural distinctiveness will often use their own linguistic variety, even, and sometimes especially, in interaction with majority group members. Maori dissidents who can speak fluent

English have nevertheless insisted on using Maori in court, making it necessary to use an interpreter. Giving a speech in a minority language to an audience made up largely of majority group monolinguals is another example of linguistically divergent behaviour. This, too, has sometimes been done to make a political point.

Accent divergence also occurs. In New Zealand, working-class men often respond to the university-educated students who join them just for the summer on the docks, in factories, or in the shearing sheds, by increasing their swearing and using a higher frequency of vernacular forms. On the other hand, people who aspire to a higher social status will diverge upwards from the speech of those from the same social class. In Liverpool, for example, teachers in some schools pronounce words like *bath* and *grass* with a back vowel more typical of southern than northern accents. So they say [ba:θ] and [gra:s] which distinguishes them from their pupils and many of their pupils' parents, who say [baθ] and [gras]. And that is often precisely the point of divergent pronunciations: they may signal the speakers' wish to distinguish themselves from their addressees.

Speech divergence does not always indicate a speaker's negative attitudes towards the addressees. Where the divergent forms are admired, divergence can be used to benefit the diverger. A small difference, such as a slight foreign accent (provided it is one which is viewed favourably), can be appealing. Brigitte Bardot and Maurice Chevalier exploited their French accents in speaking English to add to their appeal. Victor Borge's Danish nationality and accent were both well-integrated into his comedy performance to positive effect. A foreigner can also elicit help by using an accent or vocabulary which signals inadequate control of the language. If a foreign visitor sounds too much like a native speaker it may work to their disadvantage, and even arouse suspicions. An English Canadian who was fluently bilingual in French and English aroused considerable hostility when a French-speaking group he was talking with realised he could speak perfect English too. He reported that they treated him as if he was a spy. Perfect convergence has its costs.

Speakers may also deliberately diverge both from their own usual speech style and from that of their addressee(s) towards the style of a third party for special effect. This has been labelled *referee design* – the third party is 'referred to' although they are not present. People initiate such stylistic shifts for a range of reasons. When you imitate your teacher to amuse your friends, or when you adopt a prestige accent to impress your boss, you are engaging in referee design. Television adverts sometimes include accents which are not those of their audience for special effects such as humour, or to borrow the accent's prestige in order to enhance the attractiveness of the product being promoted. In New Zealand, a Scottish or North of England accent is sometimes used to exploit the stereotype of the honest and straightforward bloke whose word can be trusted. New Zealand and Australian singers similarly draw on referee design when they adopt features of overseas singers' styles, such as American post-vocalic (r), or Cockney glottal stops. Presumably they believe this will enhance the appeal of their song for their audience, and hence boost their sales. In England, young white English teenagers sometimes adopt features of Indian or Panjabi English speech, or even AAVE, 'crossing' over into the other group momentarily for special stylistic effect – to identify with their music or alternatively to mock and distance themselves from the group. Like metaphorical code-switching, with which it has much in common, referee design allows the speaker to exploit the symbolic function of language, and allude in an economical way to more than one set of values.

■ Accommodation problems

Example 9

Father: What's this? (pointing to picture)
Jo: [maus] (i.e. mouth)
Father: [maus] eh.
Jo: No daddy not say [maus], daddy say [mauθ] (i.e. daddy doesn't say [maus], daddy says [mauθ]).

It is possible to overdo convergence and offend listeners. Over-convergent behaviour may be perceived as patronising and ingratiating, as sycophantic, or even as evidence that the speaker is making fun of others. We look for possible reasons for changes in other people's speech. If the reasons appear manipulative, we are less likely to feel positive about convergence.

Listeners also react differently to different types of convergence. A Canadian speaker was more favourably rated when he accommodated in speech rate and content (by explaining unfamiliar American terms), than when he adopted a 'mild' RP accent as well. Accent accommodation was seen as going too far. People seemed to feel that by altering his accent the speaker was misleading his listeners about his 'true' identity.

In general, then, reactions to speech convergence and divergence depend on the reasons people attribute for the convergence or divergence. If divergence is perceived as unavoidable, for instance, then the reaction will be more tolerant than when it is considered deliberate. Deliberate divergence will be heard as uncooperative or antagonistic. Someone who uses English in Montreal because their French is clearly inadequate will be perceived more sympathetically than someone who, though a fluent bilingual, deliberately chooses to use English to Francophones.

Exercise 7

It has been suggested that when women and men are talking to each other, women tend to converge more than men. Is this claim consistent with the discussion of differences in women's and men's linguistic behaviour in chapter 7?

Answer at end of chapter

Example 10

Grant: The next thing he had an apoplectic fit. I didn't know what to do.
Brian: I think you have to make sure they don't swallow their tongues.

Should Brian correct Grant's use of *apoplectic* and point out he really means *epileptic*? When people come from different backgrounds or have different experiences this may cause occasional problems. When someone mispronounces a word in a conversation with you, for instance, how do you react? What if you then have to use the word yourself? Do you converge and mispronounce it too, or do you diverge and pronounce it the way you know it ought to be pronounced? An accurate interpretation of a person's speech behaviour in such cases obviously involves considering more than just the influence of the addressee. The best way of solving an accommodation problem will depend on the context. The speech accommodation or style shifting which often occurs unconsciously in casual contexts may not be appropriate in more formal settings, as we shall see in the next section, though an ingenious sociolinguist can often elicit remarkable style-shifts, even within an interview.

CONTEXT, STYLE AND CLASS

Formal contexts and social roles

Example 11

Yesterday in the Wellington District Court . . . the All Black captain, Jock Hobbs, appeared as duty solicitor. Presiding was his father, Judge M. F. Hobbs.

Etiquette required Mr Hobbs to address his father as Your Honour, or Sir, and the Bench had to address counsel as Mr Hobbs . . .

[Mr Hobbs] could not remember the last time he had to call his father Sir . . . Said the father to son, when the son announced his appearance on all matters as duty solicitor: 'I appreciate the difficulties you are labouring under, Mr Hobbs.'

Although a powerful influence on choice of style, characteristics of the addressee are not the only relevant factors. In example 3 in chapter 1, the way the businesswoman was addressed was determined largely by the relationship between the woman and her addressee in terms of relative status and solidarity. People who were very close to her used a short form of her first name (*Meg*), or an endearment. People who were less close and socially subordinate used her title and last name (*Mrs Walker*). In example 11, however, the choice of appropriate form is influenced not by the personal relationship between the participants, but by the formality of the context and their relative roles and statuses within that setting.

A law court is a formal setting where the social roles of participants override their personal relationship in determining the appropriate linguistic forms. In classrooms where a child's mother or father is the teacher, the same pattern is usually found. Children call their parents *Mrs Grady* or *Mr Davis* rather than *Mum* or *Dad*. A Catholic priest will be addressed as *Father* even by his own father during a religious ceremony. People's roles in these formal contexts determine the appropriate speech forms. Example 12 illustrates the way vocabulary varies with setting.

Example 12

Judge: I see the cops say you were pickled last night and were driving an old jalopy down the middle of the road. True?

Defendant: Your honour, if I might be permitted to address this allegation, I should like to report that I was neither inebriated nor under the influence of an alcoholic beverage of any kind.

The formal and Latinate vocabulary used by the defendant and appropriate to very formal settings – *inebriated, alcoholic beverage,* and *allegation* – contrasts for humorous effect with the inappropriately informal vocabulary used by the judge. Words such as *pickled* and *jalopy* are normally heard in much more casual contexts.

Different styles within an interview

Example 13

(a) Reading passage

There's some*th*ing strange about *that* – how I can remember every*th*ing he did: *th*is *th*ing, *th*at *th*ing, and *th*e o*th*er *th*ing. He used to carry *th*ree newspapers in his mou*th* at *th*e same time. I suppose it's *th*e same *th*ing wi*th* most of us: your first dog is like your first girl. She's more trouble *th*an she's wor*th*, but you can't seem to forget her.

(b) Minimal pairs

tin	thin
den	then
beer	bear
pin	pen

Language variation: focus on uses

In an interview between two strangers we would expect the interviewee to use a relatively careful style of speech, as discussed in chapter 7. In a social dialect survey in New York, William Labov demonstrated some ingenuity in devising ways of overriding this 'stranger effect' to elicit a wider range of styles within the interview context.

He asked his interviewees to read aloud a passage of continuous speech and a set of word lists, one of which included words such as *pin* and *pen* (called 'minimal pairs') which differed only on one pronunciation feature. Example 13 illustrates the kinds of reading material used. Both these styles were very much more carefully monitored than the speaker's 'normal' interview style. As a result the number of instances of standard variants used in these styles was considerably higher than in the careful interview style, or, to put it another way, speakers used fewer vernacular forms in these styles. One speaker, Tom, for instance, used 2 per cent vernacular forms in reading minimal pairs, 30 per cent in reading a passage, and 65 per cent vernacular forms in interview style.

The basis for the distinctions between the styles was the amount of attention people were paying to their speech. In a situation which involved two strangers, an interview schedule of questions to be answered, and a tape recorder as another member of the audience, it was relatively easy to elicit more formal styles.

Eliciting a more casual style was more of a challenge. Labov refers to a person's most relaxed style as the vernacular (using a definition of this term which was foreshadowed in chapter 4). He describes the vernacular as the style in which the minimum of attention is given to the monitoring of speech. In this sense the vernacular is a person's most basic style – the style which, if it can be captured, provides the sociolinguist with the most systematic and therefore most valuable data for analysis. In some ways it has come to represent a kind of holy grail in social dialectology.

Trying to capture this style on tape involves *the observer's paradox*, i.e. trying to capture on tape the way a person speaks when they are not being observed. This is always a methodological challenge and researchers have used a range of strategies to distract people from concentrating on their own speech. In order to elicit this style, Labov skilfully manipulated the topic of discussion within the interview. By asking questions which grabbed people's attention he managed to shift them to a less careful speech style. When people were emotionally involved in the story they were telling, they were not so aware of other factors (such as the unfamiliar interviewer and the tape recorder) which favoured a more formal style.

There has been a great deal of debate about the relationship of this style to others. While it seems unlikely that it is identical to the most relaxed style used between peers and intimates in casual contexts, it is certainly distinguishable from the more formal styles identified in the interview context. People consistently used more vernacular features in describing situations where they had been in danger of death, or recounting the details of fights they had seen, than when reading aloud or talking on more conventional topics.

Exercise 8

You should note the many ways in which the term *vernacular* is used in sociolinguistics. Go back to chapter 4 (page 75) and chapter 6 (page 138) and read the definitions provided there. Are they compatible with the way the term is used in the section above? Do these various uses have anything in common?

Answer at end of chapter

Colloquial style or the vernacular

There are other strategies besides topic manipulation which have been used in order to capture people's most relaxed or vernacular speech style. Taping groups of people rather than individuals, for instance, and choosing a very comfortable or informal setting are strategies which have been found to shift people's speech towards the vernacular. One social dialectologist collected her data from adolescents in vacant lots and adventure playgrounds, and she taped them in groups of two or three. Another taped groups of friends yarning in each other's kitchens. And Labov himself in a later study used African American interviewers to collect data from African American adolescents, generally in groups on the streets where they met. Both increasing the number of participants, and choosing a very casual setting contributed to obtaining more relaxed speech. The following examples of the vernacular were recorded in a family living-room. The person making the recording was a linguist, but also a family member.

Example 14

Trevor is recounting a dispute over tree-felling rights on a patch of leased bushland.

Trev: . . . but Frazer and we had a bloody row over some wood . . . We was up there cuttin' and Frazer come on to us you see . . . 'Oh well', 'e said, 'I suppose you can 'ave 'im [a tree].' But we already 'ad 'im, all bar a few pieces, cut up and loaded, and Frazer said 'I suppose you can have 'im,' he said, 'Yeah, but don't touch that one over there.' But we'd been passing him with the axe and 'e was only a bit of – bloody – papery – shell 'e wasn't –

Dave: 'E wasn't worth it.

Trev: No. That's why we left 'im. We'd had 'im.

This is an excerpt from one of many anecdotes about country life recounted to a small group of family and friends in the home of the speakers. Telling stories of this kind based on personal experience is a regular pastime in the speaker's small rural community in north-east Tasmania, an island off the Australian mainland. The speaker's casual style

C

Language variation: focus on uses

has a number of linguistic features, many of which also occur in informal styles of English in other English-speaking communities.

There are many such features which distinguish colloquial from more formal styles of English. Two further examples which can be found in the English of widely different regions of the world are the use of *me* (for formal *my*), e.g. *then me mate arrives*, and the use of *them* (instead of *those*) as a determiner: *there's a cross-piece in them old-fashioned doors.*

One particularly interesting feature noted in the Tasmanian informal narratives is the use of animation for objects. Note, for instance, the use of *he* to refer to the tree in example 14, and the use of *she* to refer to the axe in example 15 below. It has been suggested that *she* is often used to refer to animals or inanimate objects which are the centre of attention in the story being told. The same feature has been noted in rural, colloquial conversation in New Zealand: e.g. *she's a hard road, she was a real beauty that storm.*

Example 15

Old Kit . . . 'e had the only chopping axe John B. had. Nobody 'ad two them days y' know, in the bad old days, and John 'ad a pretty good axe . . . they got Kit entered in this Chop y' know . . . 'e was off say three or five or whatever. When they said 'Five!' 'e's no sooner [. . .] than 'e hit 'er [the block], y'know, and 'e chopped two or three six-inch nails clean off . . . 'e dug himself in too low, y' see, and 'e fetches 'er [the axe] and 'e looks at 'er, y' see . . . and 'e holds 'er round to John, and 'e's got a great big gap clean through the face of 'er, and 'e said 'CRIPES!' Hahaha! when he turned – when 'e showed it to John.

This pattern of animating objects and assigning them a gender in casual narratives has been noted in the colloquial speech of rural New Zealand men too. It is possible that calling objects *she* or *he* is characteristic only of the colloquial narratives of men, but we have no comparable data on female narratives so we can't be sure. Nor is it clear whether this feature occurs in the colloquial English of other regions. Have you heard people use it in your region?

▉ The interaction of social class and style

> **Example 16**
>
> Elizabeth's 9-year-old daughter, Lily, took a phone message for her. It read 'arriving Tuesday at 10'. 'Who was it?' she asked but Lily didn't know. 'It was a man and he sounded like a teacher' was all the information Lily could provide. Elizabeth reviewed the possibilities without any inspiration, and began to worry a little about how to cater for this unexpected guest. In the event the caller phoned again on Tuesday morning. It was the glazier who had promised to ring before arriving to put in a new window. He didn't sound at all like a teacher in his conversation with Elizabeth. She concluded that it was his careful style while dictating his message to Lily which had misled her daughter.

When we combine information about the way people from different social groups speak with information about the way people speak in different contexts, it is clear that features of social class and contextual style interact. Figure 10.2 illustrates the relationship between social class, style and linguistic variation. The structured hierarchy of the Norwich social classes is reflected in each of the distinct lines drawn on the diagram. Group 4 at the top of the graph is the lowest social group and uses the highest proportion of vernacular [in] pronunciation. Going down the graph, each social group uses fewer vernacular [in] pronunciations than the one above and more than the one below, and so the lines are clearly distinguishable. The diagram also shows that the more formal the style, the fewer vernacular [in] pronunciations (or the more standard [iŋ] pronunciations) occur.

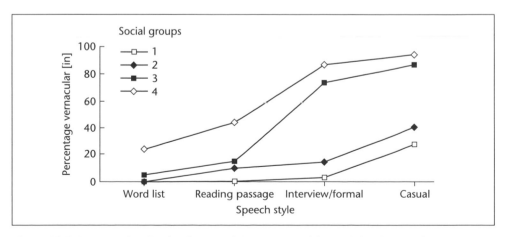

Figure 10.2 Vernacular [in] for four social groups and four styles in Norwich
Source: This diagram was modified from one in Trudgill, 1974: 92. Reproduced with permission

Language variation: focus on uses

A low frequency of vernacular [in] pronunciations or a higher frequency of standard [iŋ] pronunciations may therefore signal that the speaker belongs to a high social class, or indicate that they are speaking in a more formal context, or both. This interaction between social group membership and style seems to be very widespread. If a linguistic feature is found to occur frequently in the speech of people from lower social groups, it will often be frequent in the casual speech of those from higher social groups too. In other words, the same linguistic feature often distinguishes between speakers socially (inter-speaker variation), while within the speech of one person it distinguishes different styles (intra-speaker variation). Example 16 illustrates the effect that this overlap and interaction between stylistic features and social group features can have. As Labov has said, it may be difficult with any particular linguistic feature to distinguish 'a casual salesman from a careful pipefitter'.

Generally this two-pronged pattern involving social group and style is quite regular. The speech of each social group remains in the same relationship to other groups whatever the style. So, as figure 10.2 shows, in every style, social group 4 uses more vernacular [in] pronunciations than every other group. In fact it has been suggested that the stylistic variation derives from and echoes the variation between speakers from different social groups. When you want to shift style, the obvious way to vary your speech is to imitate the speech of another person. Often this is in response to the presence of people from the other group in the situation. In order to sound more casual, for instance, in the pub or at a party, people model their speech on that of a lower social group. In order to sound more formal in an interview or giving a formal speech, they use people from a higher or more sophisticated social group as their speech models. So when they shift styles, people often adopt the linguistic features of a different group. And, in general, the lower social groups shift their speech more as they move from one style to another than the higher social groups do – as figure 10.2 illustrates.

Hypercorrection

Example 17

I remember where he was run over, not far from our corner. He darted out about four feet before a car and he got hit hard. We didn't have the heart to play ball or cards all morning. We didn't know we cared so much for him till he was hurt.

Example 17 is another of the reading passages used by Labov in his study of New York City speech. You can doubtless guess the variable it was designed to elicit. The results for the distribution of this variable – post-vocalic [r] – over five speech styles for four social groups is probably the most widely reproduced diagram from Labov's research: see figure 10.3. The reason for its popularity is no doubt the fact that it illustrates so many fascinating points about the relationships between language use, social group membership, and style.

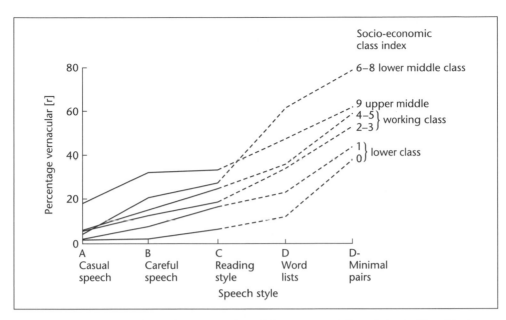

Figure 10.3 Post-vocalic [r] for range of social groups and five styles in New York
Source: From Labov, 1966: 160. Reproduced with permission

First of all, the diagram provides another example of the patterned relationships between social group and linguistic variation discussed in chapter 6. The structured hierarchy of New York social classes is reflected in each of the distinct lines drawn on the diagram. In fact, Labov comments that [r] is such a sensitive sociolinguistic variable that he could have drawn as many lines as he could distinguish social groups. Because it is a prestige variable which is spreading through the community, it stratifies the New York community very accurately and finely.

The diagram also illustrates variation in speech style. People's pronunciation of post-vocalic [r] increases as they pay more attention to their speech. Within reading style, this diagram identifies the two further degrees of formality that Labov distinguished. These involved two types of word lists, the most formal being a list of minimal pairs where the variants under study were the explicit focus of attention: e.g. *beer/bear*, *tin/thin*, *then/den*, and, in the case of *r*, *god/guard*, *pa/par*.

So post-vocalic [r] pronunciation is a very sensitive marker of class and of style in New York. Overall, the higher the social class you belong to, the more post-vocalic [r] you pronounce, and the more formal the context, the more often you pronounce post-vocalic [r] regardless of your social class.

There is an exception to this generalisation, however. The third interesting point the diagram illustrates is the tendency of group 2, the lower middle class (LMC), to pronounce [r] even more often than group 1, the upper middle class (UMC) in the two most formal styles. LMC speakers out-perform UMC speakers when they are reading

Language variation: focus on uses

isolated words. This is hypercorrect behaviour – the LMC are overdoing it. UMC speakers serve as a model for the LMC, but in the styles where they can most easily monitor their speech, the LMC go beyond the UMC norms to produce a style which can be described, perhaps somewhat ironically, as 'more correct' than the standard – 'hypercorrect' speech. Some have called it 'super-standard'.

Hypercorrect usage goes beyond the norm; it involves extending a form beyond the standard. The use of *I* rather than *me* in constructions such as *between you and I* illustrates structural hypercorrection. So does *he asked for you and I*. These examples of hypercorrect behaviour result from the insecurity introduced by Latin-based English grammars. *I* is over-extended from contexts such as *It was I who rang you last night* where one could argue it is formally and technically 'correct' (though pompous!), to contexts which appear similar but are in fact grammatically different.

Exercise 10

Comment on the following letter to the Editor. What does it suggest the speaker considers the formal, standard or correct form, and which the vernacular or casual form in the phrase *for you or I/me*?

King George VI wrote to Churchill 'It would be wrong for either you or I to be there', but I am sure that chatting over the port at Sandringham, he would have said 'for you or me' – like the most rough-hewn of us.

Answer at end of chapter

Though the pattern of interaction I have described between social group (or inter-speaker) variation and style (or intra-speaker) variation seems to be very widespread, it is not universal. In some communities, such as Tyneside, and in the town of Rades in Tunis, speakers signal stylistic and social group differences using distinct linguistic variables. In other words the linguistic features that signal their group membership are quite different from the linguistic features which reflect the kind of context in which they are speaking. In English this pattern can be found when we turn to examine the features of particular registers – the language associated with particular contexts such as finance or science, music, the law, or horse-racing. The stylistic features which identify these ways of speaking are generally distinct from social class variables, as we will see in the final section. First, however, now that we have discussed style in English, let's turn to some different languages. I will briefly consider how distinct speech styles are expressed in non-Western societies. Do all languages use the same features to signal social group membership as those used to signal different social contexts? Or are the linguistic features which mark social group membership and style quite distinct?

STYLE IN NON-WESTERN SOCIETIES

> **Example 18**
>
> When he first visited Tokyo, Neil found his Japanese was fine for reading and for talking to other young men of his own age, but in any other interactions he found himself floundering. He knew that he needed to express the appropriate degree of respect to his hosts, and to the various business contacts he was introduced to. Yet his control of the complex system of Japanese styles and honorifics was not yet good enough. He simply struggled along in a 'basic' or 'plain' style, frustrated that the subtleties of Japanese interpersonal interaction were beyond him.

Japanese is one of a number of languages with a special set of grammatical contrasts for expressing politeness and respect for others. Before deciding which style of Japanese to use, Japanese speakers assess their status in relation to their addressees on the basis of such factors as family background, gender, and age (and even one day's age difference can be important), as well as the formality of the context. They then select from plain, polite and deferential styles. The choice of appropriate style involves consideration of a range of word forms and syntax. The appropriate form of the verb, for instance, varies in different styles.

> **Example 19**
>
> (a) Sakai-ga   watashi ni chizu-o   kai- te-   kure- ta
> **Sakai-Subject me   for map-Object draw gerund-plain past
>   marker   marker   form tense**
> 'Sakai drew a map for me.'
> (b) Sakai-senpai- ga   watashi ni chizu-o
> **Sakai-respect Sub   me   for map-Obj
>   form   marker   marker**
> kai-te   kure-mashi-ta.
> **draw-gerund   polite-past tense
>   form**
> 'Mr Sakai drew a map for me.'

The basic straightforward non-deferential utterance represented by (a) contrasts with the politer style used in (b) where the polite verb ending -*mashi* is added to the verb.

Language variation: focus on uses

C

Utterances can also be modified in a variety of ways according to the attitude and rela-tionship of the speaker to the subject matter of the utterance. In (b) the speaker uses the respect form (or honorific) -*senpai* (appropriate to older colleagues) to express respect for the person mentioned. In addition to these morphological means, there are also other strategies for increasing the politeness of one's style, such as using negative construction (analogous to English *wouldn't you like to . . .*), using longer sentences, avoiding dialect words and using Chinese loan words.

Knowledge of the complexities of stylistic variation in countries like Japan and Korea reflects a person's educational level and social status. Better-educated people have greater control of the various styles. So the social status of a speaker can be deduced from the skill with which they select and use the various styles of Japanese or Korean.

Although the Islamic revolution has increased the use of reciprocal forms of address, ritual courtesy is still very important in Iranian society too. Relative status must be carefully assessed on every occasion in order to select the correct combina-tion of grammatical forms, vocabulary items and pronunciation – in other words the appropriate style for the context and the addressee. Expressing deference in Tehran Persian involves choosing from clusters of particular verb forms, as well as carefully selecting the appropriate high, neutral, or low alternative from twenty-four personal pronoun forms.

Here, too, context is a relevant factor and Iranian reading styles, in particular, con-trast dramatically with other styles of speech. In all social groups, there is a dramatic increase in the percentage of standard variants in people's reading and word-list styles, compared to their careful and casual styles. For at least some linguistic features, then, this society marks speech style differently from social group membership. The choice between the vernacular and standard variants of some sounds reflects the social context in which a person is speaking, independently of their social group membership. In these cases, the standard variants mark reading style rather than social group membership. In other communities, too, reading style contrasts markedly with other styles. Where reading aloud is not a common activity, it may be best measured along a different dimension than that of formality.

Javanese is another example which illustrates the complexity of stylistic variation which can be found in languages. As mentioned in chapter 6, the choices facing a speaker of Javanese involve two ranked social dialects, within each of which there are three stylistic levels. In other words, both social group membership and social con-text influence a speaker's linguistic choices. In addition there is also the possibility of raising any utterance an additional 'half-level' by various linguistic means. Each level involves different pronunciations, different grammatical forms, and different items of vocabulary. There are three words for 'house', for example, *omah*, *grija* and *dalem*, and five forms for 'you'. Once you have selected the appropriate stylistic level, you must follow the rules for which forms may occur with which. You cannot jump around between levels.

Example 20

Menapa	nandalem	mundhut	sekul	semanten?	3a	HIGH
Menapa	panjenengan	mendhet	sekul	semanten?	3	
Napa	sampéyan	mendhet	sekul	semonten?	2	
Napa	sampéyan	njupuk	sega	semonten?	1a	
Apa	sliramu	mundhut	sega	semono?	1b	
Apa	kowé	njupuk	sega	semono?	1	LOW
QUESTION MARKER	YOU	TAKE	RICE	THAT MUCH		

Did you take that much rice?

The sentences in this example are ordered from the most formal 'high' style (level 3a, known as *krama inggil*) to the least formal 'low' style (level 1, known as *ngoko*). Though there is a great deal of overlap – especially between half-levels – every sentence is different from each of the others, and not a single word-form is common to all of them.

Selecting the appropriate 'level' of Javanese for a particular interaction involves, as elsewhere, taking account of your relationship to the addressee in context. As elsewhere, too, solidarity (or degree of friendship) and relative status (determined by such factors as age, wealth, descent, education, and occupation) are important in assessing the relationship. The result may be that each of the participants selects a different level of Javanese. If I am an ordinary educated citizen speaking to a high government official, I will use the highest level 3a to express respect, but the official will use only level 1, *ngoko*, to me. Two very high status Javanese, on the other hand, will both use level 3 to each other. Faced with this array of levels and the social consequences of a wrong choice – insult or embarrassment, for instance – one can readily understand the popularity of Indonesian, the national language. In a society where social divisions are not so clear as they once were, Indonesian offers much simpler stylistic alternatives.

Javanese provides a graphic example of a language where the stylistic choices are much more clear-cut than in English, i.e. the co-occurrence rules can be explicitly specified. The discussion of diglossia and situational code-switching in chapter 2 provided further examples of linguistic variation motivated by contextual features. In its narrow definition, diglossia involves two distinct styles or varieties of a language – a High variety and a Low variety, distinguished by features of pronunciation, grammar and vocabulary, and appropriately used in different contexts. The broader definition of diglossia adopted by some sociolinguists includes situational switching between dialects of a language, such as a regional dialect and a standard language, or even between distinct languages. So the shift by Norwegian students from Ranamål in their village homes to standard Norwegian with less regionally marked pronunciation when

C

Language variation: focus on uses

at university is a style shift motivated by features of the context – addressee, topic and setting. Similarly, the switch from Greek at home to English at university by Maria, a linguistics student at La Trobe university in Melbourne, can equally be regarded as an example of a style switch. Situational code switching and diglossia are therefore further examples of the effect of contextual factors on linguistic behaviour.

I have illustrated that linguistic features which signal social group membership are often, but not always, signals of contextual variation too. A high level of education and familiarity with using language in more formal contexts frequently go hand-in-hand, and so it is scarcely surprising that the features which characterise each tend to overlap. However, particular pronunciations, syntactic constructions or vocabulary items may simply indicate a person's social group without also patterning for style. Conversely, linguistic features may serve primarily as markers of particular social contexts rather than particular groups. This pattern is illustrated in the final section on register differences.

Exercise 11

Is the choice between *tu* and *vous* in French (or equivalent pronouns in other languages that you are familiar with) an example of a choice between different styles? Identify the factors discussed in this chapter which may be relevant in choosing the appropriate pronoun.

Answer at end of chapter

Exercise 12

Identify the contexts in which you would expect to see or hear the following, and one feature of each which served as a linguistic clue.

(a) NO NUKES
(b) Who's a lovely little girl then eh? Who's a lovely little girl?
(c) Where any registered security interest is discharged, the person entered in the register as the secured party shall, within 10 working days of the date on which the security interest is discharged, apply to . . .
(d) txt 4 lift   b gr8 2 c u
(e) I have no desire to be a party to this on-going useless debate. I therefore wish to UNSUBSCRIBE from this list.

Answers at end of chapter

REGISTER

Example 21

In our gerontological sociolinguistic context, we would argue that when, in inter-generational encounters, contextual features trigger an elderly (or even 'aged') identity in people, they will assume communicative strategies they believe to be associated with older speakers.

This is an example of the kind of jargon which a group of specialists often develop to talk about their speciality. It could be described as an occupational style. I have used the term 'style' in earlier sections to refer to language variation which reflects changes in situational factors, such as addressee, setting, task or topic. Some linguists describe this kind of language variation as 'register' variation. Others use the term 'register' more narrowly to describe the specific vocabulary associated with different occupational groups. The distinction is not always clear, however, and many sociolinguists simply ignore it.

Styles are often analysed along a scale of formality, as in the examples from social dialect research discussed above. Registers, on the other hand, when they are distinguished from styles, tend to be associated with particular groups of people or sometimes specific situations of use. Journalese, baby-talk, legalese, the language of auctioneers, race-callers, and sports commentators, the language of airline pilots, criminals, financiers, politicians and disc jockeys, the language of the courtroom and the classroom, could all be considered examples of different registers. The term 'register' here describes the language of groups of people with common interests or jobs, or the language used in situations associated with such groups.

I will discuss just one example – sports announcer talk – to illustrate the kind of linguistic features which may distinguish different registers.

Sports announcer talk

Example 22

Cooley – steaming in now, – bowls to Waugh again, – stroking it out into the covers, – just thinking about a single, – Tucker taking a few ah stuttering steps down the wicket from the bowler's end but Waugh sending him back.

['–' marks a short pause, commas indicate non-final intonation contour.]

When people describe a sporting event, the language they use is quite clearly distinguishable from language used in other contexts. The most obvious distinguishing feature is generally the vocabulary. Terms like *silly mid on*, *square leg*, *the covers*, and *gully*, for instance, to describe positions, and *off-break*, *googly* and *leg break* to describe deliveries, are examples of vocabulary peculiar to cricket. But the grammar is equally distinctive. This is especially true of the kind of sports announcer talk which is known as 'play-by-play' description.

Play-by-play description focusses on the action, as opposed to 'colour commentary' which refers to the more discursive and leisurely speech with which commentators fill in the often quite long spaces between spurts of action. Play-by-play description is characterised by telegraphic grammar. This involves features such as syntactic reduction and the inversion of normal word order in sentences. Each feature contributes to the announcer's aim of communicating the drama of the moment. In colour commentary, by contrast, where there is more time, nouns tend to be heavily modified. In both types of commentary, as well as in the 'state of the play' score or summary, sports announcers make extensive use of linguistic formulas and routines. I will illustrate each of these features in turn.

Syntactic reduction

Example 23

From baseball or cricket commentaries.

(a) [It] bounced to second base
(b) [It's] a breaking ball outside
(c) [He's a] guy who's a pressure player
(d) McCatty [is] in difficulty
(e) Tucker [is] taking a few ah stuttering steps down the wicket from the bowler's end but Waugh [is] sending him back

---

While describing the action they are observing, sports announcers often omit the subject noun or pronoun, as in (a), and frequently omit the verb *be* as well, as utterances (b) and (c) illustrate. Utterances (d) and (e) omit only *be*. There is no loss of meaning as a result of this syntactic reduction, since the omitted elements are totally predictable in the context. The referent is unambiguous – in (a) *it* refers to the hit, and in (b) *it* could not refer to anything other than the bowler's pitch.

Syntactic inversion

Example 24

From baseball or cricket commentaries.

(a) In comes Ghouri
(b) And all set again is Pat Haden
(c) On deck is big Dave Winfield
(d) Pete goes to right field and back for it goes Jackson

Reversal or inversion of the normal word order is another feature of sports announcer talk. This device allows the announcer to foreground or focus on the action and provides him or her (but almost universally him in fact) with time to identify the subject of the action – an important piece of information for listeners.

Heavy noun modification

Example 25

From baseball or cricket commentaries.

(a) David Winfield, the 25-million-dollar man, who is hitting zero, five, six in this World Series . . .
(b) First-base umpire Larry Barnett . . .
(c) This much sought-after and very expensive fast bowler . . .

People rather than action are the focus of interest at certain points during the sports announcer's spiel. When this is the case, the subject nouns which are the focus of interest are often heavily modified both after the noun as in (a), and before the noun as in (b) and (c).

These examples are taken from cricket and baseball commentary, but similar sorts of features characterise commentaries in other sports, including soccer and rugby.

Exercise 13

Classify the following utterances from an English soccer match commentary according to which of the three syntactic features identified above they illustrate:

(a) and here's Clark, the new Chelsea skipper and a player worth every penny they paid for him . . .
(b) Dickens a marvellous through-ball
(c) combining well the two defenders
(d) pitch very slippery
(e) looking for a hat-trick remember Rush

Answers at end of chapter

Exercise 14

Tape-record a commentary from your favourite team sport and see if any of the features identified above occur. Are there any other features in your data which you consider distinguish sports commentary from everyday chat?

Routines and formulas

An interesting feature of sports commentaries, including race calling (the commentary accompanying a horse race), is the use of routines to reduce the memory burden on the speaker. The same feature has been identified in other situations where the memory burden from information which must be simultaneously processed and communicated is potentially very high, such as livestock auctions in New Zealand, tobacco auctions in the United States, and North American ice hockey commentaries. These registers are all characterised by the extensive use of oral formulas. The formulas involve a small number of fixed syntactic patterns and a narrow range of lexical items.

The following excerpts come from a race commentary by Reon Murtha, a Christchurch race commentator. He is commentating on a 2000-metre heat for the Lion Brown Championship.

Example 26

(a) a little wider on the track the favourite Race Ruler
    Twilight Time is in behind those
    Breaking up behind is Noodlum's Fella
    and he went down
    and one tipped out was My Dalrae . . .
(b) El Red the leader by two lengths from Speedy Cheval
    the favourite Race Ruler parked on the outside
    followed by Florlis Fella
    Twilight Time's up against the rail

Each of these examples is composed of a set of pre-determined formulas into which the horses' names are slotted. The whole of the play-by-play commentary – the description of the race while it is in progress – is constructed in this way.

The narrow range of syntactic and lexical choices made by the commentators can be illustrated by looking at the possible ways of communicating (a) that the race has started and (b) where the horses are positioned. These are both elements of the 'play-by-play' description of the race and both are conveyed formulaically. The 'start' formula and the 'horse locator' formula can be described as follows:

(a) Start formula:
    and they're away (and racing now)
    or
    and they're off (and racing now)

(b) The horse locator formula:
    (*horse's name*) wide out on the outside (*horse's name*)
    or
    (*horse's name*) over on the outside (*horse's name*)
    or
    (*horse's name*) parked on the outside (*horse's name*)

Quite clearly this register, too, is characterised by a very restricted range of lexical and syntactic variation. Moreover, the specific features of the formulas are not arbitrary, but motivated by the demands of the context. For example, the syntactic inversion which was noted above as a feature of baseball and cricket commentary also occurs as a feature of race-calling formulas, e.g. *one tipped out was My Dalrae*. It gives the speaker time to identify the person or horse before having to name them. The use of passives allows the speaker to follow the natural order in naming the horses. *Taro is followed by Sunny*, rather than out of order *Sunny follows Taro*.

Finally, the sound patterns of race calling are also distinctive. Race callers use particular intonation patterns or tunes as they call the race. In New Zealand and Australia, the distinctive sound pattern used by race callers has been described as a 'drone', for reasons obvious from figure 10.4.

If you have a piano available you might find it interesting to play this tune while reciting the alphabet. This will give you some idea of its effect. The New Zealand race caller's voice pitch rises by about an octave during the race, and drops rapidly back to the initial pitch after the finish. So the distinctive intonation contours used by different sports announcers in the course of their work are another feature of this easily identified linguistic register.

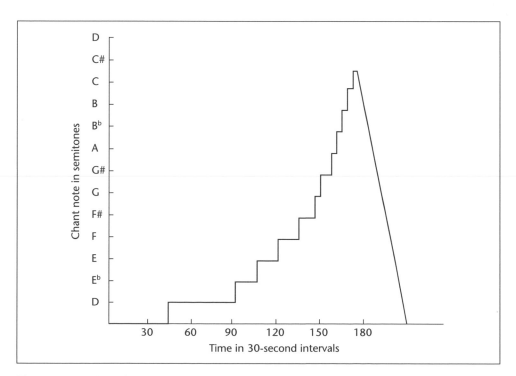

Figure 10.4 Intonation contour of a typical New Zealand race-caller's chant
Source: Modified from Kuiper and Austin 1990: 205. Reproduced with permission

Sports commentators are expected to give the impression of fluency. Pauses and hesitations in race calling, for instance, are unacceptable. Race callers must keep talking and fast! They speak at four to five syllables per second. The use of formulas enables them to convey information with the minimum demand on short-term memory. Sports commentators must also retain the listener's interest and convey the drama of the action. For this they tend to use volume and intonation – hence the dramatically rising drone used by race callers. The linguistic features which develop as characteristic of a register are clearly functionally motivated. The demands of the particular context in which the language is used determine its shape.

The specialised registers of occupational groups develop initially from the desire for quick, efficient, and precise communication between people who share experience, knowledge and skills. Bricklayers, butchers, carpenters, dentists, doctors and linguists all adopt specialised terminology to express shared meanings concisely and precisely. Over time the language of such groups develops more and more characteristics – lexical, syntactic and even phonological (as the race-caller example illustrated) – which distinguish their communications from those of other groups. Eventually these specialised registers may be very difficult for outsiders to penetrate.

Conclusion

People's styles of speech and written communication reflect and express not only aspects of their identity such as their ethnicity, age, gender, and social background, they also indicate the contexts in which language is being used. The way people talk in court, in school, at business meetings and at graduation ceremonies reflects and constitutes the formality of those contexts and the social roles people take in them. The way people write letters, emails, text messages, and blog entries similarly indicates awareness of the different audiences of these different genres. We use more relaxed language at home with those we know well. When we talk differently to babies and adults, or to people from different social backgrounds, we are adapting or accommodating our language to our audience.

Stylistic variation of this sort can be observed in all languages. In multilingual communities it is often signalled by the choice of a specific language, as well as by choice of linguistic variants within a particular language. The linguistic distinctions between styles within a language are more clear-cut in some languages, such as Javanese, Korean and Japanese, than in others, such as Tasmanian English. The reasons people choose one style rather than another can be related once again to the scales described in chapter 1. How well does the speaker know the addressee(s)? What is their relative status? How formal is the context? All these factors have proved important in the discussion of linguistic variation in this chapter. The fourth dimension introduced in chapter 1 concerned the functions of an interaction. The discussion of register differences introduced the idea that style may be determined by the function which the language is serving. This functional dimension of language and its effect on linguistic choice will be the main focus of chapter 11.

ANSWERS TO EXERCISES IN CHAPTER 10

Answer to exercise 2

You may find some of the following features, among others.

(a) High frequency vocabulary.
(b) Fewer contractions (e.g. *must not* rather than *mustn't*).
(c) Use of nouns rather than pronouns so referents are clear (e.g. *then you open the oven and you put the cake into the oven* rather than *then put it in the oven*).
(d) Shorter sentences with simple grammar.
(e) Use of tag questions like *don't you?* and *isn't it?* (which are easy to respond to).
(f) Repetition. ·

Answers to exercise 3

(a) *Radio 3.* Clues: Use of the determiner *the* before *Home Secretary.* Use of *Mr* before *David Waddington.* Use of uncontracted *was not* rather than *wasn't.*
(b) *Radio 1*: Clues: Consonant cluster reduction in word *last.* Use of familiar form *Maggie* with no title. Use of contracted form *wasn't*, and colloquial phrase *wasn't much to write home about.* Pronunciation of standard [t] as [d] inter-vocalically in *better.*
(c) *Radio 3.* Clues: Use of uncontracted *have not.* No consonant cluster reduction in words like *latest, postbox.* Use of determiner before *spokesman* and full title with first name *Detective Superintendent Ray Huntley.*

Answer to exercise 4

The papers in column 2 illustrate higher percentages of determiner deletion than those in column 1. The figures in table 10.1 support this claim.

Once again this provides evidence that the patterning of a linguistic feature reflects the social structure of the intended audience – in this case the papers' readerships.

Table 10.1 Percentage of determiner deletion in British newspapers

Newspaper	%
The Times	5
The Guardian	10
The Daily Telegraph	12
Daily Mail	73
Daily Express	79
The Mirror	80
The Sun	89

Source: From Bell 1991: 108. Reproduced with permission

Answer to exercise 5

People may converge or adapt their speed of speech, the length of their utterances, the frequency of their pauses, the grammatical patterns used, their vocabulary, the verbal fillers or pragmatic particles (such as *sort of, you know* and *you see*) that they use, their intonation, and their voice pitch. People may also converge in their pronunciation of a wide variety of different sounds, as was

Language variation: focus on uses

C

illustrated by the examples of the travel agent assistant in Cardiff and the interviewer in Norwich. In text messaging and email communication, people may converge in style, e.g. omitting greetings and sign-offs, and using shorthand spelling. There are many other possibilities too.

Answers to exercise 6

(a) Example 2: The teenage boy converges upwards in addressing his friend's mother but speech to his friend is speech to an equal.
(b) Example 3: The baby-talk example involves downward convergence by the adults to the supposed baby.
(c) Example 4 (b): The letter from an adult to a child illustrates downward convergence.
(d) Example 5: The utterance from a staff member to an elderly patient illustrates downward convergence.
(e) Example 6: This shows the newsreaders converging towards the predicted norms of their audiences, but without information on the background of the newsreaders we cannot tell whether this involves upwards or downwards convergence.
(f) Example 7: This describes June involved in both upward and downward convergence.

Answer to exercise 7

The answer must be 'it all depends'! – on which women and men and in which contexts and talking to whom. A woman who uses more standard forms when talking to an interviewer than when talking to a friend is converging towards the interviewer's speech provided that the interviewer's speech uses more standard forms than the friend's speech. Women who maintain the level of vernacular forms in speech to an interviewer that they would use in speech to a close friend could be regarded as diverging from the interviewer's standard forms. The answer must always be relative and depend on evidence of contrasting usage to different addressees or in different contexts.

Answer to exercise 8

In chapter 4 the term 'vernacular language' was discussed. In a multilingual context a vernacular language is usually a language which has not been standardised and which does not have official status. Vernaculars are generally the first languages learned by people in multilingual communities, and they are often used for a relatively narrow range of informal functions.

In chapter 6, it was pointed out that social dialectologists also use the term vernacular to refer to linguistic forms which are not used in the standard dialect. So within social dialectology, vernacular forms are non-standard forms.

In the section above, the term vernacular is used to refer to a particular style in a monolingual community – the style used in the most relaxed circumstances. Because of this association with casual speech people sometimes use the term facetiously to describe the use of swear words, as in *I'd really like you to leave me in peace now, or – to use the vernacular – bugger off.*

The various uses do have some elements of shared meaning. In monolingual communities vernacular refers to the style which is most obviously parallel to the ethnic language for a polyglot – in other words the variety learned first and used in the most relaxed circumstances. Vernacular forms are those which characterise people's most relaxed style.

Answers to exercise 9

Linguistic features of colloquial or casual style:

(a) Pronunciation features:
    [h]-dropping: e.g. *'oh well', 'e said, 'I suppose you can 'ave 'im.'*
    [in] (vs formal [iŋ]): e.g. *We was up there cuttin'.*

(b) Grammatical features:

was with plural subject *we*, e.g. *We was up there cuttin'*.

come (vs *came*): *Frazer come on to us*.

Answer to exercise 10

This is an interesting example of confusion of stylistic variation and standard usage. The writer seems to be suggesting that *either you or I* is the formal variant and therefore presumably the standard or 'correct' form. It is the form appropriately used in writing, the writer claims. Yet, in fact, 'correct English usage' here requires *you or me*, since these pronouns follow the preposition *for*. Compare, for example, *It would be wrong for us to be there* with *it would be wrong for we to be there*. This makes it clear that the object pronoun (*us, me*) is usual after a preposition rather than the subject pronoun (*we, I*).

To make matters even more complicated, however, the letter writer goes on to argue that the more standard or correct form is the one which would have been used in an informal chat between the two people concerned. The confusion arises from the Latin-based insecurity described in the previous section over when to use *me* and when to use *I*. As a result of its association with Latin-influenced forms such as *It is I*, people assume that *I* is generally more correct and formal than *me*, and so they substitute *I* for *me* in all kinds of contexts.

Answer to exercise 11

The choice between *tu* and *vous* is often, but not always, a matter of style. When talking to a group of people, *tu* is not a possibility, for instance. When addressing one person, however, the choice is often almost entirely determined by the relationship between the speaker and the addressee, and the social context in which they are speaking. Among the factors mentioned in this chapter, the age of the addressee relative to the speaker may be relevant, relative social status will generally be taken into account, and so will the formality of the context. So, for example, *tu* will generally be used to a child as well as to an intimate. *Vous* will generally be used to an older person, especially someone the speaker does not know well. *Vous* is used in more formal situations such as graduation ceremonies and in law courts. *Vous* is used to express respect – it is the polite pronoun. The various strategies which speakers use to express politeness are discussed further in chapter 11.

Answers to exercise 12

(a) NO NUKES. – **Graffiti**

Clues: alliteration, short phrase, simple syntax, colloquial abbreviation of *nuclear weapons*, capital letters, political message.

(b) Who's a lovely little girl then eh? Who's a lovely little girl? – **Baby-talk**

Clues: repetition of whole clauses, simple syntax, use of tag (*eh*), and simple vocabulary.

(c) Where any registered security interest is discharged, the person entered in the register as the secured party shall, within 10 working days of the date on which the security interest is discharged, apply to . . . – **Legal text**

Clues: passive constructions (e.g. *is discharged*), repetition of noun phrases rather than use of pronouns (e.g. *security interest*), subordinate clauses. Note that the main clause . . . *the person . . . shall . . . apply to* is both preceded by, and interspersed with, subordinate clauses which qualify it.

(d) txt 4 lift   b gr8 2 c u – **Phone text message**

Clues: minimal brief text with all redundancies eliminated, short phrases with no articles or auxiliary verbs; elimination of vowels, use of figures for words such as 'for' and 'to', and even

Language variation: focus on uses

C

for parts of words with the same sound (e.g. *gr8* for 'great'); use of single letters with sound of a whole word: *c* for 'see' and *u* for 'you'; no punctuation, no greeting and no sign off.

(e) I have no desire to be a party to this on-going useless debate. I therefore wish to UNSUBSCRIBE from this list. – **Entry in a publicly accessible email list, instance of CMC (Computer-Mediated Communication)**

Clues: lexical items such as *list*, UNSUBSCRIBE, *debate*. The capitals used in UNSUBSCRIBE are the standard means of leaving an email list. The rather formal syntax and lexis *I have no desire to be a party to, therefore*, suggests the list is probably an academic one.

Answers to exercise 13

(a) Post-noun modification of *Clark*.

(b) Syntactic reduction: the verb is omitted – it is predictably *kicks* or *provides* or something similar in meaning.

(c) Syntactic inversion: the subject *the two defenders* follows the predicate *combining well*.

(d) Syntactic reduction: the definite article *the* is omitted before *pitch* and the verb form *is* is omitted after *pitch*. Both words are totally predictable.

(e) Syntactic reduction and inversion: the unreduced sentence in normal word order would be *remember that Rush is looking for a hat-trick*.

◾ Concepts introduced

Style
Audience design
Speech accommodation
Speech convergence
Speech divergence
Referee design
Labovian methodology
Observer's paradox
Hypercorrection
Register

◾ References

The following sources provided material for this chapter:

Bell (1984, 1991, 2001) on audience design, referee design and media language
Cazden (1972) on children's language
Coupland (1981) for data on Cardiff
Douglas-Cowie (1978) on Northern Ireland
Errington (1988) on Javanese
Ferguson (1983) on baseball commentary
Giles and Smith (1979) on accommodation theory
Hatch (1983) on foreigner talk
Jahangiri and Hudson (1982) and Keshavarz (1988) on Tehrani Persian
Kuiper and Austin (1990) on race calling

Kuiper and Haggo (1984) on oral formulas
Labov (1966) on New York speech
Labov (1972a) on style
Milroy (1989) for data on Tyneside and Tunis
O'Hanlon (2006) on accents used in Australian hip-hop
Pawley (1991) on language of cricket commentary
Rampton (1995) on 'crossing'
Rickford and McNair-Knox (1994) on AAVE interviewer style
Russell (1982) on Mombasa Swahili
Trudgill (1974, 1983a) especially data on Norwich
Wolfram and Fasold (1974)

Quotations

Example 3 is an excerpt from a Monty Python sketch.
Example 8 is from Giles and Smith (1979: 53).
Example 11 is from the *New Zealand Herald*, 31 December 1986.
Example 12 is from Finegan and Besnier (1989: 431).
Examples 13 and 17 are from Labov (1966: 426).
Examples 14 and 15 are from Pawley, Syder and He (1989: 2–5).
Example 19 is modified from Inoue (1979: 287–9).
Example 20 is from Errington (1988: 90–1).
Example 21 is from Coupland, Coupland, Giles, and Henwood (1988: 25).
Example 22 is slightly edited from Pawley (1991: 3).
Examples 23, 24, 25 are from Ferguson (1983) and Pawley (1991).
Example 26 is from Kuiper and Austin (1990).
The data in exercise 4 is from Bell (1991).
The 'casual salesman' and the 'careful pipefitter' quotation is from Labov (1972a: 240).
The example in exercise 12 (e) is modified from Harris (2004: 69)

Useful additional reading

Coupland and Jaworski (1997), Section IV
Crystal (1997), Ch. 11
Downes (1998), Ch. 4
Eckert and Rickford (2001)
Giles and Smith (1979)
Meyerhoff (2006), Ch. 3
Trudgill (2000), Ch. 5
Wardhaugh (2006), Ch. 2

C

Language variation: focus on uses

11 Speech functions, politeness and cross-cultural communication

In the previous chapter, I discussed ways in which language reflects the context in which it is used. We adapt our talk to suit our audience and talk differently to children, customers and colleagues. We use language differently in formal and casual contexts. The purpose of talk will also affect its form. In this chapter I will begin by considering the range of functions language may serve, and the variety of ways in which the 'same' message may be expressed.

Why do we select one way rather than another to convey our message? Given a choice between *Mr Shaw*, *Robert*, and *Bob*, for instance, how do we decide which is appropriate? One relevant factor is politeness. In the second part of this chapter I will illustrate how considerations of politeness influence the choice between different address forms, and I will discuss the social dimensions which influence what is considered polite in different situations and communities. Being linguistically polite is often a matter of selecting linguistic forms which express the appropriate degree of social distance or which recognise relevant status or power differences.

Rules for polite behaviour differ from one speech community to another. Linguistic politeness is culturally determined. Different speech communities emphasise different functions, and express particular functions differently. How should one express gratitude for a meal in another culture? Is it possible to refuse an invitation politely? How should one greet people in different speech communities? These are the kinds of questions which will be touched on in the final section of this chapter where some examples of cross-cultural differences in the expression of speech functions are discussed.

THE FUNCTIONS OF SPEECH

Example 1

Boss: Good morning Sue. Lovely day.
Secretary: Yes it's beautiful. Makes you wonder what we're doing here doesn't it.
Boss: Mm, that's right. Look I wonder if you could possibly sort this lot out by 10. I need them for a meeting.
Secretary: Yes sure. No problem.
Boss: Thanks that's great.

This dialogue is typical of many everyday interactions in that it serves both an affective (or social) function, and a referential (or informative) function. The initial greetings and comments on the weather serve a social function; they establish contact between the two participants. The exchange then moves on to become more information-oriented or referential in function. In chapter 1, I described just these two broad functions of speech – the affective and the referential. It is possible, however, to distinguish a great variety of different functions which language serves.

There are a number of ways of categorising the functions of speech. The following list has proved a useful one in sociolinguistic research.

1. **Expressive** utterances express the speaker's feelings, e.g. *I'm feeling great today.*
2. **Directive** utterances attempt to get someone to do something, e.g. *Clear the table.*
3. **Referential** utterances provide information, e.g. *At the third stroke it will be three o'clock precisely.*
4. **Metalinguistic** utterances comment on language itself, e.g. *'Hegemony' is not a common word.*
5. **Poetic** utterances focus on aesthetic features of language, e.g. a poem, an ear-catching motto, a rhyme, *Peter Piper picked a peck of pickled peppers.*
6. **Phatic** utterances express solidarity and empathy with others, e.g. *Hi, how are you, lovely day isn't it!*

Though I have provided a very brief indication of what the function labels mean, and an example of each in the form of a single utterance, it is important to remember that any utterance may in fact express more than one function, and any function may be expressed by a stretch of discourse which doesn't exactly coincide with an utterance.

The first three functions are recognised by many linguists, though the precise labels they are given may differ. They seem to be very fundamental functions of language, perhaps because they derive from the basic components of any interaction – the speaker (*expressive*), the addressee (*directive*) and the message (*referential*). The *phatic* function is, however, equally important from a sociolinguistic perspective. Phatic communication conveys an affective or social message rather than a referential one. One of the insights provided by sociolinguists has been precisely that language is not used to convey only referential information, but also expresses information about social relationships.

Exercise 1

Identify in example 1

(a) An utterance which serves a primarily expressive function.
(b) An utterance which serves a primarily directive function.
(c) An utterance which serves a primarily referential function.

Answers at end of chapter

The categories are useful as guides for analysis, but they are not mutually exclusive. A love poem, for example, is both poetic and expressive. An advert, as the sentences in example 2 demonstrate, may be poetic, directive, amusing and possibly informative!

Example 2

(a) A Mars a day, helps you work rest and play.®

(b) Beanz Buildz Kidz.

(c) Put a tiger in your tank.

(d) San Antonio, sans delay.

® Mars slogan is a registered trademark

The list of functions provided above is not definitive or all-encompassing. Other speech function categories have been identified, often arising from the particular interests of a researcher or the focus of a particular study. Michael Halliday, for instance, identified a function of language concerned with learning, which he labelled *heuristic*, and glossed as the 'tell me why' function. The need for this function arose from his study of the acquisition of language by his son, Nigel. Many of Nigel's utterances seemed to be aimed at learning more about the world.

Other researchers have added categories to deal with promises and threats (*commissives*), and with marriage vows, bets, and declarations of war (*performatives* or declarations). Each category has its distinctive characteristics. The precise linguistic form used is crucial to bets, for instance. By uttering the words *I bet* . . . we 'perform' the bet. Similarly the precise words uttered at particular points are crucial in a wedding ceremony. So it is possible to add a variety of further categories which may prove useful and illuminating for particular analyses.

Researchers have examined the ways that particular speech functions are expressed in a variety of contexts, examining the range of linguistic forms they take. They have also been interested in the way different functions are distributed in a speech community. Who uses which forms to whom and in what contexts? To illustrate this kind of research, I will look at the directive function in more detail.

Exercise 2

Directives are linguistic utterances intended to get someone to do something. Think of five obvious and five less obvious verbal ways of getting someone to sit down.

Answer at end of chapter

▪ Directives

Example 3

Teacher: What are you doing over by the window Helen?
Helen: Looking at the birds Miss.
Teacher: And what should you be doing?
Helen: *(No answer)*
Teacher: Go and sit down now and get on with your writing.

Directives are concerned with getting people to do things. The speech acts which express directive force vary in strength. We can attempt to get people to sit down, for instance, by suggesting or inviting them to do so, or by ordering or commanding them to sit down. Orders and commands are speech acts which are generally expressed in imperative form. Polite attempts to get people to do something tend to use interrogatives or declaratives, as the following examples illustrate.

Sit down.	IMPERATIVE
You sit down.	*You* IMPERATIVE
Could you sit down?	INTERROGATIVE WITH MODAL VERB
Sit down will you?	INTERROGATIVE WITH TAG
Won't you sit down?	INTERROGATIVE WITH NEGATIVE MODAL
I want you to sit down.	DECLARATIVE
I'd like you to sit down.	DECLARATIVE
You'd be more comfortable sitting down.	DECLARATIVE

The list could go on and on. There are many ways of expressing this directive. And although we can say that in general the interrogatives and declaratives are more polite than the imperatives, a great deal depends on intonation, tone of voice and context. A gentle *sit down* may be far more polite than a thundered *I want you all sitting down now*. In a shop, utterance (a) in example 4 will be considered normal, while (b) might well be regarded as sarcastic.

Example 4

(a) Box of matches.
(b) Could you possibly give me a box of matches?

How do people decide which form to use in a particular context? What are the social factors which affect a speaker's choice of the appropriate form of directive? A number of factors have been suggested. The social distance between participants,

'I'm sorry to bother you and I hope I'm not too much trouble but could you move your foot a little either way because somehow mine seems to have got caught under yours.'

their relative status, and the formality of the context (the social dimensions which were discussed in chapter 1) are usually relevant. (These factors turn up again in the discussion of politeness in chapter 14.) People who are close friends or intimates use more imperatives, for instance. The utterances in example 5 were all produced within a family, were (almost!) all said without rancour, and caused no offence.

Example 5

(a) Roll over.
(b) Shut up you fool.
(c) Set the table, Robbie.
(d) Wash your hands for tea, children.
(e) Turn that blessed radio down.

Where status differences are clearly marked and accepted, superiors tend to use imperatives to subordinates. Teachers often use imperatives to pupils, for instance.

Example 6

(a) Open your books at page 32.
(b) Shut the door.
(c) Stop talking please.

Teachers can use very direct expressions of their meaning because of their high status relative to their pupils. On the other hand, the rights and obligations in a role relationship such as teacher–pupil are so clear-cut that teachers can also use minimally explicit forms and be confident they will be interpreted accurately as directives.

Example 7

(a) Blackboard! ('Clean the blackboard')
(b) Bus people! ('Those who get the school bus should now leave')
(c) I hear talking. ('Stop talking')

So clear-cut are the rules for classroom behaviour that it has been suggested that pupils operate with a very general rule of the form 'Scan every utterance of the teacher for directive intent.' In other words pupils consider everything the teacher says as a possible directive. New entrant Jason in example 8, however, has obviously not learned this rule yet, so his teacher's attempts to gently direct him to the appropriate behaviour are initially far too indirect.

Language variation: focus on uses

Example 8

Teacher: Jason, why have you got your raincoat on inside?
Jason: *(Smiles)*
Teacher: It's not raining inside.
Jason: *(No response)*
Teacher: What are you going to do about it?
Jason: *(No response)*
Teacher: Go and hang it up.

Formality and status may be very relevant in choosing an appropriate directive form. At a graduation ceremony the University Chancellor gave the Vice-Chancellor the directive in example 9.

Example 9

I now call on the Vice-Chancellor to read the citation for our distinguished guest.

The required action ('read the citation') is embedded as a subordinate clause in the second part of the declarative sentence, and this is a common grammatical means of expressing directives less directly and more politely. A study which looked at the directives used between medical professionals in a meeting also demonstrated the importance of relative status in determining the form of directives in a formal setting. Imperatives were overwhelmingly used by superiors to those of subordinate status. The only imperatives used 'upwards' were greeted with laughter, and regarded as humorous because they so clearly flouted this sociolinguistic rule. The general rule was that directives upwards were couched as indirect forms, such as modal interrogatives, as in example 10 (a). Others took the form of hints as illustrated by the exchange in example 10 (b).

Example 10

Medical professional of lower status to person of higher status.

(a) Could you ring his mother and find out?
(b) A. We've got a referral from Dr T. He's your neighbour Jody.
    B. OK I'll take him.

The relevance of status in a less formal context was nicely demonstrated in a study of children's directives in a New Zealand child-care centre. Relative status in the centre was determined by age and size. The oldest, biggest and strongest child used by far the most imperatives, while attempts by the other children to get him to cooperate involved less direct forms such *I think I need that now* and *Could I borrow that?*

Another factor which is relevant to the form of a directive is the routineness or reasonableness of the task. A boss might produce utterance (a) in example 11 to his mechanic when giving her a routine task. If, however, he is expecting her to do something out of the ordinary or especially difficult, he is far more likely to use a less direct form such as (b) or even a hint such as (c).

Example 11

(a) Get those brake pads in by 5 o'clock Sue. That car's needed first thing in the morning.

(b) Could you stay a bit later tonight, do you think, and finish this job?

(c) That job's taking longer than we predicted. I don't know what we'll do if it isn't ready for tomorrow.

In general, imperatives are used between people who know each other well or to subordinates. Interrogatives and declaratives, including hints, tend to be used between those who are less familiar with each other, or where there is some reason to feel the task being requested is not routine (see also the discussion of politeness in chapter 14). But there are many qualifications to these generalisations. Hints may also be used for humorous effect between people who are close friends, as example 12 illustrates.

Example 12

(a) *To someone blocking the light out.*
You make a better door than a window.

(b) *Mother to teenage son.*
I'm not sure that a couple of smelly socks in the middle of the lounge floor can be beaten as a centre piece for our dinner party. What do you think, Tim?

It has also been noted that girls and women tend to favour more polite and less direct forms of directives than males – at least in the contexts investigated. These are examples of children's utterances to each other in a play centre.

Example 13

(a) Tom: Give me that. I need it now.

(b) Seymour: Get off that car.

(c) Grant: Get out of my house.

(d) Maria: You finished with that rolling pin now?

(e) Lisa: My turn now eh?

(f) Meg: It's time for tea so you'll have to go home now.

C

Language variation: focus on uses

The forms used by the girls are clearly less direct and more polite than those used by the boys. In a study of doctors' directives to patients, male doctors typically used imperatives (e.g. *eat more fruit*), while female doctors used less direct forms (e.g. *maybe you could try fresh fruit for dessert*). There are many other influences on the form of directives: the addressee's gender is significant, for instance. Women not only use less direct forms of directive, they also receive less direct forms. Relative power or status, and social distance clearly influence the form of directives, as some of the examples above have demonstrated. There is not space to illustrate all the possible contextual influences, but you might find it interesting to investigate some of them for yourself in your own community.

Exercise 3

Consider the form of directives, i.e. how people get others to do things in your community.

(a) First make some observations in a range of different contexts, writing down the form of the directives and the situations in which they occur. Then try to make some generalisations about the reasons for any patterns you observe.

(b) Note the form of the directives used in your family by both adults and children during a different two-hour period on three different days. List the different social factors (e.g. relative status/power, degree of solidarity, degree of formality, urgency) which you consider influence the forms of the directives.

Not all communities follow the patterns I have described. In a study of a community of lower-class male migrant agricultural workers on the eastern seaboard of the United States, for instance, it was found that almost all the directives took the form of imperatives, regardless of differences in social status, social distance, the presence of outsiders and the setting or location.

Example 14

(a) Stay away from them social workers.

(b) Well if you don't want to work, get out of the field.

(c) Grab that there hand truck.

(d) Now get to it.

(e) Overseer assigns the farmworker the wrong row to hoe.
   Farmworker: Go to hell. Two times you have told me what to do – each time it's been wrong. I'm staying in this row. You put somebody else there.

The researchers in this study considered that the insecure and unpleasant work conditions of the participants accounted for the antagonism evident in many of their social interactions. Relations between the workers and their bosses were characterised by mistrust and tension on both sides. Their language reflected these social relationships in that the great majority of directives, whether from bosses to workers or vice versa, took the form of unmodified imperatives. The last section of this chapter provides further examples of differences in the way different speech communities express particular speech functions.

Clearly getting what you want from someone else requires knowledge of the rules for expressing yourself appropriately in the relevant socio-cultural context. A successful outcome can reflect a real sociolinguistic accomplishment. And even at the age of three some children have worked out that a threat can sometimes be more effective than any directive. The following example illustrates the sociolinguistic skills of both parties to this exchange.

C

Example 15

Mischa: Can I borrow your biscuit?
Jake: No, it's my lunch.
Mischa: I won't be your friend if you won't let me.
Jake: OK.
Jake gives her the biscuit but looks miserable.
Mischa: Here, it's OK you have it.
Jake: No. You won't be my friend.
Mischa starts eating.
Jake: My turn.
Mischa gives it back and they then finish the biscuit taking turns.

Jake will no doubt be a great diplomat some day!

Discussing the ways in which speech functions are expressed in different contexts has repeatedly involved considerations of politeness. Choosing the appropriate linguistic form for directives to family, friends and foreigners involves the dimensions of solidarity (or social distance) and social status (or power). These dimensions are at the heart of politeness behaviour and are discussed further in chapter 14. In the next section I will focus explicitly on linguistic politeness, using terms of address for exemplification.

Exercise 4

For the purposes of the discussion in this chapter, I have simplified and treated most utterances as if they expressed just one speech function. But when we interact we generally use language in complex ways, and this often involves expressing several functions of language simultaneously. Identify at least two functions which could be expressed simultaneously by each of the following utterances.

▶

Language variation: focus on uses

(a) Fire!
(b) Keep up that excellent work.
(c) I'd like to see Sam in my office at four.
(d) I'm very tired.

Answers at end of chapter

POLITENESS AND ADDRESS FORMS

Example 16

Israeli passenger and driver on an inter-city bus
Passenger: Turn the light on, please.
Driver: What?
Passenger: Turn the light on, please.
Driver: It disturbs me.
Passenger: I wanted to read.

This exchange between two Israelis seems very direct and blunt to most English speakers. Being polite is a complicated business in any language. It is difficult to learn because it involves understanding not just the language, but also the social and cultural values of the community. We often don't appreciate just how complicated it is, because we tend to think of politeness simply as a matter of saying *please* and *thank you* in the right places. In fact it involves a great deal more than the superficial politeness routines that parents explicitly teach their children, as the discussion of directives and expressives above suggested.

Take the word *please* for example. Children are told to say *please* when they are making requests, as a way of expressing themselves politely. But adults use *please* far less than one might suppose, and when they do, it often has the effect of making a directive sound less polite and more peremptory. Compare the pairs of utterances in example 17, for instance.

Example 17

(a1) Could you take my bags up?
(a2) Could you take my bags up, please.
(b1) Answer the phone Jo.
(b2) Please answer the phone Jo.

As always, a great deal depends on intonation and tone of voice, but clearly *please* does not necessarily increase the politeness of these directives.

This example also raises the question of what we mean by politeness. Generally speaking politeness involves taking account of the feelings of others. A polite person makes others feel comfortable. Being linguistically polite involves speaking to people appropriately in the light of their relationship to you. Inappropriate linguistic choices may be considered rude. Using an imperative such as *stop talking* or *shut that door* to a superior at work is likely to earn the office junior a reprimand. Calling the managing director *Sally* when you do not know her well and have only just started work as a stores assistant in the department is likely to be considered impolite. Making decisions about what is or is not considered polite in any community therefore involves assessing social relationships along the dimensions of social distance or solidarity, and relative power or status. We need to understand the social values of a society in order to speak politely.

These two dimensions also provide the basis for a distinction between two different types of politeness. *Positive politeness* is solidarity oriented. It emphasises shared attitudes and values. When the boss suggests that a subordinate should use first name (FN) to her, this is a positive politeness move, expressing solidarity and minimising status differences. A shift to a more informal style using slang and swear words will function similarly as an expression of positive politeness. By contrast, *negative politeness* pays people respect and avoids intruding on them. Indirect directives such as those in example 11 (b) and (c) express negative politeness. Negative politeness involves expressing oneself appropriately in terms of social distance and respecting status differences. Using title + last name (TLN) to your superiors, and to older people that you don't know well, are further examples of the expression of negative politeness.

Being polite may also involve the dimension of formality. In a formal situation the appropriate way of talking to your brother will depend on your roles in the context. If he is acting as the judge in a law court then calling him *Tom* will be considered disrespectful, while at the dinner table calling him *Your honour* will be perceived as inappropriate or humorous.

Figure 11.1 is a useful summary of the kinds of factors which were considered relevant in accounting for people's choice of appropriate address terms in British English in the 1970s. The model accounts for the forms used as ADDRESS TERMS in an utterance which could be used to attract attention, e.g. *Hey Mr Brown*, or in an utterance such as *I'm sure you will find it interesting Prime Minister*.

The diagram assumes the speaker knows the addressee's name and the first box takes account of whether the addressee is a child or an adult. Where the line between adult and child is drawn differs between communities, and even within communities for different purposes (e.g. baby-sitting, buying fireworks, marrying, owning a firearm, voting). If the addressee would be classified as a child in the relevant social interaction, then, following the minus exit from the box, the flow chart indicates FN is used in British English, e.g. *Hey Jill*. Box 2, labelled 'marked setting', refers to formal settings such as Parliament and law courts where people act in role, and where speech is governed by

C

Language variation: focus on uses

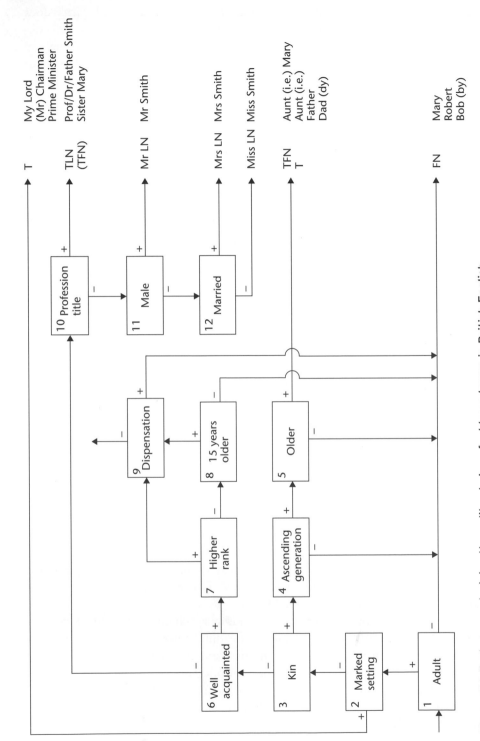

Figure 11.1 Factors constraining the polite choice of address terms in British English

Source: Reproduced from Laver 1981: 297. Reproduced with permission

relatively explicit discourse rules. Forms of address are derived from identity in the context, e.g. *Your honour*, *Prime Minister*. The boxes marked 'kin' and 'well acquainted' are self-explanatory – though who qualifies in each case will of course be culture- and context-dependent. The box marked 'higher rank' refers to social superiors or people of higher status in a hierarchy. The 'ascending generation' is the generation above the speaker – parents and parents' sisters, brothers and cousins, for instance. A 'dispensation' refers to the fact that a superior may absolve the speaker from the obligation of using TLN and permit them to use FN, e.g. *Dr Worth is far too formal. Please call me Helen.* The box marked 'profession title' refers to occupational or courtesy titles such as *Doctor*, *Professor*, *Sister* for a nun, *Father* for a priest, and so on.

Exercise 5

(a) Modify this diagram (which is based on outdated British English usage) to account for the current norms of address usage in your speech community. What are the dimensions which are relevant to determining social distance and solidarity in your community?

   (i) Is the formality of the setting ('marked setting') relevant? Consider a law court, Parliament, a formal prize giving or graduation ceremony, or a very formal annual meeting of a society or union.

   (ii) Do you use kin-titles such as *grandad* or *aunt* which indicate a person's kinship relationship to you? Is age or generation relevant in selecting kin titles? What do you call your mother's cousin, for instance, if she is the same age as you? (See chapter 13 for some discussion of cultural differences in the area of kinship.)

   (iii) Is relative status or rank relevant in selecting an appropriate term in your community? What do you call the most senior person at the place where you work or study? What do you call your equals or peers?

   (iv) What, if any, is the age difference between people which is considered relevant in determining address usage? What do you call your neighbours, for instance? Is their age relative to yours relevant? If they were twenty or thirty years older than you, would this be different? What do you call your parents' friends?

   (v) Are the elements in the diagram organised in a way which accurately reflects their relative importance in your community? Is status more important than social distance, for instance, in your community or vice versa? Would you call a friend by first name in all contexts (except marked settings) even if they were of very much higher status than you? Would you call an equal by first name on first meeting?

(b) How might such a model be extended? What, for instance, would you use to attract the attention of a stranger who had dropped something in the street? What additional address terms are available in your community (e.g. *sir*, *madam*, *dear*, *mate*) and what factors determine their usage?

Example 18

(a) *Post Office delivery man to elderly upper-class British woman.*
   Can I have your signature, my love?
(b) *Director to colleague at a meeting where first names are generally used.*
   I think it's time you let someone else contribute, Mr Morgan.

We can cause offence by treating someone too familiarly, as in (a), or by treating them too distantly as in (b). Being polite means getting the linguistic expression of social distance right as far as your addressee is concerned. This is very variable from one speech community to another. In the north of England many newspaper vendors, bus conductors and people selling railway tickets call everyone *love* regardless of how well they know them, and often regardless of their gender. By contrast mutual TLN (*Mrs Landy, Mr Duncan*) is usual between upper-working-class neighbours who live close to each other, but who are not friends and do not see each other socially. In North America it is usual to use first names to people you work with, regardless of how little or much you like them. In other English-speaking cultures mutual FN is experienced as too familiar. Mutual TLN is appropriate until you have worked together for a period of time or develop a friendship. Issues like how long do you have to know someone, or how close a friendship does it have to be, to use FN raise further complications, of course. The answers will be different for different communities.

In earlier centuries the norms were simpler. Status was the major consideration. In general, people used TLN (or an appropriate kin-term) upwards to superiors, and FN downwards to subordinates, no matter how well they knew them. Solidarity became relevant only between equals. Equals used mutual TLN with people they did not know well, and they used mutual first names to friends. In addition, between some (mainly male) people, mutual LN was the norm (*Elementary my dear Watson!*), and there was also a non-reciprocal pattern involving *madam/sir* upwards and LN downwards to subordinates (*clean that blackboard, Hadley*).

Today, however, the interaction between social status and social distance in many Western societies is more complicated. This results in a conflict of norms in two situations: (a) high status with high solidarity and (b) low status with low solidarity. If your addressee is of lower status and you know them well (ignoring for the moment the issue of how well counts as 'well'), then either way you use FN to them. But what form do they use to you? The norms conflict. Because they know you well, they could assume FN is appropriate, but their subordinate status predicts TLN. How can this dilemma be resolved? One common solution is to avoid address terms altogether. When an address term must be used, however, FN is generally used in such a situation. In other words, in many Western communities in the second half of the twentieth century, the solidarity dimension is usually given greater weight. So secretaries, for instance, generally use FN to their bosses if they have worked for them for some time. Workers use FN to the factory floor supervisor. Civil servants use FN to their policy-making bosses if they talk to them regularly.

What of the second conflicting situation? There is no problem when you do not know someone well, and they are your superior. Both factors predict that you will use TLN. But when someone is your subordinate and you don't know them well, what do you use? This is a tricky area but, in general, once again the solidarity dimension tends to win out: degree of solidarity (or social distance) is what counts. British office workers tend to use TLN to the caretaker whom they rarely see. Middle-class women generally use TLN to their cleaning women, especially when the woman is older and rarely encountered face-to-face. The following American example describes a different pattern, however, and illustrates the complexity of the factors which may be relevant.

Example 19

Interviewer: How do you address the custodian of your building?

Professor: We have a young college boy now, so I call him by his FN . . . Now our housekeeper, I call her Mrs ____, and she calls me Miss ____. Once in a great while I call her by her FN. But I want the students to know that I respect her, so in public, I call her Mrs ____. And she's not in the category of a cleaning lady. She wears a uniform and makes a vital contribution to the department.

Another factor which contributes to the assessment of social distance, and hence to the appropriate way of being polite, is the type of relationship involved. In many communities, as illustrated in example 19, transactional relationships favour TLN. Shopkeepers and customers may exchange mutual TLN even when they have known each other for a long time. Doctors and patients similarly tend to use mutual TLN. These relationships put the emphasis on the social distance dimension in that even when they are long-standing, they do not involve intimacy. To know someone 'well' involves more than just knowing them for a long time. Mutual TLN is also a marker of mutual respect, as example 19 indicates, and it may be especially relevant to express this in certain contexts. Transactional relationships are usually one-dimensional. When they shift to become more personal, they often also shift to mutual FN.

One factor which seems to override these patterns – as reflected by its primary position in figure 11.1 – is relative age. Adults use FN to children on first meeting. Young people are more likely to receive FN in any context. A young shop assistant, hairdresser, cleaner, or an office junior will receive FN from a customer or client, and will often be expected to use TLN back, especially if the person is a generation or more older.

Exercise 6

Consider the complications introduced into the interaction of solidarity and status by languages which have a choice of pronoun such as *tu* and *vous* in French, or *du* and *Sie* in German. What kind of social relationship is implied by mutual *vous* between two people?

Answer at end of chapter

Exercise 7

(a) When a subordinate is using TLN to a superior and receiving FN back, how could a change to mutual FN be achieved politely?
(b) When people are using mutual TLN who do you think has the right to suggest a move to FN?

Answers at end of chapter

Norms of Western address usage have changed over time to place more emphasis on solidarity and less on status. But this is not the case universally. In many Eastern societies, such as Japan, Korea and Indonesia, the emphasis remains on status differences. Being polite involves using language which recognises relative status very explicitly.

The Javanese example (20) discussed in chapter 10 illustrated this point. The choice of an appropriate style reflected the speaker's assessment of the relative status of the two participants. The higher the addressee's status the more complex the level of Javanese selected. As well as choosing between low style (*ngoko* or 1), middle style (*krama madya* or 2), and high style (*krama* or 3), Javanese speakers also add another dimension of politeness to the high and the low style by using high or low honorifics. These are alternative words for people, body parts, possessions, and human actions which can be used to raise the high style one notch further up (to 3a, so to speak), and the low style two notches further up (to 1a and 1b).

Being polite in Javanese is obviously a complex linguistic matter. The factors which determine the choice of appropriate level, however, include all those relevant to the choice of an appropriate address form in English (as well as some extra factors, such as the status of one's family, which is irrelevant in many English-speaking societies these days). Age, gender, kinship relationship, and social status as determined by occupation and education, are all relevant. Even the formality of the context is relevant – a Javanese speaker would use a different level to the same person when they met in the street as opposed to at a wedding. Social status, social distance or solidarity, and the degree of formality of the interaction are relevant dimensions in all societies in determining ways of speaking politely.

Though the relevant dimensions may be universal, people from different speech communities often unwittingly offend each other. The way the dimensions are expressed in speech acts and interactive rules may be the source of misunderstandings, as we shall see in the next section.

Exercise 8

Tino, a young Samoan boy who had recently arrived in New Zealand, was summoned to the office of the school principal for being repeatedly late for school. He knocked on the door of the principal's office. When he was told to come in, he walked in with hunched shoulders, scuttled over to a chair and sat down without being asked to do so by the principal. In response to the principal's questions he either said nothing or he muttered *I don't know.* He looked down at the floor throughout the interview and never met the principal's eyes. What impression do you think he gave?

Answer at end of chapter

LINGUISTIC POLITENESS IN DIFFERENT CULTURES

Example 20

Christina Paulston, a Swede, returned home after living in America for some time. One evening soon after arriving back she invited some people to dinner, including her brother and his wife. She was in the kitchen when they arrived, and when she came through into the lounge she said to her sister-in-law, in impeccable Swedish, 'do you know everyone?' An American or an English person would assume that Christina, as hostess, was checking that her sister-in-law had been introduced to anyone she had not previously met. In Sweden, however, etiquette requires a new arrival to introduce themselves to anyone they do not know. Her sister-in-law was very offended by Christina's question, assuming Christina was implying she did not know the rules for greeting people politely.

Christina encountered a cross-cultural communication problem on returning to her own native culture. The potential areas of misunderstanding are even greater when we venture into new cultures. Anyone who has travelled outside their own speech community is likely to have had some experience of miscommunication based on cultural differences. Often these relate to different assumptions deriving from different 'normal' environments. A Thai student in Britain, for example, reported not being able to understand what her hostess meant when she asked *On which day of the week would you like to have your bath?* Coming from a very hot country with a 'water-oriented culture', the notion that she might have a bath only once a week was very difficult to grasp. Learning another language usually involves a great deal more than learning the literal meaning of the words, how to put them together, and how to pronounce them. We need to know what they mean in the cultural context in which they are normally used. And that involves some understanding of the cultural and social norms of their users.

We automatically make many unconscious sociolinguistic assumptions about what people mean when they ask a particular question or make a statement. When we ask someone to introduce an honoured guest at an important formal dinner, we expect something more elaborate than *This is Dr Kennedy*. When we ask someone to dinner we assume they will know the norms concerning appropriate dress, time of arrival, and possible topics for discussion during the evening. Detailed discussion of the cat's latest operation or the innards of your new car are generally not considered appropriate, for instance.

Exercise 9

Note the assumptions about appropriate topics that operate at your family dinner table. Are there some topics which are acceptable or 'safe', and others which are 'taboo'?

Example 21

Hostess: Have another helping.
Guest: No thanks I am thoroughly fed up.

There are sociolinguistic rules for polite acceptance and refusal which differ cross-culturally. Refusing an invitation appropriately in Western culture can be a challenging task. How do you refuse a lift home from someone you don't like? How do you refuse an invitation to a meal from someone who is your social superior? An excuse is mandatory, and it needs to be plausible and reasonably specific. In some cultures there are very general vague formulas such as *I'm busy that night I'm afraid*, which are perfectly acceptable. But in many Western communities people expect to be provided with a more specific reason for a refusal. Where solidarity is the dominant social dimension, privacy is reduced and vagueness about one's activities is seen as evasive. Being polite in such contexts involves knowing how to express a range of speech functions in a culturally appropriate way.

> **Example 22**
>
> When Rebecca arrived in New Zealand from Nottingham in England, she and her family were invited to a Christmas party at a neighbour's house. *Bring a plate* she was told, and, thinking her hosts must be having a very big party if they expected to run out of plates, she obligingly brought four. Empty ones! When she arrived she was embarrassed to discover that *bring a plate* meant bring a contribution to the food. Fortunately she had some flowers with her to cover her confusion.

Rebecca's experience is not unusual. The phrase *bring a plate* is a common trap for unsuspecting new arrivals in New Zealand. A commonly quoted phrase is *Ladies a plate, gentlemen a crate*, meaning women should bring some food and men some beer.

Having accepted an invitation to dinner, what are the sociolinguistic rules which then apply? What is the appropriate linguistic formula for the beginning of the meal? *Buon appetito* in Italy, *bon appétit* in France, *smakelijk eten* in Holland, *Guten Appetit* in Germany. At a Maori gathering a prayer always precedes the meal, as it does in the rather different Liverpool household of the Catholic Boswell family portrayed in the old British TV programme *Bread*.

Then there is the problem of how you get enough to eat. In some parts of India and Taiwan, as well as in parts of the Arabic-speaking world, it is considered impolite to accept food when it is first offered. Only on the third offer is it appropriate to accept, and, correspondingly, only a third refusal is considered definitive by the offerer. There are many stories of over-replete Western visitors who had not worked out this cultural norm. On the other hand, overseas visitors who operate with such norms are likely to perceive their English hosts as ungenerous, because a second helping is offered only once. Once again the sociolinguistic norms reflect cultural values. Plying someone with food is regarded as positively polite behaviour, especially in cultures with sharp economic differences between social groups. In Western society, on the other hand, fatness is not regarded as a sign of wealth. Indeed thinness is highly valued and sociolinguistic dinner norms tend to take account of the possibility that guests are dieting.

These examples illustrate that ways of expressing the same speech act may differ quite markedly from one culture to another. These differences may seem totally random and unpredictable, but in fact they are not. They reflect the different social values and attitudes of different societies. Greeting routines, which are discussed in the next section, provide further illustrations of this point.

> **Exercise 10**
>
> At the end of a telephone conversation which he had initiated, a German professor said to his English colleague, Tom, *That is very good then. Good evening.*
>   What is odd about this form of farewell?
>
> *Answer at end of chapter*

C

Language variation: focus on uses

▨ Greetings

> ### Example 23
>
> (a) How are you?
> (b) Where are you going?
> (c) Have you eaten?
> (d) Where do you come from?
> (e) Are you married?
> (f) How much do you earn?
> (g) What do you weigh?

In different cultures each of these questions is perfectly acceptable as part of a normal greeting routine. They are formulas, and the expected answer is ritualistic. Just as a detailed blow-by-blow description of the state of your cold would be unexpected and inappropriate in response to *How are you?*, so the South-East Asian questioner does not expect a minute and specific account of your intended journey and destination. Just as *fine* is enough of an answer to the first question, so *along the way* or *just a short distance* is an appropriate and polite response to the second. Greeting formulas universally serve an affective function of establishing non-threatening contact and rapport, but their precise content is clearly culture specific.

The sociolinguistic rules governing more formal meetings are usually equally culturally prescribed. The Maori ritual of encounter, for instance, is a complex procedure. The bare structure of the ritual is represented by the following sequence of speech events.

The elements in brackets are not used on all occasions, while the other elements, however brief, are observable at any Maori formal meeting. Figure 11.2 specifies the order in which the elements occur. There are also rules governing which particular elements occur on any particular occasion. A wero, for example, is a ritual challenge which involves actions and fearsome noises, but no words. It is appropriate only in welcoming a very high-ranking visitor such as the Prime Minister or the Governor-General. The British Queen always faces a wero when she visits New Zealand.

1. (WAEREA) Protective incantation	2. (WERO) Challenge	3. KARANGA Call	4. (POOWHIRI) Action chant
5. TANGI Keening	6. WHAIKOORERO Oratory or formal speeches	7. HONGI Pressing noses	

Figure 11.2 Maori formal meeting ritual

Source: Simplified from Salmond, 1974: 201. Reproduced with permission

There are also rules about who is eligible to contribute different elements. The gender, age and status of appropriate participants is pre-determined, for instance. The wero is performed by a young man (a warrior in earlier times). The karanga is the prerogative of the oldest and most respected woman on each side. The women exchange high chanted calls of greeting and invoke the dead in a series of calls, often improvised to fit the occasion. The length of some contributions is also dependent on the occasion. The more formal and important the occasion, the more speeches (whaikoorero) for instance, and the longer they are.

Both the visitors and the hosts have to proceed through all stages of the ritual greeting (with slightly different rules for the ordering of hosts' and guests' whaikoorero or speeches in different tribes), until all have spoken. The hongi – the greeting between the two groups – is then the final stage of the formal encounter. In a long queue with the most respected elders at the front, the visitors file past the hosts. They greet each in turn by gently pressing noses and uttering a greeting such as *kia ora* or *tena koe*. The next stage in proceedings may be a discussion, a debate, or an exchange of views on an important political issue, or it may simply be time to relax. The occasion will always conclude with a meal, however.

The importance of appropriately welcoming visitors in Polynesian culture has widespread repercussions. These formal events are not isolated set pieces which Polynesian people produce for special occasions. The values they reflect pervade Polynesian culture. Maori and Samoan parents often feel uncomfortable at school meetings, for example, where the principal, with the good intention of 'dispensing with formalities', does not bother with any formal welcome or introductions. To the Polynesian parents this is getting priorities all wrong, putting business ahead of people. Welcoming someone properly, even in a relatively informal context, is very important, and sharing food is also an important sign that the occasion has been concluded appropriately.

Exercise 11

At a formal meeting where a number of new courses were being formally ratified by a group of teachers, a Maori contributor commented that the lack of discussion and the silence with which the proposals were met, would have been regarded as an ominous sign in his culture. Most of those present were Pakeha New Zealanders. Knowing that the preparatory discussion had already taken place elsewhere, they interpreted the lack of talk as a sign that all were in agreement and there were no problems. By contrast, as indicated by the Maori contributor's comment, a group of Maori people would have seen it as appropriate at this stage to welcome the proposals and explicitly record their consent to them.

When silence contrasts with speech it can be very communicative. In different cultures and contexts, silence may convey respect, consent, disagreement, attention, disapproval, anger or boredom.

For each of the contexts below there are some cultures where silence is the appropriate response, and others where talk is the appropriate response. Is silence or speech more appropriate in these contexts in your culture?

▶

C

Language variation: focus on uses

If speech is appropriate then what message does silence convey?

(a) On first meeting someone.
(b) When someone has put forward a proposal at a meeting.
(c) At the dinner table.
(d) When you are accused of wrongdoing.
(e) While listening to someone talk.

In this chapter I have discussed a number of different speech functions, and the ways in which they may be expressed, as well as some of the reasons why people express the same speech function differently on different occasions. Social context, formality, and the relationship between participants, have proved important influences in this area as elsewhere. The effect of these influences on the form of a speech act is often perceived as a matter of politeness. The relevance of social factors to the linguistic expression of politeness has therefore been another important thread throughout this chapter.

The sociolinguistic rules or appropriate ways of speaking in different communities are clearly quite distinctive in a range of areas. Speech functions are expressed differently in different communities. Being polite involves understanding the social values which govern the way social dimensions such as status, solidarity and formality are expressed. A sociolinguistic description aims to identify the different weight put on these factors in different cultures.

In the next chapter, these themes will be developed further as we examine differences in the way in which women and men express different speech functions and linguistic politeness.

ANSWERS TO EXERCISES IN CHAPTER 11

Answers to exercise 1

(a) Any of the following utterances could be categorised as primarily expressive, though the first four could probably be most usefully labelled as 'phatic' in function.
Good morning Sue.
Lovely day.
Yes it's beautiful.
Makes you wonder what we're doing here doesn't it.
Mm, that's right.
Thanks that's great.
No problem.
Had it occurred without the utterance which precedes it, the last utterance could have served as referential in function, conveying information that the task could and would be achieved in time. However, in the context of the previous utterance, it is more likely to be intended and interpreted as reassurance, i.e. expressive.
(b) An example of an utterance which serves a primarily directive function:
Look I wonder if you could possibly sort this lot out by 10.

(c) Examples of utterances which serve a primarily referential function:
Yes sure.
I need them for a meeting.

In a different context, the latter could have served as a directive, but in the context of the previous utterance, which is clearly directive, it is more likely to be intended and interpreted as informative or referential. It may also be expressive – apologising for the short notice.

Answer to exercise 2

There are an infinite number of possible utterances which could express this directive.
There are many obvious and relatively direct ways such as
sit down
please take a seat
would you please sit down?
would you mind sitting down?
could you possibly sit down?
There are also many indirect forms such as
your legs must be tired
you must be worn out
here's a seat
do you want to rest?
or even
I can't see
The last example was addressed to someone standing in front of the speaker when they should have been sitting down.

The context determines the appropriate form of a directive. Context will also often determine whether a particular utterance may be interpreted as a directive. Further examples are discussed in the next section.

Answers to exercise 4

(a) could act as an informative as well as a directive to run or get out (or to shoot!)
(b) expresses admiration (expressive) as well as encouragement to continue behaving in a particular way (directive)
(c) could be expressing a wish but is more likely to be a directive which also provides information
(d) expresses how the speaker feels, but is simultaneously informative, and could be directive if it serves as a hint that it is time to leave.

Answer to exercise 6

Mutual *vous* generally expresses some social distance between two people, so complete strangers generally use mutual *vous*, for instance.

Vous is also used non-reciprocally to express the speaker's respect for the addressee. A younger person would generally use *vous* to an older person with higher status, for instance, even if they knew them as an acquaintance. The patterns vary from one speech community to another, however, and in many communities mutual *tu* is spreading to more and more contexts.

Answers to exercise 7

The answer to both these questions for many communities is that where one person has higher status or is superior they have the right to initiate a change. The subordinate person may suggest

C

Language variation: focus on uses

a change, but in doing so they risk causing offence, since they may be regarded as trying to increase the intimacy of the relationship. This is usually to their advantage, so it is often not considered polite for them to make such a move. The superior can suggest the move with impunity, since it is to the addressee's advantage to be on closer terms with a superior. Where both participants are of equal status either may suggest or try out a move to first names, though the risk of rebuff is always present. In many English-speaking communities the move to FN between equals is now so rapid that this problem rarely arises. The issue is discussed further in the next section.

Answer to exercise 8

This is an example where cross-cultural differences in the rules of polite interaction have the potential to cause grave difficulties for the Samoan child in a New Zealand school. Non-verbal messages are particularly powerful, but also particularly vulnerable to misinterpretation. A hunched posture may be seen as an uncooperative stance, possibly expressing resentment. It is polite to wait till asked to sit down in the office of a superior. Avoiding the questioner's eyes is likely to be interpreted as evasive behaviour.

In fact these communicative patterns are culturally appropriate ways of expressing respect to a superior in Samoan culture. A bowed posture is respectful, since one must attempt to keep oneself at a lower level than the superior. This also accounts for Tino's sitting down quickly. Keeping one's eyes lowered is similarly a signal of respect. Finally it is not appropriate in Samoan culture for Tino to 'answer back'. He should hear the principal's reprimand in silence. His mono-syllabic answers reflect wariness in a situation where he is unsure how to respond appropriately. In his own culture, shame might well keep him appropriately silent in a parallel context.

Note that, by contrast, looking at people fixedly for several seconds ('staring') is not polite in British or New Zealand culture, whereas in places like Slovenia it is perfectly acceptable.

Answer to exercise 10

There are two odd features of the German professor's farewell from Tom's point of view. First there is no opportunity for Tom to respond to the professor's pre-closing formula. A pre-closing formula checks out that the other person is ready to close the conversation. It often takes the form of *is that OK then?* or *right?* to which the other person responds similarly, but with a falling intonation. The professor pre-closes with a slightly odd but recognisable formula *That is very good then.* But he then proceeds immediately to a final closing formula without giving Tom a chance to respond.

The second odd usage is the phrase *good evening. Good evening* is a greeting formula, not a farewell. *Goodbye* would be more appropriate. Note that *good night*, which closely resembles *good evening* in its form, is a farewell formula, but not one generally considered appropriate on the telephone between acquaintances. The reasons appear to be that *good night* has connotations of intimacy, or perhaps it implies that the call has been unreasonably late. The conventions of telephone behaviour are another fascinating area for cross-cultural investigation, as well as those governing greetings and farewells.

▩ Concepts introduced

Speech function
Phatic function
Directive function
Positive politeness and negative politeness
Cross-cultural communication

References

The following sources provided material for this chapter:

Brown and Gilman (1960) on address forms
Brown and Levinson (1987) on politeness
Ervin-Tripp (1972) on address forms
Geertz (1960) on Javanese
Goodwin (1980) on girls' and boys' directives
Halliday (1973, 1975) on speech functions and children's language
Holmes (1983) on teachers' directives
Hymes (1974) on speech functions
Johnston and Robertson (1993) on New Zealand address system
Laver (1981) on British address usage
Leech (1983) on politeness and pragmatics
Mooney (1980) on directives
Richards and Schmidt (1983) on cross-culturally different speech acts
Salmond (1974) on Maori greeting rituals
Searle (1976) on speech acts
Weigel and Weigel (1985) on American directives
West (1990) on doctors' directives
Wilford (1982) on children's directives

Quotations

Example 4 is from Haupt (1970: 101–2) cited in Spender (1980: 41).
Example 8 is from Holmes (1983: 110).
Example 10 is based on Mooney (1980).
Examples 13 and 15 are based on Wilford (1982).
Example 14 is from Weigel and Weigel (1985).
Example 16 is from Blum-Kulka, Danet and Gherson (1985: 135–6).
Example 19 is from Blocker (1976: 9).
Example 20 is based on Paulston (1974).

Useful additional reading

Holmes (1995)
Kiesling and Bratt-Paulston (2005), Part 2
Lakoff and Ide (2005)
Meyerhoff (2006), Ch. 5
Saville-Troike (2003), Ch. 2
Sifianou (1992)
Wardhaugh (2006), Chs 10 and 11

Language variation: focus on uses

Gender, politeness and stereotypes

In this section of the book where we are examining styles and registers, the way language is used, the relationship between language, thought and culture, and linguistic attitudes, the issue of 'women's language' is one which illustrates all these concepts. Is 'women's language' a distinct style or register of a language? Are women more polite than men? Are there any differences in the way women and men interact? How is language used to refer to women and men? What message does the language used about women convey about their status in the community? These are the questions I will address in this chapter. Chapter 7 reviewed some of the evidence that women speak differently from men. In this chapter I examine claims that women and men use language differently, and I also look at what language reveals about the way society categorises women.

WOMEN'S LANGUAGE AND CONFIDENCE

Example 1

'. . . a girl is damned if she does, damned if she doesn't. If she refuses to talk like a lady, she is ridiculed and subjected to criticism as unfeminine; if she does learn, she is ridiculed as unable to think clearly, unable to take part in a serious discussion: in some sense, as less than fully human. These two choices which a woman has – to be less than a woman or less than a person – are highly painful.'

While some social dialectologists suggested that women were status conscious, and that this explained their use of standard speech forms (see chapter 7), Robin Lakoff, an American linguist, suggested almost the opposite. She argued that women were using language which reinforced their subordinate status; they were 'colluding in their own subordination' by the way they spoke.

Social dialect research focussed on differences between women's and men's speech in the areas of pronunciation (such as [in] vs [iŋ]) and morphology (such as past tense forms), with some attention to syntactic constructions (such as multiple negation). Robin

Lakoff shifted the focus of research on gender differences to syntax, semantics and style. She suggested that women's subordinate social status in American society is indicated by the language women use, as well as in the language used about them. She identified a number of linguistic features which she claimed were used more often by women than by men, and which in her opinion expressed uncertainty and lack of confidence.

Example 2

1. Lawyer: What was the nature of your acquaintance with the late Mrs E. D.?
   Witness A: Well, we were, uh, very close friends. Uh she was even sort of like a mother to me.
2. Lawyer: And had the heart not been functioning, in other words, had the heart been stopped, there would have been no blood to have come from that region?
   Witness B: It may leak down depending on the position of the body after death. But the presence of blood in the alveoli indicates that some active respiratory action had to take place.

The speech of the two female witnesses in example 2 contrasts in that witness A uses features of what Lakoff labelled 'women's language', while witness B does not. Before I describe these features, you might like to see if your intuitions about what constitutes 'women's language' agree with Lakoff's.

Exercise 1

Consider the following sentences. Put F beside those you think were said by a woman, M beside those you think were said by a man and F/M beside those you think could have been said by either.

(a) Close the door.
(b) That's an adorable dog.
(c) Oh dear, the TV set's broken.
(d) I'll be damned there's a friend of mine!
(e) I was very tired.
(f) Won't you please get me that pencil?
(g) They did the right thing didn't they?
(h) You're damn right!
(i) I was just exhausted.
(j) My goodness, there's the Prime Minister!
(k) I was so mad.
(l) Damn it, I've lost my keys!

Answers at end of chapter

▓ Features of 'women's language'

Lakoff suggested that women's speech was characterised by linguistic features such as the following.[1] [↗ indicates rising intonation]

(a) Lexical hedges or fillers, e.g. *you know, sort of, well, you see.*
(b) Tag questions, e.g. *she's very nice, isn't she?*
(c) Rising intonation on declaratives, e.g. *it's really go͗od.*
(d) 'Empty' adjectives, e.g. *divine, charming, cute.*
(e) Precise colour terms, e.g. *magenta, aquamarine.*
(f) Intensifiers such as *just* and *so*, e.g. *I like him so much.*
(g) 'Hypercorrect' grammar, e.g. consistent use of standard verb forms.
(h) 'Superpolite' forms, e.g. indirect requests, euphemisms.
(i) Avoidance of strong swear words, e.g. *fudge, my goodness.*
(j) Emphatic stress, e.g. *it was a BRILLIANT performance.*

Many of these features are illustrated in the list of sentences in exercise 1. Lakoff's claims were based on her own intuitions and observations, but they sparked off a spate of research because they appeared to be so specific and easy to investigate.

Much of this initial research was methodologically unsatisfactory. Speech was recorded in laboratory conditions with assigned topics, and sometimes rather artificial constraints (such as a screen between the speakers). Most of the subjects were university students. Consequently it was difficult to generalise from the results to natural informal speech in the community as a whole. In addition the linguistic analysis of the data was often rather unsophisticated.

Example 3

'The final syntactic category is imperative constructions in question form, which are defined as alternatives to simple and direct ways of ordering action. They are questions which are substituted for commands. "Will you please close the door?" instead of "Close the door," is an example of an imperative in question form.'

This quotation illustrates the kind of statement which betrayed lack of linguistic expertise among these early investigators of Lakoff's claims about women's speech. No linguist would describe 'will you please close the door?' as an imperative construction, and the expression 'imperative construction in question form' confuses form and function. (It is an interrogative construction expressing directive function.) Yet this was not untypical. Many of the categorisation systems devised by non-linguists to measure features of 'women's language' seem rather odd or arbitrary to linguists. Another study, for instance, made a distinction between 'fillers' and 'hedges', with *sort of* classified as a hedge, while *well* and *you see* were described as 'meaningless particles' and assigned to the same category as 'pause fillers' such as *uh, um,* and *ah*. But this is a complicated area where form alone is never an adequate guide for classification, and function and meaning need careful analysis.

As well as lacking linguistic expertise, many researchers also missed Lakoff's fundamental point. She had identified a number of linguistic features which were unified by their *function* of expressing lack of confidence. Her list was not an arbitrary conglomeration of forms. It was unified by the fact that the forms identified were means of expressing uncertainty or tentativeness. Other researchers, however, ignored this functional coherence, and simply listed any forms that produced a statistical difference between women and men, without providing any satisfactory explanation for why these differences might have arisen. One study, for example, analysed short sections from formal speeches by American female and male college students and found they differed on a range of features including the number of prepositional phrases, such as *at the back* (women used more) and progressive verb forms, such as *was walking* (men used more). Without a theoretical framework, it is difficult to know how to interpret such apparently arbitrary differences.

Nor did Lakoff claim her list was comprehensive. But because they ignored the underlying functional coherence which unified Lakoff's list of features, many researchers treated it as definitive. The internal coherence of the features Lakoff identified can be illustrated by dividing them into two groups. Firstly, there are linguistic devices which may be used for hedging or reducing the force of an utterance. Secondly, there are features which may boost or intensify a proposition's force. Researchers who recognised this functional unifying factor included in their analysis any form which had a hedging or boosting effect on an assertion. Those who didn't tended to stick to Lakoff's list as if it had been handed down like Moses' tablets.

Exercise 2

Allocate as many as possible of the features in the list provided by Lakoff to one of the following columns.

Features which may serve as:
Hedging devices   **Boosting devices**

Answer at end of chapter

Lakoff argued that both kinds of modifiers were evidence of an unconfident speaker. Hedging devices explicitly signal lack of confidence, while boosting devices express the speaker's anticipation that the addressee may remain unconvinced and therefore supply extra reassurance. So, she suggested, women use hedging devices to express uncertainty, and they use intensifying devices to persuade their addressee to take them seriously. Women boost the force of their utterances because they think that otherwise they will not be heard or paid attention to. Thus, according to Lakoff, both hedges and boosters express women's lack of confidence.

C

Language variation: focus on uses

It is not surprising, given the range of methods used to collect and analyse the data, that the research results were often contradictory. In some studies women were reported as using more tag questions than men, for instance, while in others men used more than women. Some researchers reported that women used up to three times as many hedges as men, while others noted no gender differences. Most, but not all, claimed women used more boosters or intensifiers than men.

One pair of researchers recorded the speech of witnesses in a law court and found that male witnesses used more 'women's language' features than women witnesses with more expertise in court or higher occupational status. Example 4 illustrates this.

Example 4

Lawyer: And you saw, you observed what?

Witness C: Well, after I heard – I can't really, I can't definitely state whether the brakes or the lights came first, but I rotated my head slightly to the right, and looked directly behind Mr Z, and I saw reflections of lights, and uh, very very instantaneously after that I heard a very, very loud explosion – from my standpoint of view it would have been an implosion because everything was forced outward like this, like a grenade thrown into the room. And, uh, it was, it was terrifically loud.

Witness C is a male witness who uses a relatively high number of hedges and boosters. These researchers suggested the forms be relabelled 'powerless forms' to emphasise a point made by Lakoff herself, that the patterns she had noted were characteristic of the speech of the powerless in society rather than of women exclusively. (It is also worth noting that one could argue the witness was simply being cautious about his claims.)

Overall, however, Lakoff's claim that women used more hedging and boosting devices than men was borne out in a number of studies. But a more detailed analysis sometimes showed that these forms were not always expressing uncertainty.

◼ Lakoff's linguistic features as politeness devices

Example 5

[⟋ indicates rising intonation]
Susan is a university student. She is telling her friend and flatmate about her experiences at school.
I did my exams in sixty-three wás it.

The tag question is a syntactic device listed by Lakoff which may express uncertainty, as example 5 illustrates. Susan is uncertain about the date, and she indicates this with a tag which signals doubt about what she is asserting. This tag focusses on the referential meaning of Susan's assertion – the accuracy of the information she is giving. But tags may also express affective meaning. They may function as facilitative or positive politeness devices, providing an addressee with an easy entrée into a conversation, as illustrated in example 6.

Example 6

[↘ indicates falling intonation]
Margaret is holding a small party to introduce a new neighbour, Frank, to other people in the street. She introduces Frank to an old friend, Andrew.

Margaret: Andrew this is our new neighbour, Frank. Andrew
                   has just changed jobs, haven't you.
Andrew: Yes I am now a well-paid computer programmer instead of a poorly
                   paid administrative assistant.

Teachers, interviewers, hosts at parties and, in general, those in leadership roles who are responsible for the success of an interaction tend to use tags in this facilitative way. The host provides the guests with a topic of conversation. In example 7, the teacher makes it easy for the child to participate.

Example 7

Mrs Short is a primary school teacher working with a group of 5-year-olds. They are preparing for a nature walk by looking at pictures of birds, flowers and leaves that they hope to see on their walk.

Mrs Short: Here's a pretty one what's this one called Simon?
Simon: Mm, erm [pause]
Mrs Short: See its tail, look at its tail. It's a fantail, isn't it?
Simon: Mm a fantail. I seen one of them.

A tag may also soften a directive or a criticism as in example 8.

Example 8

Zoe and her mother Claire have just come home from the supermarket. Zoe empties the shopping basket all over the kitchen floor.

Claire: That was a bit of a daft thing to do, wasn't it?

The tag functions not to express uncertainty, but rather affectively to soften the critical comment, indicating concern for Zoe's feelings.

Tags may also be used as confrontational and coercive devices. Example 9 is an example of a tag used to force feedback from an uncooperative addressee.

Example 9

A police superintendent is interviewing a detective constable and is criticising the constable's performance:

A: . . . you'll probably find yourself um before the Chief Constable, okay?
B: Yes, Sir, yes, understood.
A: Now you er fully understand that, don't you?
B: Yes, Sir, indeed, yeah.

The tag in this exchange functions not to hedge but rather to strengthen the negative force of the utterance in which it occurs. So here we have a tag which could be classified as a boosting device. Treating all tags as signals of uncertainty is clearly misleading.

Table 12.1 summarises the patterns found in a 60,000-word corpus containing equal amounts of female and male speech collected in a range of matched contexts. It is clear that in this corpus the women used more tags than the men, as Lakoff predicted. But more interesting is the fact that women and men used them more often for different

Table 12.1 Distribution of tag questions by function and sex of speaker

Function of tag	Women %	Men %
Expressing uncertainty	35	61
Facilitative	59	26
Softening	6	13
Confrontational	–	–
Total	100	100
N	51	39

Source: Based on Holmes 1984a: 54. Reproduced with permission

functions. Women put more emphasis than men on the polite or affective functions of tags, using them as facilitative positive politeness devices. Men, on the other hand, used more tags for the expression of uncertainty.

Exercise 3

Using the contextual information together with the information provided on intonation, how would you characterise the functions of the tags in the following examples?

(a) *The teacher is talking to Sam, a pupil who is looking at a picture of a butterfly in a cocoon in a book:*
   Teacher: What's this called Sam?
   Sam: *No answer.*
   Teacher: It's a cocoon isn't it?
(b) *Conversation in kitchen between flatmates:*
   Thomas: This isn't Bridget's egg beater is it?
   Michael: No, it's ours. We still haven't found hers.
(c) *Older child 'tutor' to younger child who is reading to her:*
   Fran: That's not right is it? Try again eh.
(d) *To visitor who has called in for a chat with a group of neighbours:*
   Sally: Ray had some bad luck at the races yesterday didn't you Ray?
(e) *One friend to another in a relaxed conversation at her home:*
   Fiona: But then it would pass on to the rest of your family wouldn't it?
   Jim: No, not necessarily.

Answers at end of chapter

What has emerged from this discussion of tag questions is not peculiar to tags. Many linguistic forms have complex functions. Similar results have been found when other so-called 'hedges' such as *you know* and *I think* have been analysed. They are used differently in different contexts. They mean different things according to their pronunciation, their position in the utterance, what kind of speech act they are modifying, and who is using them to whom in what context. Like tags, they are often being used as politeness devices rather than as expressions of uncertainty.

Analyses which take account of the function of features of women's speech often reveal women as facilitative and supportive conversationalists, rather than as unconfident, tentative talkers. What is more, this image is consistent with the explanation suggested in chapter 7 for the use of more standard speech forms by many women. In using standard forms these women could be seen as responding positively to their addressees by accommodating to their speech. Women's greater use of politeness devices can be regarded as another aspect of their consideration of the addressee.

This also suggests that explanations of differences between women's and men's speech behaviour which refer only to the status or power dimension are likely to be unsatisfactory. The social distance (or solidarity dimension) is at least as influential. Many of the features which characterise women's language are positive politeness devices expressing solidarity. In the next section we will look at some evidence which suggests that the formality of the context is another relevant factor in a comparison of women's and men's use of language.

Exercise 4

A study of the language used by prospective jurors in law courts in Tucson, Arizona, identified interesting grammatical differences between women's and men's utterances. It was found that men deleted what were described as 'non-essential' words more often than women – especially in monologues. (a) is an utterance with an example of what was regarded as 'non-essential' elements deleted.

(a) I'm employed with the city of Tucson. Aah been there over 9 months.
In this utterance *I have* has been deleted before *been*.

(b) My name is Sophia K. Jacobs. I'm employed by Krable, Parsons and Dooley.
I've been employed there for 10 years as a bookkeeper an' junior accountant.
My husband is employed by (Amphitheater) school district. He's a teacher.
And he's worked there for 10 years. I have never been on a trial jury before.
I don't have any formal legal training.

(c) Herb R. Beasley, senior. President of Beasley Refrigeration Incorporated.
Do commercial refrigeration. And my wife's name is Lillian an' she works in
the office. I've never been on a trial jury and no legal training.

Utterance (b) illustrates the kind of utterances that women jurors produced. Utterance (c) illustrates the kind that male jurors typically produced. Overall in this study men deleted 'non-essential' words more often than women.

(i) Compare utterances (b) and (c). Identify places where so-called 'non-essential' elements may have been deleted.

(ii) How would you interpret the significance of this data?

(iii) What extra information would you need in order to support your preferred interpretation?

Answers at end of chapter

The data reviewed in this section has been collected in English-speaking communities. To what extent can the patterns described be generalised to different cultures? This is an interesting question which to some extent still awaits an answer, since there is not yet a great deal of research in this area. There are some indications, however, that we should be cautious in interpreting patterns observed in other cultures through Western spectacles. In a study of a Mayan community in Mexico, for instance, overall the women used more politeness devices than the men, so the pattern seemed to resemble the Western pattern. But, interestingly, the men used far fewer politeness forms to each other than to women, so male talk to males was relatively plain and unmodified. In all other contexts everyone used more politeness devices. In this community, 'men's talk' could be seen as the unusual variety rather than women's talk. Women's patterns were used in most contexts.

In Malagasy, by contrast, it is the men rather than the women who qualify and modify their utterances, and who generally use less direct language. Since indirectness is equated with politeness, Malagasy men are correspondingly considered the more polite speakers, another clear contrast with Western norms, but one which is accounted for by the specific social roles of women and men in that community. In other communities, too, factors such as social role or status are relevant to the different patterns of language use by women and men. Indeed, a study of Samoan personal narratives found that status was more important than gender in accounting for the use of certain positive politeness devices. Statusful women with a Samoan title, for instance, used fewer such devices than young untitled men. On the other hand, titled Samoan men used the highest frequency of negative politeness devices, expressing social distance. In order to interpret such patterns, researchers must look carefully not only at the relationships between women and men in different cultures, but also at the contribution of factors such as status, role, interaction patterns, and the meanings conveyed by particular patterns of linguistic behaviour in particular contexts and cultures.

INTERACTION

> ### Example 10
>
> 'A good guiding dinner party principle is given by Mrs Ian Fleming. She says that guests can be roughly divided into "shouters" and "listeners", and the best assortment is three shouters to five listeners.'

If you had to put money on the likely gender of the 'shouters' vs the 'listeners' what would you venture? Despite the widespread stereotype of women as the talkative sex, and proverbs which characterise women as garrulous ('Women's tongues are like lambs' tails; they are never still'), most of the research evidence points the other way. In a wide range of contexts, particularly non-private ones such as television interviews, staff meetings and conference discussions, where talking may increase your status, men dominate the talking time.

There are many features of interaction which have been shown to differentiate the talk of women and men in particular contexts. Mrs Fleming's distinction identifies one of them. In this section I will discuss two others: interrupting behaviour and conversational feedback.

Interruptions

The most widely quoted study on interruptions collected examples of students' exchanges in coffee bars, shops and other public places on a tape-recorder carried by one of the researchers. The results were dramatic, as table 12.2 illustrates. In same-gender interactions, interruptions were pretty evenly distributed between speakers. In cross-gender interactions, almost all the interruptions were from males.

Table 12.2 Average number of interruptions per interaction

	Interruptions %
Same-sex interaction	
Speaker 1	43
Speaker 2	57
Cross-sex interaction	
Woman	4
Man	96

Source: From Zimmerman and West 1975: 116

These researchers followed up this study with one which recorded interactions in sound-proof booths in a laboratory. The percentage of male interruptions decreased to 75 per cent in this less natural setting, but there was no doubt that men were still doing most of the interrupting. In other contexts, too, it has been found that men interrupt others more than women do. In departmental meetings and doctor–patient interactions, for instance, the pattern holds. Women got interrupted more than men, regardless of whether they were the doctors or the patients. In exchanges between parents and children, fathers did most of the interrupting, and daughters were interrupted most – both by their mothers and their fathers. And a study of pre-schoolers found that some boys start practising this strategy for dominating the talk at a very early age. Women are evidently socialised from early childhood to expect to be interrupted. Consequently, they generally give up the floor with little or no protest, as example 11 illustrates.

Example 11

A conversational interaction between a man and a woman:

Woman: How's your paper coming?
Man: Alright I guess. I haven't done much in the past two weeks.
Woman: Yeah. Know how that ⌈ can ⌉
Man: ⌊ Hey ⌋ ya' got an extra cigarette?
Woman: Oh uh sure (*hands him the pack*)
                 like my ⌈ pa- ⌉
Man: ⌊ How ⌋ 'bout a match
Woman: 'Ere ya go uh like my ⌈ pa- ⌉
Man: ⌊ Thanks ⌋
Woman: Sure. I was gonna tell you ⌈ my- ⌉
Man: ⌊ Hey ⌋ I'd really like ta' talk but
                                                                 I gotta run – see ya
Woman: Yeah.

(*The words within the square brackets were uttered simultaneously.*)

Exercise 5

Does the data in table 12.3 support the claims made above concerning women's and men's interaction patterns? Who talks most, men or women? Do the men interrupt more than the women?

What questions or qualifications would you want to raise in order to be sure you were interpreting the data accurately?

Answer at end of chapter

Table 12.3 Turns, speaking time and interruptions in seven staff meetings

Speaker	Average turns per meeting	Average no. of seconds per turn	Average 'did interrupt' per meeting	Average 'was interrupted' per meeting
Woman A	5.5	7.8	0.5	3.0
Woman B	5.8	10.0	0.0	3.0
Woman C	8.0	3.0	1.0	3.2
Woman D	20.5	8.5	2.0	7.5
Man E	11.3	16.5	2.0	2.6
Man F	32.3	17.1	8.0	6.7
Man G	32.6	13.2	6.6	6.3
Man H	30.2	10.7	4.3	5.0
Man I	17.0	15.8	4.5	2.5

Source: Modified from Eakins and Eakins (1979: 58). Reproduced with permission

---

Exercise 6

With their permission, tape-record a relaxed conversation between a small group of your friends. Include both males and females if possible. Listen to the tape and count the interruptions. Do the men interrupt more than the women? What kinds of problems arise in attempting this exercise? Discuss your findings with your friends.

Answer at end of chapter

■ **Feedback**

Example 12

Mary: I worked in that hotel for – ah 11 years and I found the patrons were really really you know good.

Jill: Mm.

Mary: You had the odd one or two ruffian'd come in and cause a fight but they were soon dealt with.

Jill: Right, really just takes one eh? To start trouble.

Mary: Yeah, and and it was mostly the younger ones.

Jill: Mm.

Mary: that would start you know.

Jill: Yeah.

Mary: The younger – younger ones couldn't handle their booze.

Jill: Mm.

Another aspect of the picture of women as cooperative conversationalists is the evidence that women provide more encouraging feedback to their conversational partners than men do.

One New Zealand study which examined the distribution of positive feedback (noises such as *mm* and *mhm*) in casual relaxed interaction between young people found that women gave over four times as much of this type of supportive feedback as men. American studies of informal speech as well as talk in classrooms and under laboratory conditions have also demonstrated that women provide significantly more encouraging and positive feedback to their addressees than men do. One researcher noted that women students were also more likely than men to enlarge on and develop the ideas of a previous speaker rather than challenge them.

In general, then, research on conversational interaction reveals women as cooperative conversationalists, whereas men tend to be more competitive and less supportive of others. Why are women's patterns of interaction different from men's? Is it because they are subordinate in status to men in most communities so that they must strive to please? Or are there other explanations?

C

Language variation: focus on uses

> ## Exercise 7
>
> Compare the transcript provided in example 11 with the one provided in example 12. Identify specific examples in these transcripts of the patterns of interaction discussed in the preceding section.
>
> *Answer at end of chapter*

Explanations

In an interesting range of this research, it is quite clearly gender rather than occupational status, social class, or some other social factor, which most adequately accounts for the interactional patterns described. Women doctors were consistently interrupted by their patients, while male doctors did most of the interrupting in their consultations. A study of women in business organisations showed that women bosses did not dominate the interactions. Males dominated regardless of whether they were boss or subordinate. The societally subordinate position of women indicated by these patterns has more to do with gender than role or occupation. For this data at least, women's subordinate position in a male-dominated society seems the most obvious explanatory factor.

Women's cooperative conversational strategies, however, may be explained better by looking at the influence of context and patterns of socialisation. The norms for women's talk may be the norms for small group interaction in private contexts, where the goals of the interaction are solidarity stressing – maintaining good social relations. Agreement is sought and disagreement avoided. By contrast, the norms for male interaction seem to be those of public referentially-oriented interaction. The public model is an adversarial one, where contradiction and disagreement is more likely than agreement and confirmation of the statements of others. Speakers compete for the floor and for attention; and wittiness, even at others' expense, is highly valued. These patterns seem to characterise men's talk even in private contexts, as will be illustrated below.

Exercise 8

If one accepts the generalisation that the goals of women's talk are often aimed at maintaining good social relations and emphasising solidarity, while men's talk is more often referentially oriented and competitive, whose norms prevail in mixed-gender informal interaction in your experience?

Answer at end of chapter

The differences between women and men in ways of interacting may be the result of different socialisation and acculturation patterns. If we learn ways of talking mainly in single gender peer groups, then the patterns we learn are likely to be gender-specific. And the kind of miscommunication which undoubtedly occurs between women and men may well be attributable to the different expectations each gender has of the function of the interaction, and the ways it is appropriately conducted. Some of these differences will be illustrated in the next section.

GOSSIP

Example 13

Three women chatting as they work

Maryanne: Well I don't know how she puts up with him.

Chris: God he's awful – a real dickhead I'm not kidding.

Maryanne: And he's so rude. He interrupts her all the time and he puts her down – even in front of her friends.

Fran: She must be nuts.

Maryanne: Exactly – but he's rolling of course. He gets two thousand dollars a shot as an after-dinner speaker.

Fran: Yeah?

Chris: (*singing*) Can't buy me love, can't buy me love!

Gossip describes the kind of relaxed in-group talk that goes on between people in informal contexts. In Western society, gossip is defined as 'idle talk' and considered particularly characteristic of women's interaction. Its overall function for women is to affirm solidarity and maintain the social relationships between the women involved.

Women's gossip focusses predominantly on personal experiences and personal relationships, on personal problems and feelings. It may include criticism of the behaviour of others, but women tend to avoid criticising people directly because this would cause discomfort. A common male reaction to this behaviour is to label it two-faced, but this is to mistake its purpose which is often to relieve feelings and reinforce shared values, rather than simply to communicate referential information. In gossip sessions women provide a sympathetic response to any experience recounted, focussing almost exclusively on the affective message – what it says about the speaker's feelings and relationships – rather than its referential content. Recordings of a women's group over a nine-month period, for instance, showed how women built on and developed each other's topics, told anecdotes in support of each other's points, and generally confirmed the attitudes and reactions of other participants.

Not surprisingly women's gossip is characterised by a number of the linguistic features of women's language described above. Propositions which express feelings are often attenuated and qualified, or alternatively intensified. Facilitative tags are frequent, encouraging others to comment and contribute. Women complete each other's utterances, agree frequently, and provide supportive feedback. The following example of shared turns from a gossip session between women who worked together at a bakery illustrates the cooperative and positive nature of their talk.

Example 14

Jill: Perhaps next time I see Brian I'll *pump* him for information. Brian tells me all

Fran: the gossip.

Jill: I know it's about six years old but

Fran: [laugh] it doesn't matter.

Jill: It doesn't matter at all.

Fran: True, true, it's the thought that counts.

The male equivalent of women's gossip is difficult to identify. In parallel situations the topics men discuss tend to focus on things and activities, rather than personal experiences and feelings. Topics like sport, cars and possessions turn up regularly. The focus is on information and facts rather than on feelings and reactions.

In a study of a parallel group of men working at the bakery, the linguistic features of the interaction were also quite different. Long pauses were tolerated and were apparently not interpreted as discouraging following a contribution, even one which seemed to invite a response. Responses frequently disagreed with or challenged the previous speaker's statements in any case, as example 15 illustrates.

C

Language variation: focus on uses

> **Example 15**
>
> Bernard: And er they're very smart.
> Con: Well, then, how come they keep getting caught all the time.
> Judd: Maybe that's why they
> Bernard: (*interrupts*) They don't. You've got to be really clever to pull one you know.

The men provided conflicting accounts of the same event, argued about a range of topics such as whether apples were kept in cases or crates, criticised each other constantly for apparently minor differences of approach to things, and changed topic abruptly. Their strategies for amusing each other were often to top or out-do the previous speaker's utterance or to put them down. In other words, their talk contrasted completely with the cooperative, agreeing, supportive, topically coherent talk of the women in exactly the same context – working in the bakery – on a different night.

The following excerpt illustrates the competitive verbal abuse which was typical of the male interaction in the bakery.

> **Example 16**
>
> Greg: Crate!
> Jim: Case!
> Greg: What?
> Jim: They come in cases Greg not crates.
> Greg: Oh same thing if you must be picky over every one thing.
> Jim: Just shut your fucking head Greg!
> Greg: Don't tell me to fuck off fuck (. . .)
> Jim: I'll come over and shut yo
> Allan: (*Laughingly using a thick-sounding voice*) Yeah I'll have a crate of apples thanks
> Greg: No fuck off Allan.
> Allan: A dozen.
> Con: (*Amused tone*) Shitpicker!

It seems possible that for men mock-insults and abuse serve the same function – expressing solidarity and maintaining social relationships – as compliments and agreeing comments do for women. This verbal sparring is reported by others who have examined all-male interaction and in some groups verbal insult is an established and ritual speech activity.

Evidence of this kind makes it easier to understand why some researchers have suggested that women and men belong to different cultural groups. It also helps explain why women and men sometimes miscommunicate.

Exercise 9

What do you think is the woman's primary aim in the conversation below? Is her focus mainly referential or social? How do you know?

Does the man interpret her intention accurately do you think? What is his primary concern?

The exchange took place at a camping ground. The man was fiddling with his radio attempting to tune in to a station; the woman was passing by and stopped to talk to him.

Example 17

Woman: You've got a radio there then.
Man: Yes (pause) I'm trying to get the weather.
Woman: I've been trying on mine but I can't get a thing.
Man: Mm.
Woman: We really need to know before we leave (pause) we're on bikes you see.
Man: Mm.
Woman: I've got a handicapped kiddie too (*pause*) we're from Hamilton and we're cycling to Taupo. (*pause*) Where are you going then?
Man: Taupo.

Answer at end of chapter

You should note once again, that most of the research referred to describes women's and men's interaction patterns in Western English-speaking communities, and most of the data comes from white middle-class adult speakers. While there is some evidence that women tend to be more supportive and men more competitive conversationalists in other cultures too, there is an increasing amount of research describing alternative patterns of interaction. In the rural Malagasy community mentioned above, women take more confrontational roles and their speech is more direct than men's. It is women who handle the bargaining necessary in the market-place, for instance, and it is the women who deal with family arguments and disagreements. Men's speech in this community is indirect and circumlocutionary. Not surprisingly, given that men hold the positions of power in the community, it is indirect allusive speech which

C

Language variation: focus on uses

Source: *New Zealand Herald*. Reproduced with permission

is most highly valued in the Malagasy community. The direct information-oriented style so highly prized in Western society would be regarded as unspeakably rude – and feminine! Clearly a community's attitudes towards different speech styles reflect the status of those who use them, a topic which will be pursued further in chapter 15. Incidentally, what assumptions did you make about the gender of the hedgehogs on page 314?

The Malagasy example leads to a consideration of the fact that there is variation within Western communities too. Generalisations are useful in the search for patterns and explanations, but it is important to remember that not all men behave like those in examples 11 and 16, and even Greg and Jim no doubt interact differently in different contexts. The next section outlines an approach which is much more dynamic in considering gendered language behaviour.

THE CONSTRUCTION OF GENDER

Example 18

Ed: he's I mean he's like a real artsy fartsy fag he's like [*indecipherable*]
      he's so gay he's got this like really high voice and wire rim glasses

---

The final section of chapter 8 considered ways in which individuals draw from a range of linguistic resources to construct particular social identities, including gender identity. We generally treat gender as 'given' and unalterable, automatically classifying every person we encounter as female or male without a moment's reflection. Sometimes, however, our assumptions are challenged and we have to re-think. In example 18, Ed criticises a man who fails to fit the established masculine norms, but, ironically, Ed's criticism uses features associated with, or 'indexing', a more feminine speech style, such as frequent use of the particle *like*, hedges such as *I mean*, and intensifiers, such as *real*, *so*, and *really*. Yet Ed is talking in a male-only context. This example clearly challenges some of the generalisations in earlier sections, and encourages a more dynamic and subtle analysis of the interaction between gender and talk.

Approaching gender identity as a construction, rather than as a fixed category, is also useful in accounting for examples where women adapt to masculine contexts, and men adapt to feminine contexts by using features which indirectly index or are associated with masculinity and femininity. Women in the police force, for instance, are sometimes advised to portray a masculine image – to wear bulky sweaters suggesting upper-body strength, and well-worn boots to suggest they are used to hard work. They also adopt a cool distant style; they don't smile much, and they talk 'tough'. Men who work in clothing shops and hairdressing salons, on the other hand, often construct a more feminine identity in these contexts than when they are in the pub or the sports club changing room. They use features which index femininity, such as affectionate terms of address and other characteristics of the cooperative discourse style associated with 'gossip'; they avoid strong swear words, and they act as responsive and facilitative conversationalists, encouraging their addressee to talk.

Example 19

Helen describes her daughter's attempt to learn to swim
Helen: she looked like a goldfish you (*laughs*) know there's a little head a – a rolling in the water (*laughs*) and legs sort of sagging in the water and breaststroking away you know

---

One of the more obvious ways in which people construct particular kinds of social identity is through their narratives of personal experience. In answer to a question about her father's health, one woman, Helen, gave her friend an account of what she had been doing all day, including the information that she had visited her father. Helen's long story constructs a very conservative gender identity for herself. She recounts that she had taken her children swimming, encouraged her younger daughter's attempts to swim (example 19 is a snippet from the story), persuaded her oldest daughter to cook her grandfather's lunch, and put her own needs consistently last. The identity constructed is 'good mother' and 'dutiful daughter'. The discourse style is characterised by interactive pragmatic particles such as *you know* and *you see*, appealing to shared experience, hedges like *sort of*, and even rather 'feminine' adjectives such as *cute, little* and *sweet* to describe her daughters. In other contexts, however, Helen constructs a more contestive and less conformist gender identity. At work, for instance, where she is a senior manager, she often challenges ideas she disagrees with, using a very assertive discourse style characterised by very few hedges and unmitigated direct questions.

In recounting her story Helen not only constructs her own gender identity, but she also presents very 'gendered' identities for her daughters. Example 19 presents Helen's youngest daughter, Andrea, as a sweet little girl, gamely swimming along with her admiring mother alongside. Andrea wasn't present when the story was told, but 4-year-old Ian was part of the audience in the next example.

Example 20

June and Mike are Ian's parents. Mary is his auntie who is visiting them after work.
Mary: Hi Ian what have you been up to today?
June: Oh he's been just terrible (*laugh*). Unbelievable. First he emptied all the kitchen cupboards before we were even out of bed – absolute chaos with everyone rushing round trying to get ready for work – pans and soap

powder all over the floor. (*General laughter*) Then he got himself into the bathroom and what does he do? He empties all my expensive bubble bath into the bath with the water running. So we've got bubbles every-where – the bathroom was just full of soap (*laugh*). Mike nearly broke his neck just trying to switch off the tap. He's just too much – a real monkey (*laugh*).

Mike: (*Laugh*) Yes he's a real little rascal – a real bad lad – eh Ian!

Exercise 10

What messages is Ian getting about his behaviour?
How are these signalled in the excerpt?

Answer at end of chapter

C

Narratives are just one means of constructing particular gender identities. Approaching the construction of gender as a process, rather than regarding gender as a given category, leads to a view of individuals as constantly 'doing' gender. As illustrated in earlier chapters, every phonological, lexical, and syntactic selection conveys social information. Ways of expressing solidarity or informality may also be gendered as well as expressed differently among different social and ethnic groups. The form that teasing or 'joshing' takes, for instance, is often quite distinctive for particular communities of practice. This approach encourages us to view every linguistic (and non-linguistic) choice as meaningful. Every time we speak, we are either reinforcing existing norms or we are challenging them. This belief explains why feminists object to sexist language.

SEXIST LANGUAGE

In 1980 an American linguist, Dwight Bolinger, published a book called *Language: the Loaded Weapon*. In it he explored the wide variety of ways in which the English language provides categories and ways of encoding experience which could be regarded as 'loaded' – in other words, carrying an implicit value judgement or manipulating responses. Alongside discussions of the language used in advertising and politics, he also considered the area of sexist language. Sexist language is one example of the way a culture or society conveys its values from one group to another and from one generation to the next.

Language conveys attitudes. Sexist attitudes stereotype a person according to gender rather than judging on individual merits. Sexist language encodes stereotyped attitudes to women and men. In principle, then, the study of sexist language is concerned with the way language expresses both negative and positive stereotypes of both women and men. In practice, research in this area has concentrated on the ways in which language conveys negative attitudes to women.

Can a language be sexist?

Feminists have claimed that English is a sexist language. At first sight it may seem odd to suggest that a language rather than its speakers are sexist. Sexism involves behaviour which maintains social inequalities between women and men. Can a language contribute to the maintenance of social inequalities between women and men?

There are a number of ways in which it has been suggested that the English language discriminates against women. Most obviously, perhaps, in the semantic area the English metaphors available to describe women include an extraordinarily high number of derogatory images compared to those used to describe men.

Example 21

The chicken metaphor tells the whole story of a girl's life. In her youth she is a *chick*, then she marries and begins feeling *cooped up*, so she goes to *hen parties* where she *cackles* with her friends. Then she has her *brood* and begins to *hen-peck* her husband. Finally she turns into an *old biddy*.

Animal imagery is one example where the images of women seem considerably less positive than those for men. Consider the negativity of *bitch*, *old biddy*, and *cow*, compared to *stud* and *wolf*. Animal imagery which refers to men often has at least some positive component (such as wiliness or sexual prowess). *Birds* are widely regarded as feather-brained and flighty! Even the more positive *chick* and *kitten* are sweet but helpless pets.

Women may also be described or referred to in terms of food imagery, which is equally insulting. Saccharine terms, such as *sugar*, *sweetie*, *honey*, are mainly, though not exclusively, used for addressing women. Less complimentary terms such as *crumpet* and *tart*, however, are restricted to female referents. They illustrate a common evolutionary pattern in the meaning of words referring to women. Terms which were originally neutral or affectionate eventually acquire negative connotations as they increasingly refer only to women and as their meanings focus on women as sexual objects. By contrast there appears to be less food imagery which is appropriate for referring only to men, though there are insulting terms such as *veg* and *cabbage*, and, according to one 11-year-old, *parsnip*, which may be used to abuse girls or boys!

> **Exercise 11**
>
> If you are familiar with a language other than English see if you can discover whether there is evidence of sexism expressed through the vocabulary and imagery of that language.

Many words reinforce a view of women as a deviant, abnormal or subordinate group. For example, English morphology – its word-structure – generally takes the male form as the base form and adds a suffix to signal 'female': e.g. *lion/lioness, count/countess, actor/actress, usher/usherette, hero/heroine, aviator/aviatrix*. This is true for a number of other European languages, such as French and German, too. The male form is the unmarked form, and therefore, it is argued, implicitly the norm. The use of an additional suffix to signal 'femaleness' is seen as conveying the message that women are deviant or abnormal.

It has also been suggested that suffixes like *-ess* and *-ette* trivialise and diminish women, and when they refer to occupations such as *authoress* and *poetess*, carry connotations of lack of seriousness. This attitude doubtless derives from the meaning of the associated diminutive suffixes in terms such as *laundrette* ('a little laundry') and *maisonette*.

'Generic' structures provide further evidence to support the claim that the English language marginalises women and treats them as abnormal. In fact, words like 'generic' *he* and *man* can be said to render women invisible.

> **Example 22**
>
> Mountainland ecosystems are fragile, and particularly vulnerable to the influence of man and his introduced animals . . . Life in the mountains is harsh. Storms are common, and temperatures are low . . . Into this scene comes *man*, with his great boots, ready to love the mountains to death.
>
> Man loves to hunt. He sees it as a tradition and a right. He believes that deer herds should be managed so he and his son after him, can hunt them. He cannot understand his brother's claim that deer diminish the range of plants. After all his brother couldn't name a single plant that deer had made extinct.

The basis for claims that English renders women invisible is the use of forms such as *he* and *man* as generic forms, as illustrated in example 22. Since these forms are also used with the specific meanings of 'third person singular male subject pronoun' and 'male human being', the satisfactoriness of their use to convey the meanings 'third person human subject pronoun', and simply 'human being' or 'humanity' has increasingly been challenged. One can see why. Reading example 22, with its references to *man*,

C

Language variation: focus on uses

319

his great boots, *his son* and *his brother*, it is difficult to believe that the writer had ever conceived of the possibility that women too might venture into the mountains.

The use of *man* as a generic form has a long history. But its generic use is no longer acceptable to many English speakers because this meaning has become overshadowed by its masculine meaning. Others avoid it as clumsy or misleading for the same reason: *man* has become increasingly ambiguous between the generic and the masculine meaning. In a sentence such as *Man loves to hunt*, for instance, readers may be genuinely unsure whether women are meant to be included or not.

It is also clear that the word *man* is associated with male images, even when it is used generically. The best-known experiment asked college students to select pictures to illustrate the chapters of a sociology textbook. Chapter titles such as Social Man, Industrial Man and Political Man evoked male images to a much greater extent than headings like Society, Industrial Life and Political Behaviour. Those who claim *man* can still be used generically are ignoring the fact that for many readers the term *man* is firmly established as meaning 'male'.

Generic *he* raises exactly the same issues, with even more challenging problems when writers want to avoid it. Attempts to solve the problem by introducing a new epicene (gender-neutral) pronoun can be traced back to the eighteenth century when grammarians were concerned not with the invisibility of women caused by generic *he*, but by the grammatical inefficiencies and confusions of gender and number it caused. More than eighty bisexual pronouns have been proposed since the eighteenth century, including *tey, thon, et, ip, ou, co, per, ne* and *hiser*.

Though generics survive in some outer-circle Englishes, there is evidence that newspapers, magazines, journals and books in countries such as the United States of America, Britain, and New Zealand, are increasingly aware of attitudes to the use of (so-called) generic *he* and *man*, and writers use a variety of strategies to avoid these terms. The magazine, *The New Zealand Women's Weekly*, for example, used only a quarter as many of these forms in 1984 as it did in 1964. An American study of a wide range of magazines and newspapers found a dramatic drop in the use of generic forms from twelve to four per 5000 words between 1971 and 1979. A study of generics in formal New Zealand Department of Labour documents revealed a drop from 98 per cent use of generic *he* in the 1960s to 7 per cent in the 1990s, with a complementary rise from 0 per cent to 81 per cent for generic *they*.

Some writers adopt the strategy of using *he* and *she* in alternate chapters or even in alternate paragraphs. Others use *she* consistently as a generic 'to even things up' or draw attention to the sexist implications of using *he*. (Note this is interesting evidence that people are not just passive language users; some demonstrate 'agency' or active engagement with language for social and political reasons.) Generic *they* is by far the most widespread solution, and it has been used by well-established authors including Shakespeare, Chesterfield, George Bernard Shaw and Doris Lessing. It was opposed virulently by some nineteenth-century grammarians who were delighted when an Act of Parliament in 1850 legislated that in all acts 'the masculine gender shall be deemed and taken to include females'. Nevertheless, *they* is nowadays the most frequently heard generic pronoun in informal speech, and it is spreading to more formal contexts too, as indicated above. Its use is not always problem-free, however, as the following example illustrates.

Example 23

Someone who, like me, is trying to eliminate gender-laden pronouns from their speech altogether can try to rely on the word 'they', but they will find themself in quite a pickle as soon as they try to use any reflexive verbal phrase such as 'paint themselves into a corner', and what is worse is that no matter how that person tries they will find that they can not extricate themself gracefully, and consequently he or she will just flail around, making his or her sentence so awkward that s/he wis/hes s/he had never become conscious of these issues of sexism. Obviously using 'they' just takes you out of the frying pan into the fire, since you have merely exchanged a male–female ambiguity for a singular plural ambiguity. The only advantage to this ploy, I suppose, is that there is/are to my knowledge, no group(s) actively struggling for equality between singular and plural.

Exercise 12

The following examples are based on material from textbooks and a newspaper. What is your reaction to them?

(a) Alone among the animals man uses language to communicate.
(b) 'Speech' wrote Benjamin Lee Whorf 'is the best show man puts on'. . . Language helps man in his thinking. The average student might hear 100,000 words a day. If he has a modest reading speed he would cover 90,000 words a day. He could easily be exposed to three quarters of a billion words a year. And anyone could easily increase that if he wanted.
(c) Man has been civilized for centuries. He no longer needs to hunt for food for his women and children.
(d) The two Oxford Union debaters most ably supported by a woman debater from Victoria made entertaining contributions.
(e) The pioneers who established the farms of this country, who toiled together with their wives and children to break in the land, knew little of what was happening in the towns.

Can you translate the sentences above into non-sexist terms? What strategies did you use?

Answers at end of chapter

Exercise 13

(a) Job adverts in New Zealand may not specify the gender of the required employee unless aspects of the job require the attributes of a particular gender: e.g. *wet-nurse, sperm-donor*. Do you think that the suffix *-man* could be regarded as generic in such adverts, or is it an example of sexist language? Consider *postman, milkman, fireman, salesman, foreman, warehouseman, storeman*. What alternatives would you suggest?

(b) Do you consider phrases like *master plan, master key* and *a princely sum* to be sexist? Why (not)?

Exercise 14

(a) Why do you think some women adopt the title *Ms* rather than *Mrs* or *Miss*?

(b) Is *Ms* used by women in your speech community? What do you think of this usage?

Answers at end of chapter

Linguistic categories are one source of evidence on a culture's values. The categories discussed in this section indicate the society's view of women in many English-speaking communities. Once those views are encoded it takes considerable time and effort to alter the language, even when social attitudes are changing. Guidelines and even legislation requiring people to use non-sexist language certainly help, but most changes take a considerable time to become established as the new norm.

The examples discussed in this chapter illustrate some of the ways in which language can provide insights about a community's perceptions and stereotypes, and aspects of its culture. Relative status may be indicated not only in the ways in which women and men use language, but also in the language used about women and men. What is more, the linguistic data supports the view that women are often assigned subordinate status by virtue of their gender alone, and treated linguistically as subordinate, regardless of their actual power or social status in a particular context. English, at least, appears to collude in the subordination of women. But can a language contribute to social repression? Can we escape the view of reality presented by the categories of our language? These are questions addressed in the next chapter.

ANSWERS TO EXERCISES IN CHAPTER 12

Answers to exercise 1

These sentences were devised to incorporate features which Lakoff suggested distinguished women's and men's speech. The precise claims were not always supported by research, as will become clear in the next section. They do indicate people's stereotypes of women's usage, however. The stereotype suggests sentences (b), (c), (f), (g), (i), (j) and (k) were produced by women while (a), (d), (e), (h) and (l) were men's utterances. The reasons for this particular division of the sentences will become apparent in the next section where the features identified by Lakoff as features of 'women's language' are listed.

Answer to exercise 2

Features which may serve as

Hedging devices	**Boosting devices**
lexical hedges	intensifiers
tag questions	emphatic stress
question intonation	
superpolite forms	
euphemisms	

The hedging devices can be used to weaken the strength of an assertion while the boosting devices can be used to strengthen it. For example, *it's a good film* can be strengthened by adding the intensifier *really* (*it's a really good film*) or weakened by adding the lexical hedge *sort of* (*it's sort of a good film*). However, some of these devices serve other functions too, as we will see below.

Answers to exercise 3

The tags in (a) and (d) are most obviously facilitative in function, offering the addressee an opportunity to contribute. The tag in (b) seems to be an uncertainty tag, asking for confirmation of an assertion. It could also be a way of encouraging talk, but this seems unlikely given the context. There are two tags in (c) and both serve a softening function. The first softens a criticism, the second softens a directive. Finally, in (e) the function of the tag is much less clear-cut. Is Fiona asking for confirmation of her claim, or is she simply facilitating more talk? One cannot be sure. More contextual information and more extensive surrounding text would probably help, but finally one might need to recognise that her tag is achieving both functions at once. A primary function is often identifiable, but not always. Different functions often overlap and classification into different types is not always straightforward.

Answers to exercise 4

(i) (c) provides more possible places for the insertion of 'non-essential' elements than (b).

(c) (I am) Herb R. Beasley, senior. (I am) President of Beasley Refrigeration Incorporated. (I or we) do commercial refrigeration. And my wife's name is Lillian an' she works in the office. I've never been on a trial jury and (I have) no legal training.

(ii) This example illustrates an important point relevant to any research – the importance in the research process of the stage of interpretation of the data. Whatever the patterns identified, they can often be interpreted in different ways. The interpretation can be influenced by the assumptions, preconceptions and attitudes of the interpreters. In this case, for instance, there are at least two possible interpretations:

1. The women jurors' speech contains more redundancy than the men's. It contains more non-essential elements.

2. Women jurors make less demand on the addressee by making things more explicit.

(iii) Information on whether deleted constructions were appropriate in the particular context would be helpful, as well as information on how much processing such deletions involved for the listener, and how much effort that processing involved. For instance, deletion tends to occur in more informal speech. In informal contexts where people know each other well, it would often be considered inappropriate and unnecessary, and possibly even insulting to close friends, to spell everything out and make it explicit. One could suggest that the men, by reducing redundancy, were trying to reduce the formality of the interaction, then. Alternatively one could argue that the women were responding more appropriately in a context that was unalterably formal.

This example illustrates nicely that *identifying* gender differences in language use is just one step in the research process. Interpreting their significance is equally important, and requires a theoretical framework which will make sense of the findings. In the preceding section Lakoff's framework, which used women's subordinate social status and relative 'powerlessness' to explain 'women's language', was contrasted with a framework which focussed on women as solidarity-oriented participants in interaction.

Answer to exercise 5

Overall the data supports the claims made. Most of the men spoke more often and for longer than most of the women. Most of the men interrupted more than the women, with only one man interrupting as little as the woman who did most interrupting. Note however that men also tended to be interrupted more than women – possibly a function of the fact that they were more often talking.

The data raises a number of questions. Man E interrupts much less than other men, for example. What differentiates him from his male colleagues? Why is woman D so much more talkative than her female colleagues? Information on relative status and interactional role might be helpful in interpreting the data further. Do high status women talk and interrupt less than low status men? Does the role of group leader or chair lead to a reduction or an increase in talk? The answers to these questions might assist considerably in interpreting the data.

Answer to exercise 6

The issue of what counts as an interruption is the first and most difficult problem. How long does overlapping speech need to be before it counts as an interruption?

It is also possible to distinguish between 'disruptive' interruptions and 'supportive' overlaps. Both overlap the current speaker's turn, but 'disruptive' interruptions throw the first speaker off course and often take over the floor, while 'supportive' overlaps generally do not. People often do not consider supportive overlaps as interruptions at all.

Another issue is the difference between what the speaker intends and what the others perceive and experience. Different participants often interpret the 'same' behaviour differently.

All these problems have obvious implications for claims about whether women or men interrupt most.

Answer to exercise 7

In example 11 there are four instances where the man interrupts the woman, and none of his providing encouragement to her to develop her topic. He does not give her an opportunity to talk about her paper. He answers her question and then, as she responds sympathetically, he interrupts with a request for a cigarette. When she begins to tell him about her paper he interrupts again with a request for a match. He interrupts her third attempt to tell him about her paper with an excuse and leaves. In example 12, on the other hand, there are five instances of encouraging feedback from Jill to Mary, as well as the confirming comment, *really just takes one eh?*

Answer to exercise 8

Your answer will no doubt be very context-dependent, and may differ for different social groups. On the evidence collected so far among middle-class white speakers it seems that male rules often predominate in a variety of mixed-gender informal interactions. However, there is also some evidence of a hybrid style – jointly constructed collaborative talk which combines some features of both male and female interaction. This style involves several speakers contributing to and developing a topic in a supportive rather than a competitive way. Interruptions and overlaps occur, but are not disruptive, and the amount of talk contributed by each gender is much more equal.

There is also some evidence that conflict between women's and men's use of language in informal contexts can result in miscommunication, as illustrated in example 17.

Answer to exercise 9

There is some evidence that the woman's conversational aims are primarily social or affective. Her opening gambit is quite obviously phatic in function. The answer is self-evident and her utterance simply indicates that she wants to talk. Despite lack of encouragement from the man she persists, and she volunteers a number of pieces of information which, though related, are not essential to her declared aim of finding out the weather forecast.

It is possible that the man simply does not want to chat. He may be feeling unsociable. Alternatively he may not recognise the 'real' function of the interaction from the woman's point of view. This conversation which the woman regards as primarily social or affective in function may be perceived by the man as essentially referential. He may genuinely assume that she only wants a weather report. This would explain his infrequent and monosyllabic responses. He may be ignoring the repeated attempts by the woman to draw him into a conversation because he is concentrating on what he thinks she is concerned about – getting the radio to work.

Answer to exercise 10

Ian is being given double messages. His behaviour is described as *terrible, bad*, and as a cause of *chaos*. But there is extensive mitigation at all levels of the discourse. The word *bad* is collocated with the friendly word *lad*, for instance. Phrases like *real monkey* and *little rascal* suggest that Ian is regarded affectionately and tolerantly, and his 'bad' behaviour is perhaps regarded as typical of a real lad. It is also clearly a source of amusement, as the laughter throughout indicates. Whatever the reaction at the time, Ian's exploits are here presented as mock-heroic. Note also that his mother answers his auntie's question on his behalf, modelling for him one way to present his day's activities, and his father invites him to agree he is *a real bad lad*, using a softening laugh and a friendly tag *eh*. So although Ian is being constructed here as a 'naughty boy', he is also presented as the hero of an amusing narrative. He is learning how boys are expected to behave.

Answers to exercise 12

The first two sentences use generic *man*. Alternative expressions that would avoid suggesting that these characteristics do not include women are perfectly possible. For example

(a) Alone among the animals human beings use language to communicate.
(b) 'Speech' wrote Benjamin Lee Whorf 'is the best show humankind puts on.' Language helps people think. The average student might hear 100,000 words a day. With a modest reading speed a student would cover 90,000 words a day. Students could easily be exposed to three quarters of a billion words a year. And anyone could easily increase that if they wanted.

Sentences (c), (d) and (e) are more subtly discriminatory. They begin using apparently non-sexist and generic terms but the maleness of the writer's image of the supposedly gender-neutral protagonist is later betrayed. This has been called 'slippage'. The solution may be to make the male image explicit or to eliminate all references to gender.

Language variation: focus on uses

(c) Human beings have been civilized for centuries. Men no longer need to hunt for food for their women and children.

or

Human beings have been civilized for centuries. They no longer need to hunt for food.

(d) The two Oxford Union male debaters most ably supported by a woman debater from Victoria made entertaining contributions.

or

The two Oxford Union debaters most ably supported by a debater from Victoria made entertaining contributions.

(e) The men who established the farms of this country, who toiled together with their wives and children to break in the land, knew little of what was happening in the towns.

or

The pioneers who established the farms of this country, who toiled to break in the land, knew little of what was happening in the towns.

Which alternative do you prefer and why?

Answers to exercise 13

(a) There are many who consider the suffix *-man* to be as sexist as generic *man* and *he*. They would advocate forms like *postie* (a well-established term in Australasia), *milk vendor, firefighter,* and *sales assistant.* Alternatives for the last three terms are more difficult to find. Some people use *-person* as an alternative to *-man* but this is not always considered a happy solution.

(b) Some argue that these phrases express a 'male as superior' or 'male as best' ideology which underlies many so-called neutral usages. It should be recognised, however, that for many people they do not have such connotations. There is some evidence that men are less likely than women to consider such phrases as sexist. It is also worth noting that when men dominated these occupations, the use of *-man* reflected reality. This argument is clearly no longer valid however.

Answers to exercise 14

(a) *Ms* was introduced by feminists as a genuine parallel to *Mr*. Like *Mr*, the term *Ms* does not signal the marital status of the person referred to, and hence does not define a woman in terms of her relationship with a man. However, despite some success, it has not achieved its intended aim. Rather than replacing *Mrs* and *Miss*, *Ms* has typically become a third term in the system of titles for women and it has developed a wide range of different meanings.

(b) Tina Chiles undertook a survey in the New Zealand cities of Wellington and Christchurch and found *Ms* was used more often in Wellington than in more conservative Christchurch. Women tended to avoid using titles if they could, but, if pushed, unmarried women preferred *Miss*. She also found a tendency for *Ms* to be more popular once women married. Her findings also confirmed earlier research indicating that *Ms* is frequently interpreted as a title for a divorced, separated or widowed woman, or a woman in a *de facto* relationship, and that for some people it signals 'feminist' or 'lesbian'.

▓ Concepts introduced

Women's language
Gossip
Construction of gender identity

Narratives
Sexist language
Generic forms

References

The following sources provided material for this chapter:

Bodine (1975) on sexist language
Bolinger (1980) on sexist language
Brown (2000) on generics in NZ Department of Labour documents
Cameron, McAlinden and O'Leary (1988) on tag questions
Chiles (2003) and Pauwels (1998) on *Ms* usage
Coates (1988) on gossip
Coates (1993) on gender and language
Crosby and Nyquist (1977) investigating Lakoff's hypotheses
Dubois and Crouch (1975) on tag questions
Eakins and Eakins (1979) on interruptions in meetings
Holmes (1984a) on tag questions
Holmes (1984b) on methodology
Holmes (1985) on miscommunication
Holmes (1990) on pragmatic particles
Hyndman (1985) on interruptions
James and Clarke (1993) on interruptions
Lakoff (1975) on women's language
McElhinny (1995) on women in the police force
McMillan, Clifton, McGrath and Gale (1977) investigating Lakoff's hypotheses
Miller and Swift (1991) on sexist language
Mulac, Lundell and Bradac (1986) for differences in linguistic forms between women and men
O'Barr and Atkins (1980) investigating Lakoff's hypotheses
Ochs (1987) for data on Samoan personal narratives
Ochs (1992) on the concept of 'indexing' gender
Pauwels and Winter (2004) on generics in varieties of English
Preisler (1986) on women's and men's language
Spender (1980) on gender and language
Stewart et al. (1990) on attitudes to sexist language
Thorne, Kramarae and Henley (1983) on language and gender
West (1984) and Woods (1988) on interaction of status and gender
West and Zimmerman (1983) on interruptions
Zimmerman and West (1975) on interruptions

Quotations

Example 1 is from Lakoff (1975: 6).
Example 2 is from O'Barr and Atkins (1980: 98–9).

C

Language variation: focus on uses

Example 3 is from McMillan, Clifton, McGrath and Gale (1977: 548).

Example 4 is from O'Barr and Atkins (1980: 99).

Example 9 is from Thomas (1989: 152).

Example 10 is Edwards and Beyfus (1969: 4).

Example 11 is from West and Zimmerman (1977: 527–8). It has been slightly edited for ease of reading.

Example 12 is from data collected for a New Zealand social dialect project. It has been edited for ease of reading.

Examples 13, 14, 15 and 16 are based on Pilkington (1989).

Example 17 is from Holmes (1985: 28).

Example 18 is from Cameron (1997: 56).

Example 19 is from Holmes (1997b).

Example 21 is from Nilsen (1972: 102).

Example 22 is from *Mountain Management*, a publication of the New Zealand Department of the Environment, 1986. It is perhaps only fair to note that deer-hunting is a predominantly male activity in New Zealand.

Example 23 is from Hofstadter (1982: 18).

Exercise 1 uses sentences from Edelsky (1977).

Exercise 4 is based on Philips and Reynolds (1987).

Paragraph (b) in exercise 12 is edited from Carroll (1965: 1–2).

▉ Useful additional reading

Coates (1993, 1996, 2003)
Eckert and McConnell-Ginet (2003)
Gibbon (1999)
Graddol and Swann (1989)
Holmes (1995)
Miller and Swift (1991)
Pauwels (1998)
Romaine (1999)
Sunderland (2006)
Talbot (1998)
Tannen (1990)

▉ Note———

1. These are all Lakoff's terms and it should be noted that many linguists would not endorse her use of terms such as 'empty', 'hypercorrect', and 'superpolite', since they consider them misleading.

13 Language, cognition and culture

> **Example 1**
> A: Why are all dumb blonde jokes one-liners?
> B: So men can remember them.

Jokes like this encode culturally specific assumptions, e.g. that *blonde* typically refers to a woman, not a man, and that the categories 'dumb blonde' and 'dumb blonde jokes' are familiar to the addressee. But the joke also challenges the assumptions of typical 'dumb blonde' jokes, in making men rather than women the butt of the humour. Feminists argue that such challenges are important because they provide alternatives to the dominant social stereotype. They help create new grooves for people's thinking habits.

Earlier chapters have demonstrated that the way a person speaks generally signals at least some social information about their background, such as what kind of social group or class they belong to. A person's ethnicity, age and gender are also often reflected in their linguistic choices. In discussing gender, it became clear that it is possible to view the relationship between social factors and language as rather more dynamic than is often assumed. Sociolinguists who adopt a social constructionist approach argue that language not only reflects and expresses our membership of social categories, it also contributes to the construction of our social identity. So, as she interacts with others in a variety of social contexts, a young woman's linguistic choices actively construct her age, class, ethnic and gender identity. She 'chooses' to portray herself as a young, working-class, Maori woman – or not – according to the linguistic features she uses.

The discussion of sexist language in chapter 12 introduced another perspective on the relationship between language and society. Language reflects society's attitudes and values, an area that is further pursued in chapter 15. But some researchers in the area of language and gender have argued that language may also *determine* what people notice, what categories they establish, what choices they believe are available, and consequently the way they behave. In other words, language may strongly influence perception and behaviour.

> **Exercise 1**
>
> Consider the phrase *routine pelvic examination* used in a book on women's health. What kind of perspective does such a phrase suggest?
>
> *Answer at end of chapter*

LANGUAGE AND PERCEPTION

Example 2

'... it has been said that "bad girls get babies, but good girls get myomata" '.

   Surgery is also indicated when ... hormone treatment has failed to control the symptoms ...

   Since many women erroneously believe that following hysterectomy, their sexual urge ceases, that coitus is not possible and that obesity is usual, the physician must explain that removal of the uterus has no side-effects ...

   ... hysterectomy is the treatment of choice when ... the patient has completed her family ...

   The operation of choice in all women under the age of 40 ... who wish to preserve their reproductive function ...'

As you may have guessed, these quotations occur in a textbook written by a (male) medical expert for medical students. But they also provide clues about the way doctors view patients. Perhaps the most obvious feature of the text is its impersonal and detached tone which is achieved through the use of agentless passive constructions (*surgery is ... indicated*) impersonal nouns (*the physician, the patient*), and formal devices such as nominalisations. So, for example, surgery *is indicated*, rather than *doctors think that people need surgery when* ... or even *I think that* ... This construction also permits the author to neatly avoid drawing attention to reasons for the failure of the treatment to control symptoms. Hysterectomy is described as the treatment *of choice*, allowing the author to avoid the issue of *whose* choice. Women are depicted as at least ignorant, if not gullible with their 'erroneous' beliefs, and primarily in their role as potential child-bearers, since invasive surgery is to be avoided as long as the woman's *reproductive function* needs to be maintained. And the opening sentence presents a patronising, if not insulting, saying as if it is common knowledge, although its technical word *myomata* (benign fibroid tumour of the uterus) indicates it could only have been produced by physicians.

THE FAR SIDE® By GARY LARSON

"Well, actually, Doreen, I rather resent being called a 'swamp thing.' ... I prefer the term 'wetlands-challenged mutant.'"

Language variation: focus on uses

C

Does this language simply reflect the social context in which it is produced, i.e. the relationship between the writer and intended audience, and its function of instruction? Or does it convey a worldview or perspective which may affect the perceptions of the students and their behaviour towards the women who consult them? Can language determine the way we perceive reality?

Exercise 2

Examine the problem page or advice column in a local or community newspaper, or google *Dear Abby* for examples.

Can you identify any of the taken-for-granted assumptions which lie beneath the advice provided?

▶

> Consider
>
> **(a)** who is the intended audience? How can you tell?
> **(b)** does the writer prescribe appropriate ways for parents, children, women, or men to behave?
> **(c)** what do the vocabulary items and the grammatical constructions suggest about the author's assumptions concerning the way the world should be arranged, or the author's attitudes to particular groups?

Verbal hygiene

Example 3

Angela: I was sitting quietly drinking my tea, minding my own business when suddenly the foreperson burst in and shouted 'what are you doing here? get back to work – you know that shipment's overdue.' Bloody cheek. I'm entitled to my tea-break!

Jim: You are. She's a vampire – but what's all this 'foreperson' stuff? I bet you wouldn't use that term for a man. Political correctness gone mad eh.

Verbal hygiene is the thought-provoking term used by Deborah Cameron to describe how people respond to 'the urge to meddle in matters of language'. It covers a wide range of activities, from writing letters to the Editor complaining about the 'deterioration' and 'abuse' of language (discussed in chapter 15), through prescriptions and proscriptions about what constitutes 'proper', 'correct' and 'acceptable' usage in a range of contexts, to using language as a political weapon. The discussion of sexist language in chapter 12 illustrated an area where feminists have enthusiastically engaged in verbal hygiene, reflecting their beliefs that achieving a change in linguistic usage is itself a worthwhile form of public, political action and consciousness raising.

As example 3 illustrates, the deliberate adoption of overtly non-sexist usages such as *foreperson* and *chairperson* often leads to accusations of 'political correctness'. While issues of political correctness extend well beyond linguistic concerns, linguistic terminology has often become the focus of the debate. The Crippled Children's Society in New Zealand now refers to itself only by its acronym CCS. The term *crippled* was an acceptable way of describing someone with a physical disability until relatively recently in New Zealand. As elsewhere, the term gradually grew to be regarded as tasteless and unacceptable, so the term *disabled* was substituted. But it was then pointed out that *disabled person* defined the individual in terms of just one characteristic, and one that was irrelevant in many contexts, such as chatting to friends or watching television. Those who work in this area now use the phrase *person with a disability.*

For those who do not suffer from a disability, and who have little contact with those who do, such changes often seem 'precious' word-mongering, substituting one euphemism for another basically because the concept itself is uncomfortable. This dismissive attitude is reflected in exaggerations such as *vertically challenged* to refer to short people, or *cosmetically different* as a way of avoiding the term *ugly*. Such constructions are an obvious source of humour, as in the transformed title of a well-known fairy tale *Melanin Impoverished and the Seven Vertically Challenged Individuals*. But for those centrally concerned, the issue is not just one of 'political correctness', as the parodists claim. It is as important as the issue of the use of *broad* or *bird* to refer to a woman, or *nigger or munt* for a person of colour. For those who are the butt of derogatory labels, linguistic interventions usefully challenge taken-for-granted offensive assumptions.

We have now reached the point where *are you being politically correct?* must be regarded as a trick question. If you say *yes*, you will be regarded as over-concerned with political orthodoxy. If you say *no*, you put yourself in the politically suspect, non-conformist camp. An ironic confirmation of the political power of language! And an indication, Deborah Cameron suggests, of the extent to which right-wing commentators have captured and redefined a phrase introduced by the liberal left.

Example 4

- All reactionaries are paper tigers.
- People of the world, unite and defeat the US aggressors and all their running dogs!
- We should check our complacency and constantly criticise our shortcomings.
- Lack of achievement in work may breed pessimism and depression, while achievement may breed pride and arrogance.

Maoist China provides many further examples of the co-option of language for political purposes. Mao was well aware of the power of language in furthering revolutionary goals, and he took control of channels of public communication, including the education system, at an early stage. The central text of the Cultural Revolution (1966–76) was a pocket compendium of *Quotations from Chairman Mao Zedong*, first produced in 1964 and labelled the *Little Red Book* by the rest of the world. These quotations came to permeate everyday life, and the phrase *da yulu zhang* 'fight a quotation war' became established in the Chinese lexicon. Quotation and counter-quotation were even heard in the market-place as people bargained for goods. Newspapers filled their columns with extracts from Mao's works and with articles stitched together around quotations from Mao. One analysis identified an average of 17 quotations from Mao on just the first two pages of *The People's Daily*, the government's official newspaper, throughout 1970. Even English language textbooks used mainly political material for exemplification. This often resulted in some odd pedagogical practices. Relatively unusual grammatical forms were introduced early, for instance, because of their widespread use in slogans such as *Long live Chairman Mao!* and *Down with capitalist imperialism!* And English–Chinese dictionaries illustrated the meaning of words such as *unemployment* with the citation 'Unemployment is increasing in the capitalist countries' and *luoshi* 'fulfil' with the sentence 'Fulfil the task of consolidating the dictatorship of the proletariat down to every grassroots organisation'!

Mao obviously believed that language had an important role to play in educating people, and in shaping their attitudes and values. To achieve this, powerful groups were established explicitly labelled *Mao Zedong Thought Propaganda Teams*. Critics argue that Mao's quotations provided an ideal method of 'brain-washing' or unfairly influencing the thinking of a huge and largely illiterate population. They consisted of short formulas which were easily remembered and repeated. They encoded a particular political position which was that of the dominant party, and which was reinforced by materials used in the education system, making it difficult to take an opposing position, and even more difficult to express such a position. Many analysts argue that Mao's revolution owed at least as much to his outstanding skills as a propagandist as to his military and political prowess. They suggest he used formulaic language to promote conformist attitudes and thinking. This approach suggests a close relationship between language and thought. How does language influence the way we perceive others, for instance?

Exercise 3

(a) What labels are used in your community to refer to
- members of ethnic or racial groups other than the majority?
- women?
- homosexual people?
- people with an intellectual disability?

A simple questionnaire asking one or two friends and family members to provide as many labels as they can for these groups usually elicits a wide range of items.

Are there any patterns concerning who uses particular labels and in what kinds of social contexts?

(b) One source of such information is the graffiti written on public walls and in toilet cubicles. A small study of toilet cubicles in one university suggested that male toilets were more likely than female to provide such data. Is this true in your community?

Terms such as *coots* and *coconuts* for ethnic minorities, and *queer* and *gay* for homosexual people provide further food for thought about the exact relationship between language, society, attitudes and perception. If language reflects society's perceptions of particular groups, then what is the implication of the vast array of derogatory terms (sometimes called *dysphemisms*) used for non-white people and homosexuals, for instance, and especially for male homosexuals? It is important to reflect on the effects such labels may have on young people's attitudes and ways of thinking about members of such groups.

WHORF

Vocabulary and cognition

Example 5

Frank: Don't throw your cigarette butts in there. It's dangerous.
Bill: Why not? The label says 'empty'.
Frank: Well there's no gasoline in them but there's plenty of explosive vapour – so watch out.

This example and those discussed in the previous sections suggest that there is a close relationship between language and perception. But what is the exact nature of this relationship? Does language constrain perception or vice-versa? Is thought independent of language or do the categories of language pre-determine what we can think about or conceive of? Do the categories we learn to distinguish as we acquire language provide a framework for ordering the world? And if so, is it possible to think outside that framework? Do different languages encode experience differently? And how can we ever tell since it seems impossible to escape from the circle?

The relationship between language, thought and 'reality' has fascinated linguists and philosophers for centuries. In recent times, the person whose name is most closely associated with investigations of the relationship between language and thought is Benjamin Lee Whorf. Whorf was an anthropological linguist who began his career as a chemical engineer working for a fire insurance company. He first investigated Native American languages as a hobby, but later studied with Edward Sapir at Yale University. In the course of processing insurance claims, he noticed that the particular words selected to describe or label objects often influenced people's perceptions and behaviour. So, as example 5 illustrates, around gasoline drums labelled as 'empty', people would smoke, or even toss in cigarette stubs, despite the fact that they were full of potentially explosive vapour.

This perception was a graphic illustration of something that Whorf had noted in his analysis of Native American languages, such as Hopi. Example 6 is a well-known quotation which summarises his position.

Example 6

'We dissect nature along lines laid down by our native languages. The categories and types that we isolate from the world of phenomena we do not find there because they stare every observer in the face; on the contrary, the world is presented in a kaleidoscopic flux of impressions which has to be organised in our minds – and this means largely by the linguistic systems in our minds. We cut nature up, organize it into concepts, and ascribe significances as we do, largely because we are parties to an agreement to organize it in this way – an agreement that holds throughout our speech community and is codified in the patterns of our language. The agreement is of course an implicit and unstated one, BUT ITS TERMS ARE ABSOLUTELY OBLIGATORY; we cannot talk at all except by subscribing to the organization and classification of data which the agreement decrees.'

Exercise 4

Make four points which counter Whorf's position as expressed in this quotation. Consider, for example, experiences which suggest that thought is independent of language: e.g. the experiences of bilinguals, responses to music, searching for *le mot juste*.

Answer at end of chapter

Linguistic determinism: the medium is the message

The strong form of the Sapir-Whorf hypothesis is generally labelled **linguistic determinism**. This holds that people from different cultures think differently *because of* differences in their languages. A native speaker of Hopi, Whorf claimed, perceives reality differently from a native speaker of English because she uses a different language. Few sociolinguists would accept such a strong claim, but most accept the weaker claim of **linguistic relativity**, that language influences perceptions, thought, and, at least potentially, behaviour.

The main problem in assessing Whorf's argument is the danger of inescapable circularity. We observe that languages differ and conclude that the thought of their speakers also differs. But the only evidence we have that their thought differs is the language they use. So investigating the relationship between language and thought is a real challenge because the most obvious way to access thought is through language. How can we test how language influences ways of thinking without using language as evidence of thought processes?

Some ingenious experiments have been devised to test the Sapir-Whorf hypothesis. If Whorf is right it should be difficult to identify colours which your language does not have a name for. But although the Dani, a New Guinea tribe, use only two colour terms (corresponding to *black* and *white*, or, more accurately, *dark* and *light*), it was found that they could recognise and distinguish between subtle shades of colours that their language had no names for (e.g. pale blue vs turquoise). This suggests that the strong form of the hypothesis can't be maintained. Other experiments suggest, however, that people remember colours that are coded in their language more easily than those which are not, and they tend to classify together coloured chips which are labelled as the 'same' colour by their language, even if objective measures like wavelength suggest they are different.

Some languages have linguistic categories which take account of the shape of objects. The form of Navaho verbs, for example, is sometimes determined by the shape of the object: e.g. long or short, thin or thick, round or not, and so on. Not surprisingly, Navaho-speaking children are typically much faster than English-speaking children in categorising blocks by shape. And given a choice of ways of putting objects into groups, Navaho children tend to group them according to shape, while English-speaking children group them according to colour. These interesting findings based on experiments with colours and shapes all support the weaker principle of **linguistic relativity**, i.e. the categories provided by a language may make it easier to draw certain conceptual distinctions.

C

Language variation: focus on uses

Exercise 5

Examine the data in table 13.1.

(i) What is the likely form of the name of number 16 in French, Chinese and Japanese?
(ii) How do you know?
(iii) What are the implications of your answer for learners of these languages?

Answers at end of chapter

Table 13.1 Names for numbers 1–6 and 10–15 in four languages

Number	English	French	Chinese	Japanese
1	one	un	yi	ichi
2	two	deux	er	ni
3	three	trois	san	san
4	four	quatre	si	shi
5	five	cinq	wu	go
6	six	six	liu	roku
10	ten	dix	shi	juu
11	eleven	onze	shi-yi	juu-ichi
12	twelve	douze	shi-er	juu-ni
13	thirteen	treize	shi-san	juu-san
14	fourteen	quatorze	shi-si	juu-shi
15	fifteen	quinze	shi-wu	juu-go

The Chinese word for eleven *shi-yi* is literally 'ten-one', and for twenty the Chinese word is *er-shi*, literally 'two-ten'. Consequently, learning to count beyond 10 is easier for Chinese-speaking children than for English-speaking children. More recently, it has even been suggested that Chinese, Japanese, and Korean children understand number concepts earlier than English and French children because of the ways their respective languages code numbers above 10. If true, this is interesting support for the idea that language facilitates particular kinds of thinking, or at least speed of processing. Like the colour experiments, this evidence suggests that the categories provided by a language may favour certain ways of perceiving 'reality' or 'the world', and make certain behaviours easier. However, we must also recognise the limitations of such evidence. Colours and numbers constitute very limited semantic fields. Is there evidence in other areas too?

Exercise 6

What kind of perception of time do the following expressions encode?
Are all the metaphors consistent?

don't waste time
we used up all our time
you've run out of time
that would save a lot of time
I've spent too much time on it
I gave her all the time available
he needs to budget for how much time it will take
they invested a lot of time in that project
how much time do we have left?
I can't devote any more time to it

Answer at end of chapter

◼ Grammar and cognition

Example 7

Suzanne Romaine comments that 'no particular language has a privileged view of the world as it "really" is. The world is not simply the way it is, but what we make of it through language. The domains of experience which are important to cultures get grammaticalized into languages.'

Grammatical categories such as tense, aspect, and gender encode aspects of reality differently in different languages. Whorf's analysis of the Hopi verb system led him to argue that the Hopi conception of time is fundamentally different from that of Western cultures. Speakers of European languages often conceive time as a road, for instance, with the future ahead and the past behind. Whorf suggested this reflects the verb tense system of Indo-European languages. Appropriately conjugating Hopi verbs, however, requires an analysis of events in terms of dynamic motion, expressed by aspect markers, rather than by tenses marking their distribution in time. This led Whorf to conclude that the Hopi think in terms of cycles of events and sets of processes rather than units of time. He even argued that Hopi was better equipped to deal with the wave processes and vibrations of modern physics than English was. These basic concepts of physics for which English needed metaphors such as waves and vibrations, were directly and obligatorily coded in the verb morphology of Hopi and this, according to Whorf, 'practically force[d] the Hopi to notice vibratory phenomena'.

In fact, later analyses of Hopi indicated that Hopi does have tenses and words for time units. But, while Whorf's detailed claims do not hold up, most sociolinguists consider that his general point is an interesting one with implications for the way speakers of different languages and cultures filter or 'cut up' reality. It is widely accepted that certain concepts may be more codable or easier to express in some languages than in others. And, as the quotation in example 7 suggests, the areas of experience which are important to cultures tend to get grammaticalised in their languages. (Something is said to be grammaticalised or grammaticised when it functions less and less like an independent lexical item, and more and more like an element in the grammatical system, such as an affix or an auxiliary verb.) To what extent, then, does culture intersect with language and cognition? It has been suggested, for instance, that communities with little techno-logical development employ the fewest colour terms, while their pronoun and noun classification systems are often much more complex than those of European languages.

C

Language variation: focus on uses

Exercise 7

Consider the potential cognitive and cultural implications of the following observations.

English people and bulls have *legs*; Spanish people have *piernas* and bulls have *patas*.

English people and horses *eat*; German people *essen* while horses *fressen*.

English has a general word *ant*; the Garo of Assam, India, have many words for different types of ant but no single-word equivalent to *ant*.

Mandarin Chinese has a single cover term for *fruit* and *nuts*. English has no such term.

In English the noun *stone* must be either singular or plural; in Chinese number is only expressed if it is relevant.

Kwakiutl speakers must indicate whether the stone is visible or not to the speaker at the time of speaking, and its position relative to the speaker or the listener.

In nineteenth-century Russian there was a distinct term *shurin* for your wife's brother; in modern Russian the phrase *brat zheny* 'brother of wife' is used.

The issues raised by these examples are discussed in the next section.

Exercise 8

Discussions of the relationship between language and thought often make the ethnocentric assumption illustrated by the 'Gina is by lingal' cartoon in chapter 2, i.e. they assume most people speak only one language. What are the implications of Whorf's ideas for bilingual and multilingual people?

Answer at end of chapter

Exercise 9

I have used the word *culture* throughout the book so far without defining it explicitly. Given the way it has been used, how would you define the meaning of *culture*?

Answer at end of chapter

LINGUISTIC CATEGORIES AND CULTURE

Native American and Australian Aboriginal languages are often cited as examples which roundly refute popular misconceptions about primitive languages, e.g. 'simple societies can't have complex grammars' (an issue touched on at the end of chapter 8). Kwakiutl, a Native American language, for example, requires a grammatical classification of nouns based on whether they are visible or not. And while French requires every noun to be assigned to one of two genders, Dyirbal, an Australian Aboriginal language, has four such categories.

Using Western criteria, the traditional nomadic lifestyle of the Aboriginal people of Australia seems very simple. Their culture, however, is thousands of years old and their languages are amongst the most interesting and grammatically complex that have been researched. Every noun in Dyirbal belongs to one of the four classes, illustrated in table 13.2. Consequently, whenever a Dyirbal speaker uses a noun in a sentence the noun must be preceded by one of the four classifiers: *bayi, balan, balam* or *bala*. Can you identify any semantic coherence between the items in the different classes?

While there is some basis in perceived shared semantic features for the allocation of Dyirbal nouns to different classes, the answer to this question is not at all obvious to those from other cultures. The general patterns Dyirbal speakers seem to use to learn the system can be summarised as follows:

I. *Bayi*: (human) males; some animals
II. *Balan*: (human) females, birds, water, fire, fighting
III. *Balam*: non-flesh food
IV. *Bala*: everything else

Table 13.2 Dyirbal noun classes

I bayi	II balan	III balam	IV bala
men	women	edible fruit	parts of the body
kangaroos	bandicoots	fruit plants	meat
possums	dogs	tubers	bees
snakes	platypus	ferns	mud
fishes	birds	cigarettes	grass
insects	spears	wine	wind
storms	water	cake	noises
the moon	fire	honey	language
fishing spears	stars		
boomerangs	sun		

Particular types of experience establish associations which determine the class membership of some items. So, for instance, fish are in class I because they are animate, and fishing implements are also in class I because they are associated with fish. This also explains why *sun* and *stars* are in the same class as *fire*. However, Dyirbal myths and cultural beliefs also make a contribution to class allocation. So, contrary to Western mythology, the moon is male and husband of the sun, which is female. Hence the moon is in class 1 with men, while the sun is in class 2 with women. Birds are believed to be the spirits of dead human females, and hence they are also in class 2. The system is of course totally automatic for Dyirbal speakers, and one should not necessarily expect a speaker to be able to explain it to an outsider. Nor should we expect the relationship between categorisation and cultural beliefs to be direct, transparent or available to reflection. After all, a German speaker would be hard pressed to explain why the word *Mädchen* meaning 'girl' is in the same category as inanimate objects such as books (*Buch*), while English speakers would have difficulty interpreting the significance of the fact that the English demonstratives *this* vs *that* code degrees of proximity to the speaker.

Even at the lexico-semantic level Aboriginal languages challenge Western preconceptions about primitive languages, as table 13.3 illustrates.

Clearly Kunwinjku has many more terms to label distinctions among kangaroos and wallabies than English does. The reasons are obvious: kangaroos are an important part of the Aboriginal people's environment. In cultures which use rice as a staple of the diet, there are distinct terms not only for different types of rice, but also for many different ways of cooking rice. Bird-watchers, skiers, geologists and gardeners are similarly able to lexically identify distinctions of importance to them. This suggests an alternative to Whorf's position, then: rather than language determining what is perceived, it is rather the physical and socio-cultural environment which determines the distinctions that the language develops.

From this perspective, language provides a means of encoding a community's knowledge, beliefs, and values, i.e. its culture. Tahitians don't make a distinction between

C

Language variation: focus on uses

Table 13.3 Kunwinjku kangaroo terms

kunj (general term covering all kangaroos and wallabies)			
Linnean and English names	Male	Female	Child
Macropus antilopinus (antilopine wallaroo)	karndakidj kalaba (large individual male)	karndayh	djamunbuk (juvenile male)
Macropus bernardus (black wallaroo)	nadjinem baark	djukerre	
Macropus robustus (wallaroo)	kalkberd kanbulerri (large male)	wolerrk	narrobad (juvenile male)
Macropus agilis (agile wallaby)	warradjangkal/kornobolo nakurdakurda (very large individual)	merlbbe/kornobolo	nakornborrh nanjid (baby)

'sadness' and 'sickness', for instance, using the same word for both. This reflects their belief that 'sadness/sickness' can be attributed to an attack by evil spirits, a belief that may initially seem odd to someone from Western culture. However, Western medical practice now recognises depression as an illness, and English uses many metaphorical terms for depression which no doubt appear just as strange to those from other cultures, e.g. *feeling blue, in low spirits, feeling down, under the weather*, and so on. The word *mate* covers a continuum from 'sick' to 'dead' in Maori, a continuum that Western culture perceives as a sharp division reflected in the use of two quite different words. But Maori culture does not make a sharp distinction between the living and the dead. The dead are considered to watch over the living and are in this sense always present. Dead kinsfolk are always explicitly referred to in any ritual, and treated as an extension of the living family.

Exercise 10

Maori kinship terminology distinguishes between siblings in different ways from English.

teina   younger sister of a female, younger brother of a male
tuakana older sister of a female, older brother of a male
tuahine sister of a male
tungane brother of a female

(i) What semantic distinctions do the translations of the Maori kinship terms suggest are important in Maori culture?
(ii) Given that these terms can also be used to refer to cousins, how would you expect to refer to your cousin Mere (Mary)?

Answers at end of chapter

Less tangible concepts such as kinship further illustrate the complexities of the relationship between language and culture. In Maori culture, relative age is very important. Even the status of the tribe or *iwi* to which you belong will be identified in *teina* and *tuakana* terms relative to other tribes. The importance of the extended family or *whānau* as an important social unit is also reflected in the kinship system. Kinship labels reflect the mutual rights and obligations of different members of the *whānau* towards each other. In rural areas of New Zealand Maori children typically grow up in close contact with their grandparents, aunties and uncles, and they may spend extended periods of time living in the households of relations other than their parents. These traditional social relationships are reflected in the use of the same term *whaea* both for a child's mother and for the mother's sisters, while the term *pāpā* refers not only to a child's father but also to his father's brothers. The same pattern holds for terms used to refer to a child's siblings and cousins; in these cases gender and relative age are semantically marked, but degree of kinship (as viewed through Western eyes) is not lexically distinguished. So the lexical labels identify those with similar social rights and obligations in relation to the speaker. Clearly, linguistic terminology here reflects important cultural relationships.

It has been suggested that all kinship systems are likely to encode distinctions based on genealogy and biology: so parenthood, marriage relationships, sex and generation are distinctions expressed in some way in most systems that have been studied. But the precise ways in which they are encoded, and the fineness of the distinctions and their cultural significance differs dramatically from one culture to another. In Njamal, an Australian Aboriginal language with no more than 100 speakers in the 1950s when the data was collected, the complex and intricate kinship system provides insights into the ways in which the tribe's activities were organised. Like Maori, Njamal has distinct terms for younger vs older siblings and younger cousins. *Maraga*, for example, refers to a younger brother or sister, and to some younger cousins. And in Njamal, there is a specific kinship term for every member of the tribe, however distantly they are related to you. This clearly indicates the importance of kinship relationships in the social organisation of the tribe.

Every Njamal person belongs to one of two distinct 'moieties' (descent groups) and in this tribe your moiety membership is determined by your father. Moiety membership is signalled explicitly throughout the kinship system, reflecting and reinforcing the fact that for Njamal people, moiety membership is a fundamental distinction of tribal life. Shared moiety membership creates obligations to care for people when they need it. Moiety membership also restricts your marriage options since you may only marry someone from the other moiety. This makes sense of the fact that some cousins have the same kinship terms as brothers and sisters, while others do not. You can marry your father's sister's children (opposite moiety), but not your father's brother's children (same moiety). Thus kinship terms signal your potential marriage partners. Again, the lexical labels serve as indicators of the complex mutual social rights and obligations of community members.

DISCOURSE PATTERNS AND CULTURE

Example 8

Robyn Kina grew up in difficult family circumstances in an Aboriginal environment in Australia. By the age of 19 she had a criminal record, reflecting a number of encounters with the police in which she had come off worst. In her mid-20s she lived with a non-Aboriginal man Tony Black, who regularly beat her up and subjected her to other horrific attacks, especially when he was drunk. During an argument one morning, Black threatened to rape Kina's 14-year-old niece who was living with them. Kina stabbed him once in the chest as he came towards her with a chair raised above his head. She was shocked to see him fall to the ground. He died in hospital shortly afterwards. Robyn Kina pleaded not guilty to murder since she had not intended to kill Black. She did not give evidence and no witnesses were called. After one of the shortest trials in Australian history, Kina was found guilty and sentenced to life imprisonment with hard labour.

The intertwining of language, culture and perception is evident when we examine research on patterns of interaction too. Cultural differences between the discourse patterns of the majority and minority culture can often have serious consequences, as the research of Diana Eades, comparing Aboriginal and non-Aboriginal Australians, demonstrates. Even, and perhaps especially, when both groups apparently use the same language, culturally different patterns of interaction can be a source of misunderstanding.

Regardless of the particular language being spoken, Aboriginal society throughout Australia places great importance on indirectness; it is important to avoid being intrusive. This involves giving other people interactional privacy, a crucial mechanism in a society where there is frequently little physical privacy. In discourse, this socio-cultural norm is reflected in a number of ways. If you want information from an Aboriginal person, it is important to follow the discourse rules. Factual information relating to location and time, and how people are related to each other, for instance, is typically elicited in Aboriginal English using a statement with rising intonation, e.g. *you were at the store?* In other words, the questioner presents a proposition for confirmation or correction. On the other hand, direct questions of this kind are not used for eliciting 'substantial' information such as important personal details, reasons for behaving in a particular way, and so on. A much less direct method is necessary in this case, with the information seeker volunteering some of their own knowledge on the topic, and then waiting patiently until the addressee is ready to respond, e.g. *I heard there was a big argument at the store yesterday*. It is important to realise that this is the normal everyday way of seeking information. Direct questions are totally inappropriate in such situations, and are likely to be responded to by silence or by a formulaic response such as *I don't remember* or *I don't know*. Answers in this case could be glossed as meaning 'This is not an appropriate way for me to provide information of that nature'. It is also important to realise that in Aboriginal society, some kinds of information are not freely shared, but may be restricted to those who have the right to it, and silence is much more common as an acceptable component of interaction than in non-Aboriginal exchanges.

Exercise 11

Five years after Robyn Kina's imprisonment for life, as described in example 8, her case was re-opened, and the Appeal court found that her conviction was the result of a mis-trial. Using the information on Aboriginal patterns of interaction provided above, suggest some reasons which might account for the mis-trial.

Answer is contained in the discussion below.

In 1992, some years after Robyn Kina was imprisoned, she was interviewed in prison by TV journalists for documentaries which raised legal and moral issues concerning victims of domestic violence who kill violent partners in situations of self-defence. The information she gave to the interviewers, David Goldie and Debbie Richards, about the horrific violence perpetrated by Black, and his threat to rape her niece, had never been presented at her trial. Consequently, the jury never knew of the provocation and need for self-defence which led to her fatal knife-attack on Black. As a result of the TV documentaries, an appeal was initiated which resulted in the quashing of Robyn Kina's murder conviction, and she was released after five years in prison. The question which puzzled people was 'why was she willing to tell a TV interviewer what happened but not her lawyers?'

The sociolinguist's answer to this question is that Robyn Kina responded to her lawyers in an Aboriginal way. She had no opportunity to establish a relationship with the lawyers, and they did not share information about themselves. Providing embarrassing details about her personal life was therefore not possible. She certainly could not handle direct questions about personal matters, and so responded with silence. At that point she did not have the ability to communicate any other way, and her lawyers knew nothing about Aboriginal ways of communicating. The approach used by the TV journalists, on the other hand, was very similar to Aboriginal ways of communicating. They established a good relationship with Kina over a period of time, shared information about themselves, used indirect strategies for eliciting her story, listened patiently and without interruption, and tolerated long silences. TV journalism does not always involve such time-consuming information-gathering strategies. Robyn Kina was lucky that this investigative TV programme placed a priority on people feeling comfortable about telling important stories.

Since non-Aboriginal norms dominate Australian society, Aboriginal people are often disadvantaged and misunderstood or misinterpreted in interaction. This is especially

C

Language variation: focus on uses

345

true in institutional contexts such as law courts where direct questions are the norm, and silence can be interpreted as evasive and even as evidence of guilt. Chapter 11 included further examples of cross-cultural differences in ways of interacting. Where there is a power imbalance between the groups involved, such differences can create serious communication problems for minority group members.

Cultures described as 'positive politeness' or solidarity-oriented cultures value involvement with others, while 'negative politeness' cultures emphasise respect and minimise intrusion (see chapter 11 for further discussion of these terms). On the basis of the description so far, Aboriginal society seems a classic negative politeness culture. In fact, however, Aboriginal society is characterised by high interactional involvement, on-going serial, open-ended conversations, and places great value on group activities which build solidarity. Things are never as simple as they seem, and the analysis of interaction patterns in Aboriginal communities raises questions about the adequacy of the simple negative/positive politeness framework.

This example also raises questions about the precise relationship between discourse and world-view. Can different discourse patterns be regarded as evidence of a different perspective on reality? Research on Aboriginal communities suggests that a feature such as a preference for indirect ways of conveying information reflects a distinctive perception of socio-cultural relationships. As Robyn Kina's behaviour illustrated, Aboriginal interactions give personal relationships priority over information-oriented goals; they prioritise the affective over the referential dimension. Indirectness is an obligatory aspect of respect for the other person when important personal information is at stake. And long, non-intrusive silences are tolerated, even when one party is clearly gathering information. It seems conceivable that preferred discourse patterns and linguistic usages may reflect and even influence a particular view of social reality and socio-cultural relationships.

LANGUAGE, SOCIAL CLASS AND COGNITION

Example 9

(a) Emmie, the daughter of a Scottish aristocratic family, was enrolled at an English 'public' (i.e. private fee-paying) boarding school in the south of England. At the end of her first month, she failed all the oral progress tests. The school assumed she lacked intellectual ability.

'This is outrageous,' her mother declared, 'she is an outstandingly intelligent young woman. What is the problem?'

'Her English is deficient; she can't communicate,' responded her form teacher. 'We can't understand a word she says.'

'Well, that's your problem,' announced Emmie's mother. 'You had better learn to!'

(b) Middle-class children do well in school.
    Working-class children don't do well in school.
    Middle-class children speak a different variety of English than working-class
    children.

Usual conclusion: working-class children should change the way they speak.
Spot the faulty logic?

The previous section provided an example of the potentially punitive social implications of culturally different ways of interacting, even when both groups are using varieties of the same language, a topic which is examined further in chapter 15. Others have been interested in whether there are possible cognitive implications where groups use different varieties of a language. Basil Bernstein was a sociologist who asked this question in the 1960s. Like many educationalists, he was concerned that British children from working-class backgrounds were not progressing well at school. It was also widely recognised that working-class children spoke English differently from middle-class children. It was easy to conclude that these two observations were related. Rather than deducing that teachers tended to favour children who used more standard varieties (an issue explored further in the next chapter), researchers began to examine features of working-class children's speech, looking for an explanation there. Unfortunately, they assumed that the kind of language working-class children used in a formal interview situation to a middle-class adult was an accurate representation of their sociolinguistic competence. In such situations, not surprisingly, the children used short, even mono-syllabic, responses which suggested to the interviewers that their linguistic resources were 'restricted'. (This issue is more fully discussed in the section on 'language deficit' in chapter 15.)

Bernstein went further, however. He suggested that a 'restricted code' might also constrain the cognitive abilities of those who used it. In other words, extending the principle of linguistic determinism, he argued that the language children use might affect what they were capable of perceiving and even their thinking abilities. I should first say that there is no research support whatsoever for such a claim. Bernstein himself no longer holds this extreme position. But unfortunately it had great appeal as a way of accounting for working-class children's lack of school success. It placed the blame on the children and their language rather than on the schools' failure to adequately identify their educational needs.

Bernstein's hypotheses forced sociolinguists to examine Whorf's claims about the relationship between language, thought and society really thoroughly. One of the benefits was a more detailed study of vernacular varieties, and a very clear recognition that dialect differences were comparatively superficial aspects of language which could not conceivably have consequences for different ways of thinking. Though Bernstein phrased his claims with care, they were often oversimplified and misinterpreted. His research appeared to support a view of working-class children as linguistically deprived, and

347

their use of vernacular forms as evidence of cognitive deficit. This is clearly nonsense. Whether you use a single or multiple negative construction, whether you mark past tense explicitly or not, which pronoun you use in the phrase *between you and I/me* – these are certainly not linguistic differences which can support an argument about cognitive deficiency. They are relatively superficial examples of language variation with no possible serious cognitive consequences.

Exercise 12

Show the set of pictures below to a friend or family member and ask them to tell you the story portrayed by the pictures. Record what they say on tape. Identify the number of nouns they used and the number of pronouns they used in telling you the story.

The point of this exercise is to provide an example of the kind of data which has been used to assess children's linguistic abilities. Picture description tasks like this have been used to compare the linguistic abilities of middle-class and working-class children. The underlying assumption in some of this testing has been that children who use more nouns have better linguistic resources than those who use more pronouns in such a task. Using nouns is being more explicit and expects less of the listener. The following (hypothetical) examples were provided by one researcher to illustrate the kinds of differences which might turn up.

1. Three boys are playing football and one boy kicks the ball and it goes through the window – the ball breaks the window and the boys are looking at it – and a man comes out – and shouts at them – because they've broken the window – so they run away – and then that lady looks out of her window – and she tells the boys off.
   No. of nouns: 13
   No. of pronouns: 6
2. They're playing football and he kicks it and it goes through there – it breaks the window and they're looking at it and he comes out and shouts at them because they've broken it – so they run away – and then she looks out and she tells them off.
   No. of nouns: 2
   No. of pronouns: 14

Recognising that these versions are parodies, it is nevertheless true that some children use more pronouns and some use more nouns in telling the story.

How might one critique the claim that using nouns is 'better' than using pronouns in such a context?

Answer at end of chapter

C

Language variation: focus on uses

Conclusion

In this chapter, I have discussed various ways in which language, thought and culture interrelate. Most sociolinguists agree that language influences our perceptions of 'reality'. There is little doubt that consistent use of pejorative terms for a group, for instance, affects people's perceptions of that group's members. This is the basis of arguments against (and legislation proscribing) sexist and racist language. There is also psycholinguistic evidence that the existence of particular categories in a language may predispose speakers to classify 'reality' in one way rather than another. So, for instance, sorting coloured items into categories is easier when our language provides distinct lexical labels for the relevant categories. Language clearly influences perception in such cases.

There is also undisputed evidence, however, that the physical and cultural environment in which it develops influences the vocabulary and grammar of a language. Languages develop the vocabulary that their speakers need, whether to label different kinds of kangaroo or to identify different ways of cooking rice. Important, frequently occurring distinctions tend to get incorporated into the grammar. The creolisation process described in chapter 4, for example, indicated that future time was initially lexically marked in Tok Pisin as *baimbai* but eventually became grammaticalised in the form of a regular prefix [bə]. Grammatical gender is another such category which often reflects both physical and culturally important distinctions, with roots deep in the mythology and belief systems of a community, as illustrated by the Aboriginal language Dyirbal. Culturally important semantic distinctions are thus typically encoded in many aspects of the structure of languages, even though current users may not always be able to consciously articulate the underlying rationale.

When cultural and social change occurs the linguistic system generally adapts. So, as noted in exercise 7, there was a distinct term *shurin* for your wife's brother in nineteenth-century Russian, while in modern Russian the phrase *brat zheny* 'brother of wife' is used. Other distinctive, precise Russian kinship terms for in-law relationships have also been replaced by broader descriptive phrases, reflecting the fact that family structures have radically changed in Russia over the last century, and it is no longer necessary to be so precise about these particular relationships.

On the other hand, the language and discourse patterns associated with a particular culture may not only reflect existing social relationships, they may also influence the way one group interacts with another, as the Robyn Kina case illustrated. When different cultures meet, conflicting discourse rules can result in miscommunication with potentially severe social consequences. As Whorf pointed out, it is important to be aware of the extent to which we may be constrained, if not trapped, by the norms of our own familiar systems of interaction. This chapter has identified some of the complex ways in which linguistic systems and specific ways of using language can provide insights into the perceptions, values, and beliefs of a community. The next chapter describes a range of ways of analysing discourse or the ways of talking which are appropriate in different social and cultural groups in different conversational and institutional contexts.

ANSWERS TO EXERCISES IN CHAPTER 13

Answer to exercise 1

A simple phrase such as *routine pelvic examination* reflects a particular perspective – that of the doctor rather than the person being examined. Pelvic examinations may be quick and unproblematic procedures for doctors, but they are not part of most people's daily routine. The word *routine* also creates the impression that there are no grounds for concern, constructing a reality in which medical examinations are everyday events and not a cause for worry. Critical discourse analysts suggest such usages betray particular attitudes and ideological positions.

Answer to exercise 4

Common sense and reflection on experience suggest the following points:

- The experience of knowing there is a word for something but not being able to find it.
- We can translate between languages.
- The same ideas can be expressed in many different ways.

Most linguists would add the following points:

- All languages have the same broad functions.
- Languages share important basic structural properties.

More philosophical, and possibly more contentious, points include the following:

- People's experiences and perceptions are more similar than different.
- We are all capable of identifying 'objective' reality.
- Human reasoning relies on universal logical principles.

You may of course have additional or different points.

Answers to exercise 5

(i)   The number 16 is called *seize* in French, *shi-liu* in Chinese and *juu-roku* in Japanese.

(ii) You should have been able to work out the Chinese and Japanese from the information provided, but if you got the correct name for 16 in French you must have learned French or used a dictionary.

(iii) The implications are discussed in the next two paragraphs.

Answer to exercise 6

These expressions suggest that English speakers perceive time as a resource; the way these expressions 'package' time reflects a view of it as a valuable and scarce commodity. Like money it can be wasted or wisely invested.

There are also a couple of examples which treat time as a gift (*devote time/give time*).

Can you think of alternative ways of encoding time?

This exercise could provide a basis for interesting cross-language and cross-cultural comparisons if you have access to appropriate data. For example, you could make a list of time-related expressions in another language you know and compare them with those used in English. Do both languages use similar or different metaphors? What does this suggest about the way time is perceived?

Answer to exercise 8

The possibility of translation indicates language cannot be a total conceptual straitjacket, and tests of bilingual children suggest they develop greater cognitive flexibility than monolinguals, but we know relatively little about the extent to which bilingual and multilingual people think differently in each language. One experiment suggested that bilinguals are more likely to assign people to stereotypes which fit categories provided by the language they are using at the time. So, for example, using English, bilinguals described an artistic person as 'unreliable', a feature which fits the English stereotype of the artist as a temperamental, intense person. Using Chinese, however, which has no such stereotype of the artist, they didn't refer to this characteristic. This suggests that the social and cultural perceptions of bilinguals may be influenced by the particular language they are using at any point.

Answer to exercise 9

In everyday use 'culture' tends to mean appreciation of the arts, literature, music, theatre and so on. But for sociolinguists and anthropologists, culture refers to whatever one needs to know or believe in order to function in a particular society. Culture is the basic 'know-how' we draw on in everyday life.

Answers to exercise 10

(i) The fact that different terms are used for same sex vs different sex siblings suggests that relative gender is important within the family in Maori culture.

   The fact that different terms are used for younger vs older siblings of the same sex suggests that relative age is important, especially between same sex siblings.

(ii) If you are female and she is younger, use *teina.*

   If you are female and she is older, use *tuakana.*

   If you are male, use *tuahine.*

Answer to exercise 12

The high value placed on explicitness reflects the norms of the school, and to some extent the priority attached to written language. Explicitness is not 'good' in any absolute sense. There are many contexts in which it would be offensive and imply lack of understanding or trust. It is possible then that different children interpret the demands of the situation and the needs of the listener differently. Telling the story to a friendly person with the pictures in front of both of you is very likely to result in pointing at the pictures and the use of more pronouns and fewer nouns. The influence of the context is therefore important, and the way it is perceived and interpreted may be different for different children. Some children may fail to recognise the game they are being expected to play. They have to pretend their listener can't see the pictures in order to justify a high proportion of nouns as opposed to pronouns. They may fail to be explicit because they cannot imagine what they can tell the interviewer about their own pictures that they don't already know.

   Since many tasks demanded of children in school require great explicitness, children who have learnt to play the game of spelling out and displaying what they know are likely to be at an advantage when faced with such tasks.

Concepts introduced

Social constructionist approach
Verbal hygiene

Sapir-Whorf Hypothesis
Linguistic determinism
Linguistic relativity
Grammaticalisation
Culture
Kinship systems
Restricted code

References

The following sources provided material for this chapter:

Bernstein (1973) for early discussion of 'restricted code'
Burling (1970) on kinship terms and Njamal in particular
Cameron (1995) on verbal hygiene and political correctness
Carroll (1956) for Whorf's writing
Eades (1994, 1996) for Robyn Kina case and features of Aboriginal culture
Evans (1998: 164) for Kunwinjku kangaroo terms
Fengyuan, Ji (1998) for analysis of influence of Maoist propaganda in China
Goodenough (1975: 167) quoted in Wardhaugh (2006: 221) for definition of culture
Green (1999) on graffiti
Harres (1993) on medical textbooks and the perspectives they suggest
Hawkins (1967–68) for the pictures and discussion used in exercise 12
Lakoff (1987) on Dyirbal data
Metge (1995) on Maori. Data checked by Mary Boyce
Miriam Meyerhoff (personal communication) on grammatic(al)isation
Stubbs (1997) for discussion of Whorf's influence on sociolinguistics
Talbot (1998: 233) cites politically correct translation of *Snow White and the Seven Dwarfs*
Wardhaugh (2006: Ch. 9) for material in exercise 9
Whitney (1998) for psycholinguistic experimental evidence on colours, numbers, bilinguals
    and stereotypes etc.

Quotations

Example 2. Quotations are from Llewellyn-Jones (1982: 205–9).
Example 4. Quotations are from Mao Zedong (1976: 72, 82, 266, 239).
Examples 5 and 6 are from Whorf's writings in Carroll (1956: 135, 213–14).
Example 7 is from Romaine (2000: Ch. 2).
Example 8 is based on Eades (1996).
Exercise 7 is based on a table in Whitney (1998: 124).
Quotation 'the urge to meddle in matters of language' is taken from the Preface in
    Cameron (1995: i).
Claim that their language 'practically force[d] the Hopi to notice vibratory phenomena' is
    from Whorf's writings (Carroll 1956: 60).

Language variation: focus on uses

C

▨ Useful additional reading

Bauer, Holmes and Warren (2005)
Cameron (1995)
Gibbon (1999), Ch. 3
Kiesling and Bratt-Paulston (2005)
Kramsch (1998)
Stubbs (1997)
Wardhaugh (2006), Ch. 9

14   Analysing discourse

Example 1

Phone rings

Lesley: 4766091

Mother: Hello (*second syllable is stressed and slightly lengthened*)

Lesley: Oh hello, how're you?

Mother: Very well thank you love and you?

Lesley: Yes thank you

Mother: That's good

At first glance, this looks like a normal telephone conversation. But a closer look at the way the discourse develops indicates that it has some unusual features. Typically when people answer the phone both parties identify themselves, often in the first turn, e.g. *hello, Janet Holmes speaking*; and the caller may respond *hi Janet, it's Mary here*. In example 1 neither Lesley nor her mother self-identify in their first turns, so we can deduce that they recognise each other's voices, and hence they can dispense with that step. (Interestingly, as speaker-ID on phones becomes more widespread such patterns may become more 'normal').

A second unusual feature relates to the first topic of the call. It is typically the caller who asks *how are you?* when they ring someone. It is the caller's prerogative to select the first topic, and *how are you?* is a frequent way of filling this slot in Western English-speaking cultures. In example 1, however, it is Lesley, the person called, who asks *how're you?* The reason for this deviation from a typical telephone turn sequence is that this is a regular or routine weekly call between mother and daughter. Lesley, the person called, knows that the 'business' of the call is simply to keep in touch and so she can safely take the lead in anticipating an appropriate first topic. Clearly, when we analyse even a short conversational exchange, we bring to bear a great deal of background knowledge about the discourse norms or rules of speaking which characterise different kinds of social interaction.

In chapter 1, I introduced four dimensions for analysing language in social inter-action (*social distance* or *solidarity, status, formality,* and *function*), and identified some important components of a speech event (*participants, setting* or *social context, topic,* and *aim* or *purpose of an interaction*). This chapter builds on those components, and introduces some further tools, especially those of the discourse analyst, for describing how people use language in different social contexts. The kinds of questions addressed in this chapter include: How do we know when the question *is it six o'clock?* is a direc-tive to switch on the television rather than a request for information? How do we know when a negative remark is a tease as opposed to an insult? How is it possible to infer the interviewer's assumptions from what is said and what is not said in a job interview? What is the difference between a disruptive interruption and a supportive overlap? And, can the tools of the discourse analyst assist in uncovering evidence of bias or even prejudice?

Discourse analysis provides a tool for sociolinguists to identify the norms of talk among different social and cultural groups in different conversational and institutional contexts, and to describe the discursive resources people use in constructing different social identities in interaction. This rather long chapter is divided into five sections, each illustrating a different approach to the analysis of discourse. These five approaches are just a selection from a wide array of ways of analysing discourse (others include genre analysis, discursive psychology, and speech act theory). But they will serve to illustrate what discourse analysis offers to the sociolinguist.

Among sociolinguists, the term 'discourse' is generally used to refer to stretches of spoken or written language which extend beyond an utterance or a sentence. Among those from other disciplines, and especially philosophers, discourse is a broader term. For these researchers, discourse is regarded as a means of structuring knowledge and social practice, and language is just one symbolic form of discourse. This very theoret-ical approach, in which discourse 'constitutes' social relations, is particularly associated with the French social theorist, Foucault. It is useful to be aware of this more theoret-ical approach to discourse, since it is widely referred to, but it is not the approach explored in this chapter. Rather, this chapter focusses on discourse as a stretch of spoken or written text and describes how it can be analysed. The first section of the chapter illustrates a pragmatic approach to the analysis of discourse.

PRAGMATICS AND POLITENESS THEORY

What is pragmatics?

Example 2

you didn't buy a paper?

What does this sentence mean? Even if we know the meaning of each of the words, realising that *paper* refers to a newspaper, and recognising that it is an interrogative structure, that is not enough to unambiguously decode its meaning. It could be interpreted as a request for information, or as a complaint, or even a rebuke, depending on the social relationship between participants and the background expectations regarding newspaper-buying in the household. Similarly, although example 3 could be treated as a declarative, a simple statement of fact, it may convey considerably more meaning, depending on who said it to whom.

Example 3

I can hear someone talking

Consider, for instance, the difference in meaning conveyed if this utterance was said by a teacher in a classroom as opposed to two police officers investigating an 'empty' house. Context is clearly crucial in interpreting what is meant, and pragmatics extends the analysis of meaning beyond grammar and word meaning to the relationship between the participants and the background knowledge they bring to a situation. Pragmatics is concerned with the analysis of meaning in interaction.

Exercise 1

Consider this brief conversational exchange.

Example 4

Lionel is lying in a hospital bed after an accident. Kirsty is visiting him.

1. Kirsty: [*pointing to the pain relief drip*] are you sure that thing's
2.   giving you enough pain relief
3. Lionel: yeah heaps
4. Kirsty: you are using it?
5. Lionel: any time I need it
6. Kirsty: you're not using it

What possible interpretations can you provide for Lionel's responses to Kirsty's questions in lines 3 and 5? What do you think Lionel intends Kirsty to understand? On what basis does she infer that he is *not* using the pain relief?

Answer at end of chapter

◼ Conversational maxims and implicatures

Example 5

Ken: what time is it?
Hana: three o'clock

This exchange between a pair of friends follows the pragmatic rules or conversational maxims that Paul Grice, a British philosopher, proposed to account for our basic assumptions about interaction. He suggested that, unless we have reason to think otherwise, we assume people are following a basic *cooperative principle* and being succinct, truthful, relevant, and clear. He formulated this proposal as four maxims of cooperative talk which can be summarised as follows:

Quantity: say as much as but no more than is necessary
Quality: do not say what you believe to be false, or that for which you lack evidence
Relation: be relevant
Manner: be clear, unambiguous, brief and orderly

In fact, of course, for many different reasons, people do not always follow these rules. They may deliberately want to mislead the other person as in example 6.

Example 6

Sally's father, Sam, has promised to give Sally a lift to the gym when she has finished her homework.

Sam: Have you finished your homework?
Sally: (*with a smile*) I've got my kit and I'm ready to go
Sam: OK we're off.

Sally does not say anything false here. But her statement implies she has fulfilled the conditions for the lift. Assuming that her answer follows the maxims, her father wrongly (as it turns out) infers that she has finished her homework.

Another common reason for not following the maxims is to avoid responsibility for saying something unpleasant. Grice gives the example of writing a job reference for someone who does not fulfil the job requirements. By commenting on irrelevant characteristics while omitting mention of skills crucial for the job, the reference writer generates the inference that the applicant does not have the required skills.

Example 7 looks like a perfectly normal conversation, but if you look carefully at Joyce's utterance, you will see that it does not actually answer Harry's question.

> **Example 7**
>
> Harry does not like lending the family car to the children. Joyce knows this but she has just lent their car to their son Dan.
> Harry: Where's the car?
> Joyce: Dan needed to do some shopping

Joyce's answer does not follow Grice's conversational maxim of relevance, and hence it generates a conversational implicature (i.e. we can infer more than is literally said). Again the addressee infers, on the basis of logic and knowledge of the world, that something additional is being conveyed to what is explicitly stated.

There has been some discussion about whether the conversational rules that Grice proposed can be considered as universals. Do the maxims apply in all cultures? In some communities, for instance, such as the Malagasy Republic, for a variety of cultural reasons people are systematically *uninformative*. So, for example, they deliberately avoid providing precise information about their relatives and friends, since by doing so they believe that they may attract the attention of evil spirits. However, since all members of the community know about this constraint, it generates no conversational implicatures. Similarly, in cultures where one does not utter the name of a person who has died, or refer to one's husband by his given name, one could say the quantity maxim is 'suspended' in such contexts.

Conversational maxims and politeness

Very often the reasons why people do not follow the conversational maxims relate to considerations of politeness, and this is where pragmatics overlaps with sociolinguistics. Politeness, as discussed in chapter 11, entails taking account of social factors, such as how well you know somebody, what their social role or relative status is in relation to yours, and the kind of social context in which you are interacting. Robin Lakoff, an American pragmatics researcher who has been called 'the mother of modern politeness theory', introduced three rules of politeness.

1. *Don't impose:*
   e.g. use modals and hedges: *I wonder if I might just open the window a little*
2. *Give options*
   e.g. use interrogatives including tag questions: *do you mind if I open the window? it would be nice to have the window open a little wouldn't it?*
3. *Be friendly*
   e.g. use informal expressions, endearments: e.g. *Be a honey and open the window darling*

The first two rules express the notion of negative politeness which was introduced in chapter 11, while the last rule relates to the concept of positive politeness. The concepts

C

Language variation: focus on uses

of negative and positive politeness are components of a theory of politeness associated with the pragmatics researchers, Brown and Levinson, referred to in chapter 11.

Brown and Levinson identified three social factors which they suggested qualified as universal influences on linguistically polite behaviour. The first two are very familiar to sociolinguists: they are *how well you know someone* and *what is their status relative to yours*. The third factor is illustrated in example 8.

Example 8

Rick makes a request to his mother in the family living room
[Pauses are indicated in tenths of a second: e.g. (0.5) is half a second]

Rick: um mum (0.5) um do you think um I could possibly just borrow your car (2)

Mother: [*frowns*]

Rick: um just for a little while (1)

Mother: um well [*frowns*]

Rick: it's just that I need to get this book to Helen tonight

---

In this example the two participants know each other well and, since the son is a young adult, the status or role difference is not huge. Both of these factors would predict that Rick's request could be expressed relatively directly. However, there is another factor which influences the way he expresses his request. He is asking a big favour; his mother's car is an expensive sports car and she does not generally allow her children to borrow it. Hence in making his request, Rick includes a number of negative politeness strategies in the form of mitigating devices or hedges (hesitation markers *um*, modal verb *could* and particle *possibly*, minimisers *just, a little*) as well as the positive politeness strategies of using an in-group identity marker (*mum*) and providing a reason for the request. In other words, simply the cost of the request (what Brown and Levinson call 'the ranking of the imposition') can influence the kind of politeness strategies which are appropriate: e.g. compare asking your best friend if you can borrow their newspaper to check the sports results, as opposed to asking to borrow their brand new mountain bike.

Exercise 2

Using the terms provided in this section, what pragmatic rule is illustrated in example 9?
   What kind of politeness is illustrated in this example?
   Would Des's comments be considered polite in your socio-cultural group?
   If not, why not?

> **Example 9**
>
> Small talk between workers in a New Zealand plant nursery at the start of the day. Des is the manager. Ros is the plant nursery worker.
>
> 1. Des: be a nice day when it all warms up a bit though
> 2. Ros: yeah (pause) it's okay today
> 3. Des: what did you get up to at the weekend?
>   anything exciting?

Answer at end of chapter

■ Sociolinguistics and politeness

> **Example 10**
>
> *Igbo proverb*
> O ji isi kota ebu ka ebu ga agba
> 'He who disturbs the hornet's nest gets stung by hornets'.
> i.e. Expect negative consequences from unwise behaviour.

The concepts of positive and negative politeness, and the idea of rules or strategies for expressing politeness, have generated a good deal of research. One area of this research has involved exploring how different speech acts are expressed appropriately and politely in different social and cultural contexts. In Nigeria, for instance, the Igbo people use proverbs as one indirect and socially acceptable way of criticising the behaviour of others. The proverb in example 10 could serve as an admonition to someone with a serious drinking problem, for instance. In some Asian cultures, it is inappropriate, and regarded as very odd, to say *thank you* for service in a shop. Chapter 11 illustrated how speech acts such as directives and requests, compliments, refusals and apologies vary cross-culturally.

Chapter 11 also illustrated a range of linguistic politeness devices including choice of pronoun (e.g. *tu/vous, du/Sie* etc.), endearment terms (e.g. *love, honey, dear*), modal verbs (e.g. *could, might, may*), and modal particles, such as *perhaps, possibly*. All these features may be relevant in the analysis of discourse in context. Sociolinguists examine the patterning of such pragmatic politeness devices in the usage of different social groups in particular social contexts, or in the construction of particular social identities. So, for example, certain pragmatic devices, or even speech acts, may be used more frequently by particular ethnic or social groups in specific contexts: e.g. until the beginning of the twenty-first century, the tag *eh* was particularly associated with conversations involving Maori people in New Zealand, and contributed to the construction of a Maori ethnic identity. It has become more widespread, however, and currently tends to signal informality and New Zealand identity, rather than Maori identity in particular. Modal

C

Language variation: focus on uses

devices are widely associated with feminine discourse in many speech communities. Patterns of minimal feedback or back-channelling (*mm, yeah, right*) in discourse also tend to pattern differently for different groups: Japanese conversationalists provide a great deal more than Anglo Americans, and Maori conversationalists tend to provide less than Pakeha in New Zealand. Among middle-class, Western people, it is often the case that women give more compliments than men, especially relating to appearance, and this can be seen as positively polite linguistic behaviour. Such devices thus become important discourse resources, for example, in conveying a particular kind of social identity, as illustrated in chapter 8. Knowing how to use them and to interpret their social significance is part of our socio-pragmatic competence (see chapter 16 for further discussion of this concept).

Politeness theory has come in for a good deal of criticism in recent years, especially from sociolinguists. Researchers studying Asian cultures, for instance, point to evidence of Western bias in what is categorised as linguistically polite, as opposed to required conventional behaviour. The use of address forms and honorifics, for example (see chapter 11), in languages such as Chinese, Japanese and Korean, is typically a matter of social convention or linguistic etiquette, rather than strategic choice. Respect or deference is encoded in certain linguistic forms which are *required* when talking to one's elders or those of higher status, for instance. While such features are typically optional in Western languages, they are entirely predictable on the basis of the social characteristics of the participants in many Asian languages.

Rather than focussing on the social distance or solidarity dimension, politeness in Asian cultures tends to emphasise socio-cultural values such as 'sincerity', 'respect' and 'consideration', and negative politeness strategies of avoidance and mitigation are favoured to express these values. So, for example, in asking a friend for a loan of some money, a Chinese speaker will typically express reluctance, and provide reasons, as ways of mitigating the request. Example 11 illustrates how a Chinese person reported that they would express such a request.

Example 11

1. Shizai bu hao yisi,
   'It's truly quite embarrassing
2. you ge shiqing xiang he ni shangliang yixia.
   but I'd like to discuss a problem with you
3. Wo erzi jiu yao qu Aodaiya shang xue le.
   My son is about to go to Australia to study
4. Xianzai qian hai mei chouji.
   Right now the money is insufficient
5. Bu zhi nimen shoutou shi bu shi fangbian?
   I was wondering if it would be convenient for you people
   to help us out'

The request is introduced with an explicit statement in line 1 indicating reluctance to impose on the addressee. Then the speaker prepares the way for his request in line 2. The next discourse move in line 3 involves providing a reason for the request, a discourse move known as a 'grounder'. The reason for the need is expressed rather obliquely, a strategy which saves the speaker's face, while it is also suggested that this is a temporary situation, *right now the money is insufficient*. Line 4 finally presents the request in a very mitigated form, using a negative politeness strategy which provides a way out for the addressee if it is not *convenient* to provide some financial help. The request thus expresses respect for the addressee and consideration for both participants' face, important values in Chinese culture.

By contrast, in other communities, such as Greek, Turkish, and Moroccan Arabic, politeness typically involves positive politeness strategies, and the expression of concern, consideration, friendliness and intimacy, rather than imposition-avoidance and distance maintenance strategies. Example 12 illustrates requests from a Greek study of politeness. In both cases, the speaker explicitly expresses positive feelings towards the addressee.

Example 12

(a) Little sister, I love you so much, give me your ear-rings. I'll look after them

(b) Mum I wish I was drinking a coffee now from your little hands

---

In Greek, the phrase *from your little hands* is a compliment on the high quality of the coffee that the mother makes.

Exercise 3

Consider B's response to A's apology in example 13.

Example 13

A.   A thousand apologies for continuously disturbing you

B.   yes you're indeed disturbing but it gives us great pleasure to see you

---

Is this a likely response to an apology for disturbing someone in your community? If so, in what contexts might it occur?

Answer at end of chapter

Recent research in the area of politeness has focussed on distinguishing 'unmarked' conventionally appropriate linguistic behaviour from 'marked' behaviour, including

Language variation: focus on uses

deliberately *impolite* utterances. So, for example, the utterances produced in the Prime Minister's Question Time in the British House of Commons are generally not regarded by the participants as inappropriate, even though they appear to be very impolite to outsiders. They are treated as perfectly appropriate by the participants in this confrontational context. Insulting comments about people's intelligence, appearance and rhetorical skills, which would cause great offence in other contexts, are regarded as normal and appropriate, as illustrated in example 14 which elicited laughter rather than outrage.

Example 14

MP: . . . having just heard the predictable routine from the Leader of the Opposition – the man of all gags and no policy – and before we
Other MPs laugh
MP: hear the predictable routine from . . .

There are a range of contexts, then, in which people deliberately adopt linguistically aggressive behaviour. Ritual insults are part of the interactional resources of many adolescent gangs, and game shows such as the British programme, *The Weakest Link*, provide further examples of contexts where intentional insults are regarded as acceptable and appropriate. Anne Robinson, the caustic host, confronts participants with utterances such as *you're a coward aren't you, pathetic, stupid, did you bribe the production team to get onto this show? who has the intellect of a flea?*

To sum up, a pragmatic approach to the analysis of language emphasises that the interpretation of meaning requires careful attention to context. Judgements about what counts as polite, friendly or impolite behaviour are very much a matter of dynamic negotiation between participants in particular social and cultural contexts. Different participants may interpret the 'same' interaction quite differently.

As this section has indicated, a good deal of pragmatics research has tended to concentrate on the analysis of speech acts, and even on features of single utterances or very short exchanges. By contrast, the ethnography of speaking framework, which is described in the next section, focusses rather on speech events as a whole, and embraces the total social and cultural setting as components in the analysis.

Exercise 4

Identify examples from TV or your own observations where sarcastic, insulting and face-threatening comments are treated as appropriate.

What pragmatic principles are involved in generating the 'rude' inferences?

What are the distinguishing features of the context (e.g. consider the relationship between the participants, setting, purpose of the interaction etc.)

Exercise 5

A good deal of the data collected by those interested in cross-cultural pragmatics consists of material elicited through questionnaires which ask people to respond to imaginary scenarios.

Here is an example.

A classmate who regularly misses class asks to borrow your notes. You would really prefer not to lend your notes to them. What would you say?

_____

_____

Identify three advantages and three disadvantages of this method of data collection.

Answer at end of chapter

ETHNOGRAPHY OF SPEAKING

Example 15

Harriet was a very decorous and proper linguist who hated to draw attention to herself or to 'break the rules' when attending events hosted by people from a culture other than her own. On one occasion, at a kava-drinking event in Vanuatu, she whispered to her more culturally experienced companion 'is it OK to leave the circle temporarily?' When he reassured her this was fine, she hastily left and could then be heard quietly vomiting behind a nearby bush!

Sociolinguists who have worked with people from different cultural backgrounds are very aware of the amount of cultural baggage that we all carry around with us. We make assumptions about what is normal and usual and appropriate and correct, and we respond with surprise, or sometimes disapproval, when somebody breaks our rules or behaves in a way that challenges our expectations. The ethnography of speaking (also known as the ethnography of communication since it embraces features of non-verbal communication too) is an approach to analysing language which has been designed to heighten awareness of culture-bound assumptions. Dell Hymes, the sociolinguist who first developed this theoretical approach, worked with the indigenous native peoples of the United States of America, and this made him very aware of the limitations of traditional approaches to describing communication systems.

The framework that Hymes developed for the analysis of communicative events involved the following components:

- *Genre* or type of event: e.g. phone call, conversation, business meeting, lesson, interview, blog

- *Topic* or what people are talking about: e.g. holidays, sport, sociolinguistics, politics
- *Purpose* or *function*: the reason(s) for the talk: e.g. to plan an event, to catch up socially, to teach something, to persuade someone to help you
- *Setting*: where the talk takes place: e.g. at home, in classroom, in an office
- *Key* or emotional tone: e.g. serious, jocular, sarcastic
- *Participants*: characteristics of those present and their relationship: sex, age, social status, role and role relationship: e.g. mother–daughter, teacher–pupil, TV interviewer, interviewee and audience
- *Message form*, code and/or channel: e.g. telephone, letter, email, language and language variety, non-verbal
- *Message content* or specific details of what the communication is about: e.g. organising a time for a football match, describing how a tap works, describing how to make rotis
- *Act sequence* or ordering of speech acts: e.g. greetings, meeting turn-taking rules, ending a telephone conversation
- *Rules for interaction* or prescribed orders of speaking: e.g. who must speak first, who must respond to the celebrant at a wedding, who closes a business meeting
- *Norms for interpretation* of what is going on: the common knowledge and shared understandings of the relevant cultural presuppositions: what we need to know to interpret what is going on: e.g. that *how are you* does not require a detailed response in most Western English-speaking societies, that it is polite to refuse the first offer of more food in some cultures.

Some of these components were introduced in chapter 1 (*setting, topic, participants, function*), and some have been referred to in other chapters (*message form* includes *register* and *variety*, for example), but some have not yet been discussed.

Explicitly identifying the components of a communicative event in this way has proved particularly useful in describing interaction in unfamiliar cultures. The framework highlights features that contrast between cultures, e.g. the different ways that legal proceedings or celebrations are conducted, or contrasts in how meetings are run. It also provides a way of analysing events that are unique to a particular culture: e.g. ritual insults in African-American Vernacular culture, formal rituals of welcome in Maori communities, or kava-drinking events in Pacific communities. Example 16 uses the ethnography of communication framework to describe a kava-drinking ceremony in Aulua, a community of South-East Malakula Island in Vanuatu.

Kava is a mild narcotic drunk in many parts of Polynesia and Melanesia. Public social kava drinking is restricted to adult males in Aulua; women may drink kava but not in the company of men. (Other parts of the country are far stricter, and forbid women from consuming kava or even witnessing its production.) Before the ceremony begins, the hosting male, or senior male of the clan, prepares the kava and the women prepare food. The hosting men stand around near the kava while the women and children sit on mats spread in a wide semi-circle. Visiting families may sit on their mats among the hosting families. Visiting males stand behind the mats until the speech starts.

Example 16

Communicative Event: a thanking feast

Genre: feast to repay workers who have donated labour to building a house

Topic: negotiable between participants

Purpose: to acknowledge or balance the work given by presenting food and kava to the appropriate workers

Setting: village green, late afternoon or evening

Key: relatively formal

Participants:

A: Senior male host

B: Other males from the hosting clan

C: Church elder

D: Serving/preparing males

E: Hosting females

F: Children from hosting families

G: Senior visiting male

H: Other visiting males

I: Visiting females

J: Visiting children

Message form: when everyone has arrived, A makes a short speech thanking the visitors for their work

Act sequence

A: Thank you speech

C: Prayer

ALL clap.

A calls on G to take the first cup of kava which is presented to them by D.

G must drink the kava in full view of the audience and standing.

When G is finished, all clap.

Then A drinks.

ALL clap

A calls on members from B and H to drink the kava in relative order of age. Members are entitled to decline, or defer for others to go ahead of them. Drinkers may specify how full the cup should be, the default is full. (It is bad form to leave kava in the cup when returned to D.) Drinkers other than A and G need not drink in front of the audience but slip back into the shadows and drink, and spit. Drinkers must thank D, but need not directly thank A.

When the first round is finished, all drinkers are invited to drink again until all the kava runs out.

C

Language variation: focus on uses

367

The analysis highlights the complexities of a communicative event in an unfamiliar culture, including the different roles that participants play and the different rules for speaking which operate. In many communities, high school children are expected to speak only when given permission. The audience in a TV studio during an interview has a very restricted role; they may laugh appreciatively and applaud at appropriate moments, but only the interviewer and interviewee are expected to speak. At a traditional English wedding ceremony, most of those involved are expected to remain as silent auditors during the core ceremony, although they may contribute to the singing of hymns or songs. Because the framework was devised to highlight features of a communicative event that people tend to take for granted, it is particularly useful for comparing speech events between different social and cultural groups.

Example 17

A wedding I attended last year took place in a garden, with a female lay celebrant who welcomed the guests, and then formally introduced the bride and groom and their families, and the officially designated speakers. The celebrant invited each of the parents to give their child into the care of the person they were marrying, and then led the bride and groom through their formal vows. She then declared them married. Next she invited previously designated speakers to make their contributions (a poem, a story, a song, and two sets of reflections about the couple). Guests were then invited to contribute spontaneously if they wished (and two did so). At the end of the ceremony the celebrant formally wished the married couple well for their future. There was modern recorded music at the beginning and the end, and a song from a friend of the bride as a contribution in the middle.

Using the ethnography of communication framework to compare this event with a more traditional European wedding generates some obvious questions about the ways that weddings are organised in different communities, such as:

- are there restrictions on the setting or the place where the core wedding ceremony may take place?
- who acts as 'organiser' or MC (master of ceremonies)?
- who are the core participants?
- who gets to speak and for how long?
- what role, if any, do the parents of the bride and groom play?
- how much flexibility is there in the words uttered at different points?
- is music an essential or an optional component? are there restrictions on the kinds of music?
- what are the unspoken assumptions about what is NOT permitted: e.g. responses to requests regarding impediments to the marriage, contributions from other than designated speakers.

Exercise 6

Compare the modern wedding described in example 17 with a traditional wedding in your culture, or with a wedding ceremony in Greek culture, or Hindu culture. (The films *Monsoon Wedding* or *My Big Fat Greek Wedding* could be used as a basis for discussion.) The components of a communicative event can be used to guide your analysis.

An ethnography of speaking approach is particularly valuable in highlighting the unnoticed 'rules' that operate in any interaction. The framework draws attention to features that participants take for granted, and which tend to go unobserved unless something goes wrong. Example 18, for instance, highlights how email, a relatively new genre, is challenging some of the established rules of polite written communication.

Example 18

Subject line: Help

hi there Derek

I desperately need help with an essay I have to do about new words in New Zealand English

can you send me something you have written that I can use – soon as possible – it is due this week

I will be very grateful . . . . . . promise!!

Louise

The participants (writer and addressee) in this example are strangers; and there is a large age and status gap. Derek is an older, respected and internationally acclaimed expert scholar in the field of New Zealand vocabulary, while Louise is a teenage high school student. There are many ways in which this example transgresses the rules of formal written communication between strangers: the casual greeting *hi there*, the use of first name, *Derek*, and the very directly encoded demands for assistance *I need help, can you send me something*, with the intensifiers and up-graders, *desperately, soon as possible*; and the coy final *promise!!* All these features suggest a close friendly relationship between the writer and addressee.

An ethnography of speaking or communication approach highlights the mismatch between various components of the components of this communicative event. This is a written communication on a serious topic, from a young student to an older professor, with the goal of eliciting assistance. All these factors suggest that formal rules of interaction should prevail. But the genre is email, and this clearly has a strong influence on what is considered permissible. Nevertheless, it is possible that the writer and addressee do not share similar rules of interaction, and that what each considers acceptable differs.

C

Language variation: focus on uses

369

In this case, Derek was not amused and Louise received not a contribution to her essay but a list of references!

Exercise 7

Using table 14.1, make some brief notes comparing the email message in example 18 with the telephone conversation in example 1.

Table 14.1 Analysing a communicative event

Components of event	Email communication	Telephone conversation
Genre		
Topic		
Purpose		
Setting		
Participants		
Key		
Message form		
Message content		
Act sequence		
Rules for interaction		
Norms for interpretation		

Insiders and outsiders

Another distinction which is highlighted by an ethnography of speaking or communication approach is the role of the researcher as an insider or an outsider in a community. There has been a great deal of discussion in sociolinguistics about the relative advantages of researching a culture from the inside, as a member of a community, as opposed to coming into a community as a researcher from outside. Early sociolinguists and anthropological linguists were typically outsiders in the cultures they researched and described. This had some advantages since it was often easier to identify ways of speaking and rules of interaction that contrasted with those they were familiar with. Researchers noticed when there was a silence where they expected to hear talk, for example, and vice versa; they noticed restrictions on speaking rights which differed from those in their own societies, and so on.

However, an outsider's evaluation of what certain utterances or exchanges 'mean' may be rather different from the evaluation of those who are insiders in the culture. It is easy to misinterpret the significance of a gesture or an utterance, or even of silence, if you assume you know what it means, and thus never question its significance. So, for example, the reasons for silence between two Cuna Indians who have just met for the first time cannot be interpreted by someone from outside the culture. Without a sound knowledge of the culture, an outsider would find it very puzzling indeed, since reassuring formulaic talk to dispel any tension is the normal means of greeting a stranger in many Western communities. For the Cuna Indians of Panama, however, a formulaic silence is an appropriate response to an ambiguous or unpredictable situation where the status of the participants is unclear.

A researcher who is an insider has an accepted role and position in the community, and so they are less likely to influence or alter the 'normal' order of events, or to cause people to be self-conscious about their behaviours. On the other hand, an insider may overlook distinctive patterns or rules of speaking and rules of interpretation which seem 'natural' to an insider, but which are quite distinctive to their community. So, for instance, the long silences which are perfectly normal between visiting neighbours in working-class Belfast attract no attention from insiders, but seem very distinctive rules of (not) speaking to an outside researcher.

Finally, it is worth pointing out that the ethnography of speaking approach also provides another way of defining the concept of the *speech community*: i.e. as a group of people who share the same rules of speaking. People who belong to the same speech community interpret events similarly, and know the norms for behaving appropriately in the regular communicative events of the community.

C

Language variation: focus on uses

Exercise 8

Using the ethnography of speaking framework describe the components of **one** of the following speech events:

A classroom lesson/university seminar
A school meeting
A children's party
A sports event
An auction
A TV advertisement
A cookery demonstration

Exercise 9

Here are five different definitions of the speech community.
  What distinguishes each from the others?

(i) John Lyons (1970: 326): all the people who use a given language (or dialect).
(ii) Dell Hymes (1962): a group who share rules of speaking and rules for the interpretation of speech performance.
(iii) Joshua Fishman (1971: 28): a community all of whose members share at least a single speech variety and the norms for its appropriate use.

▶

(iv) John Gumperz (1965): a social group which may be either monolingual or multilingual, held together by frequency of social interaction patterns and set off from the surrounding areas by weaknesses in the lines of communication.

(v) Labov (1972a: 120): the speech community is not defined by any marked agreement in the use of language elements, so much as by participation in a set of shared norms; these norms may be observed in overt types of evaluative behaviour, and by the uniformity of the abstract patterns of variation which are invariant in respect of particular levels of usage.

Answer at the end of the chapter

INTERACTIONAL SOCIOLINGUISTICS

Interactional sociolinguistics is an approach to analysing discourse which is associated with John Gumperz, another of those who has made a large contribution to the development of the field of sociolinguists. This approach shares a great deal with the ethnography of communication framework from which it developed; but an interactional sociolinguistic approach pays particular attention to the clues people use to *interpret* conversational interaction within its ethnographic context.

Interactional sociolinguists typically make use of the detailed tools of conversation analysis (see below), paying careful attention to turn-taking behaviour, hesitations, pauses, and paralinguistic behaviour (e.g. sighs, laughter, in-breaths etc.) to interpret what the speaker intended. But, unlike core conversation analysts, interactional sociolinguists also take account of the wider sociocultural context in which interactions take place. So they bring to bear their knowledge of the community and its norms in interpreting what is going on in an interaction. Consider example 19, an excerpt from a workplace interaction between a group of men in an information technology team at a company known as Trang. What sense can you make of it without some background information? (Note that the words between slanted lines ⁄ ⁄ are uttered simultaneously. This method of marking overlaps is used throughout this chapter.)

Example 19

1. Jac: do you want me to come as well?
2. Call: um hmm ⁄[laughs]⁄
3. Dud: ⁄don't wear a ⁄don't wear an Asher tie
4. Barr: [laughs] yeah you can go incognito
5. [general laughter]
6. Jac: hide in the back row
7. [general laughter]
8. Barr: just don't say anything . . .

It is clear from the laughter that the men are exchanging humorous comments, but it is almost impossible to work out exactly what is going on without a good deal more information. The team members are discussing a meeting which they plan to attend where people from other teams will be present. It is crucial to know that Jacob has been seconded to Trang from an American company, Asher Products. Dudley and Barry make humorous suggestions about the conditions under which Jacob may accompany them to a large meeting where they will interact with people from other teams. Each contribution elaborates the underlying proposition, 'you can come to the meeting only if you clearly identify as one of us'. In other words, Jacob is being asked to blend in and not advertise that he is a 'foreigner' from an outside organisation. And he clearly gets the point since he adds his own suggestion *hide in the back row* (line 6).

From an interactional sociolinguistic perspective, familiarity with the previous discourse, as well as the wider social context is clearly important to understanding what is going on here. It is also interesting from a sociolinguistic point of view that this short exchange focusses explicitly on Jacob's status as an 'outsider', and abruptly foregrounds the boundaries between Trang and Asher Products which have appeared irrelevant in the extensive technical discussion in which the participants have previously been engaged.

Contextualisation cues

In analysing any interaction from an interactional sociolinguistics perspective, the researcher looks for *contextualisation cues*, i.e. features 'by which speakers signal and listeners interpret what the activity is, how the semantic content is to be understood and *how* each sentence relates to what precedes or follows', to quote Gumperz. Contextualisation cues signal contextual presuppositions, i.e. knowledge that the speaker assumes the listener has already or information that they can work out for themselves by paying attention to features of the context. Contextualisation cues thus allow participants to infer the most likely interpretation of an utterance. They may take a range of forms. In example 19, the laughter and the teasing tone used by Dudley and Barry serve as important cues that their comments are intended to be interpreted as humorous teases, rather than serious suggestions.

In some parts of Canada, the choice between French and English for an interaction is politically loaded. At the very least, this choice may convey information about cultural identity. In example 20, the waiter tries to do his customers a favour by offering them a choice of languages.

Example 20

Three people in a Montreal café. Two are fluent bilinguals, one has only a working knowledge of French.

1. Waiter: Anglais ou français, English or French?
2. Bilingual Customers: Bien, les deux ['well both']
3. Waiter: No, mais, anglais ou français?
                         ['No, but, English or French?']

▶

Language variation: focus on uses

C

> 4. Bilingual Customers: It doesn't matter, c'est comme vous voulez
> ['Whatever you want']
> 5. Waiter: (*sigh*) OK, OK, I'll be back in a minute.

The customers refuse to choose and so force the waiter to make the choice. Here the contextualisation cues – in the form of the waiter's persistence and repetition of his question (line 3), his sigh, and his temporary abandonment of the customers – all suggest that he is very unhappy at being forced to make this choice.

In example 21, the use of strong stress and high volume serves as a contextualisation cue indicating that the speaker found the performance surprisingly good.

Example 21

[Capitals indicate higher volume and underline indicates strong stress]
Woman commenting on a gymnastics performance she has seen at her son's school
I went to the gymnastics display last night. It was <u>GOOD</u>.

Falling intonation may indicate that the speaker is providing definitive information in answer to a question.

Example 22

Jill.   Will you pick me up?
Tony.   I will. No problem.

Contextualisation cues can also take the form of discourse moves. In example 1, the telephone call, the form of the conversational opening served as a contextualisation cue which generated inferences about the relationship between the participants, and the routineness of the call. A Japanese researcher showed how the women leaders she studied used supportive moves to obtain cooperation for their directives. The supportive moves emphasised shared knowledge, and served as contextualisation cues to signal to their listeners that they saw themselves as members of the same team.

Example 23

Woman director to older male subordinate.
Miya: you know the ventilation fan? I'm thinking that we should leave it on during the daytime. The switch is inside the building. Then sorry to bother, but when you leave
Tomi: yes I [got it]
Miya: um [turn off] the switch

Miya succeeds so well in setting up the shared context and aligning herself with Tomi, her addressee, that he anticipates her directive and overlaps her articulation of it. Her supportive moves thus cue the up-coming directive and ensure he interprets her intent accurately.

Non-verbal behaviours such as facial expressions, head nods, gestures, and silences also provide very important contextualisation cues which are valuable when analysing video data. A raised eyebrow can give a very clear indication of how an utterance has been interpreted – though its precise meaning may differ between cultures. In Polynesian culture, for instance, a raised eyebrow serves as a greeting, whereas in British culture a raised eyebrow generally conveys surprise or even disbelief.

Exercise 10

In multilingual contexts, *code-switching* may serve as a strategy or contextualisation cue for conveying meaning at a covert, taken-for-granted level. What do you think are the social meanings cued by the big man's language switches between Tok Pisin and Buang described in chapter 2 (example 17).

Answer at end of chapter

Miscommunication

Miscommunication is possible between any two people, but the potential is greater when different sociolinguistic norms are involved. Interactional sociolinguists have made a valuable contribution to identifying potential sources of miscommunication between different socio-cultural groups.

Example 24

In a British cafeteria, an Indian woman, Roopa, serving behind the counter spread doom and gloom, and aroused customer resentment, simply because of the way she served the gravy. The customers heard her as peremptorily stating that they should have gravy, whether they wanted it or not. When the customers' complaints were reported to the woman she expressed surprise. She claimed she had been *offering* them gravy not pushing it on them!

When people from different language or even different dialect backgrounds interact, clashes between discourse norms are possible, with a risk of miscommunication. Using an interactional sociolinguistics approach, we can look for clues to help interpret what speakers intended to communicate in the specific context of their talk. The problem in example 24 involved a misinterpretation of contextualisation cues. Influenced by her native language, Roopa's variety of English led her to use strong stress and falling intonation on the word *gravy* when offering it to customers. These prosodic features were interpreted by speakers of other dialects of English as indicators of an assertion rather than an offer. The contextualisation cues were misread because of a clash between dialect features.

The interactional sociolinguist also tries to make explicit the presuppositions and background knowledge that people use to interpret utterances in context. In doing so the concept of a *schema* or frame is often useful. A schema is the set of expectations that we bring to an interaction, based on our previous experiences and our cultural norms. When we walk into a British shop, for example, we have certain expectations about how the interaction with the shopkeeper or check-out operator will proceed. So, unless we know them well, we don't expect a long personal conversation as we pay for our shopping. When we go to the doctor's, we expect the doctor to ask questions and to provide advice. In a job interview in Western cultures, we expect to be asked about relevant skills and to 'sell' ourselves as a suitable appointee.

The examination of cross-cultural encounters makes it clear that such schemas or frames are as culture-bound as other aspects of our interactional expertise. In example 25, for instance, the British interviewer takes it for granted that someone applying for a job will present themselves as positively as possible. He assumes the interviewee will play down his weaknesses and talk up his strengths. But it appears this is not what the interviewee considers appropriate.

Example 25

Ben is being interviewed by Neil for the job of driver/conductor with the London regional transport service. Ben is a bilingual Asian with near-native competence in English. Ben has just told the interviewer that he applied for a job as a guard at an earlier stage and failed the test. Rideway is the company where Ben currently works.

Neil: You failed the test at that stage, OK.
        And since then you've worked as a process operator.
        What do you think London Buses is going to offer you that Rideway don't offer you?

Ben: Well, quite a lot of things, for example like um . . . Christmas bonus.

Neil: Uh huh.

Ben: So many things, holidays and all that. Well we get holidays in Rideway but you er . . . get here more holidays than you get in Rideway.

N: All right.

The hidden message or 'real' intention of Neil's question *What do you think London Buses is going to offer you that Rideway don't offer you?* is something like 'What does the job mean to you and what will London buses gain by employing you?' In other words, the interviewer is inviting the candidate to 'sell' himself, and persuade him why he should be appointed to the job. Ben is expected to describe how his experience and abilities are relevant to the job or how the job will offer a challenge which he welcomes. But instead Ben responds to the surface meaning of the question and talks about the material advantages of the job to him in terms of bonuses and holidays. The interviewer's response *All right* with a low falling tone indicates that this was not an expected or preferred answer from the candidate. The candidate's honesty, combined with rather different assumptions about how personal to be or how to present one's commitment and worth, set this interview off on the wrong footing.

In New Zealand society, the Maori ethic which values humility and frowns on self-promotion sometimes disadvantages Maori operating in Pakeha contexts. If they have no one else to speak on their behalf, or testify to their strengths, people from cultures which discourage boasting may find themselves systematically overlooked when jobs and promotions are involved. A Pakeha managing director, Helen, asked Hemi, a Maori manager, about how people had reacted to his recent presentation on the company's revised objectives. Hemi responded *well I was very nervous and made some mistakes.* Fortunately Helen was experienced in cross-cultural discourse norms; she asked someone else about Hemi's presentation and discovered it had been very effective. It is easy to see, however, that someone less experienced might make inferences about Hemi's abilities or performance based on such a self-deprecating response.

An interactional sociolinguistic approach focusses, then, on the consequences of different background assumptions for interaction between groups. When expectations are not fulfilled listeners make inferences about the speaker: e.g. *she misheard, he is trying to offend, he's incompetent, she is stupid.* Very rarely do we assume that the speaker has a different set of interactional rules of speaking which account for their (from the listener's point of view) unexpected or damaging response. And, of course, since the majority group's definition of events generally takes precedence, it is typically minority group members who suffer. This point is discussed further in the section on Critical Discourse Analysis.

C

Language variation: focus on uses

Exercise 11

Consider the schemas or frames that could account for what is going on in example 26, and identify contextualisation cues which favour different interpretations.

Example 26

Claire, a policy analyst, has sought an interview with a manager, Tom, because Jared was appointed to a more senior position as acting manager which she had hoped to obtain.

1. Claire: well I just want to talk to you about it
2.   and and I suppose [*swallows*]

▶

3.		[*tut*] I just want to get some ideas on what I could do
4.		to actually be considered favourably next time
5.	Tom:	yeah I don't think it's a it's a question of er favourability
6.		I mean it was a question more practicalities
7.		more than anything else
8.		um I was in urgent need of someone to fill in and
9.		Jared had done that in the past already

Answer at end of chapter

CONVERSATION ANALYSIS (CA)

Conversation Analysis (CA) has its roots in sociology, and sociologists argue its value in demonstrating that talk *is* action. CA researchers approach communication as a jointly organised activity like dancing, or a cooperative musical.

CA is now used by researchers in many other disciplines, including sociolinguists who are interested in analysing the structure of talk, and explaining how we manage the rules of ordinary everyday conversation at the most-micro level. At the simplest level, for instance, it is noticeable that many interactions involve *adjacency pairs*, related utterances produced by two successive speakers in such a way that the second utterance is identified as a follow-up to the first.

Example 27

(a) A. Hi there
    B. Hi
(b) A. See you later
    B. Ciao
(c) A. What page are you on?
    B. Thirty-three
(d) A. Wanna come up for dinner tonight?
    B. Mm yeah thanks that'd be nice

Greetings, farewells, questions and answers, invitations and acceptances/refusals are all examples of *adjacency pairs*.

Exercise 12

Identify possible adjacency pairs in the following list of utterances and comment on any difficulties you encounter. The first step is to sort them into first pair parts and second pair parts. Then try to match them up.

Can I help you?
I'd like some juice.
Sorry I didn't mean to be rude
I haven't actually most of them are in the dishwasher
No I am fine thanks
Just be careful when you open that cupboard
Don't talk to me like that
OK thanks
Yes the bus station is the end of this street
Like what?
Well don't you boss me around
I can't understand what you're saying
Sorry but I just have to go or I'll be late
Too bad
Let me try again
When you say go to the end do you mean as far as the bus station?
You've left me all the dirty dishes again

Answer at end of chapter

Preferred and dispreferred second pair parts

The examples in exercise 12 indicate that identifying adjacency pairs is not always straightforward. As mentioned in the answer, CA looks for internal linguistic clues and paralinguistic clues to assist. So *OK* often functions as an acknowledgement of a point made, while *well* may signal that a qualification is coming next, as in example 28.

Example 28

Monica:	wasn't that a great concert
Don:	well, I was a bit tired

Though Don does not say so explicitly, the use of *well* to introduce the second part of this adjacency pair, responding to Monica's solicitation of his opinion, suggests he does not agree with her. His comment *I was a bit tired* can be interpreted as an excuse, implying that lack of attention explains his lack of appreciation.

Exercise 12 also illustrates that some first-part utterances may be followed by one of two possible types of responses: e.g. invitation-acceptance or invitation-refusal, complaint-apology or complaint-denial, and so on. In such cases, it is often possible to identify one as a preferred response, and the other as a dispreferred response. The dispreferred response is often structurally marked in some way, e.g. by an initial pause, or a delaying discourse marker such as *well* in example 28, or a fall–rise intonation contour, or some other signal that the speaker anticipates the utterance will be unwelcome from the addressee's point of view. Example 29 illustrates some of these features.

Example 29

[↓ indicates a marked falling intonation on the following word (here expressing unwillingness).]

Sara: Barbara I have to go to a lecture in a few minutes and Joan isn't back from lunch (2) could you take over the desk for me

Barbara: erm (0.5) (*tut*) well I I ↓could but it would be better if you could find someone else cos I have to leave at two

---

The verbal hesitation *erm*, the dental click (*tut*), the discourse marker *well*, the repeated *I*, and the stressed *could* (with marked falling intonation) are classic signals that a dispreferred response is coming next.

By drawing attention to the patterned nature of adjacency pairs, CA also provides a basis for accounting for instances where people deviate from these patterns. So, for example, people may insert a *side sequence* into an adjacency pair.

Example 30

A. Wanna come to a movie tonight?
    B. Depends what time
    A. 'Bout eight
B. Mm yeah thanks that'd be great

Side sequences appear to challenge the claim that an invitation is followed by an acceptance (preferred response) or a refusal (dispreferred response), but on closer examination they prove to be simply another regular pattern within what CA researchers call the 'systematics' of the organisation of turn-taking in everyday conversation. The pattern is still evident; it is just more complex. The second part of the initial adjacency pair follows the side sequence.

Exercise 13

Identify the side sequence in the exchange in example 31 and explain its purpose. Paying attention just to internal conversational clues, suggest what is conveyed by *oh* in the last line of this example.

Example 31

1. Ann: Then guess what (1) she dished up Phad Moo Sub
2. Liz: Phad Moo Sub?
3. Ann: It's a Thai dish with *meat*
4. Liz: Oh so she didn't know about Sally

Answer at end of chapter

Unlike the two previous approaches, CA emphasises that the analyst should only make use of information available from the text being analysed and should not refer to extra-textual, ethnographic information. Hence, attention to the discourse feature *oh* in this example enables the CA researcher to deduce that Liz has made an inference about Sally simply on the basis of the discourse itself. No extra contextual information is needed.

Conversational feedback

Adjacency pairs are one aspect of the systematics of turn-taking which is a focus of CA. Attention to conversational feedback is another. At times in a conversation, one person may hold the floor for a period while recounting a narrative, for instance, or describing an experience, or explaining how something works. Meanwhile the other participant typically provides evidence that they are attending to the speaker, i.e. some kind of feedback which may be verbal (*mm, uh-huh, right*) or non-verbal (head nodding, attentive gaze).

The need for verbal feedback is especially apparent in telephone conversations as example 32 illustrates.

Example 32

Dominic, aged 7, is phoning his parents to say he is about to be driven home by his host.

1. Phone: ring ring
2. Dad: hello Oxford 9128392

Language variation: focus on uses

3. Dom: ↑Dad
4. Dad: oh Dom
5. Dom: I'm comin' 'ome in ten minutes
6. Dad: you're comin' 'ome in ten minutes
7. Dom: yea
8. Dad: oh good boy y- have you enjoyed yourself?
9. Dom: yea
10. Dad: good (2)
11.   very nice (2)
12.   are you still there Dom?
13. Dom: mm
14. Dad   alright then pet (2)
15.   we'll be waitin' on you alright?
16. Dom: yea bye
17. Dad: bye

Dominic is not used to using the phone, and this is evident in a number of ways. His opening is minimal and contains no explicit greeting, and his closing *yea bye* (line 16) is also brief and not negotiated with his dad. So the expected pattern would be that Dominic would introduce the pre-closing *alright?* and his dad would respond *alright* and then Dominic would say *goodbye* and then his dad would say *goodbye*. Instead Dominic's dad finally initiates the pre-closing at line 14 *alright then pet*. This follows two attempts to hand the floor to Dominic which he does not take (at lines 10, 11), and nor does Dominic respond verbally to his dad to indicate that he is still attending, leading his dad to ask *are you still there Dom?* (line 12). Even when his dad makes the first pre-closing move *alright then pet* (line 14), Dominic does not provide the expected second part, leading his dad to try again *we'll be waitin' on you alright?* (line 15).

Attention signals in the form of verbal feedback on the phone are especially important since the speaker cannot see the listener. As CA researchers argue, careful attention to the data, including pauses, and absences, as well as instances, of feedback provide a basis for inferring that Dominic has not yet fully mastered the conversational rules of telephone interaction in his social group. There is no need to appeal to extra-linguistic evidence.

As illustrated by this brief discussion, CA studies what an utterance does in relation to preceding utterances and what its implications are for what follows. Dominic's lack of skill highlights how participants typically work together to jointly achieve conversational openings and closings, as well as decisions, interviews, and even story tellings. CA focusses on how an interaction unfolds as a sequence of actions by different participants, with the significance of an utterance highly dependent on its position in a sequence, as well as being jointly negotiated.

Interestingly, the frequency with which feedback is provided, and even the exact positioning of the feedback, differs between social and cultural groups. Mayumi, a Japanese student, recorded one of our meetings and she subsequently told me that she now understood why people commented on the high frequency with which Japanese people provide verbal feedback. She said she could scarcely hear what I was saying on the tape, firstly because of the high frequency of her own feedback, and secondly because her *hai* ('yes') often overlapped with my speech and so obscured it. By contrast, she noted that in conversations between New Zealanders, the listener's feedback is typically positioned at the end of the speaker's clauses and minimally overlaps the speech.

Exercise 14

Using a CA approach, identify evidence that Tom could be described as not playing a full conversational part in the conversation in example 33.

Example 33

Two workers have just met at the start of the day. The length of pauses or silences in seconds is indicated by the numbers in brackets: e.g. (2) = two-second pause.

1. Dan: looks like it's gonna be a nice day eh
2. Tom: *no response*
3. Dan: so you haven't done anything all week (2) eh (1)
4.   you haven't done anything exciting (3) talk to any girls?
5. Tom: no
6. Dan: oh that's all right then (2)
7.   gonna be a great day though eh (1) don't you think
8. Tom: *no response*

Answer at end of chapter

Exercise 15

Record a telephone conversation between two adults and another between two children.

(a) Identify the conversational feedback and compare the amount in the two conversations. Have the children developed adult-like proficiency in providing feedback?

(b) Paying attention to pauses, hesitations, and in-breaths, identify any evidence of conversational 'trouble' provided within either conversation.

(c) Identify any instances of overlapping speech. Do the overlaps cause problems?

▮ Interruptions and overlaps

CA researchers argue that talk 'constitutes' particular institutional realities. In other words, discourse is the very stuff of many interactions, especially in areas such as the

C

Language variation: focus on uses

law, in teaching and in business meetings. As its label implies, CA treats the pattern of ordinary conversation as primary: systematic alternation between reasonably equal turns at talking, negotiated implicitly, is regarded as the basic conversational model. Variations from this pattern often indicate a different kind of context. So, for example, when someone takes very long turns compared to others, or when one person explicitly allocates turns to others, or when someone disrupts the turns of others, this behaviour is marked by comparison with ordinary conversation. It suggests, for example, talk in a more formal or institutional context.

Example 34

Leila, the Chair, opens a meeting of her team of six in a government department. Before she speaks there is a buzz of small talk between various people around the table. [(*voc*) indicates a non-specific vocalisation; (*tut*) signifies a dental click.]

1. Leila: right we're all here let's get started (2.0) [*buzz of talk stops*]
2.   OK we're starting with plans for a meeting with the WIT ⁄group⟍
3. Eliz: ⁄worldwide information⟍ technology
4. Leila: um yes (0.5) Carol [*voc*] has um [*tut*] organised another meeting
5.   an introductory meeting for next Wednesday (0.5)
6.   Carol do you want to brief people
7. Carol: thanks yes um well the meeting is scheduled for . . .

Leila uses a typical meeting-opening discourse marker *right*, together with her declaration *we're all here let's get started* followed by a two-second pause to open the meeting. This pause, unlike those in casual conversation, is not a position in the interaction where someone else is expected to speak. As Chair, Leila has the right to the next turn after she declares the meeting open. Thereafter, despite the brief overlap between Elizabeth and Leila in lines 2 and 3 where Elizabeth expands on the acronym, the basic pattern here is that one person speaks at a time. This is the typical turn-taking pattern for orderly spoken interaction in many Western contexts, and especially in formal meetings. People are very proficient at positioning their next conversational turns precisely at a point (known as a transition-relevance place or TRP) where the previous speaker has completed their turn. In many conversations there are few or minimal overlaps; people read the syntactic, prosodic and non-verbal signals that a TRP is approaching and 'latch' their utterances to the previous speakers with great skill, while in formal meetings there are even short pauses between speaker turns.

Deviations from this one-at-a-time pattern typically generate inferences of various kinds, as example 35 illustrates. The excerpt is from a meeting of a sub-committee of the New Zealand National Museum Planning Committee. Cliff Whiting is the Maori Chief Executive Officer of the Museum. Ron Trotter is the Chair of the Planning Committee. The excerpt relates to a central issue for the Board, namely, how the museum will represent and reflect the relationship between the two major cultural groups in New Zealand, the indigenous Maori people, and the Pakeha settlers. The museum is to include within it a *marae*, a traditional Maori meeting house and surrounding area for speech-making, for which Cliff Whiting is responsible. Most traditional New Zealand marae are built by and for Maori, and located in particular tribal areas, though there are also some urban marae which are non-tribal. The planned museum marae is unusual in that it will be clearly visible and public. Cliff Whiting is responding to a statement from Ron Trotter about how he sees the museum marae as being a place where Pakeha as well as Maori will feel comfortable.

Example 35

Meeting of a small sub-committee of the New Zealand National Museum Planning Committee. Cliff Whiting is the Maori Chief Executive Officer of the Museum. Ron Trotter is the Chair of the Planning Committee.

[= indicates the utterances are neatly 'latched' to each other, i.e. there is not even the smallest pause between them. A question mark signals a rising intonation but not necessarily a question, i.e. a HRT; underline indicates strong stress; *tangata whenua* refers to the indigenous Maori people]

1. Cliff: there are two <u>main</u> (0.2) fields that have to be explored (0.2)
2. and er (0.1) the one that is <u>most</u> important is its <u>cus</u>tomary role
3. in the first place? because (0.2) marae <u>comes (on)</u> and it comes from
4. (0.4) the tangata whenua who are Maori
5. ╱(0.7) to change it╲
6. Ron: ╱but it's not just╲ for Maori=
7. Cliff: =no=
8. Ron: =it it you <u>must</u> get that if it is a Maori institution and nothing more
9. <u>this</u> (*bangs table*) marae has failed (0.2)
10. and they <u>must</u> (*bangs table*) get that idea

Cliff Whiting states that there are two fields to be explored (line 1), from which a listener might infer that he has two points to make. He speaks slowly and deliberately, with regular pauses, as is customary in formal Maori oratory. At line 8, Ron Trotter overlaps Cliff Whiting with a statement that challenges Cliff's focus on Maori. The overlap is positioned at a TRP, a point where it would be reasonable for Ron Trotter to assume Cliff Whiting had completed his turn if it were not for the fact that, firstly, Cliff has given notice that he had two points to make, and, secondly, that he is speaking slowly and deliberately with regular pauses between clauses. In these circumstances, Ron Trotter's overlap can be interpreted as a disruptive interruption especially since he proceeds to take over the floor, and to state his position with great emphasis accompanied by banging on the table. After one brief response *no* (line 7), which could be a protest, or could be agreeing with Ron Trotter's statement, Cliff Whiting is silent thereafter, and on the video of this excerpt he can be seen to physically withdraw and look down, while Ron Trotter's table banging invades his physical space.

In analysing this interaction a CA researcher typically begins by comparing it with mundane conversation in which the order, size and type of turns are relatively free. A CA analysis of this episode identifies the ways in which the participants display an orientation to different rules, namely the rules of a meeting where speakers typically expect to complete even relatively long turns without interruption. In this excerpt, then, the overlap disrupts the turn of the person who holds the floor, and in the context of the talk, this deviation from one-at-a-time talk can be interpreted as indicating disagreement.

Overlapping talk is not always disruptive, however, as example 36 illustrates. Here three colleagues construct a humorous fantasy sequence, an imaginary scenario describing an all-purpose suit which could be used by anyone unexpectedly summoned to see the Minister.

Example 36

Three colleagues are discussing the problems which arise when someone is unexpectedly summoned to see the Minister.

1.	Eve:	I think we need a ministry suit just hanging up in the cupboard
2.		↗[laughs]↘
3.	Leila:	↗you can just↘ imagine the problems with the length ↗[laughs]↘
4.	Eve:	↗it would have↘ it would have to have an elastic waist
5.		so ↗that we [laughs]↘ could just be yeah
6.	Leila:	↗[laughs] yes that's right [laughs]↘
7.	Eve:	bunched in for some and [laughs] let it out
8.	Leila:	↗laughs↘
9.	Eve:	↗out for others↘
10.	Lesley:	and the jacket would have to be ↗long to cover all the bulges↘
11.	Leila:	↗no I'm quite taken with this↘

There is a great deal of overlap between the talk and the laughter throughout this excerpt. At line 6, Leila overlaps Evelyn's utterance, and at line 11 she overlaps Lesley's utterance. Both Leila's contributions are positive *yes that's right* and *no I'm quite taken with this*, and they simply support the points being made by those she is overlapping, rather than introducing new content. There is no evidence from the prosodic or paralinguistic features that this is experienced as disruptive talk; rather the laughter and high energy of the interchange suggest this is collaborative 'all-together-now' talk, as Jennifer Coates labels it.

Overlapping talk is thus a particularly rewarding area for CA researchers since it always generates inferences of some sort based on the CA assumption that in conversations one person talks at a time. As we have seen, this is often not the case, but it has proved a fruitful starting point to account for variations from this pattern.

Exercise 16

Identify three internal clues in example 37 that a conversation analyst might use to support the inference that Clara is managing potential interactional trouble.

Example 37

Meeting in a large commercial organisation chaired by Clara, the section manager, since the usual chairperson is absent. Seth has gone to collect the minutes from the previous meeting.

1. Clara: okay well we might just start without Seth
2.   we can can review the minutes from last week
3.   when ⁄he finally comes back⟍
4. Renee: ⁄are <u>you</u>⟍ taking the minutes this week
5. Clara: [*eyebrows raised*] no I'm just <u>trying</u> to chair the meeting

---

Answer at end of chapter

■ Keeping just to the text

It is worth emphasising an important methodological point that has been briefly mentioned several times in the discussion so far: a basic characteristic of a CA approach is that you should not begin the analysis with any preconceived ideas about what will be worth examining. Unlike the ethnography of communication and the interactional sociolinguistics approaches, the analysis should not include any information from your field notes, or interviews, or the participants' reflections on the talk. The data is primary, and all relevant information should be deducible from the data, and relevant categories for analysis should arise out of the data. So, for example, you should not assume that gender or power are relevant aspects of an interaction, unless it is clear from the data that the participants perceive these as relevant dimensions in understanding what is being conveyed. For CA it is important to find evidence *in the interaction* of which of a range of possible interpretations is intended and interpreted by or oriented to by the participants. So, in example 26, in order to infer whether Claire's utterance in lines 1–3 is intended as an indirect complaint or whether she is genuinely seeking advice, a CA researcher would examine what comes before and what follows her utterance, together with attention to pauses, hesitations, false starts, intakes of breath, intonation, and similar clues, to help interpret what is going on.

Because CA researchers analyse talk in such detail, they rarely analyse very large amounts of text; rather they focus on significant excerpts in which conversationalists manage to convey often very subtle meanings. It will be evident from the discussion in previous sections that other approaches draw extensively on the methodology of CA

Language variation: focus on uses

C

for insights in analysing discourse. CA researchers pay attention to the interactional significance of even the smallest aspect of spoken interaction, such as the words *oh*, *OK* and *well*, and to the amount and frequency of feedback or minimal response signals such as *mm*, *mmhmm*, *uh huh*, *yeah*, and *right*; they attend to pauses and hesitations, vocalisations, sighs, in-drawn breaths, giggles and laughter. Whether an utterance is said 'breathily', or with laughter running through it, or in a surprised tone of voice may be very important to interpreting the meaning of what is going on. Overlaps are precisely transcribed and pauses carefully measured. The most minute aspect of interaction that allows the listener to infer social meaning is relevant to the analysis. The goal is to identify what is significant to the participants as evidenced by their interactional behaviour. CA provides a useful set of descriptive tools for discourse analysts, no matter what kind of theoretical approach they adopt.

Exercise 17

Identify one distinctive point that might be made using an *interactional sociolinguistic* approach to example 35.

Answer at end of chapter

While an interactional sociolinguistic approach tends to spotlight different socio-cultural norms, an ethnography of communication approach might establish that Ron Trotter's behaviour is considered quite appropriate in many of the majority group, male-dominated boardrooms which are his usual milieu. From the perspective of the approach discussed in the next section, Critical Discourse Analysis, Ron Trotter's behaviour could be analysed as an instance of explicitly 'doing power'. Indeed, some of those who saw the film from which the excerpt is taken interpreted his behaviour as an instance of verbal bullying. Critical Discourse Analysis is an approach which focusses precisely on the ways in which power and ideology are evident in interaction.

CRITICAL DISCOURSE ANALYSIS (CDA)

Example 38

Police Officer behind desk in police station greets a woman who approaches the desk

PO: Good morning love, what can I do for you
Woman: Good morning constable. I want to see your sergeant
           And its not 'love', it's Detective Inspector.

Critical Discourse Analysis (CDA) differs from all the previous methods of describing discourse in this chapter mainly in the stance of the analyst, which is, predictably, overtly 'critical'. Although I have often described the political and social, and especially cross-cultural, implications of each of the approaches outlined so far, they are all essentially descriptive in their starting points. CDA by contrast is explicitly concerned with investigating how language is used to construct and maintain power relationships in society; the aim is to show up connections between language and power, and between language and ideology. In example 38, the police officer's choice of the friendly, and perhaps patronising, term *love* turns out to be an inappropriate form of address for the senior police woman he is addressing. Her response makes it clear that she does not approve of this way of greeting women.

The critical discourse analyst deliberately dons a pair of critical spectacles and looks for evidence of the covert exercise of power in supposedly 'equal' interactions, or for indications of hidden ideological assumptions about 'normal' ways of doing things that disadvantage minority groups. Sexist and racist language are obvious targets for the critical discourse analyst, but CDA research has a very wide agenda, and includes the analysis of political speeches, medical textbooks, advertising and marketing strategies, and many other forms of rhetoric.

Critical discourse analysts often make use of aspects of other approaches: e.g. many use a CA approach to describe the ways in which participants manipulate the rules of conversation in order to gain a political advantage; or they may use interactional sociolinguistics to highlight the relevance of the social context in which people are operating, and the underlying connections between language, power and ideology. It is ultimately the over-arching critical stance which distinguishes CDA, rather than the precise methods used to analyse the discourse. In this section I illustrate this stance firstly by examining how CDA highlights the ways in which discourse enacts and reinforces power relationships; and secondly by illustrating the role of the critical discourse analyst in making explicit the ideological beliefs or covert assumptions which underlie some instances of discourse in society.

Power and CDA

The exchange between Ron Trotter and Cliff Whiting in example 35 transgressed the norms of polite, semi-formal meetings in many workplaces. The turn-taking norms in such meetings typically permit each participant to speak uninterrupted until they have made their points. But Ron Trotter verbally intruded into Cliff Whiting's space, cutting across his speaking turn and preventing him from making his points about different cultural ways of doing things. From a CDA perspective, it could be argued that Ron Trotter exercised unwarranted power, based on the covert assumption that his views warranted greater weight than Cliff Whiting's, perhaps because he was the Chair of the Committee to which the two participants belonged, or perhaps because he was a (male) member of the dominant cultural group whose rights he was explicitly asserting in this interchange.

Example 39 illustrates a situation where the turn-taking rules are not those of committee members supposedly treating each other as equals, but rather those of participants in an explicitly *unequal* encounter.

Example 39

A police officer is questioning a suspect about growing cannabis. The interview is aimed at establishing whether he was growing it for his own use or for sale.

1. PO: okay you also told me that you haven't got enough money to live on
2.   is that right so that's why you grow the cannabis
3.   cos you haven't got enough money
4.   isn't that what you said Sam
5. Sam: I've got enough money just to buy food and pay my way
6. PO: okay
7. Sam: but I ain't got enough money to buy my extras that I need
8. PO: okay (0.5) so where are you growing that cannabis
9. Sam: near in my own backyard
10. PO: I thought you said that place didn't belong to you
11.   it belongs to the X organisation
12. Sam: yeah well I was growing it in the backyard in there

In this unequal encounter, the police officer has the right to ask questions and to expect the suspect to answer them. In lines 1–4, the police officer first asks Sam to confirm something he has said earlier, *is that right* (line 2) and then *isn't that what you said Sam* (line 4). Sam is not given a chance to respond to the first request for confirmation (there is no pause after *is that right*), before the second proposition and request for confirmation are put to him. If you compare this interaction with a conversation with a friend, it is immediately apparent that this technique could be interpreted as badgering and even verbally bullying Sam into a response. The police officer is here challenging Sam to confirm a proposition that will form the foundation for an argument that he needs to sell the cannabis he grows in order to survive. It appears that Sam does not see the trap, since he voluntarily reveals that he is in need of money for extras above bare sustenance (line 7).

The police officer then asks another question *where are you growing that cannabis* (line 8), and when Sam responds, the police officer challenges the accuracy of his response by referring to earlier information that he has supplied which contradicts the implications of this response that the place he is growing cannabis belongs to him. In any normal conversation, Sam's use of the phrase *my own backyard* is understandable, given that it is the backyard of the place in which he is living. The police officer's challenge thus reminds us that this is a formal interview where precision about such details is a legal issue.

In later sections of this interview the police officer overtly challenges Sam with questions such as *what do you have to say Sam; come on Sam I'm asking you some straight questions; is that what you are saying?, is that right, isn't that what you said?* These features of the discourse clearly indicate that this is an unequal encounter. A CDA approach focusses on such features to demonstrate how the police officer uses verbal means to intimidate the suspect and make him feel powerless.

But power may also be enacted in more subtle ways in interactions which are apparently very urbane and democratic. Setting the agenda of a discussion, for instance, is one way of exercising influence in even a very democratic interaction. The person who decides what will be discussed and what will be excluded is subtly exercising control over the topics of talk which will be considered relevant. In a formal meeting this may take the form of a written agenda whose contents are determined by the meeting chair in advance. When there is no written agenda, the meeting chair usually exercises power by determining what topics will be discussed and who may contribute, as in example 40.

Example 40

Meeting in a large commercial organisation chaired by section manager.

1. Clara: Seth has gone to collect the minutes from the previous meeting
2.   okay shall we kick off and just go round the room um doing
3.   an update and then when Seth comes in with the minutes
4.   we need to check on any action items from our planning
5.   over to you Marlene

Here Clara's power or authority is apparent from the discourse: she determines the order of items for discussion and she allocates the first turn of talking to Marlene. Even in less formal interactions, particular participants may influence what is to be discussed: e.g. *it's time we sorted out where we are going; well I just thought we needed to talk this through a bit further*; or they may declare certain contributions irrelevant (*that's a red herring; you're way off track there*). One criterion for deciding on their relative power or influence in the context is to note whether others pay attention to their declarations.

The end of a conversation is another point where it is useful to look for evidence of power being exercised in an interaction. Example 41 is an excerpt from the end of an informal discussion between two women in a very egalitarian workplace. They have had a long exploration of a problematic issue and each has contributed equally to finding a solution. In many sections of the discussion it would be impossible to identify one woman as more influential or powerful than the other from the discourse alone. However, as the interaction draws to a close, there are some interesting linguistic clues as to who is calling the shots. Can you identify them before you read on?

C

Language variation: focus on uses

Example 41

Katie and Kelly are policy analysts in a government department. They have been discussing possible titles for an official publication.
(2) signals a 2-second pause.

1. Katie: well (2) if I think of anything further shall I say
2. Kelly: oh yeah let me know (thank) you yeah
3. Katie: are you just doing a memo now are you
4. Kelly: but I'll – yeah 'cause I've got to um (1) have it to Ruth at ten so
5. Katie: yeah well I think we've taken it a bit further than where it was before
6. Kelly: okay yes that was very helpful thank you Katie
7.   that's GREAT

This excerpt demonstrates that Katie is the person who decides it is time that the discussion should draw to a close. She signals this first with the discourse marker *well* followed by a pause, and then a statement indicating she has nothing further to say at this point. She follows this up by establishing that Kelly will take the required follow-up action *are you just doing a memo now are you* (line 3). Finally she summarises what they have achieved *I think we've taken it a bit further than where it was before* (line 5). Summary is a powerful tool for those wishing to assert their influence and authority. At the end of any meeting, the person who sums up thereby stamps their interpretation of what has been achieved on the proceedings. It is a subtle but effective way of enacting power, as a critical discourse analysis emphasises.

Exercise 18

1. Can you identify three features in Chris's use of language in example 42 which suggest Chris is refusing to conform to the community's expectations about appropriate ways of speaking in an interview with the headmaster?

Example 42

Chris is involved in an interview with the headmaster.

1. Headmaster: Why didn't you go straight down Queen Street?
2. Chris: I'm not walkin' down there with a load of coons from
3.   St Hilda's comin' out of school.
4. Headmaster: Why's that?
5. Chris: Well that's obvious, i'n it? I don' wanna get belted.
6. Headmaster: Well there isn't usually any bother in Queen Street?

7.		Is there?
8.	Chris:	No. None of us white kids usually go down there, do we?
9.		What about that bust-up in the Odeon car-park at
10.		Christmas?
11.	Headmaster:	That was nearly a year ago, and I'm not convinced
12.		you lot were as innocent as you made out.
13.		So when you got to the square, why did you wait around
14.		for quarter of an hour instead of going straight home?
15.	Chris:	I thought my mate might come down that way after work.
16.		Anyway, we always go down the square after school.

2. Did you assume Chris was a boy? Why (not)?

Answer at end of chapter

Ideology and CDA

CDA researchers aim to expose the hidden messages and especially the taken-for-granted assumptions that underlie much of our everyday discourse. Because advertisers make use of discourse to influence our behaviour – typically to persuade us to buy their product – adverts are one of the most obvious targets of CDA. Adverts appeal to their audience's emotions, their desires and fears, and to their often unexamined attitudes and beliefs.

Another focus of CDA has been discourse which is apparently neutral and informative, but which on closer examination turns out to be manipulative and even distorting. For example, in the health section of a women's magazine, and under the heading *Healthy Hint*, there was not some expert nutritional or medical advice as the heading might lead the reader to expect, but an advert for an anti-inflammatory with a '100% natural, herbal formula'. Identifying the 'advertorial' and the 'infomercial', a new genre in which a particular product is promoted in what at first appears to be an editorial or a feature article, is an area where a CDA approach is valuable.

Even more interesting, because less obvious, are the subtle ways in which our responses are manipulated in contexts which are supposedly sources of 'information', such as newspaper reports, or even textbooks – contexts where we are perhaps less aware of the underlying orientations and goals of the writers or speakers. When we don our CDA spectacles we can often identify subtle sources of bias in the way language is used in these contexts. Consider the different messages conveyed by the choice of lexical items and syntactic patterns in the following sentences reporting the 'same' incident.

> ### Example 43
>
> (a) Police shoot eleven people dead in pro-democracy demonstration.
> (b) Rioting blacks shot dead as political leaders meet.

The use of an active construction in (a) and the identification of the agent as the *police* conveys a very different impression from the passive construction in (b) where the agents have disappeared. The use of the word *rioting* in (b) could be read as implying that the shooting was justified, while the choice of *blacks* (vs *people*) objectifies those shot. Finally the inclusion of the information in (a) that the incident involved *a pro-democracy demonstration* communicates a very different message from the message conveyed in (b), where it is implied that the reason for the *rioting* is related to the meeting of political leaders.

A CDA approach focusses on the ways in which lexical choices such as *riot* vs *protest* vs *demonstration*, or *hooligans* vs *protestors* vs *demonstrators* subtly convey different ideological positions and different political sympathies. CDA researchers warn that as readers we are often unaware of the effect of such choices as we read apparently 'objective' news reports.

Even less obvious at first glance are the assumptions underlying the apparently descriptive and informative discourse of some medical textbooks. For example, the woman patient is framed rather differently in the excerpts in (a) vs (b) in example 44. (See also chapter 13, example 2, which discusses this text from another perspective.)

> ### Example 44
>
> (a) Surgery is also indicated when . . . hormone treatment has failed to control the symptoms. . . . Since many women erroneously believe that following hysterectomy . . . obesity is usual, the physician must explain that removal of the uterus has no side-effects.
> (b) Alternative treatments include radiation and birth control pills, but these are considered controversial and can cause serious complications. . . . If your doctor suggests any of these treatments, be sure to get a second opinion.

Both sentences use educated, technical vocabulary, but they address different readerships. The main clue to this is the stance expressed through the choice of grammatical structures. In (a), the use of the passive voice (*is also indicated*) removes any reference to the actor or agent, i.e. the doctor or physician, thus enabling the writer to avoid allocating explicit responsibility to the physician for the decision to undertake surgery as well as conveying an impression of clinical objectivity. And though this is a book written for medical students, they are not addressed as 'you', but rather the *physician* is referred to in the third person and presented as an expert who must correct the erroneous assumptions of *many women*.

By contrast (b) treats the women target readers as intelligent agents rather than passive, ignorant objects of surgery. They are addressed in the second person (*your doctor*), giving the impression of friendliness or solidarity. Moreover, the information provided is empowering rather than didactic: the reader is presented with alternatives, and evaluative comments, and recommended to seek a second opinion. This is a very different approach from (a).

A CDA approach seeks to identify ways in which readers or listeners are manipulated through choices of particular words and constructions to take a particular position in relation to the topic of discussion. Pronoun choices, for example, can quickly and effectively position a reader as one of 'us', observing the behaviour of 'them', thus including the reader or listener in one group while objectifying another group and distancing the reader or listener from them. In one government organisation where we did research, the employees commented that the usage of their Chief Executive Officer (CEO) changed over a period of time, subtly indicating a change of orientation. Initially when the CEO talked about 'we' and 'us', he was referring to himself and the other employees of the organisation. Five years later the terms 'we' and 'us' in the Chief Executive's discourse typically referred to him and his fellow chief executives in other government organisations. His pronoun usage betrayed the re-alignment of his loyalties, and his employees were aware that this reflected new priorities which impacted negatively on their working conditions.

In meetings between management and employees, it is often illuminating to examine the use of pronouns, and especially shifts between the referents of 'we', 'you' and 'they' in the course of a meeting. In example 45, three utterances are listed in the order they occurred in the speech of the manager of an industrial plant. It is interesting to ask who is included in 'we' in each instance.

Example 45

Plant Manager addressing large meeting between managers and employees in a context of re-structuring and down-sizing.

(a) it's been a bit over a month since we got together
(b) we have a cost reduction programme
(c) we'll try to handle any questions that you might have

In (a) 'we' is inclusive and refers to the management and the employees, but the referent of 'we' in (b) is less clear-cut. Though the company as a whole has a cost reduction programme, it is the managers who have been developing it. And by (c), it is clear that 'we' refers only to the managers while 'you' refers to the employees.

Language variation: focus on uses

One might expect that the pronoun *we* would consistently convey inclusiveness and solidarity. But context is crucial, as has been consistently demonstrated in this book. So when *we* clearly does *not* include the speaker, and refers only to the addressee(s), it may function as a distancing device, conveying a rather patronising tone, as in example 46.

Example 46

An email from a manager to her supervisors in a white collar organisation.

Hi,

When we are looking at grading positions, could we please ensure that we abide by the rules of the XB structure rather than creating grades for positions because of salary constraints. . . . If we do not grade appropriately then the responsibility for the grading system will go back to Finance and we will have to ask for a grade for each role change. This is not a position that I would like to see happen.

Thanks

Barbara

Although the manager uses *we*, she is not herself directly involved in grading positions, but only in managing those who are. Her usage thus sets up a false impression of shared responsibility and solidarity. It is similar to the usage of a nurse who asks a patient *how are we today?* or the mother who asks her child *did we have a good sleep then?* In other words *we* means 'you', and the effect is patronising rather than inclusive.

Exercise 19

Here are a set of dimensions for analysis somewhat simplified from those provided by Teun van Dijk, a well-known CDA researcher.

Access:	who has access to the place of interaction and under what conditions?
Setting:	location, place and time of interaction: who decides?
	who is favoured by the location and the time?
Participant positions and roles:	what are the relevant social role relationships and identities?
Genre:	is everyone equally familiar with the appropriate genre?
Speech acts:	what kinds of speech acts occur in the interaction?
Topics:	who selects topics? who controls topics?

Local meaning and coherence:

(a) *Levels of specificity and degree of completeness:*
e.g. what kind of information is given in most detail?
(b) *Perspective:* whose perspectives are presented in the discourse?
(c) *Implicitness: implications, presuppositions, vagueness:* what implicit assumptions underlie the discourse?
(d) *Coherence:* are there any gaps in the argument as presented?

Style: variations of syntax, lexicon and sound:

(a) *Lexical style:* do word choices betray assumptions?
(b) *Syntactic style:* do structures conceal/stress agency?
(c) *Anaphora and deictics:* do choices indicate relationships?

Rhetoric: what are the effects of metaphor, repetition, imagery, rhetorical questions, alliteration, parallelism in the discourse?
Summary: who sums up?

Consider what these questions reveal about the power dimensions underlying a university undergraduate seminar or tutorial. A recording of a seminar you have attended would be an ideal focus of analysis.

Answer at end of chapter

Exercise 20

Compare van Dijk's set of components of analysis with those used in the ethnography of speaking approach. What do the differences suggest about the different emphases of these two approaches to analysing language in context? One possible answer to this question can be found in the conclusion.

Conclusion

This chapter has provided a brief taste of just a small selection from a range of different ways of doing discourse analysis. It will be clear that discourse analysis provides useful tools for sociolinguists who are interested in describing in detail the ways of speaking and writing associated with particular social and cultural groups in social context, and, as illustrated in this chapter, it is especially valuable in highlighting sources of contrast between groups and potential areas of cross-cultural misunderstanding.

Each approach emphasises different aspects of the way discourse is used in communication. *Pragmatics* is concerned with the analysis of meaning in interaction and, from

397

the sociolinguist's perspective, the development of theories of politeness has offered a good deal of insight into the differing ways in which people use discourse in context, and especially in accounting for why discourse is not consistently brief, truthful, relevant, and clear.

The *ethnography of speaking* approach is particularly valuable when describing communicative events for a group whose cultural or social norms are not those of the majority group. The framework it provides ensures that researchers do not overlook important features of the event, and also that they do not over-emphasise aspects which are 'business as usual' for the participants. An *interactional sociolinguistics* approach similarly highlights the wider socio-cultural context within which events take place but this approach pays particular attention to the linguistic and non-linguistic clues which account for how people *interpret* conversational interaction within its ethnographic context.

The fourth approach exemplified in this chapter, *Conversation Analysis*, is a method of analysing much more than conversation, but conversation is regarded as basic. Meetings and transactional interactions are described in relation to the view of conversation as a jointly organised activity, with the significance of any utterance highly dependent on its position in a sequence. Versions of CA are typically used by researchers with a range of theoretical frameworks; they treat CA as a set of discourse analysis techniques and apply it in as much detail as they consider useful for their purposes. Researchers who adopt a *Critical Discourse Analysis* framework, for example, often use CA to highlight particular features of an interaction which exemplify how discourse constructs and maintains power relationships, and props up a particular view of 'reality'.

Norman Fairclough has argued that the widespread societal promotion of standard varieties of a language, and the related derogation of vernacular varieties, is a specific example of hegemony or domination which the critical discourse analyst should expose and challenge. This issue is discussed in the next chapter on attitudes to language. Abstract concepts like 'the standard language' and 'good grammar' are typically associated in the minds of many people with authority, hierarchy, tradition and elitism, and the 'correct' way of doing things. A CDA approach to this issue emphasises that these concepts are based on arbitrary, superficial rules of the formal standard language of a community, that they have no intrinsic status, and that they derive their significance from their association with the rich, educated and powerful members of a society. Chapter 15 picks up some of these themes and examines the contribution of attitudes to sociolinguistic realities.

ANSWERS TO EXERCISES IN CHAPTER 14

Answer to exercise 1

By stating that he is getting *enough* pain relief and that he is using it *any time he needs it*, Lionel implies that he is making use of the pain relief; but he does not actually say so explicitly. A more direct response would be *No I don't need it*. Because Lionel responds indirectly, Kirsty infers that he is not using it (line 6). People typically expect responses to be truthful and relevant, unless they have reason to suspect otherwise. Because Kirsty suspects Lionel is being 'brave' and avoiding taking pain relief, she examines his responses carefully, and correctly infers that he is not taking pain relief. In the next section, some of the bases for such pragmatic inferences are examined.

Answer to exercise 2

This exchange illustrates Lakoff's politeness rule 3 *Be friendly*. This is friendly social talk; the content is not important; the talk is primarily social or affective in function, designed to establish rapport and maintain good collegial relationships. Being friendly and engaging in social talk or 'small talk' is considered one way of being positively polite by many but not all socio-cultural groups.

Answer to exercise 3

This is an exchange between two people who know each other well in a Greek community. It is interesting to note that the responder acknowledges that the apologiser is indeed disturbing them, but then makes a positively polite comment. While this kind of response might occur jokingly between very close friends in my community, a more likely response would be 'No problem you are not disturbing us at all'.

Answer to exercise 5

Advantages include the following:

This data collection method enables the researcher to

1. collect information about a much wider range of situations and from a larger group of people than could ever easily be collected using observation or recording;
2. manipulate the social variables: e.g. to systematically vary aspects of the relationship between the participants, and the ranking of the imposition;
3. access sociolinguistic and pragmatic norms – to identify what people believe is appropriate and correct verbal behaviour in different contexts.

Disadvantages include the following:

1. People are often inaccurate in what they report. They tend to report what they think they would say rather than necessarily what they would actually say in the situation.
2. Because it is written, the data is edited, so important information about pauses, hesitations etc. which typically occur in speech are omitted.
3. Because they are writing rather than speaking, people tend to give short responses.
4. There is no information (generally) about the dynamics of an interaction, e.g. how an invitation or request is 'negotiated' between the different participants.

Answer to exercise 9

(i)   Delimiting speech communities is a task for the linguist if one adopts Lyons' definition since it involves delimiting dialects and languages. There is an implicit assumption of a monolingual community.
(ii) Hymes' definition takes account of shared cultural norms as described in the previous section.
(iii) Fishman's definition takes account of multilingual individuals and requires only one shared variety to define the community; it also takes into account shared social rules for using that variety.
(iv) Gumperz's definition includes the possibility of multilingual speech communities and, distinctively, uses density of social interaction as a criterion for delimiting the community.

C

Language variation: focus on uses

(v) Labov's definition is unusual in using shared evaluative norms about speech as the distinguishing feature of a speech community, norms which he suggests will be reflected in speech usage patterns.

Answer to exercise 10

In very broad terms, the switches between Buang and Tok Pisin cue social meanings related to solidarity vs power.

Answer to exercise 11

This is a relatively formal interview between a manager and a policy analyst in her department so we approach it with a transactional schema for workplace interviews. There are two possible sub-schemas which might be relevant. Firstly Claire could be genuinely seeking advice from Tom to help her succeed in being promoted in the future. Alternatively, or perhaps additionally, she could be making a complaint about having been passed over for someone else. The paralinguistic information that she swallows and tuts (lines 2–3) suggests she is nervous, indicating that perhaps she intends to do more than just seek advice, which is not a very face-threatening act. Her choice of the words *actually* and *favourably* (line 4) support this suggestion, since they focus on the complaint aspect of her topic. In his response Tom focusses on the word *favourably* to indicate that he disagrees with Claire's perception of what happened (line 5). Tom reframes the decision being discussed as a neutral one dictated by factors beyond his control. An interactional sociolinguistic approach would also note that he uses the speaker-oriented pragmatic hedges *I don't think* to attenuate his disagreement, and *I mean* to introduce his alternative interpretation of what had happened.

Answer to exercise 12

One set of possible pairings (i.e. others are possible too):

1A Just be careful when you open that cupboard	*Warning*
1B OK thanks	*Acknowledgement*
2A Can I help you?	*Offer/request*
2Ba I'd like some juice.	*Response to offer/request*
2Bb No I am fine thanks	*Refuse offer*
3A Don't talk to me like that	*Complaint*
3Ba Sorry I didn't mean to be rude	*Apology/response to complaint*
3Bb Like what?	*Denial/challenge*
3Bc Well don't you boss me around	*Counter-complaint*
4A I can't understand what you're saying	*Complaint*
4Ba Too bad	*Response to complain*
4Bb OK, let me try again	*Response to complaint/offer*
5A When you say go to the end do you mean as far as the bus station?	*Seek clarification*
5B Yes the bus station is the end of this street	*Clarification*
6A You've left me all the dirty dishes again	*Accusation/complaint*
6Ba I haven't actually, most of them are in the dishwasher	*Denial*
6Bb Sorry but I just have to go or I'll be late	*Admission, apology, excuse*

The list of possible B responses in examples 2, 3, 4, and 6 makes it clear that there are often alternative second parts in adjacency pairs. It is generally possible to establish which are potential second parts by attending to linguistic clues. The most obvious are references to shared lexical items (*bus station*) or items from the same lexical set (*dishes, dishwasher*), but there are more subtle clues which a CA approach highlights, such as the particles *OK* (1B, 4Bb), *well* (3Bc), and *yes* (5B).

Answer to exercise 13

The initial utterance includes the phrase *guess what* followed by a one-second pause, which can be interpreted as a signal that Ann expects Liz to make an inference, and perhaps to be shocked or surprised by what follows. Liz does not produce the expected second part indicating surprise until line 4. Thus lines 2 and 3 constitute a side sequence which serves to identify crucial information needed by Liz (namely that Phad Moo Sub is a meat dish) in order to interpret the basis on which Ann expects her to be surprised. The particle *oh* in line 4 indicates that Liz has now got the point and has made an inference (that the host did not know that Sally did not eat meat) on the basis of Ann's previous utterance.

Answer to exercise 14

Dan supplies many opportunities for Tom to contribute to the conversation: (1) by providing first parts of potential adjacency pairs, (2) by pausing at places where feedback could occur, and (3) using the invitational facilitative tag *eh*. However, Tom makes only one contribution to the conversation, a negative minimal response, *no*, in response to a direct question, *talk to any girls?*

Tom also fails to respond to remarks directly addressed to him (lines 1, 3, 7), absences which conversational analysis suggests are 'notable' in this context. Without contextual information we cannot know the reason for Tom's lack of conversational cooperation, but CA provides useful tools to identify the fact that there seems to be some conversational trouble here.

Answer to exercise 16

At least three clues suggesting interactional trouble:

1. Disruptive interruption – Renee overlaps Clara's speech by several words.
2. Volume and stress on *you* suggests a rather aggressive stance.
3. Raised eyebrow and stress on *trying* conveys implication that Renee's interruption is interpreted as unhelpful.

Answer to exercise 17

There is abundant evidence within the interaction, both verbal and non-verbal, that Cliff Whiting experiences the discursive behaviour of Ron Trotter as disruptive and problematic. How you interpret what is going on depends, however, on the theoretical perspective you adopt. An interactional sociolinguistic approach might highlight the clash of different cultural norms involved. Maori discourse norms and rules for speaking in formal contexts strictly adhere to a rule that 'one person holds the floor at a time', and a speaker is allowed to complete their turn uninterrupted. From a Pakeha perspective, interruption can be interpreted as conveying enthusiasm or passion, and this is one possible interpretation of what is going on here.

Answer to exercise 18

1. (i) Chris's use of vernacular rather than standard forms (e.g. *-in'* rather than *-ing* forms) in the relatively formal context of an interview with the Headmaster.

(ii) Chris's use of challenging tags to a superior: *i'n it? do we?*

(iii) Chris's explicit challenge to the headmaster's implication that hanging about the square is not acceptable behaviour: *anyway, we always go down the square after school.*

2. On each of these three points, Chris's behaviour fits the stereotype of male rather than female speech, as discussed in earlier chapters.

Answer to exercise 19

A detailed analysis of a transcript would take too much space, so the answer below provides just a starting point for the analysis, illustrating some points that might emerge from a consideration of the first five components of van Dijk's framework. Based on a typical scenario:

Access:	Only the teacher can book the teaching room and access the relevant teaching resources.
Setting:	The location and timing of a seminar is typically in a place more convenient to the teacher than the students (though an overarching timetable and room bookings system operated by the institution often imposes an even higher level of constraint).

Participant positions and roles: relevant identities:

Teacher, students; student presenting a paper

Teacher has the right to determine what will count as a valid contribution, declare what is relevant etc.

Genre:	The teacher is generally much more familiar than the students with the structure and discourse appropriate to a seminar.
Speech acts:	Teachers tend to use

longer, more sustained informative speech acts

evaluative speech acts

test questions (to which they know the answers)

directives

Students tend to use

short informative speech acts

information seeking questions

Topics:	The teacher typically determines the agenda and main topics for discussion

If you can record such a session, you could expand the analysis to examine how the discourse further constructs the power relations evident in the non-verbal dimensions.

You might consider, for instance, evidence of presupposed positions, beliefs, attitudes, and so on. Note, for instance, the use of particles such as *you know, of course, obviously, clearly*, which imply shared presuppositions/knowledge/experience.

Check for pronoun usage: who is *we, you, they*?

Consider who sums up and what their summary reveals about their position in relation to the topic.

◼ Concepts introduced

Pragmatics

Conversational maxims and implicatures

Ethnography of speaking

Interactional sociolinguistics

Contextualisation cues

Conversation analysis
Adjacency pairs
Critical Discourse Analysis (CDA)

References

Example 1 is from Drew and Chilton (2000: 145); it has been slightly edited for ease of reading.

Example 4 is transcribed from an episode of the popular New Zealand soap *Shortland Street* © South Pacific Pictures Serials Limited 1995.

Example 9 is from Holmes and Fillary (2000).

Example 11 is from Lee-Wong (2000: 143); it has been edited for ease of reading.

Example 12 from Kouletaki (2005: 260–2); the examples are translated from questionnaire responses provided in Greek.

Example 13 is from Sifianou (2001: 395); the example is translated from Greek.

Example 14 is from Harris (2001: 467).

Example 15 is based on a genuine incident described by the late Terry Crowley.

Example 16 was provided by Martin Paviour-Smith based on his field-working experience.

Example 19 is from Holmes and Marra (2002).

Example 20 is adapted from Heller (1982: 116–17).

Example 23 is adapted from an example in Takano (2005: 648).

Example 24 is elaborated from an account in Gumperz (1982: 173).

Example 25 is from Roberts, Davies and Jupp (1992); it has been slightly edited for ease of reading.

Example 26 is from Stubbe et al. (2003). The discussion draws in particular on observations by Maria Stubbe and Elaine Vine in the interactional sociolinguistics section.

Example 32 is from research on children's telephone conversations described in Holmes (1981).

Examples 33, 34, 36, 37, 40 and 41 are edited excerpts from the Wellington Language in the Workplace Corpus.

Example 35 is an excerpt from the New Zealand film *Getting to our Place*, transcribed by Julia de Bres. A video clip of this excerpt is available through the on-line version of the *Elsevier Encyclopedia of Language & Linguistics*.

Example 38 is from the TV series *Prime Suspect*.

Example 42 is adapted from Fairclough (1989: 68–9).

Example 43 is adapted from Lee (1992: 98ff).

Example 44 is adapted from Harres (1993). The first excerpt is from a medical textbook (Llewellyn-Jones 1982: 209); the second is from a handbook produced by the Boston Women's Health Collective (1984: 510).

Example 45 is from Tulin (1997: 108).

Example 46 is based on data from Waldvogel (2005).

The following sources also provided material for this chapter:

Drew and Heritage (1992) for the concept of 'notable absences'.

Keenan (1976) on Malagasy communicative norms.

Lee-Wong (2000) and Usami (2002) on politeness strategies in Asian cultures.

Liao and Bresnahan (1996) is the source of the scenario in exercise 5.

Language variation: focus on uses

C

Milroy (1980: 89) on silence during visits in working-class Belfast homes.

New Idea, December 2006, p. 42 was source of advert for an anti-inflammatory.

Nwoye (1989) on Igbo proverbs.

Sacks, Schegloff and Jefferson (1978) on CA.

Saville-Troike (2003) for examples of the components of the ethnography of communication.

Sherzer (1977) on the Cuna Indians.

Stubbe (1998) on minimal feedback by Maori vs Pakeha conversationalists.

Thomas (1995: 76) on the suspension of implicatures in cultures where the norm is not to refer to the dead.

van Dijk's (1998) CDA approach to text is the basis for exercise 18.

White (1989) on back-channelling by Anglo-Americans vs Japanese conversationalists.

Quotations and definitions

Definition of 'contextualisation cues' from Gumperz (1982: 131).

Igbo proverb in example 10 is taken from Nwoye (1989).

Definition of CA as jointly organised activity from Sacks (1984).

Definition of adjacency pairs from Sacks, Schegloff and Jefferson (1974).

The examples cited from *The Weakest Link* can be found on the following website: http://www.bbc.co.uk/weakestlink/about_show.shtml

Useful additional reading

Cameron (2001)

Jaworski and Coupland (1999)

Paltridge (2006)

Thomas (1995)

Thornbury (2005)

Attitudes and applications

ATTITUDES TO LANGUAGE

Example 1

Sir,

What are teachers doing today? They don't seem to know the first thing about teaching pronunciation. One mispronunciation which really galls me is when people say *LORE* instead of *law*. On radio and TV *LORE and order* is replacing *law and order* in the speech of all the announcers. Can't people see that *lore* and *law*, *saw* and *soar* are different words? Introducing these superfluous *r*s all over the place is a sign of ignorance. Yesterday my son *SOAR* a frog in the pond he tells me. Though his teacher isn't a *bore*, she appears to be a *boor* as far as teaching him which words have an *r* in them and which don't!

People who hold strong views about the way words should be pronounced illustrate nicely the themes of this chapter. The issue of whether *r* should be pronounced or not pronounced in English is an especially good example of the arbitrariness of the linguistic features which attract such attention, as we saw in chapters 9 and 10. There is nothing intrinsically good or bad about [r]-pronouncing. Yet in some communities it is regarded as an example of 'good speech', and in others [r]-pronouncing is regarded as humorous, rustic, and as evidence of lack of education. Ultimately attitudes to language reflect attitudes to the users and the uses of language, as we shall see in this chapter. There is nothing intrinsically beautiful or correct about any particular sound. *Swallow*, for example, has positive connotations when people associate the word with the bird, but if you define it as the action which follows chewing, the associations alter, and so do assessments of the word's 'beauty'. Context is all!

Some critics of [r]-less accents argue that they will disadvantage their users in the area of reading in particular. They argue that people who don't distinguish the pronunciation of *lore* and *law* or *sword* and *sawed* are storing up literacy problems for the future. It is easy to demonstrate that such fears are ill-founded. While pronunciation differences can be a help in distinguishing different meanings, they are not essential. People manage to distinguish the meanings of *son* and *sun*, *break* and *brake*, and *write*, *rite* and *right*, despite the fact that they sound the same in most accents of English. But this kind of argument, linking linguistic attitudes which are based in social prejudice to often spurious educational consequences, is surprisingly widespread. The second half of this chapter discusses these issues as one example of applied sociolinguistics.

Example 2

'Danish is not a language, but a throat disease' wrote one Norwegian respondent in reply to a 1950s postal questionnaire asking for Scandinavian people's opinions of the relative aesthetic qualities of Swedish, Danish and Norwegian.

The results of the questionnaire placed Swedish first and Danish at the bottom of the pile. These results reflected not so much the relative aesthetic qualities of the three languages as the political fortunes of the three countries associated with each. Swedish was at that time the undoubted political leader, while Danish – the former ruling power – was in a less influential political position. People's attitudes to Swedish and Danish reflected Scandinavian politics rather than any intrinsic linguistic features of the language. With the rise of Danish influence through its membership of the European Economic Community, one would expect different results from a similar questionnaire in the twenty-first century.

It has been suggested that intelligibility is also affected by attitudes. People generally find it easier to understand languages and dialects spoken by people they like or admire. A closely related point, at least for majority group members, is that people are more highly motivated, and consequently often more successful, in acquiring a second language when they feel positive towards those who use it. Clearly attitudes to language have interesting implications both for politicians and language teachers.

People generally do not hold opinions about languages in a vacuum. They develop attitudes towards languages which reflect their views about those who speak the languages, and the contexts and functions with which they are associated. When people listen to accents or languages they have never heard before, their assessments are totally random. There is no pattern to them. In other words there is no universal consensus about which languages sound most beautiful and which most ugly, despite people's beliefs that some languages are just inherently more beautiful than others.

Attitudes to language are strongly influenced by social and political factors, as was evident in the discussion in chapters 4 and 5. Language planners must take account of attitudes when they select a suitable language for development as an official or national language. Attitudes to pidgins and creoles, for instance, present major impediments to their promotion and acceptance as official languages, or for use in schools. In other countries the official status given to unpopular languages has caused problems. There have been riots in Belgium and India over language issues, and bombings and the removal of

English road signs illustrate the strength of people's feelings about the place of English in Wales. In Quebec it was found in the 1960s that French-Canadians tended to rate English-Canadian voices on tape very positively, as more intelligent, competent and likeable, for instance, than French-Canadian voices. By the 1970s, however, ratings of French-Canadians were higher, reflecting increased political awareness, and the increased self esteem that went with this. Language attitudes are very sensitive to social and political changes.

Language attitudes can have a great influence in areas such as education. Arguments in Somalia about which script should be used to write down Somali, a Cushitic language, delayed progress in increasing literacy rates for decades. The most influential factors in this debate were not the intrinsic merits of the alternative scripts, but rather people's attitudes to speakers and writers of Arabic and English and the functions for which those languages were used. Supporters of Arabic script pointed to the prestige, the religious significance, and the cultural importance of Arabic for the people of Somalia. It was claimed that some of the religious poetry written by Somalis in Arabic surpassed in its ardour and zeal similar compositions by the Arabs. Those who advocated the Latin alphabet pointed to its usefulness and the access it would give to scientific and techno-logical information. An attempt at a hybrid script, known as Osmanian script after its inventor Osman Yusuf, was tried, but failed to catch on. Finally, in 1973 a Latin script was adopted and given official status. Some saw this as a triumph for efficiency over sentiment. Others regarded it as a bureaucratic decision in favour of a culturally sterile script. Attitudes to language certainly contributed to the years of stalemate and lack of progress in selecting a script in Somalia.

Exercise 1

How could you test whether people's opinions about a language are based on the intrinsic linguistic features of the language (such as its sounds and its grammatical patterns) or derive from non-linguistic factors such as the social and political status of the speakers?

Answer at end of chapter

Overt and covert prestige

Example 3

Context: elocution class in Belfast. The pupil has just recited a poem using the local Belfast pronunciation of words like Jane. *The elocution teacher responds as follows.*

Teacher: How do you pronounce her name?
Pupil: Jane *(with an RP-like pronunciation)*
Teacher: How do you remember that?
Pupil: The rain in Spain falls mainly on the plain *(with an RP-like pronunciation)*

Prestige is a slippery concept. The meaning of overt prestige is reasonably self-evident. The standard variety in a community has overt prestige. Speakers who use the standard variety are rated highly on scales of educational and occupational status, and these ratings reflect the associations of their speech variety, which is generally held up as the 'best' way of speaking in the community. It is the variety taught in elocution classes, regardless of the pupils' native accents, as example 3 illustrates. It is overtly admired and generally identified as a model of 'good' speech by all sections of the community, regardless of the way they themselves speak. In fact it has been suggested that this agreement about the standard variety or 'best' accent is what identifies a group of people as belonging to a speech community. Regardless of variation in their own speech, they all recognise one variety as the standard or norm for the community.

Covert prestige, by contrast, is an odd term which could even be regarded as involving two contradictory ideas. How can something have prestige if its value is not publicly recognised? The term 'covert prestige' has been widely used, however, to refer to positive attitudes towards vernacular or non-standard speech varieties. Clearly such varieties are valued or they would not continue to be used. Yet when people are asked to comment on them, they rarely admit to valuing them (at least to strangers). New Yorkers, for instance, vehemently denounce New York speech. One New Yorker described it as 'incontrovertibly dumb'. After talking to many New Yorkers, Labov described the city as a 'sink of negative prestige'! Similarly in Norwich Trudgill was told 'I speak 'orrible' by men who used the local vernacular. Yet people continue to use the forms they avowedly despise. The term covert prestige was therefore introduced to explain the fact that, despite their 'official' protestations, people clearly do in fact value vernacular varieties.

In some schools in Britain, and in New Zealand too, children are taught to speak RP in elocution classes, but they would never be caught using it outside the classroom. The local accent is the only possible way of speaking to friends, workmates and family. It expresses group identity and solidarity. Not surprisingly, many people do not want to sound like Prince Andrew, the Duchess of Kent, or even the TV newsreaders.

There is also a large group of people who are not aware that they do not speak with the accent they admire and regard as the standard. Most people are surprised when they hear their own voices on tape. Some of this surprise usually relates to the pronunciations they hear themselves using. There is a story about a public speaker at a conference on speech who inveighed for some time against slipshod and sloppy pronunciations such as the use of *gonna*, for *going to*. He ended up with

> 'And I tell you I believe that this deplorable pronunciation should be opposed by all teachers and eliminated entirely, and I'm gonna make damn sure that no child in my class uses it.'

Condemned out of his own mouth with a pronunciation which is a widespread and perfectly acceptable one, he collapsed red-faced and defeated in the face of gales of laughter from his audience. Similarly, in example 4 Labov tells the sad story of how he unintentionally disillusioned a New York woman and her daughter about the way they spoke, not realising how damaging his slice of reality would be.

Example 4

'The case of Debbie S. and Mrs S. ends on an unhappy note. In the discussion of *r*, both mother and daughter insisted that they always pronounced all their *r*'s . . . They had ridiculed Speaker 2 [one of the speakers on the tape played to them] for dropping a single *r*, and they could not believe that they would make such a mistake themselves. Unwisely I played back the section of tape in which Mollie S. recited "Strawberry shortcake, cream on top, tell me the name of my sweetheart". She could hear the consistent [lack of *r*] in her speech but after a moment's thought she explained the situation as a psychological transference – she had imagined herself in her childhood setting, and had used a childish speech form. I then played a section of careful speech, the discussion of *common sense*, and also Debbie's reading of the standard text. When Mrs S. and her daughter at last accepted the fact that they regularly [omitted *r*] in their own speech, they were disheartened in a way that was painful to see. An interview which would otherwise have been an exhilarating experience for this lady and her daughter was thus terminated in a bitter disappointment for them both: and once the damage had been done, there was no way to restore their pride in their own speech.'

The realisation that we do not always speak as we had imagined can serve as a warning not to be too hasty in judging the speech of others.

Exercise 2

This exercise is intended to give you some idea of how language attitude data is collected and of the kind of results which emerge. In order to make the exercise manageable, I suggest you use just two taped voices and ask for responses from a small number of people. To obtain results you could generalise from, it would be necessary to use more voices and many more respondents.

Tape a person from your community with a local accent telling you a story from their personal experience. Then tape someone with a standard accent (such as RP in England) from the television or radio, if possible talking on a similar personal topic. Then play excerpts from the two speakers to two or three of your friends or family and ask them to rate the speakers on the following scale.

Speech rating scale
Listen to the tape and then indicate with a tick where you would place the speakers on the following scales.

►

C

Language variation: focus on uses

Speaker 1	1	2	3	4	5	
pleasant	—	—	—	—	—	unpleasant
attractive	—	—	—	—	—	unattractive
self-confident	—	—	—	—	—	un-self-confident
likeable	—	—	—	—	—	unlikeable
fluent	—	—	—	—	—	not fluent
reliable	—	—	—	—	—	unreliable
sincere	—	—	—	—	—	insincere
ambitious	—	—	—	—	—	unambitious
friendly	—	—	—	—	—	unfriendly
intelligent	—	—	—	—	—	unintelligent
good sense of humour	—	—	—	—	—	no sense of humour
leadership skills	—	—	—	—	—	no leadership skills
highly educated	—	—	—	—	—	uneducated
high status job	—	—	—	—	—	low status job

What differences are there in the ratings? How would you explain them?

Answer at end of chapter

Example 5

Ray is a West Indian teenager whose linguistic repertoire includes Patois as well as standard English with a local London accent. He has no illusions about his teacher's views about Patois, the language variety that he speaks with his friends. 'She'd rather we said nothing at all if we don't use "proper English". And as for Patois she hits the roof if she hears us using it at school. She calls it sloppy, ugly speech.'

Jamaican Creole, or Patois, which was discussed in chapters 2 and 8, is an excellent example of a code which survives because it is valued as a marker of identity by its users. We could say it has covert prestige since few Black people admit to outsiders that proficiency in Patois is greatly admired, especially among young British Blacks. As example 5 indicates, official attitudes to the language, even in the 1980s, regarded it is a deplorably deficient form of English which hindered the educational progress of Jamaican children in Britain. Teachers have described the language of their West Indian pupils as 'babyish', 'careless and slovenly', 'lacking proper grammar', and 'very relaxed like the way they walk'! In fact Patois is a language variety with a complex grammar, distinctive pronunciations, and some distinctive vocabulary items, as we saw in chapter 8. It has its own literary material. There are poets and novelists who write in Patois.

Overtly negative attitudes towards Patois reflect the depressed social position of the West Indian people in Britain rather than features of the language itself. West Indian migrants went to Britain during the 1950s and 1960s with a generally positive attitude looking for work. But Britain needed mainly unskilled workers, and as a result literate well-educated Caribbean people had to take low-paid low-status jobs. Despite this they were confident that their children would do better as a result of a good British education. Unfortunately the reality has been different. By the late 1980s, West Indian people were still working mainly in unskilled and semi-skilled jobs, earning less on average than other groups. Moreover, their children were not doing well at school. Not only were they not doing as well as children of indigenous British people, they were not even doing as well as the children of other immigrant groups in Britain, such as Greeks, Chinese and Indians. Schools have tended to blame the children and their Patois for their educational failure (a point mentioned in chapter 13 which will be discussed further below). But there is nothing linguistically inadequate about Patois. Comments about Patois are largely based on ignorance and prejudice. Most people are not aware of the full complexity of this variety since they hear very little of it. It is the fact that Patois is used by West Indian children – a low-status group in Britain – that determines attitudes towards it. Society's overt evaluation of this variety simply reflects attitudes to the low social status of West Indians in Britain.

This was clearly demonstrated in a study which asked student teachers to rate recordings of five children they had never met all talking fluently on the topic of a visit to the dentist. The listeners heard a middle-class boy, two working-class children and two West Indian children. They rated the middle-class boy most intelligent, most interesting, best behaved and friendliest. Next came the working-class children who were both rated alike. Last came the two West Indian children. Yet one of the West Indian children actually spoke twice on the tape – though the listeners did not realise this. (This is known as the 'matched guise' technique.) She spoke once in the Barbadian (West Indies) accent which she used at home with her friends and family, and once in the working-class accent she used at school. So the same girl was viewed as more intelligent, for instance, when she spoke in her working-class accent than when she was identifiable as a West Indian. Clearly, it is the associated social status of the speakers which forms the basis of people's evaluations.

In what follows I will discuss in more detail first people's attitudes to overtly valued varieties, such as standard English and the RP accent, and Standard American English (SAE), and then attitudes to covertly valued vernacular varieties, such as Patois and African American Vernacular English (AAVE).

Exercise 3

Discuss with five different people their views about the language of any immigrant group with which you are familiar. The method used to collect information on attitudes to language in exercise 2 (playing voices on a tape) tends to elicit overt norms and attitudes. With people you know well you may be able to get beyond the overt attitudes to find out how they really feel about their own speech, the

▶

Language variation: focus on uses

C

speech of other local people, the speech of immigrants, and the way the TV newsreaders speak. Do people's comments on language reflect the social status of the groups concerned, as suggested in the previous section?

Note any evidence in the comments you collect of a difference between covert and overt attitudes to language. In other words, do people criticise a variety which they nevertheless use regularly, while saying they admire a variety which they would never or very rarely use?

Attitudes to standard English and RP

Example 6

(a) 'Next to our people our language is our greatest national asset; it is the essential ingredient of the Englishness of England.'
(b) 'English ought to be the queen of the curriculum for any British child. It is one of the things that define his or her nationality.'

Standard English has an enormous legacy of overt prestige. It has been regarded as a symbol of British nationhood, as the quotations in example 6 indicate. For well over a century it has been promoted as the only acceptable variety for use in all official domains, including education. By comparison, vernacular dialects of English are downgraded. The political and social basis of these attitudes is clearly evident, however, when we remember that the elite consensus until at least the eighteenth century was that English was a decidedly inferior language, less eloquent than Latin or Greek, or even than French and Italian. Prestige codes emerge by social consensus and owe nothing to their intrinsic linguistic features.

While there is general agreement on the inferior status of vernacular dialects (whatever their covert value as solidarity markers), many people are surprised to find that standard accents of English are so highly regarded by those who don't use them. This is clearly illustrated by reactions to RP in England. When people are asked to assess RP speakers on tape they rate them as more intelligent, industrious, self-confident and determined than regional-accented speakers – even when the raters themselves speak with a regional accent. RP is rated ahead of all other accents on such criteria as communicative effectiveness, social status and general pleasantness. People who use RP accents are often taken more seriously, and RP speakers are more likely to persuade people to cooperate. And for RP-speaking women there are even further benefits. They are rated as more competent, less weak, more independent, adventurous and more feminine than non-RP speakers. (This, incidentally, provides another good reason for the fact, noted in chapter 7, that women use more prestige forms than men. Women are more positively evaluated by others when they use such forms.)

> **Example 7**
>
> 'But in England, people of education and good social position all speak pure English. In New Zealand, this harsh and horrid brogue of ours is permeating every class of society; you get it in the speech of shop-girls and on the lips of university graduates.'

Even outside Britain, RP is still an overtly admired model in many countries where English is used, such as Singapore and New Zealand. While attitudes to local varieties vary, RP often has a guaranteed place among acceptable prestige forms.

The robustness of such attitudes is remarkable. School inspectors visiting New Zealand from Britain in the 1880s described New Zealand speech as 'pure and undefiled', preserving all that was good about English pronunciation. By the turn of the century, however, a New Zealand accent which was different from RP and British regional accents began to develop. The school inspectors' reports became correspondingly less admiring and more critical. Agreeing with the letter writer in example 7, they called New Zealand English an 'objectionable colonial dialect'. Subsequently the New Zealand accent was described as 'indefensible', 'corrupt', 'degraded', and even 'hideous' and 'evil-sounding'. Given the inspectors' British origins, these views were predictable. What is rather more surprising is that many New Zealand teenagers in the 1980s and 1990s rated RP more highly than any New Zealand accent (though interestingly, by 1998, not as highly as a North American accent). One student responded to a recording of a distinctly New Zealand accent with the comment 'God help us if we all sound like this.'

Once again the social basis of these attitudes is very clear. Though there are many notable exceptions, such as the late former Prime Minister David Lange, it is still the case for most New Zealanders that a high level of education and a high-status job is associated with an accent closer to RP than to broad New Zealand English. Hence the high ratings of RP – at least on overt measures.

It should be said that there have always been a few New Zealanders who took a different view, objecting, for example, to the adoption of imported so-called 'refined' upper-class vowels. But they have been a minority. On the other hand, while RP tends to be rated highly on the status dimension, as in Britain, local accents generally score more highly on characteristics such as friendliness and sense of humour, and other dimensions which measure solidarity or social attractiveness. This evidence of the covert prestige of regional accents and vernacular varieties is discussed further in the next section.

Attitudes to vernacular forms of English

In the early section of this chapter, I discussed attitudes to British Patois, a variety used by members of the West Indian community in Britain. While attitudes are always changing, and new varieties of Black English, such as Jafaican, are said to be developing, it is still true to say that these varieties can be described as vernacular varieties which are generally condemned or ridiculed by those who consider themselves guardians of the language, and regarded ambivalently even by their users. Another example of a widely known variety of this kind is African American Vernacular English (AAVE). Astonishingly a recent study found that negative evaluations of AAVE could even be found among university students in Japan, suggesting that Japan has absorbed American racial stereotypes alongside many other American values. In the USA, AAVE has been at the centre of a debate about the role of vernacular varieties in education for at least four decades.

African American Vernacular English

Example 8

'. . . what makes me feel that blacks tend to be ignorant is that they fail to see that the word is spelled A-S-K not A-X. And when they say *aksed*, it gives the sentence an entirely different meaning. And that is what I feel holds blacks back.'

(female call-in viewer, *Oprah Winfrey Show*, 1987)

Some examples of structural differences between African American Vernacular English (AAVE) and Standard American English (SAE) were discussed in chapter 8. Most non-linguists, however, are unaware of the evidence for AAVE as a distinct and systematic variety. Consequently, criticism of AAVE has been well documented by sociolinguists for decades. As example 8 indicates, critics typically assume that AAVE use reflects ignorance rather than choice. Given the minuscule sound difference between [ask] and [aks], and the lack of logic in arguing for a particular pronunciation on the basis of a written form, it is ironic that *ask* has been a particularly frequent focus of comment. (And in fact [aks] for [ask] has a long history as a vernacular form since it can be found in the speech of the yokels in Shakespearian plays and in Chaucer's tales too.) Yet this is quite typical of the kinds of comments made about AAVE use, no matter which particular feature is selected for condemnation.

Much media use tends to confirm these negative attitudes to AAVE. African American newsreaders and movie stars typically use SAE, while those entertainers and sports celebrities who do use AAVE features tend to restrict them to more intelligible, stereo-typical features in less formal contexts. The prejudices of the wider community tend to be reinforced by such behaviour, as well as by the subtle reinforcement of negative attitudes provided by the depiction of AAVE users in TV shows and movies as less well-educated, down-at-heel and often unsavoury characters. One interesting analysis showed that the characters who used AAVE in successful Disney films such as *The Jungle Book* and *The Lion King* represented animals rather than humans. This is how stereotypes are constructed and reinforced.

Example 9

Negro Dialect
Substandard Negro Dialect
Nonstandard Negro English
Black English
Afro-American English
Ebonics
Vernacular Black English
African American Vernacular English

AAVE is a prime example of a language variety which is so politically 'hot' that it has been constantly labelled and re-labelled, as example 9 illustrates. (See chapter 13 for a discussion of political correctness and euphemism.) The term 'Ebonics' was originally coined in the 1970s, but it was revived and popularised in the 1990s when the Oakland Unified School District Board of Education passed a resolution affirming the legitimacy of Ebonics (as they labelled AAVE) as a language system, and supporting its use as a bridge to learning standard English in school. The decision created a furore and even resulted in a Senate sub-committee hearing on the status of AAVE and its role in education.

Many African American parents were unconvinced of the benefits of using AAVE and concerned that the time would be better devoted to acquiring SAE. Their letters to the newspapers and contributions on talk-back and call-in shows expressed fears that the use of AAVE in schools was just another strategy for preventing their children from achieving educational success. On the other hand, many successful African Americans asserted the importance of maintaining and giving status to AAVE, and of resisting attempts by the majority group to impose SAE on everyone.

Example 10

'Language is political. That's why you and me, my Brother and Sister, that's why we sposed to choke our natural self into the weird, lying, barbarous, unreal, white speech and writing habits that the schools lay down like holy law. Because in other words the powerful don't play; they mean to keep that power, and those who are the powerless (you and me) better shape up mimic/ape/suck-in the very image of the powerful, or the powerful will destroy you – you and our children.'

(June Jordan, poet, writer, political activist)

Adopting SAE, even for part of the time, seems a betrayal of their home dialect to many African Americans. The issue has become too politicised for the notion of a broader verbal repertoire, or the construction of different social identities, to provide a simple resolution. For many minority ethnic group members, ethnic identity is fundamental and colours or infuses everything they say and do, think and believe. From this perspective, advocating bidialectalism is perhaps like asking a woman to pretend to be a man for the duration of each working day, or vice-versa.

The Ebonics debate of the 1990s thus re-ran the familiar arguments about the social disadvantages of using AAVE. Reduced to its basic element the argument is:

If you use AAVE you won't get a good job.

But those who put forward this argument generally imply that African American children who use SAE *will* get good jobs. This is the fallacy. It is clear from the evidence provided by USA employment statistics that it is ethnicity rather than language which is the primary basis of discrimination. Moreover, those African Americans who do succeed, achieving occupations such as airline pilots and army officers, are often mistaken for service personnel in public places. The problem is racist attitudes, not linguistic deficit or even dialect difference. These issues are developed further in the next two sections.

Vernacular forms of English, users and contexts

Example 11

'Attention to the rules of grammar and care in the choice of words encourages punctiliousness in other matters . . . The overthrow of grammar coincided with the acceptance of the equivalent of creative writing in social behaviour. As nice points of grammar were mockingly dismissed as pedantic and irrelevant, so was punctiliousness in such matters as honesty, responsibility, property, gratitude, apology and so on.'

Support for so-called 'grammar' teaching often derives from the misleading association of grammar with authority, hierarchy, tradition and elitism, order and rules, as illustrated by this quotation. What is meant here is not 'grammar', but a number of arbitrary, superficial rules of formal standard English. Such advocates do their cause more harm than good. It is difficult for a sociolinguist to take seriously the suggestion that using standard grammar encourages honesty, or that the use of vernacular forms has any connection with ingratitude.

In chapter 6 we saw that the standard dialect is primarily a socially defined entity, not a linguistically defined one. Standard English is the English used by educated people with relatively high social status (generally referred to as the middle class). So, middle-class children speak standard English, and children from other social groups do not.

It is also worth emphasising a point that was illustrated in chapter 10: no one uses 100 per cent vernacular or non-standard forms. When people talk of non-standard English they are referring to the fact that particular linguistic forms occur more often in the speech of one group than another. Omission of the verb *be* in utterances such as *she not here*, the use of multiple negation, and the substitution of [d] for [ð] in words such as *the* and *then*, for instance, are all features of vernacular dialects, but people who use these forms generally know and use the standard forms too. They simply use fewer standard forms than those who come from different socio-economic or ethnic groups. Our speech also expresses and constructs our identity. The reasons that vernacular forms survive is attitudinal. As mentioned above, working-class children do not want to sound like John Major or Hillary Clinton. They do not even want to sound like their teachers, however well they get on with them. If they were to speak like their middle-class friends their families would laugh at them for sounding 'posh' or 'stuck-up' or 'prissy'.

It is also true that everyone increases their use of standard forms as the context becomes more formal. This means that middle-class children are unlikely to use any vernacular forms at all when they are asked to read aloud, for instance, whereas children from lower socio-economic groups may use some vernacular forms. The use of vernacular forms is clearly patterned and systematic, not random and haphazard. The number of standard forms in everyone's speech increases in formal contexts like school and a law court, while the number of vernacular forms increases in relaxed casual contexts such as the playground and the home. Vernacular forms express the friendliness and relaxed attitudes appropriate in casual contexts.

I have tried to show that the reasons people condemn vernacular forms are attitudinal, not linguistic. Children who use vernacular forms are not disadvantaged by inadequate language. They are disadvantaged by negative attitudes towards their speech – attitudes which derive from their lower social status and its associations in people's minds. Unfortunately, these attitudes often have unhappy educational consequences, as we shall see in the last section. First, however, a brief look at methods of collecting attitude data.

Exercise 4

Think of three ways that a sociolinguist could find out about a community's attitudes to a particular language variety. Identify one advantage or strength and one disadvantage or weakness of each method.

Answer in the next section

A note on methodology

Collecting information about attitudes to language is a tricky business. While we can use direct observation and questions to elicit overt attitudes, it is much more difficult to discover how people evaluate vernacular varieties, especially those which are overtly condemned or ridiculed in the media. There are three main ways that people have used to collect information on attitudes to language, and they have all been referred to or illustrated at various places in this book.

1. Direct observation

Sociolinguists can simply observe what people say and write to collect information about their attitudes to language. People regularly express views about language issues on the radio, on TV, on the net and in the press. Sociolinguists record people's views and collect letters from the public in newspaper and magazines as evidence of people's attitudes to language. Many of the examples in this book, such as example 9 in chapter 5, example 2 in chapter 9, and example 1 in this chapter, are instances of Letters to the Editor. They provide one kind of evidence about attitudes to language. These sources of attitude data are relatively easy to access. They can provide useful clues to language changes in progress, and suggest areas for further study. Though data collected in this way is rarely adequate for a sociolinguist to come to definitive conclusions about how widely such attitudes are shared, it can provide interesting indications of the range of attitudes held in a community. A study of attitudes to the Maori language expressed in 51 Letters to the Editor in the early 1990s, for instance, identified a range of arguments that people drew on to support their pro-Maori or anti-Maori claims. So, observation can be a useful source of information about some aspect of attitudes to language, but it rarely provides a representative picture of how widely held such views are.

2. Direct questions

Sociolinguists can ask direct questions about people's attitudes to particular languages or language varieties or even linguistic features: e.g. do you like the Welsh language? do you think Welsh sounds beautiful? do you like the sound at the beginning of the Welsh word Llandudno? These closed *yes/no* questions are easy to code so you can collect answers from large numbers of people using a written questionnaire or an interview schedule, and then count the responses easily. Written questionnaires can be anonymous and they can even be sent out to large numbers of people by post, thus accessing a large sample of the community.

Less easy to count are open questions: e.g. what do you think of the way the Queen of England speaks? what are your views about African American Vernacular English? what do you think about the pronunciation [aks] for [ask]? Answers to these questions require some analysis; they need to be categorised at least into those which are for and against, and as a result it is less easy to draw nice neat conclusions about people's views. But they also offer the possibility of eliciting richer and more interesting data since the researcher hasn't decided in advance on what the relevant dimensions of analysis will be. Using more open-ended questions, it is possible to be surprised and learn something new.

One major disadvantage of such direct approaches to collecting information about attitudes is that people may not reveal their true attitudes, especially if they feel that their views are unacceptable in the wider community. So if they secretly admire or hate Maori or Welsh or AAVE, they may not admit this to an interviewer who appears to represent a group unsympathetic to their views. Anonymous questionnaires can help in resolving this dilemma, but the response rates to written questionnaires tend to be very low, and the people who respond are often those with a particular barrow to push, i.e. a special interest in the topic. So the results will not be representative of the views of the community as a whole. Students in lecture theatres are often asked to respond to such questionnaires because they provide a captive and usually cooperative audience. But their results present the same problem; they are hardly representative of the wider community.

3. Indirect measures

A third way of collecting data on language attitudes is to use an indirect measure which elicits the respondents' attitudes without making them feel self-conscious or embarrassed. The most sophisticated form of this method is the 'matched guise' technique described above. Typically, listeners hear tapes of two people saying the same thing but speaking in two different languages or two different varieties. The listeners are unaware that the four samples they hear are produced by just two speakers. Moreover, they are asked to evaluate the personality of the speakers rather than the language variety itself. Since the personality of the speakers is constant for the pairs of voices, this cannot in principle be an influence on the responses. So since attitudes to language and its users and uses are inextricably intertwined, as this chapter has described, people's responses inevitably tell us something about their attitudes to the language. Many variations of this basic strategy have been developed involving more bilinguals and a range of varieties of languages and accents.

The most radical variation involves simply playing taped stimuli of different languages and accents to listeners and asking them to respond to the voices on a range of dimensions such as those provided in the rating scale in exercise 2. Obviously this does not hold the personality of the speakers constant, but the problems that have been identified relate not so much to variation in the personality of speakers, but rather to the problem of getting speakers who sound equally fluent and confident. Stutters and hesitations have a huge influence on people's judgements. So getting data which is truly comparable is a major challenge for this methodology.

As a footnote to this brief discussion on methods of collecting data on language attitudes, it is perhaps worth mentioning that observing what people *do* can also provide a measure of their attitudes to language. Enrolment in language classes is a good indication of a positive attitude, for example. Attending events such as plays and concerts which use the language is another. One clever study sent an invitation to an evening of Puerto Rican singing and dancing to people who had indicated positive attitudes to Puerto Rican people and to the use of Spanish in a questionnaire. They were being asked to demonstrate their commitment. Another study asked people to respond to a questionnaire in a different language each evening at the theatre and deduced people's attitudes by the numbers who responded to each request. You can probably think of some weaknesses in these methods, but they are attempts to circumvent the problem that what people tell a researcher and what they really believe are not necessarily the same.

Attitudes to language are important to sociolinguists for a variety of reasons. In chapter 4 we saw that they were important in the description of pidgin and creole languages. Social dialectologists have claimed that shared attitudes to speech or shared speech norms is the crucial criterion in defining members of the same speech community. Attitudes to vernacular varieties or the languages of disfavoured groups affect teachers' academic expectations of those who use these varieties, with implications for their academic progress. Not surprisingly, it has also been found that attitudes to the way people speak affect employers' decisions about who to hire. Clearly, attitudes to language have implications in many social spheres and illustrate well the ways in which sociolinguistic research often has an applied dimension. In the next section I will give some examples of ways in which sociolinguistic research has proved useful in the educational sphere in particular.

Exercise 5

In chapter 10, it was demonstrated that the number of standard vs vernacular forms used by people varied according to the social context. What are the educational implications of this fact?

Answer at end of chapter

SOCIOLINGUISTICS AND EDUCATION

Vernacular dialects and educational disadvantage

Many sociolinguists have been drawn into public debates about the educational implications of their research. The best-known example is probably the part sociolinguists have played in debates over the place of vernacular dialects in schools, and the claims that children who use vernacular forms are linguistically deprived or deficient.

It has been evident for some time that in many speech communities middle-class children do better at school than working-class children. They get better exam results, for instance. Similarly, though there are some exceptions, children from the mainstream culture generally have greater success in school than minority group children. In English-speaking communities, these facts have often been misleadingly linked to the fact that children from the successful groups tend to use more standard dialect forms – they use standard English – while the speech of children from the less successful groups often includes a greater frequency of vernacular forms.

This is an area where some sociolinguists have tried very hard to be helpful. Some have undertaken research to investigate the extent to which the use of vernacular forms or a distinct variety like Patois in Britain may act as a barrier to communication between teachers and pupils. Others have interpreted the results of sociolinguistic research for teachers and provided advice and recommendations for classroom practice. A widely quoted example involved the legal case in the United States which is described in example 12.

> **Example 12**
>
> In 1977 Moira Lewis was eight years old. She lived in the city of Ann Arbor in the United States in Green Road, an area where there were both rich and poor people. She went to the local school, Martin Luther King Elementary School. It was a school with mainly white children, but there were also some African American children like Moira, and a few Asian and Latino children. By the time Moira was eight, her mother was getting concerned that she was not doing well at school. She talked to some of the other African American mothers and found they were worried too. The school took the view that Moira and her African American friends were problems – they labelled them as 'learning disabled'. But Moira's mother and her friends knew better. Their kids were perfectly healthy, bright children. It was the school which was failing not the children. The mothers decided to take the school to court claiming that the teachers were not adequately providing for their children's education. The mothers won their case, and the school was required to provide a programme for Moira and her friends which gave them a better chance of educational success.

In this example the African American mothers argued that the local school was not taking proper account of their children's linguistic proficiency and educational needs. A number of sociolinguists were called as 'expert witnesses' to testify that the variety of English used by the children was a dialect distinct from Standard American English (SAE), with a distinct history and origins in a Creole which developed on American slave plantations. The judge accepted their testimony and ordered the school to take account of features of the children's dialect. He pointed out that the teachers and children could understand each other, and expressed the view that the main barriers to the children's progress took the form of unconscious negative attitudes held by the teachers to children who spoke AAVE. The steps that were taken to remedy the situation consisted mainly of in-service training for the teachers. This involved, for example, helping them distinguish between features of the children's dialect and reading errors, and suggesting ways they could help the children develop the ability to switch between AAVE and SAE.

Dialect differences can certainly lead to miscommunication, especially if vernacular dialect users do not hear a great deal of the standard dialect. In most English-speaking communities, however, as in Ann Arbor, there is little evidence that children who use vernacular forms have trouble understanding the standard English they hear on television, on radio, and from their teachers. In fact sociolinguists have demonstrated that in some communities, at least, children clearly do understand the standard dialect, since when they are asked to repeat sentences in the standard they often translate them accurately into the vernacular equivalents, as the pairs of sentences in example 13 demonstrate. The (b) sentences are the child's repetition of the (a) sentences.

Example 13

(a1) Nobody ever sat at any of those desks.
(b1) Nobody never sat at no desses.
(a2) I asked Alvin if he knows how to play basketball.
(b2) I aks Alvin do he know how to play basketball.

Translation presupposes understanding. If, as these examples suggest, understanding is not usually a major hurdle, the next question is whether anything should be done to change the speech of children who use vernacular forms.

Sociolinguists have pointed out that attempts to alter people's speech without their full cooperation are fruitless. People can change their own speech if they really want to, but teachers and parents simply waste their time correcting children's usage if the children do not want to sound different. It has been noted that when children imitate their teachers for fun, or when they role-play a middle-class person in a game or a school activity, they often produce consistently standard forms for as long as required. Motivation and free choice are crucial factors, and any attempts to teach standard dialect forms will not succeed without them.

If, however, children can see some point in being able to use standard forms consistently in certain contexts, such as job interviews, then, with the information provided by sociolinguists, teachers can provide students with guidance on which vernacular forms are most salient to listeners. Many sociolinguists believe, however, that their primary obligation is to educate the community to accept variation and vernacular forms, without condemning or stereotyping their users as uneducated and low status, rather than to train vernacular users to adopt standard speech forms. This is an area of on-going debate in educational linguistics.

Exercise 6

Can you think of any reason why a language teacher might think it was *not* their job to teach those who use vernacular forms to use standard dialect forms?

Answer at end of chapter

■ Linguistic deficit

A related area where sociolinguistic research has proved useful is in the area of educational testing. Sociolinguists have successfully demonstrated that claims that minority group children and working-class children were linguistically deprived were generally based on inadequate tests. The major contribution that sociolinguists have made in this area is to provide evidence about the effect of contextual factors on speech.

An example will serve to illustrate this point. In order to determine the extent of their vocabulary and grammar, it is usual to ask children to complete a number of language tests. At one time these tests were often administered by an adult stranger from a different social background from the child, and sometimes from a different ethnic group from the child too. As a rule each child was interviewed individually in a quiet room in the school. Children from minority and working-class backgrounds who were tested under these conditions generally did not do well. They responded monosyllabically, saying as little as possible, and escaping with relief after it was all over. Middle-class children, on the other hand, tended to do much better. They were much more willing to answer questions at length.

Sociolinguists pointed out that, although those administering them thought they were administering these tests under 'standard' and 'controlled' conditions, there were in fact some important differences in the experiences of middle-class children compared to others being tested. An adult stranger using the standard dialect would be more likely to resemble the friend of your mother or father if you were a middle-class child. If you were not a middle-class child, your experience of adults who used the standard variety would be teachers, social welfare workers, and government officials – not the sort of people a child would be likely to want to talk to for long if it could be avoided.

Example 14

Michelle came home from school after her history exam.

'How did you get on?' asked her mother. 'What did they ask you?'

'I had to write about Captain Cook,' Michelle replied.

'What did you say?' asked her mother.

So Michelle told her all the interesting stories about Captain Cook's adventures that she had recounted in her exam answer. Finally her mother interrupted, 'But didn't you mention that he was one of the first Europeans to discover New Zealand?'

'Oh no,' she replied. 'I think they know that!'

The kind of questions the interviewer asked would also be more familiar to middle-class children. Middle-class parents are much more likely to ask children to 'display what they know'. When grandma visits, for instance, little Pauline is instructed 'Tell grandma what you did on Sunday'. This kind of question is used in language tests too, e.g. 'Tell me everything you can about this picture.' To a child who is used to being asked questions like these – questions to which the questioner obviously knows the answer – such instructions are not a problem. Other children may find them puzzling and wonder if there is a catch or a trick involved. In other words, the testing conditions are not the same for all the children.

Sociolinguists were able to provide evidence that children who responded mono-syllabically in a test-interview were voluble and communicative in different contexts – with their friends, for instance. One researcher showed that the evaluative construc-tions used in story-telling by the African American teenagers he recorded were more developmentally advanced or mature than those used by the whites. In other words, claims that these children were linguistically deficient or 'had no language' or were limited to a 'restricted code' could be roundly refuted. The formality and unfamiliarity of the testing context for these children accounted for the misleading inference that they were linguistically deprived.

It was also pointed out that the language of the tests was more similar to that of the middle-class children than to that of children from other social groups. When responses to the test questions were analysed, it was found that sometimes answers which were factually correct but which used vernacular forms were marked wrong, because they didn't exactly match the form of the answers on the marking schedule. Once again evid-ence from sociolinguists was valuable in demonstrating that the children's language was linguistically systematic and well-structured and not inadequate or deficient.

Exercise 7

The following dialogue took place between an adult and an African American child in a New York school.

The black boy enters a room where there is a large, friendly white interviewer, who puts an object on the table in front of the boy and says, 'Tell me everything you can about this.' (The interviewer's further remarks are in round brackets.)

[12 seconds of silence]
(What would you say it looks like?)
[8 seconds of silence]
A space ship.
(Hmmmm.)
[13 seconds of silence]
Like a je-et.
[12 seconds of silence]
Like a plane.
[20 seconds of silence]
(What colour is it?)
Orange. *[2 seconds]* An' wh-ite. *[2 seconds]* An' green.
[6 seconds of silence]
(An' what could you use it for?)
[8 seconds of silence]
A je-et.
[6 seconds of silence]
(If you had two of them, what would you do with them?)
[6 seconds of silence]

Give one to some-body.
(Hmmm. Who do you think would like to have it?)
[10 seconds of silence]
Cla-rence.
(Mm. Where do you think we could get another one of these?)
At the store.
(Oh ka-ay!)

Can you suggest any reasons for the child's monosyllabic responses?

Answer at end of chapter

Example 15

Fifteen-year-old Alan was totally disgusted with his English teacher. 'She's not interested in our ideas', he said, 'or whether we are original or creative. All she cares about is big words! The guy who gets top marks uses a thesaurus. He just looks up the longest words he can find and sticks them in. He doesn't even know what they mean half the time!'

At secondary level (students aged 11 and above), sociolinguists have explored more specifically the ways in which the vocabulary range of middle-class children differs from that of working-class children. Through wide reading of the kinds of books that teachers approve of, and exposure to the vocabulary of well-educated adults, some children are more familiar than others with words of Graeco-Latin origin. These words – words like *education*, *exponent*, *relation* and *expression* – make up between 65 per cent and 100 per cent of the specialist vocabularies of subjects taught in secondary schools and tertiary institutions. Obviously children who are familiar with such words will be at an advantage. One study showed that between the ages of 12 and 15 massive differences developed in the oral use of such words by children from different social backgrounds.

Children who use words of Graeco-Latin origin with familiarity and confidence are clearly more likely to succeed in exams which require knowledge of such vocabulary in particular subject areas. Children from homes where adults don't read for entertainment, and where reading is not a normal everyday activity, tend to develop a different range of vocabulary – one which is of great value in many spheres of their daily lives, but of little relevance in understanding the materials they meet in secondary school textbooks.

One reason why working-class children fail in school, then, is that the odds are stacked against them. The criteria for success are middle-class criteria – including middle-class language and ways of interacting. Familiarity with the vocabulary essential to school success gives middle-class children an advantage. A second reason identified by socio-linguists is that many of the children, recognising that schools are essentially middle-class institutions, deliberately and understandably rebel against all that they represent. One very dramatic piece of evidence of this was provided by a study of male adolescent gangs in New York. The gang members were failing in school, yet many were bright, verbally skilled young men. To maintain a position as a gang leader in the Harlem district of New York, for instance, requires a quick wit and considerable verbal facility. They could trade insults with ease and respond quickly and wittily to verbal challenges. There was little doubt about their oral language abilities. Yet most of these teenage boys were three or more years behind in their reading levels, and none had a reading score above the norm for an 11-year-old. What was more, the higher their status in the gang, the lower was their reading score. The reasons are complicated, but the most basic and important one was that they did not share the school's ideas of what was worth knowing. They did not identify with the school's values, and they knew that the school did not recognise their skills and values. They felt they had been defined as outsiders from the beginning, and saw no point in conforming since there was no chance of success.

Structural differences between standard and vernacular varieties may lead to inaccur-ate assessments of children's educational potential. Differences between groups in their perceptions of the appropriate ways of talking in a variety of contexts may also lead to inaccurate evaluations of children's ability. Sociolinguists have used the information described in this book about the relationships between language and its users, and lan-guage and its uses, in order to identify the misconceptions which can disadvantage some social and ethnic groups in school.

Exercise 8

One sociolinguistic study of an African American working-class community showed that the verbal skills expected of boys and girls differ considerably. Both learn how to deal with 'analogy' questions asked by their elders. These encourage them to see parallels and connections among disparate events and to tell about them cleverly without spelling out explicitly what the links are. Allusiveness is valued, rather than explicitness, and the resulting style has been described as 'topic-associating'. Boys, however, are also encouraged to practise story-telling in competitive public arenas where adults as well as children watch and judge. How might these different cultural experiences affect the success of the children in school?

Answer at end of chapter

◼ Conclusion

This chapter has described a range of attitudes to languages and varieties of language, as well as some of the social and educational implications of such attitudes. The lin-guistic varieties of different groups and their sociolinguistic rules, or appropriate ways of speaking in different contexts, may be quite distinctive. Sociolinguistic information on the social basis of attitudes to these varieties and their uses helps explain why children from lower socio-economic groups and children from minority cultural backgrounds often do not succeed in middle-class classrooms. Sociolinguistic research can assist in identifying points of potential conflict, and suggesting alternative styles of interaction which may be more successful.

There has been space in this chapter to explore only a very small range of examples, specifically in the field of educational linguistics, where the implications and applications of sociolinguistic study may be beneficial. Reflecting on the sociolinguistic variation described in previous chapters you will be able to think of many more implications and applications of sociolinguistic research. Language planning, for example, discussed in chapter 5, is an obvious area of applied sociolinguistics. Second language learning is another area where sociolinguistic information on patterns of language use and attitudes to language has proved valuable. Sociolinguistic information can usefully illuminate many everyday interactions in a speech community. In the concluding chapter I will attempt to draw together some of the many interesting linguistic patterns which characterise the users and uses of language which have emerged in the discussion in previous chapters.

ANSWERS TO EXERCISES IN CHAPTER 15

Answer to exercise 1

One method which has been used to investigate this question is to play a range of tape-recorded speakers of different languages to a group of listeners. The listeners' reactions to languages and dialects that are familiar to them are then compared with their reactions to languages which are unfamiliar.

Using this method, it has been found that responses to a familiar language form a pattern. The pattern reflects the prestige of the speakers of the language in the community whose views are being sought. Responses to unfamiliar dialects and languages, however, form no pattern and are randomly distributed. The same is true for accents. For example, Cockney was rated tenth in a list of 10 accents played to British listeners, while it was rated third by American listeners to whom it was much less familiar. These results provide support for the claim that listeners' responses are strongly influenced by non-linguistic factors.

Answer to exercise 2

The local accent is likely to be less highly rated than the standard accent, especially by older listeners, and especially on the 'status' related features such as confidence, ambition, intelligence, leadership skills, high education and high-status job. Local accents generally gain higher ratings on solidarity related features such as sincerity, friendliness, reliability and sense of humour, and from young people.

Whatever reactions you collect, you should be able to explain them by considering social influences on people's attitudes to accents, and by taking account of the concepts of overt and covert prestige.

Answer to exercise 5

As pointed out in the preceding section, even the most well-educated speaker uses some verna-cular forms on some occasions in some contexts, so there can be no argument for the inherent superiority of standard forms for educational purposes. Conversely if a speaker can produce a standard form – even if they do not do so consistently – the argument for educational deficit based on ignorance of that form cannot hold water. Claims about the educational disadvantages of some varieties reflect attitudes to the users and functions of those varieties in context, rather than any intrinsic features of the varieties. This issue is discussed in more detail in the next section.

Answer to exercise 6

It has been suggested by some sociolinguists that schools should not identify their task in the language section of the curriculum as teaching standard forms to children who do not use them. Rather, they suggest, the teacher's task is to provide children with the means to challenge the attitudes which discriminate against their speech forms. Since there is no linguistic basis for these negative attitudes, it is argued that schools should empower children and give them the con-fidence to assert the validity of their language and the skills needed to expose the insubstantial nature of the criticisms made of vernacular forms.

On the other hand, others argue that the standard dialect is necessary for social advancement and for communicating effectively with a wider audience, at least in writing. Moreover, they claim, it is essential to use standard forms in order to be taken seriously in many social contexts, spoken and written.

Where do you stand in this debate?

Answer to exercise 7

There are many possible reasons for the child's responses. He may be unwilling to talk freely to an adult from a different ethnic group and social class. He may be frightened in a situation which he experiences as a testing situation. He may feel resentful and uncooperative in testing situations where his previous experience has been that he does not do well. He may find it diffi-cult to work out what answers are required. He may consider the questions so obvious that he suspects they are trick questions, and therefore feel uncomfortable and suspicious. Some of these possibilities are elaborated in the next section.

Note Labov's comment on this interview: 'The child is in an asymmetrical situation where anything he says can literally be held against him. He has learned a number of devices to avoid saying anything in this situation, and he works very hard to achieve this end.'

Answer to exercise 8

The boys' experience of story-telling stands them in good stead in white middle-class schools. They respond to requests to tell the teacher about an experience with a topic-focussed narrative which is accepted as a story. The teacher accepts their stories and helps develop them.

The girls have not had this kind of experience, however, and their stories tend to resemble children's responses to 'analogy' questions in their community. They draw parallels between events which have no obvious connection and expect the listener to draw out the links. But schools value explicitness, and the girls' allusive accounts of their experiences often make no sense to white middle-class teachers. The teachers think the girls are incapable of sticking to the point and constructing a coherent story. By identifying these differences in the background experiences of the children, the sociolinguist was able to account for the differences in their performance in school, and recommend ways of helping the working-class African American girls develop narrative skills.

▉ Concepts introduced

Language attitudes
Overt and covert prestige
Matched guise technique
Ebonics
Attitude methodology
Educational disadvantage

▉ References

The following sources provided material or ideas for this chapter:

Aghcyisi and Fishman (1970) on methods of collecting attitude data, and especially commitment measures.
Andrzejewski (1963) on Somali
Baker (1992)
Bayard (1990), and Bayard and Weatherall (1999) on attitudes to New Zealand English
Bourhis (1983) on Quebec
Burton (1976) on classroom discourse
Cargile et al. (2006) on attitudes to AAVE in Japan
Corson (1985) on social class and vocabulary
Crystal (1997) on Somali
Edwards (1982) on ratings of RP
Edwards, V. (1978, 1985) on attitudes to Patois
Gardner (1985) on matched guise technique
Gordon and Abell (1990) on attitudes to New Zealand English
Haugen (1966c) on attitudes to Scandinavian languages
Hirst (1974) on Graeco-Latin vocabulary
Labov (1966) on attitudes to New York speech
Labov (1972c, 1972d) on New York adolescents' speech
Ladegaard (2000) on methods of collecting attitude data
Lane (2003) on Letters to the Editor about the Maori language
Lippi-Green (1997) on attitudes to African American Vernacular English
Michaels (1981) on African American children's narrative styles
Millar (1989) on elocution lessons in Ireland
Milroy (1984) on inter-dialectal comprehension
Stubbs (1983) on classroom interaction and educational linguistics
Trudgill (1972, 1975) on attitudes to vernacular varieties of English
Trudgill and Giles (1977) on attitudes to languages, and aesthetics
Wolfram and Schilling-Estes (1998) on Ebonics

▉ Quotations

Example 1 is from the *New Zealand Listener* 1985.
Example 2 is based on Haugen (1966c: 292).

C

Language variation: focus on uses

Example 3 is based on Millar (1989).

Example 4 is from Labov (1966: 329).

Example 6(a) is from an article by the Secretary of State for Education in *The Times*, 7/11/86.

Example 6(b) is from an Editorial in *The Times*, 30/4/88.

Example 7 is from *The Triad* 1912 quoted in Gordon and Deverson (1989: 30).

Example 8 is from Lippi-Green (1997: 180).

Example 9. The list is from Wolfram and Schilling-Estes (1998: 14).

Example 10 is from Lippi-Green (1997: 186).

Example 11 is from an article by John Rae in *The Observer* (a British newspaper) cited in Cameron and Bourne (1989: 11).

Example 12 is based on material in Labov (1982).

In example 13, the sentences are from Labov (1972b).

Example 14 is adapted from Burton (1976: 30–1).

Exercise 7: the excerpt is from Labov (1972c: 184–5)

Exercise 8 is based on Hawkins (1967–68).

New York speech as 'incontrovertibly dumb': New Zealand newspaper *Dominion*, 6/11/89, p. 8.

Useful additional reading

Bauer and Trudgill (1998)

Coupland and Jaworski (1997), Part V

Downes (1998), Ch. 7

Labov (1972c, 1982)

Lippi-Green (1997)

Mesthrie et al. (2000), Ch. 11

Meyerhoff (2006) Ch. 4

Romaine (2000), Ch. 7

Saville-Troike (2003), Chs 5 and 6

Stubbs (1983)

Web-site on Ebonics: www.cal.org/ebonics/

16 Conclusion

In this final chapter I will draw together some of the themes that have run through this book. In doing this I will first discuss the notion of sociolinguistic competence – what is involved in knowing how to use language appropriately? Almost every chapter has illustrated some aspect of sociolinguistic competence, so this concept provides a useful means of reviewing the material covered.

I will then use the social scales or dimensions of analysis introduced in chapter 1, and referred to throughout the book, in order to highlight their importance in accounting for patterns of language use in different communities. Status and solidarity have repeatedly proved fundamental social dimensions in sociolinguistic analysis, though the emphasis differs in different communities according to factors such as the fluidity of group boundaries. Formality and function are equally useful concepts for illuminating linguistic variation in different speech communities. The demonstrable value of these dimensions in sociolinguistic analysis suggests they may prove universally relevant sociolinguistic tools of analysis.

The data reviewed in this book has demonstrated the rich diversity of language behaviour in different contexts and communities. The same basic components have produced myriads of linguistic mosaics throughout the world. As well as describing this variation, sociolinguists, like others who seek to understand human behaviour, also search for generalisations that reveal common human responses to particular social influences. In the final section of this chapter, I will give examples of possible sociolinguistic universals or generalisations.

SOCIOLINGUISTIC COMPETENCE

When the term linguistic competence was first proposed by Noam Chomsky, it provoked a strong reaction from one of the leading sociolinguists of the time, Dell Hymes. Chomsky defined linguistic competence as the knowledge of language of 'the ideal speaker-hearer in a completely homogeneous speech community'. Hymes argued that this idealisation was so far from the reality of most of the world's experience as to be unhelpful. From a sociolinguist's perspective, the challenge was to account for the knowledge that enabled people to use language appropriately in a range of diverse social contexts. Using language appropriately involves knowing the sociolinguistic rules for speaking in a community. It means understanding the influence of social factors on speech behaviour – which is what this book has been about. Each chapter has illustrated a different aspect of the many and varied types of knowledge which people in different communities acquire when they learn to use language appropriately in their own community. The knowledge which underlies people's ability to use language appropriately is known as their *sociolinguistic competence*.

In the first section of the book the focus was on multilingual communities. Choosing the appropriate variety or code to use in such communities involves choosing from distinctly different languages, as well as styles within a language. In multilingual communities children generally learn their ethnic language first, and later add other languages for purposes such as education, and for communication with a wider range of people in a wider range of contexts. So children gradually develop a linguistic repertoire of the linguistic codes or varieties which are appropriate in different domains in their speech communities. In Zaire, for example, as described in chapter 2, Kalala acquired standard Zairean Swahili in school, and Kingwana for communication in the market-place. The ways in which individuals exploit their linguistic repertoires by switching between different varieties can be observed particularly clearly in multilingual communities, because the varieties being switched are often distinct languages. Some of the many social meanings that can be conveyed by code-switching in multilingual communities were illustrated in the first section of the book.

The linguistic repertoire of different generations may differ. This is particularly apparent in communities where language shift is in progress. The sociolinguistic competence of an immigrant's granddaughter, for example, will usually differ markedly from that of her grandfather, as we saw in chapter 3. She may have lost the ethnic language, while developing a wider range of styles in the language of the new community. Alternatively she may have retained the ethnic language, but only for use in one or two domains. Young British Portuguese may use Portuguese only in the home and at church, for example. English will be appropriate in all other domains. There are many different social factors which contribute to the relative speed of language shift, and different factors are relevant in different communities.

The relative status and functions of different languages in multilingual communities were examined in chapters 4 and 5. Vernacular languages are the first languages people learn and in many multilingual communities the number of people who speak a particular vernacular is relatively small. A language of wider communication or lingua franca is often an essential addition to a person's repertoire. Kalala would not have got far in Bukavu with his vernacular, Shi. He needed the local variety of Swahili, Kingwana, as a lingua franca. Vernacular languages contrast with lingua francas in many ways which reflect their different functions for speakers. For the same reasons they differ from standard languages too. The factors which result in the promotion of a particular variety to the status of standard are social rather than linguistic. But, as a result, members of a speech community generally need to acquire some familiarity with a standard language as part of their sociolinguistic competence. A vernacular may be unwritten, for instance, whereas a standard will generally have a writing system. Standard languages also have more status and are used more widely than vernaculars, so there are obvious advantages to learning them. As a result of colonial expansion, and subsequent political and economic expansion, English has become a particularly widespread and influential lingua franca – an international or global language. It now serves many varied functions in different countries and takes diverse forms.

Pidgin and creole languages, which are also discussed in chapter 4, develop initially as lingua francas. Pidgins are never the only language in an individual's linguistic repertoire. They serve as a means of communication between people who don't share any variety with each other. Creoles by contrast are first languages for some individuals. Haitian Creole is not only the first language, it is the only language of most Haitians. Learning how to use a creole appropriately is as complex a task as acquiring sociolinguistic competence in any other language.

The final chapter of the first section looks at the status of languages from a macro level, rather than from the individual's point of view. National and official languages are defined in relation to states rather than social groups or individuals. They develop or are developed to serve the needs of governments and nations. Swahili in Tanzania, Hebrew in Israel, Mandarin Chinese in China and standard Norwegian in Norway are all examples of varieties which have been consciously developed to serve the many functions of the official language of their countries. The process of developing languages for such high-level functions is one of the activities of language planners, as also illustrated in chapter 5.

In the second section of the book the focus was on variation in monolingual communities. Just as the particular configuration of a person's linguistic repertoire in a multilingual community indicates their social and regional affiliations, so the range of dialects and styles used by monolinguals tells the same story. Sociolinguistic competence in a monolingual community includes learning to use the community language in a way which signals one's membership of various overlapping social groups, and enacts a range of social identities. You belong to a particular social group – whether you define it in terms of class or caste or simply group. You also live in a particular region. It is possible that both these factors are evident in your speech, but the first will almost certainly be indicated linguistically. If you live in a monolingual community, the social group to which you belong may be indicated by your pronunciation, by your grammar, or by your vocabulary – or by all of these.

You will almost certainly also indicate your gender in some aspects of the way you speak, as well as whether you are a child or an adult. We unconsciously acquire as part of our sociolinguistic competence the linguistic features which convey these social messages in our own speech community. We learn how to speak appropriately for our gender and age group, and to actively construct our social identities. Swearing and slang can be crucial indicators of group membership, for example. Ethnicity can also be signalled by the way essentially monolingual people of different ethnic backgrounds use their language. So, for instance, there are a range of linguistic features which serve as ethnic signals in English-speaking communities. A young British Black woman from

C

Language variation: focus on uses

433

the Midlands speaks differently from her white middle-class teachers. Her speech signals her ethnic identity as well as indicating her gender, age, and social background. Ethnic linguistic tags are obvious signals, but ethnicity is also often signalled by the frequency of occurrence of particular vernacular forms. We tend to notice only the ethnic markers of those who belong to minorities. The majority ethnic group is treated as the norm against which others are described. Obviously, however, the absence of specific markers of ethnicity also conveys information about a speaker's ethnic group affiliation.

We all belong to overlapping social groups. We are concurrently members of a social, an ethnic, and a regional group as well as members of a particular gender and age group. Clearly these groups do not coincide. Your particular way of speaking is constructed, mainly unconsciously, from choices among all these different possibilities. And another important factor is who you talk to. The people you interact with most often may also influence your speech – your social network of regular contacts will therefore indicate the potential range of linguistic influences on your speech. Which of these contacts actually has most effect on your speech is often best explained by referring to the social dimensions of solidarity and status, which are discussed below.

Like chapter 5 in the first section, chapter 9 at the end of section B moves away from the speech behaviour of small groups and individuals to take a broader view by focussing on language change. This chapter draws on the patterns described in the preceding chapters in order to explore the contribution of social factors to language change in a community. Linguistic change is always embedded in variation. But which variation will lead to change and which will remain stable over time? Where do changes begin? Who leads linguistic change? How do changes proceed through a community? The processes by which a particular change spreads reflect patterns of social contact. You learn the current slang from a friend who learnt it from another friend outside your group. You adopt new pronunciations, often unconsciously, in order to sound more like those you have heard using them. In established speech communities, the reasons for the successful spread of one change compared to others are predominantly social and attitudinal.

The third section of the book focussed on the uses of language rather than its users. While the second section explored the influence of features of *speakers* on the language varieties they used, in the third section the influence of other aspects of the situation on the form of language is discussed. Features of the different speech styles that people use in socially distinct situations are explored in chapter 10, for instance. Using language appropriately involves learning to take account of who you are talking to. Knowing how to speak or write to a child, for instance, as opposed to an elderly relative, or to a stranger compared to a friend – these all involve this aspect of sociolinguistic competence. The setting itself and the purpose of an interaction are further factors which influence speech style – how formal is it, for instance, or how relaxed? Uncontracted forms such as *was not* and *has not* are typical of more formal speech styles while *wasn't* and *hasn't* tend to occur in less formal speech.

Is the interaction aimed at a specialised audience or not? Sociolinguistic competence includes knowing when to speak and when to be silent, for example. So children

434

(eventually!) learn to be silent during the sermon in church, but to join in chorused responses to prayers. For some speakers, sociolinguistic competence includes knowing how to speak appropriately in a formal context such as a law court, or how to describe a cricket match for the benefit of radio listeners. The way the specialised features of such registers are moulded by their function is exemplified in chapter 10.

Sociolinguistic competence also involves knowing how to use language for different functions, such as getting things done in different contexts. The ability to use language effectively and politely to different people is important. Ways in which people demonstrate such knowledge are illustrated in chapter 11. When people from different social groups or cultures meet, their sociolinguistic norms may conflict. The result may be embarrassment or misunderstanding. Learning a foreign language in a Western classroom, for example, often seems at first to be a matter of learning the vocabulary and grammar from a book, and struggling to imitate the pronunciation of the teacher in class. But the concept of sociolinguistic competence makes it clear that much more is involved than control of the linguistic structures. Even at the early stages of learning French it is evident that social factors are relevant too. When do you use *tu* and when *vous* for instance? Who is addressed as *Madame* and who *Mademoiselle*? Learning to speak appropriately in a range of contexts is important if one wants to avoid giving offence, reducing everyone to hysterical laughter, or embarrassing others by a socio-linguistic *faux pas*.

Acquiring sociolinguistic competence in another language may be a slow and difficult process, since it involves understanding the social values that underlie the community's ways of using language. Many rules for polite interaction depend on an understanding of the social distance norms of the community. It is considered rude to say only *allo, allo* when answering the telephone in a French-speaking culture. You also need to state who you are, so the caller can 'place' you appropriately. Greeks hardly ever apologise for ringing a friend, assuming their call is a welcome token of friendship, while English people often begin with 'I hope I'm not disturbing you', reflecting a view of phone calls as intrusions, which require a negative politeness strategy in mitigation. Being polite in another language is not just a matter of using a perfect native accent and correct grammar. It also involves knowing the relative weight that the community puts on different kinds of social relationships, and how this is appropriately expressed.

Gender is another relevant factor in accounting for patterns of language use. In the middle section of the book we saw that in many communities men used more vernacular forms than women. Vernacular forms consequently index masculinity in many communities. In chapter 12, the different ways in which women and men use language in interaction are explored. Acquiring sociolinguistic competence involves recognising the different ways in which women and men interact in a community (even if one might wish to change them!). The widely held stereotype of women as unconfident speakers is challenged by a view that focusses on the politeness function of many features of women's usage. Does women's talk reflect their subordinate social position? Or do women and men unconsciously collude in the social construction of a less powerful and assertive gender identity for women than for men? A social constructionist approach provides a more dynamic way of analysing social interaction, and also draws attention to opportunities to challenge and change existing interaction patterns.

From this perspective, acquiring sociolinguistic competence is not simply a matter of absorbing appropriate rules of interaction by socialising with one's peers. The social construction of females and males is a society-wide activity, beginning with the important gender label assigned at birth, and continuing with messages about appropriately gendered ways of presenting oneself throughout one's life. Constructing an appropriate gender identity is largely an unconscious process acquired in peer group interaction as one grows. But the wider social context in which it takes place provides clues about the way society expects females and males to behave. In many communities, girls develop ways of speaking which are appropriate to second-class citizens.

There is little doubt that many English-speaking societies treat women as a group in this way, as an examination of sexist language reveals. Sexist language constructs and reinforces negative stereotypes of women, as illustrated in the last section of chapter 12 and the beginning of chapter 13. A community's attitudes to different groups are reflected in the linguistic categories which have developed over time to label those groups. As children learn the language they absorb the value judgements and affective messages as well as the referential meanings of words. Those who wish to challenge the messages must recognise their relationships to the wider societal evaluation of these groups. Changing the language is a consciousness-raising exercise which may assist in the more important and fundamental task of changing the status of oppressed groups.

Language constructs social reality. If medical textbooks represent patients as helpless, ignorant, and problematic, then the doctors who use them are likely to absorb these attitudes and behave in ways which reinforce them. They will be patronising to their patients. Chapter 13 explores the relationship between language, thought and culture, and the issue of the extent to which learning a language also involves acquiring a particular world-view. Can we escape the linguistic lenses provided by our language? Labels such as *queer* and *coconut* encode social prejudices which children absorb with the language. And while resistance is possible, it takes considerable effort to challenge and alter well-established attitudes and habitual linguistic behaviours.

If language influences cognition, children acquiring languages which make particular semantic distinctions may learn to count more quickly, or to distinguish colours or shapes more speedily than those learning different languages. If we can be influenced by sexist and racist terminology, then perhaps the structural categories provided by our language also influence our perceptions of space and time. These issues are discussed in chapter 13, as well as the influence of the environment on the language of those who occupy it. The precise balance between the influence of language on perceptions of 'reality', as opposed to the influence of 'reality' on the categories developed by language, will doubtless continue to generate debate for many more centuries. The issues involved are seen most starkly when radically different cultures come into contact. The world-views of Native Americans and Aboriginal Australians, for example, are often difficult for Westerners to comprehend. It is not surprising, then, that culturally

436

different patterns of interaction expressing different views of social relationships, rights and obligations, result in cultural clashes and miscommunication. Inevitably, it is members of the minority culture who suffer when this happens. Where cultural and social values differ, the perspective of the majority tends to define social 'reality', as chapter 13 illustrates.

Chapter 14 focusses on a specific aspect of sociolinguistic competence, our ability to manage discourse in a range of social contexts. How do we know when to respond to an insult with laughter as opposed to outrage? How do we identify the complex meanings conveyed by an indirect response such as *I am a bit tired* to a direct question such as *do you want to come to a movie tonight?* How do we know when and how much small talk to use at work, and what topics are acceptable? How do we know when *come and see me tomorrow* is an invitation as opposed to a summons? Interpreting the social meaning conveyed by talk-in-interaction, and encoding social meaning appropriately in different social contexts, are aspects of *socio-pragmatic competence*. Discourse analysis provides a way of studying this aspect of competence.

There are many different approaches to the analysis of discourse. Chapter 14 illustrates five, each of which analyses discourse from a slightly different angle. From a sociolinguistic perspective, pragmatics provides useful insights into the different ways that politeness is encoded in discourse in different socio-cultural contexts. So, pragmatic principles account for how it is possible to infer that someone is politely asking for a lift when they say *Damn I just missed my bus.* In some cultures people are expected to explicitly express their concern and interest in other people, while in other cultures such behaviour is considered intrusive. Knowing whether to invite someone into your home for a meal, how often to telephone, when to apologise and for what – these are all aspects of socio-pragmatic competence.

The ethnography of speaking framework provides a means of describing communicative events in any culture. For formal events the rules are sometimes made explicit, e.g. who may talk, in what order, about what topics, and for how long. But we acquire knowledge of the rules for less formal interactions as we grow up in a community, e.g. when to talk in school and when to keep quiet, how much talk to contribute as a dinner guest, how quickly to respond to an email from your lecturer, whether it is OK not to use your Skype camera if the other person has their camera on.

The ability to accurately interpret the social significance of what is going on is another aspect of our socio-pragmatic competence. We learn to 'read' the underlying social meaning of utterances and to make inferences about what someone 'really' means. New pupils in school, especially those from minority ethnic backgrounds, sometimes miss the point of teachers' utterances. They take literally questions which are intended as reprimands, such as *are you talking? is that Mary I see sitting on the windowsill?* And they fail to recognise *door* as an instruction to open the door for the teacher. Interactional sociolinguistics provides a way of identifying the contextualisation cues that we use to interpret the social meanings conveyed by talk in interaction.

New ways of interacting highlight the old communicative rules we use without reflection. Concepts such as adjacency pairs emphasise the fact that greetings and farewells,

437

questions and answers, are typically paired sets of utterances in many contexts. But how do these patterns work out with sms texting or real-time on-line chats using an internet messaging service? Do the rules of written communication take over? People often dispense with greetings and 'sign offs' when sending text messages. Text messages are typically minimal in content, more like the old-fashioned telegram than a letter. Feedback in simultaneous on-line internet messaging or chat room interaction is often delayed in time, and thus does not always occur in the 'correct' sequence on screen. Conversation analysis provides tools for describing what is going on as new rules or norms of inter-action emerge with the development of these new genres.

I recently sent an email to a colleague, Marion, asking *could you come and see me tomorrow about 10.30?* She replied very quickly saying *yes sure.* A couple of hours later I received another email saying *In my last three institutions if the boss asked to see you then you were in trouble, I'm not in trouble am I?* Marion was certainly not in trouble. I just needed to discuss a complicated problem that I thought she could help with. But this email exchange highlights the potential for miscommunication on the basis of assumptions and inferences we all make in interaction. I had not thought of myself as Marion's 'boss', although I was manager of the unit in which she worked. Having worked in much more hierarchical organisations, she 'read' my email as a threatening summons. The ways in which power is encoded in discourse are often subtle. In this case, reflecting on the encounter I realised that by not telling Marion the reason for the meeting, I was putting her at a disadvantage. Note too that she was required to come to my room rather than the other way round. The different approaches to discourse analysis in chapter 14 provide ways to unpack the socio-pragmatic and socio-cultural assumptions which underlie different interpretations of messages.

Chapter 15 extends the discussion of the relevance of concepts such as power and status in sociolinguistics in relation to language attitudes in particular. Children absorb attitudes from their peers and families as they grow up. The attitudes people hold towards different languages or accents are part of their sociolinguistic competence. These attitudes do not reflect any intrinsic linguistic merits or deficiencies of the lin-guistic varieties concerned. Rather they reflect the social status of those who use the varieties, or the contexts in which the varieties are customarily used. The language of the highest status group in a community is generally overtly admired and recognised as a model by the whole community. Being able to recognise the prestige variety is part of a person's sociolinguistic competence, even though they may not choose to use that variety themselves.

All members of a community need to be able to understand the standard dialect. All should have the option of producing it too, if they choose to do so. Most people acquire control of the standard variety in school, at least for written purposes. Those who do not do so may suffer the educational implications of negative attitudes to vernacular speech varieties. There is some discussion in chapter 15 of the mistaken bases for the widespread negative judgements which label as educational failures many children who speak vernacular varieties, or who use language in ways which differ from the approved norms of the middle-class school.

Using the concept of sociolinguistic competence I have reviewed the material covered in the book in a linear progression which has emphasised the links between different chapters. In the next section I will briefly show how the social scales or dimensions, introduced in chapter 1, provide another thread throughout the book.

DIMENSIONS OF SOCIOLINGUISTIC ANALYSIS

Sociolinguists are interested in identifying ways of describing and explaining the relationship between language and the social context in which it is used. In this book it has become clear that there are a number of concepts which have repeatedly proved useful in accounting for the patterns found in a wide range of societies. In particular I have made use of the following scales or dimensions introduced in chapter 1:

1. social distance/solidarity
2. status/power
3. formality
4. function – affective and referential.

Example 1

Two little Maori girls are playing 'school' in the classroom during the lunch-break. Mere is the teacher and Hine the pupil. Mere has written on the board 'It is ten o'clock. Time for work.' A little boy, Tama, puts his head in the door.
Tama: Where's Mrs McLean?
Mere: Dunno. She not here.
Tama: You sure?
Hine: Mrs McLean not here dummy!
Mere: Mrs McLean isn't around today.
[*Tama leaves at this point and Mere continues with her lesson.*]
Mere: Now Hine. You copy this carefully.
Hine: Yes Miss. I am.

This example shows Mere and Hine code-switching between standard and vernacular forms of English for a variety of reasons. Sometimes they use standard utterances with forms of the verb *be*, and sometimes they don't. As teacher, Mere uses *is*, a form of the verb *be*, in her writing on the board. As pupil, Hine uses *am*, another form of *be*, in her final reply. Both switch to utterances without *be* in addressing Tama. However, when Tama questions her response, Mere switches to standard English to emphasise what she is saying, while Hine resorts to friendly abuse!

Mere and Hine know both the standard and the vernacular forms, and they choose which to use. They choose according to the influence of the sociolinguistic dimensions

C

Language variation: focus on uses

of solidarity, status, formality and function. In the formal classroom situation acting as teacher and pupil, standard forms are appropriate (reflecting the formality and status/power dimensions). To a fellow Maori pupil, vernacular forms are appropriate (signalling solidarity). For emphasis, a switch to the standard is effective (exploiting the affective function or dimension of meaning). In the 1920s, the same social messages may have been conveyed by switching between Maori and English in these circumstances. Maori would have expressed solidarity, while English would have expressed formality and superior status.

Solidarity/social distance

The solidarity dimension has proved relevant in accounting for patterns of linguistic interaction throughout the book. How well you know someone is one of the most important factors affecting the way you talk to them. The choice between regional dialect and standard Norwegian in Norway, or between German and Italian in Sauris, or *Meg* vs *Mrs Billington* in London, may simply reflect the degree of solidarity between the speaker and addressee.

Vernacular languages are often used between people who share attitudes and values, and who may belong to the same ethnic group. In-group language is the language of solidarity. Two Paraguayans who meet in Paris will use Guaraní to signal their shared identity. Strangers with little in common are more likely to use a lingua franca or official language for communication. Vernacular forms within a language also occur more frequently in interactions where people know each other well. Standard forms often express social distance between participants. Certain speech styles are also used most often between intimates. In most cultures, positive politeness strategies are appropriate between those who know each other well, for example, or who wish to know each other better. But gossip would be inappropriate between strangers. Negative politeness strategies tend to characterise interactions between strangers – those who are socially distant.

Status/power

The status or power dimension also accounts for a variety of linguistic differences in the way people speak. You speak in a way which signals your social status and constructs your social identity in a community. Those at the top in multilingual communities usually have the widest linguistic repertoire, and they certainly speak the official language. In a monolingual community, the higher your social group, the more standard forms you are likely to use. The language of the most prestigious group is by definition the standard dialect.

The way you talk to others also signals your relationship on this dimension. Where people use non-reciprocal address forms, for instance, the reason is generally due to a status or power difference. If you call someone *Sir* and he calls you *Chris*, then he is your superior in some context. The subordinate status of women is often reflected in the non-reciprocal use of address forms. The butcher may use *dear* to his women customers, for instance, but they do not call him *dear* and he is not likely to use *dear* to the men working on the road outside. Power or status differences also explain the greater use of negative politeness forms by some speakers. You will probably use a less direct form when asking your boss for a lift, for example, than when asking your sister.

Formality

The formality dimension accounts for speech variation in different settings or contexts. The H variety in a diglossia situation is the variety used in more formal situations. Classical Arabic is not used in everyday talk. In Haiti, the L language, Haitian Creole, is the language of relaxed informal situations. Official languages are the appropriate varieties for formal government interactions and state occasions. Vernaculars are the languages of informal interaction. In monolingual communities, vernacular forms predominate in casual talk, while standard forms are more frequent in situations such as a formal interview with the school principal or the bank manager. Formal settings such as law courts, the House of Assembly or Parliament, a graduation ceremony, or a retirement dinner will require appropriate language. Formal styles of speech with distinctive pronunciation, syntax and vocabulary are the linguistic equivalent of formal dress on such occasions. Though status and solidarity are usually very important influences on appropriate language choice, the formality of the setting or speech event can sometimes override them. In court, even sisters will call each other by their formal titles, and at a wedding ceremony the language of the bride and groom is determined by the ritual occasion, not by the closeness of their relationship.

Different communities put different degrees of weight on solidarity vs status, and formality vs casualness. In a conservative, status-based community, where differences are emphasised, interactions with acquaintances may be relatively formal. In groups where friendship or how well you know someone tends to override status differences, similarities are stressed, and interactions tend towards the informal in many contexts. A group of elderly Indian upper-caste men might represent one extreme, while a group of lower-class American teenagers might represent the other.

Function

The function of an interaction can also be an important influence on its linguistic form, as we have seen throughout the book. Some interactions, such as news bulletins, sports commentaries and legal documents, are high in information content, or referential meaning. Their linguistic features are strongly influenced by the kind of information they need to convey, and the constraints of time and setting they are responding to. In other interactions, such as friendly gossip, the social or affective message may be the most important reason for the interaction. This too affects the form of the language.

Pidgin languages develop for primarily referential functions. As a result the linguistic forms found in pidgin languages are not elaborated in ways which could serve to convey social information. They are simple and minimal. The speakers have other

C

Language variation: focus on uses

441

varieties which they use with their friends for social and affective functions and to construct their social identities. People do not generally use pidgins to convey their social status, nor how much they like the addressee. Where variation develops, however, these are precisely the kinds of functions it serves. For example, it is possible to convey warmth and affection in the H variety or using standard dialect forms, but it is more often the case that people use L varieties and vernacular forms for this purpose. Similarly, while referential information can certainly be conveyed in any language or dialect, in practice, the H variety or standard dialect tends to be regarded as the most appropriate way of expressing primarily informative material, particularly for a wide audience, and especially when the information is in written form.

Language serves many functions, but in all communities the basic functions of referential and affective (or social) meaning have proved useful dimensions of analysis. Every language provides means of expressing social as well as referential meaning, and the choice between alternative ways of saying the 'same' thing frequently involves a consideration of these dimensions. Though referentially equivalent, *Oh it's you!* conveys a very different affective message from *How lovely to see you, do come in!* when you open the door to someone. It has been suggested that, at least in casual interaction, some women stress the affective rather than the referential function of talk. If this is so, the possibilities for miscommunication with those who have different norms are obvious. Similarly, different cultural groups may emphasise affective functions in contexts where others consider referential information is the primary focus. A short welcoming greeting to parents at a school meeting, for instance, may strike some groups as too perfunctory, and as indicating that the school does not value their presence. For others, a short greeting may be considered as sensible. It 'dispenses with formalities' and enables the meeting to get down to business with minimal delay.

These four dimensions thus prove valuable in analysing the range of sociolinguistic variation in many different types of speech communities and different contexts. As I suggested above, they seem to be universally useful sociolinguistic tools of analysis. In the final section of this chapter I will briefly exemplify the notion of sociolinguistic universals.

SOCIOLINGUISTIC UNIVERSALS

Sociolinguists look for general patterns in the relationship between language and society. They are interested in identifying and explaining common trends in the ways social factors account for linguistic variation in different speech communities. The generalisations they seek could be described as sociolinguistic universal tendencies. At this stage, some will be obvious from the previous discussion. You may like to try formulating some yourself before reading on.

- All speech communities have linguistic means of distinguishing different social relationships; here solidarity and status are relevant dimensions of analysis.
- All speech communities have linguistic means of distinguishing different contextual styles; formality is here the relevant dimension of analysis.

- All speech communities have linguistic means of expressing basic speech functions: potential universals here are referential and affective functions, or at a greater level of specificity, those listed on page 271.
- In all speech communities language change implies language variation, with social variation an important contributing component.

These potential sociolinguistic universals are at a high level of generality, and have been illustrated throughout the book. Before closing, however, I will also provide examples of three more specific universals that sociolinguists have developed. They are testable hypotheses derived from fundamental sociolinguistic principles. The first is one which links the solidarity and status/power dimensions. The second links the status/power dimension to the formality dimension. The third universal involves considerations of the functions of language in relation to the solidarity and status/power dimensions.

Sociolinguistic universal 1

If a particular linguistic form, such as *tu* in French, or first name in English, is used reciprocally to express solidarity between people who know each other well, the same form will be used non-reciprocally by more powerful people to their subordinates to express superior status or power.

Sociolinguistic universal 2

If a particular pronunciation or grammatical feature, such as [*h*]-*dropping* or *be* omission, is used to express a shift in style, from formal to informal for instance, the same feature will be used to signal differences in social group membership.

Sociolinguistic universal 3

Linguistic forms expressing negative politeness will be used more frequently as social distance and status/power differences between people increase.

Making such generalisations explicit means they can more easily be tested against a range of data. Do they hold for your speech community, for example?

It is easy to illustrate the first generalisation. People in many English-speaking speech communities call those that they know well by their first names in all but the most formal contexts. They use title and last name, e.g. *Mrs Davidson, Dr Boyce*, to those they know less well (socially distant addressees). This pattern is generally reciprocal. But in situations where one person is more powerful or has more social status, we find a non-reciprocal pattern. The Director calls the office junior *Jim*, but she is called *Mrs Johnson* in reply.

This is an example of a generalisation which once applied widely but which appears to be involved in a process of change. As discussed in chapter 11, for some communities, including some in America, Australia and New Zealand, the fact that people know each

443

other well may override their status or power differences – especially if the difference is not a great one. Reciprocal usage may therefore be usual even between superior and subordinate when they have known each other for some time. So while these socio-linguistic generalisations involve fundamental social dimensions such as status and solidarity, the ways in which they interact, and especially the precise ways in which they are expressed or realised will change over time. The reasons for linguistic changes are often changes in the social values of the societies concerned. In this case, the old pattern reflected an emphasis on status differences. The new pattern indicates the increasing relevance of solidarity as a factor in relationships in Western societies.

Example 1 illustrates the second generalisation. The switch from using standard to vernacular forms of *be* is one feature of a switch from formal to informal style. Mere uses standard forms when she is acting in her role as teacher in a formal classroom setting, and this vernacular grammatical feature is also a feature which distinguishes different social groups. Those from higher socio-economic groups tend not to omit *be*, while those from lower status social groups omit it some of the time. This is a common pattern, as we saw in chapter 10. The linguistic features which signal higher status are those used in more formal or careful speech styles.

Again the generalisation must be treated with caution, however. There are some linguistic features which characterise different styles, but which do not necessarily distinguish different social groups. It seems unlikely that greater use of the passive, for instance, a feature which tends to characterise more formal styles of speech, will systematically distinguish between the speech of different social classes. The generalisation seems more likely to hold with respect to features of pronunciation and morphology than features of syntax. It is also less relevant where social distinctions are relatively rigid. So in Javanese, as we saw in chapters 6 and 10, the linguistic features which characterise distinct Javanese social dialects and reflect social caste membership are distinguishable from the features which mark different styles within each dialect.

The third generalisation relates negative politeness to social distance and status/power differences between people. Negative politeness is respectful and avoids imposing on the addressee. People who do not know each other well tend to use negative politeness forms to reduce the strength of directive speech acts, for instance. Subordinates similarly soften the impact of speech acts such as requests and disagreements with appropriate negative politeness devices. In some cultures even speech acts such as invitations and informatives will be expressed with attenuated force to a stranger or a superior. We use forms such as *Would you like to sit down?* and *I wonder if you could possibly pass me that glass* when speaking to a new acquaintance or a new boss. To a friend, the direct *sit down* or *pass me that glass* would be much more likely.

Similar patterns hold in other languages and cultures. Negative politeness devices mitigate the force of speech acts such as directives to those who are socially distant or superior, while direct unadorned imperative forms characterise the language of equals with solidarity links. In Tzeltal, for instance, men use direct forms to each other. In Javanese, the most basic form of the language, *ngoko*, is used between close friends of equal rank. Differences in status and solidarity lead to the use of more elaborated forms to express the same message in a socially more appropriate way. Negative politeness devices are also extensively used in Japanese to those who are socially distant or superior in status.

These three sociolinguistic universals are presented as examples of the kinds of generalisation which sociolinguists are interested in formulating. They identify universal tendencies or trends, and so make it easier to link such trends to social trends and processes. They encapsulate an important step in the process of explaining the relationship between language and society. And that is of course the primary goal of sociolinguistics.

Tailpiece

Example 2

Robbie: What is social linguistics anyway?
Mum: It's sociolinguistics not social linguistics. Why don't you read the book and find out?
Robbie: It's too long!

In concluding this book, I must note regretfully that many topics have received only the briefest discussion, and many more have not been covered at all – despite a tolerant publisher who allowed me to stretch this book well beyond the limit initially envisaged. For example, though I have discussed the role of English as a lingua franca, and described features of a range of varieties of English, I have had very little to say about the globalisation of English, a large, and rapidly expanding topic. There are many applied sociolinguistic topics, too, that have been necessarily curtailed. Bilingual education has had no more than passing mention. The implications of sociolinguistic research for second language learning is another rich topic which has not been done justice. I can only hope that the choices I have made will serve the purpose of whetting your appetite for further reading in this area, and that having read this book you will be better equipped to understand other sociolinguistic books. A final example will serve to illustrate a number of the themes which have been discussed in this book, while also, I hope, provoking further thought.

Example 3

Brendan: That's a real neat skateboard you got there Kate.
Katherine: Yeah it's friggin' fast. Everyone wants a go on it – even my bloody mother!
Brendan: Watch it Katherine. My grandmother's here.
Katherine: Oh, will she want to borrow it too?

▉ Concepts introduced

Linguistic competence
Sociolinguistic competence
Socio-pragmatic competence
Dimensions of socio-pragmatic analysis
Sociolinguistic universals

▉ References

Chomsky (1965: 3) for a definition of linguistic competence
Hymes (1972: 269ff) on sociolinguistic competence
Universal 1 is based on Brown and Ford (1961)
Universal 2 is based on Bell (1984: 151)
Universal 3 is based on Brown and Levinson (1987)

▉ Useful additional reading

Hudson (1996)
Saville-Troike (2003)

References

Agheyisi, Rebecca and Joshua A. Fishman (1970) Language attitude studies. *Anthropological Linguistics* 12, 5: 137–57.

'Aipolo,' Anahina and Janet Holmes (1990) The use of Tongan in New Zealand: prospects for language maintenance. *Journal of Multilingual and Multicultural Development* 11, 6: 501–21.

Aitchison, Jean (2000) 3rd edn. *Language and Change: Progress or Decay?* Cambridge: Cambridge University Press.

Allan, Scott (1990) The rise of New Zealand intonation. In Allan Bell and Janet Holmes (eds), *New Zealand Ways of Speaking English*. Clevedon, Avon: Multilingual Matters, 115–28.

Andrzejewski, B. W. (1963) Poetry in Somali society. *New Society* 25: 21/3/63.

Appel, René and Pieter Müysken (1987) *Language Contact and Bilingualism*. London: Edward Arnold.

Auer, Peter (1999) From code-switching via language mixing to fused lects. *International Journal of Bilingualism* 3: 309–32.

Bailey, Charles-James N. (1973a) The patterning of language variation. In Richard W. Bailey and Jay L. Robinson (eds) *Varieties of Present-Day English*. London: Collier-Macmillan, pp. 156–86.

Bailey, Charles-James N. (1973b) *Variation and Linguistic Theory*. Washington, DC: Center for Applied Linguistics.

Baker, Colin (1992) *Attitudes and Language*. Clevedon, Avon: Multilingual Matters.

Bassett, Judith, Keith Sinclair and Marcia Stenson (1985) *The Story of New Zealand*. Auckland: Reed Methuen.

Bauer, Laurie, Janet Holmes and Paul Warren (2005) *Language Matters*. London: Palgrave.

Bauer, Laurie and Peter Trudgill (eds) (1999) *Language Myths*. London: Penguin.

Bayard, Donn (1987) Class and change in New Zealand English: a summary report. *Te Reo* 30: 3–36.

Bayard, Donn (1990) 'God help us if we all sound like this': attitudes to New Zealand and other English accents. In Allan Bell and Janet Holmes (eds) *New Zealand Ways of Speaking English*. Clevedon, Avon: Multilingual Matters, pp. 67–96.

Bayard, Donn and Ann Weatherall (1999) Identifying and evaluating accents of English: a replication study. To appear in *Proceedings of the Wellington Language and Gender Symposium*, Victoria University of Wellington, 21–22 October 1999. Wellington: Victoria University of Wellington.

Bell, Allan (1984) Language style as audience design. *Language in Society* 13, 2: 145–204.

Bell, Allan (1991) *The Language of the News Media*. Oxford: Blackwell.

Bell, Allan (2000) Maori and Pakeha English: a case study. In Allan Bell and Koenraad Kuiper (eds) *New Zealand English*. Wellington: Victoria University Press, pp. 221–48.

Bell, Allan (2001) Back in style: reworking audience design. In Penelope Eckert and John R. Rickford (eds) *Style and Sociolinguistic Variation*. Cambridge: Cambridge University Press, pp. 139–69.

Bell, Allan, Karen Davis and Donna Starks (2000) *Languages of the Manukau Region*. Auckland: Report to the Woolf Fisher Research Centre, University of Auckland.

Benton, Richard A. (1981) *Flight of the Amokura*. Wellington: New Zealand Council for Educational Research.

Benton, Richard A. (1991) The Maori language: dying or reviving. *East-West Centre Association Working Paper* No. 28. Honolulu: East-West Centre Association.

Benton, Richard A. (2001) Whose language? Ownership and control of te reo Maori in the third millennium. *New Zealand Sociology* 16, 1: 35–54.

Bernstein, Basil (1973) *Class, Codes and Control*. London: Routledge and Kegan Paul.

Blake, Renée and Meredith Josey (2003) The /ay/ diphthong in a Martha's Vineyard community: what can we say 40 years after Labov? *Language in Society* 32, 4: 451–85.

Blanc, Haim (1968) The Israeli koine as an emergent national standard. In Joshua A. Fishman, Charles A. Ferguson and Jyotirindra Das Gupta (eds) *Language Problems of Developing Nations*. New York: John Wiley, pp. 237–51.

Blocker, Dianne (1976) And how shall I address you? A study of address systems at Indiana University. *Working Papers in Linguistics*, No. 33. Austin, Texas: Southwest Educational Development Laboratory.

Blom, Jan-P. and John J. Gumperz (1972) Social meaning in linguistic structure. In John J. Gumperz and Dell Hymes (eds) *Directions in Sociolinguistics*. London: Holt, Reinhart & Winston, pp. 407–34.

Blum-Kulka, Shoshana, Brenda Danet and Rimona Gherson (1985) The language of requesting in Israeli society. In Joseph P. Forgas (ed.) *Language and Social Situations*. New York: Springer-Verlag, pp. 113–39.

Bodine, Anne (1975) Androcentrism in prescriptive grammar. *Language in Society* 4, 2: 129–56.

Bolinger, Dwight (1980) *Language: The Loaded Weapon*. London: Longman.

Bortoni-Ricardo, S. M. (1985) *The Urbanisation of Rural Dialect Speakers: A Sociolinguistic Study in Brazil*. Cambridge: Cambridge University Press.

Boston Women's Health Collective (1984) *The New Our Bodies, Ourselves: A Book by and for Women*. Boston: Simon and Schuster.

Bourhis, Richard Y. (ed.) (1983) *Conflict and Language Planning in Quebec*. Clevedon, Avon: Multilingual Matters.

Bright, William (1966) Language, social stratification and cognitive orientation. *Sociological Inquiry* 36, 2: 313–18.

Bright, William and Attipat K. Ramanujan (1964) Sociolinguistic variation and language change. In *Proceedings of the Ninth International Congress of Linguists*. The Hague: Mouton.

Brown, Penelope and Stephen Levinson (1987) *Politeness: Some Universals in Language Usage*. Cambridge: Cambridge University Press.

Brown, Roger and Albert Gilman (1960) The pronouns of power and solidarity. In Thomas A. Sebeok (ed.) *Style in Language*. Cambridge, Mass.: MIT Press, pp. 253–76.

Brown, Roger and Marguerite Ford (1961) Address in American English. *Journal of Abnormal and Social Psychology* 62: 375–85.

Brown, Tim (2000) The implementation of non-sexist language reform in the NZ public sector. Unpublished Honours terms paper. Wellington: Victoria University.

Browning, Robert (1982) Greek diglossia yesterday and today. *International Journal of the Sociology of Language* 35: 49–68.

Bryen, Diane N., Cheryl Hartman and Pearl E. Tait (1978) *Variant English*. Columbus, Ohio: Bell and Howell.

Burling, Robbins (1970) *Man's Many Voices*. New York: Holt, Rinehart and Winston.

Burton, Deirdre (1976) 'I think they know that': aspects of English language work in primary classrooms. *Nottingham Linguistic Circular* 5, 1: 22–34.

Cameron, Deborah (1995) *Verbal Hygiene*. London: Routledge.

Cameron, Deborah (1997) Performing gender identity: young men's talk and the construction of heterosexual masculinity. In Sally Johnson and Ulrike Hanna Meinhof (eds) *Language and Masculinity*. Oxford: Blackwell, pp. 47–65.

Cameron, Deborah (2001) *Working with Spoken Discourse*. London: Sage.

Cameron, Deborah and Jill Bourne (1989) *Grammar, Nation and Citizenship: Kingman in Linguistic and Historical Perspective*. University of London, Institute of Education: Department of English and Media Studies Occasional Paper No. 1.

Cameron, Deborah, Fiona McAlinden and Kathy O'Leary (1988) Lakoff in context. In Jennifer Coates and Deborah Cameron (eds) *Women in their Speech Communities*. London: Longman, pp. 74–93.

Cargile, Aaaron Castelan, Jiro Takai and José I. Rodriguez (2006) Attitudes towards African American Vernacular English: a US export to Japan? *Journal of Multilingual and Multicultural Development* 27, 6: 443–56.

Carroll, John B. (ed.) (1956) *Language, Thought and Reality: Selected Writings of Benjamin Lee Whorf*. New York: Wiley.

Carroll, John B. (1965) *Language and Thought*. Englewood Cliffs, NJ: Prentice Hall.

Cazden, Courtney B. (1972) *Child, Language and Education*. New York: Holt, Rinehart and Winston.

Chambers, Jack K. (2003) 2nd edn. *Sociolinguistic Theory*. Oxford: Blackwell.

Chambers, Jack K. and Peter Trudgill (1980) *Dialectology*. Cambridge: Cambridge University Press.

Cheshire, Jenny (1982) *Variation in an English Dialect: A Sociolinguistic Study*. Cambridge: Cambridge University Press.

Cheshire, Jenny (1989) Addressee-oriented features in spoken discourse. *York Papers in Linguistics* 13: 49–64.

Cheshire, Jenny, Paul Kerswill and Ann Williams (2005) Phonology, grammar, and discourse in dialect convergence. In Peter Auer, Frans Hinskens and Paul Kerswill (eds) *Dialect Change: Convergence and Divergence in European Languages*. Cambridge: Cambridge University Press, pp. 135–67.

Chiles, Tina (2003) Titles and surnames in the linguistic construction of women's identities. *New Zealand Studies in Applied Linguistics* 9, 1: 87–97.

Choi, Jinny K. (2005) Bilingualism in Paraguay: forty years after Rubin's study. *Journal of Multilingual and Multicultural Development* 26, 3: 233–48.

Chomsky, Noam (1965) *Aspects of the Theory of Syntax*. Cambridge, Mass.: MIT Press.

Clyne, Michael (ed.) (1982) *Multilingual Australia*. Melbourne: River Seine.

Clyne, Michael (1985) Language maintenance and shift – some data from Australia. In Nessa Wolfson and Joan Manes (eds) *Language and Inequality*. The Hague: Mouton, pp. 195–206.

Coates, Jennifer (1988) Gossip revisited: language in all-female groups. In Jennifer Coates and Deborah Cameron (eds) *Women in their Speech Communities*. London: Longman, pp. 94–122.

Coates, Jennifer (1993) 2nd edn. *Women, Men and Language*. London: Longman.

Coates, Jennifer (1996) *Women Talk: Conversation between Women Friends*. Oxford: Blackwell.

Coates, Jennifer (2003) *Men Talk: Stories in the Making of Masculinities*. Oxford: Blackwell.

Coates, Jennifer and Deborah Cameron (eds) (1988) *Women in their Speech Communities*. London: Longman.

Collins Dictionary of the English Language (1991) London: Collins.

Cooper, Robert L. (ed.) (1982) *Language Spread: Studies on Diffusion and Social Change*. Bloomington: Indiana University Press in cooperation with the Center for Applied Linguistics, Washington, DC.

Cooper, Robert L. (1989, reprinted 1996) *Language Planning and Social Change*. Cambridge: Cambridge University Press.

Corson, David (1985) *The Lexical Bar*. Oxford: Pergamon.

Coupland, Nik (1981) The social differentiation of functional language use. A sociolinguistic investigation of travel agency talk. Ph.D. dissertation. Cardiff: University of Wales Institute of Science and Technology.

Coupland, Nikolas and Adam Jaworski (1997) (eds) *Sociolinguistics: A Reader and Coursebook*. Basingstoke: Palgrave Macmillan.

Coupland, Nikolas, Justine Coupland, Howard Giles and Karen Henwood (1988) Accommodating the elderly: invoking and extending a theory. *Language in Society* 17, 1: 1–41.

Crosby, Fay and Linda Nyquist (1977) The female register: an empirical study of Lakoff's hypotheses. *Language in Society* 6: 313–22.

Crowley, Terry (1990) *From Beach-la-Mar to Bislama*. Oxford: Oxford University Press.

Crystal, David (1988) *The English Language Today*. Harmondsworth: Penguin.

Crystal, David (1997) 2nd edn. *The Cambridge Encyclopedia of Language*. Cambridge: Cambridge University Press.

Crystal, David (2000) *Language Death*. Cambridge: Cambridge University Press.

De Camp, David (1977) The development of pidgin and creole studies. In Albert Valdman (ed.) *Pidgin and Creole Linguistics*. Bloomington: Indiana University Press, pp. 3–20.

Denison, Norman (1972) Some observations on language variety and plurilingualism. In John B. Pride and Janet Holmes (eds) *Sociolinguistics*. Harmondsworth: Penguin, pp. 65–77.

Dimitropoulos, C. J. (1983) Demotic is on the march. *Language Monthly* 2.

Dorian, Nancy C. (1982) Defining the speech community to include its working margins. In Suzanne Romaine (ed.) *Sociolinguistic Variation in Speech Communities*. London: Edward Arnold, pp. 25–34.

Douglas-Cowie, Ellen (1978) Linguistic code-switching in a Northern Irish village: social interaction and social ambition. In Peter Trudgill (ed.) *Sociolinguistic Patterns in British English*. London: Edward Arnold, pp. 37–51.

Downes, William (1998) 2nd edn. *Language and Society*. London: Fontana.

Drew, Paul and Kathy Chilton (2000) Calling just to keep in touch: regular and habitualised telephone calls as an environment for small talk. In Justine Coupland (ed.), *Small Talk*. New York: Longman, pp. 137–62.

Drew, Paul and John Heritage (1992) Analyzing talk at work: an introduction. In Paul Drew and John Heritage (eds) *Talk at Work: Interaction in Institutional Settings*. Cambridge: Cambridge University Press, pp. 3–65.

Dubois, Betty Lou and Isobel Crouch (1975) The question of tag questions in women's speech: they don't really use more of them, do they? *Language in Society* 4: 289 94.

Eades, Diana (1994) A case of communicative clash: Aboriginal English and the legal system. In John Gibbons (ed.) *Language and the Law*. London: Longman, pp. 234–64.

Eades, Diana (1996) Legal recognition of cultural differences in communication: the case of Robyn Kina. *Language and Communication* 16, 3: 215–27.

Eakins, Barbara W. and R. Gene Eakins (1978) *Sex Differences in Human Communication*. Boston: Houghton Mifflin.

Eakins, Barbara W. and R. Gene Eakins (1979) Verbal turn-taking and exchanges in faculty dialogue. In Betty-Lou Dubois and Isobel Crouch (eds) *The Sociology of the Languages of American Women*. San Antonio, Texas: Trinity University, pp. 53–62.

Eastman, Carol M. (1983) *Language Planning: An Introduction*. San Francisco: Chandler and Sharp.

Eckert, Penelope and Sally McConnell-Ginet (1992) Think practically and look locally: language and gender as community-based practice. *Annual Review of Anthropology* 21: 461–90.

Eckert, Penelope and Sally McConnell-Ginet (1995) Constructing meaning, constructing selves: snapshots of language, gender, and class from Belten High. In Kira Hall and Mary Bucholtz (eds) *Gender Articulated: Language and the Socially Constructed Self*. New York: Routledge, pp. 469–507.

Eckert, Penelope and Sally McConnell-Ginet (2003) *Language and Gender*. Cambridge: Cambridge University Press.

Eckert, Penelope and John R. Rickford (eds) (2001) *Style and Sociolinguistic Variation*. Cambridge: Cambridge University Press.

Edelsky, Carole (1977) Acquisition of an aspect of communicative competence: learning what it means to talk like a lady. In Susan Ervin-Tripp and Claudia Mitchell-Kernan (eds) *Child Discourse*. London: Academic Press, pp. 225–43.

Edwards, Anne and Drusilla Beyfus (1969) *Lady Behave: A Guide to Modern Manners for the 1970s*. London: Cassell.

Edwards, John (1982) Language attitudes and their implications among English speakers. In Ellen Bouchard Ryan and Howard Giles (eds) *Attitudes towards Language Variation*. London: Edward Arnold, pp. 20–33.

Edwards, John (1985) *Language, Society and Identity*. Oxford: Blackwell.

Edwards, Viv (1978) Language attitudes and underperformance in West Indian children. *Educational Review* 30, 1: 51–8.

Edwards, Viv (1985) Expressing alienation: Creole in the classroom. In Nessa Wolfson and Joan Manes (eds) *Language and Inequality*. The Hague: Mouton, pp. 325–34.

451

Edwards, Viv (1986) *Language in a Black Community*. Clevedon, Avon: Multilingual Matters.

Eisikovits, Edina (1989a) Variation in the perfective in inner-Sydney English. *Australian Journal of Linguistics* 9: 3–20.

Eisikovits, Edina (1989b) Girl-talk/boy-talk: sex differences in adolescent speech. In Peter Collins and David Blair (eds) *Australian English*. St Lucia, Queensland: University of Queensland Press, pp. 35–54.

Errington, J. Jospeh (1988) *Structure and Style in Javanese: A Semiotic View of Linguistic Etiquette*. Philadelphia: University of Pennsylvania Press.

Ervin-Tripp, Susan M. (1968) An analysis of the interaction of language, topic and listener. In Joshua A. Fishman (ed.) *Readings in the Sociology of Language*. The Hague: Mouton, pp. 192–211.

Ervin-Tripp, Susan M. (1972) Sociolinguistic rules of address. In John B. Pride and Janet Holmes (eds) *Sociolinguistics*. Harmondsworth: Penguin, pp. 225–40.

Evans, Nicholas (1998) Aborigines speak a primitive language. In Laurie Bauer and Peter Trudgill (eds) *Language Myths*. London: Penguin, pp. 159–68.

Fairbairn-Dunlop, Peggie (1984) Factors associated with language maintenance: the Samoans in New Zealand. *New Zealand Journal of Educational Studies* 19: 99–113.

Fairclough, Norman (1989) *Language and Power*. London: Longman.

Fasold, Ralph (1984) *The Sociolinguistics of Society*. Oxford: Blackwell.

Fasold, Ralph (1990) *The Sociolinguistics of Language*. Oxford: Blackwell.

Feagin, Crawford (1979) *Variation and Change in Alabama English*. Washington, DC: Georgetown University Press.

Fengyuan, Ji (1998) Language and politics during the Chinese Cultural Revolution: a study in linguistic engineering. Ph.D. thesis. Christchurch: University of Canterbury.

Ferguson, Charles A. (1959) Diglossia. *Word* 15: 325–40. Reprinted in Pier Paolo Giglioli (ed.) 1972: *Language and Social Context*. Harmondsworth: Penguin, pp. 232–51.

Ferguson, Charles A. (1983) Sports announcer talk: syntactic aspects of register variation. *Language in Society* 12, 2: 153–72.

Finegan, Edward and Niko Besnier (1989) *Language: Its Structure and Use*. New York: Harcourt Brace Jovanovich.

Fishman, Joshua, A. (1971) *Sociolinguistics*. Rowley, Mass.: Newbury House.

Fishman, Joshua A. (1972) The relationship between micro- and macro-sociolinguistics in the study of who speaks what language to whom and when. In John B. Pride and Janet Holmes (eds) *Sociolinguistics*. Harmondsworth: Penguin, pp. 15–32.

Fishman, Joshua A. (1978) Positive bilingualism: Some overlooked rationales and forefathers. In James E. Alatis (ed.) *International Dimensions of Bilingual Education*. Washington, DC: Georgetown University Press, pp. 42–52.

Fishman, Joshua A. (2001) *Can Threatened Languages Be Saved? Reversing Language Shift, Revisited: A 21st Century Perspective*. Clevedon, Avon: Multilingual Matters.

Fishman, Joshua A. (2003) Bilingualism with and without diglossia: diglossia with and without bilingualism. In Christina Bratt Paulston and G. Richard Tucker (eds) *Sociolinguistics: The Essential Readings*. Maldon, Mass.: Blackwell.

Gal, Susan (1978) Peasant men can't get wives: language change and sex roles in a bilingual community. *Language in Society* 7, 1: 1–16.

Gal, Susan (1979) *Language Shift: Social Determinants of Linguistic Change in Bilingual Austria.* New York: Academic Press.

Gardner, Robert C. (1985) *Social Psychology and Second Language Learning: The Role of Attitudes and Motivation.* London: Edward Arnold.

Gardner-Chloros, Penelope (1997) Code-switching: language selection in three Strasbourg department stores. In Nikolas Coupland and Adam Jaworski (eds) *Sociolinguistics: A Reader and Coursebook.* Basingstoke: Palgrave Macmillan, pp. 361–75.

Garvin, Paul and Madeleine Mathiot (1956) The urbanisation of the Guaraní language. In Anthony F. C. Wallace (ed.) *Men and Cultures: Selected Papers from the Fifth International Congress of Anthropological and Ethnological Sciences.* Philadelphia: University of Pennsylvania Press, pp. 365–74.

Geertz, Clifford (1960) *The Religion of Java.* Illinois: The Free Press of Glencoe.

Getting to our Place (2000) Directed by Anna Cottrell and Gaylene Preston. Wellington, NZ: Gaylene Preston Productions.

Gibbon, Margaret (1999) *Feminist Perspectives on Language.* London: Longman-Pearson Education.

Giles, Howard (ed.) (1977) *Language, Ethnicity and Intergroup Relations.* London and New York: Academic Press.

Giles, Howard and Philip Smith (1979) Accommodation theory: optimal levels of convergence. In Howard Giles and Robert St Clair (eds) *Language and Social Psychology.* Oxford: Blackwell, pp. 45–65.

Gold, David L. (1989) A sketch of the linguistic situation in Israel today. *Language in Society* 18, 3: 361–88.

Goodenough, W. H. (1975) Cultural anthropology and linguistics. In Paul L. Garvin (ed.) *Report of the Seventh Round Table Meeting on Linguistics and Language Study.* Washington, DC: Georgetown University Press.

Goodwin, Marjorie H. (1980) Directive-response speech sequences in girls' and boys' task activities. In Sally McConnell-Ginet, Ruth Borker and Nellie Furman (eds) *Women and Language in Literature and Society.* New York: Praeger, pp. 157–73.

Gordon, Elizabeth (1997) Sex, speech and stereotypes: why women use prestige forms more than men. *Language in Society* 26, 1: 47–64.

Gordon, Elizabeth and Marcia Abell (1990) 'This objectionable colonial dialect': historical and contemporary attitudes to New Zealand speech. In Allan Bell and Janet Holmes (eds) *New Zealand Ways of Speaking English.* Clevedon, Avon: Multilingual Matters, pp. 21–48.

Gordon, Elizabeth and Tony Deverson (1985) *New Zealand English.* Auckland: Heinemann.

Gordon, Elizabeth and Tony Deverson (1989) *Finding a New Zealand Voice.* Auckland: New House.

Gordon, Elizabeth and Margaret Maclagan (1990) A longitudinal study of the *ear/air* contrast in New Zealand speech. In Allan Bell and Janet Holmes (eds) *New Zealand Ways of Speaking English.* Clevedon, Avon: Multilingual Matters, pp. 129–48.

Goyvaerts, Didier L. (1988) Indoubil: a Swahili hybrid in Bukavu. *Language in Society* 17, 2: 231–42.

Goyvaerts, Didier, Diederick Naeyaert and Muzeyi Semikenke (1983) Language and education policy in the multilingual city of Bukavu. *Journal of Multilingual and Multicultural Development* 4, 1: 47–62.

Graddol, David and Joan Swann (1989) *Gender Voices*. Oxford: Blackwell.

Green, James A. (1999) Handwriting on the stall: a study of graffiti and gender. BA Honours Research Essay. Dunedin: Otago University.

Grosjean, François (1982) *Life with Two Languages*. London and Cambridge, Mass.: Harvard University Press.

Gumperz, John J. (1965) The speech community. *Encyclopedia of the Social Sciences* 9(3): 382–6. Reprinted in Pier Paolo Giglioli (ed.) *Language and Social Context*. Harmondsworth: Penguin 1972.

Gumperz, John J. (1971) *Language in Social Groups*. Stanford: Stanford University Press.

Gumperz, John J. (1977) The sociolinguistic significance of conversational code-switching. *RELC Journal* 8, 2: 1–34.

Gumperz, John J. (ed.) (1982) *Language and Social Identity*. Cambridge: Cambridge University Press.

Gumperz, John J. and Robert Wilson (1971) Convergence and creolisation: a case from the Indo-Aryan/Dravidian border in India. In Dell Hymes (ed.) *Pidginization and Creolization of Languages*. Cambridge: Cambridge University Press, pp. 151–67.

Guy, Gregory (1988) Language and social class. In Frederick J. Newmeyer (ed.) *Linguistics: The Cambridge Survey*. IV: *Language: The Socio-Cultural Context*. Cambridge: Cambridge University Press, pp. 37–63.

Halliday, Michael A. K. (1973) *Explorations in the Functions of Language*. London: Edward Arnold.

Halliday, Michael A. K. (1975) *Learning How to Mean*. London: Edward Arnold.

Hancock, Ian (1977) Appendix: repertory of pidgin and creole languages. In Albert Valdman (ed.) *Pidgin and Creole Linguistics*. Bloomington: Indiana University Press, pp. 277–94.

Harres, Annette (1993) The representation of women in three medical texts. *Australian Review of Applied Linguistics* Series S, No. 10: 35–53.

Harris, David K. (2007) *When Languages Die: The Extinction of the World's Languages and the Erosion of Human Knowledge*. Oxford: Oxford University Press.

Harris, Sandra (2001) Being politically impolite: extending politeness theory to adversarial political discourse. *Discourse and Society* 12, 4: 451–72.

Harris, Sandra (2004) Subverting conversational repair in computer-mediated conversation. In Mike Baynham, Alice Deignan and Goodith White (eds) *Applied Linguistics at the Interface*. London: Equinox, pp. 65–77.

Hatch, Evelyn (1983) *Psycholinguistics: A Second Language Perspective*. Rowley, Mass.: Newbury House.

Haugen, Einar (1959) Planning for a standard language in modern Norway. *Anthropological Linguistics* 1, 3: 8–21.

Haugen, Einar (1965) Construction and reconstruction in language planning. *Word* 21: 188–207.

Haugen, Einar (1966a) Dialect language and nation. *American Anthropologist* 68: 922–35.

Haugen, Einar (1966b) *Language Conflict and Language Planning*. Cambridge, Mass.: Harvard University Press.

Haugen, Einar (1966c) Semicommunication: the language gap in Scandinavia. *Sociological Inquiry* 36, 2: 280–97.

Haupt, Enid (1970) *New Seventeen Book of Etiquette and Young Living*. New York: David McKay.

Hawkins, Peter R. (1967–68) Some linguistic consequences of a working-class environment. *Te Reo* 10–11: 40–51.

Heller, Monica S. (1982) Negotiations of language choice in Montreal. In John J. Gumperz (ed.) *Language and Social Identity*. Cambridge: Cambridge University Press, pp. 108–18

Hirsh, Walter (ed.) (1987) *Living Languages: Bilingualism and Community Languages in New Zealand*. Auckland: Heinemann.

Hirst, P. H. (1974) *Knowledge and the Curriculum: A Collection of Philosophical Papers*. London: Routledge and Kegan Paul.

Hofstadter, Douglas R. (1982) Metamagical themas: 'default assumptions' and their effects on writing and thinking. *Scientific American*: 247, 5: 14–21.

Holmes, Janet (1981) Hello-goodbye: an analysis of children's telephone conversations. *Semiotica* 37, 1/2: 91–107.

Holmes, Janet (1983) The structure of teacher's directives. In Jack C. Richards and Richard W. Schmidt (eds) *Language and Communication*. London: Longman, pp. 89–115.

Holmes, Janet (1984a) Hedging your bets and sitting on the fence: some evidence for hedges as support structures. *Te Reo* 27: 47–62.

Holmes, Janet (1984b) 'Women's language': a functional approach. *General Linguistics* 24, 3: 149–78.

Holmes, Janet (1985) Sex differences and miscommunication: some data from New Zealand. In John B. Pride (ed.) *Cross-Cultural Encounters: Communication and Mis-communication*. Melbourne: River Seine, pp. 24–43.

Holmes, Janet (1990) Hedges and boosters in women's and men's speech. *Language and Communication* 10, 3: 185–205.

Holmes, Janet (1995) *Women, Men and Politeness*. London: Longman.

Holmes, Janet (1997a) Maori and Pakeha English: some New Zealand social dialect data. *Language in Society* 26, 1: 65–101.

Holmes, Janet (1997b) Story-telling in New Zealand women's and men's talk. In Ruth Wodak (ed.) *Gender and Discourse*. London: Sage, pp. 263–93.

Holmes, Janet, Allan Bell and Mary Boyce (1991) *Variation and Change in New Zealand English: A Social Dialect Investigation*. Project Report to the Social Sciences Committee of the Foundation for Research, Science and Technology. Wellington, Victoria University.

Holmes, Janet and Rose Fillary (2000) Handling small talk at work: challenges for workers with intellectual disabilities. *International Journal of Disability, Development and Education* 47, 3: 273–91.

Holmes, Janet and Meredith Marra (2002) Humour as a discursive boundary marker in social interaction. In Anna Duszak (ed.), *Us and Others: Social Identities Across Languages, Discourses and Cultures*. Amsterdam/Philadelphia: John Benjamins, pp. 377–400.

Holmquist, Jonathan C. (1985) Social correlates of a linguistic variable: a study in a Spanish village. *Language in Society* 14, 2: 191–203.

Honey, John (1989) *Does Accent Matter?* London: Faber and Faber.

Horvath, Barbara (1985) *Variation in Australian English*. Cambridge: Cambridge University Press.

Hudson, Richard A. (1996) 2nd edn. *Sociolinguistics*. Cambridge: Cambridge University Press.

Hui, Saiying (1989) Pronunciation of intervocalic and final stops in New Zealand English: a pilot project. Unpublished terms project. Wellington: Victoria University.

Hymes, Dell (1962) The ethnography of speaking. In Thomas Gladwin and William C. Sturtevant (eds) *Anthropology and Human Behaviour*. Washington, DC: The Anthropology Society of Washington (Washington), pp. 13–53.

Hymes, Dell (1972) On communicative competence. In John Pride and Janet Holmes (eds) *Sociolinguistics*. Harmondsworth: Penguin, pp. 269–93.

Hymes, Dell (1974) *Foundations in Sociolinguistics*. Philadelphia: University of Pennsylvania Press.

Hyndman, Christine (1985) Gender and language differences: a small study. Unpublished terms paper. Wellington: Victoria University.

Inoue, Kyoko (1979) Japanese: a story of language and people. In Timothy Shopen (ed.) *Languages and their Speakers*. Cambridge, Mass.: Winthrop.

Jacob, Jenny (1990) *A Grammatical Comparison of the Spoken English of Maori and Pakeha Women in Levin*. Wellington: Victoria University.

Jahangiri, N. and Richard A. Hudson (1982) Patterns of variation in Tehrani Persian. In Suzanne Romaine (ed.) *Sociolinguistic Variation in Speech Communities*. London: Edward Arnold, pp. 49–63.

Jahr, Ernst Håkon (1989) Limits of language planning? Norwegian language planning revisited. *International Journal of the Sociology of Language* 80: 33–9.

James, Deborah and Sandra Clarke (1993) Interruptions, gender and power: a critical review of the literature. In Deborah Tannen (ed.) *Gender and Conversational Interaction*. Oxford: Oxford University Press, pp. 231–80.

Jamieson, Pennie (1980) The pattern of urban language loss. *Australian and New Zealand Journal of Sociology* 16, 2: 102–9.

Jaworski, Adam and Nik Coupland (eds) (1999) *The Discourse Reader*. London/New York: Routledge.

Johnston, Lorraine and Shelley Robertson (1993) 'Hey yous!' the Maori–NZE interface in sociolinguistic rules of address. *Te Reo* 36: 115–27.

Kachru, Braj (1985) Standards, codification and sociolinguistic realism: the English language in the outer circle. In Randolph Quirk and Henry G. Widdowson (eds) *English in the world*. Cambridge: Cambridge University Press.

Kachru, Braj (1992) The *Other Tongue: English Across Cultures*. Urbana: University of Illinois Press.

Kachru, Braj (1997) World Englishes, and English-using communities. *Annual Review of Applied Linguistics* 17: 66–87.

Kaplan, Robert B. and Richard B. Baldauf (2005) Language-in-Education policy and planning. In Eli Hinkel (ed.) *Handbook of Research in Second Language Teaching and Learning*. New Jersey: Lawrence Erlbaum, pp. 1013–33.

Keenan, Elenor (1976) The universality of conversational postulates. *Language in Society* 5: 67–80.

Kerswill, Paul, Eivind Torgersen and Sue Fox (2006) Innovation in Inner-London teenage speech. Paper presented at NWAV35, University of Ohio, Columbus, Ohio, November.

Kerswill, Paul and Ann Williams (2000) Creating a new town koine: children and language change in Milton Keynes. *Language in Society* 29: 65–115.

Keshavarz, Mohammad Hossein (1988) Forms of address in post-revolutionary Iranian Persian: a sociolinguistic analysis. *Language in Society* 17, 4: 565–75.

Khan, Farhat (1991) Final consonant cluster simplification in a variety of Indian English. In Jenny Cheshire (ed.) *English Around the World: Sociolinguistic Perspectives*. Cambridge: Cambridge University Press, pp. 288–98.

Kiesling, Scott F. and Christina Bratt Paulston (eds) (2005) *Intercultural Discourse and Communication*. Oxford: Blackwell.

Kirkwood, Michael (1989) *Language Planning in the Soviet Union*. London: Macmillan.

Knowles, Gerry (1987) *Patterns of Spoken English*. London: Longman.

Kochman, Thomas (1972) *Rappin' and Stylin' Out*. Urbana: University of Illinois Press.

Kouletaki, Ekaterini (2005) Women, men and polite requests: English and Greek. In Robin T. Lakoff and Sachiko Ide (eds) *Broadening the Horizon of Linguistic Politeness*. Amsterdam/Philadelphia: John Benjamins, pp. 245–74.

Kramsch, Claire (1998) *Language and Culture*. Oxford: Oxford University Press.

Kuiper, Koenraad and Paddy Austin (1990) They're off and racing now: the speech of the New Zealand race caller. In Allan Bell and Janet Holmes (eds) *New Zealand Ways of Speaking English*. Clevedon, Avon: Multilingual Matters, pp. 195–220.

Kuiper, Koenraad and Douglas Haggo (1984) Livestock auctions, oral poetry and ordinary language. *Language in Society* 13, 2: 205–34.

Labov, William (1963) The social motivation of a sound change. *Word* 19: 273–309.

Labov, William (1966) *The Social Stratification of English in New York City*. Washington, DC: Center for Applied Linguistics.

Labov, William (1972a) *Sociolinguistic Patterns*. Philadelphia: University of Pennsylvania Press.

Labov, William (1972b) *Language in the Inner City: Studies in the Black English Vernacular*. Philadelphia: University of Pennsylvania Press.

Labov, William (1972c) The logic of non-standard English. In Pier Paolo Giglioli (ed.) *Language and Social Context*. Harmondsworth: Penguin, pp. 179–215.

Labov, William (1972d) The relation of reading failure to peer-group status. In *Language in the Inner City*. Philadelphia: University of Pennsylvania Press, pp. 241–54.

Labov, William (1981) What can be learned about change in progress from synchronic description? In David Sankoff and Henrietta Cedergren (eds) *Variation Omnibus*. Edmonton: Linguistic Research Inc.

Labov, William (1982) Objectivity and commitment in linguistic science: the case of the Black English trial in Ann Arbor. *Language in Society* 11, 2: 165–201.

Labov, William (1990) The intersection of sex and social class in the course of linguistic change. *Language Variation and Change* 2, 3: 205–54.

Ladegaard, Hans J. (2000) Language attitudes and sociolinguistic behaviour: exploring attitude–behaviour relations in language. *Journal of Sociolinguistics* 4, 2: 214–33.

Lakoff, George (1987) *Women, Fire and Dangerous Things: What Categories Reveal About the Mind*. Chicago: University of Chicago Press.

Lakoff, Robin (1975) *Language and Woman's Place*. New York: Harper Colophon.

Lakoff, Robin T. and Sachiko Ide (2005) *Broadening the Horizon of Linguistic Politeness*. Amsterdam: John Benjamins.

Lane, Chris (2003) Writing a language off. Anti Maori argumentation in letters to New Zealand editors. In Phyllis M. Ryan and Roland Terborg (eds) *Language: Issues of Inequality*. México: Universidad Nacional Autónoma de México, Centro de Enseñanza de Lenguas Extranjeras.

Lass, Roger (1987) *The Shape of English*. London: Dent.

Laver, John (1981) Linguistic routines and politeness in greeting and parting. In Florian Coulmas (ed.) *Conversational Routine*. The Hague: Mouton, pp. 289–304.

Lee, David (1989) Sociolinguistic variation in the speech of Brisbane adolescents. *Australian Journal of Linguistics* 9: 51–72.

Lee, David (1992) *Competing discourses: Language and Ideology*. New York: Longman.

Leech, Geoffrey N. (1983) *Principles of Pragmatics*. London: Longman.

Lee-Wong, Song Mei (2000) *Cross Cultural Communication: Politeness and Face in Chinese Culture*. Frankfurt, Peter Lang.

Leith, Dick (1983) *A Social History of English*. London: Routledge and Kegan Paul.

Lewis, E. Glyn (1978) Bilingualism in education in Wales. In Bernard Spolsky and Robert L. Cooper (eds) *Case Studies in Bilingual Education*. Rowley, Mass.: Newbury House.

Liao, Chao Chih and Mary I. Bresnahan (1996) A contrastive pragmatic study on American English and Mandarin refusals strategies. *Language Science*, 18, 3–4: 703–27.

Linguistic Minorities Project (1985) *The Other Languages of England*. London: Routledge and Kegan Paul.

Lippi-Green, Rosina (1997) *English with an Accent*. London: Routledge.

Llewellyn-Jones, Derek (1982) *Fundamentals of Obstetrics and Gynaecology*. Vol II. London: Faber & Faber.

Lyons, John (ed.) (1970) *New Horizons in Linguistics*. Harmondsworth: Penguin.

Macafee, Caroline (1989) Qualitative insights into working-class language attitudes. *York Papers in Linguistics* 13: 191–202.

Macauley, R. K. S. (1977) *Language, Social Class and Education*. Edinburgh: Edinburgh University Press.

Macaulay, Ronald K. S. (1978) Variation and consistency in Glaswegian English. In Peter Trudgill (ed.) *Sociolinguistic Patterns in British English*. London: Edward Arnold, pp. 132–44.

Mao Zedong (1976) *Quotations from Chairman Mao Zedong*. Beijing: Foreign Languages Press.

May, Stephen (2001) *Language and Minority Rights: Ethnicity, Nationalism and the Politics of Language*. London: Longman.

Mæhlum, Brit (1990) Codeswitching in Hemnesberget – myth or reality? In Ernst Håkon Jahr and Ove Lorentz (eds) *Tromsø Linguistics in the Eighties*. Oslo: Novus, pp. 338–55.

Mæhlum, Brit (1996) Codeswitching in Hemnesberget: myth or reality? *Journal of Pragmatics* 25: 749–61.

McCallum, Janet (1978) In search of a dialect. *New Zealand Journal of Educational Studies* 13, 2: 133–43.

McColl Millar, Robert (2005) *Language, Nation and Power*. Basingstoke: Palgrave Macmillan.

McElhinny, Bonnie S. (1995) Challenging hegemonic masculinities: female and male police officers handling domestic violence. In Kira Hall and Mary Bucholtz (eds) *Gender Articulated: Language and the Socially Constructed Self*. London: Routledge, pp. 217–43.

McMillan, Julie R., A. Kay Clifton, Diane McGrath and Wanda S. Gale (1977) Women's language: uncertainty or interpersonal sensitivity and emotionality. *Sex Roles* 3, 6: 545–59.

Mesthrie, Rajend, Joan Swann, Andrea Deumert and William L. Leap (2000) *Introducing Sociolinguistics*. Edinburgh: Edinburgh University Press.

Metge, Joan (1995) *New Growth from Old: The Whānau in the Modern World*. Wellington: Victoria University Press.

Meyerhoff, Miriam (2006) *Introducing Sociolinguistics*. London: Routledge.

Michaels, Sarah (1981) Sharing time: children's narrative styles and differential access to literacy. *Language in Society* 10, 3: 423–42.

Migge, Bettina (2007) Code-switching and social identities in the Eastern Maroon community of Suriname and French Guiana. *Journal of Sociolinguistics* 11, 1: 53–73.

Mihalic, Francis (1957) *Grammar and Dictionary of Neo-Melanesian*. Westmead, New South Wales: Mission Press.

Mihalic, Francis (1971) *The Jacaranda Dictionary and Grammar of Melanesian Pidgin*. Milton, Australia: The Jacaranda Press.

Millar, Sharon (1989) Approaches to accent in the classroom. *Pre-Publications of the English Department of Odense University*. No. 51. Denmark: Odense University.

Miller, Casey and Kate Swift (1991) *Words and Women: New Language in New Times*. New York: HarperCollins.

Milroy, James and Lesley Milroy (1985) Linguistic change, social network and speaker innovation. *Journal of Linguistics* 21, 2: 339–84.

Milroy, Lesley (1980) *Language and Social Networks*. Oxford: Blackwell.

Milroy, Lesley (1982) Social network and linguistic focusing. In Suzanne Romaine (ed.) *Sociolinguistic Variation in Speech Communities*. London: Longman, pp. 141–52.

Milroy, Lesley (1984) Comprehension and context: successful communication and communication breakdown. In Peter Trudgill (ed.) *Applied Sociolinguistics*. London: Academic Press, pp. 7–31.

Milroy, Lesley (1987) *Observing and Analysing Natural Language*. Oxford: Blackwell.

Milroy, Lesley (1989) Gender as a speaker variable: the interesting case of the glottalised stops in Tyneside. *York Papers in Linguistics* 13: 227–36.

Milroy, Lesley and Matthew Gordon (2002) *Sociolinguistics: Methods and Interpretation*. Oxford: Blackwell.

Mitford, Nancy (1949) *The Pursuit of Love*. Harmondsworth: Penguin.

Mitford, Nancy and Alan S. C. Ross (1980) *Noblesse Oblige*. London: Futura.

Mooney, Maureen (1980) Directives as a speech function: an examination of the structure of directives in a New Zealand psychiatric clinic. Unpublished terms project. Wellington: Victoria University.

Mulac, Anthony, Torborg Louisa Lundell and James Bradac (1986) Male/female language differences in a public speaking situation. *Communication Monographs* 53, 2: 115–29.

Myers-Scotton, Carol (1993) *Social Motivations for Code-Switching: Evidence from Africa.* Oxford: Oxford University Press.

Myers-Scotton, Carol (1997) *Duelling Languages: Grammatical Structure in Codeswitching.* Oxford: Clarendon Press.

Myers-Scotton, Carol (2005) *Multiple Voices: An Introduction to Bilingualism.* Oxford: Blackwell.

Nation, I. S. P. (2001) *Learning Vocabulary in Another Language.* Cambridge: Cambridge University Press.

National Maori Language Survey (1998) Wellington: Te Puni Kōkiri/Ministry of Maori Development, Te Taura Whiri i te reo Māori/Maori Language Commission, and Statistics New Zealand.

Nelson, Hank (1972) *Papua New Guinea: Black Unity or Black Chaos?* Harmondsworth: Penguin.

Nichols, Patricia C. (1984) Networks and hierarchies: language and social stratification. In Cheris Kramarae, Muriel Shulz and William O'Barr (eds) *Language and Power.* London: Sage, pp. 23–42.

Nilsen, Alleen Pace (1972) Sexism in English: a feminist view. In Nancy Hofman, Cynthia Secor and Adrian Tinsley (eds) *Female Studies* VI. Old Westbury, NY: The Feminist Press, pp. 102–9.

Nwoye, Onuigbo G. (1989) Linguistic politeness in Igbo. *Multilingua* 8, 2–3: 259–75.

O'Barr, William M. and Bowman K. Atkins (1980) 'Women's language' or 'powerless language'? In Sally McConnell-Ginet, Ruth Borker and Nelly Furman (eds) *Women and Language in Literature and Society.* New York: Praeger, pp. 93–110.

Ochs, Elinor (1987) The impact of stratification and socialization on men's and women's speech in Western Samoa. In Susan U. Philips, Susan Steele and Christine Tanz (eds) *Language, Gender and Sex in Comparative Perspective.* Cambridge: Cambridge University Press, pp. 50–70.

Ochs, Elinor (1992) Indexing gender. In Alessandro Duranti and Charles Goodwin (eds) *Rethinking Context: Language as an Interactive Phenomenon.* Cambridge: Cambridge University Press, pp. 335–58.

O'Hanlon, Renae (2006) Australian hip hop: a sociolinguistic investigation. *Australian Journal of Linguistic* 26, 2: 193–209.

Orsman, Harry W. (1997) *The Dictionary of New Zealand English.* Auckland and Oxford: Oxford University Press.

Paltridge, Brian (2006) *Discourse Analysis: An Introduction.* London: Continuum.

Pandit, P. B. (1979) Perspectives on sociolinguistics in India. In William McCormack and Stephen A. Wurm (eds) *Language and Society.* The Hague: Mouton.

Paulston, Christina Bratt (1974) Linguistic and communicative competence. *TESOL Quarterly* 8, 4: 347–62.

Paulston, Christina Bratt and Tucker, G. Richard (eds) (2003) *Sociolinguistics: The Essential Readings*. Maldon, Mass.: Blackwell.

Pauwels, Anne (1998) *Women Changing Language*. London: Longman.

Pauwels, Anne and Joanne Winter (2004) Generic pronouns and gender-inclusive language reform in the English of Singapore and the Philippines. *Australian Review of Applied Linguistics* 27, 2: 50–62.

Pawley, Andrew (1991) How to talk cricket. In Robert Blust (ed.) *Currents in Pacific Linguistics: Papers in Austronesian Languages and Ethnolinguistics in Honour of George W. Grace*. Honolulu: Pacific Linguistics, pp. 339–68.

Pawley, Andrew, Frances Syder and He Fangming (1989) Tasmanian Vernacular English. *Working Paper*. Canberra: Australian National University.

Petyt, K. M. (1985) *Dialect and Accent in Industrial West Yorkshire*. Amsterdam: John Benjamins.

Philips, Susan and Anne Reynolds (1987) The interaction of variable syntax and discourse structure in women's and men's speech. In Susan U. Philips, Susan Steele and Christine Tanz (eds) *Language, Gender and Sex in Comparative Perspective*. Cambridge: Cambridge University Press, pp. 71–94.

Pilkington, Jane (1989) 'Don't try and make out that I'm nice': the different strategies that men and women use when gossiping. Unpublished term paper. Wellington: Victoria University.

Platt, John (1977) A model for polyglossia and multilingualism (with special reference to Singapore and Malaysia). *Language in Society* 6, 3: 361–78.

Pope, Jennifer (2002) The social history of a sound change on the island of Martha's Vineyard, Massachusetts: forty years after Labov. MA dissertation. University of Edinburgh.

Poplack, Shana (1980) Sometimes I'll start a sentence in Spanish y termino en Español: toward a typology of code-switching. *Linguistics* 18: 581–618.

Pragji, Usha (1980) A measure of dropped [h] in the speech of two New Zealand speakers: Marjorie Lee and George Davies. Unpublished term paper. Auckland University.

Preisler, Bent (1986) *Linguistic Sex Roles in Conversation*. Berlin: Mouton de Gruyter.

Rampton, Ben (1995) *Crossing: Language and Ethnicity among Adolescents*. London: Longman.

Reinecke, John (1964) Trade jargons and creole dialects. In Dell Hymes (ed.) *Language in Culture and Society*. New York: Holt, Reinhart and Winston, pp. 534–46.

Richards, Jack C. and Richard W. Schmidt (1983) Conversational analysis. In Jack C. Richards and Richard W. Schmidt (eds) *Language and Communication*. London: Longman, pp. 117–54.

Rickford, John R. and Faye McNair-Knox (1994) Addressee- and topic-influenced style shift. In Douglas Biber and Edward Finnegan (eds) *Sociolinguistic Perspectives on Register*. Oxford: Oxford University Press, pp. 235–76.

Roberts, Mary (1991) The New Zealand Chinese community of Wellington: aspects of language maintenance and shift. In Janet Holmes and Ray Harlow (eds) *Threads in the Tapestry of Language*. Auckland: Linguistic Society of New Zealand, pp. 31–70.

Roberts, Mary L. (2001) The effects of immigration flow on patterns of language maintenance and shift in two immigrant communities in New Zealand. *New Zealand Sociology* 16, 1: 55–78.

Roberts, Celia, Evelyn Davies and Tom Jupp (1992) *Language and Discrimination: A Study of Communication in Multi-Ethnic Workplaces*. London: Longman.

Romaine, Suzanne (1984) *The Language of Children and Adolescents*. Oxford: Blackwell.

Romaine, Suzanne (1988) *Pidgin and Creole Languages*. London: Longman.

Romaine, Suzanne (1989) *Bilingualism*. Oxford: Blackwell.

Romaine, Suzanne (1999) *Communicating Gender*. Mahwah, NJ: Lawrence Erlbaum.

Romaine, Suzanne (2000) 2nd edn. *Language in Society*. Oxford: Oxford University Press.

Romaine, Suzanne and Daniel Nettle (2000) *Vanishing Voices*. Oxford: Oxford University Press.

Rubin, Joan (1968) *National Bilingualism in Paraguay*. Janua Linguarum Series Practica 60. The Hague: Mouton.

Rubin, Joan (1985) The special relation of Guaraní and Spanish in Paraguay. In Nessa Wolfson and Joan Manes (eds) *Language and Inequality*. The Hague: Mouton, pp. 111–20.

Rubin, Joan and Björn H. Jernudd (eds) (1971) *Can Languages Be Planned?* Honolulu: University of Hawaii Press.

Russell, Joan (1982) Networks and sociolinguistic variation in an African urban setting. In Suzanne Romaine (ed.) *Sociolinguistic Variation in Speech Communities*. London: Edward Arnold, pp. 141–52.

Russell, Joan (1989) The role of vernacularisation in Tanzania: Swahili as a political tool. *York Papers in Linguistics* 13: 295–305.

Sacks, Harvey (1984) Notes on methodology. In J. Maxwell Atkinson and John Heritage (eds) *Structures of Social Action: Studies in Conversation Analysis*. Cambridge: Cambridge University Press, pp. 21–7.

Sacks, Harvey, Emanuel A. Schegloff and Gail Jefferson (1978) A simplest systematics for the organization of turn taking for conversation. In Jim Schenkein (ed.) *Studies in the Organization of Conversational Interaction*. New York: Academic.

Salmond, Anne (1974) Rituals of encounter among the Maori. In Richard Bauman and Joel Sherzer (eds) *Explorations in the Ethnography of Speaking*. Cambridge: Cambridge University Press, pp. 192–212.

Sankoff, Gillian (1972) Language use in multilingual societies: some alternative approaches. In John B. Pride and Janet Holmes (eds) *Sociolinguistics*. Harmondsworth: Penguin, pp. 33–51.

Sankoff, Gillian and Henrietta Cedergren (1971) Some results of a sociolinguistic study of Montreal French. In Regna Darnell (ed.) *Linguistic Diversity in Canadian Society*. Edmonton, Canada: Linguistic Research Inc., pp. 61–87.

Santarita, Paula and Marilyn Martin-Jones (1990) The Portuguese speech community. Unpublished paper: copy sent by author.

Sapir, Edward (1921) *Language*. New York: Harcourt, Brace and World.

Saville-Troike, Muriel (2003) 3rd edn. *The Ethnography of Communication*. Oxford: Blackwell.

Schmidt, Annette (1985) *Young People's Dyirbal: An Example of Language Death from Australia*. Cambridge: Cambridge University Press.

Schmidt, Annette (1990) *The Loss of Australia's Aboriginal Language Heritage*. Canberra: Aboriginal Studies Press.

Searle, John R. (1976) The classification of illocutionary acts. *Language in Society* 5, 1: 1–24.

Shaklee, Margaret (1980) The rise of standard English. In Timothy Shopen and Joseph M. Williams (eds) *Standards and Dialects in English*. Cambridge, Mass.: Winthrop, pp. 33–62.

Sharpe, Margaret C. and John Sandefur (1976) The creole language of the Katherine and Roper River areas, Northern Territory. In Michael Clyne (ed.) *Australia Talks: Essays on the Sociology of Australian Immigrant and Aboriginal Languages*. Pacific Linguistics Series D-No. 23. Canberra: Australian National University, pp. 63–73.

Sherzer, Joel (1977) The ethnography of speaking: a critical appraisal. In Muriel Saville-Troike (ed.) *Linguistics and Anthropology*. Washington DC: Georgetown University Press, pp. 43–57.

Shibamoto, Janet S. (1987) The womanly woman: manipulation of stereotypical and non-stereotypical features of Japanese female speech. In Susan U. Philips, Susan Steele and Christine Tanz (eds) *Language, Gender and Sex in Comparative Perspective*. Cambridge: Cambridge University Press, pp. 26–49.

Shuy, Roger (1969) Sex as a factor in sociolinguistic research. Paper presented at meeting of the Anthropological Society of Washington. Washington, DC. ERIC document; ED 027522.

Shuy, Roger W., Walter A. Wolfram and William K. Riley (1967) *Linguistic Correlates of Social Stratification in Detroit Speech*. Cooperative Research Project No. 6–1347. East Lansing, Mich.: Michigan State University.

Siebenhaar, Beat (2006) Code choice and code-switching in Swiss-German Internet Relay chat rooms. *Journal of Sociolinguistics* 10, 4: 481–506.

Siegel, Jeff (1995) How to get a laugh in Fijian: code-switching and humor. *Language in Society* 24, 1: 95–110.

Sifianou, Maria (1992) *Politeness Phenomena in England and Greece*. Oxford: Clarendon Press.

Sifianou, Maria (2001) 'Oh! How appropriate!': compliments and politeness. In Arin Bayraktaroglu and Maria Sifianou (eds) *Linguistic Politeness Across Boundaries: The Case of Greek and Turkish*. Amsterdam: John Benjamins, pp. 391–430.

Smith, Lee (1971) Language usage and code-switching among Maori bilinguals. Unpublished terms project. Wellington: Victoria University.

Sorensen, Arthur P. (1972) Multilingualism in the Northwest Amazon. In John B. Pride and Janet Holmes (eds) *Sociolinguistics*. Harmondsworth: Penguin, pp. 78–93.

Spender, Dale (1979) Language and sex differences. In *Osnabrücker Beitrage zur Sprach Theorie Spräche und Geschlecht*. 9. Osnabrück: Wilfried Wolf, pp. 38–59.

Spender, Dale (1980) *Man Made Language*. London: Routledge and Kegan Paul.

Spolsky, Bernard (1978) A model for the evaluation of bilingual education. *International Review of Education* 24, 3: 347–60.

Spolsky, Bernard (2003) Reassessing Māori regeneration. *Language in Society* 32: 553–78.

Stewart, Malcolm W., Cynthia D. Verstraate and Janet L. Fanslow (1990) Sexist language and university academic staff: attitudes, awareness and recognition of sexist language. *New Zealand Journal of Educational Studies* 25, 2: 115–25.

Stubbe, Maria (1998) Are you listening? Cultural influences on the use of supportive verbal feedback in conversation. *Journal of Pragmatics* 29: 257–89.

Stubbe, Maria, Chris Lane, Jo Hilder, Elaine Vine, Bernadette Vine, Janet Holmes, Meredith Marra and Ann Weatherall (2003) Multiple discourse analyses of a workplace interaction. *Discourse Studies* 5, 3: 351–88.

Stubbs, Michael (1983) *Language Schools and Classrooms*. London: Methuen.

Stubbs, Michael (1997) Language and the mediation of experience. In Florian Coulmas (ed.) *The Handbook of Sociolinguistics*. London: Blackwell, pp. 358–73.

Sunderland, Jane (ed.) (2006) *Language and Gender*. London: Routledge.

Survey of the Health of the Maori Language (2001). Wellington: Ministry of Maori Development, Te Puni Kōkiri.

Tagliamonte, Sali and Alex D'Arcy (2004) 'He's like she's like.' The quotative system in Canadian youth. *Journal of Sociolinguistics* 8: 493–514.

Takano, Shoji (2005) Re-examining linguistic power: strategic uses of directives by professional Japanese women in positions of authority and leadership. *Journal of Pragmatics* 37, 5: 633–66.

Talbot, Mary M. (1998) *Language and Gender: An Introduction*. Oxford: Polity Press.

Tannen, Deborah (1986) *That's Not What I Meant*. London: Dent.

Tannen, Deborah (1990) *You Just Don't Understand: Women and Men in Conversation*. New York: Morrow, Ballentine.

Thomas, Beth (1988) Differences of sex and sects: linguistic variation and social networks in a Welsh mining village. In Jennifer Coates and Deborah Cameron (eds) *Women in their Speech Communities*. London: Longman, pp. 51–61.

Thomas, Jenny (1989) Discourse control in confrontational interaction. In Leo Hickey (ed.) *The Pragmatics of Style*. London: Croom Helm, pp. 133–56.

Thomas, Jenny (1995) *Meaning in Interaction*. London: Longman.

Thornbury, Scott (2005) *Beyond the Sentence: Introducing Discourse Analysis*. Oxford: Macmillan.

Thorne, Barrie, Cheris Kramarae and Nancy Henley (eds) (1983) *Language, Gender and Society*. Rowley, Mass.: Newbury House.

Todd, Loreto (1974) *Pidgins and Creoles*. London: Routledge and Kegan Paul.

Trudgill, Peter (1972) Sex, covert prestige and linguistic change in the urban British English of Norwich. *Language in Society* 1, 2: 179–96.

Trudgill, Peter (1974) *The Social Differentiation of English in Norwich*. Cambridge: Cambridge University Press.

Trudgill, Peter (1975) *Accent, Dialect and the School*. London: Edward Arnold.

Trudgill, Peter (1983a) 2nd edn. *Sociolinguistics: An Introduction to Language and Society*. Harmondsworth: Penguin.

Trudgill, Peter (1983b) Social identity and linguistic sex differentiation. In *On Dialect*. Oxford: Blackwell.

Trudgill, Peter (1988) Norwich revisited: recent linguistic changes in an English urban dialect. *English World-Wide* 9, 1: 33–49.

Trudgill, Peter (1990) *The Dialects of England*. Oxford: Blackwell.

Trudgill, Peter (1992) *Introducing Language and Society*. Harmondsworth: Penguin.

Trudgill, Peter (1994) *Dialects*. London and New York: Routledge.

Trudgill, Peter (2000) 4th edn. *Sociolinguistics: An Introduction to Language and Society*. Harmondsworth: Penguin.

Trudgill, Peter and Howard Giles (1977) Sociolinguistics and linguistic value judgments: correctness, adequacy and aesthetics. In Frank Coppieters and Didier L. Goyvaerts (eds) *The Functions of Language and Literature Studies*. Ghent: Story-Scientia.

Tulin, Mary Fewel (1997) Talking organization: possibilities for conversation analysis in organizational behavior research. *Journal of Management Inquiry* 6, 2: 101–19.

UNESCO (1953) *The Use of Vernacular Languages in Education*. Paris: UNESCO.

Usami, Mayumi (2002) *Discourse Politeness in Japanese Conversation*. Tokyo: Hituzi Syobo.

Valdman, Albert (1988) Diglossia and language conflict in Haiti. *International Journal of the Sociology of Language* 71: 67 80.

van Dijk, Teun A. (1998) Principles of critical discourse analysis. In Jenny Cheshire and Peter Trudgill (eds) *The Sociolinguistics Reader*. Vol 2. *Gender and Discourse*. London: Arnold, pp. 367–93.

Verivaki, Maria (1991) Greek language maintenance and shift in the Greek community of Wellington. In Janet Holmes and Ray Harlow (eds) *Threads in the Tapestry of Language*. Auckland: Linguistic Society of New Zealand, pp. 71–116.

Vikør, Lars S. (1995) 2nd edn. *The Nordic Languages: Their Status and Interrelations*. Oslo: Novus Press.

Waldvogel, Joan (2005) *Email in Workplace Communication*. Unpublished Ph.D. thesis. Wellington: Victoria University of Wellington.

Wales, Katie (1994) Royalese: the rise and fall of 'The Queen's English'. *English Today* 39, 10, 3: 3–10.

Wardhaugh, Ronald (1987) *Languages in Competition*. Oxford: Blackwell.

Wardhaugh, Ronald (2006) 5th edn. *An Introduction to Sociolinguistics*. Oxford: Blackwell.

Weigel, Margaret M. and Ronald M. Weigel (1985) Directive use in a migrant agricultural community: a test of Ervin-Tripp's hypothesis. *Language in Society* 14, 63–80.

Welsh Language Board (2006) *2004 Welsh Language Use Survey*. Cardiff: Welsh Language Board.

West, Candace (1984) When the doctor is a lady: power, status and gender in physician–patient dialogues. *Symbolic Interaction* 7, 1: 87–106.

West, Candace (1990) Not just 'doctors' orders': directive-response sequences in patients' visits to women and men physicians. *Discourse and Society* 1, 1: 85–112.

West, Candace and Don Zimmerman (1977) Women's place in everyday talk: reflections on parent–child interaction. *Social Problems* 24: 521–9.

West, Candace and Don Zimmerman (1983) Small insults: a study of interruptions in cross-sex conversations between unacquainted persons. In Barrie Thorne, Cheris Kramarae and Nancy Henley (eds) *Language, Gender and Society*. Rowley, Mass.: Newbury House, pp. 103–18.

White, Sheida (1989) Backchannels across cultures: a study of Americans and Japanese. *Language in Society* 18: 59–76.

Whiteley, William, H. (1968) *Some Problems of Transitivity in Swahili*. London: SOAS.

Whiteley, William, H. (1969) *Swahili: The Rise of a National Language*. London: Methuen.

Whitney, Paul (1998) *The Psychology of Language*. Boston: Houghton Mifflin.

Wiggen, Geirr (1997) Nynorsk-Bokmål. In Hans Goebl, Peter Nelde, Zdenek Stary and Wolfgang Wölck (eds) *Contact Linguistics: An International Handbook of Contemporary Research*. Vol. 2. Berlin and New York: Walter de Gruyter, pp. 948–57.

Wilford, Judith (1982) Can I borrow your biscuit? Directive choice among children in a child care centre. Unpublished terms paper. Wellington: Victoria University.

Williams, Michael (1990) A small study of post-vocalic (r) on the Isle of Wight. Unpublished term paper. Wellington: Victoria University.

Wolfram, Walt (1991) *Dialects and American English*. Englewood Cliffs, NJ: Prentice Hall.

Wolfram, Walt (1998) Dialect awareness programs in the school and community. In Rebecca S. Wheeler (ed.) *Language Alive in the Classroom*. Westport, Conn.: Greenwood Press, pp. 47–66.

Wolfram, Walter and Ralph W. Fasold (1974) *The Study of Social Dialects in American English*. Englewood Cliffs, NJ: Prentice Hall.

Wolfram, Walt and Natalie Schilling-Estes (1998) *American English*. Oxford: Blackwell.

Woods, Nicola (1988) Talking shop: sex and status as determinants of floor apportionment in a work setting. In Jennifer Coates and Deborah Cameron (eds) *Women in their Speech Communities*. London: Longman, pp. 141–57.

Wurm, Stephen A. (1985) The status of New Guinea Pidgin (Neo-Melanesian) and attitudes towards it. In Nessa Wolfson and Joan Manes (eds) *Language and Inequality*. The Hague: Mouton, pp. 373–86.

Zimmerman, Don H. and Candace West (1975) Sex roles, interruptions and silences in conversation. In Barrie Thorne and Nancy Henley (eds) *Language and Sex: Difference and Dominance*. Rowley, Mass.: Newbury House, pp. 105–29.

Zuckermann, Ghil'ad (2003) *Language Contact and Lexical Enrichment in Israeli Hebrew*. London-New York: Palgrave Macmillan.

Appendix I   Phonetic symbols

Following Knowles (1987) I have adopted the system used by Daniel Jones for the broad transcription of RP in *The Principles of the IPA*. Each sound is identified by its symbol and a key word. The key word is given in ordinary spelling and in broad transcription. The key words have been chosen for their relative stability from one variety of English to another.

Vowels

1.	i:	reed	/riːd/
2.	i	rid	/rid/
3.	e	red	/red/
4.	a	bad	/bad/
5.	a:	shah	/ʃa:/
6.	o	cod	/kod/
7.	o:	law	/lo:/
8.	u	could	/kud/
9.	u:	mood	/mu:d/
10.	ʌ	bud	/bʌd/
11.	ə:	bird	/bə:d/
12.	ə	the	/ðə/
		about	/əbaut/
		sofa	/soufə/
13.	ei	raise	/reiz/
14.	ou	rose	/rouz/
15.	ai	rise	/raiz/
16.	au	rouse	/rauz/
17.	oi	toy	/toi/
18.	iə	beer	/biə/
19.	eə	there	/ðeə/
20.	uə	lure	/luə/

Consonants

p	pop	/pop/
b	Bob	/bob/
t	tight	/tait/
d	dead	/ded/
k	cake	/keik/
g	gag	/gag/
tʃ	church	/tʃə:tʃ/
dʒ	judge	/dʒʌdʒ/
f	fife	/faif/
v	van	/van/
θ	thirtieth	/θə:tiəθ/
ð	then	/ðen/
s	sauce	/so:s/
z	zoos	/zu:z/
ʃ	sheep	/ʃi:p/
ʒ	leisure	/leʒə/
h	hat	/hat/
m	mime	/maim/
n	noon	/nu:n/
ŋ	singing	/siŋiŋ/
l	lull	/lʌl/
r	rain	/rein/
j	yacht	/jot/
w	will	/wil/

The number of the vowels is conventional, and follows the order originally used by Jones in 1918 in his *Outline of English Phonetics* (Cambridge: Heffer), and since adopted by a number of phonetics textbooks.

In addition the following symbols have been used to represent sounds from languages other than English or to represent a greater degree of phonetic detail than the broad transcription system makes possible.

[ɲ] the palatal nasal sound heard in Spanish *señor*.

[ʔ] the glottal stop, a brief period of silence or absence of sound heard in place of medial and final [t] in some dialects.

[ʈ] a retroflex sound produced by curling the tip of the tongue so that its underside touches the ridge behind the top teeth. This sound is heard in many Indian languages.

Appendix II Preface to first edition

This book has been written for people who have never heard of sociolinguistics, but who would like to know what it is. At the end of it, I hope they will not only know what sociolinguists do and why, they might also feel like reading further about some of the topics that have interested them.

Because my aim has been to share my love of the subject with newcomers, I have made some conscious decisions about the content which would have been different for more advanced students. In selecting examples I have used a good deal of material from recent published research, but I have also used many examples which could perhaps be described as 'classics', in the sense that any sociolinguist will be familiar with them. These 'tried and true' examples will be old friends if readers progress to further reading, and should help bridge the gap between this introductory text and more sophisticated sociolinguistic books. Though I have drawn on sociolinguistic research involving a wide variety of languages, I have used a large number of English examples too. English is likely to be a very familiar language for most of my readers, and I know from experience that some points will therefore be understood more quickly and thoroughly using an English example – at least for the initial encounter with a new concept.

I have assumed that my readers will be familiar with very basic grammatical terms, but little more. The glossary at the end of the book defines more specialised grammatical terms which crop up in the text. Similarly I have used a minimum of phonetic symbols in the text, but a sociolinguist cannot avoid talking about speech sounds, and phonetic symbols are the only really satisfactory way of conveying different pronunciations. Appendix I describes the phonetic symbols I have used, with a glossary to help readers work out what they sound like.

Different people approach books differently. I have constructed this book on the assumption that most will read section A before section B, and section B before section C. The later chapters refer back to the earlier ones to some extent. However, readers who like a sense of the whole before dipping into the parts may find it helpful to read the first and the last chapters before trying the rest.

Finally, I am sure perceptive readers will be able to guess which are my own particular areas of interest within the broad area of sociolinguistics. I make no apology for that. But I hope that my enthusiasm for sociolinguistics as a whole also communicates itself, so that at least some readers will feel encouraged not only to pursue the subject further, but perhaps also to address some of the many questions about the relationship between language and society which still await answers.

Janet Holmes
Wellington, New Zealand
December 1990

Appendix III   Preface to second edition

This second edition of my textbook has provided an opportunity to respond to some of the many kind suggestions and comments that readers have sent to me over the last 10 years. I have corrected errors and clarified examples. I have expanded the text in places. I have updated the references and recommended readings. Thanks to the comments of a number of reviewers, I have also persuaded the publishers to accept a recommendation I made with the first edition, namely, to separate the exercises from their answers. In response to suggestions and requests, I have also added a number of substantial sections to the book, most obviously a new chapter on language, cognition and culture, and sections on social constructionism in the two chapters dealing with gender and language. I hope the amendments and additions increase the usefulness of the book both for students and teachers, as well as increasing its readability.

Janet Holmes
Wellington, New Zealand
June 2000

Glossary

This glossary explains the meaning of technical linguistic or other unfamilar terms which are used but not defined in this book. Terms which are explained in the text are generally not included. They can be found in the index which points to where they are discussed in the text.

affricate: a sound produced by building up air behind a complete closure at some point in the mouth, followed by a slow release which sounds like a fricative: e.g. the initial sounds in English *chin* and *chat*, *jar* and *jury*, and the initial sound in German *Zeit* are affricates.

back vowel: a vowel produced by the tongue in the back of the mouth.

case markers: affixes on words signalling their grammatical status as subject, object, possessive, etc. In Latin the *-a* on *Maria* in the sentence *Mari-a pueel-am amat* 'Mary loves the girl' marks Mary as subject while the *-am* on *puellam* signals it is the object. The *-a* is thus a subject case marker and the *-am* is an object case marker.

declarative: the normal form of a sentence used to express a statement in a language. In English the normal word order in a declarative sentence has the subject first, then the verb and then the direct object: e.g. *he has cooked the dinner.*

determiner: a broad grammatical category of words which precede nouns in English. It includes the definite article (*the*), the indefinite article (*a*, *an*) demonstrative items such as *this*, *that*, *these* and *those*, and possessives such as *my* and *your*. More formally, determiners can occur in the slot ____ (Adjective) Noun in English.

diachronic: historical. A diachronic study of a language traces changes in the language over time.

fricative: a sound made by narrowing the exit passage of air from the lungs at some point sufficiently to cause friction: e.g. [s], [z], [f], [v].

glottal stop: a brief period of silence or absence of sound caused by cutting off the air stream from the lungs at the vocal cords. It functions as a consonant in some languages. It can be heard in place of medial and final [t] in some English dialects.

imperative: the normal form of a sentence used to express a command or order in a language. In English this usually involves using the verb without any subject: e.g. *sit down, cook the dinner!*

inflections: affixes added to word roots to signal grammatical information such as number, case, gender, tense, aspect: e.g. the *-s* at the end of *books* is an inflection; so is the *-s* on *loves* in *she loves books.*

interrogative: the normal form of a sentence used to express a question in a language. In English this involves reversal of the verb and subject; e.g. *has he cooked the dinner?* and *where are you going?*

lexical item: a unit in the dictionary of a language. It may consist of more than one ortho-graphic word: e.g. *made up* is one lexical item in *she made up a story*.

lexis: vocabulary

Māoritanga: knowledge of Maori culture, vital and essential elements of Maori culture, Maoriness

marae: the traditional meeting place of a Maori tribe or sub-tribe. The term refers specific-ally to the open area where welcoming ceremonies take place for visiting groups, but it may also be used to refer to a whole complex of buildings and their surrounds, includ-ing the meeting house and dining hall.

modal items: elements which express speakers' attitudes to the truth of their assertions, or express obligation or permission. English modal verbs include *will, would, may, might, can, could, should, must*. Other modal items are words such as *perhaps, probably*, and *maybe*.

morphology: the word structure of languages and the study of word structure.

Pakeha: a non-Polynesian New Zealander, usually used to refer specifically to a New Zealander of European origin.

phonology: the sound systems of human languages and the study of sound systems.

pragmatic particles: forms which typically occur in informal speech such as *well, you see, you know, anyway, of course*, and *I think*. Their exact function is difficult to define since it varies with context. They have been described by some as 'fillers' since they give the speaker planning time in speech, and by others as 'hedges' when they soften the force of a statement or 'boosters' when they have an emphatic function.

rhotic: r-full. Rhotic accents of English are accents in which [r] is pronounced after a vowel in word final position (e.g. *start*) or before a final consonant (*start*).

semantics: the meaning expressed by human languages and the study of meaning especially word meaning and sentence meaning.

synchronic: at one point in time. A synchronic study of a language is a study at a particular point without regard for previous or succeeding states of the language.

syntax: the structure of sentences and the study of sentence structure.

tag questions: forms such as *isn't it?* and *don't they?* which may be appended to a statement. Informal tag question forms include *eh?* and *right?*. French has a tag question form *n'est-ce pas?* and German has a tag question form *nicht wahr?*

Index